GREATES...
OF ...

... they are! The largest, the longest, the deepest,
... highest, the fastest, the fattest, the oldest, the
... west, the most startling prodigies of nature, the
... ost spectacular accomplishments of man, the most
incredible records from the world of sport . . .
packed with fantastic facts and fully documented
fascinating figures . . . here it is

GIANT NEW 1977 EDITION

GUINNESS
BOOK OF
WORLD RECORDS

BY NORRIS McWHIRTER
AND ROSS McWHIRTER

**GUINNESS
RECORDS EXHIBIT**

WORLD · CIRCUS CIRCUS · LAS VEGAS · EMPIRE STATE BUILDING · N.Y.C. · HALLS ·

The high point of your
visit in New York will
be in seeing the 216
lifesize Guinness dis-
plays. In Las Vegas
the Guinness "living
museum" is the most
unusual show in town.

LARGEST FLAG: Created for New York City's Bicentennial celebration, this gigantic Stars and Stripes only "flew" on the Verrazano-Narrows Bridge for a few hours in a test hanging before it was torn apart by winds (see page 361).

1977 Edition

GUINNESS BOOK OF WORLD RECORDS

NORRIS McWHIRTER
AND ROSS McWHIRTER

BANTAM BOOKS · TORONTO · NEW YORK · LONDON

GUINNESS BOOK OF WORLD RECORDS

*A Bantam Book/published by arrangement with
Sterling Publishing Company, Inc.*

PRINTING HISTORY OF AMERICAN EDITION

American Guinness edition published October 1956
Sterling edition published April 1962

3rd edition .. September 1963	9th edition ...... May 1970
4th edition ..... January 1964	10th edition ...... April 1971
5th edition ..... October 1965	11th edition .. November 1972
6th edition .. September 1966	12th edition ...... October 1973
7th edition ..... January 1968	13th edition .. September 1974
Book Club edition.. Sept. 1969	14th edition ..... October 1975

Bantam edition / October 1963
4 printings through February 1964

Revised Bantam edition / April 1964
8 printings through February 1966

Revised and enlarged Bantam Special edition / June 1966
7 printings through July 1967

Revised and enlarged new Bantam edition / March 1968
9 printings through October 1969

Revised and enlarged new Bantam edition / May 1970
6 printings through December 1970

Revised and enlarged new Bantam edition / April 1971
17 printings through September 1972

Revised and enlarged new Bantam edition / March 1973
17 printings through December 1973

Revised and enlarged new Bantam edition / February 1974
10 printings through November 1974

Revised and enlarged new Bantam edition / February 1975
13 printings through August 1975

Revised and enlarged new Bantam edition / March 1976
10 printings through October 1976

Revised and enlarged new Bantam edition / March 1977

CONTENTS

FOREWORD

By Senator the Right Honourable the Earl of Iveagh

The book that you hold in your hands is the fifteenth American edition. It was first designed in 1956 to record the then extremes in, on and beyond the Earth—notably in human performance and of the natural world. The name "Guinness" derives from the Guinness Brewery in Dublin which is Ireland's largest Company. In Ireland people, as everywhere else, are always arguing about the largest, the longest, the heaviest, the hottest, the coldest, the wettest, the mostest, etc., and some authoritative reference work was needed to settle such arguments. We realise, of course, that much joy lies in argument, but how exasperating it can be if there is no ultimate means of finding out the correct answer. The Guinness Book has rather proved this point, since it has now succeeded to the title of the fastest selling book ever published anywhere in the world.

While the exports of Guinness Stout from Dublin to the rest of the world make the Guinness Brewery the largest exporter of beer in the world we never expected that the Guinness Book would become the runaway best seller that it now is. It is now published all over the world in fourteen different languages. We are proud to have made the world more aware of the records that it is continually setting.

All who have read the work will share our grief and shock at the brutal murder of Ross McWhirter on November 27, 1975 and will share with his twin brother and co-author the loss he and Ross's own family have suffered.

Iveagh.
[BENJAMIN GUINNESS]
EARL OF IVEAGH, Chairman
Arthur Guinness, Son & Co. (Dublin) Ltd.,
St. James's Gate Brewery, Dublin, Ireland.

September, 1976

PREFACE

This fifteenth U.S. edition has been brought up to date and provided with new illustrations. We wish to thank correspondents from most of the countries of the world for raising and settling various editorial points. Strenuous efforts have been made to improve the value of the material presented and this policy will be continued in future editions.

In 1976 two permanent Guinness World Records Exhibit Halls were opened in the Empire State Building, New York City and in Circus Circus Hotel, Las Vegas, Nevada.

NORRIS D. MCWHIRTER
General Editor

Guinness Superlatives, Ltd.,
Main Editorial Office,
2 Cecil Court,
London Road, Enfield,
Middlesex, England.

Norris (sitting) and Ross McWhirter (standing) were born identical twins on August 12, 1925, in London, England. They were both educated at Trinity College, Oxford University, where they received M.A. degrees in Economics and Law. They both served in the Royal Navy. They were both members of the Oxford University track team. They were both candidates for the Conservative Party in the 1964 General Election. They have both worked for the B.B.C., Norris as TV and radio commentator on track and field, and Ross on tennis. They wrote a joint Sunday newspaper column for more than seven years, and contributed to the *Encyclopaedia Britannica*.

Norris is married and has a son and daughter. Ross, assassinated by terrorists on the doorstep of his London suburban home on November 27, 1975, after calling for funds that would lead to the capture and execution of those responsible for indiscriminate bombings in England, leaves a wife and two sons.

IS IT A RECORD?

We are likely to publish only those records which improve upon previous records or which are newly significant in having become the subject of widespread and preferably international competitiveness.

It should be stressed that unique occurrences and interesting peculiarities are not in themselves necessarily records. Records in our sense essentially have to be both measureable and comparable. Records which are *qualified* in some way, for example, by age, day of the week, etc. cannot be accommodated in a reference work so general as the *Guinness Book of World Records*.

Claimants should send independent corroboration in the form of local or national newspaper cuttings, radio or TV coverage reports and signed authentication by independent adult witnesses or representatives of organizations of standing in their community. Signed log books should show there has been unremitting surveillance in the case of endurance events.

There has been in recent years a marked increase in efforts to establish records for sheer endurance in many activities. In the very nature of record breaking the duration of such "marathons" will tend to be pushed to greater and greater extremes and it should be stressed that marathon attempts are not without possible dangers. Organizers of marathon events would be well counselled to seek medical advice before and surveillance during marathons which involve extended periods with little or no sleep. (See below for notes on rest periods.)

Five-minute rest intervals (optional but aggregable) are *permitted* after each completed hour in marathon events except for those few "non-stop" categories in which minimal intervals may be taken only for purposes other than for resting.

If there are discrepancies between entries in one edition and another, it may be generally assumed that the *later* entry is the product of the more up-to-date research.

If an activity is one controlled by a recognized world or national governing body that body should be consulted and involved in ratifying it.

The publishers do *not* supply personnel to invigilate record attempts but reserve the right to do so.

Finally the editorial office, which is concerned with maintaining and improving the quality of each succeeding edition, is unable to perform also the function of a free general information bureau for quiz competitions and the like, by telephone or by correspondence.

TALLEST LIVING WOMAN: Sandy Allen of Shelbyville, Indiana, stands 7 feet
$5\frac{5}{16}$ inches and is still growing.

Chapter One

THE HUMAN BEING

1. Dimensions

Tallest Giants

The height of human giants is a subject in which accurate information is frequently obscured by exaggeration and commercial dishonesty. The only admissible evidence on the true height of giants is that collected in the last 100 years under impartial medical supervision. Some medical papers have, however, perpetuated fanciful, as opposed to measured, heights.

The Biblical claim that Goliath of Gath (c. 1060 B.C.) stood 6 cubits and a span (9 feet 6½ inches) suggests a confusion of units or some over-enthusiastic exaggeration by the Hebrew chroniclers. The Hebrew historian Flavius Josephus (born in 37 or 38 A.D., died after 93 A.D.) and some of the manuscripts of the Septuagint (the earliest Greek translation of the Old Testament) attribute to Goliath the quite credible height of 4 Greek cubits and a span (6 feet 10 inches).

Extreme medieval data, taken from bone measurements, invariably refer to specimens of extinct whale, giant cave bear, giant ape, mastodon, woolly rhinoceros or other prehistoric non-human remains.

Paul Topinard (1830–1911), a French anthropometrist, stated that the tallest man who ever lived was Daniel Mynheer Cajanus (1714–49) of Finland, standing 9 feet 3.4 inches. In 1872 his right femur, now in the Leyden Museum, in the Netherlands, was measured by Prof. Carl Langer of Germany and indicated a height of 7 feet 3.4 inches. Pierre Lemolt reported in 1847 that Ivan Stepanovich Lushkin (1811–44), a drum major in the Russian Imperial Regiment of Guards at Preobrazhenskiy, measured 3 arshin 9¼ vershok (8 feet 3¾ inches) and was "the tallest man that has ever lived in modern days." However, his left femur and tibia, which are now in the Museum of the Academy of Sciences in Leningrad, U.S.S.R., indicate a height of 7 feet 10¼ inches.

An extreme case of exaggeration concerned Siah Khan ibn Kashmir Khan (born 1913) of Bushehr (Bushire), Iran. Prof. D. H. Fuchs showed photographs of him at a meeting of the Society of Physicians in Vienna, Austria, in January, 1935, claiming that he was 10 feet 6 inches tall. Later, when Siah Khan entered the Imperial Hospital in Teheran for an operation, it was revealed that his actual height was 7 feet 2.6 inches.

The tallest recorded "true" (non-pathological) giant was Angus MacAskill (1825–63), born on the island of Berneray, in the Sound

TALLEST MAN: Robert Wadlow reached the height of 8 feet 11.1 inches when he was 22.4 years old. At the time, he weighed 439 lbs., after having weighed 491 lbs. He is shown here at the age of 18 with his brothers Eugene (left) and Harald (right). Robert is the one wearing glasses.

of Harris, in the Outer Hebrides, Scotland. He stood 7 feet 9 inches and died in St. Ann's, on Cape Breton Island, Nova Scotia, Canada.

Modern opinion is that the tallest recorded man of whom there is irrefutable evidence was Robert Pershing Wadlow, born in Alton, Illinois, on February 22, 1918. Weighing 8½ lbs. at birth, his abnormal growth began almost immediately. His height progressed as follows:

Age in Years	Height ft.	ins.	Weight in lbs.	Age in Years	Height ft.	ins.	Weight in lbs.
5	5	4	105	15	7	8	355
8	6	0	169	16	7	10½	374
9	6	2½	180	17	8	0½	315*
10	6	5	210	18	8	3½	—
11	6	7	—	19	8	5½	480
12	6	10¼	—	20	8	6¾	—
13	7	1¾	255	21	8	8¼	491
14	7	5	301	22.4†	8	11.1	439

* Following severe influenza and infection of the foot.
† He was still growing during his terminal illness.

Dr. C. M. Charles, Associate Professor of Anatomy at Washington University School of Medicine, in St. Louis, measured him at 8 feet 11.1 inches, on June 27, 1940. He died 18 days later, on July 15, 1940, in Manistee, Michigan, as a result of cellulitis of the feet aggravated by a poorly fitted brace. He was buried in Oakwood Cemetery, Alton, Illinois, in a coffin measuring 10 feet 9 inches in length, 32 inches in width, and 30 inches in depth. His greatest recorded weight was 491 lbs., on his 21st birthday. He weighed 439 lbs. at the time of his death. His shoes were size 37AA (18½ inches long) and his hands measured 12¾ inches from the wrist to the tip of the middle finger. His arm span was 9 feet 5¾ inches and he consumed 8,000 calories daily. At the age of 9 he was able to carry his father, the mayor of Alton, up the stairs of the family home.

Gabriel Estevao Monjane (born 1944) of Manjacaze, Mozambique, has been credited with a height of 8 feet 6 inches. This eunuchoid-infantile giant has not, however, grown since he was anthropometrically assessed by Dr. Manuel Simoes Alberto in Lourenco Marques in December, 1965. His standing height was 7 feet 10 inches.

The only other men for whom heights of 8 feet or more have been reliably reported are the nine listed next. In each case gigantism was followed by acromegaly, a disease which causes an enlargement of the nose, lips, tongue, lower jaw, hands and feet, due to renewed activity by the already swollen pituitary gland, which is located at the base of the brain.

	ft.	in.
John F. Carroll (1932–69) of Buffalo, New York	(a) 8	7¾

(a) Carroll was a victim of severe kypho-scoliosis (two-dimensional spinal curvature). The figure represents his height with assumed normal spinal curvature, calculated from a standing height of 8 feet 0 inches, measured on October 14, 1959. His standing height was 7 feet 8¼ inches shortly before his death.

TALLEST LIVING MAN: Don Koehler, born in Denton, Montana, and now living in Chicago, was photographed in Detroit, standing 8 feet 2 inches high. His twin sister is only 5 feet 9 inches.

(*Continued from page* 13)

		ft.	in.
John William Rogan (1871–1905), a black of Gallatin, Tennessee	(b)	8	6
Unnamed African acromegalic (*fl.* 1962), Nairobi, Kenya		8	3
Don Koehler (1925–*fl.* 1976) of Denton, Montana, now living in Chicago (see photo)	(c)	8	2
Bernard Coyne (1897–1921) of Anthon, Iowa		8	2
Väinö Myllyrinne (1909–63) of Helsinki, Finland	(d)	8	1.2
Louis Moilanen (1885–1913) born in Finland, died in Hancock, Michigan		8	1
Constantine (1872–1902) of Reutlingen, West Germany	(e)	8	0.8
Sulaiman 'Ali Nashnush (born 1943) of Tripoli, Libya	(f)	8	0.4

(b) Measured in a sitting position. Unable to stand owing to ankylosis (stiffening of the joints through the formation of adhesions) of the knees and hips.

(c) Some spinal curvature. Recent standing height *c.* 7 feet 10 inches. He has a twin sister who is 5 feet 9 inches tall. His father was 6 feet 2 inches tall, his mother 5 feet 10 inches. He lives a normal life.

(d) Stood 7 feet 3½ inches at the age of 21 years. Experienced a second phase of growth in his late thirties and may have stood 8 feet 3 inches at one time.

(e) Height estimated, as both legs were amputated after they turned gangrenous. He claimed a height of 8 feet 6 inches.

(f) Operation to correct abnormal growth in Rome in 1960 was successful.

Circus giants and others who are exhibited are normally under contract not to be measured and are, almost traditionally, billed by their promoters at heights up to 18 inches in excess of their true heights. Other notable examples of such exaggeration are:

Name	*Dates*	*Country*	*Claimed Height*		*Actual Height*	
			ft.	in.	ft.	in.
Gerrit Bastiaansz	1620–68	Netherlands	8	3	7	1
Cornelius Magrath	1736–60	Ireland	8	6	7	2¼
Bernardo Gigli	1736–62	Italy	8	0	7	6½
Patrick Cotter O'Brian	1760–1806	Ireland	8	7¾	7	10.86
Charles Byrne	1761–83	Ireland	8	4	7	7
Sam McDonald	1762–1802	Scotland	8	0	6	10
"Lolly"	1783–1816	Russia	8	4½	7	3
James Toller	1795–1819	England	8	6	7	6
Arthur Caley	1829–53	Isle of Man	8	4	7	6
Patrick Murphy	1834–62	Ireland	8	10	7	3.4
Martin van Buren Bates	1845–1919	U.S.	7	11½	7	2½
Chang Wu-gow	1846–93	China	9	2	7	8¾
Joseph Drazel	1847–86	Germany	8	3½	7	6.5
Paul Henoch	1852–76	Germany	8	3	7	2
Franz Winkelmeier	1867–89	Austria	8	9	7	5.7
Lewis Wilkins	1873–1902	U.S.	8	2	7	4½
John Turner	1876–1911	U.S.	8	3	7	3
Baptiste Hugo	1879–1916	France	8	10	7	6.5
Fyodor Machnov	1880–1905	Russia	9	3½	7	9.7
Frederick Kempster	1889–1918	England	8	4½	7	8½
Johnny Aasen	1890–1937	U.S.	8	0	7	0
Albert Johann Kramer	b. 1897	Netherlands	9	3½	7	8¼
Clifford Thompson	b. 1904	U.S.	8	8	7	5
Jacob Ehrlich, *alias* Jack Earle	1906–52	U.S.	8	7	7	7½
Aurelio Tomaini	1912–62	U.S.	8	4½	7	4
Henry Mullens, *alias* Henry Hite	b. 1915	U.S.	8	2	7	6¾
Rigardus Riynhout	b. 1922	Netherlands	9	1½	7	8.1
William Camper	1924–42	U.S.	8	6	7	2
Edward Evans	1924–58	England	9	3	7	8½
Poolad Gurd	b. 1927	Iran	8	2	7	3
Max Palmer	b. 1928	U.S.	8	0½	7	7
Eddie Carmel	1938–1972	Israel/U.S.	9	0⅝	7	6⅝

NOTE: The heights of John Turner, Frederick Kempster, Clifford Thompson and Max Palmer are estimated from photographs. Each of the other heights given in the last column above was obtained by an independent medical authority, the first from evidence of his leg bones.

Tallest Giantesses

Giantesses are rarer than giants but their heights are still spectacular. The tallest woman in medical history was the acromegalic giantess Jane ("Ginny") Bunford, born on July 26, 1895, at Bartley Green, Northfield, West Midlands, England. Her abnormal growth started at the age of 11 following a head injury, and on her 13th birthday she measured 6 feet 6 inches. Shortly before her death on April 1, 1922, she stood 7 feet 7 inches tall, but she had a severe curvature of the spine and would have measured about 7 feet 11 inches with assumed normal curvature. Her skeleton, now preserved in the Anatomical Museum in the Medical School at Birmingham University, has a mounted height of 7 feet 4 inches.

It was announced on February 10, 1972, that the skeleton of a medieval giantess measuring 8 feet 3 inches had been found in the Laga Mountains near Abruzzi, Italy, by archeologists but this was a hoax. Anna Hanen Swan (1846–88) of Nova Scotia, Canada, was billed at 8 feet 1 inch but actually measured 7 feet 5½ inches. In London, on June 17, 1871, she married Martin van Buren Bates (1845–1919), of Whitesburg, Letcher County, Kentucky, who stood 7 feet 2½ inches. Ella Ewing (born March, 1872) of Gorin, Missouri, was billed at 8 feet 2 inches and reputedly measured 6 feet 9 inches at the age of 10 (cf. 6 feet 5 inches for Robert Wadlow at this age). She measured 7 feet 4½ inches at the age of 23 and may have attained 7 feet 6 inches before her death in January, 1913.

Living. The tallest living woman is Sandy Allen (born June 18, 1955, in Chicago), who lives in Shelbyville, Indiana, and works in Indianapolis. In September, 1974, she measured 7 feet 5$\frac{5}{16}$ inches and is still growing. A 6½-lb. baby, her abnormal growth began soon after birth. She now weighs 421 lbs. and takes a size 16EEE shoe. She uses 6 yards of material to make a dress. (See photo on page 10.)

Shortest Dwarfs

The strictures which apply to giants apply equally to dwarfs, except that exaggeration gives way to understatement. In the same way 9 feet may be regarded as the limit toward which the tallest giants tend, so 23 inches must be regarded as the limit toward which the shortest mature dwarfs tend (cf. the average length of new-born babies is 18 to 20 inches). In the case of child dwarfs the age is often enhanced by their agents or managers.

There are many forms of dwarfism. Ateliotic dwarfs, known as midgets, suffer from a deficiency of growth hormone and are usually well proportioned. Such dwarfs tended to be even shorter when human stature was generally shorter due to lower nutritional standards. The shortest dwarfs are currently found among forms of chondrodystrophic or skeletal dwarfs such as those who have cartilage-hair hypoplasia or pseudoachondroplasia.

Midgets seldom grow to more than 40 inches tall. The most famous midget in history was Charles Sherwood Stratton, *alias* "General Tom Thumb," born on January 11, 1838. When he came into the clutches of the circus proprietor P. T. Barnum, his birth date

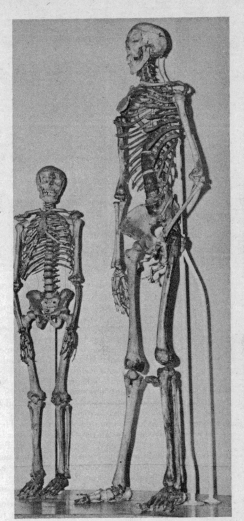

TALLEST WOMAN'S SKELETON: Jane Bunford of England stood 7 feet 7 inches.

was changed to January 11, 1832, so that when he was billed as standing 30½ inches at the age of 18 he was in fact only 12 years old. He died of apoplexy on July 15, 1883, aged 45 (not 51), and was then 3 feet 4 inches tall.

Another celebrated midget was Józef ("Count") Boruwlaski (born November, 1739) of Poland. He measured only 8 inches long at birth,

SHORTEST ADULT: Only 23.2 inches tall at age 19, this Dutch midget called "Princess Pauline" weighed 9 lbs. at her heaviest in 1895.

growing to 14 inches at the age of one year. He stood 17 inches at 6 years, 21 inches at 10, 25 inches at 15, 35 inches at 25 and 39 inches at 30. He died near Durham, England, on September 5, 1837, aged 97.

The shortest mature human of whom there is independent evidence was Pauline Musters ("Princess Pauline"), a Dutch midget. She was born at Ossendrecht on February 26, 1876, and measured 12 inches at birth. At the age of 4 she was only 15 inches tall. At the age of 9 she was 21.65 inches tall and weighed only 3 lbs. 5 oz. She died, at the age of 19, of pneumonia, with meningitis, in New York City on March 1, 1895. Although she was billed at 19 inches, she was measured shortly before her death and was found to be 23.2 inches tall. A *post mortem* examination showed her to be exactly 24 inches (her body was slightly elongated after death). Her mature weight varied from 7½ lbs. to 9 lbs. and her "vital statistics" were 18½–19–17.

The Italian girl Caroline Crachami, born in Palermo, Sicily, in 1815, was only 20.2 inches tall when she died in London, England, in 1824, aged 9. At birth she measured 7 inches long and weighed 1 lb. Her skeleton, measuring 19.8 inches, is now part of the Hunterian collection in the Museum of the Royal College of Surgeons, London.

Male. The shortest recorded adult male dwarf was Calvin Phillips, born in Bridgewater, Massachusetts, on January 14, 1791. He weighed 2 lbs. at birth and stopped growing at the age of 5. When he was 19 he measured 26½ inches tall and weighed 12 lbs. with his clothes on. He died two years later, in April, 1812, from progeria, a rare disorder characterized by dwarfism and premature senility.

William E. Jackson, *alias* "Major Mite," born on October 2, 1864, in Dunedin, New Zealand, measured 9 inches long and weighed

12 oz. at birth. In November, 1880, he stood 21 inches and weighed 9 lbs. He died in New York City, on December 9, 1900, when he measured 27 inches.

Another notable case was Max Taborsky, *alias* "Prince Kolibri," born in Vienna, Austria, in January, 1863. He measured 13.8 inches at birth and stopped growing at the age of 9. When he died, aged 25, in 1888, he stood 27.2 inches tall and weighed 11 lbs.

The shortest living mature human reported is Nruturam (born May 28, 1929), a rachitic dwarf of Naydwar, India, who measures 28 inches. The more famous circus midget Mihaly Meszaros (born October 1, 1939) of Hungary, currently billed as the "Smallest Man on Earth," stands 32⅝ inches tall.

Most Variable Stature. Adam Rainer, born in 1899 in Graz, Austria, measured 3 feet 10.45 inches at the age of 21. But then he suddenly started growing upwards at a rapid rate, and by 1931 he had reached 7 feet 1¾ inches. He became so weak as a result that he was bedridden for the rest of his life. He died on March 4, 1950, aged 51. By constant practice in muscular manipulation of the vertebrae, the circus performer Clarence E. Willard (1882–1962) of the U.S. was, at his prime, able to increase his apparent stature from 5 feet 10 inches to 6 feet 4 inches at will.

Greatest Height Differential. When Don Koehler at 8 feet 2 inches, the world's tallest living man, met Mihaly Meszaros (known as "Mishu"), at 32⅝ inches one of the world's smallest living men, the difference in their heights was 65⅝ inches. The occasion was the taping of the TV special, "The Second David Frost Presents the Guinness Book of World Records," on April 5, 1974.

Races

Tallest. The tallest race in the world is the Tutsi (also called Batutsi, Watutsi, or Watussi), Nilotic herdsmen of Rwanda and Burundi, Central Africa, whose males *average* 6 feet 1 inch, with a maximum of 7 feet 6 inches. A tribe with an average height of more than 6 feet was discovered in the inland region of Passis Manua of New Britain in December, 1956. In May, 1965, it was reported that the Crahiacoro Indians in the border district of the States of Mato Grosso and Pará, in Brazil, are exceptionally tall—certainly with an average of more than 6 feet. A report in May, 1966, specifically attributed great stature to the Kran-hacacore Indians of the Xingu region of the Mato Grosso, whose adult males reputedly averaged more than 6 feet 6 inches. In December, 1967, the inhabitants of Barbuda, Leeward Islands, were reported to have an average height in excess of 6 feet.

The Tehuelches of Patagonia, long regarded as of gigantic stature (*i.e.* 7 to 8 feet), have in fact an average height (males) of 5 feet 10 inches with a maximum of just over 6 feet 6¾ inches.

Shortest. The world's smallest known race is the Negrito Onge tribe, of whom only 12 men and 10 women survived on Little Andaman Island in the Indian Ocean by May, 1956. Few exceeded 4 feet. The smallest pygmies are the Mbuti, with an average height of 4 feet 6 inches for men and 4 feet 5 inches for women, with some

LIGHTEST HUMAN ADULT: Lucia Zarate of Mexico weighed 4.7 lbs. at the age of 17 and stood 26½ inches tall. At birth in 1863, she weighed 2½ lbs.

groups averaging only 4 feet 4 inches for men and 4 feet 1 inch for women. They live in the forests near the river Ituri in the Congo (Zaire), Africa.

Weight

Lightest Humans. The lightest recorded adult was Lucia Zarate, born in San Carlos, Mexico, on January 2, 1863. At birth she weighed 2½ lbs. This emaciated ateliotic dwarf of 26½ inches weighed 4.7 lbs. at the age of 17. She "fattened up" to 13 lbs. by her 20th birthday. She died in October, 1889.

The thinnest recorded adults of normal height are those suffering from Simmonds' disease (Hypophyseal cachexia). Losses up to 65 per cent of the original body weight have been recorded in females, with a "low" of 45 lbs. in the case of Emma Shaller (1868–1890) of St. Louis, Missouri, who stood 5 feet 2 inches tall. In cases of anorexia nervosa, weights of under 70 lbs. have been reported.

It was recorded that the American exhibitionist Rosa Lee Plemons (born 1873) weighed 27 lbs. at the age of 18. Edward C. Hagner (1892–1962), *alias* Eddie Masher, is alleged to have weighed only 48 lbs. at a height of 5 feet 7 inches. He was also known as "the Skeleton Dude." In August, 1825, the biceps measurement of Claude-Ambroise Seurat (born April 10, 1797, died April 6, 1826), of

Troyes, France, was 4 inches and the distance between his back and his chest was less than 3 inches. He stood 5 feet 7½ inches and weighed 78 lbs., but in another account was described as 5 feet 4 inches and only 36 lbs.

Heaviest Man. The heaviest medically weighed human was the 6-foot-0½-inch tall Robert Earl Hughes (born 1926) of Monticello, Illinois. An 11¼-lb. baby, he weighed 203 lbs. at 6 years, 378 lbs. at 10, 546 lbs. at 13, 693 lbs. at 18, 896 lbs. at 25, and 945 lbs. at 27. His greatest recorded weight was 1,069 lbs. in February, 1958, and he weighed 1,041 lbs. at the time of his death. His claimed waist of 122 inches, his chest of 124 inches and his upper arm of 40 inches were the greatest on record. Hughes died of uremia (condition caused by retention of urinary matter in the blood) in a trailer at Bremen, Indiana, on July 10, 1958, aged 32, and was buried in Benville Cemetery, near Mount Sterling, Illinois. His coffin, as large as a piano case measuring 7 feet by 4 feet 4 inches and weighing more than 1,100 lbs., had to be lowered by crane. It was once claimed by a commercial interest that Hughes had weighed 1,500 lbs.—a 40 per cent exaggeration.

John Lang, *alias* Michael Walker (born 1934) of Clinton, Iowa, was treated outside the Veterans' Administration Hospital in

HEAVIEST HUMAN OF ALL TIME: This is Robert Earl Hughes when he weighed only 700 lbs. He later reached a top weight of 1,069 lbs. He was buried in a coffin the size of a piano case.

Houston, Texas on January 5, 1972, because no one could get him through the doors. He was treated for extreme obesity and drug-induced bulimia (morbid desire to overeat). According to one newspaper report, he tipped the scales between 900 and 1,000 lbs. when weighed on a cattle scale. A spokesman for Christian Farms of Killeen, Texas (a religious oriented, anti-drug organization with whom Walker is affiliated) claims he reached a peak of 1,187 lbs. in the summer of 1971, at which time he was completely immobilized by his own obesity and unable to walk. Photographic evidence suggests that this weight may not have been exaggerated for a man standing 6 feet 2 inches tall but authentication of these claims is still lacking.

The only other men for whom weights of 800 lbs. or more have been *reliably* reported are listed below:

Mills Darden (1798–1857) U.S. (7 ft. 6 in.)	1,020 lbs.
John Hanson Craig (1856–94) U.S. (6 ft. 5 in.)	907 (c)
Arthur Knorr (1914–60) U.S. (6 ft. 1 in.)	900 (a)
Toubi (b. 1946) Cameroon	857½
T. A. Valenzuela (1895–1937) Mexico (5 ft. 11 in.)	850
David Maguire (1904–*fl.* 1935) U.S. (5 ft. 10 in.)	810
William J. Cobb (b. 1926) U.S. (6 ft. 0 in.)	802 (b)
Unnamed Patient (b. 1936) Richmond, Virginia (August, 1973)	800¼

(a) Gained 300 lbs. in the last 6 months of his life.
(b) Reduced to 232 lbs. by July, 1965.
(c) Won $1,000 in a "Bonny Baby" contest in New York City in 1858.

Heaviest Twins. The heaviest are the tag wrestlers Billy and Benny McCreary, *alias* Billy and Doug McGuire (born 1948) of Hendersonville, North Carolina, who, in March, 1970, weighed 640 lbs. and 660 lbs., respectively. Since becoming professional wrestlers, they have been billed at weights up to 770 lbs. They have married two Canadian sisters, Danielle (115 lbs.) and Maryce (130 lbs.). "I married the fat one," commented the fatter twin, Benny.

Heaviest Woman. The heaviest woman ever recorded was the late Mrs. Percy Pearl Washington (born Louisiana, 1926) who died in a hospital in Milwaukee, on October 9, 1972. The hospital scales registered only up to 800 lbs., but she was believed to weigh about 880 lbs. The previous weight record for a woman was set 84 years earlier at 850 lbs. although an unsubstantiated report exists of a woman, Mrs. Ida Maitland (1898–1932) of Springfield, Mississippi, who had a bust measurement of 152 inches and weighed 911 lbs. She was said to have died trying to pick a four-leaf clover.

A more reliable and better documented case was that of Mrs. Flora Mae (or May) Jackson (*née* King), a 5-foot-9-inch woman born in 1930 at Shuqualak, Mississippi. She weighed 10 lbs. at birth; 267 lbs. at the age of 11; 621 lbs. at 25; and 840 lbs. shortly before her death in Meridian, Mississippi, on December 9, 1965. She was known in show business as "Baby Flo."

Greatest Weight Differential. The greatest weight differential recorded for a married couple is 922 lbs. in the case of Mills Darden

HEAVIEST TWINS: The McCreary brothers, Benny and Billy, together weigh almost 1,500 lbs. They sometimes, in their motorcycling act, use the names Doug and Billy McGuire.

(1,020 lbs.) of North Carolina and his wife Mary (98 lbs.). Despite her diminutiveness, however, Mrs. Darden bore her husband three children before her death in 1837.

Slimming

The greatest recorded slimming feat was that of William J. Cobb (born 1926), *alias* "Happy Humphrey," a professional wrestler of Macon, Georgia. It was reported in July, 1965, that he had reduced from 802 lbs. to 232 lbs., a loss of 570 lbs., in 3 years. His waist measurement declined from 101 inches to 44 inches. In October, 1973, "Happy" was reported back to a normal 650 lbs.

The U.S. circus fat lady, Mrs. Celesta Geyer (born 1901), *alias* Dolly Dimples, reduced from 553 lbs. to 152 lbs. in 1950–51, a loss of 401 lbs. in 14 months. Her vital statistics diminished *pari passu* from 79–84–84 to a *svelte* 34–28–36. Her book "How I Lost 400 lbs." was not a best seller. In December, 1967, she was reportedly down to 110 lbs.

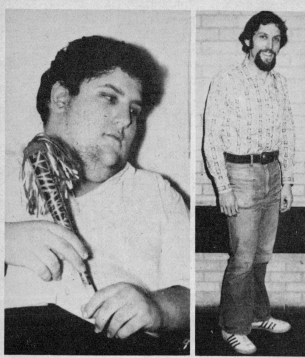

FASTEST WEIGHT LOSS: Paul Kimelman, who weighed 487 lbs. on Christmas Day, 1966, in 8 months lost 357 lbs., ending at 130 lbs. Today he tips the scales at a normal 175 lbs.

The speed record for slimming was established by Paul M. Kimelman, 21, of Pittsburgh, Pennsylvania, who from December 25, 1966, to August, 1967, went on a crash diet of 300 to 600 calories per day to reduce from 487 lbs. to 130 lbs., a total loss of 357 lbs. He has now stabilized at 175 lbs. Between February 4th and 8th, 1951, Mrs. Gertrude Levandowski of Burnips, Michigan, successfully underwent a series of operations to reduce her weight from 616 lbs. to 308 lbs.

Weight Gaining

A probable record for gaining weight was set by Arthur Knorr (born May 17, 1914), who died on July 7, 1960, aged 46, in Reseda, California. He gained 300 lbs. in the last 6 months of his life and weighed 900 lbs. when he died. Miss Doris James of San Francisco, is alleged to have gained 325 lbs. in the 12 months before her death in August, 1965, aged 38, at a weight of 675 lbs. She was only 5 feet 2 inches tall.

2. Origins

EARLIEST MAN

The earliest known primates appeared in the Paleocene period of about 70,000,000 years ago. The sub-order of higher primates, called Simiae (or Anthropoidea), evolved from the catarrhine or old-world sect nearly 30,000,000 years later in the Lower Oligocene period. During the Middle and Upper Oligocene the super-family Hominoidea emerged. This contains three accepted families, *viz.* Hominidae (bipedal, ground-dwelling man or near man), Pongidae (brachiating forest apes) and Oreopithecidae, which includes *Apidium* of the Oligocene and *Oreopithecus* of the early Pliocene. Opinion is divided on whether to treat gibbons and their ancestors as a fourth full family (Hylobatidae) or as a sub-family (Hylobatinae) within the Pongidae. Some consider that Proconsulidae should also comprise a family, although others regard the genus *Proconsul*, who lived on the open savannah, as part of another sub-family of the Pongidae.

Earliest Hominid (Near Man)

There is a conflict of evidence on the time during which true but primitive Hominidae were evolving. Fossil evidence indicates some time during the Upper Miocene (about 10,000,000 to 12,000,000 years ago). Evidence published in August, 1969, indicated that *Ramapithecus*, from the northeastern Indian sub-continent, can be dated from not less than 10,000,000 years ago and *Australopithecus*, from Eastern Africa, from 5,500,000 years (down to only a million years before the present).

Earliest Genus Homo (True Man)

The greatest age attributed to fossils of the genus *Homo* is for the remains of 8 adults and 3 children discovered in the summer of 1975 at Laetolil, Tanzania, by Dr. Mary Leakey, and dated by the University of California at Berkeley to between 3,350,000 and 3,750,000 B.C. Proof of whether or not "near man" and "true man," who had a contiguous existence, evolved from a common ancestor awaits new discoveries.

Earliest Homo Sapiens

Man (*Homo sapiens*) is a species in the sub-family Homininae of the family Hominidae of the super-family Hominoidea of the sub-order Simiae (or Anthropoidea) of the order Primates of the infra-class Eutheria of the sub-class Theria of the class Mammalia of the sub-phylum Vertebrata (Craniata) of the phylum Chordata of the sub-kingdom Metazoa of the animal kingdom.

The earliest recorded remains of the species *Homo sapiens*, variously dated from 300,000 to 450,000 years ago, in the middle Pleistocene period, were discovered on August 24, 1965, by Dr. László Vértes in a limestone quarry at Vértesszöllös, about 30 miles west of Budapest, Hungary. The remains, designated *Homo sapiens palaeo-hungaricus*, comprised an almost complete occipital bone, part of a skull with an estimated cranial capacity of nearly 1,400 cubic centimeters (85 cubic inches).

Earliest man in the Americas dates from at least 50,000 B.C. and "more probably 100,000 B.C.' according to the late Dr. Leakey after the examination of some hearth stones found in the Mojave Desert, California, and announced in October, 1970. The earliest human relic is a skull found in the area of Los Angeles, California, dated in December, 1970, to be from 22,000 B.C.

Scale of Time

If the age of the earth-moon system (latest estimate at least 4,700 million years) is likened to a single year, Handy Man appeared on the scene at about 8:35 p.m., on December 31, Britain's earliest known inhabitants arrived at about 11:32 p.m., the Christian era began about 13 seconds before midnight and the life span of a 113-year-old woman (see Oldest Centenarian) would be about three-quarters of a second. Present calculations indicate that the sun's increased heat, as it becomes a "red giant," will make life insupportable on earth in about 10,000 million years. Meanwhile there may well be colder epicycles. The period of 1,000 million years is sometimes referred to as an eon.

3. Longevity

Oldest Centenarian

No single subject is more obscured by vanity, deceit, falsehood and deliberate fraud than the extremes of human longevity. Extreme claims are generally made on behalf of the very aged rather than by them.

Many hundreds of claims throughout history have been made for persons living well into their second century and some, insulting to the intelligence, for people living even into their third. The facts are that centenarians surviving beyond their 110th year are of the extremest rarity and the present absolute limit of proven human longevity does not admit of anyone living to celebrate a 114th birthday.

It is highly significant that in Sweden, where alone proper and thorough official investigations follow the death of every allegedly very aged citizen, none has been found to have surpassed 110 years. The most reliably pedigreed large group of people in the world, the British peerage, has, after ten centuries, produced only two peers who reached their 100th birthdays. Neither one reached his 101st. However, this is possibly not unconnected with the extreme draftiness of many of their residences.

Scientific research into extreme old age reveals that the correlation between the claimed density of centenarians in a country and its regional illiteracy is 0.83 ±0.03. In late life, very old people often tend to advance their ages at the rate of about 17 years per decade. This was nicely corroborated by an analysis of the 1901 and 1911 censuses of England and Wales. Early claims must necessarily be without the elementary corroboration of birth dates. England was among the earliest of all countries to introduce local registers (1538) and official birth registration (July 1, 1837), which was made fully compulsory only in 1874. Even in the United States, where, in 1971, there were reputed to be 12,642 centenarians, 45 per cent of births occurring between 1890 and 1920 were unregistered.

Several celebrated super-centenarians are believed to have been double lives (father and son, brothers with the same names or successive bearers of a title). The most famous example is Christian Jakobsen Drackenberg allegedly born in Stavanger, Norway, on November 18, 1626, and died in Aarhus, Denmark, aged seemingly 145 years 326 days on October 9, 1772. A number of instances have been commercially sponsored, while a fourth category of recent claims are those made for political ends, such as the 100 citizens of the Russian Soviet Federative Socialist Republic (population about 132,000,000 at mid-1967), claimed in March, 1960, to be between 120 and 156. From data on documented centenarians, actuaries have shown that only one 115-year life can be expected in 2,100,000,000 lives (cf. world population was estimated to be 4,025,000,000 at mid-1975).

The height of credulity was reached on May 5, 1933, when a news agency solemnly filed a story from China with a Peking dateline that Li Chung-yun, the "oldest man on earth," born in 1680, had just died aged 256 years (sic). Recently the most extreme case of longevity claimed has been 168 years for Shirali Mislimov of Azerbaijan, U.S.S.R., who died on September 2, 1973 and was reputedly born on March 26, 1805. No interview of this man had ever been permitted to any Western journalist or scientist. He was said to have celebrated the 100th birthday of his third wife, Hartun, in 1966 and that of one of his grandchildren in August, 1973. It was reported in 1954 that in the Abkhasian Republic of Georgia, U.S.S.R., 2.58 per cent of the population was aged over 90—some 25 times the proportion in the U.S.

Dr. Zhores A. Medvedev, the exiled Soviet gerontologist, on April 30, 1974, in Washington, D.C., referring to the claims of the U.S.S.R. stated: "The whole phenomenon looks like a falsification . . . He (Stalin) liked the idea that (other) Georgians lived to be 100 or more . . . Local officials tried hard to find more and more cases for Stalin." He points out that the *average* life span in the regions claiming the highest incidence of centenarians is lower than the U.S.S.R.'s average, and that the number of centenarians claimed in the Caucasus has declined rapidly, from 8,000 in 1950 to 4,500 in 1970.

The Andean valley of Vilcabamba in Ecuador became the source of reports of extreme longevity after the 1971 census in which nine of the 819 inhabitants were recorded at ages of more than 100, of whom three were listed as over 120. The two oldest were Miguel Carpio Mendreta or Mendieta and José David Toledo, who were reputedly 122 and 140. Dr. David Davies of University College, London, supports the claim of Francisco Camacho of Sacapalka as the best candidate for the title of the world's oldest living man. Camacho's baptismal certificate is dated April 19, 1847.

Charlie Smith of Bartow, Florida obtained a Social Security card in 1955, claiming to have been born in Liberia on July 4, 1842. The

U.S. Dept. of Health, Education and Welfare states that they are "unable to disclose the type of evidence used" to determine Mr. Smith's age because such disclosure "would infringe on the confidentiality of the individual's record." The *essential* data on the ages entered for him in any of the 10 censuses from 1860 to 1950 remains undisclosed. He has a son born in 1902, and celebrated what he reckoned to be his 133rd birthday on July 4, 1975.

George Fruits, a veteran of the American Revolution, was reputedly born in Baltimore, Maryland, on February 2, 1762, and died on August 6, 1876, at Alamo, Indiana, aged 114 years.

Another American, still living, named Emma Spriggs, claims to have been born in Washington, D.C., in 1853, the daughter of a slave, but birth records are not available as proof.

Mythology often requires immense longevity; for example, Larak the god-King lived according to Sumerian mythology 28,800 years and Dumuzi even longer. The most extreme biblical claim is that for Methuselah at 969 years (Genesis V, verse 27).

OLDEST WOMAN: Delina Filkins of Herkimer County, New York, lived to the age of 113 years 214 days.

Oldest Authenticated Centenarian

The greatest authenticated age to which a human has ever lived is 113 years 214 days in the case of Mrs. Delina Filkins, *née* Ecker, who was born at Stark, Herkimer County, New York, on May 4, 1815, and died in Richfield Springs, New York, on December 4, 1928. She never wore eyeglasses. The following national records can be taken as authentic:

AUTHENTICATED NATIONAL LONGEVITY RECORDS

	Years	Days		Born	Died
U.S. (b)......	113	214	Delina Filkins (née Ecker)...	May 4, 1815	Dec. 4, 1928
Canada (a) .	113	124	Pierre Joubert	July 15, 1701	Nov. 16, 1814
Japan (e)...	112	100+	Mito Umeta (Mrs.)...........	Mar. 27, 1863	fl. July, 1975
U.K. (c)...	112	39	Alice Stevenson	July 10, 1861	Aug. 18, 1973
Morocco....	112	+	El Hadj Mohammed el Mokri (Grand Vizier)	1844	Sept. 16, 1957
Ireland	111	327	The Hon. Katherine Plunket..	Nov. 22, 1820	Oct. 14, 1932
South Africa (d) .	111	151	Johanna Booyson	Jan. 17, 1857	June 16, 1968
Czecho-slovakia...	111	+	Marie Bernatkova	Oct. 22, 1857	fl. Oct., 1968
Channel Islands	110	321	Margaret Ann Neve (née Harvey)	May 18, 1792	Apr. 4, 1903
Northern Ireland ...	110	234	Elizabeth Watkins (Mrs.)...	Mar. 10, 1863	Oct. 31, 1973
Yugoslavia .	110	150+	Demitrius Philipovitch	Mar. 9, 1818	fl. Aug., 1928
Australia (f)	110	39	Ada Sharp (Mrs.)...............	Apr. 6, 1861	May 15, 1971
U.S.S.R. (i)	110	+	Khasako Dzugayer	Aug. 7, 1860	fl. Aug., 1970
Netherlands	110	5	Baks Karnebeek (Mrs.)........	Oct. 2, 1849	Oct. 7, 1959
France	109	309	Marie Philomene Flassayer...	June 13, 1844	Apr. 18, 1954
Italy	109	179	Rosalia Spoto	Aug. 25, 1847	Feb. 20, 1957
Scotland....	109	14	Rachel MacArthur (Mrs.)....	Nov. 26, 1827	Dec. 10, 1936
Norway......	109	+	Marie Olsen (Mrs.)	May 1, 1850	fl. May, 1959
Tasmania ...	109	+	Mary Ann Crow (Mrs.)......	Feb. 2, 1836	1945
Germany (g)	108	128	Luise Schwarz	Sept. 27, 1849	Feb. 2, 1958
Portugal (j)	108	+	Maria Luisa Jorge..............	June 7, 1859	fl. July, 1967
Sweden	108	+	Anna Johansson	1865	Nov. 21, 1973
Finland......	107	221	Amalia Wallenius (Mrs.)	Aug. 6, 1867	Mar. 24, 1975
Belgium	106	267	Marie-Joseph Purnode (Mrs.).	Apr. 17, 1843	Nov. 9, 1949
Austria	106	231	Anna Migschitz.................	Feb. 3, 1850	Nov. 1, 1956
Spain (h)...	106	14	José Palido	Mar. 15, 1866	Mar. 29, 1972
Malaysia ...	106	+	Hassan Bin Yusoff..............	Aug. 14, 1865	fl. Jan., 1972
Isle of Man .	105	221	John Kneen	Nov. 12, 1852	June 9, 1958

(a) Mrs. Ellen Carroll died in North River, Newfoundland, Canada, on December 8, 1943, reputedly aged 115 years 49 days.

(b) The U.S. Veterans Administration was in March, 1974, paying pensions to 272 women attested to be widows of veterans of the Civil War (1861–65), the last soldier having died in 1959. The oldest of these widows is Angela Fleicia Virginia Davalos (Mrs. Harry Harrison Moran), who filed a claim dated 1928 with a baptismal certificate showing she was born in Morelia, Mexico, on May 17, 1856.

(c) London-born Miss Isabella Shephard was allegedly 115 years old when she died at St. Asaph, North Wales, on November 20, 1948, but her official age was believed to have been 109 years 90 days.

(d) Mrs. Susan Johanna Deporter of Port Elizabeth, South Africa, was reputedly 114 years old when she died on August 4, 1954.

(e) A man named Nakamura of Kamaishi, northern Japan, was reported to have died on May 4, 1969, aged 116 years 329 days.

(f) Reginald Beck of Sydney, was allegedly 111 years old when he died on April 13, 1928.

(g) Friedrich Sadowski of Heidelberg reputedly celebrated his 111th birthday on October 31, 1936.

(h) Juana Ortega Villarin, Madrid, Spain, allegedly 112 years in February, 1962.

(i) There are allegedly 21,700 centenarians in the U.S.S.R. compared with 7,000 in the U.S. Of these, 21,000 are ascribed to the Georgian S.S.R. or one out of every 232 people. In July, 1962, it was reported that 128, mostly male, resided in the one village of Medini.

(j) Senhora Jesuina da Conceicao of Lisbon was reputedly 113 years old when she died on June 10, 1965.

In the face of the above data the claim published in the April, 1961 issue of the Soviet Union's *Vestnik Statistiki* ("Statistical

Herald") that there were 224 male and 368 female Soviet citizens aged in excess of 120 recorded at the census of January 15, 1959, indicates a reliance on hearsay rather than evidence. Official Soviet insistence on the unrivalled longevity of the country's citizenry is curious in view of the fact that the 592 persons in their unique "over 120" category must have spent at least the first 78 years of their prolonged lives under Czarism. It has recently been suggested that the extreme ages claimed by men in Georgia, U.S.S.R., are the result of attempts to avoid military service when younger, by assuming the identities of older men.

4. Reproductivity

MOTHERHOOD

Most Children. The greatest number of children produced by a mother in an independently attested case is 69 by the first wife of Fyodor Vassilet (1816–72) a peasant of the Moscow Jurisdiction, Russia, who in 27 confinements, gave birth to 16 pairs of twins, 7 sets of triplets and 4 sets of quadruplets. Most of the children attained their majority. Mme. Vassilet became so renowned that she was presented at the court of Czar Alexander II.

Currently the highest reliably reported figure is a 32nd child born to Raimundo Carnauba and his wife Madalena, of Ceilandia,

OLDEST MOTHER: Mrs. Ruth Alice Kistler gave birth to her daughter Suzan in Glendale, California, in 1956, when she was 57 years old.

Brazil. She was married at 13 and so far has had 24 sons and 8 daughters. In May, 1972, the mother said "They have given us a lot of work and worry but they are worth it," and the father "I don't know why people make such a fuss." The figures given here are tentative, however, since no two published interviews with this family produce entirely consistent data.

Oldest. Medical literature contains extreme but unauthenticated cases of septuagenarian mothers such as Mrs. Ellen Ellis, aged 72, of Four Crosses, Clwyd, Wales, who allegedly produced a stillborn 13th child on May 15, 1776, in her 46th year of marriage. Many early cases were cover-ups for illegitimate grandchildren. The oldest recorded mother of whom there is certain evidence is Mrs. Ruth Alice Kistler (*née* Taylor), formerly Mrs. Shepard, of Portland, Oregon. She was born at Wakefield, Massachusetts, on June 11, 1899, and gave birth to a daughter, Suzan, in Glendale, California, on October 18, 1956, when her age was 57 years 129 days.

The incidence of quinquagenarian births varies widely with the highest known rate in Albania (nearly 5,500 per million).

Descendants

In polygamous countries, the number of a person's descendants soon becomes incalculable. The last Sharifian Emperor of Morocco, Moulay Ismail (1672–1727), known as "The Bloodthirsty," was reputed to have fathered a total of 548 sons and 340 daughters.

Capt. Wilson Kettle (born 1860) of Grand Bay, Port Aux Basques, Newfoundland, Canada, died on January 25, 1963, aged 102, leaving 11 children by two wives, 65 grandchildren, 201 great-grandchildren, and 305 great-great-grandchildren, a total of 582 living descendants. Mrs. Johanna Booyson (see table, page 29), of Belfast, Transvaal, was estimated to have 600 living descendants in South Africa in January, 1968.

Multiple Great-Grandparents

Theoretically a great-great-great-great-grandparent is a possibility, although, in practice, countries in which young mothers are common generally have a low expectation of life. The case of a 97-year-old woman in the U.S. was reported in June, 1973, who had four great-great-great-grandchildren among her 67 living descendants, while Hon. General Walter Washington Williams (1855–1959) of Houston, Texas, was reportedly several times a great-great-great-grandfather.

Mrs. Alice Jones Miller Eierdam (b. December 15, 1875) of St. Maries, Idaho, held her granddaughter's great-grandchild Shasta (b. November 18, 1973) in her arms. Similarly in 1973, Mrs. Alvena Dan Liming (b. January 3, 1877) sat in a six-generation photograph with her great-great-great-granddaughter Mollie Marie Rettinger (b. October 8, 1972). In April, 1975, Mrs. Hattie Brooks of Texas learned that her great-granddaughter, Mrs. Robert Alexander, had become a grandmother with the birth of Michelle Crist.

MULTIPLE BIRTHS

Highest number reported at single birth (Decaplets):
10 (2 male, 8 female), Bacacay, Brazil, April 22, 1946 (also report from Spain, 1924, and China, May 12, 1936).

Highest number medically recorded (Nonuplets):
9 (5 male, 4 female), to Mrs. Geraldine Broderick at Royal Hospital, Sydney, Australia, June 13, 1971. 2 males were stillborn. Richard (12 oz.) survived 6 days.

9 (all also died), to patient at University of Pennsylvania, Philadelphia, May 29, 1972.

Highest number surviving:
6 out of 6 sextuplets (3 males, 3 females), to Mrs. Susan Rosenkowitz (née Scoones) at Capetown, South Africa, January 11, 1974. In order of birth they were: David, Nicolette, Jason, Emma, Grant and Elizabeth. They totaled 24 lbs. 1 oz.

Quintuplets (Heaviest):
25 lbs., to Mrs. Lui Saulien, Chekiang, China, June 7, 1953.

(Most sets):
25 lbs., to Mrs. Kamalammal, Pondicherry, India, December 30, 1956.

No recorded case of more than a single set.

Quadruplets (Heaviest):
21 lbs. 9 oz. to Mrs. David Bergquist, University of Minnesota Hospital, Minneapolis (4 girls).

(Most sets):
4, to Mme. Fyodor Vassilet (d. 1872), of Moscow Jurisdiction, Russia.

Triplets (Heaviest):
26 lbs. 6 oz. (unconfirmed), Iranian case (2 male, 1 female), March 18, 1968.

(Most sets):
15, to Maddalena Granata (1839–fl. 1886), Nocera Superiore, Italy.

Twins (Heaviest):
35 lbs. 8 oz. (live-born), Warren's case (2 males), reported in The Lancet from Derbyshire, England, December 6, 1884.

27 lbs. 12 oz. (surviving), to Mrs. J. P. Haskin, Fort Smith, Arkansas, February 20, 1924.

(Most sets):
16, to Mme. Vassilet (see above).

15, to Mrs. Mary Jones (d. December 4, 1899), of Chester, England—all sets were boy and girl.

SEXTUPLETS: The Rosenkowitz sextuplets of Capetown, South Africa, were born January 11, 1974.

Multiple Births

With multiple births, as with giants and centenarians, exaggeration is the rule. Since 1900, two cases of nonuplets, five cases of octuplets, 19 cases of septuplets and at least 23 cases of sextuplets have been reported. Jamaica has the highest incidence of multiple births (*i.e.* triplet and upward) at 4 per 1,000.

It was announced by Dr. Gennaro Montanino of Rome that he had removed the fetuses of ten girls and five boys from the womb of a 35-year-old housewife on July 22, 1971. A fertility drug was responsible for this unique and unsurpassed instance of quindecaplets.

Earliest Surviving Quintuplets. The earliest set of quintuplets in which all survived were the Dionnes: Emilie (died August 6, 1954, aged 20), Yvonne (now in a convent), Cecile (now Mrs. Philippe Langlois), Marie (later Mrs. Florian Houle, died February 28, 1970) and Annette (now Mrs. Germain Allard), born in her seventh pregnancy to Mrs. Olivia Dionne, aged 25, near Callander, Ontario, Canada, on May 28, 1934 (aggregate weight 13 lbs. 6 oz. with an average of 2 lbs. 11 oz.).

Oldest Surviving Triplets. The longest-lived triplets were Faith, Hope, and Charity Caughlin, born on March 27, 1868, in Marlboro, Massachusetts. Mrs. (Ellen) Hope Daniels was the first to die on March 2, 1962, when she was 93.

Fastest. The fastest recorded natural birth of triplets was to Mrs.

LIGHTEST TWINS: Margaret and Mary Stimson, born on August 16, 1931, in England, together weighed only 2 lbs. 3 oz.

John R. Tyler of Houston, Texas, who gave birth to three girls—Linda Lee, Carol Lynn and Brenda Sue—between 2:00 p.m. and 2:03 p.m. on July 29, 1952.

Twins

Heaviest. The heaviest recorded live-born twins were two boys, the first weighing 17 lbs. 8 oz. and the second 18 lbs., born in Derbyshire, England. This was reported in a letter in *The Lancet* of December 6, 1884. The heaviest recorded surviving twins were John and Jane Haskin weighing 14 lbs. and 13¾ lbs., born to Mrs. J. P. Haskin on February 20, 1924, in Fort Smith, Arkansas.

Lightest. The lightest recorded birth weight for surviving twins is 2 lbs. 3 oz. in the case of Mary (16 oz.) and Margaret (19 oz.) born to Mrs. Florence Stimson of Peterborough, England, delivered by Dr. Macaulay, on August 16, 1931.

Oldest. The oldest recorded twins were Gulbrand and Bernt Morterud, born at Nord Odal, Norway, on December 20, 1858. Bernt died on August 1, 1960, in Chicago, aged 101, and his brother died at Nord Odal on January 12, 1964, aged 105.

Twin sisters, Mrs. Vassilka Dermendjhieva and Mrs. Vassila

SIAMESE TWINS: Born in 1811 in Siam, the twins Chang and Eng Bunker married sisters at age 32 and fathered 10 and 12 children respectively.

Yapourdjieva of Sofia, Bulgaria, allegedly celebrated their joint 104th birthday on September 27, 1966.

The chances of identical twins both reaching 100 are said to be one in 1,000 million.

"Siamese." Conjoined twins derived this name from the celebrated Chang and Eng Bunker, born at Maklong, Thailand (Siam), on May 11, 1811. They were joined by a cartilaginous band at the chest and married in April, 1843, the Misses Sarah and Adelaide Yates. They fathered ten and twelve children respectively. They died within three hours of each other on January 17, 1874, aged 62.

There is no genealogical evidence for the existence of the Chalkhurst twins, Mary and Aliza, of Biddenden, England, allegedly born in c. 1550. Daisy and Violet Hilton, born in Brighton, England, on February 5, 1908, were joined at the hip. They died in Charlotte, North Carolina, on January 5, 1969, aged 60.

The earliest successful separation of Siamese twins was performed on Prisna and Napit Atkinson (b. May, 1953, in Thailand) by Dr. Dragstedt at the University of Chicago on March 29, 1955.

The rarest form of conjoined twins is Dicephales tetrabrachius dipus (two heads, four arms and two legs) of which only one example is known to exist today—in Russia. In a Brazilian case, two girls, Juraci and Nadir Climerio de Oliveira, were born in the interior of Bahia State in 1962 and lived permanently at the Climerio de Oliveira Maternity Hospital in Salvador, sharing one intestinal and renal system until they died in 1974. The Russian pair, Masha and Dasha, were born on January 4, 1950.

BABIES

Largest. The heaviest normal newborn child recorded in modern times was a boy weighing 24 lbs. 4 oz., born on June 3, 1961, to Mrs. Saadet Cor of Cegham, southern Turkey.

A report from Dezful, southwest Iran, that Mrs. Massoumeh Valizadeh or Valli-Ullah, aged 32, had given birth to a 26 lb. 6½ oz. boy on February 7, 1972, was later officially stated to be incorrect. There is an unconfirmed report of a woman giving birth to a 27-lb.

baby in Essonnes, a suburb of Corbeil, France, in June, 1929. A deformed baby weighing 29¼ lbs. was born in May, 1939, in a hospital at Effingham, Illinois but only lived for two hours.

Most Bouncing Baby. The most bouncing baby on record was probably James Weir (1819–1821) whose headstone in the Old Parish Cemetery, Wishaw, Strathclyde, Scotland, lists him at 112 lbs., 3 feet 4 inches in height, and 39 inches around the waist at the age of 13 months.

Therese Parentean, who died in Rouyn, Quebec, Canada, aged 9, on May 11, 1936, weighed 340 lbs.

Smallest. The lowest birth weight for a surviving infant, of which there is definite evidence, is 10 oz. in the case of Marion Chapman, born on June 5, 1938, in South Shields, northwest England. She was 12¼ inches long. By her first birthday her weight had increased to 13 lbs. 14 oz. She was born unattended, and was nursed by Dr. D. A. Shearer, who fed her hourly through a fountain pen filler. Her weight on her 21st birthday was 106 lbs.

A weight of 8 oz. was reported on March 20, 1938, for a baby born prematurely to Mrs. John Womack, after she had been knocked down by a truck in East St. Louis, Illinois. The baby was taken alive to St. Mary's Hospital, but further information is lacking. On February 23, 1952, it was reported that a 6 oz. baby only 6½ inches in length lived for 12 hours in a hospital in Indianapolis. A twin was stillborn.

Longest Pregnancy. Claims of pregnancies lasting up to 413 days have been widely reported, but accurate data are bedevilled by the increasing use of oral contraceptive pills, which is a cause of amenorrhea. Some women on becoming pregnant erroneously add some preceding periodless months to their pregnancy. In the pre-pill era, English law had accepted pregnancies with extremes of 174 days (1939), and 349 days (1949).

Coincidental Birth Dates. The only verified example of a family producing five single children with coincidental birthdays is that of Catherine (1952); Carol (1953); Charles (1956); Claudia (1961) and Cecilia (1966), born to Ralph and Carolyn Cummins of Clintwood, Virginia, all on February 20th. The odds are calculable at about 3,900 million to one against which closely coincides with the world population. The odds against 5 such births occurring singly on the same date would at random be 1 to 17,748,855,000.

5. Physiology and Anatomy

A U.S. scientific publication in 1975 set a value of $5.60 on the raw materials in an average-weight human body. It may be a commentary on world inflation that a 1936 figure was 98¢. Hydrogen (63%) and oxygen (25.5%) are the commonest of the 24 elements in the human body. In 1972, four more trace elements were added—fluorine, silicon, tin and vanadium. The "essentiality" of nickel has not yet been finally pronounced upon.

SMALLEST WAIST: Mrs. Ethel Granger of England, with a 13-inch waist, has the tiniest beltline for a normal-sized person.

Bones

Longest. The thigh bone or *femur* is the longest of the 206 bones in the human body. It constitutes usually $27\frac{1}{2}$ per cent of a person's stature, and may be expected to be $19\frac{3}{4}$ inches long in a 6-foot-tall man. The longest recorded bone was the *femur* of the German giant Constantine, who died in Mons, Belgium, on March 30, 1902, aged 30. It measured 29.9 inches. The *femur* of Robert Wadlow, the tallest man ever recorded, measured approximately $29\frac{1}{2}$ inches.

Smallest. The *stapes* or stirrup bone, one of the three auditory ossicles in the middle ear, is the smallest human bone, measuring from 2.6 to 3.4 millimeters (0.10 to 0.17 of an inch) in length and weighing from 2.0 to 4.3 milligrams (0.03 to 0.065 of a grain). Sesamoids are not included among human bones.

Muscles

Largest. Muscles normally account for 40 per cent of the body weight and the bulkiest of the 639 muscles in the human body is the *gluteus maximus* or buttock muscle, which extends the thigh.

Smallest. The smallest muscle is the *stapedius*, which controls the *stapes* (see above), an auditory ossicle in the middle ear, and which is less than 1/20th of an inch in length.

Smallest Waists

Queen Catherine de Médici (1519–89) decreed a standard waist measurement of 13 inches for ladies of the French court. This was at a time when females were more diminutive. The smallest recorded waist among women of normal stature in the 20th century is a reputed 13 inches in the case of the French actress Mlle. Polaire (1881–1939) and Mrs. Ethel Granger (born April 12, 1905) of Peterborough, England, who reduced from a natural 22 inches over the period 1929–39.

Largest Chest Measurements

The largest chest measurements are among endomorphs (those with a tendency toward globularity). In the extreme case of Robert Earl Hughes of Monticello, Illinois (the heaviest recorded human), this was reportedly 124 inches, but in the light of his known height and weight a figure of 104 inches would be more supportable. Among muscular subjects (mesomorphs), chest measurements above 56 inches are extremely rare. The largest such chest measurement ever recorded is one of 67 inches in the case of Bruce Wayne Richardson of Salt Lake City, who was measured on November 7, 1975. He stands 5 feet $7\frac{1}{2}$ inches tall, weighed $206\frac{3}{4}$ lbs. and has bench-pressed 500 lbs.

Brain

The brain has 1.5×10^{10} cells each containing 10^{10} macromolecules. Each cell has 10^4 interconnections with other cells. At the age of 18 the brain loses some 10^3 cells every day but the macromolecular content of each cell is renewed 10^4 times in a normal life span.

Largest. The brain of an average adult male (30–59 years) weighs 3 lbs. 1.73 oz., falling to 2 lbs. 4.31 oz. The heaviest brain ever recorded was that of a 50-year-old white male which weighed 4 lbs. 8.29 oz., reported by Dr. Thomas F. Hegert, Chief Medical Examiner for District 9, State of Florida, October 23, 1975. The brain of Oliver Cromwell (1599–1658) reputedly weighed 4 lbs. 14.8 oz., but the size of his head in portraits does not support this extreme figure. The brain of Lord Byron, who died in Greece in 1824, aged 36, reportedly weighed 6 Neopolitan pounds (4 lbs. 3.86 oz.), but this figure also included a certain amount of blood. In January, 1891, the *Edinburgh Medical Journal* reported a case of a 75-year-old man in the Royal Edinburgh Asylum whose brain weighed 4 lbs. 0.5 oz.

Smallest. The brain of Anatole France (1844–1924), the French writer, weighed only 2 lbs. 4 oz. without the membrane, but there was some shrinkage due to old age. His brain probably weighed *c.* 2 lbs. 7.78 oz. at its heaviest.

Brains in extreme cases of microcephaly may weigh as little as 10.6 oz. (*cf.* 20 oz. for the adult male gorilla, and 16–20 oz. for other anthropoid apes).

Longest Necks

The maximum measured extension of the neck by the successive fitting of copper coils, as practiced by the Padaung or Karen people of Burma, is $15\frac{3}{4}$ inches. From the male viewpoint the practice serves the dual purpose of enhancing the beauty of the female and ensuring fidelity. The neck muscles become so atrophied that the removal of the support of the rings produces asphyxiation.

Most Fingers

In 1938, the extreme case of a baby girl with 14 fingers and 12 toes was reported by St. George's Hospital, Hyde Park, London.

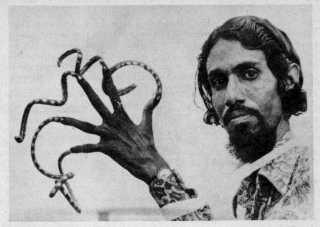

LONGEST FINGER NAILS: The length of the nails on the left hand of Murari Mohan Aditya of Calcutta, India, totals 66½ inches. The longest, on his ring finger, extends over 13 inches. He has given each nail a separate name.

Longest Finger Nails

The longest recorded finger nails were reported from Shanghai in 1910, in the case of a Chinese priest who took 27 years to achieve nails up to 22¾ inches in length. Probably the longest single nail now grown is owned by Romesh Sharma of Delhi, India. It is 22½ inches long after 10 years.

The longest known set of nails now belong to the left hand of Murari Mohan Aditya, 31, of Calcutta, India. They have grown since March, 1962 to 66½ inches. Human nails normally grow from cuticle to cutting length in from 117 to 138 days.

Longest Moustache

The longest moustache on record is that of Masuriya Din (born 1908), a Brahmin of the Partabgarh district in Uttar Pradesh, India. It grew to an extended span of 102 inches between 1949 and 1962, and costs over $30 per year in upkeep.

MOUSTACHE AT LEAST 102 INCHES LONG: The longest moustache on record belongs to Masuriya Din of India.

Touch Sensitivity

The extreme sensitivity of the fingers is such that a vibration with a movement of 0.02 of a micron can be detected. On January 12, 1963, the Soviet newspaper *Izvestia* reported the case of a totally blindfolded girl, Rosa Kulgeshova, who was able to identify colors by touch alone. Later reports confirmed in 1970 that under rigorous test conditions, this claimed ability totally disappeared.

Longest Hair

The longest recorded hair was that of Swami Pandarasannadhi, the head of the Thiruvadu Thurai monastery, India. His hair was reported in 1949 to be 26 feet in length and, being matted, he was doubtless suffering from the disease Plica caudiformis. The hair of Jane Bunford (see page 16) which she wore in two plaits, reached down to her ankles, indicating a length in excess of 8 feet.

Longest Beard

The longest beard preserved was that of Hans Langseth (1846–1927) of Norway, which measured $17\frac{1}{2}$ feet at the time of his death in 1927, after 15 years residence in the U.S. The beard was presented to the Smithsonian Institution, Washington, D.C. in 1967.

The beard of the bearded lady Janice Deveree (born in Bracken County, Kentucky, in 1842) was measured at 14 inches in 1884.

Commonest Illness

The commonest illness in the world is coryza (acute nasopharyngitis) or the common cold.

Commonest Disease

The commonest disease in the world is dental caries or tooth decay, known to afflict over 53 per cent of the population of the U.S. During their lifetime few completely escape its effects. Infestation with pinworm (*Enterobius vermicularis*) approaches 100 per cent in some areas of the world.

Rarest Disease

Medical literature periodically records hitherto undescribed diseases. Kuru, or laughing sickness, afflicts only the Fore tribe of eastern New Guinea and is 100 per cent fatal. It is transmitted by the cannibalistic practice of eating human brains.

The only recorded case of congenital agammaglobulinaemia was reported from Houston, Texas, in February, 1972. A disease as yet undescribed but predicted is podocytoma of the kidney—a tumor of the epithelial cells lining the glomerulus of the kidney.

Highest Morbidity

Rabies in humans is uniformly fatal when associated with the hydrophobia symptom. A 25-year-old woman, Candida de Sousa Barbosa of Rio de Janeiro, Brazil, was believed to be the first ever to survive the disease in November, 1968. Some sources give priority to Matthew Winkler, 6, in 1970. In 1969, all 515 cases reported were fatal.

Most and Least Infectious Diseases

The most infectious of all diseases is the pneumonic form of plague, with a mortality rate of 99.99 per cent. Leprosy transmitted by *Mycobacterium leprae* is the least infectious of communicable diseases.

Most Notorious Carrier

The most notorious of all typhoid carriers was Mary Mallon, known as Typhoid Mary, of New York City. She was the source of the 1903 outbreak with 1,300 cases. Because of her refusal to leave employment, often under assumed names, involving the handling of food, she was placed under permanent detention from 1915 until her death in 1938.

Blood Groups

The preponderance of one blood group varies greatly from one locality to another. On a world basis Group O is the most common (46 per cent), but in some areas, for example Norway, Group A predominates.

The rarest blood group on the ABO system, one of nine systems, is AB. The rarest type in the world is a type of Bombay blood (sub-type A-h) found so far only in a Czechoslovak nurse in 1961 and in a brother (Rh positive) and sister (Rh negative) named Jalbert in Massachusetts, reported in February, 1968. The brother has started a blood bank for himself.

Champion Blood Donor

Ed "Spike" Howard (1877–1946), the professional strongman from Philadelphia, during his life donated a total of 1,056 pints of blood.

Joe Thomas of Detroit was reported in August, 1970, to have the highest known count of Anti-Lewis B, the rare blood antibody. A U.S. biological supply firm pays him $1,500 per quart—an income of $12,000 per annum. The Internal Revenue regards this income as a taxable liquid asset.

Largest Vein

In the human body, the largest is the vein known as the inferior *vena cava*, which returns most of the blood from the body below the level of the heart.

Blood Transfusion

The greatest recorded blood infusion is 2,400 pints, required by a 50-year-old hemophiliac, Warren C. Jyrich, when undergoing open heart surgery at the Michael Reese Hospital, Chicago, in December, 1970.

Longest Coma

The longest period of human unconsciousness ever recorded is that of Elaine Esposito (born December 3, 1934) of Tarpon Springs, Florida. She has never stirred since an appendectomy on August 6, 1941, when she was six, in Chicago. On December 6, 1974, she had been in a coma for 33 years 4 months—a third of a century.

Temperature

Highest. Temperatures of up to 107.6°F. are induced and maintained in robust subjects undergoing pyrexial therapy. Sustained body temperatures of much over 109°F. are normally incompatible with life, although recoveries after readings of 111°F. have been noted. Marathon runners in hot weather attain 105.8°F.

In a case reported in the British medical magazine, *Lancet* (October 31, 1970), a woman following halothane anesthesia ran a temperature of 112° F. She recovered after a procainamide infusion.

A temperature of 115°F. was recorded in the case of Christopher Legge in the Hospital for Tropical Diseases, London, England, on February 9, 1934. A subsequent examination of the thermometer disclosed a flaw in the bulb, but it is regarded as certain that the patient sustained a temperature of more than 110°F.

Lowest. There are two recorded cases of patients surviving body temperatures as low as 60.8°F. Dorothy Mae Stevens (1929–74), was found in an alley in Chicago on February 1, 1951, and Vickie Mary Davis of Milwaukee, Wisconsin, at age 2 years 1 month was admitted to the Evangelical Hospital, Marshalltown, Iowa, on January 21, 1956, also with a temperature of 60.8°F. She had been found unconscious on the floor of an unheated house and the air temperature had dropped to −24°F. Her temperature returned to normal (98.4°F.) after 12 hours and may have been as low as 59°F. when she was first found.

Pulse Rate

A normal adult pulse rate is 70–72 beats per minute at rest for males, and 78–82 for females. This can increase to 200 or more during violent exercise or drop to as low as 12 in the extreme case of Dorothy Mae Stevens (see Lowest Temperature).

Heart Stoppage

The longest recorded heart stoppage is 3 hours in the case of a Norwegian boy, Roger Arntzen, in April, 1962. He was rescued, apparently drowned, after 22 minutes under the waters of the River Nideelv, near Trondheim.

The longest recorded interval in a post-mortem birth was one of at least 80 minutes in Magnolia, Mississippi. Dr. Robert E. Drake found Fanella Anderson, aged 25, dead in her home at 11:40 p.m. on October 15, 1966, and he delivered her of a son weighing 6 lbs. 4 oz. by Caesarean operation in the Beacham Memorial Hospital at 1 a.m. on October 16, 1966.

Largest Stone

The largest stone or vesical calculus reported in medical literature was one of 13 lbs. 14 oz., removed from an 80-year-old woman by Dr. Humphrey Arthure at Charing Cross Hospital, London, England, on December 29, 1952.

Fastest Reflexes

The results of experiments carried out in 1943 have shown that the fastest messages transmitted by the nervous system travel at 265 m.p.h. With advancing age, impulses are carried 15 per cent more slowly.

Most Alcoholic Person

It is recorded that a hard drinker named Vanhorn (1750–1811), born in London, England, averaged more than four bottles of ruby port per day for 23 years prior to his death at 61. He is believed to have emptied 35,688 bottles.

The youngest recorded death from alcoholic poisoning was that of an 8-year-old boy in Redon, France, in October, 1965. He worked in his uncle's bar.

Hiccoughing

The longest recorded attack of hiccoughs was that afflicting Charles Osborne (b. 1894) of Anthon, Iowa, from 1922 to date. He contracted it when slaughtering a hog. His first wife left him and he is unable to keep in his false teeth.

The infirmary at Newcastle upon Tyne, England, is recorded to have admitted a young man from Long Witton, Northumberland, on March 25, 1769, suffering from hiccoughs which could be heard at a range of more than a mile.

Sneezing

The most chronic sneezing fit ever recorded was that of June Clark, aged 17, of Miami, Florida. She started sneezing on January 4, 1966, while recovering from a kidney ailment in the James M. Jackson Memorial Hospital, Miami. The sneezing was stopped by electric "aversion" treatment on June 8, 1966, after 155 days. The highest speed at which expelled particles have been measured to travel is 103.6 m.p.h.

Loudest Snore

Research at the Ear, Nose and Throat Department of St. Mary's Hospital, London, published in November, 1968, shows that a rasping snore can attain a loudness of 69 decibels.

Yawning

In a case reported in 1888, a 15-year-old female patient yawned continuously for a period of five weeks.

Swallowing

The worst reported case of compulsive swallowing was an insane woman, Mrs. H., aged 42, who complained of a "slight abdominal pain." She was found to have 2,533 objects in her stomach, including 947 bent pins. They were removed by Drs. Chalk and Foucar in June, 1927, at the Ontario Hospital, Canada.

The heaviest object ever extracted from a human stomach was a 5-lb. 3-oz. ball of hair, from a 20-year-old woman at the South Devon and East Cornwall Hospital, England, on March 20, 1895.

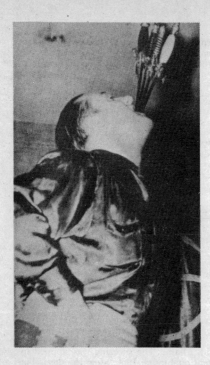

"SWALLOWS" FOUR SWORDS: Alex Linton from Ireland shows how he "swallows" four 27-inch blades at one time.

Swallowing Foreign Objects

The most extreme recorded case of coin swallowing was revealed by Sedgefield General Hospital, County Durham, England, on January 5, 1958, when it was reported that 366 halfpennies, 26 sixpences, 17 threepences, 11 pennies, and four shillings (424 coins valued at about $5) and 27 pieces of wire totaling 5 lbs. 1 oz. had been extracted from the stomach of a 54-year-old man.

Another similar case was revealed at Metropolitan Hospital, New York City, on May 25, 1976, when physicians operated on a 38-year-old, 155-lb. man who was a mental patient. In his stomach were discovered more than 300 coins (quarters, dimes, nickels, pennies and subway tokens), plus broken thermometers, can openers, parts of knives, forks, spoons, nuts, bolts, a chain and keys. The patient's esophagus and intestinal tract were not damaged, and he survived the operation.

Sword "Swallowing"

The longest length of sword able to be "swallowed" by a practiced exponent, after a heavy meal, is 27 inches. Perhaps the greatest exponent is Alex Linton, born on October 25, 1904, in Boyle,

County Roscommon, Ireland. Sandra Dee Reed (Lady Sandra) of Florida has swallowed five 30-inch blades to two-thirds of their length simultaneously.

Pill Taking

It is recorded that among hypochondriacs Samuel Jessup (born 1752), a wealthy grazier of Heckington, Lincolnshire, England, has never had a modern rival. His consumption of pills from 1794 to 1816 was 226,934, with a peak annual total of 51,590 in 1814. He is also recorded as having drunk 40,000 bottles of medicine before death overtook him at the surprisingly advanced age of 65.

Most Tattoos

Vivian "Sailor Joe" Simmons, a Canadian tattoo artist, had 4,831 tattoos on his body. He died in Toronto on December 22, 1965, aged 77.

The most decorated woman is Rusty Field (born 1944) of Aldershot, Hampshire, England, who, after 12 years under the needle of tattoo artist Bill Skuse, is within 15 per cent of totality.

Dentition

Earliest. The first deciduous or milk teeth normally appear in infants at five to eight months, these being the mandibular and maxillary first incisors. There are many records of children born with teeth, the most distinguished example being Prince Louis Dieudonné, later Louis XIV of France, who was born with two teeth on September 5, 1638. Molars usually appear at 24 months, but in Pindborg's case published in Denmark in 1970, a 6-week premature baby was documented with 8 natal teeth of which 4 were in the molar region.

Most. Cases of the growth in late life of a third set of teeth have been recorded several times. A reference to an extreme case in France of a fourth dentition known as Lison's case was published in 1896. A triple row of teeth was noted in 1680 by Albertus Hellwigius.

Most Dedicated Dentist. Brother Giovanni Battista Orsenigo of the Ospedale Fatebenefratelli, Rome, Italy, a religious dentist, conserved all the teeth he extracted in three enormous boxes during the time he exercised his profession from 1868 to 1904. In 1903, the number was counted and found to be 2,000,744 teeth.

Fire-Eating

Peter De-Valle (né Peter Ashton, April 29, 1950) blew a flame from his mouth to a distance of 19 feet 8 inches in The Rugby Cattle Market, England, on October 28, 1975.

Fire-Walking

The highest temperature endured in a fire-walk is 1,183°F. for 25 feet by "Komar" (Vernon E. Craig) of Wooster, Ohio, at the Phoenix Psychic Seminar, Arizona, on March 7, 1975. The temperature was measured by a pyrometer.

HOTTEST FIRE-WALK (left): Vernon E. Craig ("Komar") of Wooster, Ohio, endured a temperature of 1,183°F. in a 25-foot walk through hot coals. YOUNGEST FIRE-WALKER (right): 11-year-old Maikeli Masi treads on white-hot 400-degree coals in ceremony in Fiji.

The youngest person to walk on white-hot coals (of 400° F.) was Maikeli Masi, aged 11, outside the Korolevu Beach Hotel, Fiji, on December 15, 1972.

Smallest Visible Object

The resolving power of the human eye is 0.0003 of a radian or an arc of one minute (1/60th of a degree), which corresponds to 100 microns at 10 inches. A micron is a thousandth of a millimeter, hence 100 microns is 0.003937, or less than four thousandths, of an inch. The human eye can, however, detect a bright light source shining through an aperture of only 3 to 4 microns across. In October, 1972, the University of Stuttgart, West Germany reported that their student Veronica Seider (b. 1953) possessed a visual acuity 20 times better than average. She could identify people at a distance of more than a mile.

Color Sensitivity

The unaided human eye, under the best possible viewing conditions, comparing large areas of color, in good illumination, using both eyes, can distinguish 10,000,000 different color surfaces. The most accurate photo-electric spectrophotometers possess a precision probably only 40 per cent as good as this.

Color Blindness. The most extreme form of color blindness, monochromatic vision, is very rare. The highest rate of red-green color blindness exists in Czechoslovakia and the lowest rate among Fijians and Brazilian Indians. About 7.5 per cent of men and 0.1 per cent of women are color blind.

Voice

Highest and Lowest. The highest and lowest recorded notes attained by the human voice before this century were a C in *alt-altissimo* (*c''''*) by Lucrezia Agujari (1743–83), noted by the Austrian composer, Wolfgang Amadeus Mozart (1756–91) in Parma, northern Italy, in 1770, and an *A'* (55 cycles per second) by Kaspar Foster (1617–73). Since 1950 singers have achieved high and low notes far beyond the hitherto accepted extremes. Notes, however, at the bass and treble extremities of the register tend to lack harmonics and are of little musical value. Fraulein Marita Günther, trained by Alfred Wolfsohn, has covered the range of the piano from the lowest note *A''* to *C''''*. Of this range of 7¼ octaves, 6 octaves are considered to be of musical value. Mr. Roy Hart, also trained by Wolfsohn, has reached notes below the range of the piano.

Madeleine Marie Robin (1918–60), the French operatic coloratura, could produce and sustain the B flat above high C in the Lucia mad scene in *Lucia di Lammermoor*.

The highest note sung by a tenor is G in *alt-altissimo* by Louis Lavelle, coached by Mr. S. Pleeth, in *Lovely Mary Donelly*. The lowest note put into song is *D''* by the singer Tom King, of King's Langley, Hertfordshire, England. The highest note called for in singing was an *f'''' ♯*, which occurred twice in Zerbinetta's Recitative and Aria in the first (1912) version of the opera *Ariadne auf Naxos* by Richard Strauss (1864–1949). It was transposed down a tone in 1916.

Greatest Range. The normal intelligible outdoor range of the male human voice in still air is 200 yards. The *silbo*, the whistled language of the Spanish-speaking Canary Island of La Gomera, is intelligible across the valleys, under ideal conditions, at 5 miles. There is a recorded case, under freak acoustic conditions, of the human voice being detectable at a distance of 10½ miles across still water at night. It was said that Mills Darden (see Heaviest Man) could be heard 6 miles away when he shouted at the top of his voice.

Lowest Detectable Sound. The intensity of noise or sound is measured in terms of power. The power of the quietest sound that can be detected by a person of normal hearing at the most sensitive frequency of *c.* 2.750 Hz is 1.0×10^{-16} of a watt per square centimeter. One tenth of the logarithm (to the base 10) of the ratio of the power of a noise to this standard provides a unit termed a decibel. Noises above 150 decibels will cause immediate permanent deafness and at 200 decibels may be fatal, while a noise of 30 decibels is negligible.

Highest Detectable Pitch. The upper limit of hearing by the human ear has been regarded as 20,000 Hz (cycles per second), although children with asthma can often detect a sound of 30,000 cycles per second. It was announced in February, 1964, that ex-

SHOUTING RECORD BREAKER: Mrs. Margaret Featherstone informs the gentlemen at the bar that closing time is nigh.

periments in the U.S.S.R. had conclusively proved that oscillations as high as 200,000 cycles per second can be heard if the oscillator is pressed against the skull.

Shouting. At the "World" Shouting Competition at Scarborough, Yorkshire, England, held on February 17, 1973, the title was taken by Skipper Kenny Leader with 111 decibels. Mrs. Margaret Featherstone hit the feminine record of 109.7 decibels on June 12, 1974.

Longest Survival in Iron Lung

The longest recorded survival by an iron lung patient is 31 years by Lee Hale (born 1912) of Crockett, Virginia. Paul Bates of Horsham, West Sussex, England entered his 23rd year on a mechanical positive pressure respirator on August 13, 1975. During 21 years, he received 155,585,115 respirations into his lungs via his trachea.

Operations

Longest. The most protracted operations are those involving brain surgery. Such an operation lasting up to 31 hours was performed on Victor Zazueta, 19, of El Centro at San Diego Hospital, California, by Dr. John F. Alksne and his team on January 17–18, 1972.

Oldest Subject. The greatest recorded age at which a person has been subjected to an operation is 111 years 105 days in the case of James Henry Brett, Jr. (born July 25, 1849, died February 10, 1961) of Houston, Texas. He underwent a hip operation on November 7, 1960.

Youngest Subject. Babies are now increasingly operated on within minutes of birth so there is no specific record for the youngest subject.

Heart Transplants

The first human heart transplant operation was performed on Louis Washkansky, aged 55, at the Groote Schuur Hospital, Cape Town, South Africa, between 1:00 and 6:00 a.m. on December 3, 1967, by a team of 30 headed by Prof. Christiaan N. Barnard (born 1922). The donor was Miss Denise Ann Darvall, aged 25. Washkansky died on December 21, 1967.

The longest surviving heart transplant patient is Mrs. Betty Anick of Milwaukee, Wisconsin, who received her replacement heart on October 23, 1968, and was still flourishing on July 1, 1975.

Laryngectomy

On July 24, 1924, John I. Poole of Plymouth, England, then aged 33, after diagnosis of carcinoma, underwent total laryngectomy in Edinburgh, Scotland. In July, 1974, he entered his 51st year as a "neck-breather."

Earliest Appendectomy

The earliest recorded successful appendix operation was performed in 1736 by Claudius Amyand (1680–1740). He was Serjeant Surgeon to King George II (reigned 1727–60) of Great Britain.

Earliest Anesthesia

The earliest recorded operation under general anesthesia was for the removal of a cyst from the neck of James Venable by Dr. Crawford Williamson Long (1815–78), using diethyl ether ($(C_2 H_5)_2 O$), in Jefferson, Georgia, on March 30, 1842.

Surgical Instruments

The longest surgical instruments are bronchoscopic forceps which measure up to $23\frac{1}{2}$ inches over-all. Robot-retractors for abdominal surgery made by Abbey Surgical of England weigh 11 lbs. The smallest is Elliot's eye trephine which has a blade 0.078 of an inch in diameter.

Fastest Amputation

The shortest time recorded for the amputation of a leg in the pre-anesthetic era was 13 to 15 seconds by Napoleon's chief surgeon, Dominique Larrey.

Fasting

Most humans experience considerable discomfort after an abstinence from food for even 12 hours, but this often passes off after 24–48 hours. Records claimed without unremitting medical surveillance are of little value.

The longest period for which anyone has gone without solid food is 382 days by Angus Barbieri (born 1940) of Tayport, Fife, Scotland. He lived on tea, coffee, water, soda water and vitamins from June, 1965, to July, 1966, in Maryfield Hospital, Dundee, Angus, Scotland. His weight declined from 472 lbs. to 178 lbs.

Sister Therese Neuman survived 35 years on the "bread" of the Holy Eucharist at mass each morning at Konnersreuth, Germany.

Hunger Strike

The longest recorded hunger strike was one of 94 days by John and Peter Crowley, Thomas Donovan, Michael Burke, Michael O'Reilly, Christopher Upton, John Power, Joseph Kenny and Sean Hennessy in Cork Prison, Ireland, from August 11 to November 12, 1920. These nine survivors owed their lives to expert medical attention.

Fastest Talker

Extremely few people are able to speak articulately at a sustained speed above 300 words per minute. The fastest broadcaster has usually been allowed to be Gerry Wilmot, the Canadian ice hockey commentator in the post World War II period. Raymond Glendenning (1907–74) of the British Broadcasting Corp. once spoke 176 words in 30 seconds while commentating on a greyhound race. In public life the highest speed recorded is a 327-words-per-minute burst in a speech made in December, 1961, by John Fitzgerald Kennedy (1917–63), then President of the U.S. Tapes of attempts to recite Hamlet's 262-word soliloquy in under 24 seconds (655 w.p.m.) have proved indecipherable. A computer-based speech synthesis system is reported to be under development in the United States.

Human Memory

Mehmed Ali Halici of Ankara, Turkey, on October 14, 1967, recited 6,666 verses of the Koran from memory in six hours. The recitation was followed by six Koran scholars. Rare instances of eidetic memory, the ability to reproject and thus "visually" recall material, are known to science.

Highest I.Q.

On the Terman index for Intelligence Quotients, 150 represents genius level. The indices are sometimes held to be immeasurable above a level of 200, but a figure of 210 has been attributed to Kim Ung-Yong of Seoul, South Korea (born March 7, 1963). He composed poetry and spoke four languages (Korean, English, German and Japanese), and performed integral calculus at the age of 4 years 8 months on television in Tokyo on "The World Surprise Show" on November 2, 1967. Both his parents are university professors and were both born at 11 a.m. on May 23, 1934. Research into past geniuses at Stanford University, California, has produced a figure of "over 200" for John Stuart Mill (1806–73), who began to learn ancient Greek at the age of three. A similar rating has also been attributed to Emanuel Swedenborg (1688–1772) and Johann Wolfgang von Goethe (1749–1832). More than 20 per cent of the 22,000 members of the international Mensa society have an I.Q. of 161 or above on the Cattell index which is equivalent to 142 on the Terman index.

HUMAN COMPUTER: Willem Klein of the Netherlands took only $10\frac{1}{2}$ minutes to extract the 23rd root of a 200-digit number in 1975.

Human Computer

The fastest time in which anyone has succeeded by purely mental process in extracting the 23rd root of a 200-digit number is $10\frac{1}{2}$ minutes by Willem Klein (Netherlands) at the Lycée Mixte Nationalisé, Lyon, France, on March 5, 1975. He extracted the 13th root of a 100-digit number at the Zeeman Laboratory in Amsterdam, on September 19, 1975, producing the answer 47,272,683 in 5 minutes 22 seconds. Baron Herbert de Grote (born July 9, 1892) of Mexico City extracted a 9-digit root from a 300-digit number on May 15, 1975.

Memorizing Pi

The greatest number of places to which π (Pi) has been memorized is 4,000 by Robert Paige Miller (b. Dec. 6, 1960) a student at South Shore High School, Brooklyn. U.S.A. He wrote the 4,000 decimal places in a period of 7 hours on April 21, 1976. An offer to repeat the feat in reverse was declined by his two invigilators. (Note: The approximation of π at $\frac{22}{7}$ repeats after its sixth decimal place and can, of course, be recited *ad nauseam*.)

Isolation

The longest recorded period for which any volunteer has been able to withstand total deprivation of all sensory stimulation (sight, hearing and touch) is 92 hours, recorded in 1962 at Lancaster Moor Hospital, England.

The farthest distance that any human has been isolated from all other humans has been when the lone pilots of the lunar command modules were antipodal to their Apollo missions, 2,200 miles away.

MOTIONLESSNESS:
William A. Fuqua of Corpus
Christi, Texas, "froze"
standing up for 5 hours 40
minutes on December 19, 1975.

Motionlessness

The longest that any person has voluntarily remained motionless
is 5 hours 40 minutes by William A. Fuqua of Corpus Christi, Texas.
He stood astride a bicycle in Dillard's department store from 1:00 to
6:40 p.m. on December 19, 1975.

Staff Sgt. Samuel B. Moody, U.S.A.F., was punished by being
forced to stand at attention for 53 hours in Narumi prison camp,
Nagoya, Japan, in the spring of 1945. He survived to write *Reprieve
from Hell.*

Highest Temperature Endured

The highest dry-air temperature endured by naked men in U.S.
Air Force experiments in 1960 was 400°F. and for heavily clothed
men 500°F. (Steaks require only 325°F.) Temperatures of 284°F.
have been found quite bearable in Sauna baths.

Longest Dream

Dreaming sleep is characterized by rapid eye movements (called
REM). The longest recorded period of REM is 2 hours 23 minutes,
set by Bill Carskadon on February 15, 1967, at the Department of
Psychology, University of Illinois, Chicago. His previous sleep had
been interrupted.

Sleeplessness

Researches indicate that the peak of efficiency is attained between
8 p.m. and 9 p.m., and the low comes at 4 a.m.

The longest recorded period for which a person has voluntarily
gone without sleep is 288 hours (12 days) by Roger Guy English, 23,
in a waterbed showroom in San Diego, California, from 10:30 a.m.

March 20 to 10:30 a.m. April 1, 1974. His only stimulant was coffee. He has suffered hallucinations following this most ill-advised test.

It was reported that Toimi Artturinpoika Silvo, a 54-year-old port worker of Hamina, Finland, stayed awake for 32 days 12 hours from March 1 to April 2, 1967. To stay awake he walked 17 miles per day, and lost 33 lbs. during this time.

Mr. Valentine Medina (b. February 23, 1900) of Cuenca, Spain, claims he lost all desire to sleep in 1904 and has not slept since. During the day, he works on his farm and, at night, patrols the village as a watchman. "I've taken sleeping pills until I rattle," he says, "but it does no good."

Extrasensory Perception

The highest consistent performer in tests to detect powers of extrasensory perception is Pavel Stepánek (Czechoslovakia) known in parapsychological circles as "P.S." His performance in correctly naming hidden white or green cards from May, 1967, to March, 1968, departed from a chance probability yielding a Chi^2 value corresponding to $P < 10^{-50}$ or odds of more than 100 octillion to one against the achievement being one of chance. One of the two appointed referees recommended that the results should not be published.

The highest published scores in any E.S.P. test were those of a 26-year-old female tested by Prof. Bernard F. Reiss of Hunter College, New York City, in 1936. In 74 runs of 25 guesses each, she scored one with 25 all correct, two with 24, and an average of 18.24, as against a random score of 5.00. Such a result would depart from chance probability by a factor $> 10^{700}$. This produced the comment that there might be a defect in the theory of probability.

g Forces

The acceleration due to gravity (g) is 32 feet 1.05 inches per second per second at sea level at the Equator. A *sustained* force of 31 g was withstood for 5 seconds by R. Flanagan Gray, aged 39, at the U.S. Naval Air Development Center in Warminster, Johnsville, Pa., on December 5, 1958. This makes the bodyweight of a 185-lb. man seem like 5,700 lbs. The highest force endured in a dry capsule is 25 g.

The highest g force endured was 82.6 g for 0.04 of a second on a water-braked rocket sled by Eli L. Beeding, Jr., at Holloman Air Force Base, New Mexico, on May 16, 1958. He was put in the hospital for three days.

A man who fell off a 185-foot cliff has survived a *momentary* g force of 209 in decelerating from 68 m.p.h. to stationary in 0.015 of a second.

The land divers of Pentecost Island, New Hebrides, dive from 70-foot-high platforms with liana vines attached to their ankles. The resulting jerk can transmit a momentary force in excess of 100 g.

UNDERWATER LONGEST: Robert L. Foster of California, while he held his breath for a record 13 minutes 42½ seconds in a swimming pool. Record-breaking of this kind is extremely dangerous.

Electric Shock

Excluding lightning bolts, the highest reported voltage electric shock survived was one of 230,000 volts by Brian Latasa, 17, on the tower of an ultra-high voltage power line in Griffith Park, Los Angeles, November 9, 1967.

Most Durable "Ghosts"

Ghosts are not immortal and, according to the *Gazetteer of British Ghosts*, seem to deteriorate after 400 years. The most outstanding exceptions to this normal "half-life" are the ghosts of Roman soldiers three times reported still marching through the cellars of the Treasurer's House, York Minster, England, after nearly 19 centuries. The book's author, Peter Underwood, states that Britain has more reported ghosts per square mile than any other country with Borley Rectory near Long Melford, Suffolk, the site of unrivaled activity between 1863 and its destruction by fire in 1939.

Underwater

The world record for voluntarily staying underwater is 13 minutes 42.5 seconds by Robert Foster, aged 32, an electronics technician of Richmond, California, who stayed under 10 feet of water in the swimming pool of the Bermuda Palms at San Rafael, California, on March 15, 1959. He hyperventilated with oxygen for 30 minutes before his descent. The longest breath-hold without oxygen was 6 mins. 29.8 secs. by Georges Pouliquin in Paris on November 3, 1912. It must be stressed that record-breaking of this kind is *extremely* dangerous.

Chapter Two

THE ANIMAL AND PLANT KINGDOMS

ANIMAL KINGDOM (ANIMALIA)

Largest and Heaviest Animal

The largest and heaviest animal in the world, and probably the biggest creature which has *ever* existed, is the blue or sulphur-bottom whale (*Balaenoptera musculus*), also called Sibbald's rorqual. The largest accurately measured specimen on record was a female landed at an Argentine Whaling Station, South Georgia, *c.* 1912 which measured 110 feet $2\frac{1}{2}$ inches in length. Another female measuring $96\frac{3}{4}$ feet brought into the shore station at Prince Olaf, South Georgia, Falkland Islands, off Argentina, in *c.* 1931 was calculated to have weighed 183.34 tons, exclusive of blood, judging by the number of cookers that were filled by the animal's blubber, meat and bones. The total weight of the whale was believed to have been 195 tons. On the principle that the weight should vary as the cube of the linear dimensions, a 100-foot blue whale in good condition should weigh about 179 tons, but in the case of pregnant females the weight could be as much as 200 or more tons, equivalent to 35 adult bull African elephants. (See color photograph on color page A.)

Longest Animal

The longest animal ever recorded is the giant jellyfish (*Cyanea arctica*), which is found in the northwest Atlantic Ocean. One specimen washed up on the coast of Massachusetts, *c.* 1865, had a bell $7\frac{1}{2}$ feet in diameter and tentacles measuring 120 feet, thus giving a theoretical tentacular span of some 245 feet.

Tallest Animal

The tallest living animal is the giraffe (*Giraffa camelopardalis*), which is now found only in the dry savannah and semi-desert areas of Africa south of the Sahara. The tallest ever recorded was a Masai bull (*G. camelopardalis tippelskirchi*) named "George," received at Chester Zoo, England on January 8, 1959 from Kenya. His head almost touched the roof of the 20-foot-high Giraffe House when he was 9 years old. George died on July 22, 1969. Less credible heights of up to 23 feet have been claimed for bulls shot in the field.

Longest-Lived Animal

Few non-bacterial creatures live longer than humans. It would appear that tortoises are the longest-lived such animals. The greatest authentic age recorded for a tortoise is 152-plus years for a male Marion's tortoise (*Testudo sumeirii*), brought from the Seychelles to

MIGHTIEST MEMBER of the animal kingdom: The blue whale is probably the largest animal that ever lived.

Mauritius in 1766 by the Chevalier de Fresne, who presented it to the Port Louis army garrison. This specimen (it went blind in 1908) was accidentally killed in 1918. When the famous Royal Tongan tortoise "Tu'malilia" (believed to be a specimen of *Testudo radiata*) died on May 19, 1966, it was reputed to be over 200 years old, having been presented to the then King of Tonga by Captain James Cook (1728–79) on October 22, 1773, but this record lacks proper documentation.

The bacteria *Thermoactinomyces vulgaris* has been found alive in cores of mud taken from the bottom of Windermere Lake, northern England, which have been dated to 1,500 years before the present.

Smallest Animal

The smallest of all free-living organisms are pleuropneumonia-like organisms (P.P.L.O.) of the *Mycoplasma*. One of these, *Mycoplasma laidlawii*, first discovered in sewage in 1936, has a diameter during its early existence of only 100 millimicrons, or 0.000004 of an inch. Examples of the strain known as H.39 have a maximum diameter of 300 millimicrons and weigh an estimated 1.0×10^{-16} gram. Thus a 195-ton blue whale would weigh 1.77×10^{23} or 177,000 trillion times as much.

Fastest Animal

The fastest reliably measured speed of any animal is 106.25 m.p.h. for a spine-tailed swift (*Chaetura caudacuta*), reported from the U.S.S.R. in 1942. In 1934, ground speeds ranging from 171.8 to 219.5 m.p.h. were recorded by stopwatch for spine-tailed swifts over a 2-mile course in the Cachar Hills of northeastern India, but scientific tests since have revealed that this species of bird cannot be seen at a distance of 1 mile, even with standard binoculars. This bird is the fastest moving living creature and has a blood temperature of 112.5°F. Speeds even higher than a free-fall maximum of 185 m.p.h. have been ascribed to peregrine falcons (*Falco peregrinus*) in a stoop, but in recent experiments in which miniature air speedometers were fitted, the maximum recorded diving speed was 82 m.p.h.

Rarest Animal

The best claimants to the title of the world's rarest land animal are those species which are known only from a single (type) specimen. One of these is the tenrec, *Dasogale fontoynonti*, which is known only from the specimen collected in eastern Madagascar (Malagasy) and now preserved in the Paris (France) Museum of Natural History.

The pygmy opossum, believed to have been extinct for 20,000 years until a single example was caught in 1966, is no longer the rarest, as three more specimens have been discovered in Australia.

Commonest Animal

It is estimated that man shares the earth with 3×10^{33} (or 3 followed by 33 zeros) other living things. Of these, more than 75 per cent are bacteria, which scientists no longer classify as animals, but as protista.

Most Valuable

The most valuable animals in cash terms are thoroughbred race horses. *What a Pleasure* (see Chapter XII, Horse Racing) was sold in early 1976 for $8,000,000. The most valuable zoo exhibits are the Giant Pandas (*Ailuropoda melanoleuca*) for which the San Diego Zoological Gardens offered $250,000 in 1971 for a fertile pair. The most valuable exhibit is the Killer Whale (*Orcinus orca*). In September, 1975, the 6,500-lb. female "Newtka" was flown from Dallas, Texas, to Niagara Falls insured for $150,000. Trained specimens such as "Ramu" at the Windsor Safari Park in England are valued at $85,000.

Fastest Growth

The fastest growth in the animal kingdom is that of the blue whale calf. A barely visible ovum weighing 0.000035 of an ounce grows to a weight of *c.* 29 tons in $22\frac{3}{4}$ months, made up of $10\frac{3}{4}$ months gestation and the first 12 months of age. This is equivalent to an increase of 30,000 million fold.

Largest Egg

The largest egg of any living animal is that of the whale-shark (*Rhiniodon typus*). One egg case measuring 12 inches by 5.5 inches by 3.5 inches was picked up by the shrimp trawler "Doris" on June 29, 1953, at a depth of 186 feet in the Gulf of Mexico, 130 miles south of Port Isabel, Texas. The egg contained a perfect embryo of a whale-shark 13.78 inches long.

Greatest Size Difference Between Sexes

The largest female deep-sea angler fish of the species *Ceratias holboelki* on record weighed half a million times as much as the smallest known parasitic male. It has been suggested that this fish would make an appropriate emblem for Women's Lib.

Heaviest Brain

The sperm whale (*Physeter catodon*) has the heaviest brain of all living animals. The brain of a 49-foot-long bull processed aboard the Japanese factory ship, *Nissin Maru No. 1* in the Antarctic on December 11, 1949, weighed 9,200 grams (20.24 lbs.), compared to 6,900 grams (15.38 lbs.) for a 90-foot blue whale. The heaviest brain recorded for an elephant is 16.5 lbs. in the case of a 2.17-ton Asiatic cow. The normal brain weight for an adult African bull is $9\frac{1}{4}$–12 lbs.

Largest Eye

The giant squid *Architeuthis sp.* has the largest eye of any living animal. The ocular diameter may exceed 15 inches, compared to 3.93 to 4.71 inches for the largest blue whale.

Highest g Force

The highest g force encountered in nature is the 400 g endured by the 0.47-inch-long click beetle (*Athous haemorrhoidalis*), a common British species, when jack-knifing into the air to a height of $11\frac{1}{4}$ inches to escape predators. According to Dr. Glyn Evans of Manchester

(England) University, the parts of the click beetle farthest from its central pivot travel at an even greater acceleration, the brain being subjected to a peak deceleration of 2,000 g at the end of the movement.

1. Mammals (Mammalia)

Largest and Heaviest is the blue whale (see page 55). One whale, a female taken by the *Slava* whaling fleet of the U.S.S.R. in the Antarctic on March 17, 1947, measured 90 feet 8 inches in length. Its tongue and heart weighed 4.73 tons and 1,540 lbs. respectively.

Blue whales inhabit the colder seas and migrate to warmer waters in winter for breeding. Observations made in the Antarctic in 1947–8 showed that a blue whale can maintain speeds of 20 knots (23 m.p.h.) for 10 minutes when frightened. This means a 90-foot blue whale traveling at 20 knots would develop 520 horsepower. The young measure up to 28.5 feet long at birth and weigh up to 3.1 tons.

It has been estimated that there were between 17,500 and 19,000 blue whales living throughout the oceans in 1976. The species has been totally protected since 1967. Non-member countries of the International Whaling Commission (Chile and Peru) are not bound by this agreement.

The greatest recorded depth to which a whale has dived is 620 fathoms (3,720 feet) by a 47-foot bull sperm whale (*Physeter catodon*) found with his jaw entangled with a submarine cable running between Santa Elena, Ecuador, and Chorillos, Peru, on October 14, 1955. At this depth the whale withstood a pressure of 1,680 lbs. per square inch.

On August 25, 1969, a sperm whale was killed 100 miles south of Durban, South Africa, after it had surfaced from a dive lasting 1 hour 52 minutes, and inside its stomach were found two small sharks which had been swallowed about an hour earlier. These were later identified as *Scymnodon sp.*, a species found only on the sea floor. At this point from land the depth of water is in excess of 1,646 fathoms (10,476 feet) for a radius of 30–40 miles, which now suggests that the sperm whale sometimes may descend to a depth of over 10,000 feet when seeking food.

Largest on Land. The largest living land animal is the African bush elephant (*Loxodonta africana africana*). The average adult bull stands 10 feet 6 inches at the shoulder and weighs 6½ tons. The largest specimen ever recorded was a bull shot 48 miles northwest of Macusso, Angola, on November 13, 1955. Lying on its side this elephant measured 13 feet 2 inches in a projected line from the highest point of the shoulder to the base of the forefoot, indicating that its standing height must have been about 12 feet 6 inches. Other measurements included an over-all length of 33 feet 2 inches (tip of extended trunk to tip of extended tail) and a maximum bodily girth of 19 feet 8 inches. The weight was estimated at 24,000 lbs.

LARGEST LAND ANIMAL: This African bull elephant, measuring 13 feet 2 inches at the shoulder and weighing 12 tons, was shot in Angola in 1955, and is now preserved in the Smithsonian Institution, Washington, D.C.

On March 6, 1959, the mounted specimen was put on display in the rotunda of the Smithsonian Institution in Washington, D.C. (see also Shooting, Chapter 12).

Another outsized bull elephant known as "Dhlulamithi" (Taller than the Trees), reputed to stand over 12 feet at the shoulder, was shot at Fishan, east of the Lundi River, Rhodesia in August, 1967, by a South African police officer after it had strayed outside the Gona-Re-Zhou Reserve.

Smallest. The smallest recorded mammal is Savi's white-toothed pygmy shrew (*Suncus etruscus*), also called the Etruscan shrew, which is found along the coasts of the northern Mediterranean and southwards to Cape Province, South Africa. Mature specimens have a body length of only 1.32–2.04 inches, a tail length of 0.94–1.14 inches, and weigh between 0.062 and 0.09 oz.

The smallest totally marine mammal is the sea otter (*Enhydra lutris*), which is found in coastal waters off California, western Alaska and islands in the Bering Sea. Adult specimens measure 47.24–61.5 inches in total length, and weigh 55–81.4 lbs.

Fastest. The fastest of all land animals over a short distance (*i.e.* up to 600 yards) is the cheetah or hunting leopard (*Acinonyx jubatus*) of the open plains of East Africa, Iran, Turkmenia and Afghanistan, with a probable maximum speed of 60–63 m.p.h. over suitably level ground. Speeds of 71, 84 and even 90 m.p.h. have been claimed for this animal, but these figures must be considered exaggerated. Tests in London in 1937 showed that on an oval greyhound track over 345 yards a female cheetah's average speed over three runs was 43.4 m.p.h. (compare with 43.26 m.p.h. for the fastest race horse), but this specimen was not running at its best.

The fastest land animal over a sustained distance (*i.e.* 1,000 yards or more) is the pronghorn antelope (*Antilocapra americana*) of the western United States. Specimens have been observed to travel at 35 m.p.h. for 4 miles, at 42 m.p.h. for 1 mile and 55 m.p.h. for half a mile. On August 14, 1936, at Spanish Lake, Lake County, Oregon, a hard-pressed buck was timed by a car speedometer at 61 m.p.h. over 200 yards.

Slowest. The slowest moving land mammal is the ai or three-toed sloth (*Bradypus tridactylus*) of tropical America. The usual ground speed is 6 to 8 feet a minute (0.068 to 0.098 m.p.h.), but one mother sloth, speeded up by the calls of her infant, was observed to cover 14 feet in one minute (0.155 m.p.h.). In the trees, this speed may be increased to 2 feet a second (1.36 m.p.h.). (Compare these figures with the 0.03 m.p.h. of the common garden snail and the 0.17 m.p.h. of the giant tortoise.)

Tallest is the giraffe (see page 55).

Longest-Lived. No mammal can match the extreme proven age of 113 years attained by man (*Homo sapiens*). It is probable that the closest approach is among blue and fin whales (*Balaenoptera physalas*). The annual growth layers in the ears indicate an age of 90–100 years for some specimens. A bull killer whale (*Orcinus orca*) with distinctive markings, known as "Old Tom," was observed every winter from 1843 to 1930, in Twofold Bay, Eden, New South Wales, Australia.

The longest-lived land mammal, excluding man, is the Asiatic elephant (*Elephas maximus*). The greatest age that has been verified with certainty is 70 years in the case of a bull timber elephant "Kyaw Thee" (Tuskar 1342), who died in the Taunggyi Forest division, southern Shan States, Burma, in 1965. An age of 78 years has been attributed to "Modoc," the circus cow elephant, when she died at Lion Country Safari, Irvine, California, on July 17, 1975. An elephant's life span is indicated by the persistence of its teeth, which generally wear out around the 50–55th year.

Rarest Mammal is the tenrec, *Dasogale fontoynonti* (see page 57).

The rarest large mammal in the world is now the fully protected Javan rhinoceros (*Rhinoceros sondaicus*). In May, 1973, there were only 44 in the Udjung-Kulon Reserve of 117 square miles at the tip of western Java, Indonesia. There may also be a few in the Tenasserim area on the Thai-Burmese border. Among subspecies, the Bali tiger (*Pantheria tigris sondaica*) was believed to have become extinct in 1974 when only a single specimen was reported sighted in 1973. The last Arabian oryx reported in the wild was a male in the Oman desert on October 20, 1972.

Longest Hibernation. The common dormouse (*Glis glis*) spends more time in hibernation than any other mammal. The hibernation usually lasts between 5 and 6 months (October to April), but there is a record of an English specimen sleeping for 6 months 23 days without interruption.

Highest Living. The highest-living wild mammal in the world is probably the yak (*Bos grunniens*), in Tibet and the Szechwanese Alps, China, which occasionally, when foraging, climbs to an altitude of 20,000 feet. The Bharal (*Pseudois nayaur*) and the Pika or Mouse hare (*Ochotona thibetana*) may also reach this height in the Himalayas. In 1890, the tracks of an elephant were found at 15,000 feet on Mt. Kilimanjaro, Tanzania.

Largest Herd. The largest herds on record were those of the South African Springbok (*Antidorcas marsupialis*) during migration in the 19th century. In 1849, Sir John Fraser of Bloemfontein reported seeing a herd that took three days to pass through the settlement of Beaufort West, Cape Province. Another herd seen in the same province in 1888 was estimated to contain 100,000,000 head. A herd estimated to be 15 miles wide and more than 100 miles long was reported from Karree Kloof, Orange River, South Africa, in July, 1896.

Longest and Shortest Gestation Periods. The longest of all mammalian gestation periods is that of the Asiatic elephant (*Elephas maximus*), with an average of 609 days (or just over 20 months) and a maximum of 760 days (2 years and 30 days)—more than 2½ times that of a human.

The viviparous amphibian Alpine black salamander (*Salamandra atra*) can have a gestation period of up to 38 months when living above 4,600 feet in Switzerland.

The shortest gestation period is that of the American opossum (*Didelphis marsupialis*), also called the Virginian opossum, normally 12 to 13 days, but it may be as short as 8 days.

The gestation periods of the rare water opossum or Yapok (*Chironectes minimus*) of Central and northern South America (average 12–13 days) and the Eastern native cat (*Dasyurus viverrinus*) of Australia (average 12 days) may also be as short as 8 days.

Largest Litter. The greatest recorded number of young born to a wild mammal at a single birth is 32 (not all of which survived), in the case of the common tenrec (*Centetes ecaudatus*), found in Madagascar and the Comoro Islands. The average litter is 13 to 14.

LARGEST LITTER: 32 young at once is not unknown for the common tenrec.

In March, 1961, a litter of 32 was also reported for a house mouse (*Mus musculus*) at the Roswell Park Memorial Institute in Buffalo, N.Y. (average litter size 13–21). (See also Chapter 9, prolificacy records—pigs.)

Youngest Breeder. The streaked tenrec (*Hemicentetes semispinosus*) of Madagascar is weaned after only 5 days, and females are capable of breeding 3–4 weeks after birth.

Carnivores

Largest. The largest living terrestrial member of the order Carnivora is the Kodiak bear (*Ursus arctos middendorffi*), which is found on Kodiak Island and the adjacent Afognak and Shuyak islands in the Gulf of Alaska. The average adult male has a nose-to-tail length of 8 feet (tail about 4 inches), stands 52 inches at the shoulder and weighs 1,050–1,175 lbs.

In 1894, a weight of 1,656 lbs. was recorded for a male shot at English Bay, Kodiak Island, whose *stretched* skin measured 13 feet

HEAVIEST BEAR: This Peninsular brown bear, shot in Alaska in 1948, measured 10 feet long and weighed almost 1,700 lbs.

HEAVIEST POLAR BEAR: This 2,210-lb. specimen, 11 feet 1½ inches tall, was displayed at the Seattle World's Fair.

6 inches overall. This weight was exceeded by a male in the Cheyenne Mountain Zoological Park, Colorado Springs, which scaled 1,670 lbs. at the time of its death on September 22, 1955.

The Peninsular brown bear (*Ursus arctos gyas*), also found in Alaska, is almost as large, adult males measuring 7¾ feet nose-to-tail length and weighing about 1,100 lbs. A specimen 10 feet long, with an estimated weight of between 1,600 and 1,700 lbs. was shot near Cold Bay, Alaska, on May 28, 1948.

Weights in excess of 1,600 lbs. have also been reported for the male polar bear (*Ursus maritimus*), which has an average nose-to-tail length of 7¾ feet and weighs 850-900 lbs. In 1960, a polar bear allegedly weighing 2,210 lbs. was shot at the polar entrance to Kotzebue Sound, northwest Alaska. In April, 1962, the mounted specimen, measuring 11 feet 1½ inches, was put on display at the Seattle World's Fair.

The largest toothed mammal ever recorded is the sperm whale (*Physeter catodon*), also called the cachalot. The average adult bull is 47 feet long and weighs about 37 tons. The largest specimen ever to be measured accurately was a bull 67 feet 11 inches long captured off the Kurile Islands, in the northwest Pacific, by a U.S.S.R. whaling fleet in the summer of 1950.

Rarest. The rarest land carnivore is probably the Mexican grizzly bear (*Ursus nilsoni*), of which no more than 20–30 survive in a small patch of territory about 50 miles north of Chihuahua.

Smallest. The smallest living carnivore is the least weasel (*Mustela rixosa*), also called the dwarf weasel, which is circumpolar in distribution. Four races are recognized, the smallest of which is the *M. r. pygmaea* of Siberia. Mature specimens have an overall length (including tail) of 6.96–8.14 inches and weigh between 1¼ and 2½ oz.

Largest Feline. The largest member of the cat family (Felidae) is the long-furred Siberian tiger (*Pantheria tigris altaica*), also known as the Amur or Manchurian tiger. Adult males average 10 feet 4 inches in length (nose to tip of extended tail), stand 39–42 inches at the shoulder, and weigh about 585 lbs. The heaviest specimen on record was an 857-lb. Indian tiger (*Pantheria tigris*) shot in northern Uttar Pradesh by David J. Hasinger in November, 1967. It measured 10 feet 7 inches long (between taxidermist's pegs), or 11 feet 1 inch over the curves. It is now on display in the Smithsonian Institution, Washington, D.C.

The average adult African lion (*Pantheria leo*) measures 9 feet overall, stands 36–38 inches at the shoulder, and weighs 400–410 lbs. The

LARGEST CAT: This 857-lb. Siberian tiger, brought down in India in 1957, was the largest specimen ever recorded.

heaviest recorded specimen found in the wild was one weighing 690 lbs., shot near Hectorspruit, in the eastern Transvaal, South Africa, in 1936. In 1953, an 18-year-old liger (a lion-tigress hybrid) at the Zoological Gardens, Bloemfontein, South Africa, was weighed at 750 lbs. In July, 1970, a weight of 826 lbs. was reported for an 11-year-old black-maned lion named "Simba" at the Colchester Zoo, Essex, England. He died on January 16, 1973, at Knaresborough Zoo, North Yorkshire, England, and is now stuffed.

Smallest Feline. The smallest member of the cat family is the rusty-spotted cat (*Felis rubiginosa*) of southern India and Ceylon. The average adult male has an overall length of 25–28 inches (tail 9–10 inches) and weighs about 3 lbs.

Pinnipeds (Seals, Sea Lions and Walruses)

Largest. The largest of the 32 known species of pinnipeds is the southern elephant seal (*Mirounga leonina*) which inhabits the sub-Antarctic islands. Adult bulls average 16½ feet in length (snout to tip of tail), 12 feet in girth and weigh 5,000 lbs. The largest specimen on record was a bull killed in Possession Bay, South Georgia, on February 28, 1913, which measured *c.* 22½ feet in length or 21 feet 4 inches after flensing and weighed at least 9,000 lbs. There are old records of bulls measuring 25, 30 and even 35 feet, but all lack confirmation. A length of 22 feet has been reported in 1870 for the northern elephant seal (*Mirounga angustirostris*), killed on Santa Barbara Island, California, but this measurement may have been made over the curve of the body. Adult bulls average 14 feet in length. The largest elephant seal ever held in captivity is believed to have been "Goliath," a bull of the southern race, received at Carl Hagenbeck's Tierpark, Hamburg-Stellingen, Germany, in

1928 from South Georgia, Falkland Islands, who measured 20½ feet in length and weighed over 6,700 lbs. at the time of his death in 1930.

Smallest. The smallest pinniped is the Baykal seal (*Pusa sibrica*) of Lake Baykal, a large fresh-water lake near Irkutsk in southern Siberia, U.S.S.R. Adult specimens measure about 4 feet 6 inches from nose to tail and weigh about 140 lbs.

Fastest and Deepest. The highest speed measured for a pinniped is 25 m.p.h. for a California sea lion (*Zalophus californianus*). It was reported in March, 1966, that a dive of 1,968 feet had been recorded by a depth gauge attached to a Weddell seal (*Leptonychotes weddelli*) which stayed under water for 43 minutes 20 seconds in McMurdo Sound, Antarctica. The seal withstood a pressure of 875 lbs. per square inch of body area.

Longest-Lived. A female gray seal (*Halichoerus grypus*) shot at Shunni Wick in the Shetland Islands, Scotland, on April 23, 1969, was believed to be at least 46 years old, based on a count of dental annuli.

Rarest. The Caribbean or West Indies monk seal (*Monachus tropicalis*) was last seen on the beach of Isla Mujeres off the Yucatan Peninsula, Mexico, in 1962, and is now believed to be on the verge of extinction. Of sub-species, the Japanese sea lion (*Zalophus californianus japonicus*), formerly widespread in the Japanese archipelago, probably became extinct in the early 1950's.

Bats

Largest. The only flying mammals are bats (order Chiroptera), of which there are about 1,000 living species. The bat with the greatest wing span is the Kalong (*Pteropus vampyrus*), a fruit bat found in Malaysia and Indonesia. It has a wing span of up to 5 feet 7 inches and weighs up to 31.7 oz.

LARGEST BAT: The Kalong fruit bat of Malaysia and Indonesia has a wing span of up to 5 feet 7 inches.

Smallest. The smallest species of bat is the rare Kitti's hog-nosed bat (*Craseonycteris thonglongyai*) or bumblebee bat, found in the caves near Kanchanaburi, southern Thailand. It has a wing span of about 6.3 inches and weighs about 0.07 oz. It rivals the Etruscan pygmy shrew (*Suncus etruscus*) for the title of *Smallest Living Mammal*.

Fastest. Because of the great practical difficulties, little data on bat speeds has been published. The greatest speed attributed to a bat is 32 m.p.h. in the case of a free-tailed or guano bat (*Tadarida mexicana*) which flew 31 miles in 58 minutes. This speed is closely matched by the noctule bat (*Nyctalus noctula*) and the long-winged bat (*Miniopterus schreibersi*), both of which have been timed at 31 m.p.h.

Longest-Lived. The greatest age reliably reported for a bat is "at least 24 years" for a female little brown bat (*Myotis lucifugus*) found on April 30, 1960, in a cave on Mount Aeolis, East Dorset, Vermont. It had been banded at a summer colony in Mashpee, Massachusetts, on June 22, 1937.

Highest Detectable Pitch. Because of their ultrasonic echolocation bats have the most acute hearing of any land animal. Vampire bats (*Desmodontidae*) and fruit bats (*Pteropodidae*) can hear frequencies as high as 150,000 cycles per second (compare with 20,000 cycles per second for the adult human but 153,000 cycles for the bottlenosed dolphin (*Tursiops truncatus*).

Primates

Largest. The largest living primate is the eastern lowland gorilla (*Gorilla gorilla grauei*) which inhabits the lowlands of the eastern part of the Upper Congo (now Zaïre) and southwestern Uganda. The average adult bull stands 5 feet 9 inches tall (including crest) and measures 58–60 inches around the chest and weighs about 360

LARGEST PRIMATE: Gorillas measure up to 69 inches around the chest. The largest ever kept in captivity weighed "nearly 670" lbs. at times.

pounds. The greatest height (top of crest to heel) recorded for a mountain gorilla is 6 feet 2 inches for a bull shot in the eastern Congo in *c.* 1921.

The heaviest gorilla ever kept in captivity was a bull of the eastern lowlands named "Mbongo," who died in San Diego Zoological Gardens, on March 15, 1942. During an attempt to weigh him shortly before his death, the platform scales "fluctuated from 645 pounds to nearly 670." This specimen measured 5 feet 7½ inches in height and 69 inches around the chest.

The heaviest gorilla living in captivity today is the western lowland (*Gorilla gorilla gorilla*) bull "Samson" (born 1949) of Milwaukee County Zoological Park. He has weighed as much as 658 lbs. but now fluctuates between 586 and 605 lbs.

Smallest. The smallest known primate is the rare feather-tailed tree shrew (*Ptiolcercus lowii*) of Malaysia. Adult specimens have a total head and body length of 3.9–5.5 inches and a tail of 5–7.5 inches. The weight varies from 1.23 to 1.76 oz. The mouse lemur (*Microcebus murinus*) of Madagascar is approximately the same length (10.8–11.8 inches overall) but heavier, adults weighing 1.58 to 2.82 oz.

Longest-Lived. The greatest irrefutable age reported for a primate (excluding humans) is 54 years in the case of the orangutans Guas and Guarina, reported in the Philadelphia Zoo in October, 1974.

Rarest. The rarest primate is the hairy-eared mouse lemur (*Cheirogaleus trichotis*) of Madagascar, which was known, until fairly recently, only from a type specimen and two skins. However, in 1966 a live one was found on the east coast near Mananara.

Strength. "Boma," a 165-lb. male chimpanzee at the Bronx Zoo, New York City, in 1924 recorded a right-handed pull (feet braced) of 847 lbs. on a dynamometer (compare with 210 lbs. for a man of the same weight). On another occasion an adult female chimpanzee named "Suzette" (estimated weight 135 lbs.) at the same zoo registered a right-handed pull of 1,260 lbs. while in a rage. A record of a 100-pound chimpanzee achieving a two-handed dead lift of 600 pounds with ease suggests that a male gorilla could, with training, raise 1,800 pounds!

Largest and Smallest Monkeys. The largest monkey is the mandrill (*Mandrillus sphinx*) of equatorial West Africa, weighing up to 119 lbs., with a total length of 36 inches, plus tail of 3 inches. Unconfirmed weights of up to 130 lbs. have been reported.

The smallest monkey is the pygmy marmoset (*Cebuella pygmaea*) of Ecuador, northern Peru and western Brazil. Mature specimens have a maximum total length of 12 inches, half of which is tail, and weigh 1.7 to 2.81 oz. which means it rivals the mouse lemur for the title of *Smallest Living Primate.*

Most and Least Intelligent. Of sub-human primates, chimpanzees appear to have the most superior intelligence. Lemurs have less learning ability than any monkey or ape, and in some tests, are inferior to dogs and even pigeons.

LARGEST RODENT: The capybara of tropical South America measures up to 4½ feet long and can weigh as much as 174 lbs.

Longest-Lived Monkey. The greatest reliable age reported for a monkey is *c.* 46 years for a male mandrill (*Mandrillus sphinx*) named "George" of London Zoological Gardens, who died on March 4, 1916.

Rodents

Largest. The world's largest rodent is the capybara (*Hydrochoerus hydrochaeris*), also called the carpincho or water hog, which is found in tropical South America. Mature specimens have a head and body length of 3¼ to 4½ feet and weigh up to 174 lbs.

Smallest. The smallest rodent is the Old World harvest mouse (*Micromys minutus*), of which some forms weigh between 4.2 and 10.2 grams (0.15 to 0.36 of an ounce) and measure up to 5.3 inches long, including the tail. It was announced in June, 1965, that an even smaller rodent had been discovered in the Asian part of the U.S.S.R., probably a more diminutive form of *M. minutus*, but further information is lacking.

Rarest. The rarest rodent in the world is believed to be the James Island rice rat (*Oryzomys swarthi*). Four were collected on this island in the Galápagos group in the eastern Pacific Ocean in 1906. The next trace was a skull of a recently dead specimen found in January, 1966.

Fastest Breeder. The female meadow vole (*Microtus agrestis*), found in Britain, can reproduce from the age of 25 days and have up to 17 litters of 6 to 8 young in a year.

Longest-Lived. The greatest reliable age reported for a rodent is 22 years for an Indian crested porcupine (*Hystrix indica*) which died in Trivandrum Zoological Gardens, southwestern India, in 1942.

Insectivores

Largest. The largest insectivore (insect-eating mammal) is the moon rat (*Echinosorex gymnurus*) also known as Raffles' gymnure, found in Burma, Thailand, Malaysia, Sumatra and Borneo. Mature specimens have a head and body length of 10.43–17.52 inches, a tail measuring 7.87–8.26 inches, and weigh up to 3.08 lbs. Although anteaters feed on termites and other soft-bodied insects, they are not insectivores, but belong to the order Edentata which means "without teeth."

Smallest. The smallest insectivore is Savi's white-toothed pygmy shrew (see page 60).

Longest-Lived. The greatest reliable age recorded for an insectivore is 10½ years for a hedgehog tenrec (*Setifer setosus*), which died in the London Zoo in 1971. There is an unconfirmed record of a hedgehog (*Erinaceus europaens*) living for 14 years.

Antelopes

Largest. The largest of all antelopes is the rare Derby eland (*Taurotragus derbianus*), also called the giant eland, of west and north-central Africa, which may surpass 2,000 lbs. The common eland (*T. oryx*) of east and south Africa has the same shoulder height, of up to 70 inches, but is not quite so massive, although there is one record of a 65-inch bull being shot in Nyasaland (now Malawi) *c.* 1937 which weighed 2,078 lbs.

Smallest. The smallest known antelope is the Royal antelope (*Neotragus pygmaeus*) of West Africa, measuring only 10 to 12 inches at the shoulder, and weighing only 7 to 8 lbs. The slenderer Swayne's dik-dik (*Madoqua swaynei*) of Somali, East Africa, when adult, stands about 13 inches at the shoulder, weighs only 5 to 6 lbs.

LARGEST INSECT-EATING MAMMAL: The moon rat (left) of Thailand and Malaysia grows to more than 27 inches. SMALLEST ANTELOPE (right) is the Royal antelope of West Africa, which stands only 10 inches high at the shoulder.

Rarest. The rarest antelope is probably Jentink's duiker (*Cephalophus jentinki*), also known as the black-headed duiker, which is found only in a restricted area of tropical West Africa. Only one, "Alpha," a female born on December 1, 1971, is known in captivity in the Gladys Porter Zoo, Brownsville, Texas.

Deer

Largest. The largest deer is the Alaskan moose (*Alces alces gigas*). A bull standing 7 feet 8 inches at the withers, and weighing 1,800 lbs., was shot in 1897 in the Yukon Territory, Canada. Unconfirmed measurements of up to 8½ feet at the withers and 2,600 lbs. have been claimed. The record antler span is 78½ inches.

Smallest. The smallest true deer (family Cervidae) is the pudu (*Pudu mephistophiles*) of Ecuador, the male of which stands 13–15 inches at the shoulder and weighs 18–20 pounds. The smallest known ruminant is the lesser Malayan chevrotain or mouse deer (*Tragulus javanicus*) of southeastern Asia. Adult specimens measure 8–10 inches at the shoulder and weigh 6–7 lbs.

Rarest. The rarest deer in the world is Fea's muntjac (*Muntiacus feae*), which is known only from two specimens collected on the borders of Tenasserim (in Burma) and Thailand.

Oldest. The greatest reliable age recorded for a deer is 26 years 6 months and 2 days for a red deer (*Cervus elephus*), which died in the National Zoological Park, Washington, D.C., in March, 1941.

Tusks and Horns

Longest. The longest recorded elephant tusks (excluding prehistoric examples) are a pair from the eastern Congo (Zaïre) preserved in the National Collection of Heads and Horns, kept by the New York Zoological Society in Bronx Park, New York City. One measures 11 feet 5½ inches along the outside curve and the other measures 11 feet. Their combined weight is 293 lbs. A single tusk of 11 feet 6 inches has been reported, but details are lacking.

Heaviest. The greatest weight ever recorded for one elephant tusk is 258 lbs. for a specimen collected in Benin (formerly Dahomey), western Africa, and exhibited at the Paris Exposition in 1900.

Longest Horns. The longest recorded animal horn was one measuring 81¼ inches on the outside curve, with a circumference of 18¼ inches, found on a specimen of domestic Ankole cattle (*Bos taurus*) near Lake Ngami, Botswana (formerly called Bechuanaland).

The largest head (horns measured from tip to tip across the forehead) is one of 13 feet 11 inches on a wild buffalo (*Bubalus bubalus*) shot in India in 1955. The maximum for a Texas longhorn steer is 9 feet 9 inches tip to tip.

The longest recorded anterior horn of a rhinoceros is one of 62¼ inches, found on a female southern race white rhinoceros (*Ceratotherium simum simum*) shot in South Africa *c.* 1848. The interior horn

LONGEST TUSKS: Weighing 293 lbs. and measuring more than 11 feet each, this pair of elephant tusks from the Congo are in the Bronx Zoo.

measured 22¼ inches. An unconfirmed length of 81 inches has also been once reported.

Blood Temperatures

The highest mammalian blood temperature is that of the domestic goat (*Capra hircus*) with an average of 103.8°F., and a normal range of from 101.7° to 105.3°F. The lowest mammalian blood temperature is that of the spiny anteater (*Tachyglossus aculeatus*), a monotreme found in Australia and New Guinea, with a normal range of 72° to 87°F. The blood temperature of the golden hamster (*Mesocricetus auratus*) sometimes falls as low as 38.3°F. during hibernation, and an extreme figure of 29.6°F. has been reported for a myotis bat (family Vespertilionidae) during a deep sleep.

Most Valuable Furs

The highest-priced animal pelts are those of the sea otter (*Enhydra lutris*), also known as the Kamchatka beaver, which fetched up to $2,700 each before their 55-year-long protection started in 1912. The protection ended in 1967, and at the first legal auction of sea otter pelts in Seattle, Washington, on January 31, 1968, Neiman Marcus, the famous Dallas department store, paid $9,200 for four pelts from Alaska. On January 30, 1969, a New York company paid $1,100 for an exceptionally fine pelt from Alaska.

On Feb. 26, 1969, forty selected pelts of the mink-sable crossbreed "Kojah" from the Piampiano Fur Ranch, Zion, Illinois, realized $2,700 in New York City. In May, 1970, a Kojah coat costing $125,000 was sold by Neiman Marcus to Welsh actor Richard Burton for his then wife, Elizabeth Taylor.

Ambergris

The heaviest piece of ambergris (a fatty deposit in the intestine of the sperm whale) on record weighed 1,003 lbs. and was recovered from a sperm whale (*Physeter catodon*) on December 3, 1912, by a Norwegian whaling company in Australian waters. The lump was sold in London for £23,000 (then $111,780).

Marsupials

Largest. The largest of all marsupials is the red kangaroo (*Macropus rufus*) of southern and eastern Australia. Adult males or "boomers" stand 6–7 feet tall, weigh 150–175 lbs. and measure up to 8 feet 11 inches in a straight line from the nose to the tip of the extended tail. The great gray kangaroo (*Macropus giganteus*) of eastern Australia and Tasmania is almost equally large, and there is an authentic record of a boomer measuring 8 feet 8 inches from nose to tail (9 feet 7 inches along the curve of the body) and weighing 200 lbs. The skin of this specimen is preserved in the Australian Museum, Sydney, New South Wales.

Smallest. The smallest known marsupial is the rare Kimberley planigale or marsupial mouse (*Planigale subtilissima*), which is found only in the Kimberley district of Western Australia. Adult males have a head and body length of 1.75 inches, a tail length of 2 inches and weigh about 0.141 oz. Females are smaller than males.

Rarest. The rarest marsupial is the sandhill dunnart (*Sminthopsis psammophila*) also known as the narrow-footed marsupial mouse, which is known only from the type specimen collected in 1894 near Lake Amadeus, Northern Territory, Australia.

In September, 1973, a marsupial "mouse," still unnamed, of a hitherto unknown species, was trapped in the Billiatt Conservation Park, 100 miles east of Adelaide, South Australia.

Longest-Lived. The greatest reliable age recorded for a marsupial is 19 years 7 months for a South Australian wallaroo (*Macropus robustus erubescens*), which died at the New York Zoological Society (Bronx Zoo) in 1968.

Highest and Longest Jump. The greatest measured height cleared by a hunted kangaroo is a pile of timber 10 feet 6 inches high. The longest recorded leap was reported in January, 1951, when, in the course of a chase, a female red kangaroo (*Macropus rufus*) made a series of bounds which included one of 42 feet. There is an unconfirmed report of a great gray kangaroo (*Macropus canguru*) jumping nearly 44 feet 8½ inches on the flat.

DOMESTICATED ANIMALS

Horses and Ponies

Horse Population. In 1974, the world's horse population was estimated to be 72,600,000.

Age. The greatest reliable age recorded for a horse is 62 years in the case of "Old Billy" (foaled 1760), believed to be a cross between a Cleveland and an Eastern blood, who was bred by Edward Robinson of Wild Grave Farm in Woolston, Lancashire, England. In 1762 or 1763, he was sold to the Mersey and Irwell Navigation Company and remained with them in a working capacity, marshalling and towing barges, until 1819 when he was retired to a farm, where he died on November 27, 1822. The skull of this horse is preserved in the Manchester Museum, and his stuffed head is now on display in the Bedford Museum.

The greatest reliable age recorded for a pony is 54 years for a stallion owned by a farmer in central France which was still alive in 1919. In June, 1970, a Welsh pony "Chess" living on a farm near Pebbles Bay, south Wales, was reported to be 66 years old, but this claim is unconfirmed.

Largest. The heaviest horse ever recorded was "Brooklyn Supreme," a pure-bred Belgian stallion weighing 3,200 lbs. and standing 19.2 hands (6 feet 6 inches). He died on September 6, 1948, aged 20, in Callender, Iowa. In April, 1973, the Belgian mare "Wilma du Bos" (foaled July 15, 1966), owned by Mrs. Virgie Arden of Reno, Nevada, was reported to weigh slightly more than 3,200 lbs. when in foal and being shipped from Antwerp. The mare stands 18.2 hands (6 feet $\frac{2}{3}$ inches) and normally weighs about 2,400 lbs.

The tallest horse ever documented was Percheron-Shire cross "Firpon" (foaled 1959) owned by Julio Falabella which stood 21.1

TALLEST HORSE: "Firpon" stood 7 feet 1 inch high and weighed 2,976 lbs. The same height was also claimed for a Clydesdale, "Big Jim" (see next page).

TALLEST HORSE: Rival to "Firpon," the Clydesdale "Big Jim," bred in Scotland, also stood 21.1 hands.

hands (7 feet 1 inch) and weighed 2,976 lbs. He died on Recco de Roca Ranch in Argentina on March 14, 1972. A height of 21.1 hands was also claimed for the Clydesdale gelding "Big Jim" (foaled 1950), bred by Lyall M. Anderson of West Broomley, Montrose, Scotland. "Big Jim" died in St. Louis in 1957.

A claim of 21.2 hands (7 feet 1½ inches) was made in 1908 for "Morocco" of Allentown, Pennsylvania, weighing 2,835 lbs.

Smallest. The smallest breed of horse is that bred by Julio Falabella (see above). Adult specimens range from under 18 inches to 30 inches at the shoulder and weigh from 40 to 80 lbs. The upper accepted limit for the American Miniature Horse Breeders Association is 34 inches.

The smallest breed of pony is the Shetland pony, which usually measures 8–10 hands (32–40 inches) and weighs 275–385 lbs.

Heaviest Load Haul. The greatest load hauled by a pair of Clydesdale draught horses (with a combined weight of 3,500 lbs.) was 50 fire logs comprising 36,055 board-feet of lumber (143.9 tons) hauled on a sledge litter 275 yards across snow on the Nester Estate at Ewen, Michigan, on February 26, 1893.

Dogs

Oldest. Dogs of over 20 are very rare but even 34 years has been accepted by one authority. The oldest reliably reported dog in the world was "Adjutant," a black Labrador gun dog who was whelped on August 14, 1936, and died on November 20, 1963, aged 27 years 3 months, in the care of his lifetime owner, James Hawkes, a gamekeeper at the Revesby Estate, near Boston, Lincolnshire, England. Less reliable is a claim of 29 years 5 months for a Queensland "heeler," named "Bluey," who died in Melbourne, Australia, in February, 1940.

Most Popular. The breed with the most American Kennel Club new registrations for the year in 1975 was the Yorkshire terrier with 14,640. The earliest dog show was held in The Town Hall, Newcastle-on-Tyne, England, June 28–29, 1859, with 23 pointers and 27 setters.

Rarest. The rarest breed of dog may be the *Shar-pei* or *Sha-pei* or Chinese fighting dog, which is, due to restrictions on trading and ownership, extinct in China. Only 23 specimens were known to exist in January, 1976, in California, but there may be others in Korea. In March, 1974, there were no more than 50 Portuguese water dogs (*caes de agua*) known to be living.

Largest. The heaviest breed of domestic dog (*Canis familiaris*) is the St. Bernard. The heaviest example is "Schwarzwald Hof Duke" owned by Dr. A. M. Bruner of Oconomowoc, Wisconsin. He was whelped on October 8, 1964, and weighed 295 lbs. on May 2, 1969. He died in August, 1969.

Tallest. The world's tallest dog is the Great Dane "Brynbank Apollo" (kennel name "Dominic"), whelped in 1970 and measured

RARE BREED: Only 23 specimens of the Chinese fighting dog were known to exist in 1976, all in California.

by his vet on August 21, 1973, to be 39¾ inches at the shoulder. He is owned by Mrs. Iris Bates of Harlow, Essex, England.

Smallest. The smallest breed of dog is the Chihuahua from Mexico. New-born pups average 3½–4½ oz. and weigh 2–4 lbs. when fully grown, but some "miniature" specimens weigh only 16 oz.

The world's smallest fully grown dog is a Chihuahua of 10 oz. owned by Rodney M. Sprott of Clemson, South Carolina.

Strongest. The greatest load ever shifted by a dog was 4,400 lbs. pulled over a 15-foot dirt course in accordance with Sled Dog Association rules by a champion Newfoundland dog "Barbara-Allen's Bonzo Bear," owned by Elizabeth Stackhouse, on July 28, 1973, at Bothell, Washington.

In the annual 1,049-mile dog sled race from Anchorage to Nome, Alaska, the record time is 14 days 14 hours 43 minutes, by Emitt Peters in the 1975 race.

Fastest. The fastest breed of dog (excluding the greyhound and possibly the whippet) is the saluki, also called the Arabian gazelle hound or Persian greyhound. Speeds up to 43 m.p.h. have been claimed, but tests in the Netherlands have shown that it is not as fast as the present-day greyhound which has attained a measured speed of 41.7 m.p.h. on a track.

Largest Litter. The largest recorded litter of puppies is one of 23 thrown on June 9, 1944, by "Lena," a foxhound bitch owned by Commander W. N. Ely of Ambler, Pennsylvania. On February 6–7, 1975, "Careless Ann," a St. Bernard owned by Robert and Alice Rodden of Lebanon, Missouri, produced a litter of 23, of which 14 survived.

LARGEST LITTER: This foxhound shows off its litter of 23 healthy, uniform puppies.

Most Prolific. The dog who has sired the greatest recorded number of puppies was the greyhound "Low Pressure" whelped in 1957 and owned by Mrs. Bruna Amhurst of Regent's Park, London. Before he died in November, 1969, he had fathered 2,414 registered puppies, with at least 600 others unregistered.

Most Expensive. In June, 1972, Mrs. Judith Thurlow of Great Ashfield, Suffolk, England, turned down an offer of £14,000, then $33,600, for her champion greyhound "Super Rory" who was whelped in October, 1970.

The highest price ever paid for a dog is £2,000 (about $10,000 then) by Mrs. A. H. Hempton in December, 1929, for the champion greyhound "Mick the Miller" (whelped in Ireland in June, 1926, and died 1939).

"Top Dog." The greatest altitude attained by a mammal other than man is 1,050 miles by the Samoyed husky (Russian, *laika*) bitch fired as a passenger in *Sputnik II* on November 3, 1957. The dog was variously named "Kudryavka" (feminine form of Curly), "Limon-chik" (diminutive of lemon), "Malyshka," "Zhuchka" or by the Russian breed name for husky "Laika."

Top Show Dog. The record number of "Best in Show" awards won by any dog in all-breed shows is 127, compiled from January, 1957, to February, 1960, by International Champion Chik T'Sun of Caversham, owned by Mr. and Mrs. Charlie C. Venable of Marietta, Georgia.

Police Dog. The world's top police dog is "Trep" of Miami, Florida, who has sniffed out $63,000,000 worth of narcotics. In a school demonstration looking for 10 hidden packets, Trep once found 11.

Highest and Longest Jump. The canine "high jump" record is held by a German shepherd named "Crumstone Danko" owned by the De Beers mining company, who, without a springboard, scaled a wall of 11 feet 3 inches in Pretoria, South Africa in May, 1942. The longest recorded canine long jump was one of 30 feet by a greyhound named "Bang" made in jumping a gate in coursing a hare at Brecon Lodge, Gloucestershire, England, in 1849.

Ratting. James Searle's bull terrier bitch "Jenny Lind" killed 500 rats in 1 hour 30 minutes at "The Beehive" in Liverpool, England, in 1853.

Tracking. The greatest tracking feat recorded was performed by the Doberman "Sauer" trained by Detective-Sergeant Herbert Kruger. In 1925, he tracked a stock thief 100 miles across the Great Karroo, South Africa, by scent alone. "Whisky," an 8-year-old minia-ture fox terrier lost in October, 1973, by his master, truck driver Geoff Hancock, at Hayes Creek, 120 miles south of Darwin, Australia, turned up at Mambray Creek, 150 miles north of Adelaide, on June 13, 1974, having covered 1,700 miles across central Australia.

Most Pampered Dogs. A leading New York dog delicatessen catering to the topmost of the city's 470,000 dogs provides private din-ing rooms for pets riding up in chauffeured limousines. The menu includes Maryland lump crabmeat at $3.50 per 4 oz. and shrimps at 65¢ per pair. One "client" with 75 coats has a red satin-lined pearl encrusted cloak and rhinestone-trimmed sunglasses.

The German shepherd "Viking Baron von Heppeplatz" was left property worth $312,000 in the will of his master Herr George Ritt, who died in Munich, West Germany, in August, 1971.

Greatest Dog Funeral. The greatest dog funeral on record was for the mongrel dog Lazaras belonging to the eccentric, Emperor Norton I of the United States, Protector of Mexico, held in San Francisco, in 1862 which was attended by an estimated 10,000 people. There are 410 pet cemeteries in the U.S.

Cats

Oldest. Cats are longer-lived animals than dogs and there are a number of authentic records over 20 years. Information on this subject is often obscured by two or more cats bearing the same nickname. The oldest cat ever recorded was the tabby "Puss," owned by Mrs. T. Holway of Clayhidon, North Devon, England. He was 36 on November 28, 1939 and died the next day. A more recent and better documented case was that of the female tabby "Ma," owned by Mrs. Alice St. George Moore, of Drewsteignton, Devon, England. She was put to sleep on November 5, 1957, aged 34.

Heaviest. The heaviest domestic cat (*Felis catus*) on record was a 9-year-old ginger-and-white tom named "Spice," owned by Mrs. Loren C. Caddell of Ridgefield, Connecticut. He scaled 43 lbs. on June 26, 1974, but has since reduced to 35 lbs. The average weight for an adult cat is 11 lbs.

Largest Litter. The largest live litter ever recorded was one of 14 kittens born in December, 1974, to the Persian cat "Bluebell," owned by Mrs. Elenore Dawson of Wellington, South Africa. On April 23, 1972, a one-year-old seal point Siamese cat named "Seeley," owned by Mrs. Harriet Browne of Southsea, Hampshire, England, gave birth to a litter of 13 kittens, 11 of which survived. The usual litter size is between 5 and 9. In July, 1970, a litter of 19 kittens (four incompletely formed) was reportedly born by Caesarean section to "Tarawood Antigone," a brown Burmese owned by Mrs. Valerie Gane of Oxfordshire, England, but this claim has never been fully substantiated.

Most Prolific. A cat named "Dusty," aged 17, living in Bonham, Texas, gave birth to her 420th kitten on June 12, 1952.

Greatest Escape. A cat named "Gros Minou" fell from the 20th story of a high-rise apartment near Westmount, Quebec, Canada, on May 1, 1973, suffering only a pelvic fracture. In December, 1937, an R.S.P.C.A. inspector rescued a cat which had fallen down a 45-foot-deep quarry shaft on Idle Moor, Yorkshire, England, 18 months earlier.

Most Lives. "Thumper," a 2½-year-old tabby owned by Mrs.

FAT CAT, BUT NOT THE FATTEST: "Gigi" of Great Britain, at 42 lbs. is 1 lb. shy of the record.

Reg Buckett of Westminster, London, was trapped in an elevator shaft without food or water for 52 days from March 29, 1964.

Richest. Dr. William Grier of San Diego, California, died in June, 1963, leaving his entire estate of $415,000 to his two 15-year-old cats, "Hellcat" and "Brownie." When the cats died in 1965 the money went to George Washington University, Washington, D.C.

Most Valuable. In 1967, Miss Elspeth Sellar of Bromley, England, turned down an offer of 2,000 guineas (then $5,880) from an American breeder for her 2-year-old champion copper-eyed white Persian tom, "Coylum Marcus" (born March 28, 1965).

Ratting. The greatest ratter on record was probably the female tabby named "Minnie" who during a six year period, 1927 to 1933, killed 12,480 rats at the White City Stadium, London, England. The greatest mouser on record was a tabby named "Mickey," owned by Shepherd & Sons Ltd. of Burscough, Lancashire, England, which killed more than 22,000 mice during 23 years with the firm. He died in November, 1968.

Cat Population. The largest cat population is in the U.S.— 30 million. Of Britain's cat population of 4.2 million, an estimated 100,000 are "employed" by the civil service.

Rabbits

The largest breed of domestic rabbit (*Oryctolagus cuniculus*) is the Flemish giant, with a weight of 12–14 lbs. This breed measures up to 36 inches long from toe to toe, when fully extended. The heaviest specimen recorded was a male named "Floppy," who weighed 25 lbs. shortly before dying in June, 1963, aged 8. In May, 1971, a weight of 25 lbs. was also reported for a 4-year-old Norfolk Star named "Chewer," owned by Edward Williams of Attleborough, Norfolk, England.

The heaviest recorded wild rabbit is one of 6 lbs. 12 oz., shot by Derek Tooth on the Swinford Estate, Burford, Oxfordshire, England, in February, 1976.

Oldest. The greatest reliable age recorded for a domestic rabbit is 18 years for a doe which was still alive in 1947.

Most Prolific. The most prolific domestic breed is the Norfolk Star. Females produce 9 to 10 litters a year, each containing about 10 young (compare with 5 litters and 3 to 7 young for the wild rabbit). "Chewer" (see above) fathered 36,772 offspring up to July 3, 1972.

Guinea Pigs

The greatest recorded age for a domestic guinea pig (*Cavia parcellus*) is 10 years, attained in June, 1975, by a pet owned by R. Lockyer of Crayford, Kent, England. This is three times the average lifespan.

For auction prices, milk yield and prolificacy records for cattle, sheep and pigs, see Agriculture, Chapter 9.

2. Birds (Aves)

Largest. Of the 8,600 known living species, by far the largest is the North African ostrich (*Struthio camelus camelus*) which lives south of the Atlas Mountains from Upper Senegal and Niger country across to the Sudan and central Ethiopia. Male examples of this flightless or *ratite* bird reach 345 lbs. in weight and stand 9 feet tall.

The heaviest flying bird, or *carinate*, is the Kori bustard or paauw (*Otis kori*) of East and South Africa, which has a wing span up to 8 feet 4 inches. Weights up to 40 lbs. have been reliably reported for cock birds shot in South Africa, and one enormously fat specimen, killed in Transvaal *c.* 1892, was estimated to weigh 54 lbs. The mute swan (*Cygnus olor*) can also reach 40 lbs. on occasion, and there is a record from Poland of a cob weighing 49.5 lbs., which was probably too heavy to fly.

The heaviest flying bird of prey is the Andean condor (*Vultur gryphus*), which averages 20-25 lbs. as an adult. An exceptionally large specimen of the rare California condor (*Gymnogyps californianus*), now preserved in the California Academy of Sciences, Los Angeles, reputedly weighed 31 lbs.

Smallest. The smallest bird in the world is Helena's humming-bird (*Mellisuga helenae*) found in Cuba and the Isle of Pines. An average male adult has a wing span of 3 inches and weighs only 2 grams or 1/18th of an ounce (0.070 oz.). This is less than a Sphinx moth. It has an overall length of 2.28 inches, the bill and tail accounting for about 1.7 inches. The adult females are slightly larger. The bee hummingbird (*Acestrura bombus*) of Ecuador is about the same size, but is slightly heavier.

The smallest bird of prey is the 1¼-oz. Bornean falconet (*Microhierax latifrons*).

Largest Wing Span. The wandering albatross (*Diomedea exulans*) of the southern oceans has the largest wing span of any living bird, adult males averaging 10 feet 4 inches with wings tightly stretched. The largest recorded specimen was a male measuring 11 feet 10 inches caught by banders in Western Australia *c.* 1957, but some unmeasured birds may exceed 13 feet.

The only other bird reliably credited with a wing spread in excess of eleven feet is the vulture-like marabou stork (*Leptoptilus crumeniferus*) of Africa. A 12-foot specimen has been reported, and there is an unconfirmed claim of 13 feet 4 inches for a stork shot in Central Africa in the 1930's.

Most Abundant. The most abundant of all birds is the red-billed quelea (*Quelea quelea*) of the drier parts of Africa south of the Sahara with a population estimated at 10,000,000,000 of which a tenth are destroyed each year by pest control units.

The most abundant domesticated bird is the chicken, the domesticated form of the wild red jungle fowl (*Gallus gallus*) of southeast

BIRD WITH LARGEST WING SPAN: The marabou stork has a wing span of 9 feet or more—with an unconfirmed record 13 feet 4 inches. This specimen was shot in Central Africa in the 1930's.

Asia. There are believed to be about 4,000,000,000 chickens in the world, or nearly one chicken for every member of the human race.

The most abundant sea bird is Wilson's petrel (*Oceanites oceanicus*). No population estimates have been published, but the number runs into the hundreds—possibly thousands—of millions.

Rarest. Great practical difficulties attend the identification of the rarest species of bird in the wild. Three of the strongest candidates are (a) the new species of sparrow-sized honeycreeper found in late 1973 on the Hawaiian island of Maui; (b) the Mauritius kestrel, of which 7 survive; and (c) the Eskimo curlew (*Numenius borealis*), last sighted on August 7, 1972 in Massachusetts.

Longest-Lived. The greatest irrefutable age reported for any bird is 72 years in the case of a male Andean condor (*Vultur gryphus*) named "Kuzya," which died in Moskovskii Zoologicheskeii Park, Moscow, in 1964. This bird had been received there as an adult in 1892. Other records which are regarded as probably reliable include 73 years (1818–91) for a greater sulphur-crested cockatoo (*Cacatua galerita*), 72 years (1797–1869) for an African gray parrot (*Psittacus erithacus*), 70 years (1770–1840) for a mute swan (*Cygnus olor*), and 69 years for a raven (*Corvus corax*). In 1972, a southern ostrich (*Struthio camelus australis*) aged 62 years 3 months was killed in the Ostrich Abattoir at Oudtshoorn, Cape Province, South Africa.

"Jimmy," a red and green Amazon parrot owned by Mrs. Bella Ludford of Liverpool, England, was allegedly hatched in captivity on December 3, 1870, and lived 104 years in his original brass cage He died on January 5, 1975.

Fastest-Flying. The spine-tailed swift (see page 57) is the fastest bird.

The bird which presents the hunter with the greatest difficulty is the red-breasted merganser (*Mergus serrator*). On May 29, 1960, a specimen flushed from the Kukpuk River, Cape Thompson, northern Alaska, by a light aircraft recorded an air speed of 80 m.p.h. in level flight for nearly 13 seconds before turning aside.

Fastest and Slowest Wing Beat. The fastest recorded wing beat of any bird is 90 beats per second by the hummingbird (*Heliactin cornuta*) of tropical South America. This rate is probably exceeded by the bee hummingbirds *Mellisuga helenae* and *Acestrura bombus*, but figures have not yet been published.

Large vultures (family Vulturidae) can soar for hours without beating their wings, and sometimes exhibit a flapping rate as low as one beat per second.

Fastest Swimmer. Gentoo penguins (*Pygoscelis papua*) have been timed at 22.3 m.p.h. underwater, which is a respectable flying speed for some birds.

Deepest Diver. The emperor penguin (*Aptenodytes forsteri*) of the Antarctic can reach a depth of 870 feet and remained submerged for as long as 18 minutes.

Longest Flights. The greatest distance covered by a ringed bird during migration is 12,000 miles by an Arctic tern (*Sterna paradisaea*), which was banded as a nestling on July 5, 1955, in the Kandalaksha

Sanctuary on the White Sea coast of the U.S.S.R., north of Archangel, and was captured alive by a fisherman 8 miles south of Fremantle, Western Australia, on May 16, 1956.

Highest-Flying. The celebrated example of a skein of 17 Egyptian geese (*Alopochen aegyptiacus*), photographed by an astronomer from Dehra Dun, India, on September 17, 1919, as they crossed the sun at a height estimated at between 11 and 12 miles (58,080–63,360 feet), has been discredited by experts. The highest acceptable altitude is 26,900 feet by a small group of alpine choughs (*Pyrrhocorax graculus*) which followed the British expedition up Mount Everest in 1924. On May 23, 1960, a steppe eagle (*Aguila nipalensis*) and two other raptors were found dead at nearly 26,000 feet on the South Col of Mount Everest.

On three separate occasions in 1959, a radar station in Norfolk, England, picked up flocks of small passerine night migrants flying in from Scandinavia at up to 21,000 feet. They were probably warblers (*Sylviidae*), chats (*Turdidae*) and fly-catchers (*Muscicapidae*).

Most Airborne. The most airborne of all land birds is the common swift (*Apus apus*) which remains aloft for at least nine months of the year, but the sooty tern (*Sterno fuscata*) remains continuously aloft for three or four years after leaving the nesting grounds before it returns to the breeding grounds.

Most Acute Vision. Tests have shown that under favorable conditions the long-eared owl (*Asio otus*) and the barn owl (*Tyto alba*) can swoop on targets from a distance of 6 feet or more in an illumination of only 0.00000073 of a foot candle (equivalent to the light from a standard candle at a distance of 1,170 feet). This acuity is 50–100 times as great as that of human night vision. In good light and against a contrasting background a golden eagle (*Aquila chrysaetos*) can detect an 18-inch-long hare at a range of 2,150 yards (possibly even 2 miles).

Eggs—Largest. Of living birds, the one producing the largest egg is the ostrich (*Struthio camelus*). The average egg weighs 3.63 to 3.88 lbs., measures 6 to 8 inches in length, 4 to 6 inches in diameter and requires about 40 minutes for boiling. The shell is 1/16th of an inch thick and can support the weight of a 252-lb. man.

Eggs—Smallest. The smallest egg laid by any bird is the egg of Helena's hummingbird (*Mellisuga helenae*), the world's smallest bird. One measuring 0.45 of an inch long and 0.32 of an inch wide is now in the Smithsonian Institution in Washington, D.C. This egg, which weighs 0.176 oz., was collected at Boyate, Santiago de Cuba, on May 8, 1906.

Incubation. The longest incubation period is that of the wandering albatross (*Diomedea exulans*), with a normal range of 75 to 82 days. There is one case recorded of an egg of the mallee fowl (*Leipoa ocellata*) of Australia taking 90 days to hatch. Its normal incubation period is 62 days. The shortest incubation period is the 10 days of the great spotted woodpecker (*Dendrocopus major*) and the black-billed cuckoo (*Coccyzus enythropthalmus*). The idlest of cock birds are hummingbirds (family Trochilidae), eider ducks (*Somateria mollissima*) and golden pheasants (*Chrysolophus pictus*), among whom the hen bird does 100 per cent of the incubation, whereas the female common kiwi (*Apteryx australis*) leaves this entirely to the male for 75 to 80 days.

Largest Nests. The largest bird's nest on record is one 9½ feet wide and 20 feet deep, built by bald eagles (*Haliaeetus leucocephalus*) near St. Petersburg, Florida, reported in 1963 and estimated to weigh more than 2¼ tons. The incubation mounds built by scrubfowl (family Megapodidae) have, however, been measured up to 50 feet in diameter and 20 feet in height.

Longest Feathers. The longest feathers known are those of the cock birds of the Japanese long-tailed fowls, or onagadori (a strain of *Gallus gallus*) which have been bred in southwestern Japan since the mid 17th century. In 1973, a tail covert measuring 34 feet 9½ inches was reported by Masasha Kubota of Kochi, Shikoku.

Most Feathers. In a series of "feather counts" on various species of birds, a whistling swan (*Cygnus columbianus*) was found to have 25,216 feathers. A ruby-throated hummingbird (*Archilochus colubris*) had only 940, although hummingbirds have more feathers per area of body surface than any other living bird.

Champion Bird-Watcher

The world's leading bird-watcher is G. Stuart Keith, an Englishman who works at the American Museum of Natural History, New York City. Since April, 1947, his score is 5,340 species of the 8,650 known species.

Domesticated Birds

Largest Turkey. The greatest *live* weight recorded for a turkey (*Meleagris gallopavo*) is 75 lbs., reported in December, 1973, for a "holiday" turkey reared by Signe Olsen, Salt Lake City, Utah. The U.S. record for a dressed bird is 68½ lbs. in 1953.

Largest Chicken. The heaviest chicken on record is "Weirdo," a 4-year-old White Sully of 22 pounds reported in Calaveras County, California in January, 1973. "Weirdo" murdered an 18-pound son, crippled a dog, and has so far injured his owner to the extent of 8 stitches besides killing two cats. The white Sully breed was developed by Mr. Grant Sullens of West Point, California.

Most Talkative Bird. The world's most talkative bird is a male African gray parrot (*Psittacus erythacus*) named "Prudle," owned by Mrs. Lyn Logue of Golders Green, London, England, which is the reigning and unbeaten winner of the "best talking parrot-like bird" title at the National Cage and Aviary Bird Show in London for the 11 years, 1965–75. Prudle was taken from a nest in a tree about to be felled at Jinja, Uganda, in 1958.

Longest-Lived. It was reported in June, 1972, that Mrs. Kathleen Leck, 32, still had a 31-year-old canary (*Serinus canaria*) bartered by her father, Mr. Ross of Hull, in Calabar, Nigeria, when she was one.

The longest-lived domesticated bird (excluding the ostrich) is the domestic goose which normally lives about 25 years. In 1975, a gander named "George" celebrated his 48th birthday. He is owned by Mrs. Florence Hull of Thornton, Lancashire, England. A budgerigar (parakeet) named "Georgie," owned by Mrs. Elsie Ramshaw of Denaby Main, South Yorkshire, England, received an award in March, 1975, from the Newcastle and Gateshead Budgerigar Society upon reaching the ripe old age of 25 years. The largest caged budgerigar (*Melopsittacus undulatus*) population is probably that of the United Kingdom with an estimated 3½–4 million. In 1956, the population was about 7 million.

3. Reptiles *(Reptilia)*

(Crocodiles, snakes, turtles, tortoises and lizards.)

Largest and Heaviest. The largest reptile in the world is the estuarine or salt-water crocodile (*Crocodylus porosus*) of southeast Asia, northern Australia, New Guinea, the Philippines and the Solomon Islands. Adult bulls average 12–14 feet in length and scale about 1,100 lbs. In 1823 a notorious man-eater measuring 27 feet in length and weighing an estimated 4,400 lbs. was shot at Jala Jala on Luzon Island in the Philippines after terrorizing the neighborhood for many years. Its skull, the largest on record (if we exclude fossil remains) is now preserved in the Museum of Comparative Zoology at Harvard University, Cambridge, Massachusetts. Another outsized example with a reputed length of 33 feet and a maximum bodily girth of 13 feet 8 inches was shot in the Bay of Bengal, India, in 1840, but the dimensions of its skull (preserved in the British Museum of Natural History, London) suggest that it must have come from a crocodile measuring about 24 feet. In 1957, an unconfirmed length of 28 feet 4 inches was reliably reported for an estuarine crocodile shot on MacArthur Bank in the Norman River, in northwestern Queensland, Australia.

Smallest. The smallest species of reptile is believed to be *Sphaerodactylus parthenopion*, a gecko found only on the island of Virgin Gorda, British Virgin Islands in the Caribbean. It is known from 15 specimens, including some gravid females, found between August 10 and 16, 1964. The three largest females measured 0.71 of an inch from snout to vent, with a tail of approximately the same length.

It is possible that another gecko, *Sphaerodactylus elasmorhynchus*, may be even smaller. The only specimen ever discovered was an apparently mature female, with a snout-vent length of 0.67 of an inch and a tail of the same length, found on March 15, 1966, among the roots of a tree in the western part of the Massif de la Hotte in Haiti.

A species of dwarf chameleon, *Evoluticauda tuberculata*, found in Madagascar, and known only from a single specimen, has a snout-vent length of 0.71 inches and a tail length of 0.55 inches. Chameleons, however, are more bulky than geckos, and it is not yet known if this specimen was fully grown.

Fastest. The highest speed measured for any reptile on land is 18 m.p.h. by a six-lined race-runner (*Cnemidophorus sexlineatus*) pursued by a car near McCormick, South Carolina, in 1941. The highest speed claimed for any reptile in water is 22 m.p.h. by a frightened Pacific leatherback turtle (see *Largest Chelonians*).

Largest Lizard. The largest of all lizards is the Komodo monitor or Ora (*Varanus komodoensis*), a dragon-like reptile found on the Indonesian islands of Komodo, Rintja, Padar and Flores. Adult males average 8 feet in length and weigh 175–200 lbs. Lengths up to 23 feet (*sic*) have been quoted for this species, but the largest specimen to be accurately measured was a male presented to an American zoologist in 1928 by the Sultan of Bima which then taped 10 feet 0.8 inches. In 1937, this animal was put on display in the St. Louis Zoological Gardens for a short period. It then measured 10 feet 2 inches in length and weighed 365 lbs.

Oldest. The greatest age recorded for a lizard is more than 54 years for a male slow worm (*Anguis fragilis*) kept in the Zoological Museum in Copenhagen, Denmark, from 1892 until 1946.

Chelonians

Largest. The largest of all chelonians is the Pacific leatherback turtle (*Dermochelys coriacea schlegelii*). The average adult measures 6–7 feet in overall length (length of carapace 4–5 feet) and weighs between 660 and 800 lbs. The greatest weight reliably recorded is 1,908 lbs. for a specimen captured off Monterey, California, in 1961, which is now on permanent display at the Wharf Aquarium, Fisherman's Wharf, Monterey. Its length was 8 feet 4 inches overall.

The largest living tortoise is *Geochelone* (*Testudo*) *gigantea* of the Indian Ocean islands of Aldabra, Mauritius, Réunion and Seychelles (introduced 1874). Adult males sometimes exceed 350 lbs. in weight, and a specimen weighing 900 lbs. was allegedly collected in Aldabra in 1847.

Longest-Lived. Tortoises are the longest-lived of all vertebrates. Reliable records over 100 years include a common box tortoise (*Testudo carolina*) of 138 years and a European pond tortoise (*Emys orbicularis*) of 120+years. The greatest proven age of a continuously observed tortoise is 116+years for a Mediterranean spur-thighed tortoise (*Testudo graeca*) which died in Paignton Zoo, Devon, England, in 1957. On May 19, 1966, the death was reported of "Tu'imalilia" or "Tui Malela" the famous but much battered Madagascar radiated tortoise (*Testudo radiata*) reputedly presented to the King of Tonga by Captain James Cook in 1773, but this record of almost 200 years was all too probably a composite of two (or more) specimens whose lifetimes overlapped.

Slowest-Moving. Tests on a giant tortoise (*Geochelone gigantea*) in Mauritius show that even when hungry and enticed by a cabbage it cannot cover more than 5 yards in a minute (0.17 m.p.h.) on land. Over longer distances its speed is greatly reduced.

LARGEST LIVING TORTOISE: This giant tortoise, with a smaller relative, is a native of Aldabra Island in the Indian Ocean. Males may weigh up to 900 pounds.

Snakes

Longest. The longest (and heaviest) of all snakes is the anaconda (*Eunectes murinus*) of South America. In 1944, a length of 37½ feet was reliably reported for a specimen shot on the upper Orinoco River in eastern Colombia. It was provisionally measured but later recovered and escaped. Another anaconda killed on the lower Rio Guaviare, in southeastern Colombia, in November, 1956, reportedly measured 33 feet 7½ inches in length, but nothing of this snake was preserved.

In 1912 a reticulated python (*Python reticulatus*), measuring 32 feet 9½ inches, was killed near a mining camp on the north coast of the island of Celebes in the Malay Archipelago. An African rock python (*Python sebae*), measuring 32 feet 2¼ inches, was killed on the grounds of a school at Bingerville, Ivory Coast, in 1932.

The longest snake ever kept in a zoo was probably "Colossus," a female reticulated python (*Python reticulatus*) who died of tuberculosis on April 15, 1963, in the Highland Park Zoological Gardens, Pittsburgh. She measured 22 feet on August 10, 1949, when she arrived there from Singapore, and was measured at 28 feet 6 inches on November 15, 1956, when she was growing at the rate of about 10 inches per year. Her girth, before a feed, was measured at 36 inches on March 2, 1955, and she weighed 320 lbs. on June 12, 1957. She was probably at least 29 feet long at the time of her death in 1963. The longest snake living in captivity anywhere in the

LONGEST VENOMOUS SNAKE: The king cobra, 18 feet 9 inches long.

world today is a female reticulated python named "Cassius," owned by Adrian Nyoka, managing director of the Knaresborough Zoo, Yorkshire, England. This specimen (collected in Malaysia in 1972) now measures 27 feet 6 inches in length and weighs 240 pounds.

A 29-foot 6¼-inch specimen has been reported in the Keban Binatang, Djakata, Indonesia, but it is unconfirmed.

A long-standing reward of $5,000, offered by the New York Zoological Society, Bronx Zoo, New York City, for a living specimen of any snake measuring more than 30 feet has never been collected.

The longest venomous snake in the world is the king cobra (*Ophiophagus hannah*), also called the hamadryad. A specimen was collected near Port Dickson in Malaya in April, 1937, and grew to 18 feet 9 inches in the London Zoo. It was destroyed with the outbreak of war in 1939.

Shortest. The shortest known snake is the thread snake *Leptotyphlops bilineata*, found on the Caribbean islands of Martinique, Barbados and St. Lucia. It has a maximum recorded length of 4.7 inches.

The shortest venomous snake is the striped dwarf garter snake (*Elaps dorsalis*) of South Africa. Adults average 6 inches in length.

Heaviest. The heaviest snake is the anaconda (*Eunectes murinus*). The 37½-foot specimen (see *Longest Snake*) was also the heaviest, probably weighing nearly 1,000 lbs.

The heaviest venomous snake is the Eastern diamond-back rattlesnake (*Crotalus adamanteus*), found in the southeastern United States. A specimen 7 feet 9 inches in length weighed 34 lbs. Less reliable measurements of 40 lbs. for an 8-foot-9-inch specimen have been reported.

Oldest Snake. The greatest irrefutable age recorded for a snake is 39 years in the case of a common Boa (*Boa constrictor constrictor*) at Philadelphia Zoological Gardens. Named "Popeye," he was still alive on February 4, 1976. He was purchased from a London dealer in December, 1936.

Fastest-Moving. The fastest-moving land snake is probably the slender black mamba (*Dendroaspis polylepis*). On April 23, 1906, an angry black mamba was timed at a speed of 7 m.p.h. over a measured distance of 47 yards near Mbuyuni on the Serengeti Plains, Kenya. Stories that black mambas can overtake galloping horses (maximum speed 43.26 m.p.h.) are wild exaggerations, though a speed of 15 m.p.h. may be possible for short bursts over level ground.

Most Venomous. The world's most venomous snake is now believed to be the sea snake *Hydrophis belcheri* which has a venom one hundred times as lethal as that of the Australian taipan (*Oxyuranus scutellatus*). The snake abounds around Ashmore Reef in the Timor Sea, off northwestern Australia.

The most venomous land snake is probably the peninsular tiger snake (*Notechis ater niger*) found on Kangaroo Island and in the Sir Joseph Banks Group in Spencers Gulf, South Australia. It grows to a length of 4 to 5 feet and the average venom yield is sufficient to kill 300 sheep.

It is estimated that between 30,000 and 40,000 people (excluding Chinese and Russians) die from snakebite each year, 75 per cent of them in densely populated India. Burma has the highest mortality rate with 15.4 deaths per 100,000 population per annum.

Longest Fangs. The longest fangs of any snake are those of the Gaboon viper (*Bitus gabonica*), of tropical Africa. In a 6-foot-long specimen, the fangs measured 1.96 inches. A Gaboon viper bit itself to death on February 12, 1963, in the Philadelphia Zoological Gardens. Keepers found the dead snake with its fangs deeply embedded in its own back. It was the only one of that species in the zoo.

LONGEST FANGS: This Gaboon viper, with fangs almost 2 inches long, bit itself to death in 1963.

4. Amphibians (Amphibia)

(Salamanders, toads, frogs, newts, caecilians, etc.)

Largest

The largest species of amphibian is the Chinese giant salamander (*Megalobatrachus davidianus*), which lives in the cold mountain streams and marshy areas of northeastern, central and southern China. The average adult measures 39.37 inches in total length and weighs 24.2 to 28.6 lbs. One huge individual collected in Kweichow (Guizhou) Province in southern China in the early 1920's measured 5 feet in total length and weighed nearly 100 lbs. The Japanese giant salamander (*Megalobatrachus japonicus*) is slightly smaller, but one captive specimen weighed 88 lbs. when alive and 99 lbs. after death, the body having absorbed water from the aquarium.

Newt. The largest newt in the world is the pleurodele or ribbed newt (*Pleurodeles waltl*), which is found in Morocco and on the Iberian Peninsula. Specimens measuring up to 15.74 inches in total length and weighing over 1 lb. have been reliably reported.

Frog. The largest known frog is the rare Goliath frog (*Rana goliath*) of Cameroon and Spanish Guinea, West Africa. A female weighing 7 lbs. 4.5 oz. was caught in the rapids of the River Mbia, Spanish Guinea, on August 23, 1960. It had a snout-vent length of 13.38 inches and measured 32.08 inches overall with legs extended. In December, 1960, another giant frog known locally as "agak" or "carn-pnag" and said to measure 12–15 inches snout to vent and to weigh over 6 lbs. was reportedly discovered in central New Guinea, but further information is lacking. In 1969, a new species of giant frog was discovered in Sumatra.

Tree Frog. The largest species of tree frog is *Hyla vasta*, found only on the island of Hispaniola (Haiti and the Dominican Republic) in the West Indies. The average snout-vent length is about 3.54 inches, but a female collected from the San Juan River, Dominican Republic, in March, 1928, measured 5.63 inches.

Toad. The largest toad in the world is probably the marine toad (*Bufo marinus*) of tropical South America. An enormous female collected on November 24, 1965, at Miraflores Vaupes, Colombia, and later exhibited in the Reptile House at the Bronx Zoo, New York City, had a snout-vent length of 9.37 inches and weighed 2 lbs. 11¼ oz. at the time of its death in 1967.

Smallest

The smallest species of amphibian is believed to be an arrow-poison frog *Sminthillus limbatus*, found only in Cuba. Fully-grown specimens have a snout-vent length of 0.44–0.48 inches.

Newt. The smallest newt in the world is believed to be the striped newt (*Notophthalmus perstriatus*) of the southeastern United States. Adult specimens average 2.01 inches in total length.

Tree Frog. The smallest tree frog in the world is the least tree frog (*Hyla ocularis*), found in the southeastern United States. It has a maximum snout-vent length of 0.62 inches.

LARGEST TOAD (above): The South American marine toad can weigh up to 2 lbs. 11¼ oz. LARGEST AMPHIBIAN (right): The Chinese giant salamander can grow to a length of 5 feet.

Toad. The smallest toad in the world is the sub-species *Bufo taitanus beiranus*, first discovered in *c.* 1906 near Beira, Mozambique, East Africa. Adult specimens have a maximum recorded snout-vent length of 0.94 inches.

Salamander. The smallest species of salamander is the pygmy salamander (*Desmognathus wrighti*), which is found only in Tennessee, North Carolina and Virginia. Adult specimens measure from 1.45 to 2.0 inches in total length.

Longest-Lived. The greatest authentic age recorded for an amphibian is about 55 years for a male Japanese giant salamander (*Megalobatrachus japonicus*) which died in the aquarium at Amsterdam Zoological Gardens on June 3, 1881. It was brought to Holland in 1829, at which time it was estimated to be 3 years old.

Highest and Lowest. The common toad (*Bufo vulgaris*) is said to have been found at an altitude of 26,246 feet in the Himalayas, and at a depth of 1,115 feet in a coal mine.

Most Poisonous. The most active known venom is the batrachotoxin derived from the skin secretions of the kokoi (*Phyllobates latinasus*), an arrow-poison frog of the Choco in western Colombia, South America. Only about 1/100,000th of a gram (0.0000004 of an ounce) is enough to kill a man.

Longest Frog Jump. The record for three consecutive leaps is 32 feet 3 inches by a 2-inch-long South African sharp-nosed frog (*Rana oxyrhyncha*), recorded by Dr. Walter Rose of the South African Museum on Green Point Common, Cape Town, on January 16,

1954. It was named "Leaping Lena" (but later found to be a male). At the annual Calaveras County Jumping Frog Jubilee at Angels Camp, California, in 1975, "Ex Lax" made a *single* leap of 17 feet 6¾ inches for its owner Bill Moniz.

5. Fishes *(Pisces, Bradyodonti, Selachii and Marsipoli)*

Largest—Sea. The largest species of fish is the whale-shark (*Rhiniodon typus*) first discovered off Cape Town, South Africa, in April, 1828. It is not, however, the largest aquatic animal, since it is smaller than the larger species of whales (mammals). A whale-shark measuring 59 feet long and weighing about 90,000 lbs. was caught in a bamboo fish-trap at Koh Chik, in the Gulf of Siam, in 1919.

The plankton-feeding whale-shark, grayish or dark brown with white or yellow spots, is extremely docile and lives in the warmer areas of the Atlantic, Pacific and Indian Oceans. Unlike mammals, fish continue to grow with age.

The largest carnivorous fish (excluding plankton-eaters) is the great white shark (*Carcharodon carcharias*), also called the man-eater, which ranges from the tropics to temperate zone waters. In June, 1930, a specimen measuring 37 feet in length was reportedly trapped in a herring weir at White Head Island, New Brunswick, Canada, but this may have been a wrongly identified basking shark (*Cetorhinus maximus*). In May, 1948, a great white shark measuring 21 feet in length was captured after a fierce battle by fishermen off Havana, Cuba. It weighed 7,302 lbs.

LARGEST FRESH-WATER FISH (left): This European catfish measured up to 11 feet long and weighed 565 pounds. **LARGEST FISH** (above): The whale-shark (not a mammal) grows up to 59 feet long and lays the largest eggs of any living creature. (See page 58.)

The longest of the bony or "true" fishes (Pisces) is the Russian sturgeon (*Acipenser huso*), also called the Beluga, which is found in the temperate areas of the Adriatic, Black and Caspian Seas, but enters large rivers like the Volga and the Danube for spawning. Lengths up to 26 feet 3 inches have been reliably reported, and a gravid female taken in the estuary of the Volga in 1827 weighed 3,250½ lbs.

The heaviest bony fish in the world is the ocean sunfish (*Mola mola*), which is found in all tropical, sub-tropical and temperate waters. On September 18, 1908, a huge specimen was accidentally struck by the S.S. *Fiona* off Bird Island about 40 miles from Sydney, New South Wales, Australia, and towed to Port Jackson. It measured 14 feet between the anal and dorsal fins and weighed 5,017 lbs.

Largest—Fresh-water. The largest fish which spends its whole life in fresh or brackish water is the rare Pa Beuk or Pla Buk (*Pangasianodon gigas*), a giant catfish found in the Mekong River of Laos and Thailand. Adult males average 8 feet in length and weigh about 360 lbs. This size was exceeded in fresh water by the European catfish or Wels (*Silurus glanis*). In the 19th century lengths of up to 15 feet and weights up to 720 lbs. were reported for Russian specimens, but today anything over 6 feet and 200 lbs. is considered large. The arapaima (*Arapaima glanis*), also called the pirarucu, found in the Amazon and other South American rivers and often claimed to be the largest fresh-water fish, averages 6½ feet and 150 lbs. The largest "authentically recorded" measured 8 feet 1½ inches and weighed 325 lbs. It was caught in the Rio Negro, Brazil, in 1836.

Smallest—Sea. The smallest recorded marine fishes are the Marshall Islands goby (*Eviota zonura*), measuring 0.47 to 0.63 of an inch, and *Schindleria praematurus* from Samoa, measuring 0.47 to 0.74 of an inch, both in the Pacific Ocean. Mature specimens of the latter, largely transparent and first identified in 1940, have been known to weigh only 2 milligrams, equivalent to 17,750 to the ounce—the lightest of all vertebrates and the smallest catch possible for any fisherman.

Smallest—Fresh-water. The shortest recorded fresh-water fish and the shortest of all vertebrates is the dwarf pygmy goby (*Pandaka pygmaea*), almost transparent and colorless, found in streams and lakes on Luzon, the Philippines. Adult males measure only 0.28 to 0.38 of an inch long and weigh only 4 to 5 milligrams (0.00014 to 0.00017 of an ounce).

Fastest. The sailfish (*Istiophorus platypterus*) is generally considered to be the fastest species of fish, although the practical difficulties of measurement make data extremely difficult to secure. A figure of 68.1 m.p.h. (100 yards in 3 seconds) has been cited for one off Florida. The swordfish (*Xiphias gladius*) has also been credited with very high speeds, but the evidence is based mainly on bills that have been found deeply embedded in ships' timbers. A speed of 50 knots (57.6 m.p.h.) has been calculated from a penetration of 22 inches by a bill into a piece of timber, but 30 to 35 knots (35 to 40 m.p.h.) is the most conceded by some experts. Speeds in excess of 35 knots (40 m.p.h.) have also been attributed to the marlin (*Tetrapturus sp.*), the wahoo (*Acanthocybium solandri*), the great blue shark (*Prionace* *glauca*), and the bonefish (*Albula vulpes*), and the bluefin tuna (*Thunnus thynnus*) has been scientifically clocked at 43.4 m.p.h. in a 20-second dash. The four-winged flying fish (*Cypselurus heterururs*) may also exceed 40 m.p.h. during its rapid rush to the surface before take-off (the average speed in the air is about 35 m.p.h.). Record flights of 90 seconds, 36 feet in altitude and 3,640 feet in length have been recorded in the tropical Atlantic.

Longest-Lived. Aquaria are of too recent origin to be able to establish with certainty which species of fish can fairly be regarded as the longest-lived. Early indications are that it is the lake sturgeon (*Acipenser fulvescens*). One specimen 6 feet 9 inches long and weighing 215 lbs., caught in the Lake of the Woods, Kenora, Ontario, Canada, on July 15, 1953, was believed (but not by all authorities) to be 154 years old based on a growth ring count. A figure of 228 years has also been attributed by growth ring count to a mirror carp (*Cyprinus carpion*) named "Hanako" living in a pond in Higashi Shirakawa, Gifu Prefecture, Japan, but the greatest authoritatively accepted age is "more than 50 years." Great ages are also claimed for Japanese Koi fish.

The lungfish (*Protopterus*) of Central Africa has been known to estivate for 4 years. The coelacanth (*Latimeria chalumnae*), identified by Margaret Courtnenay-Latimer and J. L. B. Smith in 1938, having been landed in East London, South Africa, from the Mozambique Channel, was thought to have been extinct for 70 million years. By the end of 1975, 84 other specimens had been discovered in waters around the Comoro Islands, between Mozambique and Madagascar.

Oldest Goldfish. The exhibition life of a goldfish (*Carassius auratus*) is normally about 17 years, but much greater ages have been reliably reported. There is also a record of a goldfish living for 40 years.

Shortest-Lived. The shortest-lived fishes are probably certain species of the sub-order Cyprinodontei (killifish) found in Africa and South America which normally live about 8 months in the wild.

Deepest. The greatest depth from which a fish has been recovered is 27,230 feet in the Puerto Rico Trench (27,488 feet) in the Atlantic by Dr. Gilbert L. Voss of the U.S. research vessel *John Elliott*. The fish, taken in April, 1970, was a 6½-inch-long *Bassogigas profundissimus* and was only the fifth such brotulid ever caught. Dr. Jacques Piccard and Lieutenant Don Walsh, U.S. Navy, reported they saw a sole-like fish about 1 foot long (tentatively identified as *Chascanopsetta lugubris*) from the bathyscaphe *Trieste* at a depth of 35,802 feet in the Challenger Deep (Mariana Trench) in the western Pacific on January 24, 1960. This sighting, however, has been questioned by some authorities, who still regard the brotulids of the genus *Bassogigas* as the deepest-living vertebrates.

Most Venomous. The most venomous fish in the world are the stonefish (family Synanceidae) of the tropical waters of the Indo-Pacific. Direct contact with the spines of their fins, which contain a strong neurotoxic poison, often proves fatal.

Most Eggs. The ocean sunfish (*Mola mola*) produces up to 300,000,000 eggs, each of them measuring about 0.05 in. in diameter. The egg yield of the toothcarp, *Jordanella floridae*, of Florida, is only about 20 over a period of several days.

Most Electric. The most powerful electric fish is the electric eel (*Electrophorus electricus*), which is found in the rivers of Brazil, Colombia, Venezuela and Peru. An average-sized specimen can discharge 400 volts at 1 ampere, but measurements up to 650 volts have been recorded.

6. Starfishes *(Asteroidea)*

Largest. The largest of the 1,600 known species of starfish in terms of total diameter is the very fragile brisingid *Midgardia xandaros*. A specimen collected by the Texas A & M University research vessel *Alaminos* in the southern part of the Gulf of Mexico in the late summer of 1968, measured 54.33 inches from tip to tip but the diameter of its disc was only 1.02 inches. Its dry weight was only 2.46 ounces. The most massive species of starfish is probably the five-armed *Evasterias echinosoma* of the North Pacific. One specimen collected by a Russian expedition in the flooded crater of a volcano in Broughton Bay, Semushir, one of the Kurile Islands, in June, 1970, measured 37.79 inches in total diameter and weighed more than 11 lbs.

Smallest. The smallest known starfish is *Marginaster capreensis*, found deep in the Mediterranean, which is not known to exceed a diameter of 0.78 inches.

Deepest. The greatest depth from which a starfish has been recovered is 24,881 feet for a specimen of *Porcellanaster ivanovi*, collected by the Russian research ship *Vityaz* in the Mariana Trench, in the Pacific in 1962.

7. Arachnids *(Arachnida)*

Spiders (Order Araneae)

Largest. The world's largest known spider is the South American "bird eating" spider (*Theraphosa leblondi*). A male specimen with a body 3½ inches long and a leg span of 10 inches, when fully extended, was collected in April, 1925, at Montagne la Gabrielle, French Guiana. It weighed nearly 2 ounces.

The heaviest spider ever recorded was a female "tarantula" of the long-haired species, *Lasiodora klugi*, collected at Manaos, Brazil, in 1945. It measured 9½ inches across the legs and weighed almost 3 ounces.

Smallest. The smallest known spider in the world is *Patu marplesi* (family Symphytognathidae) of Western Samoa. The type specimen (a male found in moss at *c.* 2,000-foot altitude near Malolelei, Upolu, in January, 1956) measures 0.016 inches overall—half the size of a printed period (.).

Largest and Smallest Webs. The largest webs are the aerial ones spun by the tropical orb weavers of the genus *Nephila*, which have been measured up to 18 feet 9¾ inches in circumference.

The smallest webs are spun by spiders like *Glyphesis cottonae*, etc. which are about the size of a small postage stamp.

Most Venomous. The most venomous spider in the world is probably *Latrodectus mactans* of the Americas, which is better known as the "black widow." Females of this species (the much smaller males are harmless) have a bite capable of killing a human being, but deaths are rare. The funnel web spider (*Atrax robustus*) of Australia, the jockey spider (*Latrodectus hasseltii*) of Australia and New Zealand, the button spider (*Latrodectus indistinctus*) of South Africa, the podadora (*Glyptocranium gasteracanthoides*) of Argentina and the brown recluse spider (*Loxosceles reclusa*) of the central and southern United States have been credited with fatalities.

Rarest. The most elusive of all spiders are the primitive atypical tarantulas of the genus *Liphistius*, which are found in southeast Asia.

Fastest. The highest speed measured for a spider on a level surface is 1.73 feet per second (1.17 m.p.h.) in the case of a specimen of *Tegenaria atrica*. This is 33 times its body length per second (compare with the human record of 5½ times its body length per second).

Longest-Lived. The longest-lived of all spiders are the primitive *Mygalomorphae* (tarantulas and allied species). One mature female tarantula collected at Mazatlan, Mexico, in 1935 and estimated to be 12 years old at the time, was kept in a laboratory for 16 years, making a total of 28 years.

8. Crustaceans *(Crustacea)*

(Crabs, lobsters, shrimps, prawns, crayfish, barnacles, water fleas, fish lice, wood lice, sand hoppers and krill, etc.)

Largest. The largest of all crustaceans (although not the heaviest) is the giant spider crab (*Macrocheira kaempferi*), also called the stilt crab, which is found in deep waters off the southeastern coast of Japan. Mature specimens usually have a 12–14-inch-wide body and a claw span of 8–9 feet, but unconfirmed measurements up to 19 feet have been reported. A specimen with a claw span of 12 feet 1½ inches weighed 14 lbs. The heaviest crab is *Pseudocarcinus gigas* found in the Bass Straits, Australia, which weighs up to 30 lbs.

The largest species of lobster, and the heaviest of all crustaceans, is the American or North Atlantic lobster (*Homarus americanus*). One weighing 42 lbs. 7 oz. and measuring 3 feet from the end of the tail-fan to the tip of the claw was caught by the smack *Hustler* in a deep-sea trawl off the Virginia coast in 1934 and is now on display in the Museum of Science, Boston. Another specimen allegedly weighing 48 lbs. was caught off Chatham, Massachusetts, in 1949. Less reliable weights of up to 60 lbs. have been reported.

Smallest. The smallest known crustaceans are water fleas of the genus *Alonella*, which may measure less than 1/100th of an inch long. They are widely distributed.

LARGEST LOBSTER, measuring 3 feet end to end and weighing 42 lbs. 7 oz., can be seen at the Museum of Science in Boston.

The smallest known lobster is the cape lobster (*Homarus capensis*) of South Africa which measures 3.93–4.72 inches in total length.

The smallest crabs in the world are the aptly named pea crabs (family Pinnotheridae). Some species have a shell diameter of only 0.25 in., including *Pinnotheres pisum* which is found in British waters.

Longest-Lived. The longest-lived of all crustaceans is the American lobster (*Homarus americanus*). Very large specimens may be as much as 50 years old.

Deepest. The greatest depth from which a crustacean has been recovered is 32,119 feet for an amphiopod (order Amphiopoda) collected by the Galathea Deep Sea Expedition in the Philippine Trench in 1951. The marine crab *Ethusina abyssicola* has been taken at a depth of 14,000 feet. Amphiopods have also been collected in the Ecuadorean Andes at a height of 13,300 feet.

9. Insects *(Insecta or Hexapoda)*

Heaviest. The heaviest insect in the world is the Goliath beetle *Goliathus goliathus*, of equatorial Africa. One specimen measuring 5.85 inches in length (tip of mandible to end of abdomen) and 3.93 inches across the back, weighed 3.52 ounces. The longhorn beetles *Titanus giganteus* of South America and *Xinuthrus heros* of the Fiji Islands are also massive insects, and both have been measured up to 5.9 inches in length.

Longest. The longest insect in the world is the tropical stick-insect *Pharnacia serratipes*, females of which have been measured up to 12.99 inches in body length. The longest beetle known (excluding antennae) is the Hercules beetle (*Dynastes hercules*) of Central and South America, which has been measured up to 7.08 inches, but over half of this length is accounted for by the "prong" from the thorax. The longhorn beetle *Batocera wallacei* of New Guinea has been measured up to 10.5 inches, but 7.5 inches of this was antenna.

Smallest. The smallest insects recorded so far are the "hairy-winged" beetles of the family Trichopterygidae and the "battledore-wing fairy flies" (parasitic wasps) of the family Mymaridae. They measure only 0.008 of an inch in length, and the fairy flies have a wing span of only 0.04 of an inch. This makes them smaller than some of the protozoa (single-celled animals).

The male bloodsucking banded louse (*Enderleinellus zonatas*), ungorged, and the parasitic wasp *Caraphractus cinctus* may each weigh as little as 0.005 of a milligram, or 1/567,000 of an ounce. The eggs of the latter each weigh 0.0002 of a milligram, or 1/14,175,000 of an ounce.

Commonest. The most numerous of all insects are the springtails (order Collembola), which have a very wide geographical range. It has been calculated that the top 9 inches of soil in one acre of grassland contains 230,000,000 springtails or more than 5,000 per square foot.

Fastest-Flying. Experiments have proved that a widely publicized claim by an American entomologist in 1926 that the deer bot-fly (*Cephenemyia pratti*) could attain a speed of 818 m.p.h. was wildly exaggerated. If true, it would have generated a supersonic "pop." Acceptable modern experiments have now established that the highest maintainable air speed of any insect, including the deer bot-fly, is 24 m.p.h., rising to a maximum of 36 m.p.h. for short bursts. A relay of bees (maximum speed 11 m.p.h.) would use only a gallon of nectar in cruising 4,000,000 miles at 7 m.p.h.

Longest-Lived. The longest-lived insects are queen termites (*Isoptera*), which have been known to lay eggs for up to 50 years.

Loudest. The loudest of all insects is the male cicada (family Cicadidae). At 7,400 pulses per minute its tymbal (sound) organs produce a noise (officially described by the U.S. Department of Agriculture as "Tsh-ee-EEEE-e-ou") detectable over a quarter of a mile distance.

Southernmost. The farthest south at which any insect has been found is 77°S (900 miles from the South Pole) in the case of a springtail (order Collembola).

Largest Locust Swarm. The greatest swarm of desert locusts (*Schistocerca gregaria*) ever recorded was one covering an estimated 2,000 square miles, observed crossing the Red Sea in 1889. Such a swarm must have contained about 250,000,000,000 insects weighing about 500,000 tons.

Fastest Wing Beat. The fastest wing beat of any insect under natural conditions is 62,760 a minute by a tiny midge of the genus *Forcipomyia*. In experiments with truncated wings at a temperature of 98.6°F., the rate increased to 133,080 beats per minute. The muscular contraction-expansion cycle in 0.00045 or 1/2,218th of a second, further represents the fastest muscle movement ever measured.

Slowest Wing Beat. The slowest wing beat of any insect is 300 a minute by the swallowtail butterfly (*Papilio machaon*). Most butterflies beat their wings at a rate of 460 to 636 a minute.

Longest Ant. The longest ant in the world is the Australian bull ant (*Myrmecia gigas*). Workers of this species measure up to 1.5 inches in length.

Smallest Ant. The smallest is the thief ant (*Solenopsis fugax*), whose workers measure 0.059–0.18 of an inch.

Honey from a Hive. The greatest amount of wild honey ever extracted from a single hive is 404 lbs., recorded by Ormond R. Aebi of Santa Cruz, California, on August 29, 1974.

Largest Grasshopper. The bush-cricket with the largest wing span is the New Guinean grasshopper *Siliquofera grandis* with some females measuring more than 10 inches. The *Pseudophyllanax imperialis*, found on the island of New Caledonia, in the southwestern Pacific Ocean, has antennae measuring up to 8 inches.

Largest Dragonfly. The largest dragonfly is *Tetracanthagyne plagiata* of northeastern Borneo, which is known only from a single specimen preserved in the British Museum of Natural History, London. This dragonfly has a wing span of 7.63 inches and an overall length of 4.25 inches.

Largest Flea. The largest known flea is *Hystricopsylla scheffer schefferi*, which was described from a single specimen taken from the nest of a mountain beaver (*Aplondontia rufa*) at Puyallup, Washington, in 1913. Females measure up to 0.31 inches in length, which is the diameter of a pencil.

Flea Jumps. The champion jumper among fleas is the common flea (*Pulex irritans*). In one American experiment carried out in 1910 a specimen allowed to leap at will performed a long jump of 13 inches and a high jump of 7¾ inches. In jumping 130 times its own height a flea subjects itself to a force of 200 g. Siphonapterologists recognize about 1,830 varieties.

Largest Tick. The largest known tick is an engorged female *Amblyomma varium* from a Venezuelan sloth.

Smallest Tick. The smallest is a male *Ixodes soricis* from a British Columbian shrew.

Butterflies and Moths (**Order** Lepidoptera)

Largest. The largest known butterfly is the giant birdwing *Troides victoriae* of the Solomon Islands in the southwestern Pacific. Females may have a wing span exceeding 12 inches and weigh over 0.176 oz.

The largest moth in the world is the Hercules emperor moth (*Coscinoscera hercules*) of tropical Australia and New Guinea. Females measure up to 10½ inches across the outspread wings and have a wing area of up to 40.8 square inches. In 1948 an unconfirmed measurement of 14.17 inches was reported for a female captured near the post office at the coastal town of Innisfail, Queensland, Australia. The rare owlet moth (*Thysania agrippina*) of Brazil has been measured up to 11.81 inches in wing span, and the Atlas moth (*Attacus atlas*) of southeast Asia up to 11.02 inches, but both these species are less bulky than *C. hercules*.

Smallest. The smallest of the estimated 140,000 known species of Lepidoptera is the moth *Johanssonia acetosae*, with a wing span of 0.08 of an inch and a similar body length. The smallest known butterfly is the dwarf blue (*Brephidium barberae*) from South Africa. It is 0.55 of an inch from wing tip to wing tip.

Rarest. The rarest of all butterflies (and the most valuable) is the giant birdwing *Troides allottei*, which is found only on Bougainville in the Solomon Islands. A specimen was sold for $1,800 at an auction in Paris, on October 24, 1966.

Fastest. The highest speeds recorded for Lepidoptera are: for moths, 34.7 m.p.h. by the hawk-head moth (family Sphingidae); and for butterflies, 17 m.p.h. by the great monarch butterfly (*Danaus plexippus*) in 1966.

Most Acute Sense of Smell. The most acute sense of smell exhibited in nature is that of the male emperor moth (*Eudia pavonia*), which, according to German experiments in 1961, can detect the sex attractant of the virgin female at the almost unbelievable range of 6.8 miles upwind. This scent has been identified as one of the higher alcohols ($C_{16}H_{29}OH$) of which the female carries less than 0.0001 of a milligram.

10. Centipedes (*Chilopoda*)

Longest. The longest recorded species of centipede is a large variant of the widely distributed *Scolopendra morsitans*, found on the Andaman Islands, Bay of Bengal. Specimens have been measured up to 13 inches in length and 1½ inches in breadth.

Shortest. The shortest recorded centipede is an unidentified species which measures only 0.19 of an inch.

Most Legs. The centipede with the greatest number of legs is *Himantarum gabrielis* of southern Europe which has 171–177 pairs when adult.

Fastest. The fastest centipede is probably *Scutiger coleoptrata* of southern Europe which can travel at a rate of 19.68 inches a second or 4.47 m.p.h.

11. Millipedes (*Diplopoda*)

Longest. The longest species of millipede known are the *Graphidostreptus gigas* of Africa and *Scaphistostreptus seychellarum* of the Seychelles Islands in the Indian Ocean, both of which have been measured up to 11.02 inches in length and 0.78 of an inch in diameter.

Shortest. The shortest millipede in the world is the British species *Polyxenus lagurus*, which measures 0.082–0.15 of an inch in length.

Most Legs. The greatest number of legs reported for a millipede is 355 pairs (710 legs) for an unidentified South African species.

12. Segmented Worms *(Annelida or Annulata)*

Longest Earthworm. The longest known species of giant earthworm is *Microchaetus rappi* (= *M. microchaetus*) of South Africa. An average-sized specimen measures 4 feet 6 inches in length (25½ inches when contracted), but much larger examples have been reliably reported. In *c.* 1937 a giant earthworm measuring 22 feet in length when naturally extended and 3 inches in diameter was collected in the Transvaal, and in November, 1967, another specimen measuring 11 feet in length and 21 feet when naturally extended was found reaching over the national road (width 19 feet 8½ inches) near Debe Nek, eastern Cape Province, South Africa.

Shortest. The shortest segmented worm known is *Chaetogaster annandalei*, which measures less than 0.019 of an inch in length.

13. Mollusks *(Mollusca)*

(Squids, octopuses, snails, shellfish, etc.)

Largest. The heaviest of all invertebrate animals is the Atlantic giant squid (*Architeuthis sp.*). The largest specimen ever recorded was one measuring 55 feet in total length (head and body 20 feet, tentacles 35 feet), captured on November 2, 1878, after it had run aground in Thimble Tickle Bay, Newfoundland. Its eyes were

LONGEST EARTHWORM (left): This species measures 4 feet in length, 7 feet when naturally extended.

9 inches in diameter. The total weight was calculated to be 4,480 lbs. In 1896, Dr. DeWitt Webb recorded the remains of a cephalopod on the beach 12 miles south of St. Augustine, Florida, which belonged, he believed, to a 6–7 ton giant octopus with a tentacular span of 200 feet.

The rare Pacific giant squid (*Architeuthis longimanus*) is much less bulky, but the longest recorded specimen was one measuring 57 feet overall, with a head and body length of 7 feet 9 inches and tentacles of 49 feet 3 inches, found in Lyall Bay, New Zealand, in 1887.

Largest Octopus. The largest known octopus is the common Pacific octopus (*Octopus apollyon*). On February 18, 1973, Donald E. Hagen, a skindiver, caught a specimen in Lower Hood Canal, Puget Sound, Washington, which had a radial spread of 25 feet 7 inches and weighed 118 lbs. 10 oz. The octopus was seized at a depth of 60 feet and then "wrestled" to the surface single-handed. In 1874, a radial spread of 32 feet was reported for an octopus (*Octopus hong-kongensis*) speared in Illiuliuk Harbor, Unalaska Island, Alaska, but the body of this animal only measured 12 inches in length and it probably weighed less than 20 lbs.

Most Ancient. The longest existing living creature is *Neopilina galatheae*, a deep-sea worm-snail which had been believed extinct for about 320,000,000 years, but which was found at a depth of 11,400 feet off Costa Rica by the Danish research vessel *Galathea* in 1952. Fossils found in New York State, in Newfoundland, and in Sweden show that this mollusk was also living about 500,000,000 years ago.

Shells

Largest. The largest of all existing bivalve shells is the marine giant clam (*Tridacna gigas*), found on the Indo-Pacific coral reefs. A

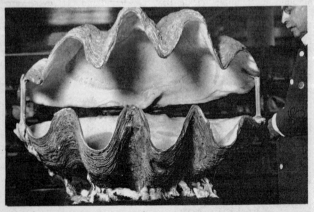

LARGEST SHELL: This giant clam shell weighs 579½ pounds.

specimen measuring 43 inches by 29 inches and weighing 579½ lbs. was collected from the Great Barrier Reef in 1917, and is now preserved in the American Museum of Natural History, New York City. Another lighter specimen was measured at 53.9 inches overall.

Smallest. Probably the smallest bivalve shell in the world is *Ammonicera rota*, found in British waters, which measures 0.02 of an inch in diameter.

Tornus unisulcatus measures 0.015 by 0.03 inches.

Rarest. The most highly prized of all molluscan shells in the hands of conchologists is the 3-inch-long white-toothed cowrie (*Cypraea leucodon*), which is found in the deep waters off the Philippines. Only three examples are known, including one at Harvard University. The highest price ever paid for a seashell is $2,510 in a sale at Sotheby's, London, on March 4, 1971, for one of the four known examples of *Conus bengalensis*. This 4-inch-long shell was trawled by fishermen in the Andaman Sea in Southeast Asia in December, 1970.

Longest-Lived. The longest-lived mollusk is probably the freshwater mussel (*Margaritifera margaritifera*) which has been credited with a potential maximum longevity of 100 years. The giant clam (*Tridacna derasa*) lives about 30 years.

Snails

Largest. The largest known species of snail is the sea hare (*Tethys californicus*) found in coastal waters off California. The average weight is 7 to 8 lbs., but a specimen has been recorded at 15 lbs. 13 oz. The largest known land snail is the African giant snail (*Achatina fulica*). In January, 1976, a huge specimen measuring 11½ inches from snout to tail, named "Geronimo" (born October, 1970), owned by Christopher Hudson of Hove, East Sussex, England, weighed 1 lb. 4½ oz.

Speed. The fastest-moving species of land snail is probably the common snail (*Helix aspersa*).

A snail's pace varies from as slow as 0.00036 m.p.h., or 23 inches per hour, up to 0.0313 m.p.h. (or 55 yards per hour) for the common garden snail (*Helix aspersa*). Tests were carried out in the United States. The snail-racing equivalent of the 4-minute mile is 24 inches in 3 minutes, which would result in a 7,920-minute or 5½-day mile.

14. Ribbon Worms *(Nemertina or Rhynchopods)*

Longest Worm. The longest of the 550 recorded species of ribbon worms, also called nemertines (or nemerteans), is the "living fishing-line worm" (*Lineus longissimus*), a highly elastic boot-lace worm found in the shallow waters of the North Sea. A specimen washed ashore at St. Andrews, Fife, Scotland, in 1864, after a severe storm, measured more than 180 feet in length, making it easily the longest recorded worm of any variety.

15. Jellyfishes *(Scyphozoa or Scyphomedusia)*

Largest and Smallest. The longest jellyfish (in fact, the longest animal) ever recorded is *Cyanea arctica*. One specimen washed up on the coast of Massachusetts, *c.* 1865, had a bell 7½ feet in diameter and tentacles measuring 120 feet, thus giving a theoretical tentacular span of some 245 feet.

Some true jellyfishes have a bell diameter of less than 0.78 of an inch.

Most Venomous. The most venomous are the box jellies of the genera *Chiropsalmus* and *Chironex* of the Indo-Pacific region, which carry a neurotoxic venom similar in strength to that found in the Asiatic cobra. These jellyfish have caused the deaths of at least 60 people off the coast of Queensland, Australia, in the past 25 years. Victims die within 1–3 minutes. A most effective defense is panty hose, outsize versions of which are now worn by Queensland life savers at surf carnivals.

16. Sponges *(Parazoa, Porifera or Spongida)*

Largest and Smallest. The largest sponges are the barrel-shaped loggerhead (*Spheciospongia vesparium*), found in the Caribbean and Florida, measuring 3½ feet high and 3 feet in diameter, and the Neptune's cup or goblet (*Poterion patera*) of Indonesia, standing up to 4 feet in height, but it is not such a bulky animal. In 1909, a wool sponge (*Hippospongia canaliculatta*) measuring 6 feet in circumference was collected off the Bahama Islands. When first taken from the water it weighed between 80 and 90 lbs., but after it had been dried and relieved of all excrescences it scaled 12 lbs. (This sponge is now preserved in the Smithsonian Institution, Washington, D.C.)

The smallest known sponge is the widely distributed *Leucosolenia blanca*, which measures 0.11 of an inch in height when fully grown.

Deepest. Sponges have been taken from depths of up to 18,500 feet.

17. Extinct Animals

Largest. The first dinosaur to be scientifically described was *Megalosaurus* ("large lizard"), a 20-foot-long bipedal theropod, in 1824. A lower jaw and other bones of this animal had been discovered before 1818 in a slate quarry at Stonesfield, near Woodstock, Oxfordshire, England. It stalked across southern England about 130,000,000 years ago. The word "dinosaur" ("fearfully great lizard") was not used for such reptiles until 1842. The longest recorded dinosaur was *Diplodocus* ("double beam"), an attenuated sauropod which wallowed in the swamps of western North America about 150,000,000 years ago. A composite skeleton of three individuals excavated near Split Mountain, Utah, and mounted in the Carnegie Museum of the Natural Sciences, Pittsburgh, measures 87½ feet in length (neck 22 feet, body 15 feet, tail 50½ feet) and stands 11 feet 9 inches at the pelvis (the highest point on the body). This animal weighed an estimated 11.63 tons in life.

The heaviest of all prehistoric animals, and the heaviest land invertebrate of all time, was probably the swamp-dwelling *Brachiosaurus* ("arm lizard") which lived from 135,000,000 to 165,000,000 years ago. Its remains have been found in East Africa, Colorado, Oklahoma and Utah and Europe. A complete skeleton excavated near Tendaguru Hill, southern Tanganyika (Tanzania) in 1909 and mounted in the Museum fur Naturkunde in East Berlin, Germany, measures 74 feet 6 inches in total length and 21 feet at the shoulder. This reptile weighed a computed 87.65 tons in life, but isolated bones have since been discovered in East Africa which indicate that some specimens may have weighed as much as 111 tons and measured over 90 feet in total length.

In the summer of 1972, the remains of another enormous sauropod, new to science, were discovered in a flood-plain bonejam in Colorado, by an expedition from Brigham Young University, Provo, Utah. Excavations are still continuing, but a study of the incomplete series of cervical vertebrae indicate that this dinosaur must have had a neck length of about 39 feet (compared with 22 feet for *Diplodocus*) and measured over 100 feet in total length when alive.

Largest Predator. The largest was thought to be *Tyrannosaurus rex*, which lived about 75,000,000 years ago in what are now Montana and Wyoming (bones found in 1900) and also in Mongolia. It measured up to 47 feet in overall length, had a bipedal height of 18½ feet, and weighed a calculated 8 tons. Its 4-foot-long skull contained serrated teeth up to 6 inches long.

It is now known that some other carnosaurs were just as large or even larger than *Tyrannosaurus*. In 1930, the British Museum Expedition to East Africa dug up the pelvic bones and part of the vertebrae of another huge carnosaur at Tendaguru Hill, Tanzania, which must have measured about 54 feet in total length when alive. During the summers of 1963–65, a Polish-Mongolian expedition discovered the remains of a carnosaur in the Gobi Desert which had 8½-foot-long forelimbs! It is not yet known, however, whether the rest of this dinosaur was built on the same colossal scale.

Longest Tusks. The longest tusks of any prehistoric animal were those of the straight-tusked elephant *Hesperoloxodon antiquus germanicus*, which lived in what is now northern Germany about 2,000,000 years ago. The average length in adult bulls was 16 feet 4¾ inches. A single tusk of a woolly mammoth (*Mammonteus primigenius*) preserved in the Franzens Museum at Brno, Czechoslovakia, measures 16 feet 5½ inches along the outside curve. In *c.* August, 1933, a single tusk of an Imperial mammoth (*Archidiskodon imperator*) measuring 16+ feet (anterior end missing) was unearthed near Post, Texas. In 1934, this tusk was presented to the American Museum of Natural History in New York City.

Heaviest Tusks. The heaviest fossil tusk on record is one weighing 330 lbs., with a girth of 35 inches, now preserved in the Museo Civico di Storia Naturale, Milan, Italy. The specimen (in two pieces) measures 11 feet 9 inches in length.

LARGEST PREHISTORIC MAMMAL: *Baluchitherium* stood over 17 feet tall and weighed nearly 22 tons.

The heaviest recorded mammoth tusks are a pair in the University of Nebraska Museum, Lincoln, Nebraska, which have a combined weight of 498 lbs. and measure 13 feet 9 inches and 13 feet 7 inches respectively. They were found near Campbell, Nebraska, in 1915.

Longest Antlers. The prehistoric giant deer (*Megaceros giganteus*), which lived in Northern Europe and Northern Asia as recently as 50,000 B.C., stood 7 feet at the shoulder and had the longest antlers of any known animal. One specimen recovered from an Irish bog had greatly palmated antlers measuring 14 feet across.

Most Brainless. The *Stegosaurus* ("plated reptile"), which measured up to 30 feet in length, 8 feet in height at the hips and weighed up to 2 tons, had a walnut-sized brain weighing only $2\frac{1}{2}$ ounces. It represented 0.004 of one per cent of its body weight, compared with 0.074 of one per cent for an elephant and 1.88 per cent for a human. It roamed widely across the Northern Hemisphere about 150,000,000 years ago, trying to remember where it had been.

Largest Mammal. The largest prehistoric mammal, and the largest land mammal ever recorded, was *Baluchitherium* (=*Indricotherium, Paraceratherium, Aceratherium, Thaumastotherium, Aralotherium* and *Benaratherium*), a long-necked hornless rhinoceros which lived in Europe and central western Asia between 20,000,000 and 40,000,000 years ago. It stood up to 17 feet 9 inches to the top of the shoulder hump (27 feet to the crown of its head), measured 35–37 feet in length and weighed nearly 22 tons. The bones of this gigantic browser were first discovered in 1907–08 in the Bugti Hills in east Baluchistan, Pakistan.

The largest known prehistoric marine mammal was *Basilosaurus* (= *Zeuglodon*) of 50,000,000 years ago. A specimen from Alabama measured 70 feet and weighed an estimated 30 tons.

Largest Flying Creature. The largest flying creature was a winged reptile (not yet named) of the order Pterosauria which glided over what is now Texas about 70,000,000 years ago. Partial remains (four wings, a neck, hind legs, and mandibles) of three specimens recently discovered in Big Bend National Park, Texas, indicate that this pterosaur must have had a wing span of at least 36 feet and that the maximum spread may have been as great as 69 feet. *Pteranodon ingens*, the previous title-holder, had a maximum expanse of 27 feet.

Largest Mammoth. The tallest extinct elephant was the mammoth *Paraelephas trogontherii* of 1 million years ago in central Europe and North America. A fragmentary skeleton found in Mosbach, West Germany, indicates a shoulder height of 14¾ feet.

Largest Dinosaur Eggs. The largest dinosaur eggs discovered were those of a *Hypselosaurus priscus* in the valley of the Durance, near Aix-en-Provence, in southern France. The eggs of this 30-foot-long sauropod, believed to be 80,000,000 years old, would have had, uncrushed, a length of 12 inches and a diameter of 10 inches.

Largest Bird. The largest prehistoric bird was the elephant bird (*Aepyornis maximus*), also known as the roc bird, which lived in southern Madagascar. It was a flightless bird standing 9 to 10 feet in height and weighing nearly 1,000 lbs. It also had the largest eggs of any known animal. One example preserved in the British Museum (Natural History), London, measures 33¾ inches around the long axis with a circumference of 28½ inches, giving a capacity of 2.35 gallons—seven times that of an ostrich egg. A more cylindrical egg preserved in the Academie des Sciences, Paris, measures 12⅞ inches by 15⅜ inches, and probably weighed about 27 lbs. with its contents. This bird may have survived until *c.* 1660. In 1974, the fossilized remains of a huge emu-like bird were discovered near Alice Springs, Australia. This bird, which lived about 10,000,000 years ago, stood more than 10 feet tall and may have been even heavier than *Aepyornis maximus*. The flightless moa *Dinornis giganteus* of North Island, New Zealand, was taller, attaining a height of over 13 feet, but probably weighed about 500 lbs.

TALLEST PREHISTORIC BIRD: The flightless moa of New Zealand, shown here in a reconstruction, stood over 13 feet tall.

In May, 1962, a single fossilized ankle joint of an enormous flightless bird was found at Gainesville, Florida. The largest actually to fly was probably the condor-like *Teratornis incredibilis*, which lived in North America about 1,000,000 years ago. Fossil remains of one of this species, discovered in Smith Creek Cave, Nevada, in 1952, indicate a wing span of 16 feet 4¼ inches, and the bird must have weighed at least 50 lbs. Another gigantic flying bird named *Osteodontornis orri*, which lived in what is now California, about 20,000,000 years ago, had a wing span of 16 feet and was probably even heavier. It was related to the pelicans and storks. The albatross-like *Gigantornis eaglesomei* has been credited with a wing span of 20 feet on the evidence of a single fossilized breastbone. It flew over what is now Nigeria between 34,000,000 and 58,000,000 years ago.

A wing span measurement of 16 feet 4¼ inches has also been reported for another flying bird named *Ornithodesmus latidens*, which flew over what is now Hampshire and the Isle of Wight, England, about 90,000,000 years ago.

Largest Marine Reptile. The largest marine reptile ever recorded was the short-necked pliosaur *Kronosaurus queenslandicus*, which swam in the seas around what is now Australia about 100,000,000 years ago. It measured about 55 feet in length, with a skull 11½ feet long. *Stretosaurus macromerus*, another short-necked pliosaur, was of comparable size. A mandible found in Cumnor, Oxfordshire, England, must have belonged to a reptile measuring at least 50 feet in length.

Largest Crocodile. The largest known crocodile was *Deinosuchus riograndensis*, which lived in the lakes and swamps of what is now Texas about 75,000,000 years ago. Fragmentary remains discovered in Big Bend National Park, Texas, indicate it must have measured at least 50 feet in total length. The less-bulky gavial *Rhamphosuchus*, which lived in northern India about 7,000,000 years ago, also reached a length of 50 feet.

Chelonians. The largest prehistoric marine turtle was *Archelon ischyros*, which lived in Kansas and South Dakota when they were shallow seas about 80,000,000 years ago. An almost complete skeleton with a carapace (shell) 6½ feet long was discovered in August, 1895, near the south fork of the Cheyenne River in Custer County, South Dakota. The skeleton, which has an overall length of 11 feet 4 inches (20 feet across the outstretched flippers), is now in the Peabody Museum of Natural History at Yale University, New Haven, Connecticut. This specimen is estimated to have weighed 6,000 lbs. when it was alive.

The fossil remains of another giant marine turtle (*Cratochelone berneyi*) which must have measured at least 12 feet in overall length when alive were discovered in 1914 at Sylvania Station, 20 miles west of Hughenden, Queensland, Australia.

The largest prehistoric tortoise was probably *Colossochelys atlas*, which lived in northern India between 7,000,000 and 12,000,000 years ago. An almost complete skeleton with a carapace 5 feet 5 inches long (7 feet 4 inches over the curve) and 2 feet 11 inches high was discovered in 1923. This animal had an overall length of 8 feet and is computed to have weighed about 2,100 lbs. when it was alive. Fossil remains of a similarly sized tortoise were recently reported from Texas.

Largest Fish. No prehistoric fish has yet been discovered that is larger than living species. The belief that the great shark *Carcharodon megalodon*, which abounded in Miocene seas some 15,000,000 years ago, measured 80 feet in length (based on ratios from fossil teeth) has now been shown to be in error. The modern estimate is that this shark did not exceed 43 feet.

Earliest Animals by Type

The earliest known primates originated about 70,000,000 years ago and were similar in form to the tarsier of Indonesia and the lemur of Madagascar. The earliest known bird was the glider *Archaeopteryx* of about 140,000,000 years ago. The earliest known mammal was a shrew-like animal between 1 and 2 inches long, whose fossilized remains, estimated to be 190,000,000 years old, were found at Pokane, in Lesotho (formerly called Basutoland), in December, 1966. The earliest known reptiles were *Hylonomus*, *Archerpeton*, *Romericus* and *Protoclepsybrops*, which all lived in Nova Scotia, Canada, about 290,000,000 years ago. The earliest amphibian and the earliest known four-legged creature was *Ichthyostega*, measuring 4 feet long, which lived in Greenland about 350,000,000 years ago. The earliest spider, *Palaeocteniza crassipes*, and the earliest insect, *Rhyniella praecursor*, a springtail, occur in a fossil peat of Middle Devonian age (about 370,000,000 years old) in Aberdeenshire, Scotland. The earliest vertebrates were agnathans, or jawless fishes, the first fragments of which occur in the Lower Ordovician period (about 480,000,000 years ago) near Leningrad, in the U.S.S.R. The most archaic living mollusk is *Neopilina galatheae*, found in 1952 off Costa Rica, belonging to a group which has survived almost unchanged for 500,000,000 years. The earliest known crustacean was the 12-legged shelled *Karagassiema*, measuring 2 feet long, found in pre-

Cambrian rock in the eastern Sayan Mountains of Siberia, U.S.S.R. This animal lived about 650,000,000 years ago.

Largest Amphibian. The largest amphibian ever recorded was the alligator-like *Eogyrinus* which lived between 280,000,000 and 345,000,000 years ago. It measured nearly 15 feet in length.

Longest Snake. The longest prehistoric snake was the python-like *Gigantophis garstini*, which inhabited what is now Egypt about 50,000,000 years ago. Parts of a spinal column discovered at El Faiyûm indicate a length of about 33 feet, which is comparable with the longest constrictors living today.

Largest Arachnid. The largest arachnid ever recorded was *Pterygotus buffaloensis*, a sea scorpion (eurypterid) which lived about 400,000,000 years ago. It grew to a length of 9 feet.

Largest Insect. The largest prehistoric insect was *Meganeura monyi*, a dragonfly that lived between 280,000,000 and 325,000,000 years ago. Fossil remains, impressions of wings, indicate that it had a wing span reaching $27\frac{1}{2}$ inches.

Largest Shelled Mollusk. The Cretaceous fossil ammonite (*Pachydiscus seppenradensis*) of about 75,000,000 years ago, had a shell measuring up to 8 feet 5 inches in diameter.

Most Southerly. The most southerly creature yet found is a fresh-water salamander-like amphibian *Labyrinthodont*, represented by a $2\frac{1}{2}$-inch piece of jawbone found near Beardmore Glacier, Antarctica, 325 miles from the South Pole, which dates from the early Jurassic period of 200,000,000 years ago. This discovery was made in December, 1967.

Protista and Microbes

Protista. Protista were first discovered in 1676 by Anton van Leeuwenhoek (1632–1723), a Dutch microscopist. Among Protista, characteristics common to both plants and animals are exhibited. The more plant-like are termed Protophyta (protophytes) and the more animal-like are placed in the phylum Protozoa (protozoans).

Largest. The largest protozoans which are known to have existed were the now extinct Nummulites, which each had a diameter of 0.95 of an inch. The largest existing protozoan is *Pelomyxa palustris*, which may attain a length of up to 0.6 of an inch.

Smallest. The smallest of all free-living organisms are the pleuro-pneumonia-like organisms (P.P.L.O.) of the *Mycoplasma*. One of these, *Mycoplasma laidlawii*, first discovered in sewage in 1936, has a diameter during the early part of its life of only 100 millimicrons, or 0.000004 of an inch. Examples of the strain known as H.39 have a maximum diameter of 300 millimicrons and weigh an estimated 1.0×10^{-15} of a gram. The smallest of all protophytes is *Micromonas pusilla*, with a diameter of less than 2 microns.

Longest-Lived. A culture of the protozoan *Euglena gracilis* has been kept alive for more than 20 years in King's College, London, England. Cysts of *Mastigamoeba* and *Oikomonas* have also been observed to live for more than 20 years.

Fastest-Moving. The protozoan *Monas stigmatica* has been measured to move a distance equivalent to 40 times its own length in a second. No human can cover even seven times his own length in a second.

Fastest Reproduction. The protozoan *Glaucoma*, which reproduces by binary fission, divides as frequently as every three hours. Thus in the course of a day it could become a "six greats grandparent" and the progenitor of 510 descendants.

Densest. The most densely existing species in the animal kingdom is the sea water dinoflagellate *Gymnodinium breve*, which exists at a density of 240,000,000 per gallon of sea water in certain conditions of salinity and temperature off the coast of Florida.

Bacteria

Largest. The largest of the bacteria is the sulphur bacterium *Beggiatoa mirabilis*, which is from 16 to 45 microns in width and which may form filaments several millimeters long.

Highest. In April, 1967, the U.S. National Aeronautics and Space Administration reported that bacteria had been discovered at an altitude of 135,000 feet (more than 25 miles).

Longest-Lived. The oldest deposits from which living bacteria are claimed to have been extracted are salt layers near Irkutsk, U.S.S.R., dating from about 600,000,000 years ago. The discovery of their survival was made on February 26, 1962, by Dr. H. J. Dombrowski of Freiburg University, West Germany, but it is not accepted internationally.

Toughest. The bacterium *Micrococcus radiodurans* can withstand atomic radiation 10,000 times greater than radiation that is fatal to the average man (i.e. 650 röntgens).

Viruses

Largest. The largest true viruses are the brick-shaped pox viruses (e.g. smallpox, vaccinia, orf, etc.), measuring *c.* 250 × 300 millimicrons (mμ) or 0.0003 of a millimeter.

Smallest. Of more than 1,000 identified viruses, the smallest is the potato spindle tuber virus measuring less than 20 mμ in diameter.

Sub- and Ultra-Viral Infective Agents

In January, 1967, evidence was announced from the Institute of Research on Animal Diseases at Compton, Berkshire, England, of the existence of a form of life more basic than both the virus and nucleic acid. It was named SF or Scrapie factor, from the sheep disease. If proven, this will become the most fundamental replicating particle known. Its diameter is believed to be not more than 7 millionths of a millimeter. Having now been cultured, it has been allocated back to its former status of an ultra-virus.

PLANT KINGDOM (*PLANTAE*)

Earliest Life. If one accepts the definition of life as the ability of an organism to make replicas of itself by taking as building materials the simpler molecules in the medium around it, life probably appeared on earth about 3,355 million years ago. This date for the earliest spheroid photosynthesizing micro-organisms (7–10 mμ in diameter) from the Lower Onverwacht strata of the South Africa-Swaziland border was announced in January, 1973.

The oldest known living life form was announced in December, 1970, by Drs. Sanford and Barbara Siegel of Harvard University, to be a microscopic organism, similar in form to an orange slice, first collected near Harlech, Merionethshire, Wales, in 1964. It has been named *Kakabekia barghoorniana* and has existed from 2,000,000,000 years ago.

Earliest Flower. The oldest fossil of a flowering plant with palm-like imprints was found in Colorado in 1953 and dated about 65,000,000 years old.

Largest Forest. The largest afforested areas are the vast coniferous forests of the northern U.S.S.R., lying mainly between latitude 55°N. and the Arctic Circle. The total wooded areas amount to 2,700,000,000 acres (25 per cent of the world's forests), of which 38 per cent is Siberian larch. The U.S.S.R. is 34 per cent afforested.

Plant Life

Rarest. Plants thought to be extinct are rediscovered each year and there are thus many plants of which specimens are known in but a single locality.

Commonest Plants. The most widely distributed flowering plant in the world is *Cynodon dactylon*, a toothed grass found as far apart as Canada, Argentina, New Zealand, Japan and South Africa.

Northernmost. The yellow poppy (*Papaver radicatum*) and the Arctic willow (*Salix arctica*) survive the latter in an extremely stunted form, on the northernmost land (83°N.).

Southernmost. The most southerly plant life recorded is seven species of lichen found in 1933–34 by the second expedition of Rear Admiral Richard E. Byrd, U.S. Navy, in latitude 86° 03′ S. in the Queen Maud Mountains, Antarctica. The southernmost recorded flowering plant is the carnation (*Colobanthus crassifolius*), which was found in latitude 67° 15′ S. on Jenny Island, Margaret Bay, Graham Land (Palmer Peninsula), Antarctica.

Highest Altitude. The *Stellaria decumbens* is the flowering plant found at the highest altitude—20,130 feet up in the Himalayas.

Deepest Roots. The greatest reported depth to which roots have penetrated is a calculated 400 feet in the case of a wild fig tree at Echo Caves, near Ohrigstad, East Transvaal, South Africa.

Largest Blooms. The mottled orange-brown and white parasitic stinking corpse lily (*Rafflesia arnoldi*) has the largest of all blooms. These attach themselves to the cissus vines of the jungle in southeast Asia. They measure up to 3 feet across and ¾ of an inch thick, and attain a weight of 15 lbs. (See color photograph on color page A.)

The largest known inflorescence is that of *Puya raimondii*, a rare Bolivian plant with an erect panicle (diameter 8 feet) which emerges to a height of 35 feet. Each of these bears up to 8,000 white blooms. In 1974, the flower-spike of an agave in Berkeley, California, was measured to be 52 feet long. (See also Slowest-Flowering Plant.)

The world's largest blossoming plant is the giant Chinese wisteria at Sierra Madre, California. It was planted in 1892 and now has branches 500 feet long. It covers nearly an acre, weighs 252 tons and has an estimated 1,500,000 blossoms during its blossoming period of five weeks, when up to 30,000 people pay admission to visit. In November, 1974, it was reported that a passion plant, owned by Dennis and Patti Carlson of Blaine, Minnesota, and fed with a hormone, had grown to a length of 600 feet.

Smallest Flowering Plant. The smallest of all flowering plants are duckweeds, seen on the surface of ponds. Of these, the rootless *Wolffia punctata* has fronds only 1/50th to 1/35th of an inch long.

Slowest-Flowering Plant. The slowest-flowering of all plants is the rare *Puya raimondii*, the largest of all herbs, discovered in Bolivia in 1870. The panicle emerges after about 150 years of the plant's life. It then dies. (See also above under Largest Blooms.)

Some agaves, erroneously called century plants, first flower after 40 years.

Largest Leaves. The largest leaves of any plant belong to the raffia palm (*Raphia raffia*) of the Mascarene Islands, in the Indian Ocean, and the Amazonian bamboo palm (*R. toedigera*) of South America, whose leaf blades may measure up to 65 feet in length with petioles up to 13 feet.

The largest undivided leaf is that of *Alocasia macrorrhiza*, found in Sabah, East Malaysia. One found in 1966 measured 9 feet 11 inches long and 6 feet 3½ inches wide, and had an area of 34.2 square feet on one side.

Most and Least Nutritive Fruit. An analysis of the 38 commonly eaten raw (as opposed to dried) fruits shows that the one with the highest calorific value is the avocado (*Persea americana*) with 741 calories per edible lb. That with the lowest value is cucumber with 73 calories per lb. Avocados probably originated in Central and South America and also contain vitamins A, C, and E and 2.2 per cent protein.

Largest Watermelon. A watermelon weighing 90 lbs. was reported at the annual summer Watermelon Cuttin' ceremony at Georgia Southern College, Macon, Georgia, on August 2, 1975.

Largest Pineapple. A pineapple weighing 16 lbs. 8 oz. was reported from a Dole Co. plantation in Mindanao, Philippines, in 1967.

Largest Cabbage. In 1865, William Collingwood of The Stalwell, County Durham, England, grew a red cabbage with a circumference of 259 inches. It reputedly weighed 123 lbs.

Largest Lemon. Mrs. Violet Philips of Cordelea, Queensland, Australia, reported in May, 1974, a lemon with a girth of 24 inches, weighing 5 lbs. 13¼ oz.

Largest Pumpkin. A pumpkin with a circumference of 9 feet, weighing 378 lbs., grown in Circleville, Ohio, won a contest in the United States in October, 1975.

Largest Squash. E. Van Wyck of Roland, Manitoba, Canada, reported a squash weighing 353 lbs. in 1971.

Largest Sugar Beet. A 35-lb. sugar beet was grown by Fritz Kuhn of Imperial Valley, California, in 1973.

Largest Mushroom. A mushroom with a circumference of 75 inches was found near the Lulualaba River, Zaïre, in 1920.

Largest Tomato. Charles Roberts of Great Britain grew a tomato weighing 4 lbs. 4 oz. in 1974. (See color photograph on color page B.)

Largest Rose Tree. A "Lady Banks" rose tree at Tombstone, Arizona, has a trunk 40 inches thick, stands 9 feet high and covers an area of 5,380 square feet, supported by 68 posts and several thousand feet of iron piping. This enables 150 people to be seated under the arbor. The original cutting came from Scotland in 1884.

Largest Rhododendron. The largest species of rhododendron is the scarlet *Rhododendron arboreum*, examples of which reach a height of 60 feet at Mangalbaré, Nepal.

Largest Aspidistra. The aspidistra (*Aspidistra elatior*) was introduced as a parlor palm to Britain from Japan and China in 1822. The biggest aspidistra in the world is one 49¾ inches tall, grown by George Munns at Perth University, Western Australia, and measured in January, 1972.

Largest Vine. The largest recorded grape vine was one planted in 1842 at Carpinteria, California. By 1900 it was yielding more than 9 tons of grapes in some years, and averaging 7 tons per year. It died in 1920.

Tallest Hedge. The world's tallest hedge is the Meikleour beech hedge in Perthshire, Scotland. It was planted in 1746 and has now attained a trimmed height of 85 feet. It is 600 yards long, and some of its trees now exceed 100 feet.

Largest Cactus. The largest of all cacti is the saguaro (*Cereus giganteus* or *Carnegiea gigantea*), found in Arizona, southeastern California, and Sonora, Mexico. The green fluted column is surmounted by candelabra-like branches rising to a height of 52 feet 5¾ inches in the case of a specimen measured on the boundary of the Saguaro National Monument, Arizona. They have waxy white blooms which are followed by edible crimson fruit. A cardon cactus

LARGEST CACTUS: The saguaro grows to a height of about 53 feet, 10 times as high as the woman standing beneath it.

in Baja California, Mexico, was reputed to reach 58 feet and a weight of 10 tons.

Worst Weeds. The most intransigent weed is the mat-forming water weed *Salvinia auriculata*, found in Africa. It was detected on the filling of Kariba Lake, in May, 1959, and within 11 months had choked an area of 77 sq. miles, rising by 1963 to 387 sq. miles. The world's worst land weeds are regarded as purple nut sedge, Bermuda grass, barnyard grass, junglerice, goose grass, Johnson grass, Guinea grass, cogon grass and lantana.

Longest Seaweed. Claims made that seaweed off Tierra del Fuego, South America, grows to 600 and even 1,000 feet in length have gained currency. More recent and more reliable records indicate that the longest species of seaweed is the Pacific giant kelp (*Macrocystis pyrifera*), which does not exceed 196 feet in length. It can grow 17¾ inches in a day.

Tallest Hollyhock. The tallest reported hollyhock (*Althaea rosea*) is one of 18 feet 6 inches, grown by Mrs. Elizabeth Shelby of 4839 North Agnes, Temple City, California, measured on June 18, 1976.

Most-Spreading. The greatest area covered by a single clonal growth is that of the wild box huckleberry (*Gaylussacia brachyera*), a mat-forming evergreen shrub first reported in 1796. A colony covering 8 acres was discovered in 1845 near New Bloomfield, Pennsylvania. Another colony, covering about 100 acres, was "discovered" on July 18, 1920, near the Juniata River in Pennsylvania. It has been estimated that this colony began 13,000 years ago.

Fourteen-Leafed Clover. A fourteen-leafed white clover (*Trifolium repens*) was found by Randy Farland near Sioux Falls, South Dakota, on June 16, 1975.

Trees

Oldest. The oldest recorded tree is a bristlecone pine (*Pinus longaeva*) designated WPN-114, which grew at 10,750 feet above sea level on the northeast face of Wheeler Peak (13,063 feet) in eastern California. During studies in 1963 and 1964 it was found to be about 4,900 years old, but was cut down with a chain saw. The oldest known *living* tree is the bristlecone pine named *Methuselah*, growing at 10,000 feet on the California side of the White Mountains, with a confirmed age of 4,600 years. In March, 1974, it was reported that this tree produced 48 live seedlings. Dendrochronologists estimate the *potential* life span of a bristlecone pine at nearly 5,500 years, but that of a "big tree" at perhaps 6,000 years. Ring count dating extends back to 6,200 B.C. by cross-dating living and dead bristlecone pine trunks. Such tree-ring datings have led archeologists to realize that some radio-carbon datings could be 800 years or more too young.

Earliest. The earliest species of tree still surviving is the maidenhair tree (*Ginkgo biloba*) of China, which first appeared about 160,000,000 years ago, during the Jurassic era. It was "re-discovered" by Kaempfer (Netherlands) in 1690, and reached England *c.* 1754. It has been grown in Japan since *c.* 1100 where it was known as *Ginkyo* (silver apricot) and is now known as *Icho.*

Largest Living Thing. The most massive living thing on earth is a California "big tree" (*Sequoiadendron giganteum*) named the "General Sherman," standing 272 feet 4 inches tall, in Sequoia National Park, California. It has a true girth of 79.1 feet (at 5 feet above the ground). The "General Sherman" has been estimated to contain the equivalent of 600,120 board feet of timber, sufficient to make 5,000,000,000 matches. The foliage is blue-green, and the red-brown tan bark may be up to 24 inches thick in parts. In 1968, the official published figure for its estimated weight was 2,145 tons.

The seed of a "big tree" weighs only 1/6,000th of an ounce. Its growth to maturity may therefore represent an increase in weight of over 250,000,000,000 fold.

Tallest. The world's tallest known species of tree is the coast redwood (*Sequoia sempervirens*), now growing indigenously only in California north of Monterey to Oregon. The tallest example is now believed to be the Howard Libbey Tree in Redwood Creek Grove, Humboldt County, California, announced at 367.8 feet in 1964 but discovered to have an apparently dead top and re-estimated at 366.2 feet in 1970. It has a girth of 44 feet. The nearby tree announced to a Senate Committee by Dr. Rudolf W. Becking on June 18, 1966, to be 385 feet proved on re-measurement to be no more than 311.3 feet tall. A coast redwood of 367 feet 8 inches, felled in 1873 near Guerneville, California, was almost exactly the same height as the Howard Libbey redwood as originally measured.

TALLEST TREE: The Howard Libbey redwood in California's Redwood Creek Grove set a record at 366.2 feet in 1970.

OLDEST LIVING THING: Bristlecone pines in California have been found to exist since the 3rd millennium B.C.

The tallest non-sequoia is a Douglas fir at Quinault Lake Park, Washington, of *c.* 310 feet.

The identity of the tallest tree of all time has never been satisfactorily resolved. A claim as high as 525 feet has been made (subsequently reduced on re-measurement, in May, 1889, to 220 feet). Currently, the accepted view is that the maximum height recorded by a qualified surveyor was 375 feet for the Cornthwaite Tree (*Eucalyptus regnans*) in Thorpdale, Gippsland, Victoria, Australia, measured in 1880. The claim that a Douglas fir (*Pseudotsuga taxifolia*) felled by George Carey in 1895 in British Columbia had a height of 417 feet and a 77-foot circumference has been called into question, though not necessarily invalidated, by a falsified photograph. The tallest Douglas fir now known is the one mentioned above of *c.* 310 feet.

Tallest Christmas Tree. The world's tallest cut Christmas tree was a 99½-foot-tall fir erected in 1975 in Lloyd Center, Portland, Oregon. It was decorated with 15,000 lights.

Greatest Girth. The Santa Maria del Tule tree, in the state of Oaxaca, in Mexico, is a Montezuma cypress (*Taxodium mucronatum*) with a girth of 112–113 feet at a height of 5 feet above the ground in 1949.

A figure of 167 feet in circumference was reported for the European chestnut (*Castanea sativa*) known as the "Tree of the 100 Horses" on the edge of Mount Etna, Sicily, Italy, in 1770.

Remotest. The tree most distant from any other is believed to be one at an oasis in the Ténéré Desert, Niger Republic. There are no other trees within 31 miles. In Feb., 1960, it survived being rammed by a truck driven by a Frenchman.

Fastest-Growing. Discounting bamboo, which is not botanically classified as a tree, but as woody grass, the fastest-growing tree is *Eucalyptus deglupta*, which has been measured to grow 35 feet in 15 months in New Guinea. The youngest recorded age for a tree to reach 100 feet is 7 years for *E. regnans* in Rhodesia, and for 200 feet is 40 years for a Monterey pine in New Zealand.

Slowest-Growing. The speed of growth of trees depends largely upon conditions, although some species, such as box and yew, are always slow-growing. The extreme is represented by a specimen of Sitka spruce which required 98 years to grow to 11 inches tall, with a diameter of less than one inch, on the Arctic tree-line. The growing of miniature trees or *bonsai* is an Oriental cult mentioned as early as *c.* 1320.

Most Expensive. The highest price ever paid for a tree is $51,000 for a single Starkspur golden delicious apple tree from near Yakima, Washington, bought by a nursery in Missouri in 1959.

Wood

Heaviest. The heaviest of all woods is black ironwood (*Olea laurifolia*), also called South African ironwood, with a specific gravity of up to 1.49, and weighing up to 93 lbs. per cubic foot.

Lightest. The lightest wood is *Aeschynomene hispida*, found in Cuba, which has a specific gravity of 0.044 and a weight of only 2¾ lbs. per cubic foot. The wood of the balsa tree (*Ochroma pyramidale*) is of very variable density—between 2½ and 24 lbs. per cubic foot. The density of cork is 15 lbs. per cubic foot.

Seeds

Largest. The largest seed in the world is that of the double coconut or Coco de Mer (*Lodoicea seychellarum*), the single-seeded fruit of which may weigh 40 lbs. This grows only in the Seychelles Islands, in the Indian Ocean.

Smallest. The smallest seeds are those of epiphytic orchids, at 35,000,000 to the ounce (*cf.* grass pollens at up to 6,000,000,000 grains per ounce). A single plant of the American ragweed can generate 8,000,000,000 pollen grains in five hours.

Most Durable. The most durable of all seeds are those of the Arctic lupin (*Lupinus arcticus*) found in frozen silt at Miller Creek in the Yukon, Canada, in July, 1954. They were germinated in 1966 and dated by the radio-carbon method to at least 8,000 B.C. and more probably to 13,000 B.C.

Mosses

The smallest of mosses is the pygmy moss (*Ephemerum*), and the longest is the brook moss (*Fontinalis*), which forms streamers up to 3 feet long in flowing water.

Fungi

Largest. The largest recorded specimen of the giant puff ball (*Lycoperdon gigantea*) was one 62 inches in diameter and 18 inches high found at Mellor, Derbyshire, England, in 1971. A flatter specimen 64 inches in diameter was recorded in New York State in 1877.

Largest Tree Fungus. The largest officially recorded tree fungus was a specimen of *Oxyporus* (*Fomes*) *nobilissimus*, measuring 56 inches by 37 inches and weighing at least 300 lbs., found by J. Hisey in Washington State in 1946.

Most Poisonous Toadstool. The yellowish-olive death cap (*Amanita phalloides*) is regarded as the world's most poisonous fungus. From 6 to 15 hours after tasting, the effects are vomiting, delirium, collapse and death. Among its victims was Cardinal Giulio de' Medici, Pope Clement VII (1478–1534).

Bamboo

Tallest. The tallest recorded species of bamboo is *Dendrocalamus giganteus*, native to southern Burma. It was reported in 1904 that there were specimens with a culm-length of 100 to 115 feet in the Botanic Gardens at Peradeniya, Ceylon.

Fastest-Growing. Some species of the 45 genera of bamboo have attained growth rates of up to 36 inches per day (0.00002 m.p.h.), on their way to reaching a height of 100 feet in less than three months.

Ferns

Largest. The largest of all the more than 6,000 species of fern is the tree-fern (*Alsophila excelsa*) of Norfolk Island, in the South Pacific, which attains a height of up to 60 feet.

Smallest. The world's smallest ferns are *Hecistopteris pumila*, found in Central America, and *Azolla caroliniana*, which is native to the U.S.

Orchids

Largest. The largest of all orchids is *Grammatophyllum speciosum*, native to Malaysia. Specimens up to 25 feet high have been recorded.

The largest orchid flower is that of *Phragmipedium caudatum*, found in tropical areas of America. Its petals are up to 18 inches long, giving it a maximum outstretched diameter of 3 feet. The flower is, however, much less bulky than that of the stinking corpse lily (see Largest Blooms).

Smallest. The smallest orchid is *Bulbophyllum minutissimum,* found in Australia. Claims have also been made for *Notylia norae,* found in Venezuela. The smallest orchid flowers are less than 0.04 inches long, borne by *Stella graminea.*

Highest-Priced. The highest price ever paid for an orchid is £1,207 10s. (then $6,000), paid by Baron Schröder to Sanders of St. Albans for an *Odontoglossum crispum* (variety *pittianum*) at an auction by Protheroe & Morris of Bow Lane, London, England, on March 22, 1906. A cymbidium orchid called "Rosanna Pinkie" was sold in the United States for $4,500 in 1952.

Parks, Zoos, Aquaria and Oceanaria

Largest Park. The world's largest park is the Wood Buffalo National Park in Alberta, Canada (established 1922), which has an area of 11,172,000 acres (17,560 square miles).

Largest Zoo. It has been estimated that throughout the world there are some 500 zoos with an estimated annual attendance of 330,000,000. The largest zoological preserve in the world is the Etosha Reserve, South-West Africa, with an area which grew between 1907 and 1970 to 38,427 square miles. (It was thus larger than Ireland.)

Largest Collection. The largest collection in any zoo is that in the Zoological Gardens of West Berlin, Germany. At January 1, 1976, the zoo had a total of 12,531 specimens from 2,315 species. This total included 1,177 mammals (260 species), 2,834 birds (711 species), 634 reptiles (303 species), 555 amphibians (99 species), 2,543 fishes (685 species) and 4,788 invertebrates (257 species).

Oldest. The oldest known zoo is that at Schönbrunn, Vienna, Austria, built in 1752 by the Holy Roman Emperor Francis I for his wife Maria Theresa. The oldest privately owned zoo in the world is that of the Zoological Society of London, founded in 1826. Its collection is housed partly in Regent's Park, London (36 acres), and partly at Whipsnade Park, Bedfordshire (541 acres, opened 1931). At the stocktaking on January 1, 1976, it was found to house 11,075 specimens—1,759 mammals, 2,255 birds, 571 reptiles and amphibians, an estimated 3,331 fish, and an estimated total of 3,159 invertebrates. Locusts, bees and ants are excluded from this figure.

The earliest known collection of animals (not a public zoo) was that set up by Shulgi, a 3rd dynasty ruler of Ur in 2094–2047 B.C. at Puzarish in southeast Iraq.

Most Valuable Zoo Animal. The most valuable land animals are giant pandas (*Ailuropoda melanoleuca*), worth $35,000. However, the trained marine mammal Killer Whales (*Orcinus orea*) in some zoos are now valued at close to $100,000.

Largest Aquarium. The world's largest is the John G. Shedd Aquarium, 12th Street and Grant Park, Chicago, completed in November, 1929, at a cost of $3,250,000. The total capacity of its display tanks is 450,000 gallons, with reservoir tanks holding

2,000,000 gallons. Exhibited are 7,500 specimens from 350 species. Salt water is brought in road and rail tankers from Key West, Florida, and a tanker barge from the Gulf of Mexico. The record attendances are 78,658 in a day on May 21, 1931, and 4,689,730 visitors in the single year of 1931.

Earliest Oceanarium. The world's first oceanarium is Marineland of Florida, opened in 1938 at a site 18 miles south of St. Augustine. Up to 7,000,000 gallons of sea water are pumped daily through two major tanks, one rectangular (100 feet long by 40 feet wide by 18 feet deep) containing 450,000 gallons and one circular (233 feet in circumference and 12 feet deep) containing 400,000 gallons. The tanks are seascaped, including coral reefs and even a shipwreck.

Largest Oceanarium. The largest salt water tank in the world is that at the Marineland of the Pacific, Palos Verdes Peninsula, California. It is 251½ feet in circumference and 22 feet deep, with a capacity of 640,000 gallons. The total capacity of the whole oceanarium is 2,200,000 gallons.

The largest marine mammal ever held in captivity was a female pacific gray whale (*Eschrichtius gibbosus*) named "Gigi," who was captured in Scammon's Lagoon, Baja California, Mexico, on March 13, 1971. Transferred to the Sea World Aquarium in Mission Bay, San Diego, California, she measured 18 feet 2 inches and weighed 4,300 pounds on arrival. She was released at sea off the San Diego coast on March 13, 1972, after she had grown to an unmanageable 27 feet and 14,000 pounds.

Chapter Three

THE NATURAL WORLD

1. Natural Phenomena

EARTHQUAKES

It is estimated that each year there are some 500,000 detectable seismic or micro-seismic disturbances of which 100,000 can be felt and 1,000 cause damage. (Note: Seismologists record all earthquake dates with the year first, based *not* on local time but on Greenwich Mean Time.)

Greatest. Using the comparative scale of Mantle Wave magnitudes (defined in 1968), the world's largest earthquake since 1930 has been the cataclysmic Alaska or Prince William Sound earthquake (epicenter Latitude 61°10′N., Longitude 147°48′W.) of 1964 March 28, with a magnitude of 8.9. The Kamchatka, U.S.S.R., earthquake (epicenter Lat. 52°45′N., Long. 159°30′E.) of 1952 November 4, and the shocks around Lebu, south of Concepción, Chile, on 1960 May 22, are both now assessed at a magnitude of 8.8. Formerly the largest earthquake during this period had been regarded as the submarine shock (epicenter Lat. 39°30′N,., Long. 144° 30′E.) about 100 miles off the Sanriku coast of northeastern Honshu, Japan, of 1933 March 2, estimated at 8.9 on the Gutenberg-Richter scale (1956).

It is possible that the earthquake in Lisbon, Portugal, of 1755 November 1, would have been accorded a magnitude of between 8.75 and 9, if seismographs, invented in 1853, had been available then to record traces. The first of the three shocks was at 9:40 a.m. and lasted for between 6 and 7 minutes. Lakes in Norway were disturbed. The energy of an earthquake of magnitude 8.9 is about 5.6×10^{24} ergs, which is equivalent to an explosion 100 times greater than the largest nuclear device ever detonated—nearly 10,000 megatons.

Worst. The greatest loss of life occurred in the earthquake in Shensi Province, China, of 1556 January 23, when an estimated 830,000 people were killed. The greatest material damage was in the earthquake on the Kwanto plain, Japan, at 11:58 a.m. of 1923 September 1, (magnitude 8.2, epicenter in Lat. 35°15′N., Long. 139°30′E.). In Sagami Bay, the sea bottom in one area sank 1,310 feet. The official total of persons killed and missing in this earthquake, called the *Shinsai* or Great 'Quake, and the resultant fires was 142,807. In Tokyo and Yokohama 575,000 dwellings were destroyed. The cost of the damage was estimated at $2,800,000,000.

HIGHEST DORMANT VOLCANO: Llullaillaco in the Andes is 22,058 feet above sea level.

VOLCANOES

The total number of known active volcanoes in the world is 455 with an estimated 80 more that are submarine. The greatest concentration is in Indonesia, where 77 of its 167 volcanoes have erupted within historic times. The name "volcano" was first applied to the now dormant Vulcano Island in the Aeolian group in the Mediterranean, and that name derives from Vulcan, Roman god of destructive fire.

Greatest Eruption. The total volume of matter discharged in the eruption of Tambora, a volcano on the island of Sumbawa, in Indonesia, April 5–7, 1815, has been estimated as 36.4 cubic miles. The energy of this eruption was 8.4×10^{26} ergs. The volcano lost about 4,100 feet in height and a crater 7 miles in diameter was formed. This compares with a probable 15 cubic miles ejected by Santorini and 4.3 cubic miles ejected by Krakatoa (see next entry). The internal pressure causing the Tambora eruption has been estimated at 46,500,000 lbs. per square inch.

Greatest Explosion. The greatest known volcanic explosion was the eruption *c.* 1470 B.C. of Thira (Santorini), a volcanic island in the Aegean Sea. It is highly probable that this explosion destroyed the centers of the Minoan civilization in Crete, about 80 miles away, with a tsunami (tidal wave) 165 feet high. Evidence was published in December, 1967, of an eruption that spewed lava over 100,000 square miles of Oregon, Idaho, Nevada and Northern California about 3,000,000 years ago.

The greatest explosion since Santorini occurred *c.* 10:00 a.m. (local time), or 3:00 a.m. G.M.T., on August 27, 1883, with an eruption of Krakatoa, an island (then 18 square miles) in the Sunda Strait between Sumatra and Java, in Indonesia. A total of 163 villages were wiped out, and 36,380 people killed by the wave it caused. Rocks were thrown to a height of 34 miles and dust fell 10 days later at a distance of 3,313 miles. The explosion was recorded four hours later on the island of Rodrigues, 2,968 miles away, as "the roar of heavy

guns" and was heard over 1/13th part of the surface of the globe. This explosion has been estimated to have had about 26 times the power of the greatest H-bomb test detonation, but was still only a fifth the size of the Santorini cataclysm (see above).

Highest—Extinct. The highest extinct volcano in the world is Cerro Aconcagua (22,834 feet), on the Argentine side of the Andes. It was first climbed on January 14, 1897, and was the highest mountain climbed until June 12, 1907.

Highest—Dormant. The highest dormant volcano is Volcán Llullaillaco (22,058 feet), on the frontier between Chile and Argentina.

Highest—Active. The highest volcano regarded as active is Volcán Antofalla (20,013 feet) in Argentina, though a more definite claim is made for Volcán Guayatiri or Guallatiri (19,882 feet), in Chile, which erupted in 1959.

Northernmost. The northernmost volcano is Beeren Berg (7,470 feet) on the island of Jan Mayen (71°05′N.) in the Greenland Sea. The island was possibly discovered by Henry Hudson in 1607 or 1608, but definitely visited by Jan Jacobsz May (Netherlands) in 1614. It was annexed by Norway on May 8, 1929. It erupted on September 20, 1970, and the island's 39 male inhabitants had to be evacuated.

The Ostenso seamount (5,825 feet), 346 miles from the North Pole (Lat. 85°10′N., Long. 133°W.), was volcanic.

Southernmost. The most southerly known active volcano is Mount Erebus (12,450 feet) on Ross Island (77°35′S.), in Antarctica. It was discovered on Janaury 28, 1841, by the expedition of Captain (later Rear-Admiral Sir) James Clark Ross (1800–62) of the British Royal Navy, and first climbed at 10 a.m. on March 10, 1908, by a British party of five, led by Professor (later Lieut.-Col. Sir) Tannatt William Edgeworth David (1858–1934).

Largest Crater. The world's largest *caldera* or volcano crater is that of Mt. Aso (5,223 feet) in Kyushu, Japan, which measures 17 miles north to south, 10 miles east to west and 71 miles in circumference. The longest lava flow, known as *pahoehoe* (twisted cord-like solidifications), is that from the eruption of Laki in southeast Iceland, which flowed 65–70 miles, covering an area of 218 square miles with 2.95 cubic miles of lava. The largest known prehistoric flow is the Roza basalt flow in North America *c.* 15,000,000 years ago, which had an unsurpassed length (300 miles), area (15,400 square miles) and volume (300 cubic miles).

GEYSERS

Tallest. The Waimangu geyser, in New Zealand, erupted to a height in excess of 1,500 feet in 1904, but has not been active since it erupted violently in 1917. Currently the world's tallest active geyser is the U.S. National Parks' Service Steamboat Geyser, in Yellowstone National Park, Wyoming, which erupted at intervals ranging from 5 days to 10 months between 1962 and 1969 to a height of 250–380 feet. The *Geysir* ("gusher") near Mt. Hekla in south-central Iceland, from which all others have been named, spurts, on occasions, to 180 feet.

Most Frequent. The most frequently erupting geyser is "Old Faithful," in Yellowstone National Park, Wyoming, whose 90- to 180-foot spire rarely varies more than 21 minutes either side of its 66-minute average.

BIGGEST GEYSER OF ALL TIME: The Waimangu geyser in New Zealand shot more than 1,500 feet high in 1904.

2. Structure and Dimensions

The earth is not a true sphere, but flattened at the poles and hence an ellipsoid. The polar diameter of the earth (7,899.809 miles) is 26.576 miles less than the equatorial diameter (7,926.385 miles). The earth also has a slight ellipticity of the equator since its long axis (about Longitude 37° W.) is 174 yards greater than the short axis. The greatest departures from the reference ellipsoid are a protuberance of 244 feet in the area of New Guinea, and a depression of 354 feet south of Sri Lanka (Ceylon) in the Indian Ocean.

The greatest circumference of the earth, at the equator, is 24,901.47 miles, compared with 24,859.75 miles at the meridian. The area of the surface is estimated to be 196,937,600 square miles. The period of axial rotation, *i.e.* the true sidereal day, is 23 hours 56 minutes 4.0996 seconds, mean time.

Earth's Structure

The mass of the earth is 6,588,000,000,000,000,000,000 tons and its density is 5.517 times that of water. The volume is an estimated 259,875,620,000 cubic miles. The earth picks up cosmic dust but estimates vary widely with 40,000 long tons a day being the upper limit. Modern theory is that the earth has an outer shell or lithosphere about 25 miles thick, then an outer and inner rock layer or mantle extending 1,800 miles deep, beneath which there is an iron-nickel core at an estimated temperature of 3,700°C. and at a pressure of 27,400 tons per square inch or 3,400 kilobars. If the iron-nickel core theory is correct, iron must be by far the most abundant element.

Rocks

The age of the earth is generally considered to be within the range 4,600 ±100 million years, by analogy with directly measured ages of meteorites and of the moon. However, no rocks of this great age have yet been found on the earth, since geological processes have presumably destroyed the earliest record.

OLDEST ROCK: This granite gneiss rock found in the Minnesota River valley is more than 3,800,000,000 years old.

Oldest. The greatest reported age for any scientifically dated rock is 3,800 ± 100 million years for granite gneiss rock found near Granite Falls in the Minnesota River valley, as measured by the lead-isotope and rubidium-uranium methods by the U.S. Geological Survey, and announced on January 26, 1975. These metamorphic samples compare with the Amitsog gneiss from Godthaab, Greenland, which is unreservedly accepted to be between 3,700 and 3,750 million years old.

Largest. The largest exposed rocky outcrop is the 1,237-foot-high Mount Augustus (3,627 feet above sea level), discovered on June 3, 1858, about 200 miles east of Carnarvon, Western Australia. It is an up-faulted monoclinal gritty conglomerate 5 miles long and 2 miles across and thus twice the size of the celebrated monolithic arkose Ayer's Rock (1,100 feet), 250 miles southwest of Alice Springs, in Northern Territory, Australia.

OCEANS

Largest. The area of the earth covered by the sea is estimated to be 139,670,000 square miles, or 70.92 per cent of the total surface. The mean depth of the hydrosphere was at one time estimated to be 12,450 feet, but recent surveys suggest a lower estimate, closer to 11,660 feet. The total weight of the water is estimated as 1.45×10^{18} tons, or 0.022 per cent of the earth's total weight. The volume of the oceans is estimated to be 308,400,000 cubic miles, compared with only 8,400,000 cubic miles of fresh water.

The largest ocean in the world is the Pacific. Excluding adjacent seas, it represents 45.8 per cent of the world's oceans and is about 63,800,000 square miles in area. From Guayaquil, Ecuador, on the east, to Bangkok, Thailand, on the west, the Pacific could be said to stretch 10,905 miles in a straight navigable line.

Longest Voyage. The longest possible great circle sea voyage is one of 19,860 miles from a point 150 miles west of Karachi, Pakistan, to a point 200 miles north of Uka, Kamchatka, U.S.S.R., *via* the Mozambique Channel, Drake Passage, and Bering Sea.

Most Southerly. The most southerly point in the oceans is 85°34′S., 154°W., at the snout of the Robert Scott Glacier, 305 miles from the South Pole, in the Pacific sector of Antarctica.

Deepest. The deepest part of the ocean was first discovered in 1951 by the British survey ship *Challenger* in the Marianas Trench in the Pacific Ocean. The depth was measured by sounding and by echo-sounder and published as 5,960 fathoms (35,760 feet). Subsequent visits to the Challenger Deep have resulted in claims by echo-sounder only, culminating in one of 36,198 feet by the U.S.S.R.'s research ship *Vityaz* in March, 1959. On January 23, 1960, the U.S. Navy bathyscaphe *Trieste* descended to 35,820 feet. A metal object, say a pound-ball of steel, dropped into water above this trench would take nearly 63 minutes to fall to the sea bed 6.85 miles below. The average depth of the Pacific Ocean is 14,000 feet.

Remotest Spot

The world's most distant point from land is a spot in the South

Pacific, approximately 48°30′S., 125°30′W., which is about 1,660 miles from the nearest points of land, namely Pitcairn Island, Ducie Island and Cape Dart, Antarctica. Centered on this spot, therefore, is a circle of water with an area of about 8,657,000 square miles—about 7,000 square miles larger than the U.S.S.R., the world's largest country (see Chapter 10).

Sea Temperature

The temperature of the water at the surface of the sea varies from —2°C. (28.5°F.) in the White Sea to 35.6°C. (96°F.) in the Persian Gulf in summer. A freak geothermal temperature of 56°C. (132.8°F.) was recorded in February, 1965, by the survey ship *Atlantis II*, near the bottom of Discovery Deep (7,200 feet) in the Red Sea. The normal sea temperature in the area is 22°C. (71.6°F.). Ice-focussed solar rays have been known to heat lake water to nearly 26.6°C. (80°F.).

Largest Sea

The largest of the world's seas (as opposed to oceans) is the South China Sea, with an area of 1,148,500 square miles. The Malayan Sea comprising the waters between the Indian Ocean and the South Pacific, south of the Chinese mainland, covering 3,144,000 square miles, is not now an entity accepted by the International Hydrographic Bureau.

Largest Gulf

The largest gulf in the world is the Gulf of Mexico, with a shoreline of 3,100 miles from Cape Sable, Florida, to Cabo Catoche, Mexico. Its area is 580,000 square miles.

Largest Bay

The largest bay in the world is the Bay of Bengal, with a shoreline of 2,250 miles from southeastern Sri Lanka (Ceylon) to Pagoda Point, Burma. Its mouth measures 1,075 miles across.

Highest Sea-Mountain

The highest known submarine mountain is one discovered in 1953 near the Tonga Trench between Samoa and New Zealand. It rises 28,500 feet from the sea bed, with its summit 1,200 feet below the surface.

Highest Wave

The highest officially recorded sea wave was measured from the U.S.S. *Ramapo* proceeding from Manila, Philippines, to San Diego, California, on the night of February 6–7, 1933, during a 68-knot (78.3 m.p.h.) gale. The wave was computed to be 112 feet from trough to crest. A stereo-photograph of a wave calculated to be 81.7 feet high was taken from the U.S.S.R.'s diesel-electric vessel *Ob'* in the South Pacific Ocean, about 370 miles south of Macquarie Island, Australia, on April 2, 1956.

The highest instrumentally measured wave was one calculated to be exactly 77 feet high, recorded by the British ship *Weather Adviser* on station Juliette in the North Atlantic at noon on March 17, 1968. Its length was 1,150 feet and its period was 15 seconds. It has been calculated on the statistics of the Stationary Random Theory that one wave in more than 300,000 may exceed the average by a factor of 4.

On July 9, 1958, a landslip caused a wave to wash 1,740 feet high along the fjord-like shore of Lituya Bay, Alaska.

"Tidal" Wave. The highest recorded seismic sea wave, or *tsunami*, was one of 220 feet which appeared off Valdez, southwest Alaska, after the great Prince William Sound earthquake of 1964 March 28. *Tsunami* (a Japanese word which is singular and plural) have been observed to travel at 490 m.p.h. Between 479 B.C. and 1967 there were 286 instances of devastating *tsunami*.

Greatest Tides. The greatest tides in the world occur in the Bay of Fundy, which separates Nova Scotia from Maine and the Canadian province of New Brunswick. Burncoat Head in the Minas Basin, Nova Scotia, has the greatest mean spring range with 47.5 feet, and an extreme range of 53.5 feet.

Extreme tides are due to lunar and solar gravitational forces affected by their perigee, perihelion, and of conjunctions. Barometric and wind effects can superimpose an added "surge" element. Coastal and sea-floor configurations can accentuate these forces.

Greatest Current. The greatest current in the oceans of the world is the Antarctic Circumpolar Current or West Wind Drift Current, which was measured in 1969 in the Drake Passage between South America and Antarctica, to be flowing at a rate of 9,500,000,000 cubic feet per second—nearly three times that of the Gulf Stream. Its width ranges from 185 to 1,240 miles and has a surface flow rate of ¾ of a knot.

Strongest Current. The world's strongest currents are the Saltstraumen in the Saltfjord, near Bodø, Norway, which reach 15.6 knots (18.0 m.p.h.). The flow rate through the 500-foot-wide channel surpasses 500,000 cu.ft./sec.

Icebergs

Largest. The largest iceberg on record was an Antarctic tabular berg of over 12,000 square miles (208 miles long and 60 miles wide) sighted 150 miles west of Scott Island, in the South Pacific Ocean, by the U.S.S. *Glacier* on November 12, 1956. This iceberg was thus larger than Belgium.

The 200-foot-thick Arctic ice island T.1 (140 square miles) was discovered in 1946, and was still being plotted in 1963.

Most Southerly Arctic. The most southerly Arctic iceberg was sighted in the Atlantic in 30°50′N., 45°06′W., on June 2, 1934.

Most Northerly Antarctic. The most northerly Antarctic iceberg was a remnant sighted in the Atlantic by the ship *Dochra* at Lat. 26°30′S., Long. 25°40′W., on April 30, 1894.

NARROWEST STRAIT: The gap between the island of Euboea and the Greek mainland is only 45 yards wide.

Tallest. The tallest on record was an iceberg carved off northwest Greenland with 550 feet showing above the surface.

Straits

Longest. The longest straits in the world are the Tartarskiy Proliv or Tartar Straits between Sakhalin Island and the U.S.S.R. mainland, running 497 miles from the Sea of Japan to Sakhalinsky Zaliv. This distance is marginally longer than the Malacca Straits, which extend 485 miles.

Broadest. The broadest straits in the world are the Davis Straits between Greenland and Baffin Island, which at one point narrow to 210 miles. The Drake Passage between the Diego Ramírez Islands, Chile, and the South Shetland Islands, is 710 miles across.

Narrowest. The narrowest navigable straits are those between the Aegean island of Euboea and the mainland of Greece. The gap is only 45 yards wide at Khalkis. The Seil Sound, Strathclyde, Scotland, narrows to a point only 20 feet wide where a bridge joins the island of Seil to the mainland and is thus said to span the Atlantic.

LAND

There is satisfactory evidence that at one time the earth's land surface comprised a single primeval continent of 80,000,000 square miles, now termed Pangaea, and that this split about 190,000,000 years ago, during the Jurassic period, into two super-continents, termed Laurasia (Eurasia, Greenland and North America) in the north and Gondwanaland, named after Gondwana, India (comprising Africa, Arabia, India, South America, Oceania and Antarctica) in the south. The South Pole was apparently in the area of the Sahara as recently as the Ordovician period of *c.* 450 million years ago.

Largest and Smallest Continents. Only 29.08 per cent, or an estimated 57,270,000 square miles, of the earth's surface is land, with a mean height of 2,480 feet above sea level. The Eurasian land mass is the largest with an area (including islands) of 21,053,000 square miles.

The smallest is the Australian mainland, with an area of about 2,940,000 square miles, which, together with Tasmania, New Zealand, New Guinea and the Pacific Islands, is described as Oceania. The total area of Oceania is about 3,450,000 square miles, including West Irian (formerly West New Guinea) which is politically in Asia.

Remotest Land. There is an unpinpointed spot in the Dzoosotoyn Elisen (desert), northern Sinkiang, China, that is more than 1,500 miles from the open sea in any direction. The nearest large town to this point is Wulumuchi (Urumchi) to its south.

Peninsula. The world's largest peninsula is Arabia, with an area of about 1,250,000 square miles.

Islands

Largest. Discounting Australia, which is usually regarded as a continental land mass, the largest island in the world is Greenland

REMOTEST ISLAND: Uninhabited Bouvet Øya was discovered in the South Atlantic in 1739, and lies about 1,050 miles from the nearest land.

(Kingdom of Denmark), with an area of about 840,000 square miles. There is some evidence that Greenland is in fact several islands overlaid by an ice-cap.

The largest island surrounded by fresh water is the Ilha de Marajó (1,553 square miles), in the mouth of the Amazon River, Brazil. The largest island in a lake is Manitoulin Island (1,068 square miles) in the Canadian (Ontario) section of Lake Huron. This island itself has on it a lake of 41.09 square miles called Manitou Lake, in which there are several islands. The largest inland island (*i.e.* land surrounded by rivers) is Ilha do Bananal, Brazil.

Remotest. The remotest island in the world is Bouvet Øya (formerly Liverpool Island), discovered in the South Atlantic by J. B. C. Bouvet de Lozier on January 1, 1739, and first landed on by Capt. George Norris on December 16, 1825. Its position is 54°26'S., 3°24'E. This uninhabited Norwegian dependency is about 1,050 miles from the nearest land—the uninhabited Queen Maud Land coast of eastern Antarctica.

The remotest inhabited island in the world is Tristan da Cunha, discovered in the South Atlantic by Tristão da Cunha, a Portuguese admiral, in March, 1506. It has an area of 38 square miles (habitable area 12 square miles) and was annexed by the United Kingdom on August 14, 1816. The island's population was 235 in August, 1966. The nearest inhabited land is the island of St. Helena, 1,320 miles to the northeast. The nearest continent, Africa, is 1,700 miles away.

Newest. The world's newest island is a volcanic one about 100 feet high, which began forming in 1970 south of Gatukai Island in the British Solomon Islands in the South Pacific.

Largest Atoll. The largest atoll in the world is Kwajalein in the Marshall Islands, in the central Pacific Ocean. Its slender 176-mile-long coral reef encloses a lagoon of 1,100 square miles.

The atoll with the largest land area is Christmas Island, in the Line Islands, in the central Pacific Ocean. It has an area of 184 square miles. Its two principal settlements, London and Paris, are 4 miles apart.

Longest Reef. The longest reef in the world is the Great Barrier Reef off Queensland, northeastern Australia, which is 1,260 geographical miles in length. Between 1959 and 1971 a large section between Cooktown and Townsville was destroyed by the proliferation of the Crown of Thorns starfish (*Acanthaster planci*).

Greatest Archipelago. The world's greatest archipelago is the 3,500-mile-long crescent of over 13,000 islands which forms Indonesia.

Northernmost Land. The most northerly land is Kaffeklubben Øyen off the northeast of Greenland, 440 miles from the North Pole, discovered in 1921, but determined only in June, 1969, to be in latitude 83° 40′ 6″. The name means "Coffee-Club Island."

The South Pole, unlike the North Pole, is on land. The Amundsen-Scott South Polar station was built there at an altitude of 9,370 feet in 1957. It is drifting bodily with the ice cap 27 to 30 feet per annum in the direction 43° W. and was replaced by a new structure in 1975.

Mountains

Highest. An eastern Himalayan peak of 29,028 feet above sea level on the Tibet-Nepal border (in an area first designated Chu-mu lang-ma on a map of 1717) was discovered to be the world's highest mountain in 1852 by the Survey Department of the Government of India, from theodolite readings taken in 1849 and 1850. In 1860 its height was computed to be 29,002 feet. On July 25, 1973, the Chinese announced a height of 8,848.1 meters or 29,032 feet 3 inches. In practice the altitude can only be justified as $29,032 \pm 25$ feet. The 5½-mile-high peak was named Mount Everest after Sir George Everest (1790–1866), formerly Surveyor-General of India. After a total loss of 11 lives since the first reconnaisance in 1921, Everest was finally conquered at 11:30 a.m. on May 29, 1953. (For details of ascents, see under Mountaineering in Chapter 12.)

The mountain whose summit is farthest from the earth's center is the Andean peak of Chimborazo (20,561 feet), 98 miles south of the equator in Ecuador. Its summit is 7,057 feet further from the earth's center than the summit of Mt. Everest. The highest mountain on the equator is Volcán Cayambe (19,285 feet), Ecuador, at Longitude 77° 58′ W.

The highest insular mountain in the world is the unsurveyed Ngga Pula, formerly Mount Sukarno, formerly Carstensz Pyramide, in Irian Jaya, Indonesia, formerly Netherlands New Guinea. According to cross-checked altimeter estimates, it is 16,500 feet high.

Highest Unclimbed. Excluding subsidiary summits, the highest separate unclimbed mountain in the world is now only the 30th highest Batura Muztagh I (Hunza Kunji I) (25,542 feet) in the Karakoram.

Largest. The world's tallest mountain measured from its submarine base (3,280 fathoms) in the Hawaiian Trough to peak is Mauna Kea (Mountain White) on the island of Hawaii, with a combined height of 33,476 feet, of which 13,796 feet are above sea level. Another mountain whose dimensions, but not height, exceed those of Mount Everest is the Hawaiian peak of Mauna Loa (Mountain Long) at 13,680 feet. The axes of its elliptical base, 16,322 feet below sea level, have been estimated as 74 miles and 53 miles. It should be noted that Cerro Aconcagua (22,834 feet) is more than 38,800 feet above the 16,000-foot-deep Pacific abyssal plain or 42,834 feet above the Peru-Chile Trench, which is 180 miles distant in the South Pacific.

Greatest Ranges. The world's greatest land mountain range is the Himalaya-Karakoram, which contains 96 of the world's 109 peaks of over 24,000 feet. The greatest of all mountain ranges is, however, the submarine mid-Atlantic range, which is 10,000 miles long and 500 miles wide, with its highest peak being Mount Pico in the Azores, which rises 23,615 feet from the ocean floor (7,615 feet above sea level).

Greatest Plateau. The most extensive high plateau in the world is the Tibetan Plateau in Central Asia. The average altitude is 16,000 feet and the area is 77,000 square miles.

Sheerest Wall. The 3,200-foot-wide northwest face of Half Dome, Yosemite, California, is 2,200 feet high, but nowhere departs more than 7 degrees from the vertical.

Highest Halites. Along the northern shores of the Gulf of Mexico for 725 miles there exist 330 subterranean "mountains" of salt, some of which rise more than 60,000 feet from bed rock and appear as the low salt domes first discovered in 1862.

Sand Dunes. The world's highest measured sand dunes are those in the Saharan sand sea of Isaouane-N-Tiferine of east-central Algeria in Lat. 26° 42′ N., Long. 6° 43′ E. They have a wave-length of nearly 3 miles and attain a height of 1,410 feet.

Depressions

Deepest. The deepest depression so far discovered is beneath the Hollick-Kenyon Plateau in Marie Byrd Land, Antarctica, where, at a point 5,900 feet above sea level, the ice depth is 14,000 feet, hence indicating a bed rock depression 8,100 feet below sea level.

The deepest exposed depression on land is the shore surrounding the Dead Sea, 1,291 feet below sea level. The deepest point on the bed of the lake is 2,600 feet below the Mediterranean. The deepest part of the bed of Lake Baykal in Siberia, U.S.S.R., is 4,872 feet below sea level.

The greatest submarine depression is a large area of the floor of the northwest Pacific which has an average depth of 15,000 feet.

Largest. The largest exposed depression in the world is the Caspian Sea basin in the Azerbaijan, Russian, Kazakh, and Turkmen republics of the U.S.S.R. and northern Iran (Persia). It is more than 200,000 square miles, of which 143,550 square miles is lake area. The preponderant land area of the depression is the Prikaspiyskaya Nizmennost', lying around the northern third of the lake and stretching inland for a distance of up to 280 miles.

Rivers

The river systems of the world are estimated to contain 55,000 cubic miles of fresh water.

Longest. The two longest rivers in the world are the Amazon (*Amazonas*), flowing into the South Atlantic, and the Nile (*Bahr-el-Nil*) flowing into the Mediterranean. Which is the longer is more a matter of definition than of measurement.

The true source of the Amazon was discovered in 1953 to be a stream named Huarco, rising near the summit of Cerro Huagra (17,188 ft.) in Peru. This stream progressively becomes the Toro, then the Santiago, then the Apurímac, which in turn is known as the Ene, and then the Tambo before its confluence with the Amazon prime tributary, the Ucayali. The length of the Amazon from this source to the South Atlantic *via* the Canal do Norte was measured in 1969 to be 4,007 miles (usually quoted to the rounded-off figure of 4,000 miles).

If, however, a vessel navigating downriver turns to the south of Ilha de Marajó through the straits of Breves and Boiuci into the Pará, the total length of the waterway becomes 4,195 miles. The Pará is not, however, a tributary of the Amazon, being hydrologically part of the basin of the Tocantins.

The length of the Nile waterway, as surveyed by M. Devroey (Belgium) before the loss of a few miles of meanders due to the formation of Lake Nasser, behind the Aswan High Dam, was 4,145 miles. This course is the hydrologically acceptable one from the source in Ruanda of the Luvironza branch of the Kagera feeder of the Victoria Nyanza *via* the White Nile (*Bahr-el-Jebel*) to the delta.

Shortest River. The strongest claimant to the title is the D River, Lincoln City, Oregon, which connects Devil's Lake to the Pacific Ocean and is 440 feet long at low tide.

Greatest Flow. The greatest flow of any river in the world is that of the Amazon, which discharges an average of 4,200,000 cubic feet of water per second into the Atlantic Ocean, rising to more than 7,000,000 "cusecs" in full flood. The lowest 900 miles of the Amazon average 300 feet in depth.

Largest Basin. The largest river basin in the world is that drained by the Amazon (4,007 miles). It covers about 2,720,000 square miles. It has about 15,000 tributaries and sub-tributaries, of which four are more than 1,000 miles long.

Longest Tributary and Sub-Tributary. The longest of all tributaries is the Madeira (part of the Amazon) with a length of 2,100 miles, which is surpassed by only 14 rivers in the whole world. The longest sub-tributary is the Pilcomayo (1,000 miles long) in South America. It is a tributary of the Paraguay (1,500 miles long), which is itself a tributary of the Paraná (2,500 miles).

Submarine River. In 1952, a submarine river 250 miles wide, known as the Cromwell current, was discovered flowing eastward 300 feet below the surface of the Pacific for 3,500 miles along the equator. Its volume is 1,000 times that of the Mississippi.

Subterranean River. In August, 1958, a crypto-river was tracked by radio-isotopes flowing under the Nile, with a mean annual flow six times greater—560,000 million cubic meters (20 million million cubic feet).

Longest Estuary. The world's longest estuary is that of the Ob', in the northern U.S.S.R., at 450 miles.

Largest Delta. The world's largest delta is that created by the Ganga (Ganges) and Brahmaputra in Bangladesh (formerly East Pakistan) and West Bengal, India. It covers an area of 30,000 square miles.

Greatest River Bores. The bore on the Ch'ient'ang-kiang (Hang-chou-fe) in eastern China is the most remarkable in the world. At spring tides, the wave attains a height of up to 25 feet and a speed of 13 knots. It is heard advancing at a range of 14 miles. The bore on the Hooghly branch of the Ganges travels for 70 miles at more than 15 knots. The annual downstream flood wave on the Mekong River of Southeast Asia sometimes reaches a height of 46 feet. The greatest volume of any bore is that of the Canal do Norte (10 miles wide) in the mouth of the Amazon.

Fastest Rapids. The fastest rapids which have ever been navigated are the Lava Falls on the Colorado River. At times of flood these attain a speed of 30 m.p.h. with waves boiling up to 12 feet high.

Lakes and Inland Seas

Largest. The largest inland sea or lake in the world is the Kaspiskoye More (Caspian Sea) in southern U.S.S.R. and Iran (Persia). It is 760 miles long and its total area is 143,550 square miles. Of the total area, 55,280 square miles (38.6 per cent) is in Iran, where the lake is named the Darya-ye-Khazar. Its maximum depth is 3,215 feet and its surface is 92 feet below sea level. Since 1930 it has diminished 15,000 square miles in area with a fall of 62 feet, while the shoreline has retreated more than 10 miles in some places. The U.S.S.R. government plans to reverse the flow of the upper Pechora River from flowing north to the Barents Sea by blasting a 70-mile-long canal with nuclear explosives into the south-flowing Kolva River so that *via* the Kama and Volga rivers the Caspian will be replenished.

The fresh-water lake with the greatest surface area is Lake Superior, one of the Great Lakes. The total area is about 31,800 square miles, of which 20,700 square miles are in the U.S. and 11,100 square miles in Ontario, Canada. It is 600 feet above sea level. The fresh-water lake with the greatest volume is Baykal (see Deepest, below) with an estimated volume of 5,750 cubic miles.

Largest Lagoon. The largest lagoon in the world is Lagoa dos Patos in southernmost Brazil. It is 158 miles long and extends over 4,110 square miles.

Lake in a Lake. The largest lake in a lake is Manitou Lake (41.09 square miles) on the world's largest lake island Manitoulin Island (1,068 square miles) in the Canadian part of Lake Huron.

Deepest. The deepest lake in the world is Ozero (Lake) Baykal in southern Siberia, U.S.S.R. It is 385 miles long and between 20 and 46 miles wide. In 1957, the Olkhon Crevice was measured to be 6,365 feet deep and hence 4,872 feet below sea level.

Underground. Reputedly the world's largest underground lake is the Lost Sea, which lies 300 feet underground in the Craighead Caverns, Sweetwater, Tennessee. Discovered in 1905, it covers an area of 4½ acres.

Highest. The highest steam-navigated lake in the world is Lago Titicaca (maximum depth 1,214 feet), with an area of about 3,200 square miles (1,850 square miles in Peru, 1,350 square miles in

Bolivia), in South America. It is 130 miles long and is situated at 12,506 feet above sea level.

There is a small unnamed lake 2 miles long near Jokpolung, Tibet, which is the true source of the Sutley River. It lies at an elevation of 22,500 feet.

Waterfalls

Highest. The highest waterfall in the world is the Salto Angel (Angel Falls), in Venezuela, on a branch of the Carrao River, an upper tributary of the Caroní, with a total drop of 3,212 feet and the longest single drop 2,648 feet. It was re-discovered in 1935 by a U.S. pilot named Jimmy Angel (died December 8, 1956), who crashed nearby on October 9, 1937. The falls, known by the Indians as Cherun-Meru, were first reported by Ernesto Sanchez La Cruz in 1910. The Auyan-Tepui plateau was first climbed on January 13, 1971.

HIGHEST WATERFALL: Angel Falls in Venezuela has a single drop of 2,648 feet, and a total fall of 3,212 feet. Note the airplane passing in front of the Falls.

Greatest. On the basis of the average annual flow, the greatest waterfall in the world is the Guairá (374 feet high), known also as the Salto dos Sete Quedas, on the Alto Paraná River between Brazil and Paraguay. Although attaining an average height of only 110 feet, its estimated annual average flow over the lip (5,300 yards wide) is 470,000 cubic feet per second. It has a peak flow of 1,750,000 cubic feet per second. The seven cataracts of Stanley Falls in the Congo (Zaïre) have an average annual flow of 600,000 cubic feet per second.

It has been calculated that, when some 5,500,000 years ago the Mediterranean basins began to be filled from the Atlantic through the Straits of Gibraltar, a waterfall 26 times greater than the Guairá and perhaps 2,625 feet high was formed.

Widest. The widest waterfalls in the world are Khône Falls (50 to 70 feet high) in Laos, with a width of 6.7 miles and a flood flow of 1,500,000 cubic feet per second.

HIGHEST WATERFALLS—BY COUNTRIES

Country	Drop in feet	Name and Location
Venezuela	3,212	Angel Falls, Carrao River
South Africa	3,110	Tugela, Natal
Norway	2,625	Utigardsfossen
United States	2,425	Yosemite, California
New Zealand	1,904	Sutherland Falls, River Arthur
Guyana	1,600	King George VI, Utshi
Australia	1,580	Wollomombi, N.S.W.
Tanzania-Zambia	1,400	Kalambo
France	1,384	Gavarnie, Gave de Pau
Brazil	1,325	Glass Fall, Iguazi
Austria	1,280	Krimmler Fälle
Congo (Zaïre)	1,259	Lofoi
Canada	1,248	Takkakaw, Yoho River, B.C.
Italy	1,033	Serio, Lombardy
Switzerland	978	Staubbach

Natural Phenomena

Longest Fjords. The world's longest "fjord" is the Nordvest Fjord arm of the Scoresby Sund in eastern Greenland, which extends inland 195 miles from the sea. The longest of Norwegian fjords is the Sogne Fjord, which extends 113.7 miles inland from Sygnefest to the head of the Lusterfjord arm at Skjolden. It averages barely 3 miles in width and has a deepest point of 4,085 feet. If measured from Huglo along the Bømlafjord to the head of the Sørfjord arm at Odda, the Hardangerfjorden can also be said to extend 113.7 miles.

Longest Glaciers. It is estimated that 6,020,000 square miles, or about 10.4 per cent of the earth's land surface, is permanently glaciated. The world's longest known glacier is the Lambert Glacier, discovered by an Australian aircraft crew in Australian Antarctic Territory in 1956–57. It is up to 40 miles wide and, with its upper section known as the Mellor Glacier, it measures at least 250 miles in length. With the Fisher Glacier limb, the Lambert forms a continuous ice passage about 320 miles long. The longest Himalayan glacier is the Siachen (47 miles) in the Karakoram range, though the Hispar and Biafo combine to form an ice passage 76 miles long.

LONGEST FJORD: The narrow Sogne Fjord in Norway extends 113.7 miles inland from the sea.

Greatest Avalanches. The greatest avalanches, though rarely observed, occur in the Himalayas, but no estimate of their volume have been published. It was estimated that 3,500,000 cubic meters (120,000,000 cubic feet) of snow fell in an avalanche in the Italian Alps in 1885. (See also Disasters.)

Natural Bridge. The longest natural bridge in the world is the Landscape Arch in Arches and Canyonlands National Park (Natural Bridge National Monument) near Moab, Utah. This natural sandstone arch spans 291 feet and is set about 100 feet above the canyon floor. In one place erosion has narrowed its section to 6 feet.

LONGEST NATURAL BRIDGE: This natural arch near Moab, Utah, spans 291 feet. Its size can be judged by the man near the left side.

Larger in mass, however, is the Rainbow Bridge, Utah, discovered on August 14, 1909, with a span of 278 feet but more than 22 feet wide.

The highest natural arch is the sandstone arch 25 miles west-northwest of K'ashih, Sinkiang, China, estimated in 1947 to be nearly 1,000 feet tall, with a span of about 150 feet.

Largest Desert. Nearly an eighth of the world's land surface is arid with an annual rainfall of less than 9.8 inches. The Sahara Desert in North Africa is the largest in the world. At its greatest length, it is 3,200 miles from east to west. From north to south it is between 800 and 1,400 miles. The area covered by the desert is about 3,250,000 square miles. The land level varies from 436 feet below sea level in the Qattara Depression, Egypt, to the mountain Emi Koussi (11,204 feet) in Chad. The diurnal temperature range in the western Sahara may be more than 80°F.

Largest Swamp. The world's largest tract of swamp is in the basin of the Pripet or Pripyat River—a tributary of the Dnieper in the U.S.S.R. These swamps cover an estimated area of 18,125 square miles.

Caves

Longest. The most extensive cave system in the world is that under the Mammoth Cave National Park, Kentucky, first discovered in 1799. On September 9, 1972, an exploration group led by Dr. John P. Wilcox, completed a connection, pioneered by Mrs. Patricia Crowther, on August 30, between the Flint Ridge Cave System and the Mammoth Cave system so making a combined system with a total mapped passageway length of 141.77 miles.

The world's largest ice caves are the Eisriesenwelt, discovered in 1879 at Werfen, Austria, with a length of 26.1 miles.

LONGEST STALACTITES: Free-hanging, 38 feet long (left) in County Clare, Ireland. (Right): Wall-supported, 195 feet long, near Málaga, Spain.

DEEPEST CAVES BY COUNTRIES

These depths are subject to continuous revisions.

Feet below entrance	Cave and mountain range	Country
3,842	Resea de la Pierre Saint-Martin, Pyrenees	France/Spain
3,743	Gouffre Berger, Sornin Plateau, Vercors	France
3,018	Abisso Michele Gortani	Italy
2,802	Grüberhornhölhe, Dachstein	Austria
2,798	Sumidero de Cellagna, Cantabria	Spain
2,651	Hölloch, Muotathal, Schwyz	Switzerland
2,467	Jaskini Snieznej, Tatras	Poland
2,463	Ghar Parau, Zagros Mountains	Iran
2,211	Kef, Toghobeit	Morocco
2,211	Poloska, Jama	Yugoslavia
2,040	Gouffre de Faour Dara	Lebanon
*2,009	Sotano del San Agustin	Mexico
1,885	Ragge favreraige	Norway
1,720	Arctomys Pot, Mt. Robson, British Columbia	Canada
1,690	Anou Boussouil, Djurdjura	Algeria
1,620	Bibina Cave, Kundiawa	Papua, New Guinea
1,454	Epos Cavern	Greece
1,350	Oumi, Senri	Japan
1,336	La Cima de Milpo	Peru
**1,312	Schachta Oktjabviskaya, Crimea	U.S.S.R.
1,184	Neffs Canyon Cave, Utah	U.S.A.
1,171	Harwood Hole	New Zealand
1,115	Izvorul Tausoarelor, Rodna	Rumania
1,053	Khazad-Dum, Tasmania	Australia
1,010	Ogof Ffynnon Ddu	Wales
642	Oxlow Cavern, Giant's Hole, Derbyshire	England
460	Carrowmore, County Sligo	Ireland

*This cave has the longest vertical pitch of 1,345 feet.
**A cave of 2,460 feet has been reported but not named in the U.S.S.R.

Longest Stalactite. The longest known stalactite in the world is a wall-supported column extending 195 feet from roof to floor in the Cueva de Nerja, near Málaga, Spain. The rather low tensile strength of calcite (calcium carbonate) precludes very long free-hanging stalactites, but one of 38 feet exists in the Poll on Ionain cave in County Clare, Ireland.

Tallest Stalagmite. The tallest known stalagmite in the world is La Grande Stalagmite in the Aven Armand cave, Lozère, France, which has attained a height of 98 feet from the cave floor. It was found in September, 1897.

Gorges

Largest. The largest gorge in the world is the Grand Canyon on the Colorado River in north-central Arizona. It extends from Marble Gorge to the Grand Wash Cliffs, over a distance of 217 miles. It varies in width from 4 to 13 miles and is up to 7,000 feet deep.

Deepest. The deepest canyon in low relief territory is Hell's Canyon, dividing Oregon and Idaho. It plunges 7,900 feet from the Devil Mountain down to the Snake River. A stretch of the Kali River in central Nepal flows 18,000 feet below its flanking summits of the Dhaulagiri and Annapurna groups. The deepest submarine canyon yet discovered is one 25 miles south of Esperance, Western Australia, which is 6,000 feet deep and 20 miles wide.

Sea Cliffs

The highest sea cliffs yet pinpointed anywhere in the world are those on the north coast of east Molokai, Hawaii, near Umilehi Point, which descend 3,300 feet to the sea at an average gradient of more than 55°.

3. Weather

The meteorological records given below necessarily relate largely to the last 125 to 145 years, since data before that time are both sparse and unreliable. Reliable registering thermometers were introduced as recently as *c.* 1820.

Greatest Temperature Ranges

The world's extremes of temperature have been noted progressively thus:

World's Highest Shade Temperatures

127.4°F.	Ouargla, Algeria	Aug. 27, 1884
130°F.	Amos and Mammoth Tank, California	Aug. 17, 1885
134°F.	Death Valley, California	July 10, 1913
136.4°F.	Al 'Aziziyah (el-Azizia), Libya*	Sept. 13, 1922†‡

World's Lowest Screen Temperatures

— 73°F.	Floeberg Bay, Ellesmere Island, Canada	1852
— 90.4°F.	Verkhoyansk, Siberia, U.S.S.R.	Jan. 3, 1885
— 90.4°F.	Verkhoyansk, Siberia, U.S.S.R.	Feb. 5 & 7, 1892
— 90.4°F.	Oymyakon, Siberia, U.S.S.R.	Feb. 6, 1933
—100.4°F.	South Pole, Antarctica	May 11, 1957
—102.1°F.	South Pole, Antarctica	Sept. 17, 1957
—109.1°F.	Sovietskaya, Antarctica	May 2, 1958
—113.3°F.	Vostok, Antarctica	June 15, 1958
—114.1°F.	Sovietskaya, Antarctica	June 19, 1958
—117.4°F.	Sovietskaya, Antarctica	June 25, 1958
—122.4°F.	Vostok, Antarctica	Aug. 7–8, 1958
—124.1°F.	Sovietskaya, Antarctica	Aug. 9, 1958
—125.3°F.	Vostok, Antarctica	Aug. 25, 1958
—126.9°F.	Vostok, Antarctica	Aug. 24, 1960

* Obtained by the National Geographical Society but not officially recognized by the Libyan Ministry of Communications.

† A reading of 140°F. at Delta, Mexico, in August, 1953, is not now accepted because of over-exposure to roof radiation. The official Mexican record of 136.4°F. at San Luis, Sonora, on August 11, 1933, is not internationally accepted.

‡ A freak heat flash struck Coimbra, Portugal, in September, 1933, when the temperature rose to 70°C. (158°F.) for 120 seconds.

The greatest recorded temperature ranges in the world are around the Siberian "cold pole" in the eastern U.S.S.R. Verkhoyansk (67°33′N., 133°23′E.) has ranged 192°F. from −94°F. (unofficial) to 98°F.

The greatest temperature variation recorded in a day is 100°F. (a fall from 44°F. to −56°F.) at Browning, Montana, on January 23–24, 1916. The most freakish rise was 49°F. in 2 minutes at Spearfish, South Dakota, from −4°F. at 7:30 a.m. to 45°F. at 7:32 a.m. on January 22, 1943.

Atmospheric Temperature

The lowest temperature ever recorded in the atmosphere is −225.4°F. at an altitude of about 50 to 60 miles, during noctilucent cloud research above Kronogård, Sweden, from July 27 to August 7, 1963.

Upper Atmosphere

A jet stream moving at 408 m.p.h. at 154,200 feet (29.2 miles) was recorded by Skua rocket above South Uist, Outer Hebrides, Scotland, on December 13, 1967.

Most Equable Temperature

The location with the most equable recorded temperature over a short period is Garapan, on Saipan, in the Mariana Islands, Pacific Ocean. During the nine years from 1927 to 1935, inclusive, the lowest temperature recorded was 67.3°F. on January 30, 1934, and the highest was 88.5°F. on September 9, 1931, giving an extreme range of 21.2 degrees F. Between 1911 and 1966 the Brazilian off-shore island of Fernando de Noronha had a minimum temperature of 65.5°F. on November 17, 1913, and a maximum of 89.6° F. on March 2, 1965, an extreme range of 24.1 degrees F.

Deepest Permafrost

The greatest recorded depth of permafrost is 4,920 feet, reported in April, 1968, in the basin of the Lena River, Siberia, U.S.S.R.

Humidity and Discomfort

Human discomfort depends not merely on temperature but on the combination of temperature, humidity, radiation and wind speed. The U.S. Weather Bureau uses a Temperature-Humidity Index, which equals two-fifths of the sum of the dry and wet bulb thermometer readings plus 15. When the THI in still air reaches 75, at least half of the people will be uncomfortable while at 79 few, if any, will be comfortable. A reading of 92 (shade temperature 119°F., relative humidity 22 per cent) was recorded at Yuma, Arizona, on July 31, 1957, but even this has been surpassed without being recorded in Death Valley, California.

Most Intense Rainfall

Difficulties attend rainfall readings for very short periods but the figure of 1.23 inches in one minute at Unionville, Maryland, at 3:23 p.m. on July 4, 1956, is regarded as the most intense recorded in modern times. The cloudburst of "near two foot . . . in less than a quarter of half an hour" at Oxford, England, on the afternoon of May 31 (Old Style), 1682, is regarded as unacademically recorded.

Cloud Extremes

The highest standard cloud form is cirrus, averaging 27,000 feet and above, but the rare nacreous or mother-of-pearl formation sometimes reaches nearly 80,000 feet. The lowest is stratus, below 3,500 feet. The cloud form with the greatest vertical range is cumulonimbus, which has been observed to reach a height of nearly 68,000 feet in the tropics. Noctilucent "clouds," a manifestation of which was observed from Hampshire, England, on June 30, 1950, are believed to pass at a height of over 60 miles.

Mirage

The largest mirage on record was that sighted in the Arctic at 83° N., 103° W. by Donald B. MacMillan in 1913. This type of mirage, known as the Fata Morgana, appeared as the same "hills, valleys, snow-capped peaks extending through at least 120 degrees of the horizon" that Peary had named Crocker Land 6 years earlier.

Lightning

The visible length of lightning strokes varies greatly. In mountainous regions, when clouds are very low, the flash may be less than 300 feet long. In flat country with very high clouds, a cloud-to-earth flash sometimes measures four miles, though in extreme cases such flashes have been measured at 20 miles. The intensely bright central core of the lightning channel is extremely narrow. Some authorities suggest that its diameter is as little as half an inch. This core is surrounded by a "corona envelope" (glow discharge) which may measure 10 to 20 feet in diameter.

The speed of a lightning discharge varies from 100 to 1,000 miles per second for the downward leader track, and reaches up to 87,000 miles per second (nearly half the speed of light) for the powerful return stroke.

Every few million strokes there is a giant discharge, in which the cloud-to-earth and the return lightning strokes flash from the top of the thunder clouds. In these "positive giants" energy of up to 3,000 million joules (3×10^{16} ergs) is sometimes recorded. The temperature reaches about 30,000° C., which is more than five times greater than that of the surface of the sun.

Waterspouts

The highest waterspout of which there is reliable record was one observed on May 16, 1898, off Eden, New South Wales, Australia. A theodolite reading from the shore gave its height as 5,014 feet. It was about 10 feet in diameter.

HOTTEST PLACE: Dallol, Ethiopia, averaged 94° over a 6-year period.

COLDEST PLACE: Soviet researchers chose this Antarctic "inaccessibility station," where the thermometer averages 72° below zero, to conduct experiments.

WEATHER RECORDS

Highest Shade Temperature: 136.4°F., Al 'Aziziyah, Libya, September 13, 1922.

Lowest Screen Temperature: —126.9°F., Vostok, Antarctica (11,500 feet above sea level), August 24, 1960[1].

Hottest Place (Annual mean):[6] Dallol, Ethiopia, 94°F., 1960–66.

Coldest Place (Annual mean): Pole of Cold (78°S., 96°E.), Antarctica, —72°F. (16 deg. F. lower than Pole).

Greatest Rainfall (24 hours): 73.62 in., Cilaos, La Réunion, Indian Ocean, March 15–16, 1952[2].

(Month): 366.14 in., Cherrapunji, Meghalaya, India, July, 1861.

(12 months): 1,041.78 in., Cherrapunji, Meghalaya, August 1, 1860 to July 31, 1861.

Greatest Snowfall (24 hours): 76 in., Silver Lake, Colorado, April 14–15, 1921[3].

(12 months): 1,224.5 in., Paradise, Mt. Rainer, Washington, February 19, 1971–February 18, 1972.

Maximum Sunshine (Year): 97%+ (over 4,300 hours), eastern Sahara.
765 days, February 9, 1967–May 17, 1969. St. Petersburg, Florida.

Minimum Sunshine: Nil at North Pole—for winter stretches of 186 days.

WETTEST PLACE: The world's biggest rain gauge is used at Mt. Waialeale, Kauai, Hawaii, the world's wettest place.

Weather Records (continued)

Barometric Pressure (Highest): 1,083.8 mb. (32 in.), Agata, Siberia, U.S.S.R., December 31, 1968.

(Lowest): 877 mb. (25.90 in.), about 600 miles northwest of Guam, Pacific Ocean, September 24, 1958[9].

Highest Surface Wind-speed:[4] 231 m.p.h., Mt. Washington (6,288 ft.), New Hampshire, April 12, 1934.

Thunder Days (Year):[5] 322 days, Bogor (formerly Buitenzorg), Java, Indonesia (average, 1916–19).

Wettest Place (Annual mean): Mt. Waialeale (5,148 ft.), Kauai, Hawaii, 451 in. (average, 1920–72).

Driest Place (Annual mean): Calama, in the Desierto de Atacama, Chile. None.

Longest Drought: c. 400 years to 1971, Desierto de Atacama, Chile.

Most Rainy Days (Year): Mt. Waialeale, Kauai, Hawaii, up to 350 days per year.

Largest Hailstones:[7] 1.67 lbs. (7½ in. diameter, 17½ in. circumference), Coffeyville, Kansas, September 3, 1970.

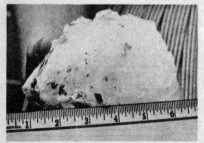

LARGEST HAILSTONE: 7½ inches across, this weighed 1.67 lbs. when it dropped on Kansas in 1970.

WINDIEST PLACE: Gales reach 200 m.p.h. at Commonwealth Bay, Antarctica.

Longest Sea Level Fogs (Visibility less than 1,000 yards): Fogs persist for weeks on the Grand Banks, Newfoundland, Canada, and the average is more than 120 days per year[8].

Windiest Place: The Commonwealth Bay, George V Coast, Antarctica, where gales reach 200 m.p.h.

---

[1] The coldest permanently inhabited place is the Siberian village of Oymyakon (63°16′N., 143°15′E.), in the U.S.S.R., where the temperature reached −96°F. in 1964.

[2] This is equal to 8,327.2 tons of rain per acre. Elevation 3,937 feet.

[3] The record for a single snowstorm is 175.4 inches at Thompson Pass, Alaska, on December 26–31, 1955. The greatest depth of snow on the ground was 25.4 feet at Paradise, Mt. Rainier, Washington, on April 17, 1972.

[4] The highest speed yet measured in a tornado is 280 m.p.h. at Wichita Falls, Texas, on April 2, 1958.

[5] At any given moment there are 3,200 thunderstorms in the world, some of which can be heard at a range of 18 miles.

[6] In Death Valley, California, maximum temperatures of over 120°F. were recorded on 43 consecutive days—July 6 to August 17, 1917. At Marble Bar, Western Australia (maximum 121°F.), 160 consecutive days with maximum temperatures of over 100°F. were recorded—October 31, 1923 to April 7, 1924. At Wyndham, Western Australia, the temperature reached 90°F. or more on 333 days in 1946.

[7] Much heavier hailstones are sometimes reported. These are usually not single but coalesced hailstones.

[8] Lower visibilities occur at higher altitudes, Ben Nevis is reputedly in cloud 300 days per year.

[9] The U.S.S. *Repose*, a hospital ship, recorded 856 mb. (25.55 in.) in the eye of a typhoon at 25°35′N., 128°20′E. off Okinawa, Japan, on September 16, 1954.

Chapter Four

THE UNIVERSE AND SPACE

LIGHT-YEAR—that distance traveled by light (speed 186,282.3960 miles per second ±3.6ft./sec., or 670,616,625.6 m.p.h., *in vacuo*) in one tropical (or solar) year (365.24219878 mean solar days at January 0, 12 hours Ephemeris time in 1900 A.D.) and is 5,878,499,780,000 miles. The unit was first used in March, 1888.

MAGNITUDE—a measure of stellar brightness such that the light of a star of any magnitude bears a ratio of 2.511886 to that of a star of the next magnitude. Thus a fifth magnitude star is 2.511886 times as bright, while one of the first magnitude is exactly 100 (or 2.511886^5) times as bright, as a sixth magnitude star. In the case of such exceptionally bright bodies as Sirius, Venus, the moon (magnitude −11.2) or the sun (magnitude −26.7), the magnitude is expressed as a minus quantity.

PROPER MOTION—that component of a star's motion in space which, at right angles to the line of sight, constitutes an apparent change of position of the star in the celestial sphere.

The universe is the entirety of space, matter and anti-matter. An appreciation of its magnitude is best grasped by working outward from the earth, through the solar system and our own Milky Way galaxy, to the remotest extra-galactic nebulae.

Meteoroids

Meteor Shower

Meteoroids are mostly of cometary origin. A meteor is the light phenomenon caused by the entry of a meteoroid into the earth's atmosphere. The greatest meteor "shower" on record occurred on the night of November 16–17, 1966, when the Leonid meteors (which recur every 33¼ years) were visible over North America. It was calculated that meteors passed over Arizona at a rate of 2,300 per minute for a period of 20 minutes from 5 a.m. on November 17, 1966.

Meteorites

Largest. When a meteoroid penetrates to the earth's surface, the remnant is described as a meteorite. This occurs about 150 times per year over the whole land surface of the earth. The largest known meteorite is one found in 1920 at Hoba West, near Grootfontein in South-West Africa. This is a block about 9 feet long by 8 feet broad, weighing 132,000 lbs.

The largest meteorite exhibited by any museum is the "Tent" meteorite, weighing 68,085 lbs., found in 1897 near Cape York, on the west coast of Greenland, by the expedition of Commander (later

Rear-Admiral) Robert Edwin Peary (1856–1920). It was known to the Eskimos as the Abnighito and is now exhibited in the Hayden Planetarium in New York City.

The largest piece of stony meteorite recovered is a piece of 3,902 lbs. which was part of a shower which struck northeast China on March 8, 1976. The oldest dated meteorites are from the Allende fall over Chihuahua, Mexico, on February 8, 1969. A piece of this has been dated to 4,610 million years—thus is several 100 million years older than the oldest dated rock on earth.

There was a mysterious explosion of about 35 megatons in Lat. 60° 55′ N., Long. 101° 57′ E., in the basin of the Podkamennaya Tunguska River, 40 miles north of Vanavar, in Siberia, U.S.S.R. at 00 hrs. 17 min. 11 sec. U.T. on June 30, 1908. The energy of this explosion was about 10^{24} ergs and the cause has been variously attributed to a meteorite (1927), a comet (1930), a nuclear explosion (1961) and to anti-matter (1965). The devastation covered an area of about 1,500 square miles, and the shock was felt more than 600 miles away.

Although the chances of being struck by a meteorite are deemed negligible, the most anxious time of day for meteorophobes is 3 p.m.

Largest Craters. Aerial surveys in Canada in 1956 and 1957 brought to light a gash, or astrobleme, $8\frac{1}{2}$ miles across near Deep Bay, Saskatchewan, possibly attributable to a very old and very oblique meteorite. There is a possible crater-like formation 275 miles in diameter on the eastern shore of Hudson Bay, where the Nastapoka Islands are just off the coast.

Evidence was published in 1963 discounting a meteoric origin for the crypto-volcanic Vredefort Ring (diameter 26 miles) to the southwest of Johannesburg, South Africa, but this claim has now been reasserted.

The largest proven crater is called Barringer Crater or Meteor Crater, formerly called Coon Butte, discovered in 1891 near Winslow, northern Arizona. It is 4,150 feet in diameter and now about 575 feet

LARGEST PROVEN CRATER: Meteor crater in northern Arizona was gouged out in about 25,000 B.C. It is 575 feet deep, almost a mile wide.

deep, with a parapet rising 130 to 155 feet above the surrounding plain. It has been estimated that an iron-nickel mass with a diameter of 200 to 260 feet, and weighing about 2,240,000 tons, gouged this crater in *c.* 25,000 B.C., with an impact force equivalent to an explosion of 30,000,000 tons of trinitrotoluene $(C_7H_5O_6N_3)$, called T.N.T.

The New Quebec (formerly the Chubb) "Crater," first sighted on June 20, 1943, in northern Ungava, Canada, is 1,325 feet deep and measures 6.8 miles around its rim.

Tektites. The largest tektite of which details have been published was one of 7.04 lbs. found *c.* 1932 at Muong Nong, Saravane Province, Laos, and is now in the Paris Museum.

Aurorae

Most Frequent. Polar lights, known as Aurora Borealis or Northern Lights in the northern hemisphere and Aurora Australis in the southern hemisphere, are caused by electrical solar discharges in the upper atmosphere and occur most frequently in high latitudes. Aurorae are visible at some time on *every* clear dark night in the polar areas within 20 degrees latitude of the magnetic poles.

Lowest Latitudes. Reliable figures exist only from 1952. Extreme cases of displays in very low latitudes were those reported at Cuzco, Peru (August 2, 1744); Honolulu, Hawaii (September 1, 1854); and, questionably, Singapore (September 25, 1909).

Altitude. The extreme height of aurorae has been measured at 620 miles, while the lowest may descend to 45 miles.

The Moon

The earth's closest neighbor in space and only natural satellite is the moon, at a mean distance of 238,855 statute miles center to center or 233,812 miles surface to surface. Its closest approach (perigee) and most extreme distance away (apogee) measured surface to surface are 216,420 and 247,667 miles respectively. It has a diameter of 2,159.6 miles and has a mass of 7.23×10^{19} long tons with a mean density of 3.34. The average orbital speed is 2,287 m.p.h.

The first direct hit on the moon was achieved at 2 minutes 24 seconds after midnight (Moscow time) on September 14, 1959, by the Soviet space probe *Lunik II* near the *Mare Serenitatis*. The first photographic images of the hidden side were collected by the U.S.S.R.'s *Lunik III* from 6:30 a.m. on October 7, 1959, from a range of up to 43,750 miles, and transmitted to the earth from a distance of 292,000 miles. The first "soft" landing was made by the U.S.S.R.'s *Lunik IX*, launched at about 11 a.m. G.M.T. on January 31, 1966. It landed in the area of the Ocean of Storms (*Oceanus Procellarum*) at 18 hours 45 minutes 30 seconds G.M.T. on February 3, 1966.

"Blue Moon." Owing to sulphur particles in the upper atmosphere from a forest fire covering 250,000 acres between Mile 103 and Mile 119 on the Alaska Highway in northern British Columbia, Canada, the moon took on a bluish color, as seen from Great Britain, on the night of September 26, 1950. The moon also appeared blue after the Krakatoa eruption of August 27, 1883 (see Volcanoes) and on other occasions.

Crater

Largest. Only 59 per cent of the moon's surface is directly visible from the earth because it is in "captured rotation" *i.e.* the period of rotation is equal to the period of orbit. The largest wholly visible crater is the walled plain Bailly, toward the moon's South Pole, which is 183 miles across, with walls rising to 14,000 feet. Partly on the averted side the Orientale Basin measures more than 600 miles in diameter.

Deepest. The deepest crater is the nearby Newton crater, with a floor estimated to be between 23,000 and 29,000 feet below its rim and 14,000 feet below the level of the plain outside. The brightest directly visible spot on the moon is *Aristarchus*.

(Left) THE EARTH AS SEEN FROM THE MOON by Apollo XI astronauts, the first to land on the moon. (Right) FIRST FOOTPRINT on the moon.

Highest Mountains

As there is no water on the moon, the heights of mountains can be measured only in relation to a reference sphere with a radius of 1,079.943 miles. Thus the greatest elevation attained by any of the 12 U.S. astronauts has been 25,688 feet, on the Descartes Highlands, by Capt. John Walter Young, U.S.N., and Major Charles M. Duke, Jr., on April 27, 1972.

Temperature Extremes

When the sun is overhead, the temperature on the lunar equator reaches 243°F. (31°F. above the boiling point of water). By sunset the temperature is 58°F., but after nightfall it sinks to −261°F.

Moon Samples

The age attributed to the oldest of the moon material brought back to earth by the *Apollo* crews has been soil-dated to 4,720 million years. The extreme figures from *Apollo XVII* samples have been modified to 4,600 and 4,500 million years, due to suspected loss of rubidium.

The Sun

Distance Extremes

The earth's 66,620 m.p.h. orbit of 584,017,800 miles around the sun is elliptical, hence our distance from the sun varies. The orbital speed varies between 65,520 m.p.h. (minimum) and 67,750 m.p.h. The average distance of the sun is 1.000000230 astronomical units or 92,955,829 miles. The closest approach (perihelion) is 91,402,000 miles, and the farthest departure (aphelion) is 94,510,000 miles. The solar system is revolving around the center of the Milky Way once in each 225 million years at a speed of 481,000 m.p.h. and has a velocity of 42,500 m.p.h. relative to stars in our immediate region such as Vega, toward which it is moving.

Temperature and Dimensions

The sun has an internal temperature of about 20,000,000°K., a core pressure of 560,000,000 tons per square inch and uses up nearly 4,500,000 tons of hydrogen per second, thus providing a luminosity of 3×10^{27} candlepower, or 1,500,000 candlepower per square inch. The sun has the stellar classification of a "yellow dwarf" and, although its density is only 1.409 times that of water, its mass is 332,946 times as much as that of the earth. It has a mean diameter of 864,940 miles. The sun with a mass of $2,096 \times 10^{27}$ tons represents more than 99 per cent of the total mass of the solar system. (K. stands for the Kelvin absolute scale of temperatures.)

Sunspots

Largest. To be visible to the *protected* naked eye, a sunspot must cover about one two-thousandth part of the sun's hemisphere and thus have an area of about 500,000,000 square miles. The largest recorded sunspot occurred in the sun's southern hemisphere on April 8, 1947. Its area was about 7,000 million square miles, with an extreme longitude of 187,000 miles and an extreme latitude of 90,000

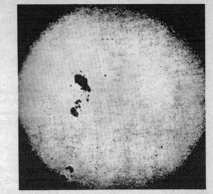

LARGEST SUNSPOTS:
The area of the spot was about 7,000 million square miles.

miles. Sunspots appear darker because they are more than 1,500°C. cooler than the rest of the sun's surface temperature of 5,660°C. The largest observed solar prominence was one measuring 70,000 miles across its base and protruding 300,000 miles, observed on June 4, 1946.

Most Frequent. In October, 1957, a smoothed sunspot count showed 263, the highest recorded index since records started in 1755 (*cf.* previous record of 239 in May, 1778). In 1943 a sunspot lasted for 200 days from June to December.

Eclipses

Earliest Recorded. The earliest extrapolated eclipses that have been identified are 1361 B.C. (lunar) and October, 2137 B.C. (solar). For the Middle East only, lunar eclipses have been extrapolated to 3450 B.C. and solar ones to 4200 B.C.

TOTAL ECLIPSE OF THE SUN: For more than 4,000 years, this has been the most spectacular natural phenomenon.

Longest Duration. The maximum possible duration of an eclipse of the sun is 7 minutes 31 seconds. The longest actually *measured* was on June 20, 1955 (7 minutes 8 seconds), seen from the Philippines. That of July 16, 2186, in the South Atlantic should last 7 minutes 28 seconds. An annular eclipse may last for 12 minutes 24 seconds. The longest totality of any lunar eclipse is 104 minutes. This has occurred many times.

Most and Least Frequent. The highest number of eclipses possible in a year is seven, as in 1935, when there were five solar and two lunar eclipses; or four solar and three lunar eclipses, as will occur in 1982. The lowest possible number in a year is two, both of which must be solar, as in 1944 and 1969.

Comets

Earliest Recorded. The earliest records of comets date from the 7th century B.C. The speeds of the estimated 2,000,000 comets vary from 700 m.p.h. in outer space to 1,250,000 m.p.h. when near the sun.

The successive appearances of Halley's Comet have been traced back to 466 B.C. It was first depicted in the Nuremberg Chronicle of 684 A.D. The first prediction of its return by Edmund Halley (1656–1742) proved true on Christmas Day, 1758, 16 years after his death. Its next appearance should be at 9:30 p.m. Greenwich Mean Time on February 9, 1986, exactly 75.81 years after the last, which was on April 19, 1910.

Closest Approach. On July 1, 1770, Lexell's Comet, traveling at a speed of 23.9 miles per second (relative to the sun), came within 1,500,000 miles of the earth. However, the earth is believed to have passed through the tail of Halley's Comet, most recently on May 19, 1910.

Largest

Comets are so tenuous that it has been estimated that even the head of one rarely contains solid matter greater than 1 kilometer in diameter. In the tail, 10,000 cubic miles contain less than a cubic inch of solid matter. These tails, as in the case of the Great Comet of 1843, may trail for 200,000,000 miles. The head of Holmes Comet of 1892 once measured 1,500,000 miles in diameter.

Comet Bennett which appeared in January, 1970, was found to be enveloped in a hydrogen cloud measuring some 8,000,000 miles.

Period

Shortest. Of all the recorded periodic comets (these are members of the solar system), the one which most frequently returns is Encke's Comet, first identified in 1786. Its period of 1,206 days (3.3 years) is the shortest established. Not one of its 48 returns (up to May, 1967) has been missed by astronomers. Now increasingly faint, it is expected to "die" by February, 1994. The most frequently observed comets are Schwassmann-Wachmann I, Kopff and Oterma, which can be observed every year between Mars and Jupiter.

Longest. The path of the comet 1910a has not been accurately determined, but it is not expected to return for perhaps 4,000,000 years.

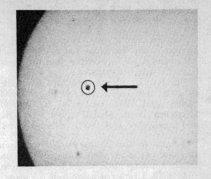

Planets

Planets (including the earth) are bodies within the solar system which revolve around the sun in definite orbits.

Largest. Jupiter, with an equatorial diameter of 88,780 miles and a polar diameter of 82,980 miles, is the largest of the nine major planets, with a mass 317.83 times and a volume 1,318 times that of the earth. It also has the shortest period of rotation, with a "day" of only 9 hours 50 minutes 30.003 seconds in its equatorial zone.

Smallest. Of the nine major planets, Mercury is the smallest with a diameter of 3,031 ±1 mile and a mass of 0.055274 earth masses or 325,100,000,000,000,000 long tons. Mercury, which orbits the sun at an average distance of 35,983,100 miles, has a period of revolution of 87.9686 days, so giving the highest average speed in orbit of 107,030 m.p.h.

Most Equable. The planet with a surface temperature closest to earth's average figure of 59°F. is Mars with a value of 55°F. for the sub-solar point at a mean solar distance of 141,636,000 miles.

Hottest. A surface temperature of *c*. 890°F. has been estimated from measurements made from Venus by the U.S.S.R. probes *Venera 7* and *Venera 8*.

Coldest. The coldest planet is, not unnaturally, the one which is remotest from the sun, namely Pluto, which has an estimated surface temperature of —360°F. (100°F. above absolute zero). Its mean distance from the sun is 3,674,488,000 miles and its period of revolution is 248.54 years. Its diameter is about 3,400 miles and it has a mass about one twentieth that of the earth. Pluto was first recorded by Clyde William Tombaugh (born February 4, 1906) at Lowell Observatory, Flagstaff, Arizona, on February 18, 1930, from photographs taken on January 23 and 29. Because of its orbital eccentricity, Pluto will move closer to the sun than Neptune between January 21, 1979, and March 14, 1999.

Nearest. The fellow planet closest to the earth is Venus, which is, at times, about 25,700,000 miles inside the earth's orbit, compared with Mars' closest approach of 34,600,000 miles outside the earth's orbit. Mars, known since 1965 to be cratered, has temperature ranging from 85°F. to —190°F. but in which infusorians of the genus *Colpoda* could survive.

Surface Features. Mariner 9 photographs have revealed a canyon in the Tithonias Lacus region of Mars which is 62 miles wider and 4,000 feet deeper than the 13-mile-wide 5,500-foot-deep Grand Canyon in Arizona.

The largest volcanic structure on Mars is Alba Patera, with a diameter of 995 miles and a height of 13,000–26,000 feet. By far the highest and most spectacular is Olympus Mons (formerly Nix Olympica) in the Tharsis region, with a diameter of 310–370 miles and a height of 75,450–95,150 feet above the surrounding plain.

Brightest and Faintest. Viewed from the earth, by far the brightest of the five planets visible to the naked eye is Venus, with a maximum magnitude of —4.4. The faintest is Pluto, with a magnitude of 15. Uranus at magnitude 5.7 is only marginally visible.

In April, 1972, the existence of a tenth or trans-Plutonian planet more than 6,000 million miles from the sun with three times the mass of Saturn was suggested, but refuted in the same year.

Densest and Least Dense. Earth is the densest planet with an average figure of 5.517 times that of water, while Saturn has an average density only about one-eighth of this value or 0.705 times that of water.

Longest "Day." The planet with the longest period of rotation is Venus, which spins on its axis once every 243.16 days, so its "day" is longer than its "year" (224.7007 days). The shortest "day" is that of Jupiter (see Largest Planet).

Conjunctions. The most dramatic recorded conjunction (coming together) of the other seven principal members of the solar system (sun, moon, Mercury, Venus, Mars, Jupiter and Saturn) occurred on February 5, 1962, when 16° covered all seven during an eclipse. It is possible that the seven-fold conjunction of September, 1186, spanned only 12°. The next notable conjunction will take place on May 5, 2000.

Satellites

Most. Of the nine major planets, all but Venus, Mercury and Pluto, have known natural satellites. The planet with the most is Jupiter, with four large and ten small moons. Jupiter's 14th moon (J-XIV) was first identified by Charles Kowal (U.S.) in October, 1975. The earth is the only planet with a single satellite. The distance of the solar system's 34 known satellites from their parent planets varies from the 5,827 miles of *Phobos* from the center of Mars to the 14,730,000 miles of Jupiter's outer satellite Sinope (Jupiter IX).

Largest and Smallest. The most massive satellite is *Ganymede* (Jupiter III) with a diameter of 3,275 miles and a mass 2.088 times that of our moon. The current estimate for the diameter of Saturn's largest moon Titan is 3,100±155 miles. The smallest is Mars' outer "moon" *Deimos* discovered on August 18, 1877, by Asaph Hall (U.S.) which has an average diameter of 7.8 miles.

Largest Asteroids. In the belt which lies between Mars and Jupiter, there are some 45,000 (only 3,100 charted) minor planets or asteroids which are, for the most part, too small to yield to diameter measurement. The largest and first discovered (by Piazzi at Palermo, Sicily, on January 1, 1801) of these is *Ceres,* with a diameter of 593 miles. The only one visible to the naked eye is *Vesta* (diameter 313 miles), discovered on March 29, 1807, by Dr. Heinrich Wilhelm Olbers, a German amateur astronomer. The closest measured approach to the earth by an asteroid was 485,000 miles, in the case of *Hermes* on October 30, 1937.

It was announced in December, 1971, that the orbit of *Toro* (discovered 1964), though centered on the sun, is also in resonance with the earth-moon system. Its nearest approach to earth is 9,600,000 miles. *Amor, Eros,* and *Ivar* are also in resonance.

Stars

Largest and Most Massive. Of those measured, the star with the greatest diameter is believed to be the cold giant star IRS5 in the Perseus spiral arm of the Milky Way, with a diameter larger than that of the entire solar system of 9,200 million miles. This was announced in January, 1973.

The *Alpha Herculis* aggregation, consisting of a main star and a double-star companion, is enveloped in a cold gas. This system, visible to the naked eye, has a diameter of 170,000 million miles. The fainter component of Plaskett's Star, discovered by J. S. Plaskett from the Dominion Astrophysical Observatory, Victoria, British Columbia, Canada, *c.* 1920, is the most massive star known with a mass *c.* 55 times that of the sun.

Smallest. The smallest known star is LP 327-186, a "white dwarf" with a diameter only half that of the moon, 100 light-years distant and detected in May, 1962, from Minneapolis. The claim that LP 768-500 is even smaller at <1,000 miles is not widely accepted. Some pulsars or neutron stars may however have diameters of only 10–20 miles.

Oldest. The sun is estimated to be about 7,500 million years old but our galaxy is estimated to be between 10,000 million and 12,000 million years old.

Farthest. The solar system, with its sun, nine principal planets, 34 satellites, asteroids and comets, was discovered in 1921 to be about 27,000 light-years from the center of the lens-shaped Milky Way galaxy (diameter 100,000 light-years) of about 100,000 million stars. The most distant star in our galaxy is therefore about 75,000 light-years distant.

Nearest. Excepting the special case of our own sun, the nearest star is the very faint *Proxima Centauri,* which is 4.28 light-years (25,200,000,000,000 miles) away. The nearest star visible to the naked eye is the southern hemisphere star *Alpha Centauri,* or *Rigel Kentaurus* (4.38 light-years), with a magnitude of —0.29. By 11,800 A.D., the nearest star will be Barnard's Star (see *Stellar Planets,* page 161) at a distance of 3.75 light-years.

Brightest. Sirius A (*Alpha Canis Majoris*), also known as the Dog Star, is apparently the brightest star of the 5,776 stars visible in the heavens, with an apparent magnitude of —1.46. It is in the constellation *Canis Major* and is visible in the winter months of the northern hemisphere, being due south at midnight on the last day of the year. Sirius A is 8.65 light-years away and has a luminosity 23 times as much as that of the sun. It has a diameter of 1,500,000 miles and a mass of 51,300,000,000,000,000,000,000,000,000 tons.

Most and Least Luminous. If all stars could be viewed at the same distance, the most luminous would be the apparently faint variable *S. Doradûs*, in the Greater Magellanic Cloud (*Nebecula Major*), which can be 300,000 to 500,000 times brighter than the sun, and has an absolute magnitude of —8.9. The faintest star detected visually is a very red star, known as LP 425–140, which is 23.5 light-years distant, with about one-millionth of the sun's brightness.

Coolest. A 16th magnitude star with a surface temperature of only about 425°C. (800°F.) was detected in *Cygnus* in 1965.

Densest. The limit of stellar density is at the neutron state, when sub-atomic particles exist in a state in which there is no space between them. Theoretical calculations call for a density of 4.7×10^{15} grams per cubic centimeter (74,400 million long tons per cubic inch) in the innermost core of a pulsar. It has been postulated that a Black Hole (see below) may progress toward a "naked singularity."

Longest Name. The longest name for any star is *Shurnarkabtîshashutu*, which is Arabic for "under the southern horn of the bull."

Constellations

The largest of the 89 constellations is *Hydra* (the Sea Serpent) which covers 1,302.844 square degrees or 6.3 per cent of the hemisphere and contains at least 68 stars visible to the naked eye (to 5.5 mag.). The constellation *Centaurus* (Centaur), ranking ninth in area embraces, however, at least 94 such stars. The smallest constellation is *Crux Australis* (Southern Cross) with an area of 68.477 square degrees compared with the 41,252.96 square degrees of the whole sky.

Brightest Super-Nova

Super-novae, or temporary "stars" which flare and then fade, occur perhaps five times in 1,000 years in our galaxy. The brightest "star" ever seen by historic man is believed to be the super-nova close to *Zeta Tauri*, visible by day for 23 days from July 4, 1054. The remains, known as the Crab Nebula, now have a diameter of about 3×10^{13} miles and are still expanding at a rate of 800 miles per second. It is about 4,100 light-years away, indicating that the explosion actually occurred in about 3000 B.C.

Stellar Planets. Planetary companions, with a mass of less than 7 per cent of their parent star, have been reported for 61 *Cygni* (1942), *Lalande 21185* (1960) *Krüger 60, Ci 2354, BD + 20° 2465* and one of the two components of 70 Ophiuchi.

A planet with 6 times the mass of Jupiter, 750 million miles from *Epsilon Eridani* (see below), was reported by Peter van de Kemp in January, 1973.

In August, 1975, van de Kemp reported that Barnard's Star (Munich 15040) possibly had two planets equivalent in mass to Jupiter and Saturn.

Listening operations ("Project Ozma") on *Tau Ceti* and *Epsilon Eridani* were maintained from April 4, 1960 to March, 1961, using an 85-foot radio telescope at Deer Creek Valley, Green Bank, West Virginia. The apparatus was probably insufficiently sensitive for any signal from a distance of 10.7 light-years to be received. Monitoring has been conducted from Gorkiy, U.S.S.R., since 1969.

Black Holes

The first tentative identification of a Black Hole was announced in December, 1972, in the binary-star X-ray source Cygnus X-1. This is a small, dark companion of some 10 solar masses, from which the escape velocity tends to *c* (the velocity of light). The critical size has been estimated to be as low as a diameter of 3.67 miles. After a star suffers gravitational collapse, neither matter nor radiation can escape from the resultant Black Hole.

The Universe

According to Einstein's Special Theory time dilatation effect (published in 1905), time slows down on a moving system at rest according to the Lorentz transformation:

$$T = T_o \sqrt{1 - \frac{v^2}{c^2}}$$

where T_o = time interval when systems are at rest relatively; c = speed of light constant; T = time measured in one system observing the other moving system; v = relative velocity.

BRIGHTEST SUPER-NOVA (left): The explosion of the Crab Nebula, which occurred in about 3000 B.C., became visible on earth by day in the year 1054 and its remains are still expanding at the rate of 800 miles per second. REMOTEST VISIBLE BODY TO NAKED EYE (right): The Great Galaxy in Andromeda is 2,200,000 light-years away.

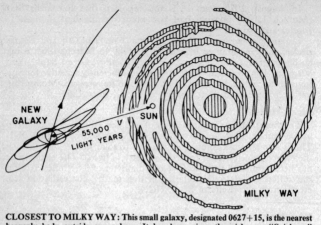

CLOSEST TO MILKY WAY: This small galaxy, designated 0627+15, is the nearest heavenly body outside our galaxy. It has been given the nickname "Snickers," because it is "like the Milky Way, only peanuts."

However, time speeds up for an object as it moves away from a body exerting gravitational force. During their mission the crew of Apollo VIII circumlunar space flight aged a net 300 microseconds more than earthlings. No formal overtime claim was lodged.

Outside the Milky Way galaxy, which possibly moves around the center of the local super-cluster of 2,500 neighboring galaxies at a speed of 1,350,000 m.p.h., there exist 10,000 million other galaxies. These range in size up to the largest known object in the universe, the radio galaxy 3C-236 in Leo Minor, announced from Westerbork Synthesis Radio Telescope, Netherlands, in August, 1974, which is 18,600,000 light-years across. The nearest heavenly body outside our galaxy is its satellite body, the ninth to be discovered, a small galaxy designated 0627 + 15, with a mass of 100,000,000 suns, which lies 55,000 ± 13,000 light-years distant. It was announced by S. Christian Simonson III of the University of Maryland, in July, 1975.

Farthest Visible Object. The remotest heavenly body clearly visible to the naked eye is the Great Galaxy in *Andromeda* (Mag. 3.47). This is a rotating nebula of spiral form, and its distance from the earth is about 2,200,000 light-years, or about 13,000,000,000,000,000,000 miles.

It is just possible, however, that, under ideal seeing conditions, Messier 33, the spiral in Triangulum (Mag. 5.79) can be glimpsed by the naked eye of keen-sighted people at a distance of 2,300,000 light-years.

Heaviest Galaxy

In April, 1971, the heaviest galaxy was found to be 41C 31:04 (a "binary" system) with a mass 45 times that of the Milky Way, thus indicating a figure of 12,000 duodecillions (1.2×10^{40}) long tons.

"Quasars"

In November, 1962, the existence of quasi-stellar radio sources ("quasars" or QSO's) was established. No satisfactory model has yet been constructed to account for the immensely high luminosity of bodies apparently so distant and of such small diameter. The diameter of 3C 446 is only about 90 light-days, but there are measurable alterations in brightness in less than one day. It is believed to be undergoing the most violent explosion yet detected, since it increased 3.2 magnitudes or 20-fold in less than one year.

"Pulsars"

The earliest observation of a pulsating radio source or "pulsar" CP 1919 by Dr. Jocelyn Bell Burnell was announced from the Mullard Radio Astronomy Observatory, Cambridgeshire, England, on February 29, 1968. The 100th was announced from Jodrell Bank, England, in June, 1973. The fastest so far discovered is NP 0532 in the Crab Nebula with a pulse of 33 milliseconds. It is now accepted that pulsars are rotating neutron stars of immense density.

Remotest Object

The greatest distance yet ascribed to a radio-detected and visibly confirmed body is to the faint blue quasar QSO OQ172 in Boötes announced in *Nature* on June 7, 1973. This object was found by Dr. Eleanor Margaret Burbidge, Director of the Royal Greenwich Observatory, Herstmonceux Castle, Sussex, England, working with the 120-inch telescope at the Lick Observatory, Santa Cruz, Calif., with Drs. E. J. Wampler, L. B. Robinson and J. B. Baldwin. The object has a stellar magnitude of 17.5 and exhibited a red-shift of $Z = 3.53$, which is consistent with a body receding at 95.5 per cent of the speed of light (177,000 miles/sec.) and a distance, on at least one model, of 15,600 million light-years or 91,700,000,000,000,000,-000,000 miles.

The interpretation of very large red-shifts exhibited by quasars is controversial. The remotest galaxy is the 22nd-magnitude 3C-123, measured in July, 1975, to have a red-shift $Z = 0.637$, indicating a distance of 8,000,000,000 light-years.

Age of the Universe

A reassessment of the three dating methods known, published by David N. Schramm in *Scientific American* in 1973, indicates an age for the universe between 10,000 and 15,000 million years with an extreme value of 20,000 million years in one method.

Rocketry and Missiles

Earliest Experiments

The origins of the rocket date from the war rockets propelled by a charcoal-saltpeter-sulphur powder, made by the Chinese as early as *c.* 1100. These early rockets became known in Europe by 1258.

The first launching of a liquid-fueled rocket (patented July 14, 1914) was by Dr. Robert Hutchings Goddard (1882–1945) (U.S.)

at Auburn, Massachusetts, on March 16, 1926, when his rocket reached an altitude of 41 feet and traveled a distance of 184 feet. The U.S.S.R.'s earliest rocket was the semi-liquid fueled GIRD-IX tested on August 17, 1933.

Most Powerful

It has been suggested that the U.S.S.R. lunar booster which blew up at Tyuratam in the summer (July ?) of 1969 had a thrust of 10,000,000 to 14,000,000 lbs. A third failure to launch the U.S.S.R. "G" class lunar booster, larger than *Saturn V*, was reported in November, 1972. A launch on May 11, 1973, may have been successful.

The most powerful rocket that has been publicized is the *Saturn V*, used for the Project Apollo and Skylab programs, on which development began in January, 1962, at the John F. Kennedy Space Center, Merritt Island, Florida. The rocket is 363 feet 8 inches tall, with a payload of 199,500 lbs. in the case of *Skylab* 1, and gulps 16.7 tons of propellant per second for $2\frac{1}{2}$ minutes. The whole assembly generates 175,600,000 h.p. and weighs up to 7,600,000 lbs. when fully loaded, as in the case of *Apollo XVII*. *Saturn V* was first launched on November 9, 1967, from Cape Kennedy, Florida.

Highest Velocity

The first space vehicle to achieve the third cosmic velocity sufficient to break out of the solar system was *Pioneer 10*. The Atlas SLV-3C launcher with a modified Centaur D second stage and a Thiokol Te-364-4 third stage left the earth at an unprecedented 32,114 m.p.h. on March 2, 1972. The highest velocity of any space vehicle has been 107,630 m.p.h. by *Pioneer 11* (now named Pioneer-Saturn) at 1:42 a.m. G.M.T. on December 2, 1974, in its fly-by 26,000 miles distant from Jupiter.

Artificial Satellites

The dynamics of artificial satellites were first propounded by Sir Isaac Newton (1642–1727) in his *Philosophiae Naturalis Principia Mathematica* ("Mathematical Principles of Natural Philosophy"), begun in March, 1686, and first published in the summer of 1687. The first artificial satellite was successfully put into orbit at an altitude of 142/588 miles and a velocity of more than 17,750 m.p.h. from Tyuratam, a site located 170 miles east of the Aral Sea on the night of October 4, 1957. This spherical satellite, *Sputnik* ("Fellow Traveler") *1*, officially designated "Satellite 1957 Alpha 2," weighed 184.3 lbs., with a diameter of 22.8 inches, and its lifetime is believed to have been 96 days, ending on January 4, 1958. It was designed under the direction of Dr. Sergey Pavlovich Korolyov (1906–66).

The heaviest object orbited is the 118-foot-long U.S. *Skylab*, weighing 99.87 tons with a capacity of 12,398 cubic feet, launched on May 14, 1973. The 442-lb. U.S. R.A.E. (radio astronomy explorer)

PROGRESSIVE ROCKET ALTITUDE RECORDS:

Height in miles	Rocket	Place	Launch Date
0.71 (3,762 ft.)	A 3-inch rocket	near London, England	April, 1750
1.24 (6,460 ft.)	Rheinhold Tiling[1] (Germany) solid fuel rocket	Osnabruck, Germany	April, 1931
3.1	OR-2 liquid-fuel rocket (U.S.S.R.)	U.S.S.R.	Nov. 25, 1933
8.1	U.S.S.R. "Stratosphere" rocket	U.S.S.R.	1935
52.46	A.4 rocket (Germany)	Peenemünde, Germany	Oct. 3, 1942
c. 85	A.4 rocket (Germany)	Heidelager, Poland ...	early 1944
118	A.4 rocket (Germany)	Heidelager, Poland ...	mid-1944
244	V-2/W.A.C. Corporal (2-stage Bumper), No. 5 (U.S.)	White Sands, N.M. ...	Feb. 24, 1949
250	M.104 *Raketa* (U.S.S.R.)......	? Tyuratam, U.S.S.R.	1954
682	Jupiter C (U.S.)	Cape Canaveral, Fla....	Sept. 20, 1956
>2,700	Farside (4 stage) (U.S.)	Eniwetok Atoll	Oct. 20, 1957
70,700	Pioneer I-B Lunar Probe (U.S.)	Cape Canaveral, Fla....	Oct. 11, 1958
215,300,000*	Luna I or Mechta (U.S.S.R.)	Tyuratam, U.S.S.R................	Jan. 2, 1959
242,000,000*	Mars I (U.S.S.R.)	U.S.S.R.	Nov. 1, 1962
887,500,000[2]	Pioneer 10 (U.S.)...............	Cape Kennedy, Fla.....	Mar. 2, 1972

* Apogee in solar orbit.

[1] There is some evidence that Tiling may shortly after have reached 31,000 ft. (5.90 miles) with a solid-fuel rocket at Wangerooge, East Friesian Islands, West Germany.

[2] Distance by April, 1976. A distance of 3,600,000,000 miles will be reached by 1987 on its way to crossing the orbit of Pluto and leaving the solar system's gravitational field.

Rocketry and Space Records

	Earth Orbits	Moon Orbits	Solar Orbits
Earliest Satellite	Sputnik I, October 4, 1957	Luna X, March 31, 1966	Luna I, January 2, 1959
Earliest Planetary Contact	Sputnik I rocket—burnt out December 1, 1957	Luna II hit moon, September 13, 1959	Venus III hit Venus, March 1, 1966
Earliest Planetary Touchdown	Discoverer XIII capsule, landed August 11, 1960	Luna IX soft landed on moon February 3, 1966	Venus VII soft landed on Venus, December 15, 1970
Earliest Rendezvous, Docking	Gemini 8 and Agena 8, March 16, 1966	Apollo X and LM 4 docked May 23, 1969	None
Earliest Crew Exchange	Soyuz IV and V, January 16, 1969	Apollo X and LM 4, May 22, 1969	None
Heaviest Satellite	34.09 tons, Apollo IV, November 9, 1967	33.98 tons, Apollo XV, July 29, 1971	15.23 tons, Apollo X rocket, May 18, 1969
Lightest Satellite	1.47 lbs. each, Tetrahedron Research Satellites (TRS) 2 and 3, May 9, 1963	150 lbs., Interplanetary Monitoring Probe IMP 6, July 19, 1967	13 lbs., Pioneer IV, March 3, 1959
Longest First Orbit	42 days, Apollo XII rocket, November 14, 1969	720 minutes, Lunar Orbiter 4, May 4, 1967	636 days, Mariner 6 (Mars Probe), February 25, 1969
Shortest First Orbit	86 min. 30.6 sec., Cosmos 169 rocket, July 17, 1967	114 min., LM 9 ascent stage (Apollo XV), August 2, 1971	195 days, Mariner 5 (Venus Probe), June 14, 1967
Longest Expected Lifetime	>1 million years, Vela 12, April 8, 1970	Unlimited, IMP 6 (see above), July 19, 1967	All unlimited
Nearest First Perigee, Pericynthion or Perihelion	63 miles, Cosmos 169 rocket, July 17, 1967	10 miles, LM 6 ascent stage (Apollo XII), November 20, 1969	50,700 miles Apollo IX rocket, March 3, 1969
Furthest First Apogee, Apocynthion or Aphelion	535,522 miles, Apollo XII rocket, November 14, 1969	4,900 miles, IMP 6 (see above), July 19, 1967	162,900,000 miles Mariner 6 (Mars Probe), February 25, 1969

The highest and lowest speeds in solar orbit are by Apollo IX rocket and Mariner 6 (see above).

NOTE:—The artificial satellite with the largest dimension is the spider-like U.S. RAE (Radio-astronomy explorer), launched into lunar orbit in June, 1973, which has antennae measuring 1,500 feet from tip to tip. Echo I and II were the brightest artificial satellites (their magnitude were about −1), and it has been claimed that Echo I became the man-made object seen by more people than any other. Its lifetime was 93 months from August 12, 1960 until it burned up in May, 1968.

B, or Explorer 49, launched on June 10, 1973, has, however, antennae 1,500 feet from tip to tip.

Earliest Successful Manned Satellites

The first successful manned space flight began at 9:07 a.m. (Moscow time), or 6:07 a.m. G.M.T., on April 12, 1961. Flight Major (later Colonel) Yuriy Alekseyevich Gagarin (born March 9, 1934) completed a single orbit of the earth in 89.34 minutes in the U.S.S.R.'s space vehicle *Vostok* ("East") *I* (10,417 lbs.).

Col. Vladimir Mikhailovich Komarov (born March 16, 1927) was launched in *Soyuz* ("Sunrise") *I* at 00:35 a.m. on April 23, 1967. The spacecraft was in orbit for about 25½ hours before crashing on the final descent after parachute failure. Komarov was thus the first man indisputedly known to have died during space flight.

Oldest and Youngest Astronauts

The oldest of the 77 people in space has been Donald Kent "Deke" Slayton (born Sparta, Washington, on March 1, 1924) who was aged 51 years 145 days when he landed from the *Apollo-Soyuz* mission on July 24, 1975. The youngest was Major (later Col.) Gherman Stepanovich Titov (born September 11, 1935) who was 25 years 329 days old when he was launched in *Vostok 2* on August 6, 1961.

First Woman in Space

The first woman to orbit the earth was Jr. Lt. (now Lt.-Col.) Valentina Vladimirovna Tereshkova (born March 6, 1937), who was launched in *Vostok VI* from Tyuratam, U.S.S.R., at 9:30 a.m. G.M.T. on June 16, 1963, and landed at 8:16 a.m. on June 19, after a flight of 2 days 22 hours 46 minutes, during which she completed over 48 orbits (1,225,000 miles) and came to within 3 miles of *Vostok V*. Her mission was variously reported to be punctuated with pleas to be brought back due to giddiness, or to be extended because of her excellent performance. She had formerly been a textile worker.

First "Walk" in Space

The first person to leave an artificial satellite during orbit was Lt.-Col. Aleksey Arkhipovich Leonov (born May 30, 1934), who left the Soviet satellite *Voshkod* ("Sunrise") *II* at about 8:30 a.m. G.M.T. on March 18, 1965. Lt.-Col. Leonov was "in space" for about 20 minutes, and for 12 minutes 9 seconds he "floated" at the end of a line 16 feet long.

Longest Manned Space Flight

The longest time spent in the weightlessness of space has been 84 days 1 hour 15 minutes 30.8 seconds by the third crew to man the U.S. *Skylab* space station (*Skylab 4*): Lt. Col. Gerald Paul Carr, U.S.M.C., Lt. Col. William Reid Pogue, U.S.A.F., and Dr. Edward George Gibson from November 16, 1973, to February 8, 1974. During this time they became the most traveled humans of all time with a total of 34,469,696 miles. *Skylab* had been launched on May 14, 1973. During the 1,214 orbits with an apogee of 283 miles, the crew temporarily grew 1 inch each in stature.

Splashdown Record

The most accurate recovery from space was the splashdown of *Gemini IX* on June 6, 1966, only 769 yards from the U.S.S. *Wasp* in the western Atlantic.

Extra-Terrestrial Vehicles

The first wheeled vehicle landed on the moon was the Soviet *Lunokhod I* which began its earth-controlled travels on November 17, 1970. It moved a total of 6.54 miles on gradients up to 30 degrees in the Mare Imbrium and did not become non-functioning until October 4, 1971.

The lunar speed and distance record was set by the *Apollo XVI* Rover with 11.2 m.p.h. and 22.4 miles.

Highest Lunar Landing

See *Highest Mountains*, page 154.

Duration Record on the Moon

The crew of *Apollo XVII*'s lunar exploration module *Challenger*, Capt. Eugene Andrew Cernan, U.S.N. and Dr. Harrison H. "Jack" Schmitt, were on the lunar surface for 74 hours 59½ minutes from December 11 to 14, 1972. They collected a record 253 lbs. of rock and soil during their 22 hour 5 minute "extra-vehicular activity." Schmitt was the 12th and last man on the moon.

Most Expensive Project

The total cost of the U.S. manned space program up to and including the lunar mission of *Apollo XVII* has been estimated at $25,541,400,000. The cost of the U.S.S.R. space program from 1958 to September, 1973, has been estimated, however, at $45,000,000,000. The cost of the space shuttle programs to 1990 is estimated to be $42,800,000,000.

Chapter Five

THE SCIENTIFIC WORLD

Elements

All known matter in the solar system is made up of chemical elements. The total of naturally occurring elements so far detected is 94, comprising, at ordinary temperature, two liquids, 11 gases and 81 solids. The so-called "fourth state" of matter is plasma, when negatively charged electrons and positively charged ions are in flux.

Lightest and Heaviest Sub-Nuclear Particles

The first sub-nuclear particle postulated was the electron in 1897. Since then, 19 other stable particles have been identified, of which 16 have anti-particles, together with 43 baryon resonances, 16 meson resonances, 6 strange mesons, 3 S-wave interactions, and 5 psions, making a total of 108. Their mass varies from zero, in the case of the graviton, photon (discovered 1902), electron neutrino (June, 1956) and muon neutrino (1962), up to 3,684 MeV, in the case of the Psi prime discovered in 1974. The lifetimes of particles range from "stable" down to that of the baryon resonance Delta (3230), discovered in 1966, at 1.4×10^{-24} seconds.

Least Stable Particles

The least stable or shortest-lived nuclear particles discovered are the rho prime meson (announced on January 29, 1973), and the three baryon resonances N (3030), Δ (2850), and Δ (3230), all lasting 1.6×10^{-24} second. The discovery of the quark was claimed at Haverah Park, near Harrogate, North Yorkshire, by researchers from Leeds University, England, on May 23, 1973, but is not internationally accepted.

Newest Particles

The particles Psi 3105 and Psi 3695 were announced on November 15 and 22, 1974, from the Stanford Linear Accelerator Center, California. In January, 1975, a neutral particle Psi 4100 with a lifetime of 10^{-23} second was announced.

Fastest Particles

A search for the existence of super-luminary particles, named tachyons (symbol T+ and T−), with a speed *in vacuo* greater than c. the speed of light, was instituted in 1968 by Dr. T. Alvager and Dr. M. Kriesler of Princeton University. Such particles would create the conceptual difficulty of disappearing before they exist.

The 106 Elements

There are 94 known naturally occurring elements comprising at ordinary temperatures, two liquids, 11 gases and 81 solids, of which 72 are metallic. To date, a further 12 transuranic elements (Elements 95 to 106) have been synthesized.

Commonest (lithosphere)
46.60 per cent by weight

Oxygen (O)
Discovered by Scheele (Germany-Sweden), 1771

Commonest (atmosphere)
78.09 per cent by volume

Nitrogen (N)
Discovered by Priestley (G.B.) *et al.*, 1772

Commonest (extra-terrestrial)
90 per cent of all matter

Hydrogen (H)
Discovered by Cavendish (G.B.), 1776

Rarest (of the 94)
1/100th oz. in earth's crust

Astatine (At)
Discovered by Corson (U.S.) *et al.*, 1940

Lightest
0.005611 lb. per cubic foot

Hydrogen (H)
Discovered by Cavendish (G.B.), 1776

Lightest (Metal)
33.29 lb. per cubic foot

Lithium (Li)
Discovered by Arwedson (Sweden), 1817

Densest
1,410 lb. per cubic foot

Osmium (Os)
Discovered by Tennant (G.B.), 1804

Heaviest (Gas)
0.6256 lb. per cubic foot

Radon (Em 222)
Discovered by Dorn (Germany), 1900

NEWEST SUB-ATOMIC PARTICLES have been discovered at the Stanford Linear Accelerator Center.

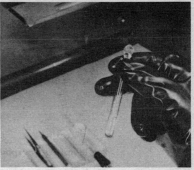

MOST EXPENSIVE SUBSTANCE: This is Californium 252, worth $100 per tenth of a microgram, according to the U.S. Atomic Energy Commission.

Newest[1]
    Announced Sept. 9, 1974

Purest
    99.99999999 per cent purity (1967)

Hardest
    Diamond Isotope, Knoop value 8,400

Most Expensive
    Sold in 1968 for $1000 per μg.

Most Stable
    Half-life of 2.2×10^{21} years

Least Stable
    Half-life of 2.4×10^{-21} seconds

Most Isotopes
    30

Least Isotopes
    3 (confirmed)

Most Ductile
    1 oz. drawn to 43 miles

Highest Tensile Strength
    3.9×10^8 lb. force per square inch

Lowest Melting Point
    −271.72°C. under pressure of 26 atmospheres

Element 106
    Discovered by Ghiorso (U.S.) et al., 1974

Germanium (Ge)
    Discovered by Winkler (Germany), 1886

Carbon (C)
    Prehistoric

Californium (Cf)
    Discovered by Seaborg (U.S.) et al., 1950

Tellurium (Te 130)
    Discovered by von Reichenstein (Hungary), 1782

Helium (He 5)
    Discovered by Ramsay (G.B.), 1895

Xenon (Xe)
    Discovered by Ramsay and Travers (G.B.), 1898

Hydrogen (H)
    Discovered by Cavendish (G.B.), 1776

Gold (Au)
    ante 3000 B.C.

Boron (B)
    Discovered by Gay-Lussac (France) et al., 1808

Helium (He)
    Discovered by Ramsay (G.B.), 1895

---

[1] On June 17, 1976, the discovery of three new super-heavy Elements 116 and eka-actinides 124 and 126 was announced by Robert V. Gentry, Thomas Cahill, J. William Nelson, Robert Flocchini and T. A. Carlsson, all of the United States. Nuclei of these were found by Gentry as trace elements from pleochroic haloes in inclusions in Madagascan mica in monazite. Preliminary data for the presence of Elements 114 and eka-actinides 125 and 127 were also announced, together with the possibility of evidence of the earlier presence of Element 116.

Highest Melting Point
3,417° ± 10°C.

Most Poisonous
1 µg. or microgram (1 thirty-millionth of an oz.) inhaled or swallowed will cause cancer. With a half-life of 23,640 years, toxicity is retained for a thousand centuries.

Tungsten (W)
Discovered by J. J. & F. d'Elhuyar (Spain), 1783
Plutonium (Pu)
Discovered by Seaborg (U.S.) *et al.*, 1940

Chemical Compounds

It has been estimated that there are more than 4 million described chemical compounds.

Most Refractory	
Tantalum Carbide ($TaCo_{88}$)	Melts at 4,010° ± 75°C.
Most Refractory (plastics)	
Modified Polymides	482°C. for short periods
Lowest Expansion	
Invar metal (Ni-Fe alloy with C and Mn)	2.3×10^{-6} of a centimeter per cm. per one degree C.
Highest Tensile Strength	
Sapphire whisker Al_2O_3	6×10^6 lb. force per square inch
Highest Tensile Strength (plastics)	
Polyvinyl alcoholic fibers	1.5×10^5 lb. force per square inch
Most Magnetic	
Cobalt-copper-samarium Co_3Cu_2Sm	10,500 oersted coercive force
Least Magnetic Alloy	
Copper nickel alloy CuNi	963 parts Cu to 37 parts Ni
Most Pungent	
Vanillaldehyde	Detectable at 2×10^{-8} milligram per liter of air
Sweetest	
In-proxy-2-amino-4-nitro-benzene	5,600 × as sweet as 1 per cent sucrose
Bitterest	
Bitrex or Benzyl diethyl ammonium benzoate	200 × as bitter as quinine sulphate
Most Acidic[1]	
Perchloric acid ($HClO_4$)	pH value of normal solution tends to zero
Most Alkaline	
Caustic soda (NaOH) and potash (KOH) and tetra-methylammonium hydroxide ($N[CH_3]_4OH$)	pH value of normal solution is 14

[1]The most powerful acid assessed on its power as a hydrogen-ion donor is a solution of antimony pentafluoride in fluosulphonic acid ($SbF_6 + FSO_3H$).

Highest Specific Impulse

    Hydrogen with liquid fluorine   447 lb. force per second per lb.

Most Poisonous

    Thiopentone (a barbiturate)   Intracardiac injection will kill in 1 to 2 seconds

Finest Powder

Particulate matter of 25 to 40 Å was reportedly produced by an electron beam evaporation process at the Atomic Energy Establishment, Harwell, England, in October, 1972. The paper was published by Dr. P. RamaKrishnan.

Most Absorbent Substance

The U.S. Department of Agriculture Research Service announced on August 18, 1974, that "H-span" or Super Slurper, composed of one half starch derivative and one fourth each of acrylamide and acrylic acid, can, when treated with iron, retain water 1,300 times its own weight.

Smelliest Substance

The most evil-smelling substance, of the 17,000 smells so far classified, must be a matter of opinion, but ethyl mercaptan (C_2H_5SH) and butyl seleno-mercaptan (C_4H_9SeH) are powerful claimants, each with a smell reminiscent of a combination of rotting cabbage, garlic, onions and sewer gas.

Most Expensive Perfume

The retail prices of the most expensive perfumes tend to be fixed at public relations rather than economic levels. The most expensive ingredient in perfume is pure French middle note jasmine essence at £2,900 ($6,960) per kilogram or £82.20 ($197) per ounce.

Most Powerful Fuel

The greatest specific impulse of any rocket-propulsion fuel combination is 447 lbs./f./sec. per lb. produced by liquid fluorine and hydrogen. This compares with a figure of 300 for liquid oxygen and kerosene.

Most Potent Poison

The rickettsial disease, Q-fever, can be instituted by a *single* organism but is only fatal in 1 in 1,000 cases. Effectually the most poisonous substance yet discovered is the toxin of the bacterium *Pasteurella tularensis*. About 10 organisms can institute tularemia, variously called alkali disease, Francis disease or deerfly fever, and this is fatal in 50 to 80 cases in 1,000.

Most Powerful Nerve Gas

In the early 1950s, substances known as V-agents notably VX, 300 times more toxic than phosgene ($COCl_2$) used in World War I, were developed at the Chemical Defence Experimental Establishment, Porton Down, Wiltshire, England, which are lethal at 1 milligram per man. Patents were applied for in 1962 and published in February, 1974.

Drugs

Most Powerful. The most potent and, to an addict, the most expensive of all naturally derived drugs is heroin, which is a chemically processed form of opium from the juice of the unripe seed capsules of the white poppy (*Papaver somniferum*). An ounce, which suffices for up to 1,800 hypodermic "fixes," may sell for up to $10,000 in the U.S., affording a 70,000 per cent profit over the raw material price in Turkey. The most potent analgesic drug is Etorphine or M-99, announced in June, 1963, by Dr. K. W. Bentley and D. G. Hardy of Reckitt & Sons Ltd. in Hull, Yorkshire, England. The drug has almost 10,000 times the potency of morphine.

The most powerful synthetically manufactured drug is d-Lysergic Acid Diethylamide tartrate (LSD–25, $C_{20}H_{25}N_3O$) first produced in 1938 for common cold research and as a hallucinogen by Dr. Albert Hoffmann (Swiss), on April 16–19, 1943.

Most Prescribed. The benzodiazepine group tranquilizing drug Valium, discovered by Hoffman–La Roche, is the world's most widely used drug. In 1973, there were an estimated 47,000,000 prescriptions in the U.S. alone.

Drink

Most Alcoholic

The strength of liquor is gauged by degrees proof. In the U.S., proof spirit is that mixture of ethyl alcohol (C_2H_5OH) and water which contains one half its volume of alcohol of a specific gravity of 0.7939 at 60°F., referred to water at 60°F. as unity. Pure or absolute alcohol is thus 200 proof. A "hangover" is due to toxic congenerics such as amyl alcohol ($C_5H_{11}OH$).

The highest strength spirits which can be produced are raw rum and some Polish vodkas, up to 194 proof or 97.2 per cent alcohol. The strongest drink sold commercially is Polish White Spirit Vodka, produced by the State Spirits Monopoly of Poland. This is 160 proof.

Beer

Strongest Beer. The world's strongest and most expensive beer is EKU Kulminator Urtyp Hell from Kulmbach, West Germany, which retails for up to $1.70 for a ½-pint bottle. It is 13.2 per cent alcohol by volume at 20°C. with an original gravity of 1117.6°.

Weakest Beer. The weakest liquid ever marketed as beer was a sweet ersatz beer which was brewed in Germany by Sunner, Colne-Kalk, in 1918. It had an original gravity of 1,000.96°.

Liqueurs

The most expensive liqueur in France is the orange-flavored *Le Grand Marnier Coronation* at 44 francs ($10.50) per bottle.

Ancient *Chartreuse* (before 1903) has been known to sell for more than $42.00 per liter bottle. An 1878 bottle was sold for this price in 1954.

CHAMPAGNE BOTTLES range in size from the Nebuchadnezzar of 16 liters, down to the little ¼ bottle, which is only 1/64th as large.

The most expensive brandy sold is *Grande Fine Champagne Arbellot* 1749 which retails at Fauchon's in Paris at 667 francs (about $160) per bottle.

Wine

Oldest Vintage. The oldest datable vintage of any wine has been a bottle of *Steinwein* 1540 from Wurzburg am Main, West Germany, salvaged from the cellars of King Ludwig of Bavaria, sold by Ehrmann's of Grafton Street, London, and described as "dark, feeble but definitely alive."

Most Expensive. The highest price ever paid for a bottle of wine of any size is $14,200 for a bottle of 1806 Château Lafite-Rothschild, a red Bordeaux, purchased at auction in New Orleans, Louisiana, by a Texas oilman, David I. Lyons.

Greatest Wine Auction

The largest single sale of wine took place at Christies' of King Street, St. James, London, on March 25–26, 1976, when 31,000 bottles of Bordeaux wines were auctioned for £1,760,000.

Largest Bottles

The largest bottle normally used in the wine and spirit trade is the Jeroboam or double magnum, with a capacity of up to 4 liters (8.45 pints), which is used only for liqueur brandy and champagne. A complete set of Monopole champagne bottles from the ¼ bottle, through the ½ bottle, bottle, magnum, Jeroboam, Rehoboam, Methuselah, Salmanazer and Balthazar, to the Nebuchadnezzar, which has a capacity of 16 liters (33.8 pints), is equivalent to 20 bottles.

Smallest Bottles

The smallest bottles of liquor sold are the 24 minim bottles of

Precious Stone Records

	Largest	Largest Cut Stone	Other Records
Diamond (pure crystallized carbon)	3,106 metric carats (over 1¼ lbs.) —*The Cullinan*, found by Capt. M. F. Wells, Jan. 26, 1905, in the Premier Mine, Pretoria, South Africa.	530.2 metric carats. Cleaved from *The Cullinan* in 1908, in Amsterdam by Jak Asscher and polished by Henri Koe. Known as *The Star of Africa* No. 1 and now in the British Royal Sceptre.	Diamond is the *hardest* known naturally occurring substance, being 90 times as hard as the next hardest mineral, corundum (Al_2O_3). The peak hardness value on the Knoop scale is 8,400 compared with an average diamond of 7,000. The rarest colors for diamond are blue (record—44.4 carat *Hope* diamond) and pink (record—24 carat presented by Dr. John Thoburn Williamson to H.M. The Queen of the U.K. in 1958). Auction record: $1,050,000 for a 69.42-carat stone bought by Cartier and sold to Richard Burton at $1,200,000 for Elizabeth Taylor on Oct. 24, 1969. The largest still un-cut diamond is *The Star of Sierra Leone* found at Kono, Sierra Leone, Africa, on Feb. 14, 1972, weighing 969.1 carats. It was sold for an undisclosed amount below its reserve of some $2,600,000 in February, 1973, to Harry Winston (N.Y.). Tiffany & Co. put a $5,000,000 price on their canary yellow diamond of 1877 for one day on November 17, 1972. Miss Debbie Reynolds wore a tiara, owned by Harry Winston (N.Y.C.), valued at $4,500,000 in New York on September 25, 1973. In November, 1975, a top blue-white uncut gem was quoted at £1,428 ($2,856) per carat.
Emerald (green beryl) $[Be_3Al_2(SiO_3)_6]$	125-lb. crystal (up to 15¾ inches long and 9¾ inches in diameter) from a Ural, U.S.S.R. mine.	2,680-carat unguent jar carved by Dionysio Miseroni in the 17th century owned by the Austrian Government. 1,350 carats of *gem* quality, the *Devonshire* stone from Muso, Colombia.	A necklace of eight major emeralds and one pendant emerald of 75.63 carats with diamonds was sold by Sotheby's in Zurich, Switzerland, on November 24, 1971 for £436,550 (then $1,050,000). The Swiss customs at Geneva confirmed the existence of a hexagonal emerald of about 20,000 carats, thus possibly worth more than $100,000,000.
Sapphire (blue corundum) (Al_2O_3)	2,302-carat stone found at Anakie, Queensland, Australia, in c. 1935, now a 1,318-carat head of President Abraham Lincoln (1809–65).	1,444-carat black star stone carved from a 2,097-carat stone in 1953–55 into a bust of General Dwight David Eisenhower (1890–1969).	*Note:* Both the sapphire busts are in the custody of the Kazanjian Foundation of Los Angeles.
Ruby (red corundum) (Al_2O_3)	3,421-carat broken stone reported found in July, 1961 (largest piece 750 carats).	1,184-carat natural gem stone of Burmese origin.	Since 1955 rubies have been the world's most precious gem attaining a price of up to $10,000 per carat by 1969. The ability to make corundum prisms for laser technology up to over 12 inches in length must now have a bearing on the gem market.

Scotch whisky marketed by the Cumbrae Supply Co. of Scotland. They contain $\frac{1}{20}$ of a fluid ounce and retailed in 1975 for the equivalent of 60 cents.

Champagne Cork Flight

The longest distance for a champagne cork to fly from an untreated and unheated bottle 4 feet from level ground is 94 feet by David Jon Wiener at San Diego, California, on August 25, 1973.

Gems

Most Precious. From 1955, the value of rubies rose, due to a drying up of supplies from Ceylon and Burma. A flawless natural ruby of good color was carat for carat more valuable than emerald, diamond or sapphire and, in the case of a 6-carat ruby, brought $30,000. The ability to produce very large corundum prisms of 12 inches or over in length in the laboratory for use in lasers must now have a bearing on the gem market.

Largest. The largest recorded stone of gem quality was a 520,000-carat (229-lb.) aquamarine ($Al_2Be_3[Si_6O_{18}]$) found near Marambaia, Brazil, in 1910. It yielded over 200,000 carats of gem quality stones.

Rarest. Only two stones are known of the pale mauve gem Taaffeite ($Be_4Mg_4Al_{16}O_{32}$), first discovered in a cut state in Dublin,

HIGHEST-PRICED DIAMOND ever sold at auction (left) was this 69.42-carat flawless diamond ring which sold to Cartier's, New York, for $1,050,000, and which was almost immediately resold to actor Richard Burton for his wife, in October, 1969. The previous record was $385,000 for a necklace. **LARGEST DIAMOND** (right): The Star of Africa No. 1 in the British Royal Sceptre was cut, with 74 facets, from the $1\frac{1}{4}$-pound Cullinan diamond.

Records for other Precious Materials

	Largest	Where Found	Notes on Present Location, etc.
Pearl (Molluscan concretion)	14 lbs. 1 oz., 9¼ in. long by 5½ in. in diameter—*Pearl of Lao-tze*	At Palawan, Philippines, May 7, 1934, in shell of giant clam.	In a San Francisco bank vault. It is the property since 1936 of Wilburn Dowell Cobb and was valued at $4,080,000 in July, 1971.
Opal ($SiO_2 NH_2O$)	220 troy oz. (yellow-orange) Gem stone: 17,700 carats (*Olympic Australis*)	Andamooka, South Australia, Jan., 1970. Coober Pedy, South Australia, Aug., 1956.	The Andamooka specimen was unearthed by a bulldozer.
Crystal (SiO_2)	70 tons (piezo-quartz crystal) Ball: 106¼ lbs., 12⅜ in. diameter, the *Warner* sphere	Kazakhstan, U.S.S.R., Sept., 1958. Burma (originally a 1,000-lb. piece).	*Note:* There is a single rock crystal of 1,728 lbs. placed in the Ural Geological Museum, Sverdlovsk, U.S.S.R., November, 1968. Smithsonian Institution Museum (U.S. National Museum) in Washington, D.C.
Topaz [$(Al_2, OH, F) SiO_4$]	596 lbs. Gem stone: 7,725 carats	Minas Gerais, Brazil.	American Museum of Natural History, New York City, since 1951.
Amber (coniferous fossil resin)	33 lbs. 10 oz.	Reputedly from Burma, acquired in 1860.	Bought by John Charles Bowing (d. 1893) for £300 in Canton, China. Natural History Museum, London, since 1940.
Turquoise [$CuAl_6(PO_4)_4 (OH)_8 4H_2O$]	218 lbs.	Riverside County, California, January 17, 1975.	Found by Chester Jastromb and Kenneth Casper. Original weight was probably c. 250 lbs.
Jade [$NaAl(Si_2O_6)$]	Submarine boulder of 5 tons (valued at $180,000)	Off Monterey, California. Landed June 5, 1971.	Jadeite can be virtually any color. The less precious nephrite is [$Ca_2 (Mg, Fe)_5 (OH)_2 (Si_4 O_{11})_2$]
Marble (Metamorphosed $CaCO_3$)	100.8 tons (single slab)	Quarried at Yule, Colorado.	A piece of over 50 tons was dressed from this slab for the coping stone of the Tomb of the Unknown Soldier in Arlington National Cemetery, Virginia.
Nuggets—Gold (Au)	7,560 oz. (472½ lbs.) (reef gold) *Holtermann Nugget*	Beyers & Holtermann Star of Hope Gold Mining Co., Hill End, N.S.W. Australia, Oct. 19, 1872.	The purest large nugget was the *Welcome Stranger*, found at Moliagul, Victoria, Australia, which yielded 2,248 troy oz. of pure gold from 2,280½ oz.
Silver (Ag)	2,750 lbs. troy	Sonora, Mexico	Appropriated by the Spanish Government before 1821.

Ireland, in November, 1945. The larger of the two examples weighs 0.84 of a carat. There are minerals of which only single examples are known.

Hardest. The hardest of all gems, and the hardest known naturally occurring substance, is diamond, which is, chemically, pure carbon. Diamond is 90 times as hard as the next hardest mineral, corundum (Al_2O_3), and those from Borneo, in Indonesia, and New South Wales, Australia, have a particular reputation for hardness. Hardnesses are compared on Mohs' scale, on which talc is 1, a fingernail is $2\frac{1}{2}$, window glass 5, topaz 8, corundum 9, and diamond 10. Diamonds average 7,000 on the Knoop scale, with a peak value of 8,400. This index represents a micro-indentation index based on kilograms per one hundredth of a square millimeter $(kg/(mm^2)^{-2})$.

Densest Gem Mineral. The densest of all gem minerals is stibotantalite $[(SbO)_2 (Ta,Nb)_2 O_6]$, a rare brownish-yellow mineral found in San Diego County, California, with a density of 7.46 grams per c.c.

Telescopes

Earliest. Although there is evidence that early Arabian scientists understood something of the magnifying power of lenses, the first use of lenses to form a telescope has been attributed to Roger Bacon (*c.* 1214–92) in England. The prototype of modern refracting telescopes was completed by Johannes Lippershey for the Netherlands government on October 2, 1608.

Largest Reflector. The largest telescope in the world is the 236.2-inch telescope sited on Mount Semirodriki, near Zelenchukskaya in the Caucasus Mountains, U.S.S.R., at an altitude of 6,830 feet. The mirror, weighing 78 tons, was completed in November, 1967, was assembled by October, 1970. Regular observations were begun on February 7, 1976, after 16 years work. The overall weight of the 260-foot-long assembly is 946 tons. Being the most powerful

LARGEST TELESCOPE: The mirror of this Russian reflector is 236.2 inches in diameter and weighs 78 tons.

HIGHEST OBSERVATORY ON EARTH: This observatory of the University of Denver is situated at 14,100 feet, on Mount Evans, Colorado.

of all telescopes, its range, which includes the location of objects down to the 25th magnitude, represents the limits of the observable universe. Its light-gathering power would enable it to detect the light from a candle at a distance of 15,000 miles.

Largest Refractor. The largest refracting (*i.e.* magnification by lenses) telescope in the world is the 62-foot-long 40-inch telescope completed in 1897 at the Yerkes Observatory, Williams Bay, Wisconsin, and belonging to the University of Chicago. In 1900, a 49.2-inch refractor 180 feet in length was built for the Paris Exposition, but its optical performance was too poor to justify attempts to use it.

Solar

The world's largest solar telescope is the 480-foot-long McMath telescope at Kitt Peak National Observatory near Tucson, Arizona. It has a focal length of 300 feet and an 80-inch heliostat mirror. It was completed in 1962 and produces an image measuring 33 inches in diameter.

Highest Observatory

The highest-altitude observatory in the world is the University of Denver's High Altitude Observatory at an altitude of 14,100 feet, opened in 1973, on Mount Evans, Colorado. The principal instrument is a 24-inch Ealing Beck reflecting telescope.

Radio-Telescopes

Largest. The first $3,000,000 installment for the building of the world's largest and most sensitive radio-telescope was included by the National Science Foundation in its federal budget for the fiscal year 1973. The instrument termed the VLA (Very Large Array) will be Y-shaped with each arm 13 miles long with 27 mobile antennae on rails. The site selected will be 50 miles west of Socorro in the Plains of San Augustin, New Mexico, and the completion date will be 1979 to 1981 at a total cost of $74,000,000.

Largest Steerable Dish. The world's largest trainable dish-type radio-telescope is the 328-foot diameter, 3,360-ton assembly at the Max Planck Institute for Radio Astronomy of Bonn in the Effelsberger Valley, West Germany; it became operative in May, 1971. The cost of the installation, begun in November, 1967, was DM36,920,000 ($14,760,000). The earliest fully steerable radio-telescope was the 82-foot dish at Dwingeloo, Netherlands, completed in May, 1956. It was announced in June, 1974, that the University of Manchester Mark V radio-telescope project at Meiford, Powys, Wales, for a 375-foot instrument had been abandoned when cost estimates surpassed $40,800,000.

The world's largest dish-type radio-telescope is the partially-steerable ionospheric assembly built over a natural bowl at Arecibo, Puerto Rico, completed in November, 1963, at a cost of about $9,000,000. It has a diameter of 1,000 feet and the dish covers $18\frac{1}{4}$ acres. Its sensitivity was raised by a factor of 1,000 and its range to the edge of the observable universe at some 15,000 million light-years by the fitting of new aluminum plates at a cost of $8,800,000. Rededication was on November 16, 1974.

The RATAN-600 radio-telescope being built in the northern Caucasus, U.S.S.R., will have mirror dishes on a 1,968.5-foot perimeter.

Planetaria

The ancestor of the planetarium is the rotatable Gottorp Globe, built by Andreas Busch in Denmark between 1654 and 1664 to the orders of Duke Frederick III of Holstein's court mathematician Olearius. It is 34.6 feet in circumference, weighs 4 tons and is now preserved in Leningrad, U.S.S.R. The stars were painted on the inside.

The earliest optical installation was not until 1923 in the Deutsches Museum, Munich, by Zeiss of Jena, Germany.

The world's largest planetarium, with a diameter of $82\frac{1}{2}$ feet, is in Moscow, U.S.S.R.

Photography

Cameras

Largest. The largest camera ever built is the 27-ton Rolls-Royce camera built for Product Support (Graphics) Ltd. of Derby, England, completed in 1959. It measures 8 feet 10 inches high, 8 feet 3 inches wide and 35 feet long. The lens is a 63″ f15 Cooke Apochromatic. Its value after improvements in 1971 is in excess of $240,000.

Smallest. Apart from cameras built for intra-cardiac surgery and espionage, the smallest camera that has been marketed is the circular Japanese "Petal" camera with a diameter of 1.14 inches and a thickness of 0.65 of an inch. It has a focal length of 0.47 inch. The BBC-TV program *Record Breakers* showed prints from this camera on December 3, 1974.

EARLY PHOTOGRAPH: This positive print of a diamond window pane in Wiltshire, England, was made from the oldest photographic negative in existence (1835).

Earliest. The earliest photograph was taken in the summer of 1826 by Joseph Nicéphore Niépce (1765–1833), a French physician and scientist. It showed the courtyard of his country house at Gras, near St. Loup-de-Varennes. It probably took eight hours to expose and was taken on a bitumen-coated polished pewter plate measuring $7\frac{3}{4}$ inches by $6\frac{1}{2}$ inches.

One of the earliest photographs taken was one of a diamond window pane in Lacock Abbey, Wiltshire, England, taken in 1835 by William Henry Fox Talbot (1800–1877), the inventor of the negative-positive process.

The world's earliest aerial photograph was taken in 1858 by Gaspard Félix Tournachon (1820–1910), *alias* Nadar, from a balloon near Villacoublay, on the outskirts of Paris.

Most Expensive. The most expensive range of camera equipment is the F-1 35 mm. system of Canon Camera Co., Inc., of Tokyo. The 40 lenses offered range from the Fish Eye 7.5-mm. F/5.6 to the FL 1200-mm. F/11, while the accessories available number 180. The total cost of the range would exceed $30,000. A Thomas Sutton wet-plate camera, *c.* 1865, was sold at auction at Sotheby's for $26,400 on March 8, 1974.

Fastest. In 1972, Prof. Basor of the U.S.S.R. Academy of Sciences published a paper describing an experimental camera with a time resolution of 5×10^{-13} of a second or $\frac{1}{2}$ a picosecond. The fastest production camera in the world is the Imacon 600 manufactured by John Hadland (P.I.) Ltd. of Bovingdon, Hertfordshire, England, which is capable of 600 million pictures per second, with the maximum framing rate 600 million frames per second. Uses include lasar, ballistic, detonic, plasma and corona research.

Numeration

In dealing with large numbers, scientists use the notation of 10 raised to various powers, to eliminate a profusion of zeros. For example, 19,160,000,000,000 miles would be written 1.916×10^{13} miles. Similarly, a very small number, for example, 0.0000154324 of a gram, would be written 1.54324×10^{-5} gram (g.). Of the prefixes used before numbers the smallest is "atto-," from the Danish *atten* for 18, indicating a million million millionth part (10^{-18}) of the unit, and the highest is "exa-" (Greek, *hexa*=six), indicating a quintillion (10^{18}) fold.

Numbers

Prime Numbers. A prime number is any positive integer (excluding 1) having no integral factors other than itself and unity, *e.g.* 2, 3, 5, 7, or 11. The lowest prime number is 2. The highest known prime number is $2^{19937}-1$ (a number of 6,002 digits of which the first five are 43,154 and the last three, 471), received by the American Mathematical Society on March 18, 1971, and calculated on an I.B.M. 360/91 computer in 39 minutes 26.4 seconds by Dr. Bryant Tuckerman at Yorktown Heights, New York.

Perfect Numbers. A number is said to be perfect if it is equal to the sum of its divisors other than itself, *e.g.* $1+2+4+7+14=28$. The lowest perfect number is 6 ($1+2+3$). The highest known, and the 24th so far discovered, is $(2^{19937}-1) \times 2^{19936}$ which has 12,003 digits, of which the first three are 931, and the last three are 656. It is a consequence of the highest known prime (see above).

Highest. The highest generally accepted named number in the system of successive powers of ten is the centillion, which is 10 raised to the power 600, or 10^{303} in the U.S. system. The number Megiston written with symbol ⑩ is a number too great to have any physical meaning. The highest named number outside the decimal notation is the Buddhist *asankhyeya*, which is equal to 10^{140} or 100 quinto-quadragintillions.

The number 10^{100} (10 duotrigintillion) is designated a Googol, a term devised by Dr. Edward Kasner of the U.S. (d. 1955). Ten raised to the power of a Googol is described as a Googolplex. Some conception of the magnitude of such numbers can be gained when it is said that the number of atoms in some models of the observable universe probably does not exceed 10^{85}. Factorial 10^{85} (written $10^{85}!$) approximates to 10 to the power of $43 + 85 \times 10^{85}$.

The largest number to have become sufficiently well known in mathematics to have been named after its begetter is the Skewes number which approximates 10 to the power 10 to the power 10 to the power 3^4, obtained by Prof. Stanley Skewes, Ph.D., now of Cape Town University, South Africa, and published in a paper in 1933 concerning the occurrence of prime numbers.

Most Primitive. The most unnumerate people are the Nambiquara of the northwest Mato Grosso section of Brazil who lack any system of numbers. They do, however, have a verb which means "they are two alike."

LONGEST SLIDE RULE:
Constructed by mathematics
teacher Clarence Hay and
two of his students, this
lengthy problem solver is
39 feet long.

Earliest Measures. The earliest known measure of weight is the *beqa* of the Amratian period of Egyptian civilization *c.* 3800 B.C. found at Naqada, Egypt. The weights are cylindrical with rounded ends from 188.7 to 211.2 grams (6.65–7.45 oz.). The unit of length used by the megalithic tomb-builders in Britain *c.* 2300 B.C. appears to have been 2.72 ± 0.003 feet.

Smallest Units

The shortest unit of length is the atto-meter, which is 1.0×10^{-16} of a centimeter. The smallest unit of area is a "shed," used in subatomic physics and first mentioned in 1956. It is 1.0×10^{-48} of a square centimeter. A "barn" is equal to 10^{24} "sheds." The reaction of a neutrino occurs over the area of 1.0×10^{-43} of a square centimeter.

Most Accurate Version of "Pi." The greatest number of decimal places to which *pi* (π) has been calculated is 1,000,000 by the French mathematicians, Jean Guilloud and Mlle. Martine Bouyer, achieved on May 24, 1973, on a CDC 7600 computer, but not verified until September 3, 1973. The published value to a million places was 3.141592653589793 . . . (omitting the next 999,975 places) . . . 5779458151. This has been described as the world's most boring 400-page book.

In 1897, the State legislature of Indiana came within a single vote of declaring that *pi* should be *de jure* 3.2.

Square Root of Two. The greatest accuracy was an enumeration to 1,000,082 places by Jacques Dutka of Columbia University, New York City, announced in October, 1971, after a $47\frac{1}{2}$-hour run on a computer.

Longest Slide Rule

The world's longest slide rule is one 39 feet in length, completed on March 24, 1976, by Clarence T. Hay, Randy R. Meyer and Jeff H. Meyer of Huron Heights Secondary School, Newmarket, Ontario, Canada.

Time Measure

Longest. The longest measure of time is the *kalpa* in Hindu chronology. It is equivalent to 4,320 million years. In astronomy a cosmic year is the period of rotation of the sun around the center of the Milky Way galaxy, *i.e.* about 225,000,000 years. In the Late Cretaceous Period of *c.* 85 million years ago, the earth rotated faster so resulting in 370.3 days per year, while in Cambrian times some 600 million years ago, there is evidence that the year contained 425 days.

Shortest. Owing to variations in the length of a day, which is estimated to be increasing irregularly at the average rate of about 2 milliseconds per century, due to the moon's tidal drag, the second has been redefined. Instead of being 1/86,400th part of a mean solar day, it is now reckoned as 1/31,556,925.9747th part of the solar (or tropical) year at 1900 A.D., January 0 at 12 hours, Ephemeris time. In 1958 the second of Ephemeris time was computed to be equivalent to $9,192,631,770 \pm 20$ cycles of the radiation corresponding to the transition of a cesium 133 atom when unperturbed by exterior fields. The greatest diurnal change recorded has been 10 milliseconds on August 8, 1972, due to the most violent solar storm recorded in 370 years of observation. In a nano-second (1.0×10^{-9} of a second) light travels 11.8 inches. The new reckoning of the second took place in 1960.

Physical Extremes (Terrestrial)

Temperatures

Highest. The highest man-made temperatures yet attained are those produced in the center of a thermonuclear fusion bomb, which are of the order of 300,000,000° to 400,000,000°C. Of controllable temperatures, the highest effective laboratory figure reported is 50,000,000°C. for 2/100ths of a second, by Prof. Lev A. Artsimovich at Tokamuk, U.S.S.R., in 1969. At very low particle densities, even higher figures are obtainable. Prior to 1963, a figure of 3,000 million °C. was reportedly achieved in the U.S.S.R. with Ogra injection-mirror equipment.

Lowest. The lowest temperature reached is 5×10^{-7} degree Kelvin, achieved by Professor A. Abragam (b. 1914) in collaboration with M. Chapellier, M. Goldman, and Vu Hoang Chau at the Centre d'Etudes Nucléaires, Saclay, France, in 1969. Absolute or thermodynamic temperatures are defined in terms of ratios rather than as differences reckoned from the unattainable absolute zero, which on the Kelvin scale is −273.15°C. or −459.67°F. Thus the lowest temperature ever attained is 1 in 546×10^8 of the melting point of ice (0°C. or 273.15°K. or 32°F.).

The lowest equilibrium temperature ever attained is 0.0003°K. by nuclear refrigeration in a 3-lb. copper specimen by Prof. Olli V. Lounasmaa (born 1920) and his team at the Helsinki University of Technology, Otaniemi, Finland, on April 17, 1974.

Highest Pressures

The highest sustained laboratory pressures yet reported are of 5,000,000 atmospheres (7.25 × 10⁷ lbs. force per square inch), achieved in the U.S.S.R. and announced in October, 1958. Using dynamic methods and impact speeds of up to 18,000 m.p.h., momentary pressures of 75,000,000 atmospheres (548,000 tons per square inch) were reported from the U.S. in 1958.

Highest Vacuum

The highest vacuums obtained in scientific research are of the order of 1.0×10^{-16} of an atmosphere. This compares with an estimated pressure in interstellar space of 1.0×10^{-19} of an atmosphere. At sea level there are 3×10^{19} molecules per cubic centimeter in the atmosphere, but in interstellar space there are probably less than 10 per c.c.

Fastest Centrifuge

The highest man-made rotary speed ever achieved and the fastest speed by any earth-bound object is 4,500 m.p.h. by a swirling tapered 6-inch carbon fiber rod in a vacuum at Birmingham University, England, reported on January 24, 1975.

Highest Note

The highest note yet attained is one of 60,000 megahertz (60 GHz) (60,000,000,000 vibrations per second), generated by a "laser" beam at the Massachusetts Institute of Technology, Cambridge, Massachusetts, in September, 1964.

FASTEST CENTRIFUGE: This machine in Birmingham, England, can spin a 6-inch rod at 4,500 m.p.h.

Highest Frequency

In November, 1974, at the U.S. National Bureau of Standards, Boulder, Colorado, D. Jennings, K. M. Evenson and F. R. Peterson measured a frequency of $147.915850 \times 10^{12}$ Hz, or close to 150 Terahertz. This was generated by a helium-xenon laser.

Loudest Noise

The loudest noise created in a laboratory is 210 decibels or 400,000 acoustic watts reported by NASA in October, 1965. The noise came from a 48-foot steel and concrete horn at Huntsville, Alabama. Holes can be bored in solid material by this means.

Most Powerful Sound System

The world's most powerful sound system is that installed at the Ontario Motor Speedway, California, in July, 1970. It has an output of 30,800 watts, connectable to 355 horn-speaker assemblies and thus able to communicate the spoken word to 230,000 people above the noise of 50 screaming racing cars.

Quietest Place

The "dead room," measuring 35 feet by 28 feet, in the Bell Telephone System Laboratory at Murray Hill, New Jersey, is the most anechoic room in the world, eliminating 99.98 per cent of reflected sound.

Finest Balance

The most accurate balance in the world is the Sartorius Model 4108, manufactured in Göttingen, West Germany, which can weigh objects of up to 0.5 grams (about .018 oz.) to an accuracy of 0.01 μg or 0.00000001 g, which is equivalent to little more than one-sixtieth of the weight of ink on this period dot (.).

Lowest Viscosity

The California Institute of Technology announced on December 1, 1957, that there was no measurable viscosity, *i.e.* perfect flow, in liquid helium II, which exists only at temperatures close to absolute zero ($-273.15°$C. or $-459.67°$F.).

Lowest Friction

The lowest coefficient of static and dynamic friction of any solid is 0.02, in the case of polytetrafluoroethylene ((C_2F_4)n), called P.T.F.E. —equivalent to wet ice on wet ice. It was first manufactured in quantity by E. I. du Pont de Nemours & Co. Inc. in 1943, and is marketed as Teflon.

At the University of Virginia a 30-lb. rotor magnetically supported has been spun at 1,000 revolutions per second in a vacuum of 10^{-6} mm. of mercury pressure. It loses only one revolution per second per day, thus spinning for years.

Longest Siphon

The longest siphon ever constructed was one with a pull of 35.1 feet, built on No. 2 Chimney, Ringsend Power Station, Dublin City, Ireland, on July 16, 1964 by A. G. Kelly. The discovery that water can be siphoned through a greater height than the barometric pressure column has been patented.

Most Powerful Electric Current

The most powerful electric current generated is that from the Zeus capacitor at the Los Alamos Scientific Laboratory, New Mexico. If fired simultaneously the 4,032 capacitors would produce for a few microseconds twice as much current as that generated elsewhere on earth.

Strongest Magnet

The heaviest magnet in the world is one measuring 196 feet in diameter, with a weight of 40,000 tons, for the 10 GeV synchrophasotron in the Joint Institute for Nuclear Research at Dubna, near Moscow, U.S.S.R. Intermagnetics General Corporation announced in 1975 plans for a 180 kG vanadium-gallium magnet.

Strongest and Weakest Magnetic Fields

The strongest recorded magnetic fields are ones of 10 megagauss (10,000,000 gauss), fleetingly produced by explosive flux compression devices, reported in 1968. The first megagauss field was announced in March, 1967.

The strongest steady magnetic field yet achieved is one of 225,000 gauss in a cylindrical bore of 1.25 inches, using 10 megawatts of power, called the "IJ" magnet, designed by D. Bruce Montgomery, which was put in operation at the Francis Bitter National Magnet Laboratory at Massachusetts Institute of Technology, Cambridge, Massachusetts, in 1964.

The weakest magnetic field measured is one of 1.6×10^{-10} gauss in the heavily shielded room at the Francis Bitter National Magnet Laboratory, at M.I.T., Cambridge, Massachusetts. It is used for research into the very weak magnetic fields generated in the heart and brain.

Most Powerful Microscopes

The world's most powerful microscope was announced by Dr. Lawrence Bartell and Charles Ritz of the University of Michigan in July, 1974, with an image magnification of 260 million fold. It uses an optical laser to decode holograms produced with 40 Kev radiation and has produced photographs of electron clouds of atoms of neon and argon.

Finest Cut

Biological specimens embedded in epoxy resin can be sectioned by a glass knife microtome under ideal conditions, to a thickness of 1/875,000th of an inch or 290 Ångström units.

Sharpest Objects

The University of California Medical Center, San Francisco, announced in July, 1974, the ultimate in sharpness—glass electrodes more than 200 times slimmer than a diamond phonograph stylus. These can be used for exploring the cells in the eye. The points are 0.05 μm.

LARGEST ATOM SMASHER: The National Accelerator Laboratory in Illinois has a 1.24-mile diameter and cost $250,000,000.

Most Powerful Particle Accelerator

The 1.24-mile diameter proton synchroton at the Fermi National Accelerator Laboratory at Weston, Illinois, is the largest and most powerful "atom-smasher" in the world. An energy of 400 GeV was attained on December 14, 1972. Plans to double the energy to nearly 1 Tera electron volts were begun in 1971 by means of a second ring of superconducting magnets, but only one sixth of this has so far been authorized.

The $76,800,000 CERN intersecting storage rings (ISR) project near Geneva, Switzerland, started on January 27, 1971, using two 28 GeV proton beams and is designed to yield the equivalent of 1,700 GeV or 1.7 Tev (1.7 million million electron volts) in its center of mass experiments.

Wind Tunnels

The world's largest wind tunnel is a low-speed tunnel with a closed test section measuring 40 feet by 80 feet, built in 1944, at Ames Research Center, Moffett Field, California. The tunnel encloses 900 tons of air and cost approximately $7,000,000. The maximum volume of air that can be moved is 60,000,000 cubic feet per minute. On July 30, 1974, NASA announced an intention to increase it in size to 80 by 120 feet for 345-m.p.h. speeds with a 135,000-h.p. system.

The most powerful is the 216,000-h.p. installation at the Arnold Engineering Test Center at Tullahoma, Tennessee. The highest mach number attained with air is mach 27 at the plant of the Boeing Company, Seattle, Washington. For periods of microseconds, shock mach numbers of the order of 30 have been attained in impulse tubes at Cornell University, Ithaca, N.Y.

Largest Bubble Chamber

The largest bubble chamber in the world is the $7,000,000 installation completed in October, 1973, at Weston, Illinois (see p. 189). It is 15 feet in diameter and contains 7,259 gallons of liquid hydrogen at a temperature of −247°C. (−412.6°F.) with a super-conducting magnet of 30,000 gauss.

Shortest Wavelength

On April 15, 1974, I.B.M. researchers E. Spillar and A. Segmüller announced that X-rays with a wavelength of only 1.54 Ångström units (6,000 millionths of an inch) had been harnessed in a device which may become a "light pipe" to guide X-rays to required locations.

Longest-Lived Electric Battery

A battery kept in the Clarendon Laboratory, University of Oxford, England, has been causing a suspended bob to be electro-statically attracted a few times a second alternately by two small bells since 1840 when it was made by the London firm of scientific apparatus makers, Watkins and Hill. It produces about 2 kV at 10^{-8}A and is an example of the so-called "dry column" associated with the names of Marechaux, de Luc, Behrens and Zamboni. The only known use of this form of battery in this century was for an infra-red viewer in the 1939–45 war.

Most Durable Light

The electric light *bulb* was demonstrated in 1860, by Heinrich (later Henry) Goebel (1818–93) of Springe, Germany in New York and first perfected to a commercial success by Thomas A. Edison in Menlo Park, New Jersey, on October 21, 1879. The average bulb lasts for 750 to 1,000 hours. There is some evidence that a carbide filament bulb burning in the Fire Department, Livermore, South Alameda County, California, has been burning since 1901.

Fastest Switch

An electric device that can be switched in less than 10 billionths of a second (10^{-11} sec.) was announced on January 18, 1973. It utilizes the prediction of the English physicist, Brian Josephson (b. 1940) in 1962 that ultra-thin insulators can be made superconductive.

Brightest Light

The brightest steady artificial light sources are "laser" beams, with a luminosity exceeding the sun's 1,500,000 candles per square inch by a factor of well in excess of 1,000. Of continuously burning sources, the most powerful is a 200-kilowatt high pressure xenon arc lamp of 600,000 candle-power, reported from the U.S.S.R. in 1965.

In May, 1969, the U.S.S.R. Academy of Sciences announced blast waves traveling through a luminous plasma of inert gases heated to 90,000°K. The flare-up for up to 3 microseconds shone at 50,000 times the brightness of the sun, *viz.* 75,000 million candles per square inch.

The synchrotron radiation emitted through a 4 inch by $\frac{1}{10}$ inch slit in the SPEAR high energy physics plant at the end of the 2-mile-long Stanford Linear Accelerator, California, has been described as the world's most powerful light beam.

The most powerful searchlight ever developed was one produced during the 1939–45 war by the General Electric Company Ltd. at the Hirst Research Centre in Wembley, Greater London, England. It had a consumption of 600 kilowatts and gave an arc luminance of 300,000 candles per square inch and a maximum beam intensity of 2,700,000,000 candles from its parabolic mirror (diameter 10 feet).

"Laser" Beams

The first illumination of another celestial body was achieved on May 9, 1962, when a beam of light was successfully reflected from the moon by the use of an optical "maser" (microwave amplification by stimulated emission of radiation) or "laser" (light amplification by stimulated emission of radiation) attached to a 48-inch telescope at the Massachusetts Institute of Technology, Cambridge, Massachusetts. The spot was estimated to be 4 miles in diameter on the moon. A "maser" beam is focused into a liquid nitrogen-cooled ruby crystal. Its chromium atoms are excited into a high energy state in which they emit a red light which is allowed to escape only in the direction desired. The maser was devised in 1958 by Dr. Charles Hard Townes (born 1915) of Bell Telephone Laboratories. Such a flash for 1/5,000th of a second can bore a hole through a diamond by vaporization at 10,000°C., produced by 2×10^{23} photons.

Computers

The modern computer was made possible by the invention of the paint-contact transistor by John Bardeen and Walter Brattain, announced in July, 1948, and the junction transistor by R. L. Wallace, Morgan Sparks and Dr. William Shockley in early 1951.

Oldest Computer

The oldest operative computer in Britain and probably in the world is Witch, built at Harwell in 1949–50 and last in service at The Polytechnic, Wolverhampton, from where it was transferred in 1973 to the Museum of Science and Industry, Birmingham, England, in full operational condition. It has 827 "Dekatron" cathode tubes.

Largest Computer

The world's most powerful computer is the Control Data Corporation CDC 7600 first delivered in January, 1969. It can perform 36 million operations in one second and has an access time of 27.5 nano-seconds. It has two internal memory cores of 655,360 and 5,242,880 characters (6 bits per character) supplemented by a Model 817 disc file of 800,000,000 characters. The cost is up to $15,000,000, depending on peripherals.

The most capacious storage device is the IBM 3850 mass storage device, introduced in 1976, with a memory capacity of 4×10^{15} bits. The Burroughs Corporation $30 million ILLIAC IV at the NASA Ames Research Center, Moffett Field, California comprises 64 separate computing elements in tandem.

Chapter Six

THE ARTS AND ENTERTAINMENT

Painting

Earliest

Evidence of Paleolithic art in a cave was found in 1834 at Chaffaud, Vienne, France, by Brouillet when he recognized an engraving of two deer on a piece of flat bone from the cave, dating to about 20,000 B.C. The number of stratigraphically-dated examples of cave art is very limited. The oldest known dated examples came from La Ferrassie, near Les Eyzies in the Périgord region, where large blocks of stone engraved with animal figures and symbols were found in the Aurignacian II layer (*c.* 25,000 B.C.).

Largest

Panorama of the Mississippi, completed by John Banvard (1815–91) in 1846, showing the river scene for 1,200 miles in a strip probably 5,000 feet long and 12 feet wide, was the largest painting in the world, with an area of more than 1.3 acres. The painting is believed to have been destroyed when the rolls of canvas, stored in a barn at Cold Spring Harbor, Long Island, New York, caught fire shortly before Banvard's death on May 16, 1891.

The largest painting now in existence is probably *The Battle of Gettysburg*, completed in 1883, after 2½ years of work, by Paul Philippoteaux (France) and 16 assistants. The painting is 410 feet long, 70 feet high and weighs 11,792 lbs. It depicts the climax of the Battle of Gettysburg, in south-central Pennsylvania, on July 3, 1863. In 1964, the painting was bought by Joe King of Winston-Salem, North Carolina, after being stored by E. W. McConnell in a Chicago warehouse since 1933.

The largest "Old Master" is *Il Paradiso*, painted between 1587 and 1590 by Jacopo Robusti, *alias* Tintoretto (1518–94), and his son Domenico on Wall "E" of the Sala del Maggior Consiglio in the Palazzo Ducale (Doge's Palace) in Venice, Italy. The work is 72 feet 2 inches long and 22 feet 11½ inches high and contains more than 100 human figures.

Smallest

The smallest paintings in the world are those executed in oil with a 4 or 5 sable-hair brush on pinheads $\frac{1}{32}$ to $\frac{1}{4}$ inch in diameter by Gerard Legare of British Columbia, Canada.

Most Valuable

The portrait of "Mona Lisa" (*La Gioconda*) by Leonardo da Vinci (1452–1519) in the Louvre, Paris, was assessed for insurance

HIGHEST PRICE PAID AT AUCTION: "Portrait of Juan de Pareja" (sometimes known as "The Slave of Velázquez") sold for $5,544,000 in 1970 to the Wildenstein Gallery of New York. Velázquez painted it in 1649 "by way of exercise" before attempting a portrait of the Pope.

purposes at $100,000,000 for its move for exhibition in Washington, D.C., and New York City, from December 14, 1962, to March 12, 1963. However, insurance was not concluded because the cost of the closest security precautions was less than that of the premiums. It was painted in *c.* 1503–07 and measures 30.5×20.9 inches. It is believed to portray Mona (short for Madonna) Lisa Gherardini, the wife of Francesco del Gioconda of Florence. The husband is said to have disliked it and refused to pay for it. Francis I, King of France, bought the painting for his bathroom for 4,000 gold florins or 492 ounces of gold (now equivalent to $69,000) in 1517.

HIGHEST PRICED PAINTINGS—PROGRESSIVE RECORDS

Price	Painter, title, sold by and sold to	Date
$32,500	Correggio's *The Magdalen, Reading* (in fact spurious) to Elector Friedrich Augustus II of Saxony.	1746
$42,500	Raphael's *The Sistine Madonna* to Elector Friedrich Augustus II of Saxony.	1759
$80,000	Van Eyck's *Adoration of the Lamb*, 6 outer panels of Ghent altarpiece by Edward Solby to the Government of Prussia.	1821
$123,000*	Murillo's *The Immaculate Conception* by estate of Marshall Soult to the Louvre (against Czar Nicholas I) in Paris.	1852
$350,000	Raphael's *Ansidei Madonna* by the 8th Duke of Marlborough to the National Gallery, London.	1885
$500,000	Raphael's *The Colonna Altarpiece* by Sedelmeyer to J. Pierpoint Morgan.	1901
$514,400	Van Dyck's *Elena Grimaldi-Cattaneo* (portrait) by Knoedler to Peter Widener (1834–1915).	1906
$514,400	Rembrandt's *The Mill* by 6th Marquess of Lansdowne to Peter Widener.	1911
$582,500	Raphael's smaller *Panshanger Madonna* by Joseph (later Baron) Duveen (1869–1939) to Peter Widener.	1913
$1,572,000	Leonardo da Vinci's *Benois Madonna* to Czar Nicholas II in Paris.	1914
$2,300,000*	Rembrandt's *Aristotle Contemplating the Bust of Homer* by Mrs. Alfred Erickson to New York Metropolitan Museum of Art.	1961
$5,000,000–	Leonardo da Vinci's *Ginevra de' Benci* by Prince Franz Josef II of Liechtenstein to National Gallery, Washington.	
$6,000,000		1967
$5,544,000*	Velázquez *Portrait of Juan de Pareja*, sometimes known as *The Slave of Velázquez* by the Earl of Radnor (U.K.) to Wildenstein Gallery, New York.	1970

* indicates price at auction, otherwise prices were by private treaty.

Highest Price

Auction Price. The highest price ever bid in a public auction was $5,544,000 for a portrait by Diego Velázquez, of his mulatto assistant and servant, called variously *Portrait of Juan de Pareja* and *The Slave of Velázquez*, painted in Rome in 1649, and sold on November 27, 1970, at Christie's salesrooms, London, to the Wildenstein Gallery of New York. When the same painting was sold at Christie's at auction in 1801, it went for 39 guineas (about $200). It remained in the possession of the Earls of Radnor from 1811 until 1970.

Miniature Portrait. The highest price ever paid for a portrait miniature is $169,260 by an anonymous buyer at a sale held by Christie's, London, on June 8, 1971, for a miniature of Frances Howard, Countess of Essex and Somerset, by Isaac Oliver, painted *c.* 1605. This miniature, sent for auction by Lord Derby, measured $5\frac{1}{8}$ inches in diameter.

Modern Painting. The highest price paid for a modern painting is $2,000,000 paid by the Australian National Gallery in Canberra for *Blue Poles* by Jackson Pollock (U.S.) (1912–56) on September 21, 1973. This is also the highest price ever paid for any American painting.

Living Artist. The highest price paid for paintings in the lifetime of the artist is $1,950,000 paid for the two canvases *Two Brothers* (1905) and *Seated Harlequin* (1922) by Pablo Diego José Francisco de Paula Juan Nepomuceno Crispin Crispiano de la Santisima Trinidad Ruiz y Picasso (1881–1973), born in Spain. This was paid by the Basle City government to the Staechelin Foundation to enable the Basle Museum of Arts to retain the paintings after an offer of $2,560,000 had been received from the U.S. in December, 1967.

Most Prolific Artist. Picasso was the most prolific of all painters. In a career that lasted 78 years, it has been estimated that he produced about 13,500 paintings or designs, 100,000 prints or engravings, 34,000 book illustrations, and 300 sculptures or ceramics. His lifetime work has been valued at $690,000,000.

Most Prolific Portrait Painter. Herman H. Simms (born in Cincinnati in 1920), who works at Disneyland, Anaheim, California, painted 9,803 water-color portraits in the year 1973.

Drawing. The highest price ever attached to any drawing was £804,361 ($2,252,210) for the cartoon *The Virgin and Child with St. John the Baptist and St. Anne*, measuring $54\frac{1}{4}$ inches by $39\frac{1}{4}$ inches, drawn in Milan, probably in 1499–1500, by Leonardo da Vinci (1452–1519) of Italy. The National Gallery (London) retained possession in 1962, after three U.S. bids of over $4,000,000 were reputed to have been made for the cartoon.

Largest Mobile

The most massive recorded mobile is *Quest* by Jerome Kirk, installed at TRW Inc., Redondo Beach, California, in September, 1968. It is a 32-foot-long pivotal mobile weighing 5.98 tons. The term "mobile" was coined to contrast with "stabile" sculpture by Marcel Duchamp in 1932.

Largest Mosaic

The world's largest mosaic is on the walls of the central library of the Universidad Nacional Autónomao de México, Mexico City. There are four walls; the two largest measuring 12,949 square feet each represent the pre-Hispanic past.

Murals

Earliest. The earliest known murals on man-made walls are those at Çatal Hüyük in southern Anatolia, Turkey, dating from *c.* 5850 B.C.

Largest. The largest logo and mural painting in the world is the American Revolution Bicentennial symbol on the curved roof of the Arizona Veterans Memorial Coliseum, Phoenix, Arizona. It occupies 110,000 square feet, or more than 2½ acres. It will be painted over in 1977. After being outlined with the aid of a computer, it took 45 man-days, under the supervision of its designer John M. Glitsos, to apply the necessary 870 gallons of patriotic red, white and blue paint on August 18–26, 1973.

A ground mural, measuring 1,400 feet long by 100 feet wide, named Yellow Brick Road—Leisure Time, painted on a disused runway near the Tamiami Stadium, South Dade, Florida, was completed on March 18, 1976.

Museums

Oldest. The oldest museum in the world is the Ashmolean Museum in Oxford, England, built in 1679.

OLDEST MUSEUM: The Ashmolean Museum was built in Oxford, England, in 1679.

Largest. The largest museum in the world is the American Museum of Natural History between 77th and 81st Streets on Central Park West, New York City. Founded in 1874, it comprises 19 interconnected buildings with 23 acres of floor space.

Largest Gallery

The world's largest art gallery is the Winter Palace and the neighboring Hermitage in Leningrad, U.S.S.R. One has to walk 15 miles to visit each of the 322 galleries, which house nearly 3,000,000 works of art and archeological remains.

Upside Down Duration Record

The longest period of time for which a modern drawing has hung upside down in a public gallery unnoticed is 47 days. This occurred to *Le Bateau*, by Henri Émile Benoît Matisse (1869–1954) of France, in the Museum of Modern Art, New York City, between October 18 and December 4, 1961. In this time 116,000 people had passed through the gallery.

Sculptures

Earliest. The earliest known examples of sculpture are the so-called Venus figurines from Aurignacian sites, dating to *c*. 25,000–22,000 B.C., *e.g.* the famous Venus of Willendorf from Austria and the Venus of Brassempouy (Landes, France). A piece of ox rib found in 1973 at Pech de l'Aze, Dordogne, France, in an early Middle Paleolithic layer of the Riss glaciation *c*. 105,000 B.C. appears to have several intentionally engraved lines on one side.

Largest. The world's largest sculptures are the mounted figures of Jefferson Davis (1808–89), Gen. Robert Edward Lee (1807–70) and Gen. Thomas Jonathan ("Stonewall") Jackson (1824–63), covering 1.33 acres on the face of Stone Mountain, near Atlanta, Georgia. They are 90 feet high and took from 1958 to May, 1970, to sculpt. Roy Faulkner was on the mountain face for 6 years with a thermo-jet torch, working with the sculptor, Walker Kirtland Hancock.

When completed the world's largest sculpture will be that of the Indian chief Tashunca-Uitco, known as Crazy Horse, of the Oglala tribe of the Dakota or Nadowessioux (Sioux) group. He is believed to have been born in about 1849, and he died at Fort Robinson, Nebraska, on September 5, 1877. The sculpture was begun on June 3, 1948, near Mount Rushmore, South Dakota. A projected 561 feet high and 641 feet long, it will require the removal of 6,500,000 tons of stone and is the life work of one man, Korczak Ziolkowski. It is estimated that the work will take until at least 1978.

Most Expensive. The highest price ever paid for a sculpture is the $750,000 given at Sotheby Parke-Bernet Galleries, New York, on May 1, 1974, for Constantin Brancusi's polished bronze *Negresse Blonde* of 1926.

The highest price paid for the work of a living sculptor is $260,000 given at Sotheby Parke-Bernet Galleries, New York, on March 1, 1972, by Fischer Fine Arts of London, England, for the 75-inch wooden carving *Reclining Figure* by Henry Moore (born Castleford,

LARGEST SCULPTURE: Three Confederate figures—Jefferson Davis, Robert E. Lee and Stonewall Jackson—are being carved on Stone Mountain, Georgia. Note the size of the workmen (top left).

West Yorkshire, England, July 30, 1898), sold by Cranbrook Academy, Bloomfield Hills, Michigan.

The highest price paid for a work of art from an ancient civilization is $260,000 given by the Metropolitan Museum of Art, New York City, for the 18th dynasty turquoise glazed Egyptian faience $9\frac{7}{8}$-inch figure of Pharaoh Amenhotep III (*c.* 1410–1320 B.C.) at Sotheby Parke-Bernet, on May 2, 1972.

Ground Figures. In the Nazca Desert, south of Lima, Peru, there are straight lines (one more than 7 miles long), geometric shapes and plants and animals drawn on the ground by still unknown persons between 100 B.C. and 700 A.D. for an uncertain but probably religious or astronomical purpose. They were first detected from the air *c.* 1928.

Hill Figures. In August, 1968, a 330-foot-tall figure was found on a hill above Tarapacár, Chile.

Language

Earliest. Anthropologists have evidence that the truncated pharynx of Neanderthal man precluded his speaking anything akin to a modern language any more than an ape or a modern baby. Cro-Magnon man of 40,000 B.C. had however developed an efficient vocal tract. Clay tablets of the neolithic Danubian culture discovered in December, 1966, at Tartaria, Moros River, Rumania have been dated to the fifth or fourth millennium B.C. The tablets bear symbols of bows and arrows, gates and combs. In 1970, it was announced that writing tablets bearing an early form of the Elamite language dating from 3,500 B.C. had been found in southeastern Iran. The scientist, Alexander Marshack (U.S.), maintains that marked Upper Paleolithic artifacts, such as a Cro-Magnon bone from 30,000 B.C. in the Musée des Antiquités Nationales, outside Paris, with 69 marks with 24 stroke changes, are not random but of possibly lunar or menstrual cycle significance.

Oldest. The written language with the longest continuous history is Egyptian from the earliest hieroglyphic inscriptions on the palette of Narmer, dated to *c.* 3100 B.C., to Coptic used in churches at the present day, more than 5,000 years later. Hieroglyphs were used until 394 A.D., and thus may be overtaken by Chinese characters as the most durable script in the 21st century.

Oldest Words in English. Recent research indicates that several river names in Britain date from pre-Celtic times (*ante* 550 B.C.). These include Ayr, Hayle and Nairn. This ascendant, Indo-Germanic tongue, which was spoken from *c.* 3000 B.C. on the Great Lowland Plain of Europe, now has only fragments left in Old Lithuanian, from which the modern English word *elanr* derives. The word *land* is traceable to the Old Celtic *landa* (a heath), and therefore must have been in use on the continent before the Roman Empire grew powerful in the 6th century B.C.

Commonest. The language spoken by more people than any other is Northern Chinese, or Mandarin, by an estimated 68 per cent of the population (575,000,000 people) in 1975. The so-called national language (*Guoyu*) is a standardized form of Northern Chinese (*Beifanghua*) as spoken in the Peking area. This was alphabetized into *zhuyin zimu* of 39 letters in 1918. In 1958, the *pinyin* system, using a Latin alphabet, was introduced.

The next most commonly spoken language and the most widespread is English, with an estimated 360,000,000 in mid-1975. English is spoken by 10 per cent or more of the population in 34 sovereign countries. Today's world total of languages and dialects still spoken is about 5,000 of which some 845 come from India.

Rarest. There are believed to be 20 or more languages, including 6 North American Indian languages, in which no one can converse, because there is only one speaker left alive. Eyak is still spoken in southeast Alaska by two aged sisters when they meet.

Most Complex. The following extremes of complexity have been noted: Chippewa, the North American Indian language of Minnesota, has the most verb forms with up to 6,000; Tillamook, the North American Indian language of Oregon, has the most prefixes with 30; Tabassaran, a language in Daghestan, U.S.S.R., uses the most noun cases with 35; the Eskimo language uses 63 forms of the present tense and simple nouns have as many as 252 inflections.

In Chinese, the *Chung-wen Ta Tz'u-tien* Dictionary lists 49,905 characters. The fourth tóne of "i" has 84 meanings, varying as widely as "dress," "hiccough" and "licentious." The written language provides 92 different characters for "i⁴." The most complex written character in Chinese is that representing the sound of thunder which has 52 strokes and is somewhat surprisingly pronounced *ping*. The most complex in current use consists of 36 strokes representing a blocked nose and less surprisingly pronounced *nang*.

Rarest and Commonest Sounds. The rarest speech sound is probably the sound written ř in Czech which occurs in very few languages and is the last sound mastered by Czech children. In the southern Bushman language !xo, there is a click, articulated with both lips, which is written ⊙. The *l* sound in the Arabic word *Allah*, in some contexts, is pronounced uniquely in that language. The commonest sound is the vowel *a* (as in the English father); no language is known to be without it.

Most and Least Regular Verbs. Esperanto was first published by Dr. Ludwig Zamenhof (1859–1917), of Warsaw, in 1887 without irregular verbs. It is now estimated from textbook sales to have a million speakers. Swahili has a strict 6-class pattern of verbs and no verbs which are irregular to this pattern. According to more daunting grammars published in West Germany, English has 194 irregular verbs, though there are arguably 214.

Largest Vocabulary. The English language contains about 490,000 words, plus another 300,000 technical terms, the most in any language, but it is doubtful if any individual uses more than 60,000.

Greatest Linguist

According to some uncompleted and hence as yet unpublished researches, the most proficient linguist in history was Sir John Bowring (1792–1872), who was said to be able to read 200 languages and speak 100.

The greatest living linguist is probably Georges Schmidt (b. Strasbourg, France, in 1915) of the United Nations Translation Department in New York City, who can reputedly speak fluently in 30 languages and has been prepared to embark on the translation of 36 others.

Alphabets

Oldest. The development of the use of an alphabet in place of pictograms occurred in the Sinaitic world between 1700 and 1500 B.C. This western Semitic language developed the consonantal system based on phonetic and syllabic principles.

Longest and Shortest. The language with most letters is Cambodian with 72 (including useless ones). Rotokas, spoken in the center of Bougainville Island in the South Pacific, has least with 11 (just a, ~~b~~, e, g, i, k, o, p, ř, t and u). Amharic has 231 formations from 33 basic syllabic forms, each of which has seven modifications, so this Ethiopian language cannot be described as alphabetic.

Most and Least Consonants and Vowels. The language with most consonants is the Caucasian mountain language, Ubyx, with 80 and that with the least is Rotokas (see above) with only 6 consonants. The language with the most vowels is Sedang, a central Vietnamese language with 55 distinguishable vowel sounds. The languages with the least (2 vowels) are the Caucasian languages Abaza and Kabardian. The Hawaiian word for "certified" has 8 consecutive vowels—hooiaioia. The English record is 6 in the musical term *euouae*. The Estonian word jäääärne, meaning "the edge of the ice," has the same vowel four consecutive times. The Latin genitive for Aeneas' island consists solely of 6 vowels—Aeaeae.

Oldest and Youngest Letters. The oldest letter is o, unchanged in shape since its adoption in the Phoenician alphabet *c.* 1300 B.C. The newest letters in the English alphabet are j and v, which are of post-Shakespearean use, *c.* 1630. There are now some 65 alphabets in use.

Largest Letter. The largest permanent letters in the world are the giant 600-foot letters spelling READYMIX on the ground in the Nullarbor near East Balladonia, Western Australia. This was constructed in December, 1971.

In sky-writing (normally at *c.* 8,000 feet) a 7-letter word may stretch for 6 miles in length and can be read from 50 miles. The world's earliest example was over Epsom racecourse, England, on May 30, 1922, when Cyril Turner "spelt out" "London Daily Mail" from an S.E.5A biplane.

Longest Words

World. The longest word ever to appear in literature occurs in *The Ecclesiazusae*, a comedy by Aristophanes (448–380 B.C.). In the Greek it is 170 letters long but transliterates into 182 letters in English, thus: lopadotemachoselachogaleokranioleipsanodrimhypo-trimmatosilphioparaomelitokatakechymenokichlepikossyphophatto-peristeralektryonopteкephalliokigklopeleiolagoiosiraiobaphetragano-pterygon. The term describes a fricassee of 17 sweet and sour ingredients, including mullet, brains, honey, vinegar, pickles, marrow (the vegetable) and ouzo (a Greek drink laced with anisette).

English. The longest word in the Oxford English Dictionary is floccipaucinihilipilification (alternatively spelt in hyphenated form with "n" in seventh place), with 29 letters, meaning "the action of estimating as worthless," first used in 1741, and later by Sir Walter Scott (1771–1832). Webster's Third International Dictionary lists among its 450,000 entries pneumonoultramicroscopicsilicovolcano-coniosis (45 letters), the name of a miner's lung disease.

The nonce word used by Dr. Edward Strother (1675–1737) to describe the spa waters at Bristol was aequeosalinocalcalinocera-ceoaluminosocupreovitriolic (52 letters).

The longest regularly formed English word is praetertranssub-stantiationalistically (37 letters), used by Mark McShane in his novel *Untimely Ripped*, published in 1963. The medical term hepaticocholangiocholecystenterostomies (39 letters) refers to the surgical creations of new communications between gall bladders and hepatic ducts and between intestines and gall bladders. The longest in common use is disproportionableness (21 letters).

Longest Chemical Name. The longest chemical term is that describing Bovine NADP-specific Glutamate Dehydrogenase, which contains 500 amino acids and a resultant name of some 3,600 letters.

Longest Palindromic Words. The longest known palindromic word (same spelling backwards as forwards) is *saippuakauppias* (15 letters), the Finnish word for a soap-seller. The longest in the English language is *redivider* (nine letters), while another nine-letter word, *Malayalam*, is a proper noun given to the language of the Malayali people in Kerala, southern India. The nine-letter word *ROTAVATOR* is a registered trademark belonging to Howard Machinery Ltd., of England. The contrived chemical term *detartrated* has 11 letters, as does *kinnikinnik* (sometimes written *kinnikkinnik*, a 12-letter palindrome), the word for the dried leaf and bark mixture which was smoked by the Cree Indians of North America.

Some baptismal fonts in Greece and Turkey bear the circular 25-letter inscription NIΨON ANOMHMATA MH MONAN OΨIN meaning "wash (my) sins not only (my) face."

The longest palindromic composition devised is one of 5,023 words completed by Jeff Grant of Hastings, New Zealand in March, 1976. It begins "Evils nag apart—Lunacy a war. A few erase . . ." and hence predictably ends ". . . Are we far away? Can ultra pagans live?"

Commonest Words. In written English, the most frequently used words are in order: the, of, and, to, a, in, that, is, I, it, for *and* as. The most used in conversation is I. The commonest letter is "e" and the commonest initial letter is "T."

Most Meanings. The most overworked word in English is the word "set" which has 58 noun uses, 126 verbal uses and 10 as a participial adjective.

Most Homophones. The most homophonous sounds in English are *air* and *sōl* which, according to the researches of Dora Newhouse of Los Angeles, both have 38 homophones. The homophone with the most variant spellings is *air*, with aire, are, ayr, e'er, eir, ere, err, erre, eyre, heir, eire, eyr *and* ore.

Most Accents. The word with most accents is the French word *hétérogénéité*, meaning heterogeneity. An atoll in the Pacific Ocean 320 miles east southeast of Tahiti is named Héréhérétué.

Worst Tongue-Twisters. The most difficult tongue-twister is deemed by Ken Parkin of Teesside to be "The sixth sick sheik's sixth sheep's sick"—especially when spoken quickly.

Perhaps more difficult is the Xhosa (from Transkei, South Africa) for "The skunk rolled down and ruptured its larynx": "Iqaqa laziqikaqika kwaze kwaqhawaka uqhoqhoqha." The last word contains three "clicks." A European rival is the vowelless *Strch prst skrz krk*, the Czech for "stick a finger in the throat."

Longest Abbreviation. The longest known abbreviation is S.O.M.K.H.P.B.K.J.C.S.S.D.P.M.W.D.T.B., the initials of the Sharikat Orang-Orang Melayu Kerajaan Hilir Perak Berkerjasama-Serkerjasama Kerama Jimat Chermat Serta Simpanan Dan Pinjam Meminjam Wang Dengan Tanggonan Berhad. This is the Malay name for the Lower Perak Malay Government Servants' Co-operative Thrift and Loan Society Limited, in Telok Anson,

LONGEST PLACE NAME IN USE: A 57-letter Maori name for a hill in New Zealand. In 1959 the first letter in the third line was changed from "A" to "O".

Perak State, West Malaysia (formerly called Malaya). The abbreviation for this abbreviation is not recorded.

Longest Acronym. The longest acronym is ADCOMSUBORD-COMPHIBSPAC (22 letters), used in the U.S. Navy to denote the Administrative Command; Amphibious Forces, Pacific Fleet, Subordinate Command.

Longest Anagrams. The longest non-scientific English words which can form anagrams are the 17-letter transpositions "misrepresentation" and "representationism."

Longest Sentence. A sentence of 1,300 words appears in *Absalom, Absalom* by William Faulkner, and one of 3,153 words with 86 semicolons and 390 commas occurs in the *History of the Church of God* by Sylvester Hassell of Wilson, North Carolina, c. 1884. Some authors such as James Joyce (1882–1941) eschew punctuation altogether. The first 40,000 words of the *Gates of Paradise* by George Andrzeyevski (Panther) appear to lack any punctuation.

The longest sentence recorded ever to have gotten past the editor of a major newspaper is one of 1,030 words in the TV column by Clarence G. Peterson, which appeared in the August 19, 1970 edition of the *Chicago Tribune*.

The Report of the President of Columbia University, 1942–43, contained a sentence of 4,284 words.

Most Prepositions at End of Sentence. The sentence claimed to possess the most prepositions at the end is a protest of a child against an Australian bedtime story book: "Mommy, what did you bring that book which I didn't want to be read to out of from about 'Down Under' up for?"

Place Names

Longest. The official name for Bangkok, the capital city of Thailand, is Krungt'ep. The full name is however: Krungthep Mahanakhon Bovorn Ratanakosin Mahintharayutthaya Mahadilokpop Noparatratchathani Burirom Udomratchanivetmahasathan Amornpiman Avatarnsathit Sakkathattiyavisnukarmprasit (167 letters) which, in the most scholarly transliteration, emerges with 175 letters.

The longest name now in use is Taumatawhakatangihangakoauauotamatea(turipukakapikimaungahoronuku)pokaiwhenuakitanatahu, the unofficial 85-letter version of the name of a hill (1,002 feet above sea level) in the Southern Hawke's Bay district of North Island, New Zealand. This Maori name means "the place where Tamatea, the man with the big knee who slid, climbed and swallowed mountains, known as Land-eater, played on his flute to his loved one." The official version has 57 letters (1 to 36 and 65 to 85).

Shortest. The shortest place names in the world are the French village of Y (population 143), so named since 1241, in the Somme, the Norwegian village of Å (pronounced "Aw"), the Swedish place Å in Vikholandet, U in the Caroline Islands of the Pacific, and the Japanese town of Sosei which is alternatively called Aioi or O-o and even O. There was once a 6 in West Virginia. Today in the U.S., there are seven two-lettered place names, including Ed and Uz, both in Kentucky.

Personal Names

Earliest. The earliest personal name which has survived is possibly N'armer, the father of men (Menes), the first Egyptian pharaoh, which dates from before 3100 B.C.

Longest. The longest name used by anyone is Adolph Blaine Charles David Earl Frederick Gerald Hubert Irvin John Kenneth Lloyd Martin Nero Oliver Paul Quincy Randolph Sherman Thomas Uncas Victor William Xerxes Yancy Zeus Wolfeschlegelsteinhausenbergerdorffvoralternwarengewissenhaftschaferswessenschafewarenwohlgepflegeundsorgfaltigkeitbeschutzenvonangreifendurchihrraubgierigfeindewelchevoralternzwolftausendjahresvorandieerscheinenvanderersteerdemenschderraumschiffgebrauchlichtalsseinursprungvonkraftgestartseinlangefahrthinzwischensternartigraumaufdersuchenachdiesternwelchegehabtbewohnbarplanetenkreisedrehensichundwohinderneurassevonverstandigmenschlichkeitkonntefortpflanzenundsicherfreuenanlebenslanglichfreudeundruhemitnichteinfurchtvorangreifenvonandererintelligentgeschopfsvonhinzwischensternartigraum, Senior, who was born at Bergedorf, near Hamburg, Germany, on February 29, 1904. On printed forms, he uses only his eighth and second Christian names and the first 35 letters of his surname. He lives in Philadelphia, and has recently shortened his surname to Wolfe+590, Senior.

The longest Christian or given name on record is Napuamahalaonaonekawrehiwehionakuahiweanenawawakehoonkakehoaalekeeaonanainananiakeao' Hawaiikawao (94 letters), in the case of Miss Dawn Lee of Honolulu, so named in February, 1967. The name means "the abundant, beautiful blossoms of the mountains and valleys begin to fill the air with their fragrance throughout the length and breadth of Hawaii."

Shortest. The single-letter surname O, of which 13 examples appear in the Brussels telephone directory, besides being the commonest single-letter name, is the one obviously causing the most distress to those concerned with the prevention of cruelty to computers. There are two one-letter Burmese names: E (calm), pronounced "aye," and U (egg), pronounced "oo." U used before the name means "uncle."

Most Christian Names. The French composer Louis Jullien (1812–1860) had 36 Christian names, because all 36 members of a Philharmonic Society insisted on being godfathers.

Mr. Brian Brown of Wolverhampton, England, in February, 1974, had his daughter christened Maria Sullivan Corbett Fitzsimmons Jeffries Hart Burns Johnson Willard Dempsey Tunney Schmeling Sharkey Carnera Baer Braddock Louis Charles Walcott Marciano Patterson Johansson Liston Clay Frazier Foreman Brown. He added, "I hope she will marry a boxer."

Most Versions. D. H. de Neveu of San Jose, California (born in Milwaukee, Wisconsin, January 17, 1933) has collected 121 incorrect spellings of his surname. The Zulu ruler, Hzilikazi (b. *c.* 1795) had his name chronicled in 324 spellings, according to researches by Dr. R. Kent Rasmussen.

Commonest. The commonest surname in the world is the Chinese name Chang which is borne, according to estimates, by between 9.7 per cent and 12.1 per cent of the Chinese population, so indicating even on the lower estimate that there are at least some 75,000,000 Changs—more than the entire population of all but 7 of the 154 other sovereign countries of the world.

The commonest surname in the English-speaking world is Smith. There are 671,550 nationally insured Smiths in Great Britain, of whom 7,081 are plain John Smith, and another 22,550 are John plus one or more given-name Smiths. There were an estimated 2,382,509 Smiths in the United States in 1973.

There are, however, estimated to be 1,600,000 persons in Britain with M', Mc or Mac (Gaelic "son of") as part of their surnames. The commonest of these is Macdonald which accounts for about 55,000 of the Scottish population.

Most Contrived Name. The palm for the most determined attempt to be last in the local telephone directory must now be awarded to Zachary Zzzzra of San Francisco. He outdid the

MOST CONTRIVED NAME: Zachary Zzzzra of San Francisco comes last in the hearts of his countrymen.

previous entrant who was a mere Zeke Zzzypt of Chicago. In September, 1970, Zero Zzyzz (rhymes with "fizz") was ousted from last place in the Miami directory by Vladimir Zzzyd (rhymes with "outdid"). In Los Angeles, a private company surpassed all, being the ZZZZZZZZ Co.

The Written Word

Texts and Books

Oldest. The oldest known written text is the pictograph expression of Sumerian speech, dating from *c.* 3500 B.C. In 1952, some clay tablets of this writing were unearthed from the Uruk IV level of the Sumerian temple of Inanna (*c.* 3300 B.C.) at Erech (called Uruk in Sumerian), now Warka, Iraq. The earliest known vellum document dates from the 2nd century A.D.; it contains paragraphs 10 to 32 of Demosthenes' *De Falsa Legatione*. Demosthenes died in the 4th century B.C.

Oldest Printed. The oldest surviving printed work is a Korean scroll or *sutra*, printed from wooden blocks found in the foundations of the Pulguk Sa pagoda, Kyongju, Korea, on October 14, 1966. It has been dated no later than 704 A.D. It was claimed in November, 1973, that a 28-page book of Tang dynasty poems at Yonsei University, Korea, was printed from metal type *c.* 1160.

Oldest Mechanically Printed. It is generally accepted that the earliest mechanically printed book was the 42-line Gutenberg Bible, printed at Mainz, Germany, in *c.* 1455 by Johann zum Gensfleisch zur Laden, called "zu Gutenberg" (*c.* 1398–*c.* 1468). Recent work on watermarks published in 1967 indicates a copy of a surviving printed Latin grammar was made from paper made in *c.* 1450. The earliest exactly dated printed work is the Psalter completed on August 14, 1457, by Johann Fust (*c.* 1400–1466) and Peter Schöffer (1425–1502), who had been Gutenberg's chief assistant.

Manuscripts. The highest price ever paid is £219,780 (then $527,472) paid at Sotheby's in Zurich, Switzerland, on November 5, 1975, for the autograph manuscript of Maimonides, the great Jewish philosopher. This was a study, written in *c.* 1160, on the rabbinical law *Mishna Torah*, from the collection of David Sassoon, bought by the Hebrew University of Jerusalem.

Largest. The largest book in the world is *The Little Red Elf*, a story in 64 verses by William P. Wood, who designed, constructed and printed the book. It measures 7 feet 2 inches high and 10 feet across when open. The book is at present on show in a cave at the foot of Beinn Ruadh ("The Red Elf Cave"), Ardentinny, near Dunoon, Scotland.

Largest Publication. The largest publication in the world is the 1,112-volume set of *British Parliamentary Papers* of 1800–1900 by Irish University Press in 1968–1972. A complete set weighs 3.64 tons, costs $65,000 and would take 6 years to read at 10 hours per day. The binding of the edition involved the death of 34,000 Indian goats and $39,000 worth of gold ingots. The total print run was 500 sets.

SMALLEST BOOK:
This type catalogue,
published in Scotland in
1975, is only 0.1131 inches
in height. It was printed
with moveable metal type.

Smallest. The smallest book printed with moveable metal type (not by a microphotographic process) is a type catalogue of 3 point Gill Titling, cast by Riscatype of Monmouth, Wales. It measures 2.9 mm. by 2.9 mm. (.1131 × .1131 inches) and is bound in red calfskin vellum to a thickness of 1.5 mm. (.059 inches). It was published by Gleniffer Press, Paisley, Scotland, in 1975.

Shortest. The shortest correspondence on record was that between Victor Marie Hugo (1802–85) and his publisher, Hurst and Blackett, in 1862. The author was on holiday and anxious to know how his new novel *Les Misérables* was selling. He wrote "?". The reply was "!".

Most Valuable. The most valuable printed books are the three surviving perfect vellum copies of the Gutenberg Bible (see above). The Library of Congress copy, bound in three volumes, was obtained in 1930 from Dr. Otto Vollbehr, who paid about $330,000 for it. During 1970, a paper edition in the hands of the New York book dealer, H. P. Kraus, was privately bought for $2,500,000. Only 48 examples (many missing some of the 324 pages) of the *c.* 200 printed have survived. The most recent discoveries were in Mons, France, in 1950, and Immenhausen, West Germany, in 1958.

Highest-Priced Printed Document. The highest price ever paid for a broadsheet was $404,000 for one of the 16 known copies of *The Declaration of Independence*, printed in Philadelphia in 1776 by Samuel T. Freeman & Co., and sold to a Texan in May, 1969.

Longest Novel. The longest important novel ever published is *Les hommes de bonne volonté* by Louis Henri Jean Farigoule (born August 26, 1885), *alias* Jules Romains, of France, in 27 volumes in 1932–46. The English version, *Men of Good Will*, was published in 14 volumes in 1933–46 as a "novel-cycle." The novel *Tokuga-Wa Ieyasu* by Sohachi Yamaoka has been serialized in Japanese daily newspapers since 1951. When completed it will run to 40 volumes.

Encyclopaediae

Earliest. The earliest known encyclopaedia was compiled by Speusippas (*post* 408–*c*. 388 B.C.), a nephew of Plato, in Athens, *c*. 370 B.C.

Most Comprehensive. The most comprehensive present day encyclopaedia is the *Encyclopaedia Britannica*, first published in Edinburgh, Scotland, in December, 1768. A group of booksellers in the U.S. acquired reprint rights in 1898 and complete ownership in 1899. In 1943, the *Britannica* was given to the University of Chicago. The current 30-volume 15th edition contains 33,141 pages and 43,000,000 words from 4,277 contributors. It is now edited in Chicago and in London.

Largest. The largest encyclopaedia ever compiled was the *Great Standard Encyclopaedia* of Yung-lo ta tien of 22,937 manuscript books (370 still survive), written by 2,000 Chinese scholars in 1403–08.

Largest Dictionary

The largest dictionary now published is the 12-volume Royal quarto *The Oxford English Dictionary* of 15,487 pages published between 1884 and 1928 with a first supplement of 963 pages in 1933 with a further 3-volume supplement, edited by R. W. Burchfield, in which the second and third volumes, covering H-Z will appear before the end of 1977. The work contains 414,825 words, 1,827,306 illustrative quotations and reputedly 227,779,589 letters and figures.

Bible

Oldest. The oldest known Bible is the *Codex Vaticanus*, written in Greek *ante*-350 A.D., and preserved in the Vatican Museum, Rome.

The earliest Bible printed in English was edited by Miles Coverdale (*c*. 1488–1569), printed in 1535 at Marberg in Hesse, Germany. The New Testament in English had, however, been printed by William Tyndale in Cologne and in Worms, Germany, in 1525.

Longest and Shortest Books. The longest book in the Authorized Version (King James) of the Bible is the Book of Psalms, while the longest book, including prose, is the Book of the Prophet Isaiah, with 66 chapters. The shortest is the Third Epistle of John, with 294 words in 14 verses. The Second Epistle of John has only 13 verses but 298 words.

Longest Psalm, Verse, Sentence and Name. Of the 150 Psalms, the longest is the 119th, with 176 verses, and the shortest is the 117th, with two verses. The shortest verse in the English Authorized Version of the Bible is verse 35 of Chapter XI of the Gospel according to St. John, consisting of the two words "Jesus wept." The longest is verse 9 of Chapter VIII of the Book of Esther, which extends to a 90-word description of the Persian empire. The total number of letters in the Bible is 3,566,480. The total number of words depends on the method of counting hyphenated words, but is usually given as between 773,692 and 773,746.

The word "and" appears 46,227 times, according to Colin McKay Wilson (U.K.) of the Salvation Army.

The longest personal name is Maher-shalal-hash-baz, the symbolic name of the second son of Isaiah (Isaiah, Chapter VIII, verses 1 and 3). Longer by 2 letters is the title in the caption of Psalm 22, in Hebrew, sometimes rendered Al-'Ayyeleth Hash-Shahar (20 letters).

Most Prolific Writers

The most prolific writer for whom a word count has been published was Charles Hamilton, *alias* Frank Richards (1875–1961), the Englishman who created Billy Bunter. At the height of his career in 1908 he wrote the whole of the boys' comics *Gem* (founded 1907) and *Magnet* (founded 1908) and most of two others, totaling 80,000 words a·week. His lifetime output has been put at 100,000,000 words. He enjoyed the advantages of electric light rather than candlelight, and of being unmarried.

The champion of the goose-quill era was Józef Ignacy Kraszewski (1812–1887) of Poland, who produced more than 600 volumes of novels and historical works.

The greatest number of novels published by any author is 904 by Kathleen Lindsay (Mrs. Mary Faulkner) (1903–1973) of Somerset West, Cape Province, South Africa. She wrote under six pen names, two of them masculine.

From 1932 to 1973, the British novelist John Creasey (1908–73) wrote under his own name and 13 *aliases*, 564 books totaling more than 40,000,000 words. Previously, he had received a probable record 743 rejection slips.

Enid Mary Blyton (Mrs. Derrell Waters) (1900–68) of England, completed 600 titles of children's stories, many of them brief, with 59 in the single year 1955. They have been translated into a record 128 languages.

Fastest Novelist. The world's fastest novelist was Erle Stanley Gardner (1889–1970), the popular mystery writer who created Perry Mason. He dictated up to 10,000 words per day and worked with his staff on as many as seven novels simultaneously. His sales on 140 titles reached 170,000,000 by his death.

The British novelist John Creasey (see above) had an output of 15 to 20 novels per annum, with a record of 22. He once wrote two books in a week with a half-day off.

Fastest Playwright. British writer (Richard) Edgar (Horatio) Wallace (1875–1932) began his play *On the Spot* on a Friday and finished it by lunchtime on the following Sunday. This included the stage directions and, unusually, after the production the prompt copy was identical to his original. The shortest time in which he wrote a novel was in the case of *The Three Oaks Mystery* which he started on a Tuesday and delivered typed to his publishers on the following Friday.

Earliest Authoress

The earliest recorded authoress was Princess Enheduanna, daughter of King Sargon of Akkad, Iraq, whose 153-verse religious poem *Nin-me-shar-ra* was published *c.* 2300 B.C.

Oldest Authoress

The oldest authoress in the world is Mrs. Alice Pollock (*née* Wykeham-Martin) (b. July 2, 1868) of Haslemere, Surrey, England, whose book "Portrait of My Victorian Youth" (Johnson Publications) was published in March, 1971, when she was aged 102 years 8 months.

Youngest Authoress

The youngest recorded commercially-published author is Dorothy Straight (born May 25, 1958) of Washington, D.C., who wrote *How the World Began* in 1962, aged 4. It was published in August, 1964, by Pantheon Books, New York.

Highest-Paid Writer

The highest rate ever offered to a writer was $30,000 to Ernest Miller Hemingway (1899–1961) for a 2,000-word article on bull-fighting by *Sports Illustrated* in January, 1960. This was a rate of $15 per word. In 1958, a Mrs. Deborah Schneider of Minneapolis,

OLDEST AND YOUNGEST AUTHORESSES: Mrs. Alice Pollock had her latest book published in 1971 when she was more than 102 years old. Dorothy Straight, of Washington, D.C., had her first book published at the age of 4.

TOP-SELLING AUTHOR (left): Agatha Christie wrote 80 novels in her lifetime (as well as the longest-running play) and her books sell in the U.K. alone in paperback about 1½ million copies a year. LEAST SUCCESSFUL AUTHOR (right): William Gold has earned only 50 cents after 18 years of unceasing labor.

Minnesota, wrote 25 words to complete a sentence in a competition for the best blurb for Plymouth cars. She won from about 1,400,000 entrants the prize of $500 every month for life. On normal life expectations she would collect $12,000 per word. No known anthology includes Mrs. Schneider's deathless prose.

Top-Selling Author

Among writers of fiction, sales alone of over 300,000,000 have been claimed for Georges Simenon (Belgium) and for the British authoress Dame Agatha Christie (née Agatha Mary Clarissa Miller), later Lady Mallowan (formerly Mrs. Archibald Christie) (1890–1976). Her 80 crime novels have been translated into 103 languages.

Least Successful Author

The world's declared least successful writer is William A. Gold (born London, June 29, 1922). After 18 years of unremitting work involving over 3,000,000 words (including 8 full-length books written to completion and 7 novels) he struck "pay dirt" with a 50-cent remittance from a newspaper in Canberra, Australia, on May 24, 1974. Until this bonanza his closest approach to success had been the publication in 1958 of a 150-word book review in the *Workers Education Association Bulletin* in Adelaide, Australia, on the clear understanding that it would be published only if he did not demand a fee.

Most Rejections

The greatest recorded number of publishers' rejections for a manuscript is 80 for "World Government Crusade" by Gilbert Young (born 1906). His public meeting in Bath, England, in support of his parliamentary candidacy as a World Government Candidate, however, drew a crowd of one.

Highest Printings

The world's most widely distributed book is the Bible, portions of which have been translated into 1,399 languages. This compares with 222 languages for Lenin. It has been estimated that between 1800 and 1950 some 1,500,000,000 Bibles were printed, of which 1,100,000,000 were handled by Bible Societies. The total distribution of complete Bibles by the United Bible Societies of the United States in the year 1972 was 5,519,909.

It has been reported that 800,000,000 copies of the red-covered booklet *Quotations from the Works of Mao Tse-tung* were sold or distributed between June, 1966, when possession became virtually mandatory in China, up to September, 1971, when their promoter, Marshal Lin Piao, was killed. The name of Mao Tse-tung (born December 26, 1893) means literally "Hair Enrich-East."

On March 13, 1953, it was announced that 672,058,000 copies of the works of Marshal Iosif Vissarionovich Dzhugashvili, *alias* Stalin (1879–1953), had been sold or distributed in 101 languages.

The total disposal through non-commercial channels by Jehovah's Witnesses of the 190-page hardbound book, *The Truth That Leads to Eternal Life*, published by the Watchtower Bible and Tract Society of Brooklyn, New York, on May 8, 1968, reached 74,000,000 in 91 languages by April, 1975.

Best Sellers

The world's all-time best selling book is the annual reference work, *The World Almanac & Book of Facts*, first published in 1868, and currently edited by George E. Delury. Its cumulative sale to October, 1976, is estimated at 36,000,000 copies, increasing by 1,100,000 each year.

The authors who have written the fastest selling title are Norris Dewar McWhirter (born August 12, 1925) and his twin brother Alan Ross McWhirter (killed November 27, 1975), editors and compilers of the *Guinness Book of World Records*, first published from 107 Fleet Street, London, England, in October, 1955. In July, 1976, global sales in 14 languages had reached 28,500,000 copies.

Self-Produced. Mrs. Carla Emery of Kendrick, Idaho, has written, printed, published and distributed 18,000 copies of her 628-page *Old Fashioned Recipe Book* up to May, 1975.

Slowest Seller. The accolade for the world's slowest selling book (known in publishing as slooow-sellers) probably belongs to David Wilkins' Translation of the New Testament from Coptic into Latin, published by Oxford University Press in 1716 in 500 copies. Selling an average of one each 139 days it was in print for 191 years.

Fiction. The novel with the highest sales has been *Valley of the Dolls* (first published in March, 1966) by Jacqueline Susann (1921–1974) with a worldwide total of 19,300,000 copies by May, 1976. Within the first six months after paperback publication by Bantam in 1967, some 6,800,000 copies were sold.

MOST SUCCESSFUL SLOGANEER: Jack Gasnick "invented" this slogan in 1929 and has sold 50 million buttons of it since 1950.

Longest Literary Gestation

The standard German dictionary *Deutsches Wörterbuch*, begun by the brothers Grimm in 1854, was finished in 1971. *Acta Sanctorum*, begun by Jean Bolland in 1643, arranged according to saints' days, reached the month of November in 1925, and an introduction for December was published in 1940.

Post Cards. The top-selling post card of all time was said to be a drawing by Donald McGill (1875–1962) with the caption: He: "How do you like Kipling?" She: "I don't know, you naughty boy, I've never Kippled." It sold about 6,000,000. Between 1904 and his death McGill sold more than 350,000,000 cards to users and deltiologists (picture post card collectors). See the color photograph on color page E.

The world's first post cards were issued in Vienna on October 1, 1869. Pin-up girls came into vogue in 1914 having been pioneered in 1900 by Raphaël Kirchner (1876–1917). The most expensive on record were ones made in ivory for an Indian prince which involved the killing of 60 elephants.

Most Successful Sloganeer. "Think Mink" invented by Jack Gasnick (b. 1918) in 1929 has sold in metal, celluloid and ribbon 50,000,000 since 1950. His *"Cross at the Green . . . not in Between Enterprises"* of New York City has sold 55,000,000 buttons, badges and tabs and 40,000,000 other pieces.

Poetry

Poets Laureate. The earliest official Poet Laureate was John Dryden (1631–1700), appointed in April, 1668. It is recorded that Henry I (1100–1135) had a King's versifier named Wale. The youngest Poet Laureate was Laurence Eusden (1688–1730), who received the bays on December 24, 1718, at the age of 30 years and 3 months. The greatest age at which a poet has succeeded is 73 in the case of William Wordsworth (1770–1850) on April 6, 1843. The longest-lived Laureate was John Masefield, O.M., who died on

May 12, 1967, aged 88 years 11 months. The longest which any poet has worn the laurel is 41 years 322 days, in the case of Alfred (later the 1st Lord) Tennyson (1809–92), who was appointed on November 19, 1850, and died in office on October 6, 1892.

Longest Poem. The longest poem ever written was the *Mahabharata* which appeared in India in the period *c.* 400 to 150 B.C. It runs to 220,000 lines and nearly 3,000,000 words. The longest poem ever written in the English language appears to be one on the life of King Alfred by John Fitchett (1766–1838) of Liverpool, England, which ran to 129,807 lines and took 40 years to write. His editor, Robert Riscoe, added the concluding 2,585 lines.

Shortest Poem. The shortest poem in the *Oxford Dictionary of Quotations* is *On the Antiquity of Microbes* and consists of the 3 words: "Adam, Had 'em."

Largest Publishers

The largest publisher in the world is the U.S. Government Printing Office in Washington, D.C. The Superintendent of Documents Division dispatches more than 150,000,000 items every year. The annual list of new titles and annuals is about 6,000.

Fastest Publishing

The shortest interval between the receipt of a manuscript and the publication of a book is 66½ hours, in the case of *The Pope's Journey to the United States—the Historic Record*, a paperback of 160 pages, costing 75 cents, written by 51 editors of the strike-bound *New York Times* and published by Bantam Books, Inc. of New York City. It was printed by the W. F. Hall Printing Co. of Chicago. The first article reached the publishers at 1:30 p.m. on October 4, 1965, and completed copies came off the printers' presses at 8:00 a.m. on October 7, 1965.

Largest Printers

The largest printers in the world are R. R. Donnelly & Co. of Chicago. The company, founded in 1864, has plants in seven main centers, and has turned out $250,000,000 worth of work per year from 180 presses, 125 composing machines and more than 50 binding lines. Nearly 18,000 tons of inks and 450,000 tons of paper and board are consumed every year.

Largest Print Order

The initial print order for the 49th Automobile Association (England) Members' Handbook (1976–77) was 3,700,000 copies. The total print run since 1908 has been 67,710,000.

Most Durable Typesetter

James Donohue (1884–1974) typeset an estimated 200,000,000 words of *The Anglo-Celt* newspaper in Cavan, Ireland, from 1898 to 1967.

Largest Cartoon

The largest cartoon ever exhibited was one covering five stories

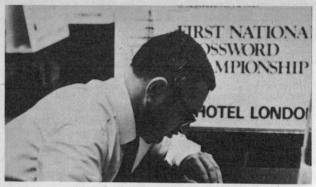

FASTEST CROSSWORD SOLVER: In a contest Roy Dean solved a difficult
puzzle from the London "Times" in 3¾ minutes.

(50 feet by 150 feet) of a University of Arizona building, drawn by
Peter A. Kesling for Mom 'n' Dad's Day, 1954.

Longest-Lived Comic Strip
The most durable newspaper comic strip has been the Katzen-
jammer Kids (Hans and Fritz) created by Rudolph Dirks, first published in the *New York Journal* on December 12, 1897, and currently
drawn by Joe Musial. The earliest strip was Little Bear by Jim Lyons
(b. 1876), which first appeared in the *San Francisco Examiner* in 1894.
The most widely syndicated is Blondie, which appears in 1,600
newspapers in 50 countries.

Autographs
Earliest. The earliest English sovereign whose handwriting is
known to have survived is Edward III (1327–1377). The earliest full
signature to have survived is that of Richard II (dated July 26, 1386).
The Magna Carta does not bear even the mark of King John (reigned
1199–1216), but carries only his seal. An attested cross of King
Canute (1016–1035) has survived.

Most Expensive Autographs. The highest price ever paid on
the open market for a single letter is $51,000, paid in 1927 for a
letter written by Button Gwinnett (1732–77), one of the three men
from Georgia to sign the Declaration of Independence on July 4,
1776. Such an item would probably attract bids of up to $250,000
today.

If one of the six known signatures of William Shakespeare (1564–
1616) were to come on the market or if a new one were discovered
the price would doubtless set a record.

Letters
Longest. The longest personal letter based on word count is one
of 720,000 words written in 9 months by Boyd Cabanaw of Bartles-
ville, Oklahoma, to irritate his cousin Andrew L. Cairns of Minnesota, on July 11, 1974.

To the Editor. The longest recorded letter to an editor was one of 13,000 words (a third of a modern novel) written to the editor of the *Fishing Gazette* by A.R.I.E.L. and published in 7-point type spread over two issues in 1884.

Crossword Puzzles

The earliest crossword was one with 32 clues invented by Arthur Wynne (born Liverpool, England) and published in the *New York World* on December 21, 1913.

Largest. The largest crossword ever published was one with 2,631 clues across and 2,922 clues down, compiled by Hank Koval, assistant producer of A.B.C.'s *Let's Make a Deal*, between February 22, 1974, and October 1, 1975. It measures 16.66 square feet and is published by Price/Stern/Sloan Publishers Inc. of Los Angeles, California.

The largest crosswords regularly published are "Mammoth" crosswords based on grids of 73 by 73 (5,329 total) squares with up to 828 clues by First Features Ltd., Hastings, England, since May 1, 1970. Edward Akenhead, *The Times* (London) Crossword Editor, succeeded in 1971 in including in a puzzle the word "honorifieabili-tudinitatibus."

Fastest Solution. The fastest recorded time for completing *The Times* (London) crossword under test conditions is 3 minutes 45.0 seconds by Roy Dean, 43, of Bromley, Kent, in the BBC "Today" radio studio on December 19, 1970.

Slowest. In May, 1966, *The Times* of London received an announcement from a Fijian woman that she had just succeeded in completing their crossword No. 673 in the issue of April 4, 1932.

Oldest Map

The oldest known map of any kind is a clay tablet depicting the Euphrates River flowing through northern Mesopotamia (Iraq), dated *c.* 3800 B.C.

The earliest printed map in the world dates from Isodore of Sevillés *Etymologarum* of 1472.

The least informative map is Sheet 281 of the 1:2500 scale map of Siteki, published by the Swaziland Government Public Work Department, which consists of a single diagonal line. Copies can be obtained from P.O. Box 58, Mbabane, Swaziland.

Birthday Cards

The most parsimonious recorded use of a birthday card is one which has shuttled 82 times between C. R. Findley of Vancouver, British Columbia, Canada, and Douglas Bohn of Seattle, Washington, since November, 1933.

Christmas Cards

The greatest number of personal Christmas cards sent out is believed to be 62,824 by Werner Erhard of San Francisco, California, in December, 1975.

Libraries

Earliest. The earliest public library was the Zaluski Library, opened in Warsaw, Poland, in 1747.

Largest. The largest library in the world is the Library of Congress (founded on April 24, 1800), on Capitol Hill, Washington, D.C. By 1973, it contained more than 74,000,000 items, including 16,466,899 books and pamphlets. The buildings contain 35 acres of floor space and 327 miles of book shelves.

The tallest library is the University of Massachusetts Library, Amherst, Mass., with 28 stories and a height of 296 feet 4 inches, opened in May, 1973.

The Lenin State Library in Moscow, U.S.S.R. (founded 1862), claims to house 27,000,000 books, but this total is understood to include periodicals.

The largest non-statutory library in the world is the New York Public Library (founded 1895) on Fifth Avenue, New York City, with a floor area of 525,276 square feet and 80 miles of shelving. Including 83 branch libraries, its collection embraces 8,605,610 volumes, 10,683,105 manuscripts, and 317,183 maps.

Overdue Books. It was reported on December 7, 1968, that a book on febrile diseases (London, 1805, by Dr. J. Currie) checked out in 1823 from the University of Cincinnati Medical Library was returned by the borrower's great-grandson Richard Dodd. The fine was calculated as $22,646, but waived.

Newspapers

Most. The U.S. had 1,768 English-language daily newspapers on January 1, 1975. They had a combined net paid circulation of 61,877,197 copies per day at September 30, 1974. The peak year for U.S. newspapers was 1910, when there were 2,202. The leading newspaper readers in the world are the people of Sweden, where 515 newspapers were sold for each 1,000 of the population in 1967–68.

Oldest. The oldest existing newspaper in the world is the Swedish official journal *Post och Inrikes Tidningar*, founded in 1644. It is published by the Royal Swedish Academy of Letters. The oldest existing commercial newspaper is the *Haarlems Dagblad/Oprechte*

Haarlemsche Courant, published in Haarlem, in the Netherlands. The *Courant* was first issued as the *Weeckelycke Courante van Europa* on January 8, 1656, and a copy of issue No. 1 survives.

Largest. The most massive single issue of a newspaper was *The New York Times* of Sunday, October 17, 1965. It comprised 15 sections with a total of 946 pages, including about 1,200,000 lines of advertising. Each copy weighed $7\frac{1}{2}$ lbs. and sold for 50 cents locally.

The largest page size ever used has been 51 inches by 35 inches for *The Constellation*, printed in 1859 by George Roberts as part of the Fourth of July celebrations in New York City.

The smallest recorded page size has been 3 inches by $3\frac{3}{4}$ inches, as used in the *Daily Banner* of Roseburg, Oregon (25 cents per month), an issue of which, dated February 2, 1876, survives.

Highest Circulation. The first newspaper to achieve a circulation of 1,000,000 was *Le Petit Journal*, published in Paris, which reached this figure in 1886, when selling at 5 centimes (fractionally more than one cent) per copy.

The claim exercised for the world's highest circulation is that by the *Asahi Shimbun* (founded 1879) of Japan with a figure which attained more than 11,171,790 copies in March, 1976. This, however, has been achieved by totaling the figures for editions published in various centers with a morning figure of 6,851,397 and an evening figure of 4,320,393.

The highest circulation of any evening newspaper is that of the *Evening News*, established in London in 1881. The latest figure is 577,457 copies per issue (average for July 1 to December 31, 1975), with an average readership of 1,694,000.

Most Read. The newspaper which achieves the closest to a saturation circulation is *The Sunday Post*, established in Glasgow, Scotland, in 1914. In 1975, its total estimated readership of 4,601,000 represented more than 77 per cent of Scotland's entire population aged 15 and over.

Periodicals

Largest Circulation. The largest circulation of any weekly periodical is that of *TV Guide*, which, in 1974, became the first magazine in history to sell 1,000 million copies in a year. The 1975 weekly average was 19,426,263.

In its 30 international editions the *Reader's Digest* (established February, 1922) circulates 29,150,000 copies monthly, in 13 languages, including a U.S. edition of more than 17,750,000 copies.

Oldest. The oldest continuing periodical in the world is the *Philosophical Transactions of the Royal Society*, which first appeared on March 6, 1665.

Advertising Rates. The highest price asked for advertising for a single page has been $84,100 for a four-color back cover of the now-defunct *Life* magazine (circulation 8,500,000 per week) from January, 1969, to January, 1971. The current record is $64,995 for a four-color page in *Reader's Digest* in January, 1976.

The highest expenditure ever incurred on a single advertisement in a periodical is $1,028,410 by the Bicentennial Commission of Pennsylvania for a detachable 48-page insert in the March, 1976, issue of the U.S. edition of the *Reader's Digest*.

The world's highest newspaper advertising rate is 21,438,000 yen ($70,745) for a full page in both morning and evening editions of the *Asahi Shimbun* of Tokyo.

Music

Instruments

Oldest. The world's oldest surviving musical notation is a heptonic scale deciphered from a clay tablet by Dr. Duchesne-Guillemin in 1966–67. The tablet has been dated to *c.* 1800 B.C. and was found at a site in Nippur, Sumeria, now Iraq. Also dated *c.* 1800 B.C. is an Assyrian love song to a Ugarit god, reconstructed for an 11-string lyre from a tablet of notation and lyric at the University of California, Berkeley, on March 6, 1974. Musical history is, however, able to be traced back to the 3rd millennium B.C., when the yellow bell (*huang chung*) had a recognized standard musical tone in Chinese temple music. Whistles and flutes made from perforated phalange bones have been found at Upper Paleolithic sites of the Aurignacian Period (*c.* 25,000–22,000 B.C.), *e.g.* at Istallosko, Hungary, and in Molodova, U.S.S.R.

Earliest Piano. The earliest pianoforte in existence is one built in Florence, Italy, in 1720, by Bartolommeo Cristofori (1655–1731) of Padua, and now preserved in the Metropolitan Museum of Art, New York.

Grandest Piano. The grandest grand piano was one of 1¼ tons, 11 feet 8 inches long, made by Chas. H. Challen & Son Ltd. of London in 1935. The longest bass string measured 9 feet 11 inches and the tensile stress on the 726-lb. frame was 3.3 tons.

Organs. The largest and loudest musical instrument ever constructed is the Auditorium Organ in Atlantic City, New Jersey. Completed in 1930, this heroic instrument has two consoles (one with seven manuals and another movable one with five), 1,477 stop controls and 33,112 pipes ranging in tone from $\frac{3}{16}$ of an inch to the 64-foot tone. It is powered with blower motors of 365 horse-power, cost $500,000 and has the volume of 25 brass bands, with a range of seven octaves. It is now only partially functional.

The world's largest church organ is that in Passau Cathedral, Germany. It was completed in 1928 by D. F. Steinmeyer & Co. It has 16,000 pipes and five manuals.

The world's only five-manual electric organ was installed in Carnegie Hall, New York City, in September, 1974.

The grand organ at John Wanamaker's department store in Philadelphia, installed in 1911, was enlarged until by 1930 it had six manuals and 30,067 pipes including a 64-foot tone Gravissima.

The loudest organ stop in the world is the Ophicleide stop of the Grand Great in the Solo Organ in the Atlantic City Auditorium (see above). It is operated by a pressure of 100 inches of water (3½ lbs.

per square inch) and has a pure trumpet note of earsplitting volume, more than six times the volume of the loudest locomotive whistles.

Youngest Organist. Henry Alban Chambers was appointed organist at Leeds' Cathedral, West Yorkshire, England, in 1913 at the age of 11.

Oldest Organist. The longest recorded career as an organist is 76 years in the case of Warren F. Acker, Mus.D., of Allentown, Pennsylvania (born March 30, 1883), who began his career as an organist in the Ebenezar Evangelical Church in 1900 and was "still going good" in 1976.

Organ Marathons. The longest church organ recital ever sustained was one of 90 hours by Frank Hughes at Wesley College Chapel, Dublin, Ireland on October 31–November 4, 1975.

The duration for playing an electric organ is 200 hours by Vince Bull of Scunthorpe, England, at the Comet Hotel, Scunthorpe, finishing on June 28, 1976. The last record on the discontinued category of non-stop organ playing (without 5-minute rest breaks) was 53 hours 36 minutes by Bonni Golde at Castleford, West Yorkshire, England on June 25–28, 1974.

The longest recorded non-stop harmonium (small organ) marathon is 72 hours by Iain Stinson and John Whiteley, both of the Royal Holloway College, at Englefield Green, Surrey, England, on February 6–9, 1970.

Accordion Marathon. Tony Bellus played an electric accordion for 53 hours at the Holiday Inn, Oakbrook Terrace, Illinois, December 11–13, 1975.

String Instruments. The largest stringed instrument ever constructed was a pantaleon with 270 strings stretched over 50 square feet, used by George Noel in 1767.

Largest Guitar. The largest and presumably also the loudest playable guitar in the world is one 8 feet 10 inches tall, weighing 80 lbs. and with a volume of 16,000 cubic inches (*cf.* the standard 1,024 cubic inches) built by The Harmony Company of Chicago and completed in April, 1970. It carries a $15,000 price tag, and is now on display at the Guinness World Records Exhibit Hall in New York City. (A duplicate is being prepared for the Guinness Museum in Las Vegas.)

The most expensive standard-sized guitar is the German chittara battente, built by Jacob Stadler (dated 1624), which sold for £10,500 ($25,200) at Christie's, London, on June 12, 1974.

Largest Double Bass. The largest bass viol ever constructed was an octo-bass 10 feet tall, built *c.* 1845 by J. B. Vuillaume (1798–1875) of France. Because the stretch was too great for any musician's finger-span, the stopping was effected by foot levers. It was played in London in 1851.

Most Valuable Violin. The highest recorded price for a violin is the $250,000 (£104,166) paid by a private buyer to Harry A. Duffy for the Cessole Stradivarius of 1716 in December, 1972. On this valuation the "Messie" Stradivarius in the Ashmolean Museum at Oxford, England, is now worth some £200,000 ($460,000). An inventory of 700 known or recorded string instruments made by Antonio Stradivari (1644–1737) is contained in the *Violin Iconography* by Herbert K. Goodkind. Those made between 1720 and 1730 reached a "tonal zenith."

Underwater Violinist. The only violinist to surmount the problems of playing the violin under water has been Mark Gottlieb. Submerged in the Evergreen State College swimming pool in Olympia, Washington, in March, 1975, he gave a submarine rendition of Handel's Water Music. He is still working on both his bow speed and his *detaché*. (See color photograph on color page F.)

Most Durable Fiddler. Otto E. Funk, 62, walked 4,165 miles from New York City to San Francisco, playing his Hopf violin every step of the way westward. He arrived on June 16, 1929, after 183 days on the road.

Brass Instruments. The largest recorded brass instrument is a tuba standing 7½ feet tall, with 39 feet of tubing and a bell 3 feet 4 inches across. This contrabass tuba was constructed for a world tour by the band of John Philip Sousa (1854–1932), the "march king," *c.* 1896–98, and is still in use. This instrument is now owned by a circus promoter in South Africa.

Longest Alphorn. The longest alphorn is 32 feet 9½ inches long, reported from Aschau bei Kraiburg, Bavaria, West Germany. It requires three blowers.

Largest Drum. The largest drum in the world is the Disneyland Big Bass Drum with a diameter of 10 feet 6 inches and a weight of

LARGEST TUBA (left): This 7½-foot-tall giant uses 39 feet of tubing. LARGEST GUITAR (below): Priced at $15,000, this 8-foot-10-inch-tall guitar made by the Harmony Company of Chicago must be played by two musicians.

450 lbs. It was built in 1961 by Remo, Inc., of North Hollywood, California, and is mounted on wheels and towed by a tractor.

Most Players for an Instrument. The greatest number of musicians required to operate a single instrument was the six required to play the gigantic orchestrion, known as the Apollonican, built in 1816 and played until 1840.

Orchestras

Most. The greatest number of professional orchestras maintained in one country is 94 in West Germany. The total number of symphony orchestras in the U.S., including "community" orchestras, was estimated to be 1,436, including 31 major and 95 metropolitan orchestras, as of June, 1976.

Largest. The vastest "orchestras" ever recorded were those assembled on Band Day at the University of Michigan, Ann Arbor. In some years between 1958 and 1965 the total number of instrumentalists reached 13,500.

On June 17, 1872, Johann Strauss the younger (1825–99) conducted an orchestra of 2,000, supported by a choir of 20,000, at the World Peace Jubilee in Boston, Massachusetts. The number of violinists was more than 350.

Largest Marching Band. The largest on record was one of 1,976 musicians and 54 drill majors, flag bearers and directors who marched 2 miles down Pennsylvania Avenue, Washington, D.C., in President Nixon's Second Inaugural Parade, January 20, 1973.

Greatest Classical Attendance. The greatest attendance at any classical concert was an estimated 150,000 for a presentation by the New York Philharmonic Orchestra, conducted by Andre Kostelanetz, at Sheep Meadow in Central Park, New York City, on July 29, 1975.

Pop Festival Attendance. The greatest estimated attendance was 600,000 for a rock festival at Watkins Glen, New York, on July 28, 1973. Billed as a "day of music in the country," it resulted in at least one death, 150 persons hospitalized (some from an overdose of drugs) and one of the worst traffic jams in New York State history. It ended with a drenching thunderstorm.

Highest and Lowest Notes. The extremes of orchestral instruments (excluding the organ) range between a handbell tuned to g′′′′′ or 6,272 cycles per second, and the sub-contrabass clarinet, which can reach $C_{,,}$ or 16.4 cycles per second. The highest note on a standard pianoforte is 4,186 cycles per second which is also the violinist's limit. In 1873, a sub double bassoon able to reach $B_{,,,}\sharp$ or 14.6 cycles per second was constructed, but no surviving specimen is known. The extremes for the organ are g′′′′′ (the sixth G above middle C) (12,544 cycles per sec.) and $C_{,,,}$ (8.12 cycles per sec.) obtainable from ¾-inch and 64-foot pipes, respectively.

Composers

Most Prolific. The most prolific composer of all time was probably Georg Philipp Telemann (1681–1767) of Germany. He composed 12 complete sets of services (one cantata every Sunday) for a year, 78 services for special occasions, 40 operas, 600 to 700 orchestral suites, 44 Passions, plus concertos and chamber music.

The most prolific symphonist was Johann Melchior Molter (c. 1695–1765) of Germany, who wrote 169. Joseph Haydn (1732–1809) of Austria, wrote 104 numbered symphonies, some of which are regularly played today.

Most Rapid. Among classical composers the most rapid was Wolfgang Amadeus Mozart (1756–91) of Austria, who wrote 1,000 operas, operettas, symphonies, violin sonatas, divertimenti, serenades, motets, concertos for piano and many other instruments, string quartets, other chamber music, masses and litanies, of which only 70 were published before he died, aged 35. His opera *The Clemency of Titus* (1791) was written in 18 days and three symphonic masterpieces, *Symphony No. 39 in E flat major, Symphony in G minor* and the *Jupiter Symphony in C*, were reputedly written in the space of 42 days in 1788. His overture to *Don Giovanni* was written in full score at one sitting in Prague in 1787 and finished on the day of its opening performance.

National Anthems

The oldest national anthem is the *Kimigayo* of Japan, in which the words date from the 9th century. The anthem of Greece constitutes the first four verses of the Solomos poem, which has 158 verses. The shortest anthems are those of Japan, Jordan and San Marino, each with only four lines. The anthems of Bahrain and Qatar have no words at all.

Longest Rendering

"God Save the King" was played non-stop 16 or 17 times by a German military band on the platform of Rathenau Railway Station, Brandenburg, on the morning of February 9, 1909. The reason was that King Edward VII was struggling inside the train to get into his German Field-Marshal uniform before he could emerge.

Longest Symphony

The longest of all single classical symphonies is the orchestral symphony No. 3 in D minor by Gustav Mahler (1860–1911) of Austria. This work, composed in 1895, requires a contralto, a women's and a boys' choir and an organ, in addition to a full orchestra. A full performance requires 1 hour 34 minutes, of which the first movement alone takes 45 minutes.

The Symphony No. 2 (the Gothic, now renumbered as No. 1), composed in 1919–22 by Havergal Brian (1876–1972), has been performed only twice, on June 24, 1961, and October 30, 1966.

The total *ensemble* included 55 brass instruments, 31 woodwind, six kettledrummers playing 22 drums, four vocal soloists, four large mixed choruses, a children's chorus and an organ. The symphony is continuous and required, when played as a recording on November 27, 1967, 100 minutes. Havergal Brian wrote an even vaster work based on Shelley's *Prometheus Unbound* lasting 4 hours

LONGEST CLASSICAL SYMPHONY: One work by Gustav Mahler (left) lasts more than 1½ hours. HIGHEST-PAID MUSICIANS: Jan Paderewski (middle) made $5 million playing the piano; while Fritz Kreisler (right) made $3 million with his violin.

11 minutes but the full score has been missing since 1961. He wrote 27 symphonies, 4 grand operas and 7 large orchestra works between 1948 when he was 72 and 1968.

The symphony *Victory at Sea* written by Richard Rodgers and arranged by Robert Russell Bennett for NBC-TV in 1952 lasted for 13 hours.

Longest Piano Composition

The longest non-repetitious piece for piano ever composed was the Opus Clavicembalisticum by Kaikhosru Shapurji Sorabji (born 1892). The composer himself gave it its only public performance on December 1, 1930, in Glasgow, Scotland. The work is in 12 movements with a theme and 49 variations and a passacaglia with 81 and a playing time of 2¾ hours.

The longest musical composition of any kind is all 40,320 possible permutations of the C major scale for piano and organ. The score is a complete print-out in 16 volumes named *Sadist Factory* by its organizer, Philip Crevier. The premiere was in Trinity College Chapel, Hartford, Connecticut, on August 9–13, 1973. It took 9 players exactly 100 hours to reach the best part—the end.

Longest Silence

The most protracted silence in a modern composition is one entitled *4 minutes 33 seconds* in a totally silent *opus* by John Cage (U.S.). Commenting on this trend among modern composers, Igor Fyodorovich Stravinsky (1882–1971) said that he now looked forward to their subsequent compositions being "works of major length."

Highest-Paid Musicians

Pianist. The highest-paid classical concert pianist was Ignace Jan Paderewski (1860–1941), Prime Minister of Poland in 1919–21, who accumulated a fortune estimated at $5,000,000, of which $500,000 was earned in a single season in 1922–23.

Liberace (born 1919 in West Allis, Wisconsin) earns more than $2,000,000 for each 26-week season with a peak of $138,000 for a

YOUNGEST OPERA SINGER was Ginetta La Bianca (left) who made her debut before she was 16. **WEALTHIEST SINGER** (right) was Enrico Caruso, the Italiah tenor, who left an estate of $9,000,000 when he died in 1921 at the age of 48. His recording of "Vesti la giubba" from "I Pagliacci" was the first to sell a million copies (see page 240).

single night's performance at Madison Square Garden, New York City, in 1954.

Violinist. The Austrian-born Fritz Kreisler (1875–1962) is reputed to have received more than $3,000,000 during his career.

Drummer. The most highly paid drummer, or indeed "side man" of any kind, is Bernard ("Buddy") Rich (born 1917), in the band of Harry James, at more than $75,000 per annum.

Singers. Of great fortunes earned by singers, the highest on record are those of Enrico Caruso (1873–1921), the Italian tenor, whose estate was about $9,000,000, and the Italian-Spanish coloratura soprano Amelita Galli-Curci (1889–1963), who received about $3,000,000. In 1850, up to $653 was paid for a single seat at the concerts given in the U.S. by Johanna ("Jenny") Maria Lind (1820–87), later Mrs. Otto Goldschmidt, the "Swedish Nightingale." She had a range of nearly three octaves, of which the middle register is still regarded as unrivaled.

While no agreement exists as to the identity of history's greatest singer, there is unanimity on the worst. The excursions of the soprano Florence Foster Jenkins (1868–1944) into lieder and even high coloratura culminated on October 25, 1944, in her sell-out concert at Carnegie Hall, New York. The diva's (already high) high F was said to have been made higher in 1943 by a crash in a taxi. It is one of the tragedies of musicology that Madame Jenkins' *Clavelitos*, accompanied by Cosme McMoon, was never recorded for posterity.

Opera

Longest. The longest of commonly performed operas is *Die Meistersinger von Nürnberg* by Wilhelm Richard Wagner (1813–83) of Germany. A normal uncut performance of this opera as performed by the Sadler's Wells company between August 24 and September 19, 1968, entailed 5 hours 15 minutes of music. An opera, *The Life and Times of Joseph Stalin*, performed in 7 acts at the Brooklyn Academy of Music on December 14–15, 1973, required 13 hours 25 mins. Act 7 was deemed by some to be the best.

Shortest. The shortest opera written was *The Deliverance of Theseus* by Darius Milhaud (born September, 1892), first performed in 1928, which lasts for 7 minutes 27 seconds.

Aria. The longest single aria, in the sense of an operatic solo, is Brünnhilde's immolation scene in Wagner's *Götterdämmerung*. A well-known recording has been precisely timed at 14 minutes 46 seconds.

Opera House—Largest. The largest opera house in the world is the Metropolitan Opera House, Lincoln Center, New York City, completed in September, 1966, at a cost of $45,700,000. It has a capacity of 3,800 seats in an auditorium 451 feet deep. The stage is 234 feet in width and 146 feet deep. The tallest opera house is one housed in a 42-story building on Wacker Drive in Chicago.

Opera Houses—Most Tiers. The Teatro della Scala (La Scala) in Milan, Italy, shares with the Bolshoi Theatre in Moscow, U.S.S.R., the distinction of having the greatest number of tiers. Each has six, with the topmost in Moscow being termed the Galurka.

Opera Singers—Youngest and Oldest. The youngest opera singer in the world has been Jeanette Gloria (Ginetta) La Bianca, born in Buffalo, New York, on May 12, 1934, who made her official debut as Rosina in *The Barber of Seville* at the Teatro dell'Opera, Rome, on May 8, 1950, aged 15 years 361 days, but who appeared as Gilda in *Rigoletto* at Velletri, Italy, 45 days earlier. Miss La Bianca was taught by Lucia Carlino and managed by Angelo Carlino.

The tenor Giovanni Martinelli sang Emperor Altoum in *Turandot* in Seattle, Washington, on February 4, 1967, when aged 81.

Bells

Oldest. The oldest bell is reputed to be that found in the Baby-lonian Palace of Nimrod in 1849 by Mr. (later Sir) Austen Henry Layard (1817–94). It dates from *c.* 1000 B.C.

Largest Carillon. The largest carillon in the world is planned for completion in 1976 in a 300-foot tower on the riverfront in Cincinnati, Ohio, with 83 bells.

HEAVIEST BELL: Tsar Kolokol, 216 tons and cracked (on the side not seen), has stood in the Kremlin, Moscow, since 1836.

Heaviest. The heaviest bell in the world is the Tsar Kolokol, cast in 1733 in Moscow, U.S.S.R. It weighs 216 tons, measures 22 feet 8 inches in diameter, is over 19 feet high, and its greatest thickness is 24 inches. The bell is cracked, and a fragment, weighing about 12 tons, is broken from it. The bell has stood on a platform in the Kremlin, in Moscow, since 1836.

The heaviest bell in use is the Mingun bell, weighing 90½ tons, in Mandalay, Burma, which is struck by a teak boom from the outside. The heaviest swinging bell in the world is the Petersglocke in Cologne Cathedral, Germany, which was cast in 1923. It has a diameter of 11 feet 1¾ inches and weighs 25 tons.

The heaviest tuned bell is the bourdon bell of the Laura Spelman Rockefeller Memorial carillon in Riverside Church, New York City. It weighs 40,926 lbs. and is 10 feet 2 inches in diameter.

Bell Ringing. Eight bells have been rung to their full "extent" (a complete "Bob Major" of 40,320 changes) only once without relays. This took place in a bell foundry at Loughborough, Leicestershire, England, beginning at 6:52 a.m. on July 27, 1963, and ending at 12:50 a.m. on July 28, after 17 hours 58 minutes. The peal was composed by Kenneth Lewis of Altrincham, Cheshire, and the eight ringers were conducted by Robert B. Smith, aged 25, of Marple, Cheshire. Theoretically it would take 37 years 355 days to ring 12 bells (maximus) to their full extent of 479,001,600 changes.

The greatest number of peals (minimum of 5,040 changes, all on tower bells) rung in a year is 209 by Mark William Marshall of Ashford, Kent, England, in 1973. The late George E. Fearn rang 2,666 peals from 1928 to May, 1974.

Song

Oldest. The oldest is the *chadouf* chant, which has been sung since time immemorial by irrigation workers on the man-powered treadwheel Nile water mills (or *saqiyas*) in Egypt. The English song *Sumer is icumen in* dates from *c.* 1240.

Top Songs of All Time. The most frequently sung songs in English are *Happy Birthday to You* (based on the original *Good Morning to All*, by Mildred and Patty S. Hill of New York, published in 1936 and in copyright until 1996); *For He's a Jolly Good Fellow* (originally the French *Malbrouk*), known at least as early as 1781, and *Auld Lang Syne* (originally the Strathspey *I fee'd a Lad at Michaelmass*), some words of which were written by Robert Burns (1759–96). *Happy Birthday* was sung in space by the Apollo IX astronauts on March 8, 1969.

Top Selling Sheet Music. Sales of three non-copyright pieces are known to have exceeded 20,000,000, namely *The Old Folks at Home*, *Listen to the Mocking Bird* (1855) and *The Blue Danube* (1867). Of copyright material, the two top-sellers are *Let Me Call You Sweetheart* (1910, by Whitson Friedman) and *Till We Meet Again* (1918, by Egan Whiting) each with some 6,000,000 by 1967.

Most Successful Song Writers. In terms of sales of single records, the most successful of all song writers have been John Lennon and Paul McCartney of The Beatles. Between 1962 and 1970 they wrote 30 songs which sold more than 1,000,000 records each.

Hymns

Earliest. There are believed to be more than 500,000 Christian hymns in existence. "Te Deum Laudamus" dates from about the 5th century, but the earliest exactly datable hymn is the French one "Jesus soit en ma teste et mon entendement" from 1490, translated into the well-known "God be in my head" in 1512.

Longest and Shortest. The longest hymn is "Hora novissima tempora pessima sunt; vigilemus" by Bernard of Cluny (12th century), which runs to 2,966 lines. In English the longest is "The Sands of Time are Sinking" by Mrs. Anne Ross Cousin, *née* Cundell (1824–1906), which is in full 152 lines, though only 32 lines in the Methodist Hymn Book. The shortest hymn is the single verse in Long Metre "Be Present at our Table, Lord," anonymous but attributed to "J. Leland."

Most Prolific Hymnists. Mrs. Frances Jan Van Alstyne, *née* Crosby (U.S.) (1820–1915) wrote more than 8,000 hymns although she had been blinded at the age of 6 weeks. She is reputed to have knocked off one hymn in 15 minutes. Charles Wesley (1707–88) wrote about 6,000 hymns. In the seventh (1950) edition of *Hymns Ancient and Modern* the works of John Mason Neale (1818–66) appear 56 times.

Longest Hymn-in. The Cambridge University Student Methodist Society (England) sang through the 984 hymns in the Methodist Hymn Book in 45 hours 42 minutes, and completed 1,000 hymns with 16 more requests in 88 minutes on February 7–9, 1969, in the Wesley Church, Cambridge.

Theatre

Origins. Theatre as we know it has its origins in Greek drama performed in honor of a god, usually Dionysus. The earliest amphitheatres date from the 5th century B.C. The largest of all known *orchestras* is one at Megalopolis in central Greece, where the auditorium reached a height of 75 feet and had a capacity of 17,000.

Oldest. The oldest indoor theatre in the world is the Teatro Olimpico in Vicenza, Italy. Designed in the Roman style by Andrea di Pietro, *alias* Palladio (1508–80), it was begun three months before his death and finished in 1582 by his pupil Vicenzo Scamozzi (1552–1616). It is preserved today in its original form.

Largest. The largest building used for theatre is the National People's Congress Building (*Ren min da hui tang*) on the west side of Tian an men Square, Peking, China. It was completed in 1959 and covers an area of 12.9 acres. The theatre seats 10,000 and is occasionally used as such, as in 1964 for the play "The East Is Red."

The largest regular theatre is the Radio City Music Hall in Rockefeller Center, New York City. It seats more than 6,200 people and the average annual attendance is more than 8,000,000. The stage is 144 feet wide and 66 feet 6 inches deep, equipped with a revolving turntable 43 feet in diameter and three elevator sections, each 70 feet long.

The greatest seating capacity of any theatre in the world is that of the "Chaplin" (formerly the "Blanquita") in Havana, Cuba. It was opened on December 30, 1949, and has 6,500 seats.

Largest Amphitheatre. The largest amphitheatre ever built is the Flavian amphitheatre or Colosseum of Rome, Italy, completed in 80 A.D. Covering 5 acres and with a capacity of 87,000, it has a maximum length of 612 feet and maximum width of 515 feet.

Longest Runs

The longest continuous run of any show is of *The Mousetrap* by Agatha Christie (later Lady Mallowan). This thriller opened at the Ambassadors Theatre (capacity 453), London, on November 25, 1952, and moved after 8,862 performances "down the road" to St.

Martin's Theatre, London, on March 25, 1974. Its 9,478th performance was on August 21, 1975, and surpasses even the former composite record of *The Drunkard* in Los Angeles, which ran from 1932 to 1953, and was revived as a musical.

The greatest number of performances of any theatrical presentation is more than 25,000 in the case of *The Golden Horseshoe Revue*—a 45-minute show staged at Disneyland Park, Anaheim, California. The show was first put on on July 17, 1955. The three main performers Fulton Burley, Bert Henry and Betty Taylor play as many as five houses a day.

The Broadway record is 3,242 performances by *Fiddler on the Roof*, which opened on September 22, 1964, and closed on July 3, 1972. Paul Lipson played Tevye 1,811 times during which he had ten "wives" and 58 "daughters." The world gross earnings reached $64,300,000 on an original investment of $375,000.

The off-Broadway musical show *The Fantasticks* by Tom Jones and Harvey Schmidt achieved its 6,668th performance as it entered its 17th year at the Sullivan Street Playhouse, Greenwich Village, New York City, on May 3, 1975. It has been played in a record 3,788 productions in 55 countries.

One-Man Show. The longest run of one-man shows is 849 by Victor Borge in his *Comedy in Music* from October 2, 1953, to January 21, 1956, at the Golden Theater, New York City.

The world aggregate record for one-man shows is more than 1,700 performances of *Brief Lives* by Roy Dotrice (born Guernsey, England, May 5, 1923) including 400-straight at the Mayfair Theatre, London, ending on July 20, 1974. He was on stage for more than 2½ hours per performance of this 17th-century monologue, and required 3 hours for makeup and 1 hour for removal, thus aggregating 40 weeks.

Shortest Runs. The shortest run on record was that of *The Intimate Revue* at the Duchess Theatre, London, on March 11, 1930. Anything which could go wrong did. With scene changes taking up to 20 minutes apiece, the management scrapped seven scenes to get the finale on before midnight. The run was described as "half a performance." In a number of Broadway productions, the opening and closing nights have coincided.

Of the many Broadway and off-Broadway shows for which the opening and closing nights coincided the most costly was *Kelly*, a musical costing $700,000 which suffered its double ceremony on February 6, 1965.

Longest Play. The 15th-century Cornish cycle of mystery plays was revived in English in July, 1969, at Earthwork Theatre, St. Piran's Round, Piran near Perranporth, Cornwall, by the Drama Department of Bristol University. Three parts, *Origo Mundi*, *Passio*, and *Resurrectio*, ran for 12 hours with two intermissions.

Shakespeare. The first all-amateur company to have staged all 37 of Shakespeare's plays was The Southsea Shakespeare Actors, Hampshire, England, when in October, 1966, they presented *Cymbaline*. The amateur director throughout was K. Edmonds Gateloy, M.B.E. Ten members of the Abbey Theatre Company, St.

LONGEST CHORUS LINE: Stretching across the 144-foot-wide stage at Radio City Music Hall in New York City, the Rockettes are 36 girls strong.

Albans, Hertfordshire, England, completed a dramatic reading of all the plays, 154 sonnets and five narrative poems in 37 hours 52 minutes on October 11–12, 1975. The longest is *Hamlet*, with 4,042 lines and 29,551 words, 1,242 words longer than *Richard III*.

Cabaret. The highest night-club fee in history was $100,000 collected by Liza Minnelli for the New Year's Eve show at The Colonie Hill Club, Long Island, New York, on January 1, 1975. Patrons paid $150 per seat.

Longest Chorus Line. The world's longest permanent chorus line was formed by the Rockettes in the Radio City Music Hall, New York City, which opened in December, 1932. The 36 girls danced precision routines across the 144-foot-wide stage.

Ice Shows. Holiday on Ice Production Inc., founded by Morris Chalfen in 1945, stages the world's most costly live entertainment with its seven productions playing simultaneously in several of 75 countries drawing 20,000,000 spectators paying $40,000,000 in a year. The total number of skaters and other personnel exceeds 900.

Shortest Criticism. The shortest dramatic criticism in theatrical history was that attributed to Wolcott Gibbs (died 1958), writing about the farce "Wham!" He wrote the single word "Ouch!"

Most Ardent Theatregoer. The highest recorded number of paid theatre attendances is 3,000 shows in 23 years from March 28, 1953 to June 19, 1976, by John Iles of Salisbury, Wiltshire, England. He estimates he has traveled 123,037 miles and seen 98,729 performances to March 28, 1976.

Radio Broadcasting

Origins. The earliest description of a radio transmission system was written by Dr. Mahlon Loomis (born New York State, 1826) on July 21, 1864, and demonstrated between two kites at Bear's Den, Loudoun County, Virginia, in October, 1866. He received a U.S. Patent entitled Improvement in Telegraphing, in 1872.

Earliest Patent. The first patent for a system of communication by means of electro-magnetic waves, numbered No. 12039, was granted on June 2, 1896, to the Italian-Irish Marchese, Guglielmo Marconi (1874–1937). The first permanent wireless installation was at The Needles on the Isle of Wight, Hampshire, England, by Marconi's Wireless Telegraph Co., Ltd., in November, 1896.

A prior public demonstration of wireless transmission of speech was given in the town square of Murray, Kentucky, in 1892 by Nathan B. Stubblefield. He died, destitute, on March 28, 1928.

Earliest Broadcast. The first advertised broadcast was made on December 24, 1906, by Prof. Reginald Aubrey Fessenden (1868–1932) from the 420-foot mast of the National Electric Signalling Company at Brant Rock, Massachusetts. The transmission included the *Largo* by Georg Friedrich Händel (1685–1759) of Germany. Fessenden had achieved the broadcast of highly distorted speech as early as November, 1900.

Transatlantic Transmissions. The earliest transatlantic wireless signals (the letter S in Morse Code) were received by Marconi,

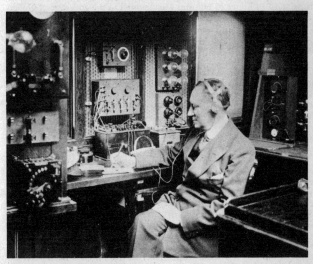

EARLIEST RADIO PATENT: Guglielmo Marconi received a patent for his electro-magnetic wave communication system on June 2, 1896.

George Stephen Kemp and Percy Paget from a 10-kilowatt station at Poldhu, Cornwall, England, at Signal Hill, St. John's, Newfoundland, Canada, at 12:30 p.m. on December 12, 1901. Human speech was first heard across the Atlantic in November, 1915, when a transmission from the U.S. Navy station at Arlington, Virginia, was received by U.S. radio-telephone engineers up in the Eiffel Tower, Paris.

Earliest Antipodal Reception. Frank Henry Alfred Walker (born November 11, 1904) on the night of November 12, 1924, received on his homemade 2-valve receiver on 75 meters at Crown Farm, Surrey, England, signals from Marconi's yacht *Electra* (call sign ICCM) which was then in Australian waters.

Earliest Radio-Microphone. The first radio-microphone, which was in essence also the first "bug," was devised by Reg Moores of Great Britain in 1947, and first used in the ice show *Aladdin* at Brighton Sports Stadium, England, in September, 1949.

Most Stations. The country with the greatest number of radio broadcasting stations is the U.S. In 1974, there were 7,426 authorized, of which 4,305 were AM and 2,413 FM. The balance broadcast television signals.

The country with the highest number of ham stations is Japan, with 286,247 in March, 1975.

Longest Broadcast. The longest radio broadcast was by Radio Station ELBC, Monrovia, on November 23, 1961, when a transmission of 14 hours 20 minutes was devoted to the coverage of Queen Elizabeth II's visit to Liberia.

The longest continuous broadcast has been one of 208 hours 32 minutes by Jim Humphries of WETE, Knoxville, Tennessee, from March 27 to April 5, 1974.

Highest Listener Response. The highest recorded response to a radio show occurred on November 27, 1974, when on a 5-hour talk show on WCAU, Philadelphia, Howard Sheldon, the astrologist, registered a total of 388,299 calls on the "Bill Corsair Show."

Television

Invention. The invention of television, the instantaneous viewing of distant objects, was not an act but a process of successive and interdependent discoveries. The first commercial cathode ray tube was introduced in 1897 by Karl Ferdinand Braun (1850–1918), but was not linked to "electric vision" until 1907 by Boris Rosing of Russia in St. Petersburg (now Leningrad). The earliest public demonstration of television was given on January 27, 1926, by John Logie Baird (1888–1946) of Scotland, using a development of the mechanical scanning system suggested by Paul Nipkov in 1884. A patent application for the Iconoscope (No. 2,141,059) had been filed on December 29, 1923, by Vladimir Kosma Zworykin (born in Russia in 1889, became a U.S. citizen in 1924), and a short-range transmission of a model windmill had been made on June 13, 1925, by C. Francis Jenkins in Washington, D.C.

Earliest Service. The first high-definition television broadcasting service was opened from Alexandra Palace, London, N.22, on November 2, 1936, when there were about 100 sets in the United Kingdom. A television station in Berlin, Germany, began low-definition broadcasting on March 22, 1935. The transmitter burned out in August, 1935.

Most Transmitters and Sets. In 1975, the total estimated number of television transmitters in use or under construction was 19,870 serving 363,770,000 sets (91 for each 1,000 of the world population). Of these, about 121,000,000 were estimated to be in use in the U.S. where 99 per cent of the population is reached. The number of color sets in the U.S. has grown from 200,000 in 1960 to 57,000,000 (47 per cent of all sets) by mid-1975.

Transatlantic Transmission. The first transatlantic transmission by satellite was achieved at 1 a.m. on July 11, 1962, *via* the active satellite *Telstar I* from Andover, Maine, to Pleumeur Bodou, France. The picture was of Frederick R. Kappell, chairman of the American Telephone and Telegraph Company, which owned the satellite. The first "live" broadcast was made on July 23, 1962, and the first woman to appear was the *haute couturière*, Ginette Spanier, directrice of Balmain, Paris, the next day. On February 9, 1928, the image of John Logie Baird and a Mrs. Howe was transmitted from Station 2KZ at Coulsdon, Surrey, England, to Station 2CVJ, Hartsdale, New York.

Greatest Audience. The greatest number of viewers for a televised event is an estimated 1,000,000,000 for the live and recorded transmissions of the XXth Olympic Games in Munich, from August 26 to September 11, 1972.

Largest TV Prizes. The greatest amount won by an individual in TV prizes was $264,000 by Teddy Nadler on quiz programs in the United States up to September, 1958. He reportedly had to pay $155,000 in federal and state taxes, and remained unemployed thereafter.

On July 24, 1975, WABC-TV, New York City, transmitted the first televised Grand Tier draw of the State Lottery in which the winner took the grand prize of $1,000,000. This was, of course, taxable.

Highest Hourly Rate. The world's highest-paid television performer based on an hourly rate is Perry Como (born Pierino Como, Canonsburg, Pennsylvania, on May 18, 1912), who began as a barber. In May, 1969, he signed a contract with N.B.C. to star in four one-hour video specials at $5,000,000. At the rate of $1,250,000 per hour, he was paid $20,833 per minute. The contract required him to provide and pay supporting artists.

Largest Contracts. The largest TV contract ever signed was one for $34,000,000 in a three-year no-option contract between Dino Paul Crocetti (Dean Martin, b. June 7, 1917) and N.B.C. Currently,

LARGEST CONTRACTS: Dean Martin (left) signed a three-year contract for $34,000,000. Johnny Carson (right) is paid $3,000,000 each year for 40 weeks' work.

television's highest-paid performer is Johnny Carson, the host of the *Tonight* show. His current three-year N.B.C. contract calls for annual payments of some $3,000,000 for forty 4-day weeks with 12 weeks' vacation.

The top-paid woman performer is Barbara Walters, formerly of N.B.C., who was signed by A.B.C. in May, 1976, for about $1,000,000 per year to co-host the *Evening News.*

Longest Program. The longest pre-scheduled telecast on record was one of 163 hours 18 minutes by GTV9 of Melbourne, Australia, covering the Apollo XI moon mission July 19–26, 1969.

Most Televised Performer. Lucille Ball (born Jamestown, New York, 1911) starred in 495 TV shows of *I Love Lucy* (179), *The Lucy Show* (156), *Here's Lucy* (144) and 16 "*Specials*," totaling $255\frac{1}{2}$ hours screen time in the 23 years, 1951–74.

Most Durable Show. The world's most durable TV show is N.B.C.'s *Meet the Press*, first transmitted on November 6, 1947, and weekly since September 12, 1948. It was originated by Lawrence E. Spivak, who until 1975 appeared weekly as either moderator or panel member.

Most Prolific Scriptwriter. The most prolific television writer in the world is the Rt. Hon. Lord Willis (b. January 13, 1918), who in the period 1949–74 has created 21 series, 20 plays, and 21 feature films. His total output since 1945 can be estimated at 15,000,000 words.

Highest TV Advertising Rates. The highest TV advertising rate was $250,000 per minute for N.B.C. network prime time on

July 30, 1974, during the transmission of Paramount Pictures *The Godfather*, bought by the network for $10,000,000.

Motion Pictures

Earliest. The greatest impetus in the development of cinematography came from the inventiveness of Etienne Jules Marey (1830–1903) of France in the 1870's.

The earliest demonstration of a celluloid cinematograph film on a screen was given at 44 Rue de Rennes, Paris, France, on March 22, 1895, by Auguste Marie Louis Nicolas Lumière (1862–1954) and Louis Jean Lumière (1864–1948), French brothers. The film was entitled *La Sortie des Ouvriers de l'Usine Lumière*, taken probably in August or September, 1894, outside the factory gates at Lyons. Louis Aimé Augustin Le Prince, according to evidence in *The Shell Book of Facts*, achieved dim moving outlines on "white-washed walls" at the Institute for the Deaf, Washington Heights, New York City, as early as 1885.

The earliest sound-on-film motion picture was achieved by Eugenè Augustin Lauste (b. Paris, January 1, 1857) who patented his process on August 11, 1906 and produced a workable system using a string galvanometer in 1910 in London. The event is more usually attributed to Dr. Lee de Forest (1873–1961) in New York City, on March 13, 1923. The first all-talking picture was *Lights of New York*, shown at the Strand Theatre, New York City, on July 6, 1928.

EARLIEST CINEMATO-GRAPH: Louis Lumière, with one of the Lumière Brothers' first projectors.

Highest Production. Japan annually makes the most full-length films, with 923 films of 4,921 feet or more completed in 1970, compared with 396 films of 11,155 feet or more approved by the censor in India in 1970. This compares, however, with Japan's production of 1,000 films in 1928. The average seat price in Japan is 70 yen (20 cents).

Movie-Going. The people of Taiwan go to the movies more often than those of any other country in the world, with an average of 66 attendances per person per year according to the latest data. The Soviet Union has the most movie theatres in the world, with 147,200 in 1970, including those projecting only 16 mm. film.

The most persistent known moviegoer is Paul Morgan, 92, a retired car paint-sprayer. Since 1949, he has attended the Rio Cinema Theatre in Miami, Florida, every day (including Sundays) although the program is not changed more than three times a week. The manager states Mr. Morgan is always "first in line."

Most Movie Theatre Seats. The Falkland Islands (off South America's Straits of Magellan) and the Cook Islands (in the South Pacific) have more seats per total population than any other country, with 250 for each 1,000 inhabitants. The least number are in the Central African Republic which has two theatres, hence one seat for each 4,100 inhabitants.

MOST OSCARS: Walt Disney won a total of 29 Oscars, plaques and certificates for his movies. Here he is shown with four Oscars awarded to him in 1954.

Oldest Theatre. The earliest was the "Electric Theatre," part of a tented circus in Los Angeles. It opened on April 2, 1902. The oldest building designed as a movie theatre is the Biograph Cinema in Wilton Road, Victoria, London. It was opened in 1905 and originally had seating accommodation for 500 patrons. Its present capacity is 700.

Largest Theatre. The largest open-air movie theatre in the world is in the British Sector of West Berlin, Germany. One end of the Olympic Stadium, converted into an amphitheatre, seats 22,000 people.

Most Expensive Film. The most expensive film ever made is *War and Peace*, the U.S.S.R. government adaptation of the masterpiece of Tolstoy directed by Sergei Bondarchuk (born 1921) over the period 1962–67. The total cost has been officially stated to be more than $96,000,000. More than 165,000 uniforms had to be made. The re-creation of the Battle of Borodino involved 120,000 Red Army "extras" at 3 rubles ($3.30) per month. The film runs for 6 hours 13 minutes.

The highest price ever paid for film rights is $5,500,000, paid on February 6, 1962, by Warner Brothers for *My Fair Lady*, which cost $17,000,000, thus making it the most expensive musical film made up to that time.

Longest Film. The longest film ever shown is *The Human Condition*, directed in three parts by Masaki Kobayashi of Japan. It lasts 8 hours 50 minutes, excluding two breaks of 20 minutes each. It was shown in Tokyo in October, 1961, at an admission price of 250 yen (70 cents).

The longest film ever released was * * * * by Andy Warhol (b. Cleveland, Ohio, 1931), which lasted 24 hours. It proved, not surprisingly, except reportedly to its creator, a commercial failure, and was withdrawn and re-released in 90-minute form as *The Loves of Ondine*.

Highest Earnings by an Actor. The greatest earnings by any actor in cinema history is reputedly paid to Charles Bronson. Press stories maintain that his fee is $20,000 per day whether or not he is before the camera, $2,500 per hour overtime, plus a box office percentage in some films amounting to a potential $2,000,000.

Highest Box Office Gross. The film with the highest world gross earnings (amount paid by theatre owners) is *Jaws*, released in June, 1975, which in its first 78 days grossed $124,000,000 in North America alone. The film, based on a novel by Peter Benchley, cost some $8,000,000 to make. (See color photo on color page C.)

Largest Studios. The largest complex of film studios are those of Universal City, Los Angeles. The back lot contains 561 buildings. There are 34 sound stages.

Oscars. Walter (Walt) Elias Disney (1901–1966) won more "Oscars"—the awards of the Academy of Motion Picture Arts and Sciences, instituted on May 16, 1929, for 1927–28—than any other person. His total was 17 Oscars plus 12 certificates and plaques for a

THREE OSCARS: Katharine Hepburn won the Best Actress award in 1933, 1967, and 1968.

total of 29 awards from 1931 to 1969. The films with most awards have been *Ben Hur* (1959) with 11, followed by *Gone with the Wind* (1939) and *West Side Story* (1961) both with 10. The film with the highest number of nominations was *All About Eve* (1950) with 14. It won four.

The only performer to win three Oscars for her starring roles has been Katharine Hepburn (born November 9, 1909), in *Morning Glory* (1933), *Guess Who's Coming to Dinner* (1967) and *The Lion in Winter* (1968). All three Oscars are on display at the Guinness World Records Exhibit Hall in New York City.

Oscars are named after Oscar Pierce of Texas. When the figurines were first delivered to the executive offices of the Academy of Motion Picture Arts and Sciences, the Executive Secretary exclaimed, "Why, they look just like my uncle Oscar." And the name stuck.

Phonograph

The phonograph was first described on April 30, 1877, by Charles Cros (1842–88), a French poet and scientist. The first successful machine was realized by Thomas Alva Edison (1847–1931), who gained his first patent on February 19, 1878 for a machine constructed by his mechanic, John Kryesi. It was first demonstrated on December 7, 1877.

The first practical hand-cranked, wax-coated-cylinder phonograph was manufactured in the United States by Chichester Bell and

Charles Sumner Tainter in 1886. The forerunner of the modern disc phonograph was patented in 1887 by Emile Berliner (1851–1929), a German immigrant to the U.S. Although a toy machine based on his principle was produced in Germany in 1889, the gramophone was not a serious commercial competitor to the cylinder phonograph until 1896.

The country with the greatest number of record players is the U.S. with more than 61,200,000 by Dec., 1971. A total of more than half a billion dollars is spent annually on 500,000 juke boxes in the U.S.

Sales in the U.S. of discs and tapes reached $2,200,000,000 in 1974, which includes sales for L.P.'s, cassettes and cartridges.

The sale of units was $94,000,000.

Oldest Record. The oldest record in the British Broadcasting Corporation's library is an Edison solid-wax cylinder, recorded in Edison's laboratory and dated June 26, 1888. The B.B.C. library, the world's largest, contains over 750,000 records, including 5,250 with no known matrix. The library also contains a collection of early Berliner discs.

The earliest jazz record made was *Indiana* and *The Dark Town Strutters Ball*, recorded for the Columbia label in New York City, on or about January 30, 1917, by the Original Dixieland Jazz Band, led by Dominick (Nick) James La Rocca (born April 11, 1889). This was released on May 31, 1917. The first jazz record to be

FIRST PLATINUM DISC awarded to Bing Crosby to commemorate the sale of 200,000,000 of his records in 1960. He received a second platinum disc in 1970 after 300,650,000 of his records had been sold. (See page 240.)

released was the O.D.J.B.'s *Livery Stable Blues* (recorded February 24), backed by *The Dixie Jazz Band One-Step* (recorded February 26), released by Victor on March 7, 1917.

Smallest Record. The smallest functional record is one 1⅜ inches in diameter of "God Save the King" of which 250 were made by HMV Record Co. in 1924.

Most Successful Recording Artist. On June 9, 1960, the Hollywood Chamber of Commerce presented Harry Lillis (*alias* Bing) Crosby, Jr. (born May 2, 1904, at Tacoma, Washington) with a platinum disc to commemorate his 200,000,000th record sold from 2,600 singles and 125 albums he had recorded. On September 15, 1970, he received a second platinum disc when 300,650,000 records had been sold by Decca. It is estimated that his global lifetime sales on 179 labels in 28 countries totaled 400,000,000.

His first commercial recording was *I've Got the Girl* recorded on October 18, 1926 (master number W142785 (Take 3) issued on the Columbia label). The greatest collection of Crosbiana owned by Bob Roberts of Chatham, Kent, England, includes 1,677 records.

The greatest recorded success in a single year has been the sale of 13,700,000 albums in 1966 by an ex-Army trumpeter, Herb Alpert (born in Los Angeles, March 31, 1937), with his Tijuana Brass band.

Most Successful Group. The singers with the greatest sales of any group were The Beatles. This group from Liverpool, England, comprised George Harrison (born February 25, 1943), John Ono (formerly John Winston) Lennon (born October 9, 1940), James Paul McCartney (born June 18, 1942) and Richard Starkey, *alias* Ringo Starr (born July 7, 1940). Between February, 1963, and January, 1973, their sales were estimated at 545,000,000 in singles equivalents. The 40,000-strong Beatles Fan Club was closed down on March 31, 1972.

Golden Discs

Earliest. The first recorded piece to sell a million copies and become a "golden disc" was a performance by Enrico Caruso (born Naples, Italy, 1873 and died 1921) of the aria *Vesti la giubba* (*On with the Motley*) from the opera *I Pagliacci* by Ruggiero Leoncavallo (1858–1919), the earliest version of which was recorded on November 12, 1902. (See photo page 224.)

The first single recording to surpass the million mark was Alma Gluck's rendition of *Carry Me Back to Old Virginny* on the Red Seal Victor label on a 12-inch single-faced (later backed) record (No. 74420).

The first literally golden disc was one sprayed by RCA Victor for presentation to Glenn Miller (1904–44) for his *Chattanooga Choo Choo* on February 10, 1942.

Most. The only *audited* measure of million-selling records within the U.S. is certification by the Recording Industry Association of America (R.I.A.A.) introduced March 14, 1958. Out of the 1,607 R.I.A.A. gold-record awards made to August 1, 1975, the most have

RECORD RECORD-BREAKERS (left): As singers and disc sellers, The Beatles broke many records in 1963-73. MOST GOLD RECORDS: Elvis Presley (right) has been awarded 28 gold records—more than any other individual.

gone to The Beatles with 38 (plus one with Billy Preston) as a group. Paul McCartney has an additional 9 more awards both on his own and with the group Wings.

The most awards to an individual is 28 to Elvis Aron Presley (born at Tupelo, Mississippi, January 8, 1935), spanning 1958 to August 1, 1975.

Youngest. The youngest age at which an artist has achieved sales of 1,000,000 copies of a record is 6 years by Osamu Minagawa of Tokyo, Japan, for his single *Kuro Neko No Tango* (*Black Cat Tango*) released on October 5, 1969.

Most Recorded Songs. Two songs have each been recorded between 900 and 1,000 times in the U.S. alone—*St. Louis Blues*, written in 1914 by W. C. (William Christopher) Handy (born Florence, Alabama, in 1873 and died 1958), and *Stardust*, written in 1927 by Hoagland ("Hoagy") Carmichael (born Bloomington, Indiana, November 22, 1899).

Biggest Sellers. The greatest seller of any record to date is *White Christmas* by Irving Berlin (born Israel Bailin, at Tyumen, Russia, May 11, 1888). First recorded in 1941, it reached 135,000,000 by December, 1974.

The highest claim for any "pop" record is an unaudited 25,000,000 for *Rock Around the Clock*, copyrighted in 1953 by the late

Max Friedman and James E. Myers, under the name of Jimmy De Knight, and recorded on April 12, 1954, by Bill Haley and the Comets.

Fastest Seller. The fastest-selling record of all time is *John Fitzgerald Kennedy—A Memorial Album* (Premium Albums), an L.P. recorded on November 22, 1963, the day of Mr. Kennedy's assassination, which sold 4,000,000 copies at 99 cents in six days (December 7–12, 1963), thus ironically beating the previous speed record set by the humorous L.P. *The First Family* about the Kennedys in 1962–63.

Long-Players. The best-selling L.P. is the 20th Century Fox album *Sing We Now of Christmas*, issued in 1958 and re-entitled *The Little Drummer Boy* in 1963. Its sales were reported to be more than 14,000,000 by November, 1972.

Carole King's *Tapestry* has been in *Billboard's* Top 100 list in the period 1970–75, selling 13 million copies on the Ode label and grossing $65,000,000.

The all-time best-seller among long-playing records of musical film shows is the *Sound of Music* sound-track album, released by RCA Victor on March 2, 1965, with over 19,000,000 to January 1, 1973.

The first classical long-player to sell a million was a performance featuring the pianist Harvey Lavan (Van) Cliburn, Jr. (born in Kilgore, Texas, July 12, 1934) of the *Piano Concerto No. 1* by Pyotr Ilyich Tchaikovsky (1840–93) of Russia. This recording was made in 1958 and sales reached 1,000,000 by 1961, 2,000,000 by 1965 and about 2,500,000 by January, 1970.

LONGEST STAY IN BEST-SELLER CHART: "Billboard" carried one of Johnny Mathis' albums for 490 weeks. **MOST RECORDINGS:** Lata Mangeshker of India has recorded at least 25,000 songs.

LOUDEST POP GROUP: England's "The Who" cranked out 120 decibels of sound in May, 1976.

The longest long-playing record is the 137-disc set of the complete works of William Shakespeare (1564–1616). The recordings, which were made in 1957–64, cost £260 12s. 6d. ($729.75) per set, and are by the Argo Record Co. Ltd., London. The Vienna Philharmonic's playing of Wagner's "Ring" covers 19 L.P.'s, was 8 years in the making and requires 14½ hours playing time.

Best-Seller Chart Duration Record. The longest stay in *Billboard's* best-seller chart has been 490 weeks from late 1958 to July, 1968, for the Columbia album *Johnny's Greatest Hits* by Johnny Mathis.

The first album ever to enter the *Billboard* list at No. 1 is *Captain Fantastic and the Brown Dirt Cowboy* by Elton John (born Reg Dwight) in June, 1975.

Best-sellers' charts were first published in *Billboard* on July 27, 1940.

Most Recordings. Miss Lata Mangeshker (born 1928) has reportedly recorded between 1948 and 1974 not less than 25,000 solo, duet and chorus-backed songs in 20 Indian languages. She frequently has 5 sessions in a day and has "backed" 1,800 films to 1974.

Highest Gross and Audience. The highest gross take for an individual pop recording group is $309,000 paid by a record 56,800 for a concert by the British group Led Zeppelin at Tampa Stadium, Florida, on May 5, 1973. There were also 6,000 "gatecrashers."

Loudest Pop Concert. The amplification for *The Who* at Charlton Athletic Football Ground, London, England, on May 31, 1976, provided by a Tasco P.A. system, had a total power of 76,000 watts from eighty 800 W Crown D.C. 300 A Amplifiers and twenty 600 W Phase Linear 200's. The readings at 50 yards from the front of the sound system were 120 decibels.

TALLEST INHABITED BUILDING: The Sears Tower dominates the Chicago skyline, standing 1,454 feet tall. Two TV antennas bring the total height to 1,800 feet.

Chapter Seven

THE WORLD'S STRUCTURES

Earliest Structures

The earliest known human structure is a rough circle of loosely piled lava blocks found in 1960 on the lowest cultural level at the Lower Paleolithic site at Olduvai Gorge in Tanganyika (now part of Tanzania). The structure was associated with artifacts and bones and may represent a work-floor, dating to *circa* 1,750,000 B.C.

The earliest evidence of *buildings* yet discovered is that of 21 huts with hearths of pebble-lined pits and delimited by stake holes, found in October, 1965, at the Terra Amata site in Nice, France. Originally dated to 300,000 B.C., they are now thought to belong more likely to the Acheulián culture of 120,000 years ago. Excavation carried out between June 28 and July 5, 1966, revealed one hut with palisaded walls having axes of 49 and 20 feet.

The oldest free-standing structures in the world are now believed to be the megalithic temples at Mgarr and Skarba in Malta and Ggantija in Gozo, dating from *c.* 3250 B.C.

1. Buildings for Working

Largest Buildings

Commercial. The greatest ground area covered by any building in the world is that by the Ford Parts Redistribution Center, Brownstown Township, Michigan, enclosing a floor area of 3,100,000 square feet or 71.16 acres. It was opened on May 20, 1971, and employs 1,400 people. The fire-control system comprises 70 miles of pipelines with 37,000 sprinklers.

The building with the largest cubic capacity in the world is the Boeing Company's main assembly plant at Everett, Washington, completed in 1968. The building, constructed for the manufacture of Boeing 747 jet airliners, has a maximum height of 115 feet and has a capacity of 200 million cubic feet.

Scientific. The most capacious scientific building in the world is the Vehicle Assembly Building (VAB) at Complex 39, the selected site for the final assembly and launching of the Apollo moon spacecraft on the Saturn V rocket, at the John F. Kennedy Space Center (KSC), near Cape Canaveral (formerly Cape Kennedy), Florida. It is a steel-framed building measuring 716 feet in length, 518 feet in width and 525 feet high. The building contains four bays, each with its own door 460 feet high. Construction began in April, 1963, by the Ursum Consortium. Its floor area is 343,500 square feet (7.87 acres) and its capacity is 129,482,000 cubic feet. The building was "topped out" on April 14, 1965, at a cost of $108,700,000.

Administrative. The largest ground area covered by any office building is that of the Pentagon, in Arlington, Virginia. Built to

TALLEST STRUCTURES IN THE WORLD—PROGRESSIVE RECORDS

Height in feet	Structure	Location	Material	Building or Completion Dates
204	Dioser step pyramid (earliest Pyramid)	Saqqâra, Egypt	Tura limestone	c. 2650 B.C.
294	Pyramid of Meidun	Meidun, Egypt	Tura limestone	c. 2600 B.C.
c. 336	Snefru Bent pyramid	Dahshûr, Egypt	Tura limestone	c. 2600 B.C.
342	Snefru North Stone pyramid	Dahshûr, Egypt	Tura limestone	c. 2600 B.C.
480.9[1]	Great Pyramid of Cheops (Khufu)	El Gizeh, Egypt	Tura limestone	c. 2580 B.C.
525[2]	Lincoln Cathedral, Central Tower	Lincoln, England	lead sheathed wood	c. 1307–1548
489[3]	St. Paul's Cathedral	London, England	lead sheathed wood	1315–1561
465	Minister of Notre Dame	Strasbourg, France	lead sheathed wood	1420–1439
502[4]	St. Pierre de Beauvais	Beauvais, France	vosges sandstone	–1568
475	St. Nicholas Church	Hamburg, Germany	vosges sandstone	1846–1874
513	Cologne Cathedral	Cologne, West Germany	vosges sandstone	1823–1880
485	Rouen Cathedral	Rouen, France	cast iron	1876
555[5]	Washington Memorial	Washington, D.C.	stone	1848–1884
985.9[6]	La Tour Eiffel	Paris, France	steel	1887–1889
1,046	Chrysler Building	New York City	steel and concrete	1929–1930
1,250[7]	Empire State Building	New York City	steel and concrete	1929–1930
1,572	KWTV Television Mast	Oklahoma City	steel	Nov. 1954
1,610[8]	KSWS Television Mast	Roswell, N. Mex.	steel	Dec. 1956
1,619	WGAN Television Mast	Portland, Maine	steel	Sept. 1959
1,676	WTVM-& WRBL-TV Mast	Cape Girardeau, Missouri	steel	June 1960
1,749	KFVS Television Mast	Columbus, Georgia	steel	May 1962
1,749	WBIR-TV Mast	Knoxville, Tennessee	steel	Sept. 1963
2,063	KTHI-TV Mast	Fargo, North Dakota	steel	Dec. 1963
2,117.3	Warszawa Radio Mast	Plock, Poland	galvanized steel	May 1974

[1] Original height. With loss of pyramidion (topmost stone) height now 449 ft. 6 in.

[2] Fell in a storm.

[3] Struck by lightning and destroyed in August, 1561.

[4] Fell April, 1573, shortly after completion.

[5] Sinking at a rate of 5 inches per year since 1884.

[6] Original height. With addition of T.V. antenna in 1957, now 1,052 ft. 4 in.

[7] Original height. With addition of T.V. tower on May 1, 1951, now 1,472 ft. On October 11, 1972, it was revealed that the top 15 stories might be replaced by 33 to give the old champion 113 stories and a height of 1,494 feet.

[8] Fell in gale in 1960.

LARGEST OFFICE BUILDINGS: Even though the Wall Street district of New York City includes many skyscrapers, they are dwarfed by the twin towers of the World Trade Center, built on the banks of the Hudson River. Each building has a rentable space of 4,370,000 square feet, 21,800 windows and 104 elevators.

house the U.S. Defense Department's offices, it was completed on January 15, 1943, and cost about $83,000,000. Each of the outermost sides of the Pentagon is 921 feet long and the perimeter of the building is about 1,500 yards. The five stories of the building enclose a floor area of 6,500,000 square feet. During the day 29,000 people work in the building. The telephone system of the building has more than 44,000 telephones connected by 160,000 miles of cable and its 220 staff members handle 280,000 calls a day. Two restaurants, six cafeterias and ten snackbars and a staff of 675 form the catering department of the building. The corridors measure 17 miles in length and there are 7,748 windows to be cleaned.

Office. The largest office buildings in the world are the twin towers comprising the World Trade Center in New York City, with a total of 4,370,000 square feet (100.32 acres) of rentable space in each. The taller tower is 1,350 feet high.

Fair Hall. The largest fair hall is in Hanover, West Germany, completed on April 1, 1970, at a cost of DM 55,000,000($16,500,000) with dimensions of 1,180 feet by 885 feet and a floor area of 877,500 square feet.

Tallest Buildings

The tallest inhabited building in the world is the Sears Tower, the national headquarters of Sears Roebuck & Co. on Wacker Drive, Chicago, with 110 stories, rising to 1,454 feet and completed in 1974. Its gross area is 4,400,000 square feet (101.0 acres). It was topped out on May 4, 1973, surpassing the World Trade Center in New York in height, at 2:35 p.m. on March 6, 1973, with the first steel column reaching the 104th story. The addition of two TV antennae brought the total height to 1,800 feet. The building's population is 16,700, served by 103 elevators and 18 escalators. It has 16,000 windows.

Most Stories. The plans for the 1,610-foot Barrington Space Needle, Barrington, Illinois, call for 120 stories—ten more than the Sears Tower and the World Trade Center (see above).

Skyscrapers of up to 3,000 feet in height with 400 stories are now regarded as feasible by the "suspend-arch" principle developed by the U.S. engineer Chelazzi.

Habitations

Greatest Altitude. The highest inhabited buildings in the world are those in the southern Tibetan herders' settlement of Baruduksum, at 21,200 feet.

The Buddhist monastery at Hanle Kashmir, India, at 16,840 feet, is inhabited the year round.

A formerly occupied 3-room dwelling was discovered in April, 1961, at 21,650 feet on Cerro Llullaillaco (22,058 feet), on the Argentine-Chile border, believed to date from the late pre-Columbian period *c.* 1480.

Northernmost. The most northerly habitation in the world is the Danish scientific station set up in 1952 in Pearyland, northern Greenland, more than 900 miles north of the Arctic Circle. The U.S.S.R. and the U.S. have maintained research stations on Arctic ice floes, which have drifted close to the North Pole. The U.S.S.R.'s "North Pole 15," which drifted 1,250 miles, passed within 1¼ miles of the North Pole in December, 1967. The 1969 Pearyland research group from Britain reported signs of Eskimo habitation above the 83rd latitude N. apparently dating from earlier than 1000 B.C.

Southernmost. The most southerly permanent human habitation is the United States' Scott-Amundsen Base at the South Pole (see page 135), completed in 1957 and replaced in 1975.

Largest Embassy. The largest embassy in the world is the U.S.S.R. embassy on Bei Xiao Jie, Peking, China, in the northeastern corner of the Northern walled city. The whole 45-acre area of the old Orthodox Church mission (established 1728), now known as the *Bei guan*, was handed over to the U.S.S.R. in 1949.

Plants

Atomic. The largest atomic plant in the world is the Savannah River Project, South Carolina, extending 27 miles along the river and over a total area of 315 square miles. The plant, comprising 280 permanent buildings, cost $1,400,000,000. Construction was started in February, 1951, and by September, 1952, the labor force had reached 38,500. The present operating strength is 8,500.

Underground. The world's largest underground factory was the Mittelwerk Factory, near Nordhausen in the Kohnstein Hills, south of the Harz Mountains, Germany. It was built with concentration camp labor during World War II and had a floor area of 1,270,000 square feet and an output of 900 V-2 rockets per month.

Tallest Chimney. The world's tallest chimney is the $5,500,000 International Nickel Company's stack, 1,245 feet 8 inches tall, at

Copper Cliff, Sudbury, Ontario, Canada, completed in 1970. It was built by Canadian Kellogg Ltd. and the diameter tapers from 116.4 feet at the base to 51.8 feet at the top. It weighs 38,390 tons and became operational in 1971.

The world's most massive chimney is one of 1,148 feet at Puentes, Spain, built by M. W. Kellogg Co. It contains 20,600 cubic yards of concrete and 2,900,000 lbs. of steel and has an internal volume of 6,700,000 cubic feet.

Largest Cooling Tower. The largest cooling tower in the world is adjacent to the nuclear power plant at Uentrop, West Germany, completed in 1976, which is 590 feet tall.

Largest Garage. The world's largest garage (as opposed to parking lot) is at O'Hare Airport, Chicago, with 6 levels and a capacity for 9,250 cars. It is operated by Allright Auto Parks, Inc., the world's largest parking company.

The largest private garage ever built was one for 100 cars at the Long Island, New York, mansion of William Kissam Vanderbilt (1849–1920).

The world's largest parking lot is believed to be that at the Lakewood Center, California, with a capacity of 12,500 cars.

Largest Hangars. The largest hangar is the Goodyear Airship hangar at Akron, Ohio, which measures 1,175 feet long, 325 feet wide and 200 feet high. It covers 364,000 square feet (8.35 acres) and has a capacity of 55,000,000 cubic feet.

The largest single fixed-wing aircraft hangar is the Lockheed-Georgia engineering test center at Marietta, Georgia, measuring 630 feet by 480 feet (6.94 acres) completed in 1967. The maintenance hangar at Frankfurt/Main Airport, West Germany, covers slightly less area but has a frontage of 902 feet. The cable-supported roof has a span of 426.5 feet.

LARGEST HANGAR: The Goodyear Airship hangar at Akron, Ohio, covers 364,000 sq. ft. and has a capacity of 55,000,000 cu. ft.

Delta Air Lines' jet base, on a 140-acre site at Hartsfield International Airport, Atlanta, Georgia, has 36 acres under its roof.

Largest Sewerage Works. The largest single sewerage works is the West-Southwest Treatment Plant, opened in 1940 on a site of 501 acres in Chicago. It serves an area containing 2,940,000 people. It treated an average of more than 835,000,000 gallons of wastes per day in 1973. The capacity of its sedimentation and aeration tanks is 1,600,000 cubic yards.

Largest Glass Greenhouse. The largest glasshouse is 826 feet long and 348 feet wide, covering 6.5 acres at Brough, East Yorkshire, England, completed in 1971. A total of 420 tons of glass was used in glazing it.

Grain Elevator. The world's largest single-unit grain elevator is that operated by the C-G-F Grain Company at Wichita, Kansas. Consisting of a triple row of storage tanks, 123 on each side of the central loading tower or "head house," the unit is 2,717 feet long and 100 feet wide. Each tank is 120 feet high, with an inside diameter of 30 feet, giving a total storage capacity of 20,000,000 bushels of wheat. The largest collection of elevators in the world is at Thunder Bay, Ontario, Canada, on Lake Superior, with a total capacity of 103,900,000 bushels.

Wooden Buildings. The oldest wooden building in the world is the Temple of Horyu (Horyu-ji), built at Nara, Japan, in 708–715 A.D. The largest wooden building in the world is the Daibutsuden, built also at Nara in 1704–11. It measures 285.4 feet long, 167.3 feet wide and 153.3 feet tall.

The world's largest timber building is the asbestos fiber storage building completed in 1971 at Deception Bay, Quebec Roverie, Canada. It measures 760 feet long with a clear span of 305 feet, and is 144 feet high.

2. Buildings for Living

Castles and Forts

Earliest. Castles in the sense of unfortified manor houses existed in all the great early civilizations, including that of ancient Egypt from 3000 B.C. Fortified castles in the more accepted sense only existed much later. The oldest in the world is that at Gomdan, in the Yemen, which originally had 20 stories and dates from before 100 A.D.

Largest. The largest citadel in the world is the Qila (Citadel) at Halab (Aleppo) in Syria. It is oval in shape and has a surrounding wall 1,230 feet long and 777 feet across. It dates, in its present form, from the Humanid dynasty of the 10th century A.D.

The largest inhabited castle in the world is the British Royal residence of Windsor Castle at New Windsor, Berkshire. It is primarily of 12th-century construction and is in the form of a waisted parallelogram, 1,890 feet by 540 feet. The total area of Dover Castle (England), however, covers 34 acres with a width of 1,100

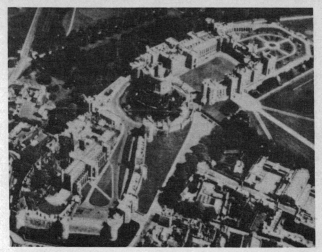

LARGEST INHABITED CASTLE is Windsor Castle, home of Queen Elizabeth of England.

feet and a curtain wall of 1,800 feet, or, if underground works are taken in, 2,300 feet.

The largest ancient castle in the world is Prague Castle, Czechoslovakia, originating in the 9th century. It is a very oblong irregular polygon with an axis of 1,870 feet and an average traverse diameter of 420 feet, with a surface area of 18 acres.

The most massive keep in the world is that in the 13th-century château at Coucy-le-Château-Auffrique, in the Department of Aisne, France. It is 177 feet high, 318 feet in circumference and has walls over 22½ feet in thickness. It was leveled to its foundations by the Germans in 1917.

The walls of Babylon, north of Al Hillah, Iraq, built in 600 B.C. were up to 85 feet in thickness.

Largest Palace. The largest palace in the world is the Imperial Palace (*Gu gong*) in the center of Peking (*Bei jing*, the northern capital), China, which covers a rectangle 1,050 yards by 820 yards, an area of 177.9 acres. The outline survives from the construction of the third Ming emperor Yong le of 1307–20, but due to constant rearrangements most of the intramural buildings are 18th century. These consist of 5 halls and 17 palaces of which the last occupied by the last Empress was the Palace of Accumulated Elegance (*Chu xia gong*) until 1924.

The largest residential palace in the world is the Vatican Palace, in the Vatican City, an enclave in Rome, Italy. Covering an area of 13½ acres, it has 1,400 rooms, chapels and halls, of which the oldest date from the 15th century.

The world's largest moats are those which surround the Imperial Palace in Peking. In plans drawn by French sources they appear to measure 54 yards wide and have a total length of 3,600 yards.

Apartments

Largest. The largest private apartment building is Dolphin Square, London, covering a site of 7½ acres. The building occupies the four sides of a square enclosing gardens of about 3 acres. Dolphin Square contains 1,220 separate and self-contained flats, an underground garage for 300 cars with filling and service station, a swimming pool, 8 squash courts, a tennis court and an indoor shopping center. It cost £1,750,000 ($8,750,000) to build in 1936 but was sold to Westminster City Council for £4,500,000 ($12,600,000) in January, 1963. Its nine stories house 3,000 people.

The Hyde Park development in Sheffield, Yorkshire, England, comprises 1,322 dwellings and an estimated population of 4,675 persons. It was built between 1959 and 1966.

Tallest. The tallest block of apartments in the world is Lake Point Towers of 70 stories, 645 feet high in Chicago.

Hotels

Largest. The hotel with the most rooms in the world is the Hotel Rossiya in Moscow, U.S.S.R., with 3,200 rooms providing accommodation for 5,350 guests. It would thus require more than 8½ years to spend one night in each room. In addition, there is a 21-story "Presidential" tower in the central courtyard. The hotel employs about 3,000 people and has 93 elevators. The ballroom is reputed to be the world's largest. Muscovites are not permitted as residents while foreigners are charged 16 times more than the low rate charged to officials of the U.S.S.R. It opened in 1967.

The largest commercial hotel building in the world is the Waldorf Astoria, on Park Avenue, between 49th and 50th Streets, New York City. It occupies a complete block of 81,337 square feet (1.87 acres) and reaches a maximum height of 625 feet 7 inches. The Waldorf Astoria has 47 stories and 1,900 guest rooms and maintains the largest hotel radio receiving system in the world. The Waldorf can accommodate 10,000 people at one time and has a staff of 1,700. The restaurants have catered for parties up to 6,000 at a time. The coffee-makers' daily output reaches 1,000 gallons. The electricity bill is about $360,000 each year. The hotel has housed six heads of state simultaneously and has both a resident gynecologist and mortician.

Tallest. The world's tallest hotel, measured from the street level of its main entrance to the top, is the 723-foot-tall 70-story Peachtree Center Plaza in Atlanta, Georgia, which was "topped" out on October 2, 1975, and opened in January, 1976. The $50,000,000, 1,100-room hotel is operated by Western International Hotels and owned by Portman Properties.

Most Expensive. The world's costliest hotel accommodation is the Celestial Suite on the ninth floor of the Astroworld Hotel,

TALLEST HOTEL: Opened
in January, 1976, Atlanta's
70-story Peachtree Plaza is
723 feet tall from street to top.

Houston, Texas, which is rented for $2,500 a day. It makes the
official New York City Presidential Suite in the Waldorf Astoria at
$450 a day seem positively lower middle class.

MOST COSTLY HOTEL ROOM: The bathroom in the Celestial Suite of the
Astroworld Hotel, Houston, which rents for $2,500 a day.

LARGEST HOUSE: Biltmore House in Asheville, North Carolina, has 250 rooms and was originally surrounded by 119,000 acres. When it was built by a Vanderbilt in the early 1890's, it cost $4,100,000, but today is worth $55,000,000.

Spas

The largest spa in the world measured by number of available hotel rooms is Vichy, Allier, France, with 14,000 rooms. Spas are named after the watering place in the Liège province of Belgium where hydropathy was developed from 1626. The highest French spa is Barèges, Hautes-Pyrénées, at 4,068 feet above sea level.

Barracks

The oldest purpose-built barracks in the world are believed to be Collins Barracks, formerly the Royal Barracks, Dublin, Ireland, completed in 1704 and still in use.

Largest House

The largest private house in the world is 250-room Biltmore House in Asheville, North Carolina. It is owned by George and William Cecil, grandsons of George Washington Vanderbilt II (1862–1914). The house was built between 1890 and 1895 in an estate of 119,000 acres, at a cost of $4,100,000, and is now valued at $55,000,000 with 12,000 acres.

The most expensive private house ever built is The Hearst Ranch at San Simeon, California. It was built 1922–39 for William Randolph Hearst (1863–1951), at a total cost of more than $30,000,000. It has more than 100 rooms, a 104-foot-long heated swimming pool, an 83-foot-long assembly hall and a garage for 25 limousines. The house would require 60 servants to maintain it.

The world's most expensive town house is the former home of the English Lord Brougham in Grafton Street, City of Westminster,

England. It was sold to the Irish Life Assurance Co. on August 28, 1973, for £3,350,000 ($8,040,000), and is now rented by Henry Ford II.

The world's most expensive penthouse apartment is a 4-story penthouse at the top of Galleria International on East 57th Street in New York City. With 4 main bedrooms, a 22-foot swimming pool, library, sauna and several solariums, it was on the market in March, 1976, for $3,500,000.

3. Buildings for Entertainment

Largest Circus. The world's largest permanent circus is Circus Circus, Las Vegas, Nevada, opened on October 18, 1968, at a cost of $15,000,000. It covers an area of 129,000 square feet capped by a 90-foot-high tent-shaped flexiglass roof. (See Circus Stunt records, Chapter 11.)

The new Moscow Circus, completed in 1968, has a seating capacity of 3,200.

Night Clubs

Oldest. The oldest night club (*boîte de nuit*) is "Le Bal des Anglais" at 6 Rue des Anglais, Paris 5*me*, France. It was founded in 1843.

Largest. The largest night club in the world is that in the Imperial Room of the Concord Hotel in the Catskill Mountains, New York, with a capacity of 3,000 patrons.

In the more classical sense the largest night club in the world is "The Mikado" in the Akasaka district of Tokyo, Japan, with a seating capacity of 2,000. It is "manned" by 1,250 hostesses, some

LARGEST CIRCUS: Circus Circus in Las Vegas, Nevada, built for $15 million in 1968 is covered by a 90-foot-high tent-shaped flexiglass roof.

LARGEST STADIUM: Up to 4,000 gymnasts perform for 240,000 spectators in
Strahov Stadium in Prague.

of whom earn $10,300 per annum. Binoculars are essential to an
appreciation of the floor show.

Loftiest. The highest night club is Altiteque 727 on the 49th
floor of the Royal Bank of Canada Building, Place Ville Marie,
Montreal. It is 617 feet above street level.

Lowest. The lowest night club is the "Minus 206" in Tiberias,
Israel, on the shores of the Sea of Galilee. It is 676 feet (206 meters)
below sea level. An alternative candidate is "Outer Limits," opposite
the Cow Palace, San Francisco, which was raided for the 151st time
on August 1, 1971. It has been called both "The Most Busted Joint"
and "The Slowest to Get the Message."

Largest Stadiums

The world's largest stadium is the Strahov Stadium in Praha
(Prague), Czechoslovakia. It was completed in 1934 and can
accommodate 240,000 spectators for mass displays of up to 40,000
Sokol gymnasts.

The largest football stadium in the world is the Maracaña Municipal Stadium in Rio de Janeiro, Brazil, which has a normal capacity
of 205,000, of whom 155,000 may be seated. A crowd of 199,854 was
accommodated for the World Cup soccer final between Brazil and
Uruguay on July 16, 1950. A dry moat, 7 feet wide and over 5 feet
deep, protects players from spectators and *vice versa*. The stadium also
has facilities for indoor sports, such as boxing, and these provide
accommodation for an additional 32,000 spectators.

The largest covered stadium in the world is the Azteca Stadium, Mexico City, opened in 1968, which has a capacity of 107,000, of whom nearly all are under cover.

Largest One-Piece Roof. The transparent acryl glass "tent" roof over the Munich Olympic Stadium, West Germany, measures 914,940 square feet in area. It rests on a steel net supported by masts, and cost $57,600,000. The roof of longest span in the world is the 680-foot diameter of the Louisiana Superdome (see below). The major axis of the elliptical Texas Stadium, completed in 1971 at Irving, Texas, is, however, 784 feet 4 inches.

Largest Indoor Arena. The world's largest indoor stadium is the 13-acre $173,000,000 273-foot Superdome in New Orleans, Louisiana, completed in May, 1975. Its maximum seating capacity for conventions is 97,365—for football, 76,791. Box suites rent for $35,000, excluding the price of admission. A gondola with six 312-inch TV screens produces instant replay (see page 275).

Largest Amusement Resort

The largest amusement resort is Disney World on 27,443 acres of Orange and Osceola Counties, 20 miles southwest of Orlando in central Florida. It was opened on October 1, 1971. This $400,000,000 investment attracted 10,700,000 visitors in its first year.

The most attended resort in the world is Disneyland, Anaheim, California, where the total number of visitors reached 137,267,000 by April 1, 1975.

LARGEST AMUSEMENT RESORT: Cinderella's Castle is one of the many attractions at Disney World, on 27,443 acres near Orlando, Florida.

LARGEST FERRIS WHEEL: The Riesenrad in Prater Park, Vienna, Austria, has a diameter of 197 feet.

Fairs

Earliest. The earliest major international fair was the Great Exhibition of 1851 in the Crystal Palace, Hyde Park, London, which in 141 days attracted 6,039,195 admissions.

Largest. The largest fair grounds were for the New York World's Fair, covering 1,216½ acres of Flushing Meadow Park, Queens, New York City, in 1939 and 1940. There were 25,817,265 admissions. An attendance of 51,607,037 was recorded for the 1964–65 Fair held on the same grounds.

Record Attendance. The record attendance for any fair was 65,000,000 for Expo '70 held on an 815-acre site at Osaka, Japan, from March to September 13, 1970. It made a profit of more than $30,000,000.

Ferris Wheel. The original Ferris Wheel, named after its constructor, George W. Ferris (1859–96), was erected in 1893 at the Midway, Chicago, at a cost of $385,000. The wheel was 250 feet in diameter, 790 feet in circumference, weighed 1,070 tons, and carried 36 cars each seating 60 people, making a total of 2,160 passengers. The structure was removed in 1904 to St. Louis, and was eventually sold as scrap for $1,800. In 1897, a Ferris Wheel with a diameter of 300 feet was erected for the Earls Court Exhibition, London. The largest wheel now operating is the Riesenrad in Prater Park, Vienna, Austria, with a diameter of 197 feet. It was built in 1896 and carried 15,000,000 people in its first 75 years.

Largest and Fastest Roller Coaster. The maximum speeds claimed for roller coasters tend to be exaggerated for commercial reasons. The world's highest are the 110-foot-high "The Racer" in Chapultepec Park, Mexico City, and "The Screamin' Eagle" at Eureka, Missouri. Even the highest roller coaster of all-time, the 120-foot-high "Blue Streak" (now demolished) in Woodcliffe Pleasure Park, Poughkeepsie, New York, could produce only 57 m.p.h.

The longest roller coaster is "The Comet" at Crystal Beach Park, Ontario, Canada, with a 4,800-foot track.

TALLEST ROLLER COASTER: "The Screamin' Eagle," which cost $3 million, is located in Six Flags Over Mid-America amusement park near St. Louis, Missouri. It is 110 feet tall at its highest point and has a single drop of 92 feet. Cars are said to reach a speed of 62 m.p.h. during a circuit.

Pleasure Beach

The largest pleasure beach in the world is Virginia Beach, Virginia. It has 28 miles of beach front on the Atlantic and 10 miles of estuary frontage. The area embraces 255 square miles and contains 134 hotels and motels.

Longest Pleasure Pier

The longest pleasure pier in the world is Southend Pier at Southend-on-Sea in Essex, England. It is 1.34 miles in length, and was first opened in August, 1889, with final extensions made in 1929. It is decorated with more than 75,000 lamps. The peak attendance was 5,750,000 in 1949–50.

Bars

The largest beer-selling establishment in the world is the Mathäser, Bayerstrasse 5, Munich, West Germany, where the daily sale reaches 84,470 pints. It was established in 1829, was demolished in World War II, rebuilt by 1955, and now seats 5,500 people. Consumption at the Dube beer halls in the Bantu township of Soweto, Johannesburg, South Africa, may, however, be higher on some Saturdays when the average of 6,000 gallons (48,000 pints) is far exceeded.

Longest Bar. The longest bar with beer pumps was built in 1938 at the Working Men's Club, Mildura, Victoria, Australia. It has a counter 287 feet in length, served by 32 pumps. Temporary bars have been erected of greater length. The Falstaff Brewing Corp. put up a temporary bar 336 feet 5 inches in length on Wharf St., St. Louis, Missouri, on June 22, 1970.

Wine Cellar. The largest wine cellars in the world are at Paarl, those of the Ko-operative Wijnbouwers Vereeniging (K.W.V.), near Cape Town, in the center of the wine district of South Africa. They cover an area of 25 acres and have a capacity of 36,000,000 gallons. The largest blending vats have a capacity of 54,880 gallons, and are 17 feet high and 26 feet in diameter.

4. Towers and Masts

Tallest Structure

The tallest structure in the world is the guyed Warszawa Radio mast at Konstantynow near Gabin and Plock in Poland, which is 2,117 feet 4½ inches tall, or more than four-tenths of a mile. The mast was completed on May 18, 1974, and put into operation on July 22, 1974. Work had begun in 1970. It was designed by Jan Polak and weighs 550 tons. The mast is so high that anyone falling off the top would reach terminal velocity, and hence cease to be accelerating, before hitting the ground. It recaptured for Europe a record held in the United States since the Chrysler Building surpassed the Eiffel Tower in 1929.

Tallest Tower

The tallest self-supporting tower (as opposed to a guyed mast) in the world is the $44,000,000 CN Tower in Metro Centre, Toronto, Canada. It rises to 1,815 feet 5 inches. Excavation began on February 12, 1973, for the 130,000-ton structure of reinforced, post-tensioned concrete. A 400-seat restaurant revolves in the 7-floor Sky Pod at 1,140 feet, from which the visibility extends to 74½ miles.

The tallest tower built before the era of television masts is the Tour Eiffel (Eiffel Tower), in Paris, France, designed by Alexandre Gustave Eiffel (1832–1923) for the Paris exhibition and completed on March 31, 1889. It was 985 feet 11 inches tall, now extended by a TV antenna to 1,052 feet 4 inches, and weighs 8,091 tons. The maximum sway in high winds is 5 inches. The whole iron edifice, which has 1,792 steps, took 2 years, 2 months, and 2 days to build and cost 7,799,401 francs 31 centimes.

The architects André and Jan Polak put forward a design in February, 1969, for a tower 2,378.6 feet in height to be erected at La Défense in Paris.

5. Bridges

Oldest. Arch construction was understood by the Sumerians as early as 3200 B.C., and a reference exists to a Nile bridge in 2650 B.C. The oldest surviving datable bridge in the world is the slab stone single-arch bridge over the River Meles in Smyrna (now Izmir), Turkey, which dates from *c.* 850 B.C.

Longest Suspension. The world's longest single span bridge is the Verrazano-Narrows Bridge stretching across the entrance to New York Harbor from Staten Island to Brooklyn. Work on the $305,000,000 project began on August 13, 1959, and the bridge was opened to traffic on November 21, 1964. It measures 6,690 feet

LONGEST SINGLE SPAN BRIDGE: The Verrazano-Narrows Bridge, whose main span is 4,260 feet long, straddles the mouth of New York Harbor.

between anchorages and carries two decks, each with six lanes of traffic. The center span is 4,260 feet and the tops of the main towers (each 690 feet tall) are 1⅝ inches out of parallel, to allow for the curvature of the earth.

The Mackinac Straits Bridge between Mackinaw City and St. Ignace, Michigan, is the longest suspension bridge in the world measured between anchorages (8,344 feet) and has an overall length, including viaducts of the bridge proper measured between abutment faces, of 19,205 feet 4 inches. It was opened in November, 1957 (dedicated June 28, 1958) at a cost of $100 million and has a main span of 3,800 feet.

The main span of the £50 million ($100 million) Humber Estuary Bridge, England, will be the longest in the world at 4,626 feet when completed in 1977. Work began on July 27, 1972. Work on the double-deck railroad Akashi-Kaikyo bridge linking Hinshu and Shikoku, Japan, is expected to start in late 1975 for completion in 1988. The main span will be 5,840 feet in length with an overall suspended length with side spans totaling 11,680 feet.

Longest Cantilever. The Québec Bridge (Pont de Québec) over the St. Lawrence River in Canada has the longest cantilever span of any in the world—1,800 feet between the piers and 3,239 feet overall. It carries a railway track and two roadways. Begun in 1899, it was finally opened to traffic on December 3, 1917, at a cost of Can. $22,500,000 and 87 lives.

Longest Steel Arch. The longest steel arch bridge in the world will be the New River Gorge bridge near Fayetteville, West Virginia, due to be completed in 1976, with a span of 1,700 feet.

LONGEST BRIDGE SPANS IN THE WORLD—BY TYPE

	feet		opening
Suspension	4,626	Humber Estuary, England	1977
Cantilever	1,800	Québec Railway, Québec, Canada	1917
Steel Arch	1,700	New River George, Fayetteville, W. Virginia	1976
Covered bridge	1,282	Hartland, New Brunswick, Canada	1899
Continuous truss	1,232	Astoria, Columbia River, Oregon	1966
Cable-stayed	1,500	Second Hooghly, Calcutta, India	1977
Chain suspension	1,114	Hercilio Luz, Florianopolis, Brazil	1926
Concrete arch	1,000	Gladesville, Sydney, Australia	1964
Plate and box girder	984	Rio Niterói, Rio de Janeiro, Brazil	1974

Railroad. The longest railroad bridge in the world is the Huey P. Long Bridge, Metairie, Louisiana, with a railroad section 22,996 feet (4.35 miles) long. It was completed on December 16, 1935, with a longest span of 790 feet.

It is sometimes claimed that the Yangtse River Bridge completed in 1968 in Nanking, China, is the world's longest railroad bridge if the rail deck of 4.16 miles is added to the road deck (2.79 miles) to total 6.95 miles.

Floating. The longest floating bridge in the world is the Second Lake Washington Bridge in Seattle, Washington. Its total length is 12,596 feet and its floating section measures 7,518 feet (1.42 miles). It was built at a cost of $15,000,000, and completed in August, 1963.

Highest. The highest bridge in the world is the bridge over the Royal Gorge of the Arkansas River in Colorado. It is 1,053 feet above the water level. It has a main span of 880 feet and was constructed in 6 months, ending on December 6, 1929. The highest railroad bridge in the world is at Fades, outside Clermont-Ferrand, France. It was built in 1901–09 with a span of 472 feet and is 435 feet above the River Sioule.

Widest. The bridge with the widest roadway is the Crawford Street Bridge in Providence, Rhode Island, with a width of 1,147 feet.

The widest long-span bridge is the 1,650-foot-span Sydney Harbour Bridge, Australia, which is 160 feet wide. It carries two electric overhead railroad tracks, 8 lanes of roadway and a cycleway and footway. It was officially opened on March 19, 1932.

The River Roch in England is bridged for a distance of 1,460 feet where the culvert passes through the center of Rochdale, Greater Manchester, and this is sometimes claimed as a breadth.

Deepest Foundation. The deepest foundations of any structure are those of the 3,323-foot-span Ponte de 25 de Abril (formerly Ponte de Salazar), which was opened on August 6, 1966, at a cost of $75,000,000, across the Rio Tejo (the River Tagus), at Lisbon, Portugal. One of the 625-foot-tall towers extends 260 feet down.

Covered. The longest covered bridge in the world is that at Hartland, New Brunswick, Canada, measuring 1,282 feet, completed in 1899.

Longest Bridging. The world's longest bridging is the second Lake Pontchartrain Causeway, opened on March 23, 1969, joining Lewisburg and Metairie, Louisiana. Its length is 126,055 feet (23.87 miles). It was completed at a cost of $29,900,000 and is 228 feet longer than the adjoining First Causeway completed in 1956.

The longest railroad viaduct in the world is the rock-filled Great Salt Lake Viaduct, carrying the Southern Pacific Railroad 11.85 miles across the Great Salt Lake, Utah. It was opened as a pile and trestle bridge on March 8, 1904, and converted to rock fill in 1955–1960.

The longest stone arch bridging in the world is the 3,810-foot-long Rockville Bridge north of Harrisburg, Pennsylvania, with 48 spans containing 219,520 tons of stone and completed in 1901.

PROGRESSIVE RECORD OF WORLD'S LONGEST BRIDGE SPANS

Feet	Location	Type	Completion
121	Martorell, Spain	Stone Arch	219 B.C.
142	Nera River, Lucca, Italy	Stone Arch	14 A.D.
170	Trajan's Bridge, Danube River	Timber Arch	104
251	Trezzo, Italy	Stone Arch	1377
390	Wettingen, Switzerland	Timber Arch	1758
408	Schuylkill Falls, Philadelphia, Pa.	Suspension	1816
449	Union Bridge, Berwick, England	Chain	1820
580	Menai Straits, Wales	Chain	1826
870	Fribourg, Switzerland	Suspension	1834
1,010	Wheeling-Ohio Bridge	Suspension	1849
1,043	Lewiston Bridge, Niagara River	Suspension	1851
1,057	Covington-Cincinnati Bridge (rebuilt 1898)	Suspension	1867
1,268	Clifton Bridge, Niagara Falls	Suspension	1869
1,595½	Brooklyn Bridge, New York City	Suspension	1883
1,706	Forth Bridge, Scotland	Cantilever	1889
1,800	Québec Bridge, Canada	Cantilever	1917
1,850	Ambassador Bridge, Detroit	Suspension	1929
3,500	George Washington Bridge, New York City	Suspension	1931
4,200	San Francisco Golden Gate	Suspension	1937
4,260	Verrazano-Narrows Bridge, New York City	Suspension	1964
4,626	Humber Estuary, England	Suspension	1977

Longest Aqueduct. The greatest of ancient aqueducts was the Aqueduct of Carthage in Tunisia, which ran 87.6 miles from the springs of Zaghouan to Djebel Djougar. It was built by the Romans during the reign of Publius Aelius Hadrianus (117–138 A.D.). By 1895, 344 arches still survived. Its original capacity has been calculated at 8,400,000 gallons per day. The triple-tiered aqueduct

GREATEST ROMAN AQUEDUCT: The top tier of the triple-tiered Pont du Gard near Nîmes, France, extends 855 feet from bank to bank of the River Gard.

LONGEST BIG SHIP CANAL: The Suez Canal was first opened on November 16, 1869, after 10 heroic years of construction.

Pont du Gard, built in 19 A.D. near Nîmes, France, is 160 feet high. The tallest of the 14 arches of the Aguas Livres Aqueduct, built in Lisbon, Portugal, in 1748, is 213 feet 3 inches.

The world's longest aqueduct, in the modern sense of a water conduit, is the California State Water Project aqueduct, completed in 1974 to a length of 826 miles, of which 385 miles is canalized.

6. Canals

Relics of the oldest canals in the world, dated by archeologists to 5000 B.C., were discovered near Mandali, Iraq, early in 1968.

Longest. The largest canalized system in the world is the Volga-Baltic Canal opened in April, 1965. It runs 1,850 miles from Astrakhan up the Volga, *via* Kuybyshev, Gor'kiy and Lake Ladoga, to Leningrad, U.S.S.R. The longest canal of the ancient world was the Grand Canal of China from Peking to Hangchow. It was begun in 540 B.C. and not completed until 1283 by which time it extended for 1,107 miles. The estimated work force at one time reached 5,000,000. Having been allowed by 1950 to silt up to the point that it was in no place more than 6 feet deep, it is now, however, plied by ships of up to 2,240 tons.

The Beloye More (White Sea)-Baltic Canal from Belomorsk to Povenets, in the U.S.S.R., is 141 miles long with 19 locks. It was completed with the use of forced labor in 1933 and cannot accommodate ships of more than 16 feet in draught.

The world's longest big ship canal is the Suez Canal, linking the Red and Mediterranean Seas, opened on November 16, 1869, but inoperative from June, 1967, to June, 1975. The canal was planned by the French diplomatist Ferdinand de Lesseps (1805–1894) and work began on April 25, 1859. It is 100.6 miles in length from Port Said lighthouse to Suez Roads, 197 feet wide. The work force was 8,213 men and 368 camels.

Busiest. The busiest big ship canal is the Panama, first transited on August 15, 1914. In 1974, there were a record 14,304 oceangoing transits. The largest liner to transit is *Queen Elizabeth* 2 on March 25, 1975, for a toll of $42,077.88. The ships with the greatest beam to transit have been the *Acadia Forest* and the *Atlantic Forest*, each of 106.9 feet. The lowest toll was 36 cents for the swimmer Richard Halliburton in 1928. The fastest transit has been 4 hours 38 minutes by the destroyer U.S.S. *Manley*.

Seaway. The world's longest artificial seaway is the St. Lawrence Seaway (189 miles long) along the New York State-Ontario border from Montreal to Lake Ontario, which enables 80 per cent of all ocean-going ships, and bulk carriers with a capacity of 26,000 tons, to sail 2,342 miles from the North Atlantic, up the St. Lawrence Estuary and across the Great Lakes to Duluth, Minnesota, on Lake Superior (602 feet above sea level). The project cost $470,000,000 and was opened on April 25, 1959.

Irrigation. The longest irrigation canal in the world is the Karakumskiy Kanal, stretching 528 miles from Haun-Khan to Ashkhabad, Turkmenistan, U.S.S.R. In September, 1971, the navigable length was reported to have reached 280 miles. The length of the $925,000,000 project will eventually reach 930 miles.

Locks

Largest. The world's largest single lock connects the Schelde with the Kanaaldok system at Zandvliet, west of Antwerp, Belgium. It is 1,640 feet long and 187 feet wide and is an entrance to an impounded sheet of water 11.2 miles long.

Deepest. The world's deepest lock is the John Day Dam lock on the Columbia River, Oregon and Washington, completed in 1963. It can raise or lower barges 113 feet and is served by a 1,100-ton gate.

HIGHEST DAM: When completed in 1979, the Nurek dam in the U.S.S.R. will be 1,017 feet high.

Highest Lock Elevator. The world's highest lock elevator is the Arzwiller-Saint Louis, France, lift completed in 1969 to replace 17 locks on the Marne-Rhine canal system. It drops 146 feet over a ramp 383.8 feet long on a 41° gradient.

Largest Cut. The Gaillard Cut (known as "the Ditch") on the Panama Canal is 270 feet deep between Gold Hill and Contractor's Hill with a bottom width of 500 feet. In one day in 1911 as many as 333 dirt trains each carrying 400 tons left this site. The total amount of earth excavated for the whole Panama Canal was 9,980,000 tons, which total will be raised by the further widening of the Gaillard Cut to 500 feet.

7. Dams

Earliest. The earliest dam ever built was the Sadd al-Kafara, 7 miles southeast of Helwan, Egypt. It was built in the period 2950–2750 B.C. and had a length of 348 feet and a height of 37 feet.

Most Massive. Measured by volume, the largest dam in the world is the Tarbela Dam, across the Indus River in the Hazara District, Pakistan. The total expenditure on the 470-foot-tall, 9,000-foot-long construction surpassed $815 million including the $623 million contract awarded to the Impregilo Consortium. The total volume of the dam is 159,000,000 cubic yards.

Largest Concrete. The world's largest concrete dam, and the largest concrete structure in the world, is the Grand Coulee Dam on the Columbia River, Washington. Work on the dam was begun in 1933, it began working on March 22, 1941, and was completed in 1942, at a cost of $56,000,000. It has a crest length of 4,173 feet and is 550 feet high. It contains 10,585,000 cubic yards of concrete, and weighs about 21,600,000 tons. The hydroelectric power plant (now being extended) will have a capacity of 9,771,000 kilowatts.

Highest. The highest dam in the world is the Grand Dixence in Switzerland, completed in September, 1961, at a cost of $372,000,000. It is 932 feet from base to rim, 2,296 feet long and the total volume of concrete in the dam is 7,792,000 cubic yards.

The earth-fill Nurek dam on the Vakhsh-Amu Darya River, U.S.S.R., will be 1,017 feet high, have a crest length of 2,390 feet and a volume of 70,806,000 cubic yards. Work began in 1961, but the completion date has so far slipped from 1967 to 1979.

The concrete Ingurskaya dam in western Georgia, U.S.S.R., was planned to have a final height of 988 feet, a crest length of 2,390 feet but may be completed only to 892 feet.

Longest. The longest river dam is the 62-foot-high Kiev dam on the Dnepr River, U.S.S.R., which was completed in 1964 to a length of 33.6 miles. In the early 17th century, an impounding dam of moderate height was built in Lake Hungtze, Kiangsu, China, to a reputed length of 62 miles.

The longest sea dam in the world is the Afsluitdijk stretching 20.195 miles across the mouth of the Zuider Zee in two sections of 1.553 miles (mainland of North Holland to the Isle of Wieringen) and 18.641 miles (Wieringen to Friesland). It has a sea-level width of 293 feet and a height of 24 feet 7 inches.

Largest Reservoir

The most voluminous man-made reservoir is Bratsk reservoir on the Angara River, U.S.S.R., with a volume of 137,214,000 acre-feet. The dam was completed in 1964.

The world's largest artificial lake measured by surface area is Lake Volta, Ghana, formed by the Akosombo dam, completed in 1965. By 1969, the lake had filled an area of 3,275 square miles with a shoreline 4,500 miles in length.

The completion in 1954 of the Owen Falls Dam near Jinja, Uganda, across the northern exit of the White Nile River from the lake, Victoria Nyanza, marginally raised the level of that lake by adding 166,000,000 acre-feet, and technically turned it into a reservoir with a surface area of 17,169,920 acres (26,828 square miles).

The most grandiose reservoir project planned is the Xingu-Araguaia river scheme in central Brazil for a reservoir behind a dam at Ilha da Paz with a volume of 780,000 million cubic yards extending over 22,800 square miles. A dam at Obidos on the Amazon would produce a 744-mile-long back-up and a 68,400-square-mile reservoir at an estimated cost of $3,000,000,000.

Largest Polder

The largest of the five great polders in the old Zuider Zee, Netherlands, will be the 149,000-acre (232.8 square-mile) Markerwaard. Work on the 66-mile-long surrounding dyke was begun in 1957. The water area remaining after the erection of the 1927–32 dam (20 miles in length) is called IJssel Meer, which will have a final area of 487.5 square miles.

Largest Levees

The most massive levees ever carried out are the Mississippi levees begun in 1717 and vastly augmented by the U.S. Government after the disastrous floods of 1927. These extend for 1,732 miles along the main river from Cape Girardeau, Missouri, to the Gulf of Mexico and comprise more than 1,000,000,000 cubic yards of earthworks. Additional levees on the tributaries comprise an additional 2,000 miles.

8. Tunnels

Longest. The world's longest tunnel of any kind is the New York City-West Delaware water supply tunnel begun in 1937 and completed in 1944. It has a diameter of 13 feet 6 inches and runs for 105 miles from the Rondout Reservoir in the Catskill Mountains into the Hillview Reservoir, near the northern city line of New York City.

Subway. The world's longest continuous vehicular tunnel is the London Transport Board underground railway line from Morden to East Finchley, *via* Bank, in London. In use since 1939, it is 17 miles 528 yards long. The diameter of the tunnel is 12 feet and the station tunnels 22.2 feet.

Bridge-Tunnel. The world's longest bridge-tunnel system is the Chesapeake Bay Bridge-Tunnel, extending 17.65 miles from the Delmarva Peninsula to Norfolk, Virginia. It cost $200,000,000, took 42 months to complete, and opened on April 15, 1964. The longest bridged section is Trestle C (4.56 miles long) and the longest tunnel is the Thimble Shoal Channel Tunnel (1.09 miles).

Canal-Tunnel. The world's longest canal-tunnel is that on the Rove Canal between the port of Marseilles, France, and the Rhône River, built in 1912–27. It is 4.53 miles long, 72 feet wide and 50 feet high, involving 2,250,000 cubic yards of excavation.

Railroad. The world's longest main-line tunnel is the Simplon II Tunnel, completed after 4 years' work on October 16, 1922. Linking Switzerland and Italy under the Alps, it is 12 miles 559 yards long. Over 60 were killed boring this and the Simplon I (1896–1906), which is 22 yards shorter. Its greatest depth below the surface is 7,005 feet.

LONGEST BRIDGE-TUNNEL stretches 17.65 miles across four man-made islands in Chesapeake Bay between the Delmarva Peninsula, Va., and the Virginia mainland.

Sub-aqueous. The world's longest sub-aqueous railroad tunnel will be the Seikan Rail Tunnel (33.49 miles), 328 feet beneath the sea bed of the Tsugaru Strait between Tappi Saki, Honshu, and Fukushima, Hokkaido, Japan. It is due to be completed in 1979 at a cost of $552,000,000. Tests started on the sub-aqueous section (14.5 miles) in 1963 and construction in June, 1972.

Currently the world's longest sub-aqueous rail tunnel is the Shin Kanmon Tunnel, completed in May, 1974, which runs 11.55 miles from Honshu to Kyushu, Japan.

Road. The world's longest road tunnel is 7.2 miles long under Mont Blanc (15,771 feet) from Pèlerins, near Chamonix, France, to Entrèves, near Courmayeur in Valle d'Aosta, Italy, on which work began in January, 1959. The holing through was achieved on August 14, 1962, and it was opened to traffic on July 16, 1965, after an expenditure of $63,840,000. The 29½-foot-high tunnel with its carriageway of two 12-foot lanes is expected to carry 600,000 vehicles a year. There were 23 deaths during tunneling.

The largest diameter road tunnel in the world was blasted through Yerba Buena Island in San Francisco Bay. It is 76 feet wide, 58 feet high and 540 feet long. Up to 35,000,000 vehicles pass through on its two decks every year.

Sub-aqueous. The world's longest sub-aqueous road tunnel is the New Kanmon Tunnel, completed in May, 1974, which runs 11.6 miles from Honshu to Kyushu, Japan.

Irrigation. The longest irrigation tunnel in the world is the 51.5-mile-long Orange-Fish Rivers Tunnel, South Africa, begun in 1967, at an estimated cost of $150,000,000. The boring was completed in April, 1973. The lining, to a minimum thickness of 9 inches, will give a completed diameter of 17 feet 6 inches. The total work force at times exceeded 5,000 men. Some of the access shafts in the eight sections descend more than 1,000 feet.

Tunneling. The records for rapid tunneling were set on March 18, 1967, in the 8.6-mile-long Blanco Tunnel, in Southern Colorado,

LONGEST IRRIGATION TUNNEL: The Orange-Fish Rivers Tunnel in South Africa runs 51½ miles to this opening.

when the "mole" (giant boring machine) crew advanced the 10-foot diameter heading 375 feet in one day, and on June 26, 1972, in the 20½-foot diameter Navajo Tunnel 3 project, in New Mexico, with an advance of 247 lineal feet.

9. Specialized Structures

Seven Wonders of the World

The Seven Wonders of the World were first designated by Antipater of Sidon in the 2nd century B.C. They included the Pyramids of Giza, built by three Fourth Dynasty Egyptian Pharaohs, Hwfw (Khufu or Cheops), Kha-f-Ra (Khafre, Khefren or Chephren) and Menkaure (Mycerinus) near El Giza (El Gizeh), southwest of El Qahira (Cairo) in Egypt (once the United Arab Republic). The Great Pyramid ("Horizon of Khufu") was built c. 2580 B.C. Its original height was 480 feet 11 inches (now, since the loss of its topmost stones or pyramidion, reduced to 449 feet 6 inches) with a base line of 756 feet and thus covering slightly more than 13 acres. It has been estimated that a permanent work force of 4,000 required 30 years to maneuver into position the 2,300,000 stone blocks averaging 2¾ tons each, totaling about 7,225,000 tons and a volume of 90,700,000 cubic feet. A cost estimate published in December, 1974, indicates that today it would require 405 men working 6 years at a cost of $1,130,000,000.

Of the other six wonders, only fragments remain of the Temple of Artemis (Diana) of the Ephesians, built c. 350 B.C. at Ephesus, Turkey (destroyed by the Goths in 262 A.D.), and of the Tomb of King Mausolus of Caria, built at Halicarnassus, now Bodrum, Turkey, c. 325 B.C. No trace remains of the Hanging Gardens of Semiramis, at Babylon, Iraq (c. 600 B.C.); the 40-foot-tall marble, gold and ivory statue of Zeus (Jupiter), by Phidias (5th century B.C.) at Olympia, Greece (lost in a fire at Istanbul); the 117-foot-tall statue by Chares of Lindus of the figure of the god Helios (Apollo), called the Colossus of Rhodes (sculptured 292–280 B.C., destroyed by an earthquake in 224 B.C.); or the 400-foot-tall lighthouse built by Sostratus of Cnidus during the 3rd century B.C. (destroyed by an earthquake in 1375 A.D.) on the island of Pharos (Greek, *pharos*= lighthouse), off the coast of El Iskandarîya (Alexandria), Egypt.

Pyramids

Largest. The largest pyramid, and the largest monument ever constructed, is the Quetzalcóatl at Cholula de Rivadabia, 63 miles southeast of Mexico City. It is 177 feet tall and its base covers an area of nearly 45 acres. Its total volume has been estimated at 4,300,000 cubic yards, compared with 3,360,000 cubic yards for the Pyramid of Cheops (see above). The pyramid-building era here was between the 2nd and 6th centuries A.D.

Oldest. The oldest known pyramid is the Djoser step pyramid at Saqqâra, Egypt, constructed to a height of 204 feet of Tura limesone c. 2650 B.C. The oldest New World pyramid is that on the island of La Venta in southeastern Mexico built by the Olmec people c. 800 B.C. It is 100 feet tall with a base diameter of 420 feet.

TALLEST STATUE (left): The female figure called "Motherland" on a hill outside Volgograd, U.S.S.R., is 270 feet high from base to tip of sword. TALLEST MONUMENTAL COLUMN (right): This 570-foot-tall column near Houston, Texas, commemorates the Battle of San Jacinto.

Tallest Totem Pole

The tallest totem pole in the world is 173 feet tall raised on June 6, 1973 at Alert Bay, British Columbia, Canada. It tells the story of the Kwakiutl and took 36 man-weeks to carve.

Tallest Barber's Pole

The world's tallest barber pole is 50 feet 3 inches high, erected on November 1, 1973, on Walker Road, Alexander, New York.

Tallest Flagpole

The tallest flagpole ever erected was outside the Oregon Building at the 1915 Panama-Pacific International Exposition in San Francisco. Trimmed from a Douglas fir, it stood 299 feet 7 inches in height. The tallest unsupported flagpole in the world is a 220-foot-tall metal pole weighing 28,000 lbs., erected in 1955 at the U.S. Merchant Marine Academy in King's Point, New York. The pole, built by Kearney-National Inc., tapers from 24 inches to $5\frac{1}{2}$ inches at the jack.

Tallest Statue. The tallest free-standing statue in the world is that of the "Motherland," an enormous female figure on Mamayev Hill, outside Volgograd, U.S.S.R., designed in 1967 by Yevgenyi Vuchetich, to commemorate victory in the Battle of Stalingrad (1942–43). The statue from its base to the tip of a sword clenched in her right hand measures 270 feet.

The U.S. sculptor Felix de Welton has announced a plan to reproduce the Colossus of Rhodes in a 308-foot version.

Near Bamiyan, Afghanistan, there are the remains of the recumbent Sakya Buddha, built of plastered rubble, which was "about 1,000 feet long" and is believed to date from the 3rd or 4th century A.D.

Obelisks

Oldest. The longest an obelisk has remained *in situ* is that at Heliopolis, near Aswan, Egypt, erected by Senusret I *c.* 1750 B.C.

Largest. The largest standing obelisk in the world is that in the Piazza of St. John in Lateran, Rome, erected in 1588. It came originally from the Circus Maximus (erected 357 A.D.) and before that from Heliopolis, Egypt (erected *c.* 1450 B.C.). It is 110 feet in height and weighs 504 tons.

Tallest Columns

The tallest columns in the world are the thirty-six fluted pillars of Vermont marble on the colonnade of the Education Building, Albany, New York. Each one measures 90 feet tall and 6½ feet in base diameter.

The tallest load-bearing stone columns are those measuring 69 feet in the Hall of Columns of the Temple of Amun at Al Karnak, the northern part of the ruins of Thebes, the Greek name for the ancient capital of Upper Egypt. They were built in the 19th dynasty in the reign of Rameses II in *c.* 1270 B.C.

Monuments

Tallest. The world's tallest monument is the stainless steel Gateway Arch in St. Louis, Missouri, completed on October 28, 1965, to commemorate the westward expansion after the Louisiana Purchase of 1803. It is a sweeping arch of stainless steel, spanning 630 feet and rising to a height of 630 feet, and costing $29,000,000. It was designed in 1947 by Eero Saarinen (died 1961). (See photo on next page).

The tallest monumental column in the world commemorates the battle of San Jacinto (April 21, 1836), on the bank of the San Jacinto River near Houston, Texas. General Sam Houston (1793–1863) and his force of 743 Texan troops killed 630 Mexicans (out of a total force of 1,600) and captured 700 others, with the loss of nine men killed and 30 wounded. Constructed in 1936–39, at a cost of $1,500,000, the tapering column is 570 feet tall, 47 feet square at the base, and 30 feet square at the observation tower, which is surmounted by a star weighing 220 tons. It is built of concrete, faced with buff limestone, and weighs 35,150 tons.

TALLEST MONUMENT: This Gateway Arch at the edge of the Mississippi River in St. Louis was designed by Eero Saarinen, is 630 feet high, and has a span of 630 feet.

Largest Prehistoric. The largest megalithic prehistoric monuments in Britain are the 28½-acre earthworks and stone circles of Avebury, Wiltshire, rediscovered in 1646. The earliest calibrated date in the area of this neolithic site is *c.* 4200 B.C. The whole work is 1,200 feet in diameter with a 40-foot ditch around the perimeter and required an estimated 15 million man-hours of work. The largest trilithons exist at Stonehenge, to the south of Salisbury Plain, Wiltshire, with single sarsen blocks weighing over 45 long tons and requiring over 550 men to drag them up a 9° gradient. The dating of the ditch was, in 1969, revised to 2180 B.C. ±105. Whether Stonehenge was a lunar calendar or an eclipse-predictor remains debatable.

Largest Earthworks. The largest earthworks in the world carried out prior to the mechanical era were the Linear Earth

Boundaries of the Benin Empire in the Mid-Western state of Nigeria. These were first reported in 1903 and partially surveyed in 1967. In April, 1973, it was estimated that the total length of the earthworks was probably between 4,000 and 8,000 miles with a total of almost 600,000,000 cubic yards of earth moved.

Largest Tomb

The largest tomb in the world is that of Emperor Nintoku (died *c.* 428 A.D.) south of Osaka, Japan. It measures 1,594 feet long by 1,000 feet wide by 150 feet high.

Ziggurat (Temple Tower)

The largest surviving ziggurat (from the verb *zigguratu*, Babylonian, to build high) is the Ziggurat of Ur (now Muqqayr, Iraq) with a base 200 feet by 150 feet built to at least three stories of which only the first and part of the second now survive to a height of 60 feet. It was built by the Akkadian King Ur-Nammu (*c.* 2113–2006 B.C.) to the moon god Nanna.

Largest Dome

The world's largest dome is the Louisiana Superdome in New Orleans. It has an outside diameter of 680 feet.

The largest dome of ancient architecture is that of the Pantheon, built in Rome in 112 A.D., with a diameter of 142½ feet.

Docks

Largest Drydock. The largest drydock in the world is that at Nigg Bay, Cromarty Firth, Highland, Scotland, completed in 1973 for the construction of North Sea oil-drilling platforms. It measures 1,000 feet by 600 feet with a depth of 43 feet over sill.

The largest shipbuilding drydock in the world is the Belfast Harbour Commission and Harland and Wolff building dock at Belfast, Northern Ireland. It was excavated to a length of 1,825 feet and a width of 305 feet, and could accommodate tankers of

LARGEST DOME: Crowning the Superdome in New Orleans, this dome has an outside diameter of 680 feet.

1 million d.w.t. Work began on January 26, 1968, and was completed on November 30, 1969, and involved the excavation of 400,000 cubic yards. (See also *Largest Crane.*)

A drydock under construction at Port Rashid, Dubai, Persian Gulf, due for completion in 1978, will measure 1,722 feet by 328 feet.

Largest Dock Gate. The worlds largest dock gate is that at Nigg Bay, Cromarty Firth, Scotland (see above), first operated in March, 1974. It measures 408 feet long, 50 feet high, with a 4-foot-thick base, and is made of reinforced concrete. With its sill, quoins and roundheads, it weighs a total of 17,882 tons.

Largest Floating Dock. The world's largest floating dock is under construction at Genoa, Italy, with a lifting capacity of 110,000 tons. It has an overall length of $1,149\frac{1}{2}$ feet, a clear width of $215\frac{1}{2}$ feet, and a 49-foot draught.

Longest Jetty

The longest deep-water jetty in the world is the Quai Hermann du Pasquier at Le Havre, France, with a length of 5,000 feet. Part of an enclosed basin, it has a constant depth of water of 32 feet on both sides.

Longest Pier

The world's longest pier is the Dammam Pier in El Hasa, Saudi Arabia, on the Persian Gulf. A rock-filled causeway 4.84 miles long joins the steel trestle pier 1.80 miles long, which joins the Main Pier (744 feet long), giving an overall length of 6.79 miles. The work was begun in July, 1948, and completed on March 15, 1950.

Longest Breakwater

The world's longest breakwater system is that which protects the Ports of Long Beach and Los Angeles, California. The combined length of the four breakwaters is 43,602 feet (8.26 miles) of which the Long Beach section, built between 1941 and February, 1949, is the longest at 13,350 feet (2.53 miles). The north breakwater at Tuticorin, Madras Province, Southern India, on which construction began in 1968, extends to 13,589 feet.

Lighthouses

Brightest. The lighthouse with the most powerful light in the world is Créac'h d'Ouessant lighthouse, established in 1638 and last altered in 1939 on l'Île d'Ouessant, Finistère, Brittany, France. It is 163 feet tall and, in times of fog, has a luminous intensity of up to 490,500,000 candles.

The lights with the greatest visible range are those 1,092 feet above the ground on the Empire State Building, New York City. Each of the four-arc mercury bulbs has a rated candlepower of 450,000,000, visible 80 miles away on the ground and 300 miles away from aircraft. They were switched on on March 31, 1956.

Tallest. The world's tallest lighthouse is the steel tower 348 feet tall near Yamashita Park in Yokohama, Japan. It has a power of 600,000 candles and a visibility range of 20 miles.

MOST POWERFUL LIGHTHOUSE (above): On the coast of Brittany, France, the Créac'h d'Ouessant, built in 1638, has a light equal to almost 500,000,000 candles. LONGEST STAIRS (right): Built of wood, these 3,875 steps at a power station in Norway are 4,101 feet long.

Remotest. The most remote lighthouse is The Smalls, about 16 sea miles (18.4 statute miles) off the Dyted coast of Wales.

Windmills

The earliest recorded windmills are those used for grinding corn in Iran (Persia) in the 7th century A.D.

The oldest Dutch mill is the towermill at Zedden, Gelderland, built *c.* 1450.

The largest Dutch windmill is the Dijkpolder in Maasland, built in 1718. The sails measure 95¾ feet from tip to tip.

The tallest windmill in the Netherlands is De Walvisch in Schiedam built to a height of 108 feet in 1794.

Waterwheel

The largest waterwheel is the Mohammadieh Noria wheel at Hama, Syria, with a diameter of 131 feet. It dates from Roman times.

Longest Stairs

The world's longest stairs are reputedly at the Mar power station, Overland, western Norway. Built of wood in 1952, these are 4,101 feet in length, rising in 3,875 steps at an angle of 41° inside the pressure shaft. The length of a very long, now discontinuous, stone stairway in the Rohtang Pass, Manali, Kulu, Northern India, is still under investigation.

Largest Windows

The largest sheet of glass ever manufactured was one of 538.2 square feet, or 65 feet 7 inches by 8 feet 2½ inches, exhibited by the Saint

Gobain Company in France at the *Journées Internationales de Miroiterie* in March, 1958. The largest windows in the world are the three in the Palace of Industry and Technology at Rond-point de la Défense, Paris, with an extreme width of 715.2 feet and a maximum height of 164 feet.

Longest Fence

The longest fence in the world is the dingo-proof fence enclosing the main sheep areas of Queensland, Australia. The wire fence is 6 feet high, goes one foot underground, and stretches for 3,437 miles.

Largest Doors

The largest doors in the world are the four in the Vehicle Assembly Building near Cape Canaveral (Kennedy), Florida, with a height of 460 feet. (See *Largest Buildings—Scientific*.)

Longest Wall

The Great Wall of China, completed during the reign of Shih Huang-ti (246–210 B.C.), has a main-line length of 2,150 miles with a further 1,780 miles of branches and spurs, with a height of from 15 to 39 feet and up to 32 feet thick. It runs from Shanhaikuan, on the Gulf of Pohai, to Chiayukuan in Kansu and was kept in repair up to the 16th century.

Cemetery

The world's largest cemetery is one in Leningrad, U.S.S.R., which contains over 500,000 of the 1,300,000 victims of the German army's siege of 1941–42.

The largest crematorium is at the Nikolo-Arkhangelskoye Cemetery, East Moscow, completed to a British design in March, 1972. It has seven twin furnaces and several Halls of Farewell for atheists.

Largest Garbage Dump

Reclamation Plant No. 1, Fresh Kills, Staten Island, which opened in March, 1974, is the world's largest sanitary landfill. In its first 4 months, 500,000 tons of refuse from New York City was dumped on the site by 700 barges.

Tallest Fire Ladder

The world's tallest mobile fire ladder is a 250-foot-tall turntable ladder built in 1962 by Magirus, a German firm.

Largest Inflatable Building

The Goodyear Tire and Rubber Co. of Topeka, Kansas, has a plastic addition to their warehouse 600 feet long, and 120 feet high, inflated by 14 fans.

Largest Tent

The largest field tent ever erected covered an area of 188,368 square feet (4.32 acres), put up by the firm of Deuter from Augsburg, Germany, for the 1958 "Welcome Expo" in Brussels, Belgium.

GREATEST ADVERTISING SIGN EVER ERECTED: In the Citroën sign which appeared on the Eiffel Tower from 1925 to 1936, the letter "N" alone measured over 68 feet in height.

Largest Nudist Camp

The oldest nudist camp is Der Freilichtpark, Klingberg, West Germany, established in 1903. The largest such camp in the world is the Centre Helio-Marin, Montalivet, near Bordeaux, France. Extending over 1¼ miles of coast and covering 420 acres, it has 1,200 chalets and 50,000 visitors per year.

Tallest Scaffolding

The greatest scaffolding structure ever erected was one 486 feet high, using 142 miles of tubing, for the reconstruction of Guy's Hospital, London, in 1971.

Largest Vat

The world's largest vat is named "Strongbow," used by H. P. Bulmer Ltd., a cider company in Hereford, England. It measures 64½ feet in height, 72½ feet in diameter, and has a capacity of 1,956,000 gallons.

Advertising Signs

Largest. The greatest advertising sign ever erected was the electric Citroën sign on the Eiffel Tower, Paris. It was switched on on July 4, 1925, and could be seen 24 miles away. It was in six colors with 250,000 lamps and 56 miles of electric cables. The letter "N" which terminated the name "Citroën" between the second and third levels measured 68 feet 5 inches in height. The whole apparatus was taken down after 11 years in 1936.

The world's largest neon advertising sign was owned by the Atlantic Coast Line Railroad Company at Port Tampa, Florida.

It measured 387 feet 6 inches long and 76 feet high, weighed 175 tons and contained about 4,200 feet of red neon tubing. It was demolished on February 19, 1970.

Broadway's largest current billboard is 11,426 square feet in area—equivalent to 107 feet by 107 feet. The world's largest working sign was in Times Square between 44 & 45th Streets, New York City, in 1966. It showed two 42½-foot-tall "bottles" of Haig Scotch Whisky and an 80-foot-long "bottle" of Gordon's Gin being "poured" into a frosted glass.

Highest. The highest advertising sign in the world are the four Bank of Montreal logos atop the 72-story 935-foot-tall First Canada Place building in Montreal. Each sign, built by Claude Neon Industries Ltd., measures 20 feet by 22 feet, and was lifted into place by helicopter.

The tallest free-standing advertising sign is the 188-foot-high 93-foot-wide sign of the Stardust Hotel, Las Vegas, Nevada, completed in February, 1968. It uses 25,000 light bulbs and 2,500 feet of neon tubing, and has letters up to 22 feet tall.

Largest Bonfire

A bonfire 107 feet 10 inches high was built at College Station, Texas, on Thanksgiving Eve, 1969.

Tallest Fountain

The world's tallest fountain is at Fountain Hills, Arizona, built at a cost of $1,500,000 for McCulloch Properties, Inc. At full pressure of 375 pounds per square inch and at a rate of 7,000 gallons a minute, the 560-foot column of water weighs more than 9 tons. The nozzle speed achieved by the three 600 h.p. pumps is 46.7 m.p.h.

LARGEST FOUNTAIN (left): This 560-foot-high column in Fountain Hills, Arizona, uses 7,000 gallons a minute. DEEPEST PENETRATION (right): The Loffland rig dug a hole deeper than Mt. Everest is high.

10. Borings and Mines

Deepest. Man's deepest penetration into the earth's crust is under Rig No. 32 gas well at No. 1 Bertha Rogers Field, Washita County, Oklahoma. After 503 days of drilling, the Loffland Brothers Drilling Co. reached 31,441 feet (5.95 miles) on April 3, 1974. The hole temperature at the bottom was 475° F. A conception of the depth of this hole can be gained by the realization that it was sufficient in depth to lower the CN Tower down it 17 times.

The most recent in a succession of announcements from the U.S.S.R. of intentions to drill down 15 kilometers (49,213 feet) was in February, 1972, from the Baku Scientific Research Institute. A depth of 21,620 feet has been reached at the Kura River Valley site in Southern Azerbaijan.

The deepest recorded drilling into the sea bed by the *Glomar Challenger* of the U.S. Deep Sea Drilling Project is one of 4,265 feet, and the deepest site is one 20,483 feet below sea level.

PROGRESSIVE RECORDS IN DEEP DRILLING

Depth in ft.	Location	Date
2,000	Szechwan, China	c. 150 B.C.
5,735	Schladebach, Germany	1886
6,570	Schladebach, Germany	1893
7,230	Schladebach, Germany	1909
8,046	Olinda, Calif.	1927
8,523	Big Lake, W. Texas	1928
9,280	Long Beach, Calif.	1929
9,753	Midway, Calif.	1930
10,030	Rinconfield, Calif.	1931
10,585	Vera Cruz, Mexico	1931
10,944	Kettleman Hills, Calif.	1933
11,377	Belridge, Calif.	1934
12,786	Gulf McElroy, W. Texas	1935
15,004	Wasco, Calif.	1938
15,279	Pecos County, W. Texas	1944
16,246	S. Coles Levee, Calif.	1944
16,655	Brazos County, Texas	1945
16,668	Miramonte, Calif.	1946
17,823	Caddo County, Oklahoma	1947
18,734	Ventura County, Calif.	1949
20,521	Sublette County, Wyoming	1949
21,482	Bakersfield, Calif.	1953
22,570	Plaquemines, Louisiana	1956
25,340	Pecos County, W. Texas	1958
25,600	St. Bernard Parish, Louisiana	1970
28,500	Pecos County, W. Texas	1972
30,050	Beckham County, Oklahoma	1972
31,441	Washita County, Oklahoma	1974

Oil Fields

Largest. The largest oil field in the world is the Ghawar Field, Saudi Arabia, developed by ARAMCO, which measures 150 miles by 22 miles. It has been asserted that the Groningen gas field in the Netherlands is the largest yet discovered.

As of April 1, 1975, the area of the designated parts of the United Kingdom's continental shelf was 223,550 square miles, with total recoverable reserves of 3,000 to 4,500 million tons of oil and 44,000,000 million cubic feet of gas. Gas was first discovered in the West Sole Field in October, 1965, and oil in the Forties Field in November, 1970. The most productive field is expected to be Brent (found in July, 1971) with 22,000,000 tons per year attainable by 1981.

Greatest Gusher. The most prolific wildcat recorded is the 1,160-foot-deep Lucas No. 1, at Spindletop, about 3 miles south of Beaumont, Texas, on January 10, 1901. The gusher was heard more than a mile away and yielded 800,000 barrels during the 9 days it was uncapped. The surrounding ground subsequently yielded 142,000,000 barrels.

Greatest Flare. The greatest gas fire ever burnt at Gassi Touil in the Algerian Sahara from noon on November 13, 1961 to 9:30 a.m. on April 28, 1962. The pillar of flame rose 450 feet and the smoke 600 feet. It was eventually extinguished by Paul Neal ("Red") Adair, aged 47, of Austin, Texas, using 550 lbs. of dynamite. His fee was understood to be about $1,000,000.

Largest Gas Tank. The world's largest gas tank is that at Fontaine l'Evêque, Belgium, where disused mines have been adapted to store up to 500 million cubic meters (17,650 million cubic feet) of gas at ordinary pressure. Probably the largest conventional gas tank is that at Wien-Simmering, Vienna, Austria, completed in 1968, with a height of 274 feet 8 inches and a capacity of 10.59 million cubic feet.

Well

The world's deepest water well is the Stensvad Water Well 11-W1 7,320 feet deep drilled by the Great Northern Drilling Co. Inc. in Rosebud County, Montana, in October–November, 1961.

The Thermal Power Co. geothermal steam well begun in Sonoma County, California in 1955 is now down to 9,029 feet.

The largest hand-dug well is one 32 feet in diameter, 100 feet in circumference and 109 feet deep dug in 1877–78 in Greensburg, Kansas.

The highest recorded flow rate of any artesian well is 20,000 gallons per minute, certified in 1973 for a well 20 miles northwest of Orlando, Florida, by the Wekiva River.

Mines

Earliest. The earliest known mining operations were in the Ngwenya Hills of the Hhohho District of northwestern Swaziland, where hematite (iron ore) was mined for body paint *c.* 41,000 B.C.

Deepest. The world's deepest mine is the Western Deep Levels Mine at Carletonville, South Africa. A depth of 12,600 feet (2.38 miles) was attained in May, 1975. At such extreme depths where the rock temperatures reach 131°F., refrigerated ventilation is necessary. The other great hazard is rock bursts due to the pressures.

Gold. The largest gold-mining area in the world is the Witwatersrand gold field extending 30 miles east and west of Johannesburg, South Africa. Gold was discovered there in 1886 by George Harrison and by 1944 more than 45 per cent of the world's gold was mined there by 320,000 Bantu and 44,000 Europeans. Currently 78 per cent of the free world's supply comes from this area. Production reached a peak in 1970 of 1,102 tons.

The largest gold mine in area is East Rand Proprietary Mines of South Africa, whose 8,785 claims cover 12,100 acres. The largest, by volume extracted, is Randfontein Estates Gold Mine Co. Ltd. with 170 million cubic yards—enough to cover Manhattan Island to a depth of 8 feet. The main tunnels if placed end to end would stretch a distance of 2,600 miles.

Richest. The richest gold mine has been Crown Mines with nearly 49.9 million ounces and still productive. The richest in yield per year was West Driefontein which averaged more than 2,500,000 ounces per year until disrupted in November, 1968, by flooding. The only large mine in South Africa yielding more than one ounce per ton milled is Free State Geduld.

Iron. The world's largest iron mine is at Lebedinsky, U.S.S.R., in the Kursk Magnetic Anomaly which has altogether an estimated 20,000 million tons of rich (45–65 per cent) ore and 10,000,000 million tons of poorer ore in seams up to 2,000 feet thick. The world's greatest reserves are, however, those of Brazil, estimated to total 58,000 million tons, or 35 per cent of the world's total surface stock.

Copper. Historically the world's most productive copper mine has been the Bingham Canyon Mine, Utah, belonging to the Kennecott Copper Corporation with over 9,000,000 tons in the 65 years 1904–68. Currently the most productive is the Chuquicamata mine of the Anaconda Company 150 miles north of Antofagasta, Chile, with more than 330,000 tons.

The world's largest underground copper mine is at El Teniente, 50 miles southeast of Santiago, Chile, with more than 200 miles of underground workings and an annual output of nearly 11,000,000 tons of ore.

Silver, Lead and Zinc. The world's largest lead, zinc and silver mine is the Kidd Creek Mine of Texasgulf Canada Ltd., located at Timmins, Ontario, Canada.

Since 1970, the world's leading lead mine has been the Vibernum Trend in southeast Missouri with 489,397 tons in 1972, from which is extracted some 10 per cent of the world's output of lead.

The world's largest zinc smelter is the Cominco Ltd. plant at Trail, British Columbia, Canada, which has an annual capacity of 263,000 tons of zinc and 800 tons of cadmium.

Tungsten. The largest tungsten mine with published output figures is the Union Carbide mine in Mount Morgan, near Bishop, California. Opened in 1937, it has a capacity of about 2,000 tons per day and a work force of 420.

Excavation

The world's largest excavation is the Bingham Canyon Copper Mine, 30 miles south of Salt Lake City, Utah. From 1906 to mid-1975 the total excavation has been 3,500,000,000 tons over an area of 2.81 square miles to a depth of 2,490 feet. This is seven times the amount of material moved to build the Panama Canal. Three shifts of 900 men work around the clock with 39 electric shovels, 62 locomotives, 97 dump trucks and 18 drilling machines for the 28 tons of explosive used daily. The record daily extraction is 504,167 tons on October 13, 1974.

Manual Excavation. Even by comparison with mechanical excavation, prodigies have been performed by manual excavation. The earthworks of the North Kiangsu irrigation canal in Anhwei Province, China, were recently dug without any mechanical plant. At known work rates in China, the labor force must have been on the order of 4,000,000. The work force used to construct the Grand Canal in China in the 6th and 7th centuries A.D. may have been closer to 5,000,000.

Strip Mine. The world's largest open cast mine is the Fortuna-Garsdorf lignite mine near Bergheim, West Germany.

Quarries

The world's deepest open pit is the Kimberley Open Mine in South Africa (the "Big Hole") dug over a period of 43 years (1871 to 1914) to a depth of nearly 1,200 feet and with a diameter of about 1,500 feet and a circumference of nearly a mile, covering an area of 36 acres. Some 3.36 tons (14,504,566 carats) of diamonds were extracted from the 28,000,000 tons of earth dug out. The inflow of water has now made the depth 845 feet to the water surface. The "Big Hole" was dug by pick and shovel.

Largest Stone. The largest mined slab of quarried stone on record is one of 2,016 tons of slate at Spouterag Quarry, Longdale Valley, Cumbria, England, in May, 1969.

Dump Heap

The world's largest artificial heap is the sand dump on the Randfontein Estates Gold Mines, South Africa, which comprises 42 million long tons of crushed ore and rock waste and has a volume six times that of the Great Pyramid.

Chapter Eight

THE MECHANICAL WORLD

1. Ships

Earliest. Evidence of seafaring between the Greek mainland and the island of Melos to trade obsidian *c.* 7250 B.C. was published in 1971. Oars found in bogs at Magle Mose, Sjaelland, Denmark, and Star Carr, Yorkshire, England, have been dated to the 8th millennium B.C.

The oldest surviving boat is the 142-foot-long 44.8-ton Nile boat buried near the Great Pyramid of Khufu, Egypt, *c.* 2515 B.C., and now reassembled.

Earliest Power Vessels

The earliest experiments with marine steam engines date from those on the Seine River in France, in 1775. Propulsion was first achieved when the Marquis Jouffroy d'Abbans ascended a reach of the Saône River near Lyons, France, in 1783, in the 180-ton paddle steamer *Pyroscaphe*.

The tug *Charlotte Dundas* was the first successful power-driven vessel. She was a paddlewheel steamer built in Scotland in 1801–02 by William Symington (1763–1831), using a double-acting condensing engine constructed by James Watt (1736–1819).

The earliest regular steam run was by the *Clermont*, built by Robert Fulton (1765–1815), a U.S. engineer, which maintained a service from New York to Albany from August 17, 1807.

The oldest operational steam-driven vessel in the world is a 50-foot 54-ton Bristol-built dredger, *Bertha*, designed by I. K. Brunel in 1844 and now afloat at Exeter, England. G. H. Pattinson's 40-foot steam launch, raised from Ullswater, Cumbria, England, in 1962, and now on Lake Windermere, may date from a year or two earlier.

Earliest Turbine

The first turbine ship was the *Turbinia*, built in 1894, at Wallsend-on-Tyne, Northumberland, England, to the design of the Hon. Sir Charles Algernon Parsons (1854–1931). The *Turbinia* was 100 feet long and of 44½ tons displacement with machinery consisting of three steam turbines totaling about 2,000 shaft horsepower. At her first public demonstration in 1897 she reached a speed of 34.5 knots (39.7 m.p.h.).

Atlantic Crossings

Earliest. The earliest crossing of the Atlantic by a power vessel, as opposed to an auxiliary-engined sailing ship, was a 22-day voyage, begun in April, 1827, from Rotterdam, Netherlands, to the West Indies by the *Curaçao*. She was a 127-foot wooden paddle boat of

438 tons, built in Dundee, Angus, Scotland, in 1826, and purchased by the Dutch Government for the West Indian mail service. The earliest Atlantic crossing entirely under steam (with intervals for desalting the boilers) was by H.M.S. *Rhadamanthus* from Plymouth, England, to Barbados in 1832. The earliest crossing of the Atlantic under continuous steam power was by the condenser-fitted packet ship *Sirius* (703 tons) from Queenstown (now Cobh), Ireland, to Sandy Hook, New Jersey, in 18 days 10 hours on April 4–22, 1838.

Fastest. The fastest Atlantic crossing was made by the *United States* (then 51,988, later 38,216, gross tons), former flagship of the United States Lines. On her maiden voyage between July 3 and 7, 1952, from New York City, to Le Havre, France, and Southampton, England, she averaged 35.59 knots, or 40.98 m.p.h., for 3 days 10 hours 40 minutes (6:36 p.m. G.M.T. July 3, to 5:16 a.m. July 7) on a route of 2,949 nautical miles from the Ambrose Light Vessel to the Bishop Rock Light, Isles of Scilly, Cornwall, England. During this run, on July 6–7, 1952, she steamed the greatest distance ever covered by any ship in a day's run (24 hours)—868 nautical miles, hence averaging 36.17 knots (41.65 m.p.h.). Her maximum speed was 41.75 knots (48 m.p.h.) on a full power of 240,000 shaft horse-power. The s.h.p. figure was only revealed by the U.S. Defense Department in 1968.

Submerged. The fastest disclosed submerged Atlantic crossing is 6 days 11 hours 55 minutes by the U.S. nuclear-powered submarine *Nautilus*, which traveled 3,150 miles from Portland, Dorset, England, to New York City, arriving on August 25, 1958.

Most Crossings

Between 1856 and June, 1894, Captain Samuel Brooks (1832–1904) crossed the North Atlantic 690 times—equal to 2,437,712 statute miles. In 1850–51 he had sailed in the brig *Bessie* as an able-bodied seaman around Cape Horn to Panama, coming home to Liverpool as her master. His lifetime sailing distance was at least 2,513,000 miles.

John Hunter, boatswain of the container vessel *Sea-Land Mclean*, made 45 North Atlantic crossings and steamed 328,500 miles in the year from October 6, 1972 to October 7, 1973.

English Channel Crossing by Boat

Bernard Thomas crossed the English Channel from England to France in 13½ hours on July 18, 1974, in a Teifi coracle of willow cane and hazel sapling measuring 4 feet 6 inches long by 3 feet wide.

Pacific Crossing

The fastest crossing of the Pacific Ocean (Kobe, Japan, to Seattle, Washington, or equivalent) is 4 days 21 hours 24 minutes by the containership *Sea-Land Commerce* (50,315 tons) on May 27, 1973. On July 6, 1973, she completed the 4,840 nautical miles from Yokohama, Japan, to Long Beach, California at a higher average, 33.27 knots.

Northernmost

The farthest north ever attained by a surface vessel is 86° 39' N. in 47° 55' E. by the drifting U.S.S.R. icebreaker *Sedov* on August 29, 1939. She was locked in the Arctic ice floes from October 23, 1937, until freed on January 13, 1940.

Southernmost

The farthest south ever reached by a ship was achieved on February 15, 1913, when the *Fram* reached latitude 78° 41' S., off the Antarctic coast.

Largest Passenger Liner

When in operation, the *Queen Elizabeth* (82,998 but formerly 83,673 gross tons), of the Cunard fleet, was the largest passenger vessel ever built and also had the largest displacement of any liner in the world. She had an overall length of 1,031 feet and was 118 feet 7 inches in breadth. She was powered by steam turbines which developed 168,000 h.p. The *Queen Elizabeth's* normal sea speed was 28½ knots (32.8 m.p.h.). Her last passenger voyage ended on November 15, 1968. In 1970, she was removed to Hong Kong to serve as a floating marine university and renamed *Seawise University*. On January 9, 1972, she caught fire in three places simultaneously and was gutted.

Since the retirement of the longest (1,035 feet) and largest (66,348 gross tons) active liner, the *France*, the world's largest active liner has become R.M.S. *Queen Elizabeth 2* of 66,851 gross tons and an overall length of 963 feet, completed for the Cunard Line Ltd. in 1969. She set a "turnaround" record of 8 hours 3 minutes at New York on May 17, 1972. In her 92-day world cruise to 26 ports on five continents (January 10 to April 12, 1977) the price of the Trafalgar and Queen Anne suites will be $110,000.

LONGEST AND MOST EXPENSIVE PASSENGER LINER: The "France," a two-class ship, cost $81,250,000, on launching in 1961. She was retired in early 1975.

PROGRESSIVE LIST OF WORLD'S LARGEST LINERS

Gross Tonnage	Name	Propulsion	Overall Length in Feet	Dates
1,340	Great Western (U.K.)................	Paddle wheels......	236	1838–1856
1,862	British Queen (U.K.)................	Paddle wheels......	275	1839–1844
2,360	President (U.K.)......................	Paddle wheels......	268	1840–1841
3,270	Great Britain (U.K.)................	Single screw	322	1845–1937
4,690	Himalaya (U.K.).....................	Single screw	340	1853–1927
18,914[b]	Great Eastern (U.K.)................	Paddles and screw	692	1858–1888
10,650	City of New York (later Harvard, Pittsburgh) (U.S.)	Twin screw..........	528	1888–1923
17,274	Oceanic (U.K.)	Twin screw..........	705	1899–1914
20,904	Celtic (U.K.)	Twin screw..........	700	1901–1933
21,227	Cedric (U.K.)	Twin screw..........	700	1903–1932
23,884	Baltic (U.K.)	Twin screw..........	726	1904–1933
31,550	Lusitania (U.K.)	4 screws	790	1907–1915
31,938	Mauretania (U.K.)	4 screws	787	1907–1935
45,300	Olympic (U.K.)	Triple screw	892	1911–1935
46,328	Titanic (U.K.)........................	Triple screw	882	1912–1912
52,022	Imperator (Germany) (later Berengaria) (U.K.)	4 screws	919	1913–1938
54,282[1]	Vaterland (later Leviathan) (Germany)	4 screws	950	1914–1938
56,621	Bismarck (later Majestic) (Germany)	4 screws	954	1914–1940
79,280[2]	Normandie (France) (later U.S.S. Lafayette)	4 screws	1,029	1935–1946
80,774[3]	Queen Mary (U.K.)	4 screws	1,019.5	1936–
83,673[4]	Queen Elizabeth (U.K.)............	4 screws	1,031	1940–1972

[1] Listed as 59,957 gross tons under U.S. registration, 1922–31, but not internationally accepted as such.

[2] Gross tonnage later raised by enclosure of open deck space to 83,423 gross tons.

[3] Later 81,237 gross tons. Now at Pier J, Long Beach, California.

[4] Later 82,998 gross tons. Later sold to U.S. interests, was named *Seawise University* when gutted by fire.

[b] Originally 22,500 tons.

Fastest Warship

The world's fastest warship is the 100-ton U.S. Navy test vehicle SES-100B, which attained a speed of 82.3 knots (94.7 m.p.h.) across St. Andrew Bay, Panama City, Florida, on May 23, 1975.

Largest Battleship

The Japanese battleships *Yamato* (sunk southwest of Kyushu by U.S. planes on April 7, 1945) and *Musashi* (sunk in the Philippine Sea by 11 bombs and 16 torpedoes on October 24, 1944) were the largest battleships ever commissioned, each with a full load displacement of 72,809 tons. With an overall length of 863 feet, a beam of 127 feet and a full-load draught of 35½ feet, they mounted nine 18.1-inch guns in three triple turrets. Each gun weighed 181 tons and was 75 feet in length, firing a 3,200-lb. projectile.

The largest battleship now is the U.S.S. *New Jersey*, with a full-load displacement of 59,000 tons and an overall length of 888 feet. She was the last fire support ship on active service in the world and was decommissioned on December 17, 1969.

Largest Aircraft Carrier

The warship with the largest full-load displacement in the world is the $811 million aircraft carrier U.S.S. *Nimitz* at 91,400 tons. She is 1,092 feet in length overall and has a speed well in excess of

FASTEST WARSHIP: This U.S. Navy test vehicle reached a speed of 94.7 m.p.h. in 1975.

30 knots. U.S.S. *Enterprise* is, however, 1,123 feet long and thus still the longest warship ever built. When completed, the U.S.S. *Dwight D. Eisenhower* will have cost $1,000,000,000.

Most Landings. The pilot who has made the greatest number of deck landings is British Royal Navy Capt. Eric M. Brown, C.B.E., D.S.C., A.F.C., with 2,407. Capt. Brown, who retired in 1970, flew a record 325 types of aircraft during his career and also set a world record with 2,721 catapult launchings.

Most Powerful Cruiser

The Fleet Escort Ships (formerly cruisers) with the greatest fire power are the three Albany class ships, U.S.S. *Albany*, *Chicago* and *Columbus* of 13,700 tons and 673 feet overall. They carry 2 twin Talos and 2 twin Tartar surface-to-air missiles and an 8-tube Asroc launcher.

The largest cruiser was the U.S.S. *Newport News* of 21,500 tons full load, commissioned on January 29, 1949, and since then extensively modified as a flagship.

Fastest Destroyer

The highest speed attained by a destroyer was 45.02 knots (51.84 m.p.h.) by the 3,750-ton French destroyer *Le Terrible* in 1935. She was powered by four Yarrow small-tube boilers and two geared turbines giving 100,000 shaft horsepower. She was removed from the active list at the end of 1957.

Submarines

Largest. The world's largest submarine will be the nuclear-powered submarine U.S.S. *Trident* (now SSBN 726), due to be commissioned in 1979, with 24 Trident missiles of 6,000 miles range and a submerged displacement of 15,000 tons. The U.S.S.R. Delta II

LARGEST CAR FERRY: The 502-foot-long "Norland," operating in the North Sea out of Hull, England, can accommodate up to 520 cars at one time.

class submarines, first reported in November, 1973, with 16 SSN 8 missiles, due in late 1976, may be substantially larger.

Fastest. The world's fastest submarines are the U.S. Navy's teardrop hulled nuclear vessels of the *Los Angeles* class. They have been listed officially as capable of a speed of "30 plus knots" but the true figure is believed to be dramatically higher. The first 4 were commissioned in 1975–76, with an additional 19 by 1979–80.

Deepest. The two U.S. Navy vessels able to descend 12,000 feet are the 3-man *Trieste II* (DSV 1) of 303 tons, recommissioned in November, 1973, and the DSV 2 (Deep submergence vessel) U.S.S. *Alvin*. The *Trieste II* was reconstructed from the record-breaking bathyscaphe *Trieste*, but without the Krupp-built sphere, which enabled it to descend to 35,820 feet.

Largest Fleet. The largest submarine fleet in the world is that of the U.S.S.R. Navy or *Krasni Flot*, which numbers 232 boats, of which 167 (44 nuclear, 123 diesel) are attack boats, and 65 (44 nuclear, 21 diesel) are cruise missile boats.

Largest and Longest Tanker

The world's largest and longest tanker and ship of any kind is the 542,400-ton *Batilus* completed for Shell in June, 1976, in St. Nazaire, France. She is 1,312.3 feet long with a 206.6-foot beam, has a draft of 93.5 feet, and is capable of a speed of 16.7 knots (19.3 m.p.h.) powered by a 63,900-h.p. engine. Her sister ship *Bellamya* should join her in December, 1976. This leaves the 484,337-ton Japanese *Nissei Maru* in third place.

Some idea of the length of these ships can be conveyed by the thought that it would take a golfer, standing on the stem, a full-powered drive and a chip shot to reach the stern.

Largest Cargo Vessel

The largest vessel in the world capable of carrying dry cargo is the Swedish ore/oil carrier *Svealand* of 282,450 deadweight tons with a length of 1,109 feet and a beam of 184 feet. She is owned by Angt. A/B Tirfing and was completed in 1973.

Fastest-Built. During the Second World War "Liberty Ships" of prefabricated welded steel construction were built at seven shipyards on the Pacific coast, under the management of Henry J. Kaiser (1882–1967). The record time for assembly of one ship of 7,200 gross tons (10,500 tons deadweight) was 4 days 15½ hours. In January, 1968, some 900 Liberty ships were still in service.

Most Successful Trawler

The greatest tonnage of fish ever landed from any trawler in a year is 4,169 tons in 1969 from the British freezer stern trawler *Lady Parkes* owned by Boston Deep Sea Fisheries Ltd. (est. 1894).

Most Powerful Tug

The world's largest and most powerful tug is now the *Smit Rotterdam*, built to handle large oil tankers, rated at 22,000 h.p. and with a bollard pull in excess of 150 tons. She has an overall length of 256 feet and a beam of 49 feet.

Largest Car Ferry

The world's largest car and passenger ferry is the 502-foot-long MV *Norland* (12,998 g.r.t.), which made its maiden voyage on June 10, 1974. She can carry 520 cars, has a service speed of 18½ knots and was built by A. G. Weser of Bremen, West Germany.

Largest Hydrofoil

The world's largest naval hydrofoil is the 212-foot-long *Plainview* (310 tons full load), launched by Lockheed Shipbuilding and Construction Company at Seattle, Washington, on June 28, 1965. She has a service speed of 50 knots (57 m.p.h.).

Three 185-ton hydrofoils, carrying 250 passengers and 8 cars at 40 knots ply the Malmö-Copenhagen crossing, between Sweden and Denmark. They were built by Westermoen Hydrofoil Ltd. of Mandal, Norway.

A 500-ton-wing ground effect vehicle capable of carrying 990 tons has been reported in the U.S.S.R.

Most Powerful Dredger

The world's most powerful dredger is the 470-foot-long *Prins der Netherlanden*. Using two suction tubes, she can dredge 22,040 tons of sand from a depth of 115 feet in less than one hour.

Most Powerful Icebreaker

The world's most powerful icebreaker is the U.S.S.R.'s atomic-powered icebreaker *Arktika*, able to go through ice 7 feet thick at 4 knots (4.6 m.p.h.). She completed trials in December, 1974.

The largest converted icebreaker is the 1,007-foot-long S.S. *Manhattan* (43,000 s.h.p.), which was converted by the Humble Oil Co. into a 150,000-ton icebreaker with an armored prow 69 feet 2 inches long. She made a double voyage through the Northwest Passage in arctic Canada to Alaska from August 24 to November 12, 1969. The Northwest Passage was first navigated in 1906.

The Norwegian shipbuilders, Aker of Oslo, announced in May, 1975, plans for a 250,000-d.w.t., 121,000-h.p. semi-submarine icebreaker capable of smashing through ice 12½ feet thick.

Largest Cable Ship

The world's largest cable-laying ship is the American Telephone & Telegraph Co.'s German-built *Long Lines* (11,200 gross tons), completed by Deutsche Werft of Hamburg, Germany, in April, 1963, at a cost of $19,040,000. She has a fully-laden displacement of about 17,000 tons, measures 511 feet 6 inches overall and is powered by twin-turbine electric engines.

Largest Whale Factory

The largest whale factory ship is the U.S.S.R.'s *Sovietskaya Ukraina* (32,034 gross tons), with a summer deadweight of 46,000 tons, completed in October, 1959. She is 714.6 feet in length and 84 feet 7 inches in the beam.

Wooden Ships

The heaviest wooden ship ever built was the *Richelieu*, 333 feet 8 inches long, of 8,534 tons, launched in Toulon, France, on December 3, 1873.

The longest modern wooden ship ever built was the New York-constructed *Rochambeau* (1867–72) formerly the *Dunderberg*, which measured 377 feet 4 inches overall.

The biblical length of Noah's Ark was 300 cubits or, at 18 inches to a cubit, 450 feet.

Sailing Ships

Largest. The largest sailing vessel ever built was the *France II* (5,806 gross tons), launched at Bordeaux in 1911. The *France II* was a steel-hulled, five-masted barque (square-rigged on four masts and fore and aft rigged on the aftermost mast). Her hull measured 418 feet overall. Although principally designed as a sailing vessel with a stump top-gallant rig, she was also fitted with two steam engines. She was wrecked in 1922.

LONGEST DUGOUT CANOE: This 20-ton Kauri wood Maori war canoe, built in New Zealand in 1940, is 117 feet long and seats more than 70 paddlers.

FULL RIGGED SEVEN-MASTED SHIP was unique. Built in Massachusetts, she served only 5 years before being lost at sea.

The only 7-masted sailing vessel ever built was the 375.6-foot-long *Thomas W. Lawson* (5,218 gross tons), built at Quincy, Massachusetts, in 1902. She was lost in the English Channel on December 15, 1907.

Largest Junks. The largest junk on record was the seagoing *Cheng Ho* of *c.* 1420, with a displacement of 3,100 tons and a length variously estimated at from 300 feet to 440 feet. It was believed to have 9 masts.

A river junk 361 feet long, with treadmill-operated paddlewheels, was recorded in 1161 A.D. In *c.* 280 A.D. a floating fortress 600 feet square, built by Wang Chün on the Yangtze, took part in the Chin-Wu river war. Modern junks do not, even in the case of the Chiang-su traders, exceed 170 feet in length.

Longest Day's Run Under Sail. The longest day's run by any sailing ship was one of 465 nautical miles (535.4 statute miles) in 23 hours 17 mins. by the *Champion of the Seas* (2,722 registered tons) on her maiden voyage on December 11–12, 1854. She was on passage in the south Indian Ocean under Capt. Alex. Newlands, running before a northwesterly gale. She averaged 19.97 knots.

The highest speed by a sailing merchantman is 22 knots (25.3 m.p.h.) in 4 consecutive watches, by *Lancing* (ex *La Péreire*) when "running her easting down" on a passage to Melbourne in 1890–91. She was the last 4-masted full-rigged ship (36 sails) and at 405 feet the longest. Her main and mizzen masts were 203 feet from keelson to truck with yards 98 feet 9 inches across. In February, 1916, she sighted Cape Wrath, Scotland, 6 days 18 hours out of New York.

Slowest Voyage. Perhaps the slowest passage on record was that of the *Red Rock* (1,600 tons), which was posted missing at Lloyd's of London after taking 112 days for a 950-mile passage across the Coral Sea from February 20 to June 12, 1899, at an average speed of less than 0.4 of a knot.

Largest Sails. The largest spars ever carried were those in the British Royal Navy battleship *Temeraire*, completed at Chatham, Kent, on August 31, 1877. The fore and main yards measured 115 feet in length. The mainsail contained 5,100 feet of canvas, weighing 2 tons, and the total sail area was 25,000 square feet.

Deepest Anchorage

The deepest anchorage ever achieved is one of 24,600 feet in the mid-Atlantic Romanche Trench by Capt. Jacques-Yves Cousteau's research vessel *Calypso*, with a 5½-mile-long nylon cable, on July 29, 1956.

Largest Propeller

The largest ship's propeller ever cast has been one for the Kuwaiti oil tanker *Al Rawdatain* (328,000 d.w.t.), being built at Chantiers Naval de la Ciotat, France. It weighs 82.13 tons, has a diameter of 31 feet 8 inches and was constructed by Heliphoc of Marseilles, France, in 1976.

Wrecks

The largest ship ever wrecked has been the tanker *Bravery* of 275,000 d.w.t. which ran aground off Ushant Island, N.W. France, on January 24, 1976.

The oldest wreck to be salvaged has been a 45-foot merchant vessel which had sunk in 100 feet of water off Kyrenia, Cyprus, *c.* 250 B.C. It was spotted in 1965 and was raised after 7 years of work.

The oldest shipwreck ever found is one of a Cycladic trading vessel, located off the islet of Dhakos, near the Greek island of Hydra, reported in May, 1975, and dated to 2450 B.C. ± 250.

Greatest Roll

The ultimate in rolling was recorded in heavy seas off Coos Bay, Oregon, on November 13, 1971, when the U.S. Coast Guard motor lifeboat *Intrepid* made a 360-degree roll.

Largest Oil Platforms

The largest fixed-leg drilling platforms are four Forties Field platforms. The overall height from below the mud line to the top of the drilling rig is 686 feet. Each weighs 57,000 tons. Their foundation piles penetrate 330 feet into the sea bed and so are the deepest foundations in the world.

The world's most massive oil platform is Shell-Exxon's 230,000-ton deadweight Condeep Brent B Field platform, built in Stavanger, Norway, and positioned in June, 1975. The tallest platform under construction is one 750 feet in height, being built by Redpath Dorman Long for Shell-Exxon at Methil, Fife, Scotland, which was moved to the Brent Field in April, 1976.

The concrete production and storage platform for the Ninian Field, under construction at Loch Kishorn, Scotland, will have an overall height of 820 feet and will in 1977, when moved to its station, become the heaviest mobile object ever constructed with a ballasted weight of some 672,000 tons.

2. Road Vehicles

Coaches. Before the advent of the Macadam road surfaces in *c.* 1815 coach-riding was slow and hazardous. The zenith in speed was reached on July 13, 1888, when J. Selby, Esq., drove the "Old Times" coach 108 miles from London to Brighton and back with 8 teams and 14 changes in 7 hours 50 minutes to average 13.79 m.p.h. Four-horse carriages could maintain a speed of 21¼ m.p.h. for nearly an hour.

CARS

Earliest Automobile. The earliest car of which there is record is a two-foot-long model constructed by Ferdinand Verbiest (died 1687), a Belgian Jesuit priest, described in his *Astronomia Europaea*. His model was possibly inspired either by Giovanni Branca's description of a steam turbine, published in 1629, or by writings on "fire carts" during the Chu dynasty (*c.* 800 B.C.) in the library of the Emperor Khang-hi of China, to whom he was an astronomer during the period *c.* 1665–80.

A 3-wheeled model steam locomotive was built at Redruth, Cornwall, England, by William Murdoch (1754–1839) in 1785–6.

The earliest mechanically-propelled passenger vehicle was the first of two military steam tractors completed in Paris in 1769 by Nicolas Joseph Cugnot (1725–1804). This reached about 2¼ m.p.h. Cugnot's second, larger tractor, completed in 1771, today survives in the *Conservatoire National des Arts et Métiers* in Paris.

The first true internal-combustion-engined vehicle was built by a Londoner, Samuel Brown, whose 4-h.p. 2-cylinder-engined carriage climbed Shooters Hill, Blackheath, Kent, England, in May, 1826.

Earliest Gasoline-Driven Cars. The first successful gasoline-driven car, the Motorwagen, built by Karl-Friedrich Benz (1844–1929) of Karlsruhe, ran at Mannheim, Germany, in late 1885. It was a 560-lb. 3-wheeler reaching 8–10 m.p.h. Its single-cylinder chain-drive engine (bore 91.4 mm., stroke 150 mm.) delivered 0.85 h.p. at 200 r.p.m. It was patented on January 29, 1886. Its first 1-kilometer road test was reported in the local newspaper, the *Neue Badische Landeszeitung*, of June 4, 1886, under the heading "Miscellaneous." Two were built in 1885 of which one has been preserved in "running order" at the Deutsches Museum, Munich.

Most Durable Car. An automotive writer, Boyd Eugene Taylor of Atlanta, Georgia, in 1956 surpassed the 1,000,000 mile mark in his 1936 Ford 2-door car. The "clock" on its 11th trip around showed (1 million and) 37,000 miles.

Earliest Registrations. The world's first plates were probably introduced by the Parisian police in France in 1893. The first American plates were in 1901 in New York State. Registration plates were introduced in Britain in 1903. The original A1 plate was secured by the 2nd Earl Russell (1865–1931) for his 12-h.p. Napier. This plate, willed to Mr. Trevor Laker of Leicester, was sold in August, 1959, for £2,500 ($7,000) in aid of charity. It was reported in April, 1973, that a number plate changed hands in a private sale for £14,000 ($35,000).

FASTEST CAR: A top speed of 631.367 m.p.h. was set in this car with Gary Gabelich at the wheel.

Fastest Cars

Rocket-Engined. The highest speed attained by any wheeled land vehicle is 631.367 m.p.h. over the first measured kilometer by *The Blue Flame*, a liquid natural gas-powered 4-wheeled vehicle driven by Gary Gabelich on the Bonneville Salt Flats, Utah, on October 23, 1970. Momentarily Gabelich exceeded 650 m.p.h. The tires were made by Goodyear. The car was powered by a liquid natural gas/hydrogen peroxide rocket engine delivering 22,000 lbs.s.t. maximum, and theoretically capable of 900 m.p.h.

The building of a 745-m.p.h. racing car, the Nikitin *Khadi-9*, by the Institute of Automotive Transport, Kharkov, Ukraine, U.S.S.R., was announced in May, 1973, with a design speed of 745 m.p.h. Since then, nothing has been heard of this project.

Jet. The highest speed attained by any jet-engined car is 613.995 m.p.h. over a flying 666.386 yards by the 34-foot-7-inch-long 9,000-lb. *Spirit of America—Sonic I*, driven by Norman Craig Breedlove (born March 23, 1938, Los Angeles) on Bonneville Salt Flats, Utah, on November 15, 1965. The car was powered by a General Electric J79 GE-3 jet engine, developing 15,000 lbs. static thrust at sea level.

Wheel-Driven. The highest speed attained is 429.311 m.p.h. over a flying 666.386 yards by Donald Malcolm Campbell (1921–67), a British engineer, in the 30-foot-long *Bluebird*, weighing 9,600 lbs., on the salt flats at Lake Eyre, South Australia, on July 17, 1964. The car was powered by a Bristol-Siddeley 705 gas-turbine engine developing 4,500 s.h.p. Its peak speed was *c.* 445 m.p.h. It was rebuilt in 1962, after a crash at about 360 m.p.h. on September 16, 1960.

Piston-Engined. The highest speed attained is 418.504 m.p.h. over a flying 666.386 yards by Robert Sherman Summers (born April 4, 1937, Omaha, Nebraska) in *Goldenrod* at Bonneville Salt Flats, Utah, on November 12, 1965. The car, measuring 32 feet long and weighing 5,500 lbs., was powered by four fuel-injected Chrysler Hemi engines (total capacity 27,924 c.c.) developing 2,400 b.h.p.

In 1974, Sarron Enterprises announced its intention to break the sound barrier on an 18-mile stretch at Lake Eyre, South Australia, with the 34-foot-long, 16-wheeled *Mach 1*, driven by Johnny Conway. The car, costing $A500,000, was to be powered by 36 2.5-liter engines yielding a total of 14,760 b.h.p.

Fastest Racing Car. The world's fastest racing car yet produced was the Porsche 917/30 Can-Am car powered by a 5,374-c.c. flat 12 turbo-charged engine developing 1,100 b.h.p. On the Paul Ricard circuit near Toulon, France, in August, 1973, Mark Donohue (U.S.) reached a speed of 257 m.p.h. The two models built took 2.2 seconds to go from 0 to 60 m.p.h., 4.3 seconds from 0 to 100 m.p.h., and 12.6 seconds from 0 to 200 m.p.h. In 1973, the UOP Shadow Can-Am car's 8.1-liter turbo-charged Chevrolet V-8 engine developed 1,240 b.h.p.

FASTEST RACING CAR: The Porsche 917/30 Can-Am car (left) has reached a speed of 257 m.p.h. on a road circuit in France.

Fastest Production Car. The fastest production road cars are the Lamborghini Countach and the Ferrari BB Berlinetta Boxer, both capable of 186 m.p.h. Various detuned track cars have been licensed in some countries for road use, but these are not purchasable production models.

Fastest Truck. The U.S. stock truck class A diesel record was set on the Bonneville Salt Flats, Utah, on September 9, 1975, when Harold Miller, 26, and Larry Lange, 38, drove their 17,500-lb. rig, powered by a 1,150 cu. in. Cummins turbo-charged diesel engine, to a speed of 132.154 m.p.h.

Longest in Production

The longest any car has been in production is 42 years (1910–52), including wartime interruptions, in the case of the Jowett "Flat Twin," produced in Britain.

The Ford Model T production record of 15,007,033 cars (1908–1927) was surpassed by the Volkswagen "Beetle" series when their 15,007,034th car since May, 1938, came off the production line on February 17, 1972. Production by May, 1976, had reached 18,700,000.

Largest Car

Of cars produced for private road use, the largest ever was the Bugatti "Royale," type 41, known as the "Golden Bugatti," of which only six (not seven) were made at Molsheim, France, by the Italian, Ettore Bugatti, and some survive. First built in 1927, this machine has an 8-cylinder engine of 12.7-liter capacity, and measures over 22 feet in length. The hood is over 7 feet long. (See color photograph on color page D.)

The blood-red 1933 Model J Victoria Duesenberg custom-built for Greta Garbo measures 24 feet overall.

A special Cadillac bought by King Khalid of Saudi Arabia in December, 1975, built by the Wisco Corporation of Ferndale, Michigan, is 25 feet 2 inches long and weighs 7,800 lbs. Its cost was believed to be "several times" that of a standard Cadillac.

LONGEST CAR: This custom-built Cadillac is over 25 feet long.

LONGEST LIMOUSINE: The British-made Travelall can carry 18 people.

The longest present-day limousine is the Stageway Coaches Inc. (U.K.) 10-door Travelall 18-seat model, measuring 25 feet 4⅛ inches overall.

The heaviest standard production car is the U.S.S.R.'s Zil 114, which weighs 7,000 lbs.

(For cars not intended for private use, see *Largest Engines*.)

Most Expensive Used Cars

The greatest price paid for a used car is $280,000 for a Rolls-Royce Phantom by an undisclosed Kentucky coal merchant from Chas. Schmitt & Co. of St. Louis, Missouri, reported on November 30, 1974. The car had "one previous owner, chauffeur-driven" and was part of a job lot of 7 Rolls-Royces. The previous owner was Queen Juliana of the Netherlands.

The greatest collection of vintage cars is the William F. Harrah Collection of 1,700, estimated to be worth more than $4,000,000, in Reno, Nevada. Mr. Harrah is still looking for a Chalmer's Detroit 1909 Tourabout, an Owen car of 1910–12, and a Nevada Truck of 1915.

Most Expensive Special Car

The most expensive car ever built is the Presidential 1969 Lincoln Continental Executive delivered to the U.S. Secret Service on October 14, 1968. It has an overall length of 21 feet 6.3 inches with a

MOST EXPENSIVE CAR:
Costing $500,000, this
Presidential Lincoln
Continental Executive (1969)
was rented by Ford Motor
Co. to the U.S. Secret
Service for President
Nixon's use at $5,000
per year. It weighs
12,000 lbs. including its
armor plate of 2 tons.

13-foot-4-inch wheelbase and, with the addition of two tons of
armor plate, weighs 12,000 lbs. The cost for research, development
and manufacture was estimated at $500,000, but it is rented for a
mere $5,000 per annum. Even if all four tires were to be shot out
it can travel at 50 m.p.h. on inner rubber-edged steel discs.

Most Expensive Production Model

The most expensive standard car now available is the Mercedes
600 six-door Pullman, which sells for £45,000 ($90,000).

Most Inexpensive. The cheapest car of all-time was the 3-h.p.
U.S. 1908 Browniekar, made for children, but designed by the Mora
Motor Co. for road use, which sold for $150. The Kavan of 1905,
also of U.S. manufacture, was listed at $200. The early models of the
King Midget cars were sold in kit form for self-assembly for as little
as $100 as late as 1948.

Largest Engines

Cars are compared on the basis of engine capacity. Distinction is
made between those designed for normal road use and machines
specially built for track racing and outright speed records.

The highest engine capacity of a production car was 13½ liters
(824 cubic inches), in the case of the Pierce-Arrow 6–66 Raceabout

of 1912–18, the Peerless 6–60 of 1912–14 and the Fageol of 1918. The largest currently available is the V8 engine of 500.1 cubic inches (8,195 c.c.), developing 235 b.h.p. net, used in the 1972 Cadillac Fleetwood Eldorado.

The largest car ever used was the "White Triplex," sponsored by J. H. White of Philadelphia. Completed early in 1928, after two years' work, the car weighed about 4½ tons and was powered by three Liberty V12 aircraft engines with a total capacity of 81,188 c.c., developing 1,500 b.h.p. at 2,000 r.p.m. It was used to break the world speed record, but crashed at Daytona, Florida, on March 13, 1929.

The world's most powerful piston-engine car is "Quad A1." It was designed and built in 1964 by Jim Lytle and was first shown in May, 1965, at the Los Angeles Sports Arena. The car features 4 Allison V12 aircraft engines with a total of 6,840 cu. in. (112,087 c.c.) displacement and 12,000 horsepower. The car has 4-wheel drive, 8 wheels and tires, and dual 6-disc clutch assemblies. The wheelbase is 160 inches. It weighs 5,860 lbs. and has 96 spark plugs and 96 exhaust pipes.

The most powerful road car in the world has been the private 27,000-c.c. Merlin-engined Rolls-Royce coupé owned by the transmission expert John Dodd of Epsom, Surrey, England, and built by Paul Jameson. It exceeded 200 m.p.h. on many occasions on European roads.

The largest racing car was the "Higham Special," which first raced at Brooklands racing circuit, Surrey, England, in 1923, when driven by its owner, Count Louis Vorow Zborowski, the younger (killed 1924). J. G. Parry Thomas renamed the car "Babs" and used it to break the land speed record when it was powered by a V12 Liberty aircraft engine with a capacity of 27,059 c.c., developing 400 to 500 b.h.p. at 2,000 r.p.m. The car was wrecked, and Thomas killed, during an attempt on this record at Pendine Sands, South Wales, on March 3, 1927.

Gasoline Consumption

The world record for fuel economy on a closed circuit course (one of 14.076 miles) was set by Ben Visser (U.S.) in a highly modified 90.8 cu. in. 1959 Opel Caravan Station Wagon in the annual Shell

Research Laboratory contest at Wood River, Illinois, driven by Ben and Carolyn Visser on October 2, 1973, with 451.90 ton-miles per gallon and 376.59 miles on one gallon of gasoline. The tire pressure was 200 lbs. per square inch and the maximum speed was 12 m.p.h.

A Morris Mini-Minor, fitted with a 62-gallon tank was driven from Oxford, England, 1,900 miles to Moscow, U.S.S.R., by Lionel Harrison, Mayor of Oxford, and E. A. Ferguson, September 23–29, 1961, without refueling.

Gas Station Pumping

The highest gallonage sold through a single pump is claimed by the Downtown Service Station, Auckland, New Zealand, for dispensing 7,399.3 Imperial gallons (8,886.3 U.S. gallons) in 24 hours on November 24, 1974.

Most Massive Vehicle

The most massive vehicle ever constructed is the Marion 8-caterpillar crawler used for conveying *Saturn V* rockets to their launching pads at the John F. Kennedy Space Center, Cape Canaveral, Florida. It measures 131 feet 4 inches by 114 feet and cost $12,300,000. The loaded train weight is 9,000 tons. Its windshield wipers with 42-inch blades are the world's largest. Two vehicles were built.

Buses

Earliest. The first municipal motor bus service in the world was inaugurated on April 12, 1903, between the Eastbourne railway station and Meads, East Sussex, in England.

Longest Route. The longest regularly scheduled bus route is Greyhound's "Supercruiser" Miami-to-San Francisco route over 3,240 miles in 81 hours 50 minutes (average speed of travel 39.59 m.p.h.). The total Greyhound fleet numbers 5,500 buses.

Longest. The longest buses in the world are the 76-foot-long articulated buses, with 121 seats, built by the Wayne Corporation of Indiana for use in the Middle East.

Largest Truck

The world's largest truck is the Rotinoff Tractor Super Atlantic with a 400-b.h.p. Rolls-Royce engine. In May, 1958, one of these hauled the first of 12 atomic power station heat-exchangers at Bradwell, Essex, England. The gross train weight was 412.5 tons.

Largest Dump Truck

The world's largest dump truck is the Terex Titan 33–19 manufactured by the Terex Division of the General Motors Corporation. It has a loaded weight of 604.7 and a capacity of 350 tons. When unloading, its height is 56 feet. The 16-cylinder engine delivers 3,300 h.p. The fuel tank holds 1,560 gallons. It went into service in November, 1974.

Largest Bulldozer

The world's most powerful bulldozer is the 152½-ton VCON V220 diesel electric bulldozer, completed by the Marion Power Shovel

LARGEST DUMP TRUCK: 56 feet high when unloading, this Terex Titan truck can carry a 350-ton load.

Co., Inc. of Dallas, Texas, in 1975. The blade is 26 feet wide and can push 90 cubic yards of earth. The machine is 52 feet long and $23\frac{1}{2}$ feet high, with 500 h.p. on each of the four 10-foot 2-inch diameter wheels.

LARGEST BULLDOZER: The VCON V220 is 52 feet long and carries a 26-foot-wide blade.

Largest Tractor

The most powerful tractor in the world is the 160-ton K-205 Pacemaker with a 1,260-horsepower rating. It is built by R. G. Le Tourneau, Inc., of Longview, Texas.

Fastest Trailer

The world record for towing a house trailer in 24 hours is 1,689 miles (average speed 70.395 m.p.h.) by a Ford Zodiac Mark IV, towing a Sprite Major 5-berth trailer, 16 feet long and weighing 1,680 lbs., at Monza Autodrome near Milan, Italy, on October 15–16, 1966. The drivers were Ian Mantle, John Risborough and Michael Bowler, all of Great Britain.

The longest trailer tour on record is one of 68,000 miles carried out in a 1966 Commer Highwayman through 69 sovereign countries between December 27, 1966 and October 20, 1971, by Sy Feldman, his wife Christine, and two sons, Greg and Tim.

Largest Road Load

The world's record road load is one of 400 tons when a reactor was moved from Avila Beach for 10 miles to Diablo Canyon, California, in November, 1970. The conveyance called "Atlas," built by the Bigge Drayage Co., itself weighs 211 tons and has 192 wheels in 16 groups of twelve.

In 1973, a trucker, Floyd Veach (U.S.) drove a rig more than 300 feet long with 7 trailers and 114 wheels loaded with 347 tons of logs 33 miles down a Montana gravel trail in 18 hours.

Largest Tires

The world's largest tires are manufactured in Topeka, Kansas, by the Goodyear Co. for giant dump trucks. They are 11 feet 11 inches

LARGEST TIRES: Each of the ten tires on this Terex Titan dump truck is almost 12 feet tall and weighs 7,800 lbs.

ONLY AMPHIBIOUS CIRCUMNAVIGATION OF THE WORLD: In this jeep, "Half-Safe," Ben Carlin (Australia) arrived in London after crossing the English Channel on one leg of his journey across the Atlantic.

in diameter and weigh 7,834 pounds. A tire 17 feet in diameter is believed to be the practical upper limit.

Amphibious Vehicle

The only circumnavigation of the world by an amphibious vehicle was achieved by Ben Carlin (Australia) in an amphibious jeep called "Half-Safe." He completed the leg across the English Channel from France on August 24, 1951, and the complete circumnavigation on May 8, 1958. He covered 39,000 miles by land and 9,000 miles by river and sea.

Largest Taxi Fleet and Longest Journey

The largest taxi fleet was that of New York City, which amounted to 29,000 cabs in October, 1929, compared with the present figure of 12,500, plus an equal number of "gypsy" cabs.

The longest taxi journey on record was begun from the Tarabya Hotel, Istanbul, Turkey, by Joseph Murphy, who, on October 18, 1969, wanted to get to 13 Hasebury Road, Edmonton, London, England. The mileage driven by Mustafa Aray was 2,098½ miles.

Longest Skid Marks

The longest recorded skid marks on a public road were 950 feet long, left by a Jaguar car involved in an accident on the M.1 near Luton, Bedfordshire, England, on June 30, 1960. Evidence given in the High Court case *Hurlock v. Inglis and others* indicated a speed "in excess of 100 m.p.h." before the application of the brakes.

The skid marks made by the jet-powered *Spirit of America*, driven by Craig Breedlove, after the car went out of control at Bonneville Salt Flats, Utah, on October 15, 1964, were nearly 6 miles long.

Driving in Reverse

Charles Creighton (1908–70) and James Hargis of Maplewood, Missouri, drove their Ford Model A 1929 roadster in reverse from New York City to Los Angeles (3,340 miles), July 26–August 13, 1930, *without* stopping the engine once. They arrived back in New

York on September 5, again in reverse, thus completing 7,180 miles in 42 days.

Garage Work

The fastest time recorded for taking out a car engine and replacing it is 52 seconds for a Mini-car by a Royal Air Force team of 5 from Wattisham, England, at Colchester, England, on August 3, 1974.

Lawn Mowers

Largest. The widest gang mower on record is one of 15 overlapping sections manufactured by Lloyds & Co. of Letchworth Ltd., Hertfordshire, England, used by The Jockey Club to mow 2,500 acres on Newmarket Heath. Its cutting width is 41 feet 6 inches and has a capacity, with a 15 m.p.h. tractor, of up to 70 acres per hour.

WIDEST MOWER: This 15-section machine can mow 70 acres per hour, moving at 15 m.p.h.

Longest Tow

The longest tow on record was one of 4,759 miles from Halifax, Nova Scotia, to Canada's Pacific coast, when Frank J. Elliott and George A. Scott of Amherst, Nova Scotia, persuaded 168 passing motorists in 89 days to tow their Model T Ford (in fact, engineless) to win a $1,000 bet on October 15, 1927.

MOTORCYCLES

Earliest. The earliest internal-combustion-engined motorized bicycle was a wooden machine built in 1885 by Gottlieb Daimler (1834–1900) of Germany at Bad Canstatt and first ridden by Wilhelm Maybach (1846–1929). It had a top speed of 12 m.p.h. and developed one-half of one horsepower from its single cylinder 264-c.c. four-stroke engine at 700 r.p.m. The earliest factory which made motorcycles in quantity was opened in 1894 by Henry and Wilhelm Hildebrand and Alois Wolfmüller at München (Munich), Germany. In its first two years this factory produced over 1,000 machines, each having a water-cooled 1,488-c.c. twin-cylinder four-stroke engine developing about 2.5 b.h.p. at 600 r.p.m.

Fastest Motorcycle. The fastest standard motorcycle ever produced is the Dunstall Kawasaki, powered by a four-cylinder

1,100-c.c. engine developing 85 b.h.p. Road test marks have been 138 m.p.h. (mean) and 147.4 m.p.h. (one way).

Fastest Track Motorcycle. The fastest racing motorcycle ever built has been the 750-c.c. 117-b.h.p. Suzuki 3-cylinder 2-stroke, produced in 1974 and tested at 190 m.p.h. (see also *Motorcycle Racing*, Chapter 12).

Largest Motorcycle. The largest motorcycle ever put into production was the 1,488-c.c. Hildebrand-Wolfmüller (see above).

Seventeen men from the Huntington Park (California) Elks stunt-and-drill team mounted and rode a 1,200-c.c. Harley Davidson on April 16, 1974. The total weight for the 400-yard ride at 17–20 m.p.h. was 3,036 lbs.

Most Expensive Motorcycle. The most expensive motorcycle in current production is the Dunstall Kawasaki (see above) produced in Erith, Kent, England. In May, 1976, it retailed for £2,430 ($4,250).

BICYCLES

Earliest. The first design for a machine propelled by cranks and pedals, with connecting rods, has been attributed to Leonardo da Vinci (1452–1519) or one of his pupils, dated *c.* 1493.

The first machine of such design actually built was in 1839–40 by Kirkpatrick Macmillan (1810–78) of Dumfries, Scotland. It is now in the Science Museum, London.

Smallest Bicycle. The world's smallest wheeled rideable bicycle is one with 2⅜-inch wheels, weighing 2 lbs., built and ridden by Charlie Charles at Circus Circus Hotel, Las Vegas, Nevada. It is in the Guinness Exhibits in that hotel.

SMALLEST BICYCLE: Charlie Charles rides this bicycle in his act in Las Vegas.

Longest Bicycle. The longest tandem bicycle ever built is the $1\frac{1}{4}$-ton Vestergaard multipede built at Koege, Denmark, in April, 1976. It seats 34 and measures 72 feet in length.

Largest Tricycle. The largest tricycle ever made was manufactured in 1897 for the Woven-Hose and Rubber Company of Boston, Massachusetts. Its side wheels were 11 feet in diameter and it weighed over 2,000 lbs. It could carry eight riders.

Tallest Unicycle. The tallest unicycle ever mastered is one 34 feet 5 inches tall, ridden by Daniel K. Haynes, 17, in Hamilton, Ohio, August 22, 1974. Walter Nilsson (U.S.) set a duration record when in 1934 he completed a 3,306-mile journey across the United States from New York to San Francisco in 117 days on an $8\frac{1}{2}$-foot-high unicycle. The unicycle marathon record is 81 miles in 21 hours by Michael Boss, 13, Robert Nock, 12, and Richard Nock, 11, of Fairview Park, Ohio, August 20–21, 1974.

3. Railroads

Earliest. Railed trucks were used for mining as early as 1550 at Leberthal, Alsace, near the French-German border, and at the Broseley colliery, Salop (Shropshire), England, in October, 1605, but the first self-propelled locomotive ever to run on rails was built by Richard Trevithick (1771–1833) and demonstrated over 9 miles with a 10-ton load and 70 passengers in Penydarren, Glamorganshire, Wales, on February 21, 1804.

The earliest established railway to have a steam-powered locomotive was the Middleton Colliery Railway, set up by an Act of June 9, 1758, running between Middleton Colliery and Leeds Bridge, Yorkshire, England. This line went over to the use of steam locomotives (gauge 4 feet 1 inch), built by Matthew Murray (1765–1826), in 1812. The Stockton and Darlington Railway, Cleveland, England, which ran from Shildon through Darlington to Stockton, opened on September 27, 1825. The 7-ton *Locomotion I* (formerly *Active*) could pull 48 tons at a speed of 15 m.p.h. It was designed and driven by George Stephenson (1781–1848).

The first regular steam passenger run was inaugurated over a one-mile section on the $6\frac{1}{4}$-mile track from Canterbury to Whitstable, Kent, England, on May 3, 1830, hauled by the engine *Invicta*.

The first electric railway was Werner von Siemen's 600-yard-long Berlin electric tramway opened for the Berlin Trades Exhibition on May 31, 1879.

Fastest

Electric. The world rail speed record was set by the U.S. Federal Railroad Administration LIMRV (Linear Induction Motor Research Vehicle), built by the Garrett Corporation, on the 6.2-mile-long Pueblo, Colorado, test track, when it attained a speed of 234.2 m.p.h. on March 28, 1974.

Steam. The highest speed ever ratified for a steam locomotive is 126 m.p.h. over 440 yards by the London & North Eastern Railway

4-6-2 No. 4468 *Mallard*, which hauled seven coaches weighing 268.8 tons gross, down Stoke Bank, near Essendine, between Grantham, Lincolnshire, and Peterborough, Northamptonshire, England, on July 3, 1938. Driver Duddington was at the controls with Fireman T. Bray. The engine suffered severe damage. On June 12, 1905, a speed of 127.06 m.p.h. was claimed for the "Pennsylvania Special" near Ada, Ohio.

PROGRESSIVE RAILROAD SPEED RECORDS

Speed m.p.h.	Engine	Place	Date
29.1	The Rocket (Stephenson).........	Liverpool-Manchester, England	10.8.1829
56.75	*Lucifer*.................................	Madeley Bank, Staffordshire, England	11.13.1839
85.1	Compressed air train	Kingstown (now Dun Laóghaire) to Dalkey, Ireland	8.19.1843
89.48	Crampton No. 604	France...............................	6.21.1890
98.4*	*Philadelphia & Reading R. Engine 206*	Skillmans to Belle Mead, New Jersey	7.—*1890*
102.8*	*N.Y. Central & Hudson River Railway*	Grimesville, N.Y.	5.9.1893
112.5*†	*Empire State Express No. 999*...	Crittenden West, N.Y.	5.11.1893
90.0	Midland Rly. 7 ft. 6 in. single...	Melton Mowbray, Nottingham, England	3.—1897
130*	*Burlington Route*	Siding to Arion, Iowa............	1.— 1899
101.0	Siemens und Halske Electric	near Berlin, Germany.........	1901
120.0*‡	*Savannah, Florida and Western Rly. mail train*	Screven, Florida..................	3.1. 1901
124.89	Siemens und Halske Electric..	Marienfeld-Zossen, nr. Berlin	10.6. 1903
128.43	Siemens und Halske Electric..	Marienfeld-Zossen, nr. Berlin	10.23. 1903
130.61	Siemens und Halske Electric..	Marienfeld-Zossen, nr. Berlin	10.27. 1903
143.0	Kruckenberg (propeller-driven)	Karstädt-Dergenthin, Ger. ...	6.21.1931
150.9	Co-Co S.N.C.F. No. 7121......	Dijon-Beaune, France	2.21.1953
205.6	Co-Co S.N.C.F. No. 7107......	Facture-Morceux, France	3.28.1955
205.6	Bo-Bo S.N.C.F. No. 9004	Facture-Morceux, France	3.29.1955
235	*Aérotrain* (jet aero engine and rockets)	Gométz le Chatel, France	12.4 1967
234.2	LIMRV (see above)...............	Pueblo, Colorado	3.28.1974

* Not internationally regarded as authentic.

† Later alleged to be unable to attain 82 m.p.h. on this track when hauling 4 coaches.

‡ 5 miles in 2½ minutes alleged, but Supt. W. E. Symons stated that no stop-watches were used.

Fastest Regular Run. The fastest point-to-point schedule in the world is that of the "New Tokaido" service of the Japanese National Railways from Osaka to Okayama, inaugurated on March 15, 1972. The train covers 99.9 miles in 58 minutes, averaging 103.3 m.p.h. The maximum speed with a 1,066.5-ton, 16-car train is 159 m.p.h.

Longest Non-stop Run. The world's longest daily non-stop run is that on Amtrak's "Silver Meteor," 1,377 miles from New York City to Miami, Florida. The 659-mile section between Richmond, Virginia, and Jacksonville, Florida, is run entirely without stops.

Most Powerful Locomotive. The world's most powerful steam locomotive, measured by tractive effort, was No. 700, a triple-articulated or triplex 2-8-8-8-4 six-cylinder engine which the Baldwin Locomotive Co. built in 1916 for the Virginian Railway. It had a tractive force of 166,300 lbs. working compound and 199,560 lbs. working simple.

The greatest horsepower generated by an engine was by the

Northern Pacific 2-8-8-4 built in 1929 with 45,500 h.p., but a tractive effort of 140,000 lbs.

Probably the heaviest train ever hauled by a single engine was one of 17,100 tons made up of 250 freight cars stretching 1.6 miles by the *Matt H. Shay* (No. 5014), a 2-8-8-8-2 engine which ran on the Erie Railroad from May, 1914, until 1929.

Steepest Grade

The world's steepest standard gauge gradient by adhesion is 1:11, between Chedde and Servoz on the electric Chamonix line of the South Eastern region of the French National Railways.

Busiest Railroad

The world's most crowded rail system is the Japanese National Railways, which in 1971 carried 16,495,000 passengers daily. Professional pushers are employed in the Tokyo subway to squeeze in passengers before the doors can be closed. Among articles reported lost in the crush in 1970 were 419,929 umbrellas, 250,630 eyeglasses and hats, 172,106 shoes, and also an assortment of false teeth and artificial eyeballs.

The world's busiest station is reputedly the main Moscow Station, U.S.S.R., which in 1972 handled some 2,740,000 daily.

Widest and Narrowest Gauges

The widest gauge in standard use is 5 feet 6 inches. This width is used in India, Pakistan, Bangladesh, Sri Lanka, Argentina and Chile. In 1885, there was a lumber railway in Oregon with a gauge of 8 feet.

The narrowest gauge in use is 1 foot 3 inches on the Ravenglass

HIGHEST TRAIN TRACK: This stretch of track at La Cima, Peru, is 15,806 feet above sea level.

& Eskdale Railway, Cumbria, England (7 miles), and the Romney, Hythe & Dymchurch line in Kent, England (14 miles).

Longest Straight Length. The longest straight in the world is on the Commonwealth Railways Trans Australian line over the Nullarbor Plain from Mile 496 between Nuringa and Loongana, Western Australia, to Mile 793 between Ooldea and Watson, South Australia, 297 miles dead straight although not level.

Highest Track

The highest standard gauge (4 feet 8½ inches) track in the world is on the Peruvian State Railways at La Cima, on the Morococha Branch at 15,806 feet above sea level. The highest point on the main line is 15,688 feet in the Galera tunnel.

Longest Line

The world's longest run is one of 5,799 miles on the Trans-Siberian Line between Moscow and Nakhodka in the Soviet Far East. There are 97 stops. The new Baykal-Amur Magistral (BAM) northern line is expected to be open in 1983, and will cut 310 miles off the route around the southern end of Lake Baykal.

Most Countries by Train in a Day

Dr. Kurt Kauffmann of Lucerne, Switzerland, celebrated his 76th birthday on February 19, 1976, by traveling by train in 8 countries—West Germany, Austria, Liechtenstein, Switzerland, France, Luxembourg, Belgium and the Netherlands.

Freight Trains

Longest. The longest and heaviest freight train on record was one about 4 miles in length, consisting of 500 coal cars with three 3,600-h.p. diesels pulling, with three more placed 300 cars from the front on the Iaeger, West Virginia, to Portsmouth, Ohio, stretch of 157 miles on the Norfolk and Western Railway on November 15, 1967. The total weight was more than 47,000 tons.

Greatest Load. The heaviest single piece of freight ever conveyed by rail was a 1,230,000-lb. 106-foot-tall hydrocracker reactor which was carried from Birmingham, Alabama, to Toledo, Ohio, on November 12, 1965.

In 1974, a 16th-century church at Most, Czechoslovakia, weighing 9.980 long tons, was moved on rails 800 yards at less than one one-hundredth m.p.h.

Most Expensive Freight Rate. In accordance with British Rail regulations the correct charge for a domestic animal accompanying a passenger is the same as the 2nd class child fare. Thus in traveling from Paddington, London, to Plymouth (225¾ miles) a Miss Harries on May 7, 1968, had to pay 30s. 6d. ($4.27) for a budgerigar weighing 1 oz. This was equivalent to more than £238 ($666) per ton-mile.

Stations

Largest. The world's biggest railroad station is Grand Central Terminal, New York City, built 1903–13. It covers 48 acres on two levels with 41 tracks on the upper level and 26 on the lower. On average, more than 550 trains and 180,000 people per day use it, with a peak of 252,288 on July 3, 1947.

Highest. The highest station in the world on standard gauge railways is Condor, Bolivia, at 15,705 feet on the Rio Mulato-to-Potosí line.

Waiting Rooms. The world's largest waiting rooms are in Peking Station, Changan Boulevard, Peking, China, opened in September, 1959, with a capacity of 14,000.

Longest Platform. The longest railroad platform in the world is the Kharagpur platform, West Bengal, India, which measures 2,733 feet in length. The State Street Center subway platform staging in "The Loop" in Chicago, measures 3,500 feet in length.

Subways

The most extensive and oldest (opened January 10, 1863) underground railway system in the world is that of the London Transport Executive, with 252 miles of route, of which 77 miles is bored tunnel and 24 miles is "cut and cover." This whole system is operated by a staff of 18,000 serving 279 stations. The 591 trains comprising 4,138 cars carried 638,750,000 passengers in 1975. The record for a day is 2,073,134 on VE Day, May 8, 1945. The greatest depth is 221 feet near Hampstead. The record for touring 277 stations (all at that time) was 15 hours precisely, by Leslie V. R. Burwood on September 3, 1968.

The busiest subway in the world is operated by the New York City Transit Authority with a total of 230.8 miles of track and 2,081,810,464 passengers in 1970, a new high. The stations are close set and total 462. The record for traveling the whole system is 21 hours 8½ minutes by Moyer Wiesen and Charles Emerson on October 8, 1973.

There are 67 underground railway systems in the world today.

Monorail

Highest Speed. The highest speed ever attained on rails is 3,090 m.p.h. (Mach 4.1) by an unmanned rocket-powered sled on the 6.62-mile-long captive track at the U.S. Air Force Missile Development Center at Holloman, New Mexico, on February 19, 1959. The highest speed reached carrying a chimpanzee is 1,295 m.p.h.

The highest speed attained by a tracked hovercraft is 235 m.p.h. by the jet-powered *L'Aérotrain*, invented by Jean Bertin.

Model Train

The non-stop duration record for a model train is 273.84 miles by a Rover-Hornby *Princess* hauling 6 bogie coaches over 23,570 circuits at Mevagissey, Cornwall, England, from July 31 to August 8, 1973. It took 194 hours 27 minutes and the scale speed was 107 m.p.h.

4. Aircraft

Note.—The use of the Mach scale for aircraft speeds was introduced by Prof. Acherer of Zürich, Switzerland. The Mach number is the ratio of the velocity of a moving body to the local velocity of sound. This was first employed by Dr. Ernst Mach (1838–1916) of Austria in 1887. Thus Mach 1.0 equals 760.98 m.p.h. at sea level at 15° C. (59°F.) and is assumed, for convenience, to fall to a constant 659.78 m.p.h. in the stratosphere, *i.e.* above 11,000 meters (36,089 feet).

Earliest Flight. The first controlled and sustained power-driven flight occurred near Kill Devil Hill, Kitty Hawk, North Carolina, at 10:35 a.m. on December 17, 1903, when Orville Wright (1871–1948) flew the 12-h.p. chain-driven *Flyer I* at an airspeed of 30–35 m.p.h., a ground speed of less than 8 m.p.h. and an altitude of 8–12 feet for 12 seconds, watched by his brother Wilbur (1867–1912) and three members of the Coast Guard and two others. Both brothers, from Dayton, Ohio, were bachelors because, as Orville put it, they had not the means to "support a wife as well as an airplane." The plane is now in the Smithsonian Institution, Washington, D.C.

The first man-carrying powered airplane to fly, but not entirely under its own power, was a monoplane with a hot-air engine built by Félix du Temple de la Croix (1823–90), a French naval officer, and piloted by a young sailor who made a short hop after taking off, probably down an incline, at Brest, France, *c.* 1874. The first hop by a man-carrying airplane entirely under its own power was made when Clément Ader (1841–1925) of France flew in his *Eole* for about 164 feet at Armainvilliers, France, on October 9, 1890.

Cross-Channel Flight. The earliest flight across the English Channel by an airplane was made on July 25, 1909, when Louis Blériot (1872–1936), of France, flew his *Blériot XI* monoplane, powered by a 23-h.p. Anzani engine, from Les Baraques, France, to a meadow near Dover Castle, England, in 37 minutes, after taking off at 4:41 a.m.

Transatlantic Flight. The first crossing of the North Atlantic by air was made by Lt.-Cdr. (later Rear Admiral) Albert C. Read (1887–1967) and his crew (Stone, Hinton, Rodd, Rhoads and Breese) in an 84-knot Curtiss flying boat NC-4 of the U.S. Navy, from Newfoundland, Canada, *via* the Azores, to Lisbon, Portugal, on May 16 to 27, 1919. The whole flight of 4,717 miles originating from Rockaway Air Station, Long Island, N.Y., on May 8, required 53 hours 58 minutes, terminating at Plymouth, England, on May 31.

The first non-stop transatlantic flight was achieved from 4:13 p.m. G.M.T. on June 14, 1919, from Lester's Field, St. John's, Newfoundland, 1,960 miles to Derrygimla bog near Clifden, County Galway, Ireland, at 8:40 a.m. June 15, when Capt. John William Alcock, D.S.C. (1892–1919), and Lt. Arthur Whitten Brown (1886–1948) flew across in a Vickers *Vimy*, powered by two Rolls-Royce *Eagle* engines. Both men were given knighthoods on June 29, 1919, when Alcock was only 26 years 227 days old. They won a £10,000 (then $50,000) prize given by a London newspaper.

The first solo transatlantic flight was achieved by Capt. (later Colonel) Charles A. Lindbergh (1902–74), who took off in his 220-h.p. Ryan monoplane *Spirit of St. Louis* at 12:52 p.m. G.M.T. on May 20, 1927, from Roosevelt Field, Long Island, New York. He landed at 10:21 p.m. G.M.T. on May 21, 1927, at Le Bourget airfield, Paris, France. His flight of 3,610 miles lasted 33 hours 29½ minutes and he won a prize of $25,000.

The transatlantic flight speed record is 1 hour 54 minutes 56.4 seconds by Major James V. Sullivan, 37, and Major Noel F. Widdifield, 33, flying a Lockheed SR-71A eastwards on September 1, 1974. The average speed, slowed by refueling by a KC-135 tanker aircraft, for the New York-London stage of 3,461.53 miles was 1,806.963 m.p.h.

Transpacific Flight. The first transpacific flight was made from Oakland Field, California, to Eagle Farm, Brisbane, Australia, *via* Honolulu, Hawaii, and Suva, Fiji, by Captain Charles Kingsford-Smith and C. T. P. Ulm (pilots), accompanied by Harry Lyon (navigator) and James Warner (radio operator), from May 31 to June 9, 1928. The flying time for the 7,389 miles was 83 hours 38 minutes. The aircraft used, a Fokker F. VIIB-3m named "Southern Cross," is preserved and displayed at Eagle Farm airport.

Fastest Circumnavigation (flights longer than the Tropic of Cancer). The fastest circumnavigation of the globe was achieved by three U.S.A.F. B-52 Stratofortresses, led by Maj.-Gen. Archie J. Old, Jr., from Castle Air Force Base, Merced, California, on January 16, arriving 45 hours 19 minutes later at March Air Force Base, Riverside, California, on January 18, 1957, after a flight of 24,325 miles.

The commercial flight record was set by a Pan-Am Boeing 747 SP (Capt. Walter H. Mullikin) from New York to Delhi to Tokyo to New York, May 1–3, 1976, in 46 hours 50 seconds for the 23,230.3 miles (see page 442).

Jet-Engine Flight. Proposals for jet propulsion date back to Captain Marconnet (1909) of France and Henri Coanda of Rumania, and to the turbojet proposals of Maxime Guillaume in 1921. The earliest test bed run was that of the British Power Jets Ltd.'s experimental W.U. (Whittle Unit) on April 12, 1937, invented by Flying Officer (now Air Commodore Sir) Frank Whittle (born June 1, 1907), who had applied for a patent on jet propulsion in 1930.

The first flight by an airplane powered by a turbojet engine was made by the Heinkel He 178, piloted by Flug Kapitan Erich Warsitz, at Marienehe, Germany, on August 27, 1939. It was powered by a Heinkel S-3b engine (834-lb. s.t. as installed with long tailpipe) designed by Dr. Hans von Ohain and first tested in August, 1937.

Supersonic Flight. The first supersonic flight was achieved on October 14, 1947, by Capt. (now Brigadier-General) Charles ("Chuck") E. Yeager (born February 13, 1923), U.S.A.F. ret., over Edwards Air Force Base, Muroc, California, in a U.S. Bell XS-1 rocket plane ("Glamorous Glennis"), with Mach 1.015 (670 m.p.h.) at a height of 42,000 feet.

PLANE WITH LARGEST WINGS: Howard Hughes' mammoth flying boat with a wing span of 320 feet, flew only 1,000 yards when tested in 1947 and never flew again. It had 8 engines and weighed 190 tons.

Planes

Largest. The aircraft with the largest wing span ever constructed was Howard R. Hughes' H.2 *Hercules* flying boat, which rose 70 feet into the air in a test run of 1,000 yards off Long Beach Harbor, California, on November 2, 1947. The 8-engined 190-ton aircraft had a wing span of 320 feet and a length of 219 feet. It never flew again. The craft cost $40,000,000, and was piloted by Howard Hughes himself on its one run.

Heaviest. The greatest weight at which an airplane has taken off is 820,700 lbs., achieved by the prototype Boeing Model 747-200B (747B) commercial transport at Edwards Air Force Base, California, in November, 1970. The basic plane weighed 320,000 lbs., the remaining weight representing fuel, flight test equipment and an artificial payload of sand and water. The 747B has a wing span of 195 feet 8 inches, is 231 feet 4 inches long. It is structurally capable of accepting 4 Pratt & Whitney JT9D-7O turbofans, giving a total thrust of 208,000 lbs. or 4 Rolls-Royce RB. 211-524 turbofans, giving a total thrust of 212,000 lbs. In the latter case its permitted maximum take-off weight is 820,000 lbs.

Most Powerful. The third Boeing E-4A, advanced airborne command post version of the Boeing 747B transport, flew for the first time on June 6, 1974, powered by four General Electric F103-GE-100 turbofan engines with a total thrust of 210,000 lbs.

Lightest. The lightest powered plane ever flown is the Birdman TL-1, a single seat monoplane designed and built by Emmet M. Tally III of Daytona Beach, Florida, and first flown on January 25, 1975. It has a wing span of 34 feet, an empty weight of 100 lbs. and a normal take-off weight of 288 lbs. It is powered by a 15-h.p. Tally M.C. 101DT single cylinder two-stroke engine driving a pusher propeller, and has a maximum speed of 60 m.p.h. and a range of 200 miles on 4 gallons of fuel. The pilot sits on an open seat. Many more Birdmans are being built from kits supplied by Mr. Tally's company.

The lightest and smallest twin-engined airplane is the MC10 Cricri single-seat monoplane designed and built by Michel Colomban of Rueil-Malmaison, France, and first flown on July 19, 1973, by 68-year-old Robert Buisson. It has a wing span of 16 feet

SMALLEST TWIN-ENGINED PLANE: The French Cricri weighs only 139 lbs. when empty, and can fly at a speed of 130 m.p.h.

$4\frac{3}{4}$ inches, an empty weight of 139 pounds and a take-off weight (including the pilot) of 375 pounds. Two 9-h.p. Rowena two-stroke engines give it a maximum speed of 130 m.p.h. and a range of 248 miles. The Cricri is aerobatic.

Smallest. The smallest airplane ever flown is the Stits *Skybaby* biplane, designed by Ray Stits, and flown at Riverside, California, on May 26, 1952. It was 9 feet 10 inches long, with a wing span of 7 feet 2 inches, and weighed 452 lbs. empty. Powered by an 85-h.p. Continental C85 engine, it had a top speed of 185 m.p.h.

SMALLEST AIRPLANE: Ray Stits' "Skybaby" was only 9 feet 10 inches long. It could fly at speeds up to 185 m.p.h.

Bombers

Heaviest. The world's heaviest bomber is the 8-jet sweptwing Boeing B-52H Stratofortress, which has a maximum takeoff weight of 488,000 lbs. It has a wing span of 185 feet and is 157 feet 6¾ inches in length, with a speed of over 650 m.p.h. The B-52 can carry 2 Hound Hog thermonuclear missiles or 24 750-lb. bombs under its wings and 84 500-lb. bombs in the fuselage giving a total bomb load of 60,000 lbs. Alternatively, it can carry a total of 20 SRAM nuclear short-range attack missiles. The 10-engined Convair B-36J, weighing 205 tons, has a greater wing span, at 230 feet, but is no longer in service. It had a top speed of 435 m.p.h.

Fastest. The world's fastest operational bombers are the French Dassault Mirage IV, which can fly at Mach 2.2 (1,450 m.p.h.) at 36,000 feet; the American General Dynamics FB-111A, which also flies above Mach 2.5; and a swing-wing Russian Tupolev bomber known to NATO as "Backfire," which has an estimated over-target speed of Mach 2.25–2.5 and a range of up to 6,000 miles.

Most Expensive. Although estimated costs vary widely for the U.S. B-1 supersonic Mach 2.2 bomber, rolled out on December 23, 1974, it is clearly the most expensive aircraft ever produced. An estimate of $43,900 million for 244 was published in 1970—a cost of $180,000,000 per plane.

Airliners

Largest. The highest capacity jet airliner is the Boeing 747, "Jumbo Jet," first flown on February 9, 1969, which in November, 1970, set a record for gross takeoff weight with 820,700 lbs. and has a capacity of from 362 to 500 passengers with a maximum speed of 608 m.p.h. Its wing span is 195.7 feet and its length, 231.3 feet. It entered service on January 21, 1970.

MOST EXPENSIVE PLANE: Each of the 244 U.S. B-1 supersonic bombers built in 1974 cost the taxpayer $180 million.

Fastest. The U.S.S.R.'s Tu-144 supersonic airliner, with a capacity of 140 passengers, first flew on December 31, 1968. With a design ceiling of 65,000 feet, it "went" supersonic on June 5, 1969. It first exceeded Mach 2 on May 26, 1970, and attained 1,565.8 m.p.h. (Mach 2.37) at 59,000 feet in late December, 1971. During later flight trials it attained Mach 2.4 (1,585 m.p.h.).

The Tu-144 opened the first scheduled supersonic airline service on December 26, 1975, with 2 return flights weekly between Moscow and Alma-Ata, U.S.S.R. (2,190 miles) carrying freight and mail. It was expected to enter passenger service in the second half of 1976 at an average speed of 1,245 m.p.h.

Largest Cargo Compartment. The largest cargo compartment of any aircraft is the 39,000 cubic feet of the Guppy 201 manufactured by American Aero Spacelines, which was put into service in September, 1971. The compartment is more than 25 feet in diameter.

LARGEST CARGO AIRCRAFT: The cargo compartment of the Guppy 201 aircraft has a total volume of 39,000 cubic feet.

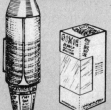

Highest Speed

The official air speed record is 2,070.102 m.p.h. by Col. Robert L. Stephens and Lt.-Col. Daniel André (U.S.) in a Lockheed YF-12A over Edwards Air Force Base, California, on May 1, 1965, over a 9–15 mile course.

The fastest fixed-wing aircraft in the world was a North American Aviation X-15A-2, which flew for the first time (after modification) on June 28, 1964, powered by a liquid oxygen and ammonia rocket propulsion system. Ablative materials on the airframe enabled a temperature of 3,000°F. to be withstood. The landing speed was 210 knots (242 m.p.h.) momentarily. The highest speed attained was 4,534 m.p.h. (Mach 6.72) when piloted by Major William J. Knight, U.S.A.F. (b. 1930) on October 3, 1967. An earlier version piloted by Joseph A. Walker (1920–66) reached 354,200 feet (67.08 miles) also over Edwards Air Force Base, California, on August 22, 1963. The program was suspended after the final flight of October 24, 1968.

The U.S. Air Force Lifting Body X-24B is expected to reach supersonic speeds between Mach 5 and Mach 10.

PROGRESSIVE FIXED-WING AIRCRAFT SPEED RECORDS

m.p.h.	Mach No.	Pilot	Date
2,111	3.19	J. A. Walker	May 12, 1960
2,196	3.31	J. A. Walker	Aug. 4, 1960
2,275	3.50	R. M. White	Feb. 7, 1961
2,905	4.43	R. M. White	Mar. 7, 1961
3,074	4.62	R. M. White	Apr. 21, 1961
3,300	4.90	J. A. Walker	May 25, 1961
3,603	5.27	R. M. White	June 23, 1961
3,614	5.25	J. A. Walker	Sept. 12, 1961
3,620	5.30	F. S. Petersen	Sept. 28, 1961
3,647	5.21	R. M. White	Oct. 11, 1961
3,900	5.74	J. A. Walker	Oct. 17, 1961
4,093	6.04	R. M. White	Nov. 9, 1961
4,104	>6.06	J. A. Walker	June 27, 1962
4,250	6.33	W. J. Knight	Nov. 18, 1966
4,534	6.72	W. J. Knight	Oct. 3, 1967

$>$ more than

Fastest Jet. The world's fastest jet aircraft is the Lockheed SR-71 reconnaissance aircraft (a variant of the YF-12A, above) which first flew on December 22, 1964, and is reportedly capable of attaining a speed of 2,200 m.p.h. and an altitude ceiling of close to 100,000 feet. The SR-71 has a span of 55.6 feet and a length of 107.4 feet and weighs 170,000 lbs. at takeoff. Its reported range is 2,982 miles at Mach 3 at 78,750 feet. Only 27 are believed to have been built and 9 had been lost by April, 1969.

The fastest Soviet jet aircraft in service is the Mikoyan MIG-25 *alias* E-266 fighter (code name "Foxbat") with a speed of Mach 3.2 (2,110 m.p.h.). It is armed with air-to-air missiles known to N.A.T.O. as "Acrid."

Fastest Biplane. The fastest recorded biplane was the Italian Fiat C.R.42B, with 1,010-h.p. Daimler-Benz DB601A engine, which attained 323 m.p.h. in 1941. Only one was built.

Fastest Piston-Engined Aircraft. The fastest speed at which a piston-engined plane has ever been measured was for a cut-down privately owned Hawker *Sea Fury* which attained 520 m.p.h. in level flight over Texas in August, 1966, piloted by Mike Carroll (d. 1969) of Los Angeles. The official record is 482.462 m.p.h. over Edwards Air Force Base, California, by Darryl C. Greenamyer, 33, in a Grumman F8F-2 Bearcat on August 16, 1969.

Fastest Propeller-Driven Aircraft. The Soviet Tu-114 turbo-prop transport is the world's fastest propeller-driven airplane. It has achieved average speeds of more than 545 m.p.h. carrying heavy payloads over measured circuits. It is developed from the Tupolev Tu-95 bomber, known in the West as the "Bear," and has 14,795-horsepower engines. The Republic XF-84H prototype U.S. Navy fighter which flew on July 22, 1955, had a top design speed of 670 m.p.h., but was abandoned.

Largest Propeller

The largest aircraft propeller ever used was the 22-foot 7½-inch diameter Garuda propeller, fitted to the Linke-Hofmann R II built in Breslau, Germany, which flew in 1919. It was driven by four 260-h.p. Mercedes engines and turned at only 545 r.p.m.

PROGRESSIVE FIXED-WING AIRCRAFT ALTITUDE RECORDS

Feet	Miles	Pilot	Date
136,500	25.85	R. M. White	Aug. 12, 1960
169,600	32.13	J. A. Walker	Mar. 30, 1961
217,000	41.11	R. M. White	Oct. 11, 1961
246,700	46.72	J. A. Walker	Apr. 30, 1962
246,700	46.72	R. M. White	June 21, 1962
314,750	59.61	R. M. White	July 17, 1962
347,000	65.88	J. A. Walker	July 19, 1963
354,200	67.08	J. A. Walker	Aug. 22, 1963

Greatest Altitude

The official altitude record by an aircraft which took off from the ground under its own power is 118,897 feet (22½ miles) by Aleksandr Fedotov (U.S.S.R.) in a Mikoyan E-266 (MIG-25) aircraft, powered by two 24,250-lb. turbojet engines on July 25, 1973.

The greatest recorded height by any pilot without a pressure cabin or even a pressure suit has been 49,500 feet by British Squadron Leader G. W. H. Reynolds, D.F.C., in a Spitfire Mark 5C over Libya in 1942.

Flight Duration

The flight duration record is 64 days, 22 hours, 19 minutes and 5 seconds, set by Robert Timm and John Cook in a Cessna 172 "Hacienda." They took off from McCarran Airfield, Las Vegas, Nevada, just before 3:53 p.m. local time on December 4, 1958, and landed at the same airfield just before 2:12 p.m. on February 7, 1959. They covered a distance equivalent to six times around the world with continued refueling without landing.

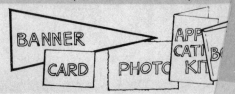

SHORTEST FLIGHT: The "Islander" makes a 2-minute flight between two Orkney Islands in Scotland—with a following wind in 69 seconds.

The record for duration without refueling is 84 hours 32 minutes, set by Walter E. Lees and Frederic A. Brossy in a Bellanca monoplane with a 225-h.p. Packard Diesel engine, at Jacksonville, Florida, May 25–28, 1931.

Longest Scheduled Flight. The longest scheduled non-stop flight is the thrice weekly Pan Am New York City-Tokyo Flight 801 (6,754 statute miles) of 13 hours 40 minutes, inaugurated on April 26, 1976. The Boeing 747 SP carries 44 1st-class and 222 economy-class passengers. The return flight takes 11 hours 30 minutes. The inaugural flight of the 747 SP around the world also set a record (see page 314).

Shortest Scheduled Flight. The shortest scheduled flight is made by Loganair between the Orkney Islands (Scotland) of Westray and Papa Westray, which has been flown since September, 1967. Though scheduled for 2 minutes, in favorable wind conditions it is accomplished in 69 seconds by Captain Andrew Alsop.

Most Take-Offs and Landings. Tony Cattle and David R. Shevloff in a Cessna 172 took off and landed at 65 airfields in southern England in 16 hours 19 minutes in daylight on June 19, 1974.

Longest-Standing Air Record

The earliest airplane record listed by the Fédération Aéronautique Internationale as still unbeaten is for a speed of 391.072 m.p.h. over a 100-km. closed circuit in a piston-engined Macchi-Castoldi sea-plane, set by G. Cassinelli of Italy on October 8, 1933. The plane had 24 cylinders in a 2,400-h.p. Fiat AS6 engine.

OLD PILOTS: Mrs. Harry Francklin (left) flew a plane over Salem, Oregon, when she was 100 years old. Walter Davies (right) of England received his private pilot's license at the age of 71.

Youngest and Oldest Pilots

The youngest age at which anyone has ever qualified as a military pilot is 15 years 5 months in the case of Sgt. Thomas Dobney (born May 6, 1926) of the British Royal Air Force. He had lied about his age (14 years) on induction.

Miss Betty Bennett took off, flew and landed solo at the age of 10 on January 4, 1952, in Cuba. Rory Kay of Oxford, England, qualified for his private pilot's license on his 17th birthday at 0900 hours on June 10, 1974.

The world's oldest pilot in March, 1976, was probably Cecile Raymond Sinclair (born April 8, 1888) of Muskegon, Michigan, aged 87 years 11 months. She first soloed in 1915. Maurice Tabiteau of Issey les Moulineaux, Seine, France, is also believed to have been born in 1888. Glenn E. Messer of Birmingham, Alabama, has been flying "steady" since May 13, 1911. Theodore Julius Caesar of Tuakau, New Zealand, was issued his private pilot's license on March 25, 1974, aged 74 years 359 days.

Airports

Largest. The world's largest airport is the Dallas/Fort Worth Airport, Texas, which extends over 17,500 acres in the Grapevine area opened in January, 1974, at an initial cost of $700,000,000. The present 3 runways and 4 terminal buildings are planned to be extended to 9 runways and 13 terminals with 260 gates with an ultimate capacity of 60,000,000 passengers per year.

The area of the Montreal airport will be 18,500 acres.

Busiest. The world's busiest airport is the Chicago International Airport, O'Hare Field, with a total of 690,419 movements and

37,123,000 passengers in fiscal year 1975. This represents a takeoff or landing every 45.68 seconds around the clock.

The busiest landing area ever has been Bien Hoa Air Base, South Vietnam, which handled more than 1,000,000 takeoffs and landings in 1970. The world's largest "helipad" was An Khe, South Vietnam, which serviced U.S. Army and Air Force helicopters.

Highest and Lowest. The highest airport in the world is El Alto, near La Paz, Bolivia, at 13,599 feet above sea level. Ladakh airstrip in Kashmir has, however, an altitude of 14,270 feet. The highest landing ever made was at 19,947 feet on Dhaulagri in the Nepal Himalayas by a Pilatus Porter, named *Yeti*, supplying the 1960 Swiss Expedition. The lowest landing field is El Lisan on the east shore of the Dead Sea, 1,180 feet below sea level. The lowest international airport is Schiphol, Amsterdam, Netherlands, at 13 feet below sea level.

Longest Runway. The longest runway in the world is 7 miles in length (of which 15,000 feet is concreted) at Edwards Air Force Base on the bed of Rogers Dry Lake at Muroc, California. The whole test center airfield extends over 65 square miles. In an emergency, an auxiliary 12-mile strip is available along the bed of the Dry Lake.

The world's longest civil airport runway is one of 15,502 feet (2.93 miles) at Salisbury, Rhodesia, completed in 1969.

Helicopters

Fastest. A Bell YUH-1B Model 533 compound research helicopter, boosted by two auxiliary turbojet engines, attained an unofficial speed record of 316.1 m.p.h. over Arlington, Texas, in April, 1969. The world's speed record for a pure helicopter is 220.885 m.p.h. by a Sikorsky S-67 Blackhawk, flown by test pilot Kurt Cannon (1934–74), between Milford and Branford, Connecticut, on December 19, 1970.

FASTEST HELICOPTER: The Sikorsky S-67 Blackhawk can fly 220.885 m.p.h.

Largest. The world's largest helicopter is the Soviet Mil Mi-12 ("Homer"), also known as the V-12, which set an international record by lifting a payload of 88,636 lbs. to a height of 7,398 feet on August 6, 1969. It is powered by four 6,500-h.p. turboshaft engines, and has a span of 219 feet 10 inches over its rotor tips with a fuselage length of 121 feet 4½ inches and weighs 115.7 tons.

Highest. The altitude record for helicopters, still subject to confirmation, is 40,820 feet by an Aerospatiale SA 315 B Lama over France on June 21, 1972.

The highest landing has been at 23,000 feet below the southeast face of Everest in a rescue sortie in May, 1971.

Autogyros

The autogyro or gyroplane, a rotorcraft with an unpowered rotor turned by the airflow in flight, preceded the practical helicopter with engine-driven rotor. Juan de la Cierva (Spain) made the first successful autogyro flight with his model C.4 (commercially named an *Autogiro*) at Getafe, Spain, on January 9, 1923. On December 6, 1955, Dr. Igor B. Bensen (U.S.) flew his very simple open-seat Gyro-Copter and then made his design available in kit form to amateur builders and pilots.

Dr. Bensen holds the straight-line distance record of 82.77 miles, set in his B.8M Gyro-Copter on May 15, 1967. Wing Commander

RECORD-SETTING AUTOGYRO: Dr. Igor Bensen has flown his Gyro-Copter a record distance of 82.77 miles.

ALTITUDE RECORDBREAKER: Kenneth Wallis of Great Britain flew his auto-gyro to an altitude of 15,220 feet in 1968. He also set speed records in 1969 and 1974.

Kenneth H. Wallis (G.B.) flew his WA-116, with a 72-h.p. McCulloch engine, to a record altitude of 15,220 feet on May 11, 1968, and to a record speed of 111.2 m.p.h. over a 3-km. (1.86-mile) straight course on May 12, 1969. Awaiting confirmation is his distance record of 416 miles over a 100-km. (62-mile) closed circuit set in another WA-116 in July, 1974, and a straight-line distance record of 543 miles, set in September, 1975.

Flying Boat

The fastest flying boat ever built has been the Martin XP6M-1 Seamaster, the U.S. Navy 4-jet-engined minelayer, flown in 1955–59 with a top speed of 646 m.p.h. In September, 1946, the Martin JRM-Two *Mars* flying boat set a payload record of 68,327 lbs.

The official flying-boat speed record is 566.69 m.p.h., set by Nikolai Andrievsky and a crew of two in a Soviet Beriev M-10, powered by two Al-7 turbojets, over a 15.25-km. course on August 7, 1961. The M-10 holds all 12 records listed for jet-powered flying boats, including an altitude of 49,088 ft. set by Georgiy Buryanov and crew over the Sea of Azov on September 9, 1961.

Human-Powered Flight

The greatest distance achieved in human-powered flight is 1,171 yards in the 80-foot span *Jupiter* by Flight Lt. John Potter of the British Royal Air Force in 1 minute 47.4 seconds on June 29, 1972. He achieved 1,355 yards unofficially in 2 minutes 15.5 seconds on June 16, 1972.

Balloons

The earliest recorded balloon was a hot-air model invented by Father Bartholomeu de Gusmão (*né* Lourenço) (b. Santos, Brazil, 1685), which was flown indoors at the Casa da India, Terreiro do Pago, Portugal, on August 8, 1709.

Distance Record. The record distance traveled is 1,896.9 miles by H. Berliner (Germany) from Bitterfeld, Germany, to Kirgishan in the Ural Mountains, Russia, on February 8–10, 1914.

Col. Thomas L. Gatch's lost balloon *Light Heart* was sighted some 3,000 miles from the takeoff point, Harrisburg, Pennsylvania, on February 19, 1974.

The official duration record is 87 hours aloft by H. Kaulen (Germany) set on December 13–17, 1913.

For hot-air ballooning the world's distance record is 337.2 miles in 16 hours 16 minutes by Matt Wiederkehr, 43, in a Raven S-55A from St. Paul, Minnesota, to Butte, Nebraska, on March 7, 1974. The altitude record is 45,837 ft. by Julian Nott and co-pilot Felix Pole (both G.B.) over Bhopal, India, in *Daffodil II*, a 375,000-cu. ft. Cameron A-375 balloon on January 25, 1974. The largest hot-air balloon ever built is the U.K. Cameron A-500 of 500,000 cu. ft. capacity *Gerard A. Heineken*, first flown on August 18, 1974. The endurance record is 18 hours 56 minutes from Dorset, England, to Angers, France, on November 21–22, 1975, by Don Cameron and a crew of two.

LARGEST HOT-AIR BALLOON is the British Cameron A-500, which has a capacity of 500,000 cu. ft.

Highest Manned. The greatest altitude reached in a manned balloon is the unofficial 123,800 feet by Nicholas Piantanida (1933–66) of Bricktown, New Jersey, from Sioux Falls, South Dakota, on February 1, 1966. He landed in a cornfield in Iowa.

The official record is 113,740 feet by Commander Malcolm D. Ross, U.S.N.R., and the late Lt.-Commander Victor E. Prather, U.S.N., in an ascent from the deck of U.S.S. *Antietam* on May 4, 1961, over the Gulf of Mexico.

Highest Unmanned. The highest altitude attained by an unmanned balloon was 170,000 feet, by a Winzen Research balloon of 47,800,000 cubic feet, launched at Chico, California, in October, 1972.

The unmanned plastic GHOST balloon, launched on November 11, 1971, at Christchurch, New Zealand, is presumed to have come down on its 744th day of flight in the South Atlantic.

Largest. The largest balloon ever to fly is one with an inflated volume of 52,600,000 cu. ft., built by Winzen Research Inc., flown from Palestine, Texas, on June 1, 1975, to a height of 145,000 feet with a payload of 1,905 lbs.

Airships

The earliest flight of an airship was by Henri Giffard from Paris in his coal-gas 88,300-cu. ft. 144-foot-long rigid airship on September 24, 1852.

The largest non-rigid airship ever constructed was the U.S. Navy ZPG 3-W. It had a capacity of 1,516,300 cubic feet, was 403.4 feet long and 85.1 feet in diameter, with a crew of 21. It first flew on July 21, 1958, but crashed into the sea in June, 1960.

The largest rigid airship ever built was the German *Graf Zeppelin II* (LZ130), with a length of 803.8 feet and a capacity of 7,062,100 cubic feet. She made her maiden flight on September 14, 1938 and in May and August, 1939, made radar spying missions in British air space. She was dismantled in April, 1940. Her sister ship, the *Hindenburg*, was 5.6 feet longer.

LARGEST NON-RIGID AIRSHIP: The Navy's ZPG 3-W, 403.4 feet long and 85.1 feet in diameter, had a capacity of more than 1½ million cubic feet. It flew from 1958 to 1960.

The most people ever carried in an airship was 207 in the U.S. Navy *Akron* in 1931. The transatlantic record is 117 by the German *Hindenburg* in 1937.

The distance record for airships is 3,967.3 miles, set by the German *Graf Zeppelin*, captained by Dr. Hugo Eckener between October 29 and November 1, 1928.

Hovercraft

The inventor of the ACV (air-cushion vehicle) is Christopher S. Cockerell (born June 4, 1910), a British engineer who had the idea in 1954, published his Ripplecraft Report 1/55 on October 25, 1955, and patented it on December 12, 1955. The earliest patent relating to an air-cushion craft was taken out in 1877 by John I. Thornycroft (1843–1928) of Chiswick, London. The first flight by a hovercraft was made by the 4½-ton Saunders Roe SR-N1 at Cowes, Isle of Wight, on May 30, 1959. With a 1,500-lb. thrust Viper turbojet engine, this craft reached 68 knots in June, 1961. The first hovercraft public service was opened across the Dee Estuary, Great Britain, by the 60-knot 24-passenger Vickers-Armstrong VA-3 in July, 1962.

The largest is the $3,600,000 Westland SR-N4, weighing 224 tons, first run on February 4, 1968. It has a top speed of 77 knots powered by 4 Bristol Siddeley Marine Proteus engines with 19-foot propellers.

The U.S. Navy's Bell Aerospace 2K SES (Surface Effect Ship) Weapons' Test Platform prototype is expected to weigh 3,140 tons and measure about 250 feet by 110 feet.

The greatest altitude at which a hovercraft is operating is on Lake Titicaca, Peru, where, since 1975, an HM2 Hoverferry hovers 12,506 feet above sea level.

The longest hovercraft journey was one of 5,000 miles through 8 West African countries between October 15, 1969, and January 3, 1970, by the British Trans-African Hovercraft Expedition.

Greatest Load. The heaviest object moved by "hover-flotation" is 784 tons carried by Mears Construction, Ltd., in February, 1975, for Shell Française near Bordeaux, France. Plans are being made to move another storage tank of 1,954 tons.

Model Aircraft

The world record for altitude is 26,929 feet by Maynard L. Hill (U.S.) on September 6, 1970, using a radio-controlled model. The speed record is 213.70 m.p.h. by V. Goukoune and V. Myakinin (both U.S.S.R.) with a radio-controlled model at Klementyeva, U.S.S.R., on September 21, 1971. The record duration flight is one of 25 hours 44 minutes 8 seconds by Myakinin with a radio-controlled glider, September-October, 1973.

The first model helicopter to fly across the English Channel was an 11-lb. model Bell 212 radio-controlled helicopter piloted by Dieter Ziegler for the 32 miles between Ashford, Kent, England, and Ambleteuse, France, on July 17, 1974.

Paper Airplane

The flight duration record for a paper aircraft over level ground is 15.0 seconds by William Harlan Pryor in the Municipal Auditorium, Nashville, Tennessee, on March 26, 1975. A paper plane was reported and witnessed to have flown 1¼ miles after thrown by "Chick" C. O. Reinhart from a 10th-story office window at 60 Beaver Street, New York City, across the East River to Brooklyn, New York, in August, 1933. It was helped by a thermal updraft from a coffee-roasting plant.

5. Power Producers

Largest Power Plant

The world's largest power station is the U.S.S.R.'s hydro-electric station at Krasnoyarsk on the Yenisey River, U.S.S.R., with a power of 6,096,000 kilowatts. Its third generator turned in March, 1968, and the twelfth became operative by December, 1970. The turbine hall completed in June, 1968, is 1,378 feet long. The reservoir backed up by the dam was reported in November, 1972, to be 240 miles long.

The largest non-hydro-electric generating plant in the world is the 2,500,000 kilowatt Tennessee Valley Authority installation at Paradise, Kentucky, with an annual consumption of 8,150,000 tons of coal a year. Its total cost: $189,000,000.

WORLD'S LARGEST HYDRO-ELECTRIC GENERATING PLANTS— PROGRESSIVE LIST

Ultimate Kilowattage	First Operational	Location	River
38,400	1898	De Cew Falls No. 1 (old plant)	Welland Canal
132,500	1905	Ontario Power Station	Niagara
403,900	1922	Sir Adam Beck No. 1 (formerly Queenston-Chippawa)	Niagara
1,641,000	1942	Beauharnois, Quebec, Canada	St. Lawrence
2,100,000	1955	Kuybyshev, U.S.S.R.	Volga
2,161,000*	1941	Grand Coulee, Washington	Columbia
2,543,000	1958	Volgograd, U.S.S.R.	Volga
4,500,000	1964	Bratsk, U.S.S.R.	Angara
6,096,000	1968	Krasnoyarsk, U.S.S.R.	Yenisey
6,400,000	—	Sayano-Shushensk, U.S.S.R.	Yenisey
10,710,000†	—	Itaipu, Brazil-Uruguay	Uruguay

*Ultimate long-term planned kilowattage will be 9,780,000 upon completion of the "Third Powerplant" with capacity of 7,200,000 kilowatts.

†Ultimate kilowattage.

Atomic Power

The world's first atomic pile was built in an abandoned squash court at the University of Chicago. It "went critical" on December 2, 1942.

The world's largest atomic power station is the Ontario Hydro's Pickering station which in 1973 attained full output of 2,160 MW.

FIRST MAJOR TIDAL POWER STATION: Built on the Rance estuary in Brittany, France, it has an annual output of 544,000,000 kWh.

Largest Reactor

The largest single atomic reactor in the world is the 1,098 MW Brown's Ferry Unit 1 General Electric boiling-water-type reactor located on the Wheeler Reservoir near Decatur, Alabama, which became operative in 1973. The Grand Gulf Nuclear Station at Port Gibson, Mississippi, will have a capacity of 1,290 MW in 1979.

Largest Generator

Generators in the 2,000,000 kW (or 2,000 MW) range are now in the planning stages both in the U.K. and the U.S. The largest under construction is one of 1,300 MW by the Brown Boveri Co. of Switzerland for the Tennessee Valley Authority.

Biggest Blackout

The greatest power failure in history struck seven northeastern U.S. states and Ontario, Canada, on November 9–10, 1965. About 30,000,000 people in 80,000 square miles were plunged into darkness. Only two were killed. In New York City the power failed at 5:27 p.m. Supplies were eventually restored by 2 a.m. in Brooklyn, 4:20 a.m. in Queens, 6:58 a.m. in Manhattan and 7 a.m. in the Bronx.

Tidal Power Station

The world's first major tidal power station is the *Usine marèmotrice de la Rance*, officially opened on November 26, 1966, at the Rance estuary in the Golfe de St. Malo, Brittany, France. (See photo, above.) Built in five years, at a cost of $75,600,000, it has a net annual output of 544,000,000 kilowatt-hours. The 880-yard barrage contains 24 turbo-alternators. This harnessing of the tides has imperceptibly slowed the earth's rate of revolution. The $1,000,000,000

Passamaquoddy project for the Bay of Fundy between Maine and New Brunswick, Canada, is not expected to be operative before 1978.

Geo-Thermal Power Plant

The world's longest geo-thermal power plant is the Pacific Gas and Electric Co. 396,000-kW (1973) plant at Big Geysers Resort, Sonoma County, California.

Biggest Boiler

The largest boilers ever designed are those ordered in the U.S. from the Babcock & Wilcox Company, with a capacity of 1,330 MW, so involving the evaporation of 9,330,000 lbs. of steam per hour.

Largest Turbines

The largest turbines are those rated at 820,000 h.p. with an overload capacity of 1,000,000 h.p., 32 feet in diameter, with a 449-ton runner and a 350-ton shaft, for the Grand Coulee "Third Power Plant" (see *Progressive List*).

Largest Gas Turbine

The largest gas turbine in the world is that installed at the Krasnodar thermal power station in August, 1969, with a capacity of 100,000 kilowatts. It was built in Leningrad, U.S.S.R.

Largest Pump Turbine

The world's largest integral reversible pump turbine was made by Allis-Chalmers for the $50,000,000 Taum Sauk installation of the Union Electric Co. in St. Louis, Missouri. It has a rating of 240,000 h.p. as a turbine and a capacity of 1,100,000 gallons per minute as a pump. The Tehachapi Pumping Plant in California, completed in 1972, pumps 18,300,000 gallons per minute over 1,700 feet up.

Largest Gas Works

The flow of natural gas from the North Sea is diminishing the manufacture of gas by the carbonization of coal and the reforming process using petroleum derivatives. The most productive gas works currently are at the oil-reforming plant at Greenwich, England, with an output of 420.5 million cu. ft. per day.

Oldest Steam Engine

The oldest steam engine in working order is the 1812 Boulton & Watt 26-h.p. 42-inch bore beam engine on the Kennet & Avon Canal at Great Bedwyn, Wiltshire, England. It was restored by the Crofton Society in 1971.

Most Powerful Jet Engine

The world's most powerful jet engine was the General Electric GE4/J5 turbojet which attained a thrust of 69,900 lbs., with afterburning, on November 13, 1969. The Pratt & Whitney JT 90D-X turbofan first run on January 15, 1972, has a thrust of 62,000 lbs. at 23° F. The thrust of the Thiokol XLR99-RM-2 rocket motor in each of the three experimental U.S. X-15 aircraft was 56,880 lbs. at

LARGEST SOLAR FURNACE: This plant in the Pyrenees Mountains of France has 63 steerable mirrors that convert the sun's rays into heat as high as 6,735 degrees F.

sea level, reaching 70,000 lbs. at peak altitudes. The Rolls-Royce RB 211-22B powered the Lockheed L-1011-1 Tristar, from April, 1972, and develops 42,000 lbs. The -22X version (45,000 lbs.) may be developed for the L-1011-2.

Solar Power Plant

The largest solar furnace in the world is the Laboratoire de L'Energie Solaire, at Odiello in the eastern Pyrenees, France. It consists of an array of 63 steerable mirrors with a total area of 30,515 square feet or seven-tenths of an acre which can generate a heat of 3,725°C. (6,735°F.).

LARGEST PRESS: With its 50,000-ton capacity, this closed-die forging press is the world's most powerful production machine.

6. Engineering

The earliest machinery still in use is the *dâlu*—a water-raising instrument known to have been in use in the Sumerian civilization which originated *c.* 3500 B.C. in Lower Iraq.

Largest Press

The world's two most powerful production machines are forging presses in the U.S. The Loewy closed-die forging press, in a plant leased from the U.S. Air Force by the Wyman-Gordon Company at North Grafton, Massachusetts, weighs 10,600 tons and stands 114 feet 2 inches high, of which 66 feet is sunk below the operating floor. It has a rated capacity of 50,000 tons, and went into operation in October, 1955. The other similar press is at the plant of the Aluminum Company of America at Cleveland, Ohio. There has been a report of a press in the U.S.S.R. with a capacity of 82,500 tons, at Novo Kramatorsk.

The Bêché and Grohs counterblow forging hammers, manufactured in West Germany, are rated at 66,120 tons.

Lathe

The world's largest lathe is the 72-foot-long 431-ton giant lathe built by the Dortmunder Rheinstahl firm of Wagner, in Germany, in 1962. The face plate is 15 feet in diameter and can exert a torque of 289,000 feet per lb. when handling objects weighing up to 225 tons.

Excavator

Largest. The world's largest excavator is the 14,325-ton bucket wheel excavator being assembled at the open cast lignite mine of Hambach, West Germany, with a rating of 260,000 cubic yards per 20-hour working day. It is 690 feet in length and 269 feet tall. The wheel is 222 feet in circumference with 6.5 cubic yard buckets.

Dragline Excavator

The Ural Engineering Works at Ordzhonikdze, U.S.S.R., completed in March, 1962, has a dragline known as the ES–25(100) with a boom of 100 meters (328 feet) and a bucket with a capacity of 31.5 cubic yards. The world's largest walking dragline is the Bucyrus-Erie 4250W with an all-up weight of 13,440 tons and a bucket capacity of 220 cubic yards on a 310-foot boom. This, the largest mobile land machine, is now operating on the Central Ohio Coal Company's Muskingon site in Ohio.

Blast Furnace

The world's largest blast furnace is one with an inner volume of 176,570 cubic feet at the Krivoi Rog Iron and Steel Works, Ukraine, U.S.S.R., completed in December, 1974, with an annual capacity of 4,480,000 tons.

Largest Forging. The largest forging on record is one 53 feet long weighing 396,000 lbs. forged by Bethlehem Steel for the Tennessee Valley Authority nuclear power plant at Brown Ferry, Alabama, in November, 1969.

Longest Pipelines

Oil. The longest crude oil pipeline in the world is the Interprovincial Pipe Line Company's installation from Edmonton, Alberta, to Buffalo, New York, a distance of 1,775 miles. Along the length of the pipe 13 pumping stations maintain a flow of 8,280,000 gallons of oil per day.

The eventual length of the Trans-Siberian Pipeline will be 2,319 miles, running from Tuimazy through Omsk and Novosibirsk to Irkutsk. The first 30-mile section was opened in July, 1957.

The world's most expensive pipeline is the Alaska pipeline running 798 miles from Prudhoe Bay to Valdez. By completion of the first phase in 1977 it will have cost at least $6,000 million. The pipe is 48 inches in diameter.

The longest submarine pipeline is the Ekofisk-Emden line stretching 260 miles under the North Sea, completed in July, 1975.

Natural Gas. The longest natural gas pipeline in the world is the TransCanada Pipeline which by 1974 had 5,654 miles of pipe up to 42 inches in diameter.

Largest Oil Tank

The largest oil tank ever constructed is the Million Barrel Ekofisk Oil Tank completed in Norway in 1973 and implanted in the North Sea. It measures 92 × 92 × 82 meters (301.8 ft. sq., 269 ft. high) and contains 8,800 tons of steel and 222,200 tons of concrete. Its capacity of 209,272 cu. yds. is equivalent to 1.42 times the amount of oil which escaped from the *Torrey Canyon*, in the largest oil spill from a ship.

LARGEST OIL TANK: Planted in the North Sea, this tank can hold more than 200,000 cubic yards of oil.

LARGEST PADLOCK:
Manufactured in England,
this model weighs 100 pounds.

Largest Cat Cracker

The world's largest catalyst cracker is the American Oil Company's installation at its refinery in Texas City, Texas, with a capacity of 4,000,000 gallons per day.

Largest Padlock

The largest padlock manufactured is ERA No. 1212 Close Shackle Clever Lock produced by J. E. Reynolds of Willenhall, England. It weighs 100 lbs.

Smallest Monkeywrench

The smallest standard ratchet monkeywrench is the No. 0 model made by the precision engineers, Leytool Ltd. of London E.10, England, with a head outside diameter of $\frac{1}{2}$ inch and a width of $\frac{1}{4}$ inch.

Largest Nut

The largest nuts ever made weigh 3,304 lbs. each and have an outside diameter of $43\frac{1}{4}$ inches and a 26-inch thread. Known as the Pilgrim Nuts, they are manufactured by Doncaster Moorside Ltd. of Oldham, England, for securing propellers.

Largest Valve

The world's largest valve is the 14-foot diameter Pratt-Triton XL butterfly valve made in Aurora, Illinois, for water and power systems.

Fastest Printer

The world's fastest printer is the Radiation Inc. electro-sensitive system at the Lawrence Radiation Laboratory, Livermore, California. Recording of up to 30,000 lines per minute each containing 120 alphanumeric characters is attained by controlling electronic pulses through chemically impregnated recording paper which is rapidly moving under closely spaced fixed styli. It can thus print the wordage of the whole Bible (773,692 words) in 65 seconds—3,333 times as fast as the world's fastest typist.

Highest Ropeway

The highest and longest aerial ropeway in the world is the Teleferico Mérida (Mérida téléphérique) in Venezuela, from Mérida City (5,379 feet) to the summit of Pico Espejo (15,629 feet), a rise of 10,250 feet. The ropeway is in four sections, involving 3 car changes in the 8-mile ascent in one hour. The fourth span is 10,070 feet in length. The two cars work on the pendulum system—the carrier rope is locked and the cars are hauled by means of three pull ropes powered by a 230-h.p. motor. They have a maximum capacity of 45 persons and travel at 32 feet per second (21.8 m.p.h.).

The longest single-span ropeway is the 13,500-foot-long span from the Coachella Valley to Mt. San Jacinto (10,821 feet), California, opened on September 12, 1963.

Largest Cable Cars

The largest cable cars in the world are those at Squaw Valley, California, with a capacity of 121 persons. Built by Carrosseriewerke A.G. of Aarburg, Switzerland, they had their first run on Dec. 19, 1968. The breaking strain on the 7,000-foot cable is 312 tons.

Fastest Passenger Elevators

The fastest domestic passenger elevators in the world are the express elevators to the 103rd floor or 1,340-foot level of the 110-story, 1,454-foot-tall Sears Tower in Chicago. They operate at a speed of 1,800 feet per minute, or about 20.45 m.p.h.

Much higher speeds are achieved in the winding cages of mine shafts. A hoisting shaft 6,800 feet deep, owned by Western Deep Levels Ltd. in South Africa, winds at speeds of up to 40.9 m.p.h.

First and Longest Escalators

The name "escalator" was registered in the U.S. on May 28, 1900, but the earliest "Inclined Elevator" was installed by Jesse W. Reno on the pier at Coney Island, New York, in 1896.

The longest escalators are on the Leningrad Underground, U.S.S.R., which have a vertical rise of 195 ft.

The world's longest "moving sidewalks" are those installed in 1970 in the Neue Messe Centre, Dusseldorf, West Germany, which measure 738 feet between comb plates.

Largest Transformer

The world's largest single-phase transformers are rated at 1,500,000 kVa of which 8 are in service with the American Electric Power Service Corporation. Of these, 5 step down from 765 to 345 kV.

Transmission Lines

Longest. The longest span between pylons of any power line in the world is that across the Sogne Fjord, Norway, between Rabnaberg and Flatlaberg. Erected in 1955 by the Whitecross Co. Ltd. of Warrington, England, as part of the high-tension power cable from Refsdal power station at Vik, it has a span of 16,040 feet and a weight of 13 tons. In 1967, two further high-tensile steel/aluminum lines 16,006 feet long, and weighing 37 tons, manufactured by Whitecross and British Insulated Callender's Cables Ltd., were erected there.

Highest. The world's highest are those across the Straits of Messina, with towers of 675 feet (Sicily side) and 735 feet (Calabria) and 11,900 feet apart.

Highest Voltages. The highest voltages now carried are 800,000 volts from Volgograd to the Donbas Basin, U.S.S.R. The Swedish A.S.E.A. Company has been experimenting with a possible 1,000,000 volt A.C./D.C. transmission line.

Longest Conveyor Belt

The world's longest single-flight conveyor belt is one of 9 miles installed near Uniontown, Kentucky, by Cable Belt Ltd. of Camberley, Surrey, England. It has a weekly capacity of 140,000 tons of coal on a 42-inch-wide 800-feet-per-minute belt and forms part of a 12½-mile long system.

The world's longest multi-flight conveyor is one of 62 miles between the phosphate mine near Bucraa and the Atlantic port of El Aaiun, Spanish West Africa, built by Krupps and completed in 1972. It has 11 flights of between 5.6 and 6.8 miles in length and is driven at 10.06 m.p.h.

LONGEST CONVEYOR: This multi-flight belt in the Spanish Sahara extends 62 miles and travels at just over 10 m.p.h.

Smallest Tubing

The smallest tubing in the world is made by Accles and Pollock, Ltd., of Warley, England. It is of pure nickel with an outside diameter of 0.0005 of an inch, and was announced on September 9, 1963. The average human hair measures from 0.002 to 0.003 of an inch in diameter. The tubing, which is stainless, can be used for the artificial insemination of mosquitoes and "feeding" nerves, and weighs only 5 ounces per 100 miles.

Longest Wire Rope

The longest wire rope ever spun in one piece was one measuring 46,653 feet (8.83 miles) long and $3\frac{1}{8}$ inches in circumference, with a weight of $31\frac{1}{2}$ tons, manufactured by British Ropes Ltd., of Doncaster, England.

The heaviest reported is one 7 inches in circumference and 3.94 miles long, weighing 90.72 tons, made by Martin-Black & Co. (Wire Ropes) Ltd., at Coatbridge, Strathclyde, Scotland, in 1973.

Largest Radar Installations

The largest of the three installations in the U.S. Ballistic Missile Early Warning System is that near Thule, Greenland, 931 miles from the North Pole, completed in 1960 at a cost of $500,000,000. Its sister stations are at Cape Clear, Alaska, completed in July, 1961, and a $115,000,000 installation at Fylingdales Moor, Yorkshire, England, completed in June, 1963. The largest scientific radar installation is the 21-acre ground array at Jicamarca, Peru.

Most Powerful Cranes

The world's most powerful crane is the Japanese twin-boomed floating crane *Musashi*, completed in 1975, with a capacity of 3,050 tons.

The most powerful crane ships are the pipe-layer *Blue Whale*, the *Ocean Builder I* and the *Thor*, used in North Sea oil development work. Each has a rated capacity of 2,200 tons.

The most powerful gantry crane is the 92.3-foot-wide Rahco (R. A. Hanson Disc. Ltd.) gantry crane at the Grand Coulee Dam Third Powerplant, which was tested to lift a load of 2,500 tons in 1975. It successfully lowered a 3,944,000-lb. generator rotor with an accuracy of $\frac{1}{32}$ of an inch.

Greatest Lift

The heaviest lifting operation in engineering history was of the 41,000-ton roof of the Velodrome in Montreal, Canada, in 1975. It was raised by jacks some 4 inches to strike its centering.

Tallest Mobile Crane

The tallest is the 924-ton Rosenkranz K10001 with a lifting capacity of 1,102 tons and a combined boom and jib height of 663 feet. It is carried on 10 trucks, each limited to 75 feet 8 inches and an axle weight of 130 tons. It can lift 33.6 tons to a height of 525 feet.

Time Measurer

The most accurate time-keeping devices are the twin atomic hydrogen masers installed in 1964 in the U.S. Naval Research Laboratory, Washington, D.C. They are based on the frequency of the hydrogen atom's transition period of 1,420,450,751,694 cycles per second. This enables an accuracy to within one second per 1,700,000 years.

Clocks

Oldest. The earliest mechanical clock, that is, one with an escapement, was completed in China in 725 A.D. by I'Hsing and Liang Ling-tsan.

The oldest surviving working clock is the faceless clock dating from 1386, or possibly earlier, at Salisbury Cathedral, Wiltshire, England, which was restored in 1956 having struck the hours for 498 years and ticked more than 500,000,000 times. Earlier dates, ranging back to c. 1335, have been attributed to the weight-driven clock in Wells Cathedral, Somerset, England, but only the iron frame is original. A model of Giovanni de Dondi's heptagonal astronomical clock of 1348–64 was completed in 1962.

Largest. The world's most massive clock is the Astronomical Clock in Beauvais Cathedral, France, constructed between 1865 and 1868. It contains 90,000 parts and measures 40 feet high, 20 feet wide and 9 feet deep. The Su Sung clock, built in China at Khaifeng in 1088–92, had a 22-ton bronze armillory sphere for $1\frac{2}{3}$ tons of water. It was removed to Peking in 1126 and was last known to be working in its 40-foot-high tower in 1136.

Most Accurate. The most accurate and complicated clock in the world is the Olsen clock, installed in the Copenhagen Town Hall, Denmark. The clock, which has more than 14,000 units, took 10 years to make and the mechanism of the clock functions in 570,000 different ways. The celestial pole motion of the clock will take 25,753 years to complete a full circle, the slowest moving designed mechanism in the world. The clock is accurate to 0.5 seconds in 300 years.

Public Clocks. The largest four-faced clock in the world is that on the building of the Allen-Bradley Company of Milwaukee, Wisconsin. Each face has a diameter of 40 feet $3\frac{1}{2}$ inches with a minute hand 20 feet in overall length.

The tallest four-faced clock in the world is that of the Williamsburgh Savings Bank, Brooklyn, New York City. It is 430 feet above street level.

Watches

Oldest. The oldest watch (portable clockwork timekeeper) is one made of iron by Peter Henlein (or Hele) in Nürnberg (Nuremberg), Bavaria, Germany, c. 1504 and now in the Memorial Hall, Philadelphia, Pennsylvania. The earliest wrist watches were those of Jacquet-Droz and Leschot of Geneva, Switzerland, dating from 1790.

 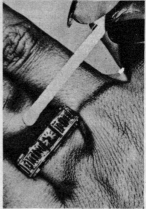

MOST EXPENSIVE POCKET WATCH (left): The Swiss "Grande Complication" retails for $45,000. SMALLEST WATCH (right): Just over a half inch long, the dial of this watch is not much larger than a match head.

Smallest. The smallest watches in the world are produced by Jaeger Le Coultre of Switzerland. Equipped with a 15-jeweled movement, they measure just over half-an-inch in length and three-sixteenths of an inch in width. The movement, with its case, weighs under a quarter of an ounce.

Most Expensive. Excluding watches with jeweled cases, the most expensive standard man's pocket watch is the Swiss *Grande Complication* by Audemars-Piguet, which retails for $45,000.

On June 1, 1964, a record £27,500 ($77,000) was paid for the Duke of Wellington's watch made in Paris in 1807 by Abraham Louis Bréguet, at the salesrooms of Sotheby & Co., London, by the dealers Messrs. Ronald Lee for a Portuguese client.

The most expensive men's wrist watch *and* jeweled case is one created by Piaget Watch Corporation and sold by Van Cleef & Arpels, valued at $47,500. (See color photograph on color page E).

Chapter Nine

THE BUSINESS WORLD

In this chapter, the pound sterling has been converted, unless otherwise noted, at the fixed mean rate of £1 = $1.75 for mid-1976, and at the prevailing rates for earlier dates.

1. Commerce

Oldest Industry

Agriculture is often described as "the oldest industry in the world," whereas in fact there is no evidence that it was practiced before *c.* 11,000 B.C. The oldest known industry is flint knapping, involving the production of chopping tools and hand axes, dating from about 1,750,000 years ago. Salt panning is of comparable antiquity.

Oldest Company. The oldest company in the world is the Faversham Oyster Fishery Co. of England, referred to in an Act of Parliament of 1930 as existing "from time immemorial," *i.e.* from before 1189.

Greatest Assets. The business with the greatest amount in physical assets is the Bell System, which comprises the American Telephone and Telegraph Company, with headquarters at 195 Broadway, New York City, and its subsidiaries. The group's total assets on the consolidated balance sheet at December 31, 1975, were valued at $80,156,000,000. The plant involved included 118,460,000 telephones. The number of employees is 939,000. A total of 20,109 attended the annual meeting in April, 1961, thereby setting a world record.

The first company to have assets in excess of $1 billion was the United States Steel Corporation with $1,400,000,000 at the time of its creation by merger in 1900.

The manufacturing company with the greatest total assets employed is Imperial Chemical Industries, Ltd., with headquarters in England. It had £2,412,000,000 ($5,547,600,000) on December 31, 1974. Its staff and payroll averaged 201,000 during the year. The company, which has 458 U.K. and overseas subsidiaries, was formed in 1926 by the merger of four concerns—British Dyestuffs Corporation Ltd.; Brunner, Mond & Co. Ltd.; Nobel Industries Ltd.; and United Alkali Co. Ltd.

Greatest Sales and Capital. The first company to surpass the $1 billion mark in annual sales was the United States Steel Corporation in 1917. Now there are 137 corporations with sales exceeding $2,500,000,000 (82 U.S., 40 European, 11 Japanese and 2 Canadian). The list is headed by Exxon (New York) with $42,061,336,000 in 1974.

Greatest Profit and Loss. The greatest net profit made by an industrial company in a year is $3,142,000,000 by Exxon in 1974. The greatest loss ever sustained by a commercial concern in a year was $431,200,000 by the Penn Central Transportation Co. in 1970— a rate of $13.67 per second.

The greatest loss recorded by *any* enterprise in a year is £309,700,000 ($712,310,000) by the Post Office in the United Kingdom in 1974–75.

Biggest Work Force. The greatest payroll of any single civilian organization in the world is that of the U.S.S.R. National Railway system with a total work force of 1,996,600.

Largest Take-Over. The largest take-over in world commercial history has been the bid of £438,000,000 ($1,051,200,000) by Grand Metropolitan Hotels Ltd., England, for the brewers Watney Mann on June 17, 1972.

Largest Write-Off. The largest reduction of assets in corporate history was the $800,000,000 write-off of Tristar aircraft development costs announced on November 23, 1974.

Advertising Agency

The largest international single-name advertising agency in the world is J. Walter Thompson Co., which in 1975 had total worldwide billings of $900,100,000.

A higher figure of $900,800,000 in 1975 was reported for Dentsu of Japan, but this is not believed to be comparable since revenues are not wholly derived from agency work, but from local media brokerage accounts.

Biggest Advertiser

The world's biggest advertiser is Sears Roebuck and Co., with $378,266,000 spent in 1975, excluding its catalogue.

Aircraft Manufacturer

The world's largest aircraft manufacturer is the Boeing Company of Seattle, Washington. The corporation's sales totaled $3,718,853,000 in 1975, and it had 67,900 (down from a 120,500 top) employees and assets valued at $1,175,133,000 on December 31, 1975.

Cessna Aircraft Company of Wichita, Kansas, produced 7,673 civil aircraft (55 models) in 1975, with total sales of $492,000,000. The company has produced more than 127,000 aircraft since Clyde Cessna's first was built in 1911. The record year for Cessna was 1965–66 with 7,922 aircraft completed.

Airlines

Largest. The largest airline in the world is the U.S.S.R. State airline "Aeroflot," so named since 1932. This was instituted on February 9, 1923, with the title of Civil Air Fleet of the Council of Ministers of the U.S.S.R., abbreviated to "Dobrolet." It operates 1,300 aircraft over about 435,000 miles of routes, employs 400,000 people and carried 90,000,000 passengers in 1974 to 67 countries.

The commercial airline carrying the greatest number of passengers in 1975 was United Air Lines (formed 1931), with 29,927,192 passengers. The company had 49,609 employees and a fleet of 365 jet planes.

Oldest. The oldest existing airline is Koninklijke-Luchtvaart-Maatschappij N.V. (KLM) of the Netherlands, which opened its first scheduled service (Amsterdam-London) on May 17, 1920, having been established in 1919. One of the original constituents of B.O.A.C., Aircraft Transport and Travel Ltd., was founded in 1918 and merged into Imperial Airways in 1924. Delag (Deutsche Luftschiffahrt A.G.) was founded at Frankfurt am Main on November 16, 1909, and started a scheduled airship service in June, 1910.

Aluminum Producer

The world's largest producer of primary aluminum is Alcan Aluminium Limited, of Montreal, Quebec, Canada. With its affiliated companies, it had an output of 2,016,000 tons and record consolidated revenues of $2,312,538,000 in 1975. The company's principal subsidiary, the Aluminium Company of Canada, Ltd., owns the largest aluminum smelter in the western world, at Arvida, Quebec, with a capacity of 440,000 tons per annum.

Art Auctioneering

The largest and oldest firm of art auctioneers is Sotheby Parke-Bernet of London and New York, founded in 1744. Their turnover in 1973–74 was $216,762,480.

The highest total of any single day's sale has been $9,595,639 at Christie of London's jewel sale in the Hotel Richemond, Geneva, Switzerland, on November 21, 1973.

Barbers

The largest barbering establishment is Norris of Houston at 3200 Audley, Houston, Texas, which employs 60 barbers.

Bicycle Factory

The 64-acre plant of Raleigh Industries Ltd. at Nottingham,

LARGEST BICYCLE FACTORY: This plant at Nottingham, England, was scheduled to make more than 2 million bicycles in 1975.

England, is the largest factory in the world producing complete bicycles, components, wheeled toys and baby carriages. The factory employs 10,000 and in 1975 had targets to make 850,000 wheeled toys and more than 2,000,000 bicycles.

Bookshop

The world's largest single bookshop is that of W. & G. Foyle, Ltd., of London, W.C.2. First established in 1904 in a small shop in Islington, the company is now at 119–125 Charing Cross Road, which has an area of 75,825 square feet. The largest single display of books in one room in the world is in the Norrington Room at Blackwell's Bookshop, Oxford, England. This subterranean adjunct was opened on June 16, 1966, and contains 160,000 volumes on 2½ miles of shelving in 10,000 square feet of selling space.

Brewery

The oldest brewery is the Weihenstephan Brewery in Freising, near Munich, West Germany, founded in 1040.

The largest single brewer is Anheuser-Busch, Inc. of St. Louis. In 1973, the company sold 34,097,000 barrels, the greatest annual volume ever produced by a brewing company. The company's St. Louis plant covers 95 acres and has a capacity of 10,500,000 barrels.

The largest brewery on a single site is Adolph Coors Co. of Golden, Colorado, which is scheduled to produce 13,500,000 barrels in 1976.

Arthur Guinness Son & Co., Ltd., founded in 1759, is the largest exporter of beer, ale and stout in the world. Exports of Guinness from the Republic of Ireland in the 52 weeks ending March 13, 1976, were 978,200 bulk barrels (1 bulk barrel = 36 Imperial gallons) which is equivalent to 1,465,998 half-pint glasses per day.

LARGEST SINGLE BOOKSHOP DISPLAY is the Norrington Room of Blackwell's of Oxford which contains 160,000 volumes.

Brickworks

The largest brickworks in the world is the London Brick Company plant at Stewartby, Bedford, England. The works, established in 1898, now cover 221 acres and produce 17,000,000 bricks and brick equivalent every week.

Car Manufacturer

The largest car manufacturing company in the world (and largest manufacturer of any kind) is General Motors Corporation of Detroit. During its peak year of 1975, worldwide sales totaled $35,724,911,215. Its assets at December 31, 1975, were valued at $21,664,884,594. Its total 1975 payroll was $10,028,000,000 to an average of 681,000 employees. The greatest total of dividends ever paid for one year was $1,514,240,066 by General Motors for 1973.

Largest Plant. The largest single automobile plant in the world is the Volkswagenwerk, Wolfsburg, West Germany, with 47,000 employees and a capacity of 4,000 vehicles daily. The surface area of the factory buildings is 356 acres and that of the whole plant, with 43.5 miles of rail sidings, is 4,991 acres.

Greatest Salesman. The all-time record for automobile salesmanship in individual units sold is 1,425 in 1973, by Joe Girard of Detroit, Michigan, winner of the Number One Car Salesman title every year since 1966. His commissions in 1973 totaled $189,000. His 1974 total was 1,376 units.

Chemical Company

The world's largest chemical company is Imperial Chemical Industries Ltd. (See *Greatest Assets*, page 341.)

Chocolate Factory

The world's largest chocolate factory is that built by Hershey Foods Corp. of Hershey, Pennsylvania, in 1905. It now has 2,000,000 square feet of floor space.

Computer Company

The world's largest computer firm is International Business Machines Corporation (I.B.M.) which, in a 1975 court decision, was held to have a 36.7 per cent share in the value of "electronic computers and peripheral equipment, except parts" based on 1971 shipments. In 1975, assets were $15,530,476,314, with a working capital of $4,751,829,045.

Department Stores

The largest department store chain, in terms of number of stores, is J. C. Penney Company, Inc., founded in Wyoming, in 1902. The company operates 2,051 retail establishments in the U.S., Belgium and Italy, with net selling space of 57,800,000 square feet. Its turnover was $7,679,000,000 in the year ending January 1, 1976, the twentieth consecutive year of record sales.

LARGEST MEN'S STORE: Barney's in New York City, founded in 1923 in a 20-foot store front, now stretches the length of a city block. Its 100,000 square feet of space houses 23 departments stocking a million items, including 200,000 suits. It employs 200 tailors.

Largest Single Store. The world's largest store is R. H. Macy & Co. Inc. at Broadway and 34th Street, New York City. It has a floor space of 50.5 acres, and 11,000 employees who handle 400,000 items. The sales of the company and its subsidiaries totaled $1,297,672,000 in 1975. Mr. Rowland Hussey Macy's sales on his first day at his fancy goods store on 6th Avenue, on October 27, 1858, were recorded as $11.06.

Most Profitable. The department store with the fastest-moving stock in the world is the Marble Arch store of Marks & Spencer Ltd. at 458 Oxford Street, London, England. The figure of more than $575-worth of goods per square foot of selling space per year is believed to have become an understatement when the selling area was raised to 72,000 square feet in October, 1970. The company has 253 branches in the U.K. and nearly 6,000,000 square feet of selling space. It now has branches in Continental Europe and Canada.

Distillery

The world's largest distilling company is Distillers Corporation-Seagrams Limited of Canada. Its sales in the year ending July 31, 1975, totaled $1,930,786,000, of which $1,629,764,000 were from sales by Joseph E. Seagram & Sons, Inc. in the United States. The group employs about 17,000 people, including about 12,500 in the United States.

The largest of all Scotch whisky distilleries is Carsebridge at Alloa, Clackmannanshire, Scotland, owned by Scottish Grain Distillers Limited. This distillery is capable of producing more than 20,000,000 proof gallons per annum. The largest establishment for blending and bottling Scotch whisky is owned by John Walker & Sons Limited at Kilmarnock, Strathclyde, where over 2,500,000 bottles are filled each week. "Johnnie Walker" is the world's largest-selling brand of Scotch whisky. The world's largest-selling brand of gin is Gordon's.

Drug Store Chain

The largest chain is that of Boots The Chemists, which has 1,290 retail branches. The firm was founded in England by Jesse Boot (1850–1931), the 1st Baron Trent.

Fisheries

The world's highest recorded catch of fish was 65,600,000 metric tons in 1972. Peru had the largest ever national haul with 12,160,000 metric tons in 1970, comprising mostly anchoveta.

The world's largest fishmongers are MacFisheries, a subsidiary of Unilever Ltd., England, with 271 retail outlets in April, 1976.

Largest Net. The largest net yet manufactured is one that can fish 8,800,000 cubic yards per hour, announced in West Germany in March, 1974.

Games Manufacturer

The largest manufacturer of games is probably Parker Bros. Inc. of Salem, Massachusetts. The company's top-selling item is the real estate game "Monopoly," acquired in 1935. Almost 80,000,000 sets were sold by July, 1974. The print of "money" by the company for all its games is $18,500,000,000,000 per year, more than the total of real paper money printed in the entire world. The streets are named after those in Atlantic City, New Jersey, where the game's then unemployed inventor, Charles Darrow (1889–1967), spent his vacations. Parker also makes the "Guinness Game of World Records."

The longest game of Monopoly approved by the Monopoly Marathon Records Documentation Committee is 1,008 hours by relays of 34 people in Denver, Colorado, from June 18 to July 31, 1974. The longest game by four players is 264 hours by Ray Kessinger, Tom Lashbrook, Tony Stanaro, and Kirk Hamiltons in Pinole, California, from December 26, 1974, to January 5, 1975.

The Milton Bradley Company of Springfield, Massachusetts, claims to be larger than Parker Bros. but its sales of games are not segregated from sales of toys and school supplies, and Parker Bros., since it became part of General Mills, does not issue a separate statement, so exact comparisons are impossible.

General Merchandise

The largest general merchandising firm in the world is Sears, Roebuck and Co. (founded by Richard W. Sears in the North Redwood railroad station in Minnesota in 1886) of Chicago. The net sales were $12,306,229,080 in the year ending January 31, 1974, when the corporation had 840 retail stores and 2,785 catalogue, retail and telephone sales offices and independent catalogue merchants in 15 countries, and total assets valued at $10,427,431,000.

Grocery Stores

The largest grocery chain in the world is Safeway Stores Incorporated, Oakland, California, with sales in 1975 amounting to $9,716,889,000 and total current assets valued at $880,114,000 as of January 3, 1976. The company has 2,451 stores totaling 51,800,000 square feet. The total payroll covers 126,964 people.

Hotels

The top revenue-earning hotel business is Holiday Inns, Inc., with 1975 revenues of $916,973,000 from 1,710 inns in 44 countries. The business was founded by Charles Kemmons Wilson with his first inn on Summer Avenue in Memphis, Tennessee, in 1952.

Insurance

The company with the highest volume of insurance in force in the world is the Prudential Insurance Company of America, Newark, New Jersey, with $232,000,000,000.

Largest Association. The largest single association in the world is the Blue Cross, the medical insurance organization, with a membership at January 1, 1975, in the U.S. and Canada of 87,648,185. Benefits paid out exceeded $5,300,000,000 in 1974.

Largest Life Policy. The largest life insurance policy ever written was one of $25,000,000 for James Derrick Slater (born March 13, 1929), chairman of Slater, Walker Securities, the City of London investment bankers. The existence of the policy was made known on June 3, 1971.

Marine Insurance. The largest marine insurance loss ever was the 125,000 grt VLCC (Very Large Crude Carrier) *Olympic Bravery*, insured at Lloyds of London and valued at £25,000,000 ($50,000,000), which ran aground off Ushant, France, on January 24, 1976. The 77,000 grt LNG (Liquid Natural Gas) Carrier *Mostefa Ben Boulaid*, owned by the Compagnie Nationale Algerienne de Navigation Algeria, is currently insured for $140,000,000.

Highest Life Insurance Pay-out. Linda Mullendore, wife of a murdered Oklahoma rancher, received some $14,000,000 as of November 14, 1970, the largest pay-out on a single life. Her husband paid $300,000 in premiums in 1969.

Mineral Water

The world's largest mineral water firm is Source Perrier near Nîmes, France, with an annual production of more than 1,800,000,000 bottles, of which more than 340,000,000 come from the single spring near Nîmes, 640,000,000 from Contrexéville, and 100,000,000 from Vichy. The French drink 50 liters of mineral water per person per year.

Oil Company and Refinery

The world's largest oil company is the Exxon Corporation (formerly Standard Oil Company (New Jersey)), with 135,500 employees and assets valued at $32,839,398,000 on January 1, 1976. The world's largest refinery is the Amuya Bay refinery in Venezuela, operated by Lagoven with a capacity of 35,200,000 tons.

Paper Mill

The world's largest paper mill is that established in 1936 by the Union Camp Corporation at Savannah, Georgia, with an output of 1,002,967 tons in 1974.

Popcorn Plant

The largest popcorn plant is the House of Clarks Ltd. of Dagenham, Essex, England (instituted in 1933), which in 1975–76 produced 65,000,000 packets of "Butterkist."

Public Relations

The world's largest public relations firm is Hill and Knowlton, Inc. of 633 Third Avenue, New York City, and ten other U.S. cities. The firm employs a full-time staff of over 500 and also maintains offices in 27 cities overseas.

The world's pioneer public relations publication is *Public Relations News*, founded by Mrs. Denny Griswold in 1944. It now has readers in 77 countries.

Publishing

The publishing company generating most net revenue is Time, Inc., of New York City with $910,700,000 in 1975. The largest book publishing concern in the world is the Book Division of McGraw-Hill, Inc., of New York City, with sales of $251,600,000 in 1975.

Restaurant Chain

The largest restaurant chain is that operated by F. W. Woolworth and Co., with 2,074 (mostly lunch counters) in six countries.

Shipbuilding

In 1975 there were 9,433,264 gross tons of ships, excluding sailing ships, barges, and vessels of less than 100 tons, completed throughout the world, excluding the U.S.S.R., Rumania and China (mainland). Japan completed 3,332,981 gross tons (35.33 per cent of the world's total).

The world's leading shipbuilding firm in 1975 was the Ishikawa-jima-Harima Heavy Industries Co. of Japan, which launched 82 ships of 2,385,090 gross tons from five shipyards.

Shipping Line

The largest shipping owner and operator is the Royal Dutch/Shell Group, which on December 31, 1975, owned and managed 154 ships of 14,766,002 deadweight tons and had on charter 158 ships of 17,471,215 deadweight tons. Additionally the fleet has 11 gas carriers owned or on charter with a combined capacity of 950,543 cubic yards.

Shoe Shop

The largest shoe shop in the world is that of Lilley & Skinner, Ltd. at 360-366 Oxford Street, London, W.1. The shop has a floor area of 76,000 square feet, spread over four floors. With a total staff of more than 180 people it offers, in ten departments, a choice of 125,000 pairs of shoes. Every week, on average, over 45,000 people visit this store.

Shopping Center

The world's largest shopping center is the Lakewood Center, California, with a gross building area of 2,451,438 square feet on a 165-acre site. There is parking for 12,500 cars.

The world's first shopping center was "Suburban Square" in Ardmore, Pennsylvania, built in 1928.

Soft Drinks

The world's top-selling soft drink is Coca-Cola with over 165,000,000 sold per day at the end of 1975 in more than 130 countries. "Coke" was invented by Dr. John S. Pemberton of Atlanta, Georgia, in 1886, and the company was formed in 1892.

Steel Company

The world's largest producer of steel is Nippon Steel of Tokyo, Japan, which produced 38,480,000 metric tons of steel, steel products and pig iron in 1974. The Fukuyama Works of Nippon Kokan has a capacity of more than 16,000,000 metric tons per annum.

Tobacco Company

The world's largest tobacco company is the British American Tobacco Company Ltd. (founded 1902) of London. The group's net assets were £1,742,260,000 ($4,007,200,000) at September 30, 1975. Group turnover for 1974–75 was £4,261,790,000 ($9,802,117,000). The group has 128 factories and over 240,000 employees.

The world's largest cigarette plant is the $200,000,000 Philip Morris plant at Richmond, Virginia, which opened in October, 1974. It employs 2,700 people producing 200,000,000 cigarettes a day.

Toy Manufacturer

The world's largest toy manufacturer is Mattel Toys of Hawthorne, California, founded in 1945. Its sales in 1975 were $340,881,000.

Toy Store

The world's biggest toy store is F.A.O. Schwarz, 745 Fifth Avenue at 58th Street, New York City, with 50,000 square feet on three floors; also 17 branch stores with a further 140,000 square feet.

Wine Company

The oldest champagne firm is Ruinart Père et Fils, founded in 1729. The oldest cognac firm is Augier Frères & Cie., established in 1643.

LAND

The world's largest land owner is the United States Government, with a holding of 760,532,000 acres (1,094,581 square miles), which is nearly the area of India.

Land Values

Highest. Currently the most expensive land in the world is that in the City of London. The freehold price on small prime sites reached £1,950 ($4,875) per square foot in mid-1973. The 600-foot National Westminster Bank on a 2¼-acre site off Bishopsgate has become pro rata the world's highest valued building. At rents of £15 ($36) per square foot on 500,000 net square feet and on 18-year purchase, it was worth £135,000,000 ($3,240,000,000). The value of the whole site of 6½ acres was £225,000,000 ($562,500,000).

In February, 1964, a woman paid $510 for a triangular piece of land measuring 3 inches by 6½ inches by 5¾ inches at a tax lien auction in North Hollywood, California—equivalent to $365,182,470 per acre.

The real estate value per square meter of the two topmost French vineyards has not been recently estimated. Recent reports of astronomical prices in Hong Kong were due to a journalist's confusion between U.S. dollars and Hong Kong dollars (worth only one-fifth as much).

Greatest Auction

The greatest auction ever was that at Anchorage, Alaska, on September 11, 1969, for 179 tracts of 450,858 acres of the oil-bearing North Slope, Alaska. An all-time record bid of $72,277,133 for a 2,560-acre lease was made by the Amerada Hess Corporation-Getty Oil consortium. The bid indicated a price of $28,233 per acre.

Highest Rent. The highest recorded rentals are about £24 ($55.20) per square foot for office accommodation in the prime areas of the City of London in mid-1975. This does not include land taxes or services. For main thoroughfare ground floor bankers' premises, figures as high as £46 ($105.80) per square foot were under negotiation.

STOCK EXCHANGES

The oldest Stock Exchange in the world is that in Amsterdam, in the Netherlands, founded in 1602. There were 138 throughout the world as of June 22, 1976.

Highest Value

The highest price quoted was for a share of F. Hoffmann-La Roche of Basel, Switzerland, worth 101,000 Swiss francs ($38,486) on April 23, 1976.

New York Stock Exchange Records

The highest index figure on the Dow Jones average (instituted October 8, 1896) of selected industrial stocks at the close of a day's trading was 1,051.70 on January 11, 1973, when the average of the daily "highs" of the 30 component stocks was 1,067.20.

The old record trading volume in a day on the New York Stock Exchange of 16,410,030 shares on October 29, 1929, the "Black Tuesday" of the famous "crash" was not surpassed until the first 20-million-share day (20,410,000) was achieved on April 10, 1968, and the ticker tape fell 47 minutes behind. The record for a day's trading is 44,512,860 shares on February 20, 1976.

The largest transaction on record "share-wise" was on March 14, 1972, for 5,245,000 shares of American Motors at $7.25 each.

The Dow Jones industrial average, which had reached 381.71 on September 3, 1929, plunged 30.57 points in the day, on its way to the Depression's lowest point of 41.22 on July 8, 1932. The total lost in security values was $74,000 million. World trade slumped 57 per cent from 1929 to 1936.

The greatest paper loss in a year was $209,957,000,000 in 1974.

The record daily increase of 28.40 on October 30, 1929, was beaten on August 16, 1971, when the Dow Jones index increased 32.93 points.

The record dollar value for one block was $76,135,026 for 730,312 shares of American Standard Class A Preferred shares at $104.25 a share.

The largest deal "value-wise" was for two 2,000,000 blocks of Greyhound shares at $20 each sold to Goldman, Sachs and Salomon Brothers, on February 9, 1971.

The highest price for a seat on the New York Stock Exchange was $625,000 in 1929. The lowest 20th century price was $17,000 in 1942.

Largest New Issue

The largest security offering in history was one of $1,375,000,000 in American Telephone and Telegraph Company stock in a rights offer on 27,500,000 shares of convertible preferred stock on June 2, 1971.

Greatest Appreciation

It is impossible to state categorically which shares have enjoyed the greatest appreciation in value. Spectacular "growth stocks" include International Business Machines Corporation (I.B.M.), in which 100 shares, costing $5,250 in July, 1932, grew to 13,472 shares with a market value of $5,813,200 on March 30, 1973. In addition, $497,300 were paid in dividends.

The Winnebago Co., makers of mobile homes, went public in 1965 when its shares sold for $12.50. By April, 1972, $5,250 worth of its shares were worth $5,241,600.

Largest Equity

The greatest aggregate market value of any corporation is $33,500,000,000, given the closing price of $206⅝ on December 31, 1975, for I.B.M., multiplied by the 149,533,813 shares outstanding. (See *Greatest Appreciation*.)

Largest Investment House

The largest investment company in the world, and also once the world's largest partnership (124 partners before going public in 1959),

LARGEST ANIMAL on land or sea, the blue whale can grow to a length of 110 feet. This specimen in the British Museum measures 91 feet long.

LARGEST BLOOM: The Stinking Corpse Lily of Southeast Asia bears blooms up to 3 feet across which weigh up to 15 lbs.

A

LARGEST TOMATO: Charles Roberts of East Sussex, England, grew this tomato which tipped the scales at 4 lbs. 4 oz.

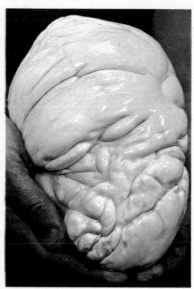

LARGEST PEARL: This 14-lb. 1-oz. baroque pearl is valued at $4,080,000 by its owner, Wilburn Dowell Cobb of San Francisco. A replica is on display in each of the Guinness World Record Exhibit Halls.

B

BIGGEST MONEY-MAKER: The movie version of Peter Benchley's novel "Jaws," released in June, 1975, grossed $124,000,000 in its first 78 days of release.

SMALLEST VIOLIN: This fully functional violin is only 2 inches long. It was made by Morris Samskin of Brooklyn, New York.

MOST-BLADED KNIFE:
The Year Knife holds a
blade for each year since the
birth of Christ. After the
year 2000 A.D., there will
be no more space for new
blades.

LARGEST CAR: This 1931 Type 41 "Royale" Bugatti, called the "Golden Bugatti,"
was over 22 feet long. Only six were made.

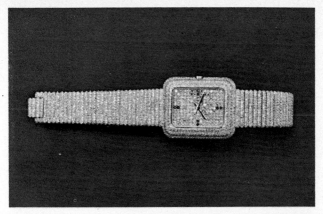

MOST EXPENSIVE WRIST WATCH: This jeweled case watch, created by the Piaget Watch Corporation for sale by Van Cleef & Arpels, New York, is valued at $47,500.

TOP-SELLING POST CARD: Between 1904 and 1962 this post card, created by Donald McGill, sold more than 350,000,000 copies.

TALLEST PAGODA: The Shwe Dogon Pagoda in Rangoon, Burma, stands 326 feet tall.

UNDERWATER VIOLINIST: Mark Gottlieb of Olympia, Washington, practices his submarine version of Handel's Water Music.

F

DOMINO MASTER: Bob Speca (standing in front of white post) set a new record for domino tumbling in the spring of 1976 when he set up and tumbled 22,221 dominoes, one by one, with one push.

MOST VORACIOUS SMOKER: Scott Case smoked 110 cigarettes at once in Los Angeles in April, 1974.

SPEED SKATER: Sheila Young, 1973 world cycling champion and a gold medalist in the 1976 Winter Olympics, set a new record mark for 500 meters in 1976.

MOST CAREER GOALS: For the greater part of his 20-year career, Pelé has averaged a goal a match. His total before he came to play in the United States in 1975 was 1,216.

H

is Merrill Lynch, Pierce, Fenner & Smith, Inc. (founded January 6, 1914) of New York City. It has 19,246 employees, 302 offices, 1,400,000 separate accounts and assets of $4,900,000,000. The firm is referred to as "We" or "We, the people" or "The Thundering Herd."

Largest Bank

The International Bank for Reconstruction and Development (founded December 27, 1945), the United Nations "World Bank" at 1818 H Street N.W., Washington, D.C., has an authorized share capital of $27,000 million. There were 127 members with a subscribed capital of $25,581,300,000 on March 31, 1976. The International Monetary Fund in Washington, D.C., has 128 members with total quotas of SDR29,211,400,000 ($33,885,000,000) on March 31, 1976.

LARGEST BANK: The U.N. "World Bank" in Washington, D.C., has an authorized share capital of $27,000,000,000.

The private bank with the greatest deposits is the Bank of America National Trust and Savings Association, of San Francisco, with $50,662,777,000 on December 31, 1974. Its total resources on that date were $60,376,458,000.

The bank with the most branches internationally is Barclays Bank of England (with Barclays Bank International and other subsidiary companies) with nearly 5,000 branches in 70 countries (3,075 in the U.K.) at the end of 1974.

Largest Bank Building

The world's tallest bank building is the Bank of Montreal's First Bank Tower, Toronto, Canada, which has 72 stories and stands 935 feet high. The largest bank vault in the world, measuring $350 \times 100 \times 8$ feet and weighing 984 tons, is in the Chase Manhattan Building, New York City, completed in May, 1961. Its six doors weigh up to 44.7 tons apiece, but each can be closed by the pressure of a forefinger.

Most Directorships

The record for directorships was set in 1961 by Hugh T. Nicholson, formerly senior partner of Harmand Banner & Co., London, who, as a liquidating chartered accountant, became a director of all 451 companies of the Jasper group in 1961 and had 7 other directorships.

MANUFACTURED ARTICLES

Largest Antique

The largest antique ever sold has been the London Bridge in March, 1968. The sale was made by Ivan F. Luckin of the Court of Common Council of the Corporation of London to the McCulloch Oil Corporation of Los Angeles, California, for $2,460,000. Over 10,000 tons of elevational stonework were re-assembled at a cost of $6,900,000 at Lake Havasu City, Arizona, and "re-dedicated" on October 10, 1971.

Armor

The highest price paid for a suit of armor is £25,000 (equivalent to $125,000 at that time) paid in 1924 for the Pembroke suit of armor, made in the 16th century for the 2nd Earl of Pembroke.

Largest Beds

In Bruges, Belgium, Philip, Duke of Burgundy, had a bed 12½ feet wide and 19 feet long erected for the perfunctory *coucher officiel* ceremony with Princess Isabella of Portugal in 1430. The largest bed in existence is the Great Bed of Ware, dating from *c.* 1580, from the Crown Inn, Ware, Hertfordshire, England, now preserved in the Victoria and Albert Museum, London. It is 10 feet 8½ inches wide, 11 feet 1 inch long and 8 feet 9 inches tall. The largest bed currently marketed is the Super Size Diplomat bed, 9 feet wide and 9 feet long, sold in England for £1,260 ($2,200), including tax.

The world's most massive bed is the four-poster slate bed in Penrhyn Castle, Bangor, Wales, which measures 7 feet 3 inches in length, 6 feet 2 inches in width and weighs 2,070 lbs.

Beer Cans

Beer cans date from a test marketing by Krueger Beer of Richmond, Virginia, in 1935. The largest collection is claimed by John F. Ahrens of Mt. Laurel, New Jersey, with over 10,000 *different* cans by July, 1976.

Stuffed Bird

The highest price ever paid for a stuffed bird is £9,000 ($23,400). This was given on March 4, 1971, in the salesrooms of Sotheby & Co., London, by the Iceland Natural History Museum for a specimen of the Great Auk (*Alca impennis*) in summer plumage, which was taken in Iceland *c.* 1821; this particular specimen stood 22½ inches high. The Great Auk was a flightless North Atlantic seabird, which was finally exterminated on Eldey, Iceland, in 1844, becoming extinct through hunting.

Carpets and Rugs

Earliest. The earliest carpet known (and still in existence) is a white bordered black hair pelt from Pazyryk, U.S.S.R., dated to the 5th century B.C. now preserved in Leningrad. Of ancient carpets the largest on record was the gold-enriched silk carpet of Hashim (dated 743 A.D.) of the Abbasid caliphate in Baghdad, Iraq. It is reputed to have measured 180 feet by 300 feet.

Largest. The world's largest carpet now consists of 88,000 square feet (over two acres) of maroon carpeting in the Coliseum exhibition hall, Columbus Circle, New York City. This was first used for the International Automobile Show on April 28, 1956.

Most Expensive. The most magnificent carpet ever made was the Spring carpet of Khusraw made for the audience hall of the Sassanian palace at Ctesiphon, Iraq. It was about 7,000 square feet of silk and gold thread, encrusted with emeralds. It was cut up as booty by a Persian army in 635 A.D. and from the known realization value of the pieces must have had an original value of some $2,400,000,000.

It was reported in March, 1968, that a 16th-century Persian silk hunting carpet was sold "recently" to an undisclosed U.S. museum by one of the Rothschild family for "about $600,000."

The highest price ever paid at auction for a carpet is the $150,000 given at Sotheby Parke-Bernet, New York City, on December 9, 1972, for an early Louis XIV French Savonnerie carpet measuring 18 ft. 6 ins. by 12 ft. 7 ins. and dating from the third quarter of the 17th century. It was woven under the administration of Simon Lourdet.

Most Finely Woven. The most finely woven carpet known is one with more than 2,490 knots per square inch from a fragment of an Imperial Mughal prayer carpet of the 17th century, now in the Altman collections in the Metropolitan Museum of Art, New York City.

Ceramics

The auction record for any ceramic object is £420,000 ($1,008,000) for the 16¼-inch Ming blue and white bottle dated 1403–24 acquired by Mrs. Helen Glatz, a London dealer, at Sotheby Parke-Bernet on April 2, 1974.

Chair

The largest chair is claimed to be an American ladderback, located outside the Hayes and Kane furniture store, Bennington, Vermont, which is 19 feet 1 inch tall and weighs 2,200 lbs.

The highest price ever paid for a single chair is $85,000 for the John Brown Chippendale mahogany corner chair attributed to John Goddard of Newport, Rhode Island, and made c. 1760. This piece was included in the collection of Mr. Lansdell K. Christie dispersed by Sotheby Parke-Bernet, New York City, on October 21, 1972.

Chandelier

The largest chandelier, named "Walküre," designed by Pietro Canta, a Milanese sculptor, was completed in October, 1974, for a client in Borneo. It measures 52 feet 5 inches in circumference and 14 feet 9 inches in height, with 900 bulbs and 15,000 crystal pieces.

Christmas Wrapping

The largest wrapping ever constructed was one 42 feet in length and 7 feet in diameter built in December, 1972, for the Christmas showroom display of Cleales Ltd. Garage, Station Road, Saffron

MOST EXPENSIVE CHAIR: This Chippendale chair, made in mid-18th century, sold for $85,000 in 1972.

Walden, Essex, England. The wrapping concealed a Ford Escort car and took two weeks to build with a metal frame covered with pliofilm and colored paper sheets.

Cigars

Largest and Most Expensive. The largest cigar in existence is one 5 feet 4½ inches long and 10¾ inches in circumference, made by Abraham & Gluckstein, London, England, and now housed at the Northumbrian University Air Squadron.

LONGEST CIGAR: Made by Fonseca of Havana, Cuba, in 1926 this 8½-foot-tall, 400-lb. tobacco monster is no longer in existence.

The largest standard brand of cigar in the world is the 9¾-inch-long "Partagas Visible Immensas." The Partagas factory in Havana, Cuba, manufactures special gift cigars 19.7 inches long for gift purposes, which retail in Europe for more than $12 each.

The most expensive cigar in the world is the Monte Cristo "A," which retails in Great Britain at a suggested £3.75 ($6.56), including tax.

Most Voracious Smoker. The only man to master the esoteric art of smoking 14 full-size cigars while simultaneously whistling, talking or giving bird imitations is Simon Argevitch of Oakland, California. He did this in New York on September 25, 1973.

Scott Case smoked 110 cigarettes simultaneously for 30 seconds at the Oddball Olympics in Los Angeles in May, 1974.

Cigarettes

Consumption. The heaviest smokers in the world are the people of the U.S. where about 607,000 million cigarettes (an average of 4,300 per adult) were consumed at a cost of about $13,000,000,000 in 1975.

Largest Collection. The world's largest collection of cigarettes is that of Robert E. Kaufman, M.D., of 950 Park Avenue, New York City 10028. In April, 1975, he had 6,705 different brands of cigarettes from 163 countries. The oldest brand represented is "Lone Jack," made in the U.S. in *c.* 1885. Both the longest and shortest (see next page) are represented.

LARGEST CIGARETTE COLLECTION: Dr. Robert E. Kaufman of New York (left) shows some of the 6,705 different brands he owns. He has cigarettes from 163 countries. RAREST PACK is the Riga packet (right) celebrating the 700th anniversary of that Latvian city.

Cigarette Packs. The world's largest collection of cigarette packs is that of Niels Ventegodt of Copenhagen, Denmark. He had 52,021 different packets from 210 countries by March, 1974. The countries supplying the largest numbers were the United Kingdom (6,861) and the United States (3,981). The earliest is the Finnish "Petit Canon" packet for 25, made by Tollander & Klärich in 1860. The rarest is the Latvian 700-year-anniversary (1201–1901) Riga packet, believed to be unique.

Most Popular. The world's most popular cigarette is "Marlboro," a filter cigarette made by Philip Morris, which sold 136,000,000,000 in 1975.

Longest and Shortest. The longest cigarettes ever marketed were "Head Plays," each 11 inches long and sold in packets of five in the U.S. in about 1930, to save tax. The shortest were "Lilliput" cigarettes, each 1¼ inches long and ⅛ inch in diameter, made in Great Britain in 1956.

Cigarette Lighter. The most expensive cigarette lighter is made by Alfred Dunhill Ltd. of St. James's, Greater London, and costs £4,090 ($7,157). It is a platinum-cased Rollagas lighter with diamond-cut crocodile pattern finish mounted with 157 brilliant-cut diamonds.

MOST EXPENSIVE TABLE LIGHTER: This 18-carat lighthouse table lighter, set on an island of amethyst, sells for $56,875.

Cigarette Cards. The earliest known and most valuable cigarette card is that bearing the portrait of the Marquess of Lorne published in the United States *c.* 1879. The only known specimen is in the Metropolitan Museum of Art, New York City.

The earliest dated cigarette cards were those of the four U.S. Presidential candidates of 1880, produced by Thomas H. Hall of New York City. The most expensive card is the John Peter ("Honus") Wagner card in the American Tobacco Co. Baseball Player series of 1912, withdrawn because Wagner was opposed to smoking. Examples are now worth $250.

Finest Cloth

The finest of all cloths is Shahtoosh (or Shatusa), a brown-gray wool from the throats of Indian goats. It is sold by Neiman-Marcus of Dallas, at $108 per linear foot and is both more expensive and finer than vicuña.

Credit Card Collection

The largest collection of credit cards is one of 793, all different, by Walter Cavanagh (b. 1943) of Santa Clara, California. The cost of acquisition was nil.

Largest Curtain

The largest curtain ever built was the bright orange-red 4-ton 185-foot-high curtain suspended 1,350 feet above and across the Rifle Gap, Grand Hogback, Colorado, by the Bulgarian-born sculptor Christo (*né* Javacheff) 36, on August 10, 1971. It blew apart in a 50-m.p.h. gust of wind 27 hours later. The total cost of displaying this work of art was $750,000.

Dinner Service

The highest price ever paid for a silver dinner service is $579,600 for the Berkeley Louis XV Service of 168 pieces, made by Jacques Roettiers between 1736 and 1738, sold at the salesrooms of Sotheby & Co., London, in June, 1960.

Dolls

The highest price paid at auction for dolls is £16,000 ($36,800) for a pair of William and Mary painted wooden dolls in original clothes 22 inches high at Sotheby's, London, on April 19, 1974. After an export license was refused, they were purchased, after a public subscription, by the Victoria and Albert Museum, London.

Most Expensive Dress

The most expensive dress ever sold by a Paris couturier was one by Pierre Balmain (directrice, Ginette Spanier) to a non-European royal personage for $11,250 in 1971.

Fabric

The oldest surviving fabric discovered from Level VIA at Çátal Hüyük, Turkey, has been radio-carbon dated to 5900 B.C.

The most expensive fabric obtainable is an evening-wear fabric 40 inches wide, hand embroidered and sequinned on a pure silk ground in a classical flower pattern. It has 194,400 tiny sequins per yard, and is designed by Alan Hershman of London; it cost $323.75 per yard in May, 1976.

Largest Fireworks

The most powerful firework obtainable is the Bouquet of Chrysanthemums *hanabi*, marketed by the Marutamaya Ogatsu Fireworks Co. Ltd., of Tokyo, Japan. It is fired to a height of over 3,000 feet from a 36-inch caliber mortar. Their chrysanthemum and peony flower shells produce a spherical flower with "twice-thrice changing colors," 2,000 feet in diameter.

The world's lowest firework was George Plimpton's 40½-inch 720-lb. Roman candle "Fat Man," which was supposed to break the record over Long Island, N.Y., in February, 1975. Instead, it sizzled, hissed and exploded, leaving a crater 10 feet deep.

Flags

Largest. The largest flag in the world was the Stars and Stripes designed by The Great American Flag Company of Warren, Vermont, to be displayed on the Verrazano-Narrows Bridge, New York City, on July 3, 1976, as part of the celebration of the Bicentennial of the American Revolution. It measured 193 by 366½ feet (1.64 acres), weighed about 1½ tons, with 15-foot-wide stripes, and stars 11 feet in diameter. It was torn apart after a few hours during a test hanging on June 28, 1976. (See photo on page 2.) The previous recordholder, owned by the J. L. Hudson Company of Detroit, was last displayed on June 14, 1976, and has been donated to the Smithsonian Institution, Washington, D.C.

Oldest. The oldest national flag in the world is that of Denmark (a large white cross on a red field), known as the Dannebrog ("Danish Cloth"), dating from 1219, adopted after the Battle of Lindanissa in Estonia, now part of the U.S.S.R. The crest in the center of the Austrian flag has its origins in the 11th century, while that of Malta dates from 1090. The origins of the Iranian flag, with its sword-carrying lion and sun are obscure, but "go beyond the 12th century."

The study of flags is known as vexicollogy.

Largest Float

The largest float used in any street carnival is the 200-foot-long dragon *Sun Loon* used in Bendigo, Victoria, Australia. It has 65,000 mirror scales. Six men are needed to carry its head alone.

Furniture

The highest price ever paid for a single piece of furniture is £240,000 ($552,000) for a French Louis XVI ormolu mounted ebony *bureau plat* and *cartonnier* 5 feet 4½ inches high by 3 feet 1½ inches wide at Sotheby Parke-Bernet, London, on December 13, 1974.

The largest item of furniture is the Long Sofa—a wooden bench for old seafarers—measuring 236 feet in length, at Oscarshamn, Sweden.

Glass

The most priceless example of the art of glass-making is usually regarded as the Portland Vase which dates from late in the first

HIGHEST-PRICED HAT (top): Worn by Napoleon it sold for almost $30,000 in 1970. **MOST-BLADED KNIFE** (left): The Year Knife now has 1,976 blades. It was built in 1822 with 1,822 blades and each year another blade was added. After the year 2000 there will be no more space for new blades. See color photo on color page D.

century B.C. or 1st century A.D. It was made in Italy and was in the possession of the Barberini family in Rome from at least 1642. It was eventually bought by the Duchess of Portland in 1792, but smashed while in the British Museum in 1847. A copy executed by John Northwood in 1876 was sold for £30,000 ($69,000) by Sotheby Parke-Bernet, London, on July 14, 1975.

LARGEST JIG-SAW PUZZLE: Covering more than 1,000 square feet and composed of 1,020 large pieces, this gigantic puzzle was put together in Trafalgar Square, London, in 1975.

Gold Plate

The world's highest auction price for a single piece of gold plate is £40,000 ($112,000) for a 20.4-oz. George II teapot made by James Ker of Edinburgh, for the King's Plate horserace for 100 guineas at Leith, Scotland, in 1736. The sale was by Christie's of London on December 13, 1967, to a dealer from Boston, Massachusetts.

The gold coffin of the 14th century B.C. Pharaoh Tutankhamun, discovered by Howard Carter on February 16, 1923, in Luxor, western Thebes, Egypt, weighed 2,448 pounds.

Gun

The highest price ever paid for a single gun is £125,000 ($312,500) given by the London dealers, F. Partridge, for a French flintlock fowling piece made for Louis XIII, King of France, in *c*. 1615 and attributed to Pierre le Bourgeoys of Lisieux, France (d. 1627). This piece was included in the collection of the late William Goodwin Renwick (U.S.) sold by Sotheby and Co., London, on November 21, 1972.

Most Expensive Hat

The highest price ever paid for a hat is 165,570 francs (including tax) ($29,471) at an auction by Maitres Liery, Rheims et Laurin, France, on April 23, 1970, for one last worn by Emperor Napoleon I (1769–1821) on January 1, 1815. It was bought by Moët et Chandon, a champagne house.

Most Expensive Jade

The highest price ever paid for an item in jade is 1,250,000 Swiss Francs ($390,625) for a necklace set with 31 graduated beads of Imperial green jade. This was sold by Christie's at the Hotel Richemond, Geneva, Switzerland, on May 9, 1973. The highest price paid for a single piece of jade sculpture is £71,000 ($177,500) for a massive Ming jade buffalo sold by Sotheby's on March 15, 1973.

Largest Jig-Saw Puzzle

The largest jig-saw puzzle ever made is one 35 feet 11 inches by 30 feet 8½ inches, built with 1,020 large pieces for The National Children's Home and first assembled in Trafalgar Square, London, on March 31, 1975. It was cut by fret saw by Lance Corporal M. P. J. Marson of the British Royal Engineers. The *Festival of Britain* jigsaw by Efroc Ltd., now in Montserrat, though of much less area, contains an estimated 40,000 pieces.

Knife with Most Blades

The penknife with the greatest number of blades is the Year Knife made by the world's oldest firm of cutlers, Joseph Rodgers & Sons Ltd., of Sheffield, England, whose trademark was granted in 1682. The knife was built in 1822 with 1,822 blades, but now has 1,976, and will continue to match the year of the Christian era until 2000 A.D., beyond which there will be no further space. (Also see color photograph on page D.)

LARGEST PAPER CUP:
This giant Dixie Cup, made of rolls of cardboard, and wrapped in paper, stands 6 feet tall, is 4¾ feet across the mouth, and can hold 569 gallons of lemonade. It is now on display at the Guinness Exhibit Hall in New York City.

Matchbox Labels

The oldest matchbox label is that of John Walker, Stockton-on-Tees, Cleveland, England, in 1827. Collectors of labels are phillumenists, of bookmatch covers philliberumenists, and of matchboxes cumyxaphists. Several labels, such as the Byron Match from Roche & Co., Marseilles, France, and the Canadian Allumettes Frontenac from the Eddy Match Co., are unique. Both of these are in the Frank J. Mrazik Collection in Quebec, Canada.

Sheerest Nylon

The lowest denier nylon yarn ever produced is the 6 denier used for stockings exhibited at the Nylon Fair in London in February, 1956. The sheerest stockings normally available are 9 denier. An indication of the thickness is that a hair from the average human head is about 50 denier.

Paperweight

The highest price ever paid for a paperweight is £8,500 ($20,040) at Sotheby & Co., London, on March 16, 1970, for a 19th-century Clichy Lily-of-the-Valley glass weight. The earliest paperweights were made in Italy in the 15th century.

Pens

The most expensive writing pens are the 18-carat pair of pens (one fiber-tipped and one ballpoint) capped by diamonds of 3.88 carats sold by Alfred Dunhill Ltd. (See *Cigarette Lighter*) for £9,943 ($22,969) the pair (including taxes).

Most Expensive Pipe

The most expensive smoker's pipe is the Charatan *Summa cum Laude* straight-grain briar root pipe available in limited number in New York City at $2,500.

Most Expensive Pistols

The highest price paid for a pair of pistols at auction is the £78,000 ($178,400) given by the London dealer Howard Ricketts at Sotheby Parke-Bernet, London, on December 17, 1974, for a pair of English Royal flintlock holster pistols made *c.* 1690–1700 by Pierre Monlong. They were sent for sale by Anne, Duchess of Westminster.

Porcelain

The highest price ever paid for a single piece of English porcelain is £32,000 (about $77,000) for a Chelsea Boar's Head (of the red anchor period) sold at Sotheby's, London, on November 13, 1973.

The record for English pottery is £15,015 ($30,030) for a Staffordshire 18th-century salt-glaze pew group sold at Christie's, London, on December 15, 1975.

Largest and Longest Ropes

The largest rope ever made was a coir fiber launching rope with a circumference of 47 inches, made in 1858 for the British liner *Great Eastern* by John and Edwin Wright. It consisted of four strands, each of 3,780 yards.

The longest fiber rope ever made without a splice was one of 10,000 fathoms (11.36 miles) of 6½-inch circumference manila by Frost Brothers (now British Ropes Ltd.) in London in 1874.

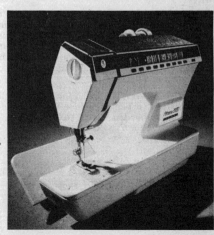

SEWING MACHINE: The earliest practical domestic sewing machine was invented by Isaac M. Singer (1811-75) of Pittstown, N.Y., in 1851. The first electronic home sewing machine (shown here), called Athena 2000, was manufactured by The Singer Co.

MOST EXPENSIVE SHOES: Lined with mink and with gold spikes, these golf shoes sell for $6,500 a pair. One shoe is on display at the Guinness Exhibit Hall in New York City, and its mate at the Guinness Exhibit in Las Vegas, Nevada.

Most Expensive Shoes

The most expensive standard shoes obtainable are the mink-lined golf shoes with 18-carat gold embellishments and ruby-tipped gold spikes by Stylo Matchmakers International Ltd. of Northampton, England, which retail for £2,700 ($6,500) per pair.

The largest shoes ever sold, excluding those made for cases of elephantiasis, are a pair of size 42 built for the giant, Harley Davidson, of Avon Park, Florida.

Silver

The highest price ever paid for any kind of silver is 2,000,000 Swiss Francs ($727,272) for a pair of Jardinières and stands by Thomas Germain of Paris, dated *c.* 1727, sold by Christie's in Geneva, Switzerland, on November 11, 1975. In the same place, on April 27, 1976, a pair of silver soup tureens and covers by Germain made 1.8 million Swiss Francs, which with a 14 per cent commission was equivalent to $780,000.

English Silver. The highest price for English silver is £115,000 ($276,000) for a pair of unique Queen Anne chandeliers by John Bodington of London, dated 1703 and 1704. The pair was sold at Christie's on June 27, 1973.

Snuff Box

The highest price ever paid for a snuff box is $205,475 paid by Kenneth Snowman of Wartski's in a sale at Christie's in London on June 26, 1974. This was for a gold and lapis lazuli example uniquely signed by Juste-Oreille Meissonnier (d. 1750), the French master goldsmith, and dated Paris, 1728. It was made for Marie-Anne de Vaviere-Neubourg, the wife of Charles II of Spain, and measures 3¼ by 2¼ inches.

Apostle Spoons

The highest price ever paid for a set of 12 apostle spoons is £70,000 ($161,000) paid by Mrs. How in a sale at Christie's, London, on June 26, 1974. They are Elizabethan silver-gilt spoons, made by Christopher Wace in 1592, and are known as the "Tichborne Celebrities."

Sword

The highest price recorded for a sword is $70,000 at Sotheby Parke-Bernet, New York, on May 31, 1973, for a 30.4-inch-long Koto Tachi Japanese sword blade by Hoe Saketsugu, dated 1312. It should be noted that prices as high as £60,000 ($150,000) have been reported in Japan for important swords by master Japanese swordsmiths, such as the incomparable 13th-century master Masamune.

Tablecloth

The world's largest tablecloth is one 219 yards long by 2 yards wide double damask, made by John S. Brown & Sons Ltd. of Belfast, Northern Ireland, and shipped to a royal palace in the Middle East. There was also an order for matching napkins for 450 places.

Tapestry

Earliest. The earliest known examples of tapestry-woven linen are three pieces from the tomb of Thutmose IV, the Egyptian pharaoh, which date from 1483 to 1411 B.C.

Most Expensive. The highest price paid for a set of tapestries is £200,000 ($560,000) for four Louis XV pieces at Sotheby & Co., London, on December 8, 1967.

Largest. The largest single piece of tapestry ever woven is "Christ in His Majesty," measuring 72 feet by 39 feet, designed by Graham Vivian Sutherland (b. August 24, 1903), for an altar hanging in Coventry Cathedral, West Midlands, England. It cost $29,400, weighs $\frac{4}{5}$ of a ton, and was delivered from Pinton Frères of Felletin, France, on March 1, 1962.

Longest. The longest of all antique tapestries is Queen Matilda of England's famous Bayeux tapestry of embroidery, a hanging 19½ inches wide by 231 feet in length. It depicts events of the period 1064–66 in 72 scenes and was probably worked in Canterbury, Kent, in *c.* 1086. It was "lost" from 1476 until 1724.

Earliest Tartan

The earliest evidence of tartan is the so-called Falkirk tartan, found stuffed in a jar of coins in Bells Meadow, north of Callendar Park, Scotland. It is a dark and light brown pattern and dates from *c.* 245 A.D. The earliest reference to a specific named tartan has been to a Murray tartan in 1618 although Mackay tartan was probably worn earlier.

Time Capsule

The building of the world's largest time capsule was begun on April 10, 1975, in Harold Keith Davisson's front yard at Seward,

Nebraska. It will be 20 feet by 8 feet by 6 feet (960 cubic feet) and will be opened *c.* A.D. 2025. It will contain *inter alia* a (by then) vintage Chevrolet Vega automobile (1975 model) and a copy of the *Guinness Book of World Records*.

Urn or Vase

The most expensive urn or vase is the Greek urn painted by Euphronios and thrown by Euxitheos in *c.* 530 B.C., which was bought by the Metropolitan Museum of Art, New York City, for $1,300,000 in August, 1972, in a private transaction.

Largest Wig

The largest wig yet made is that made by Bergman of Fifth Avenue in New York City in 1975, which measured 15 feet in length. Made for *Vogue* magazine, it now is a permanent part of the Guinness World Records Exhibit Hall in the Empire State Building.

Wreaths

The most expensive wreath on record was that sent to the funeral of President Kennedy in Washington, D.C. on November 25, 1963, by the civic authority of Paris. It was handled by Interflora Inc. and cost $1,200. The only rival was a floral tribute sent to the Mayor of Moscow in 1970 by Umberto Formichello, general manager of Interflora, which is never slow to scent an opportunity.

The largest wreath ever constructed was 25 feet 6 inches in diameter and weighed 1,008 lbs., made by the Teleflower conference at Rotorua, New Zealand, on February 27, 1975.

Writing Paper

The most expensive writing paper in the world is that sold by Cartier, Inc., on Fifth Avenue, New York City, at $8,000 per 100 sheets with envelopes. It is of handmade paper from Finland with deckle edges and a "personalized" portrait watermark. Second thoughts and misspellings can be costly.

2. Agriculture

Origins. It has been estimated that only 21 per cent of the world's land surface is cultivatable and that only two-fifths of this is cultivated.

Evidence adduced in 1971 from Nok Nok Tha and Spirit Cave, Thailand, tends to confirm that plant cultivation and animal domestication was part of the Hoabinhian culture *c.* 11,000 B.C.

The earliest attested evidence for the cultivation of grain comes from Ali Kosh, Iran, and Jericho, *c.* 7000 B.C. Goats were domesticated at Asiab, Iran, by *c.* 8050 B.C. and dogs at Star Carr, North Yorkshire, by *c.* 7700 B.C. The earliest definite date for sheep is *c.* 7200 B.C. at Argissa-Magula, Thessaly, Greece, and for pigs and cattle *c.* 7000 B.C. at the same site. The earliest date for horses is *c.* 4350 B.C. from Dereivka, Ukraine, U.S.S.R.

Reindeer may have been domesticated as early as *c.* 18,000 B.C., but definite evidence is lacking.

Farms

The largest farms in the world are collective farms in the U.S.S.R. These have been reduced in number from 235,500 in 1940 to only 39,000 in 1969, and have been increased in size so that units of over 60,000 acres are not uncommon.

The pioneer farm of Laucidio Coelho near Campo Grande, Mato Grosso, Brazil, *c.* 1901 was 3,358 square miles (2,150,000 acres) with 250,000 head of cattle at the time of his death in 1975.

Largest Wheat Field. The world's largest single wheat field was probably one of more than 35,000 acres, sown in 1951 near Lethbridge, Alberta, Canada.

Largest Hop Field. The largest hop field in the world is one of 790 acres at Toppenish, Washington, owned by John I. Haas, Inc., the world's largest hop growers, with hop farms in British Columbia (Canada), California, Idaho, Oregon and Washington, with a total net area of 3,765 acres.

Largest Vineyard. The world's largest vineyard extends over the Mediterranean façade between the Rhône and the Pyrenees in the departments (provinces) of Aude, Hérault, Gard and Pyrénées-Orientales. It has an area of 2,075,685 acres of which 52.3 per cent is *monoculture viticole*.

Largest Cattle Station. The world's largest cattle station is Alexandra Station, Northern Territory, Australia, selected in 1873 by Robert Collins, who rode 1,600 miles to reach it. It now has 82 wells, a staff of 90 and originally extended over 7,207,608 acres. The

LARGEST HOP FIELD: Covering 790 acres at Toppenish, Washington, this field is owned by the world's largest growers of hops.

present area is 6,500 square miles which is stocked with 60,000 shorthorn cattle. Until 1915 the Victoria River Downs Station, Northern Territory, was over three times larger, with an area of 22,400,000 acres (35,000 square miles).

Largest Sheep Station. The largest sheep station in the world is Commonwealth Hill, in the northwest of South Australia. It grazes between 70,000 and 90,000 sheep, about 700 cattle and 25,000 uninvited kangaroos, in an area of 4,080 square miles (2,611,200 acres). The largest sheep move on record occurred when 27 horsemen moved a mob of 43,000 sheep 40 miles from Barcaldine to Beaconsfield Station, Queensland, Australia, in 1886.

Largest Chicken Ranch. The world's largest chicken ranch is the 600-acre "Egg City," in Moorpark, California, established by Jules Goldman in 1954. Some 2,000,000 eggs are laid daily by 4,500,000 chickens. The manure sale totals $72,000 per annum.

Largest Turkey Farm. The turkey farm of Bernard Matthews Ltd., centered at Great Litchingham, Norfolk, England, has 700 workers tending 4,000,000 turkeys.

Mushroom Farm. The largest mushroom farm in the world is Butler County Mushroom Farm, Inc., founded in 1937 in a disused limestone mine near West Winfield, Pennsylvania. It has 975 employees working underground, in a maze of galleries 110 miles long, producing about 40,000,000 lbs. of mushrooms per year.

Crop Yields

Wheat. Crop yields for highly tended small areas are of little significance. The greatest recorded wheat yield is 86.10 cwt. per acre from 28.53 acres by Brian Reynolds of Stanaway Farm, Otley, Suffolk, England, in 1974, using Maris Huntsman winter wheat.

Barley. A yield of 82.61 cwt. per acre of Clermont Spring Barley was achieved in 1972 by John Graham of Kirkland Hall, Wigton, Cumbria, England, from a 13.52-acre field.

Potato. In 1968, it was reported that Tom Cooke of Funtington, West Sussex, England, dug 1,190 lbs. 10 oz. of potatoes from six seed potatoes.

Sugar Beet. The highest recorded yield for sugar beet is 62.4 tons per acre by Andy Christensen and Jon Giannini in the Salinas Valley, California.

Dimensions and Prolificacy

Cattle. Of heavyweight cattle the heaviest on record was a Hereford-Shorthorn named "Old Ben," owned by Mike and John Murphy of Miami, Indiana. When he died at the age of 8, in February, 1910, he had attained a length of 16 feet 2 inches from nose to tail, a girth of 13 feet 8 inches, a height of 6 feet 4 inches at the forequarters and a weight of 4,720 lbs. The stuffed and mounted steer is displayed in Highland Park, Kokomo, Indiana, as proof to all who would otherwise have said "there ain't no such animal."

The highest recorded birthweight for a calf is 225 lbs. from a British Friesian cow at Rockhouse Farm, Bishopston, Swansea, West Glamorgan, Wales, in 1961.

On April 25, 1964, it was reported that a cow named "Lyubik" had given birth to seven calves at Mogilev, U.S.S.R. A case of five live calves at one birth was reported in 1928 by T. G. Yarwood of Manchester, Lancashire, England. The lifetime prolificacy record is 30 in the case of a cross-bred cow owned by G. Page of Warren Farm, Wilmington, Sussex, England, which died in November, 1957, aged 32. A cross-Hereford calved in 1916 and owned by A. J. Thomas of West Hook Farm, Marloes, Pembrokeshire, Wales, produced her 30th calf in May, 1955, and died in May, 1956, aged 40.

Pigs. The highest recorded number of piglets in one litter is 34, thrown on June 25–26, 1961, by a sow owned by Aksel Egedee of Denmark. This record was equalled by a litter of 34 in England in 1955, but 30 of the piglets were born dead.

The heaviest pig ever recorded is "Big Boy," a hog of 1,904 lbs., bred by B. Liles and H. A. Sanders of Black Mountain, North Carolina, weighed on January 5, 1939.

The highest recorded weight for a piglet at weaning (8 weeks) is 81 lbs. for a boar, one of 9 piglets farrowed on July 6, 1962, at Kettle Lane Farm, Trowbridge, Wiltshire, England.

Sheep. The highest recorded birthweight for a lamb is 38 lbs., in the case of a lamb delivered in 1975 at Clearwater, Miner County, near Howard, Kansas, but neither this lamb nor the ewe survived. A case of eight lambs at a birth was reported by D. T. Jones of Priory Farm, Monmouthshire, Wales, in June, 1956, but none lived.

A case of a sheep living to 26 years was recorded in flock book records by H. Poole, Wexford, Ireland.

Egg-Laying

A Rhode Island Red named "Penny" laid 20 eggs in 7 days and 7 in one day on September 11, 1971. It is owned by Mrs. Treena White of Ashton Clinton, Buckinghamshire, England.

The highest authenticated rate of egg-laying by a hen is 361 eggs in 364 days by a Black Orpington in an official test at Taranki, New Zealand, in 1930. The heaviest egg *reported* is one of 16 ounces, with double yolk and double shell, laid by a white Leghorn at Vineland, New Jersey, on February 25, 1956. The largest *recorded* was one of "nearly 12 ounces" for a 5-yolked egg, 12¼ inches around the long axis and 9 inches around the shorter axis, laid by a Black Minorca at Mr. Stafford's Damsteads Farm, Mellor, Lancashire, England, in 1896.

The highest claim for the number of yolks in a chicken's egg is 9, reported by Mrs. Diane Hainsworth of Hainsworth Poultry Farms, Mount Morris, New York, in July, 1971.

The highest weight claimed for a duck's egg is 17 ounces, by *Cecilia*, owned by Mrs. I. Grimsmo of Pine River, Minnesota, in May, 1972.

Milk Yields

The world lifetime record yield of milk is 340,578 lbs. at 3.3 per cent butter fat by the Holstein cow "Or-Win Masterpiece Riva," owned by Willard and Gary Behm at Adrian, Michigan, up to April 10, 1975.

The greatest recorded yield for one lactation (365 days) is 50,759 lbs. by "Mowry Prince Corinne," a Holstein at Roaring Springs, Pennsylvania, ending on December 8, 1974.

The probable record milk yield in a day is 198¼ lbs. by R. A. Pierson's British Friesian "Garsdon Minnie" in 1948.

The highest recorded milk yield for any goat is 7,546 lbs. in 365 days by "Waiora Frill Q*," bred by Mr. and Mrs. E. L. Collins of Swanson, Auckland, New Zealand, in 1972.

The U.S. record (305 days only) is 5,750 pounds, made in 1960 by "Puritan Jon's Jennifer II," a Toggenberg purebred doe.

Butter Fat

The world record butter fat yield in a lifetime is 13,607 lbs. from 308,569 lbs. by the Brown Swiss cow named "Ivetta" (1954–71) in the herd of W. E. Naffziger of Pekin, Illinois, in 4,515 days.

The world's lactation (365-day) yield record is 1,956 lbs. from 31,870 lbs. of milk at 6.14 per cent by Vincent A. Machin's "Crookgate Aylwinia 7" at Penley, England, ending on July 7, 1973. This is sufficient to produce 2,386 lbs. of butter.

Cheese

The most active cheese-eaters are the people of France, with an annual average in 1969 of 29.98 lbs. per person. The world's biggest producer is the United States with a factory production of 998,800 tons in 1970.

TOP BULL: "Joe's Pride," was sold to a Canadian Company in 1974 for $2½ million.

Oldest. The oldest and most primitive cheeses are the Arabian *kishk*, made of the dried curd of goat's milk. There are today 450 named cheeses of 18 major varieties, but many are merely named after different towns and differ only in shape or the method of packing. France has 240 varieties.

Most Expensive. The most expensive of all cheeses in the country of origin is the ewe's milk Laruns cheese in the Béarn area of France, which is marketed in Paris, at times, for 38 francs per kilogram ($3.55 per lb.). In the U.S., imported Brie from France may cost $5.80 per lb. retail.

Largest. The largest cheese ever made was a cheddar of 34,591 lbs., made in 43 hours, January 20–22, 1964, by the Wisconsin Cheese Foundation for exhibition at the New York World's Fair. It was transported in a specially designed 45-foot-long refrigerated tractor trailer "Cheese-Mobile."

Livestock Prices

Note: Some exceptionally high livestock auction prices are believed to result from collusion between buyer and seller to raise the ostensible price levels of the breed concerned.

Bull. The highest price ever paid for a bull is $2,500,000 for the beefalo (⅜ buffalo, ⅜ charolais, ¼ Hereford) "Joe's Pride," sold by D. C. Basolo of Burlingame, California, to the Beefalo Cattle Co. of Canada in Calgary, Alberta, on September 9, 1974.

Cow. The highest price ever paid for a cow is $122,000 for the Holstein-Friesian "Tara Hills Pride Lucky Barb," by Pride Barb Syndicate of Ontario at Amenia, N.Y., on November 11, 1972.

Sheep. The highest price ever paid for a sheep is $A36,000 ($52,800) for a Merino ram from John Collins & Sons, Mount Bryan, South Australia, by Mr. Perce L. Puckridge of White River, Port Lincoln, South Australia.

The highest price ever paid for wool is $A46 per kilogram ($29 per lb.) for a bale of superfine Merino fleece from the Launceton, Tasmania, Australia, sales in February, 1973, paid by Mr. C. Stephen of Mount Morriston estate.

Pig. The highest price ever paid for a pig is $38,000 for a champion Duroc owned by Forkner Farms, Horton, Missouri, by Soga-No-Yo Swine Farms, Hiratosuka, Japan, at Austin, Minnesota, on September 11, 1973.

Horse. The highest price ever paid for a farm horse is $47,500 paid for the 7-year-old Belgian stallion *Farceur*, by E. G. Good at Cedar Falls, Iowa, on October 16, 1917.

Donkey. Perhaps the lowest price ever for livestock was at a sale at Kuruman, Cape Province, South Africa, in 1934, where donkeys were sold for less than 4d. (4 cents) each.

Turkey. The highest price ever paid for a turkey is $1,600 for a 44-lb. bird bought at the Pasadena Rodeo Show, Texas, from Billy R. Petty, Jr., on September 25, 1975.

Sheep Shearing

The highest recorded speed for sheep shearing in a working day was that of G. Phillips, who machine-sheared 694 lambs (average 77.1 per hour) in 9 hours at Tymawr Farms, Libanus, Powys, Wales, on June 25, 1975. The hand-shearing record for a 9-hour day is 350, set in 1899.

The feminine record is held by Mrs. Pamela Warren, aged 21, who machine-sheared 337 Romney Marsh ewes and lambs at Puketutu, near Piopio, New Zealand, in January, 1972.

The sheep shearer with the largest lifetime total is believed to be LaVor Taylor (b. February 27, 1896) of Ephraim, Utah, who, with annual totals varying between 8,000 and 22,000 sheep, sheared 510,000 head in 60 years.

Piggery

The world's largest piggery is at Sljeme, Yugoslavia, which is able to process 300,000 pigs in a year. Even bigger units may exist in Rumania, but details are lacking.

Chicken Plucking

The fastest recorded time for plucking chickens was set in the 1975 contest at Masaryktown, Florida, on October 4, when a team of four women (Sammie Alexsuk, Lottie Nemcovitc, Irene Walker and Janice Oravec) plucked 12 birds naked in 47.8 seconds. Leaving a single feather produces the cry "Fowl!"

Hand Milking

Andy Faust at Collinsville, Oklahoma, in 1937, achieved 120 gallons in 12 hours.

Chapter Ten

THE HUMAN WORLD

1. Political and Social

The land area of the earth is estimated at 57,270,000 square miles (including inland waters), or 29.08 per cent of the world's surface area.

Largest Political Division

The British Commonwealth of Nations, a free association of 36 independent sovereign states together with their dependencies, covers an area of 13,095,000 square miles and had an estimated population of 952,000,000 in 1975.

COUNTRIES

The total number of separately administered territories in the world is 223, of which 158 are independent countries. Of these, 32 sovereign and 49 non-sovereign are insular countries. Only 26 sovereign and 1 non-sovereign countries are entirely without a sea-board. Territorial waters vary between extremes of 3 miles (*e.g.* Australia, France, Ireland, United Kingdom and the U.S.) up to 200 miles (*e.g.* Argentina, Ecuador, El Salvador and Panama).

Largest. The country with the greatest area is the Union of Soviet Socialist Republics (the Soviet Union), comprising 15 Union (constituent) Republics with a total area of 8,649,500 square miles, or 15.0 per cent of the world's total land area, and a total coastline (including islands) of 66,090 miles. The country measures 5,580 miles from east to west and 2,790 miles from north to south.

Smallest. The smallest independent country in the world is the State of the Vatican City (Stato della Città del Vaticano), which was made an enclave within the city of Rome, Italy, on February 11, 1929. It has an area of 108.7 acres.

The maritime country with the shortest coastline is Monaco with 3.49 miles excluding piers and breakwaters.

The smallest colony in the world is Pitcairn Island with an area of 960 acres (1.5 square miles) and a population of 82 in December, 1973.

The world's smallest republic is Nauru, less than 1 degree south of the equator in the Western Pacific. It became independent on January 31, 1968, has an area of 5,263 acres (8.2 square miles) and a population of 7,000 (latest estimate, mid-1974).

The official residence, since 1834, of the Grand Master of the Order of the Knights of Malta totaling 3 acres and comprising the Villa del Priorato di Malta on the lowest of Rome's seven hills, the 151-foot Aventine, retains certain diplomatic privileges and has

SMALLEST INDEPENDENT COUNTRY: Vatican City, a 108.7-acre enclave within Rome, also has a zero birth rate.

accredited representatives to foreign governments. Hence, it is sometimes cited as the smallest state in the world.

On January 19, 1972, the two South Pacific atolls of North and South Minerva (400 miles south of Fiji) were declared to be a sovereign independent Republic under international law by Michael Oliver, formerly of Lithuania.

Frontiers

Most. The country with the most frontiers is the U.S.S.R., with 15—Norway, Finland, Poland, Czechoslovakia, Hungary, Rumania, Turkey, Iran (Persia), Afghanistan, Mongolia, People's Republic of China, North Korea. Japan and the U.S. (territorial waters) may be added.

France, if all her Departments d'outre-mer are included, may, if her territorial waters are extended, have 22 frontiers.

Longest. The longest *continuous* frontier in the world is ' at between Canada and the U.S., which (including the Great Lakes boundaries) extends for 3,987 miles (excluding 1,538 miles with Alaska).

Shortest. The "frontier" of the Holy See in Rome measures 2.53 miles.

Most Frequently Crossed. The frontier which is crossed most frequently is that between the U.S. and Mexico. It extends for 1,933 miles and has more than 120,000,000 crossings every year. The Sino-Soviet frontier, broken by the Sino-Mongolian border, extends for 4,500 miles with no reported figures of crossings.

Sole Frontier. The largest country entirely surrounded by another is Lesotho which has a common boundary only with South Africa.

Most Impenetrable Boundary. The 858-mile-long "Iron Curtain," dividing the Federal Republican (West) and the Democratic Republican (East) parts of Germany, utilizes 2,230,000 land mines and 50,000 miles of barbed wire, in addition to many watchtowers containing detection devices. The whole 270-yard-wide strip occupies 133 square miles of East German territory.

POPULATIONS

Estimates of the human population of the world have largely hinged on the accuracy of the component figure for the population of the People's Republic of China, which has published no census since that of July 30, 1953. On August 25, 1974, the Hsinhua Official News Agency announced that the figure was "nearly 800,000,000"— at least 29 million lower than the U.N. estimate.

The world total at mid-1975 can be estimated to be 3,967 million, giving an average density of 75.9 people per square mile of land (including inland waters). This excludes Antarctica and uninhabited island groups. The daily increase in the world's population was running at 203,250 in 1974–75. It is estimated that about 238 were born and about 97 died every minute in 1974–75. The world's population has doubled in the last 48 years and is expected to double again in the next 36 years.

WORLD POPULATION—PROGRESSIVE MID-YEAR ESTIMATES

Date	Millions	Date	Millions
4000 B.C.	85	1960	2,982
1 A.D.	c. 200–300	1970	3,632
1650	c. 500–550	1971	3,706
1750	750	1972	3,782
1800	960	1973	3,860
1850	1,240	1974	3,950
1900	1,650	1975	4,005
1920	1,862	2000	6,493*
1930	2,070	2007	7,600
1940	2,295	2070	25,000**
1950	2,486		

* U.N. Forecasts made on medium variants.

**Some demographers maintain that the figure will (or must) stabilize at 10,000 to 15,000 million, but above 8,000 million during the 21st century.

It is now estimated that the world's population in the year 2000 will be more than 6,000 million. The present population "explosion" is of such a magnitude that it has been fancifully calculated that, *if* it were to continue unabated, there would be one person to each square yard by 2600 A.D. and humanity would weigh more than the earth itself by 3700 A.D. It is estimated that 75,000,000,000 humans have been born and died in the last 600,000 years.

Largest. The country with the largest population in the world is the People's Republic of China. The mid-1975 U.N. estimate was 824,000,000 (see above). The rate of natural increase is now believed to be 16 per 1,000 or 35,000 per day.

Smallest. The independent state with the smallest population is the Vatican City or the Holy See (see *Smallest Country*), with 880 inhabitants at January 1, 1966, and a zero birth rate.

MOST DENSELY POPULATED SPOT: Hong Kong Island has 200,000 people per square mile, and one section has 1,400,000 per square mile.

Densest. The most densely populated territory in the world is the Portuguese province of Macau (or Macao), on the southern coast of China. It has an estimated population of 266,000 (mid-1974) in an area of 6.2 square miles, giving a density of 42,900 per square mile.

Of territories with an area of more than 200 square miles, Hong Kong (398¼ square miles) contains 4,249,000 people (estimate mid-1974), giving the territory a density of 10,663 per square mile. Hong Kong is only the transcription of the local pronunciation of the Peking dialect version of Xiang gang (a port for incense). About 80 per cent of the population lives in the urban areas of Hong Kong Island (Victoria) and Kowloon, a peninsula of the mainland, and the density there is greater than 200,000 per square mile. On the Wah Fu estate, there are 55,000 people living on 24 acres, giving an unsurpassed spot density of more than 1,466,000 per square mile. In 1959 it was reported that in one house designed for 12 people the number of occupants was 459, including 104 in one room and 4 living on the roof. Hong Kong is now the most populous of all colonies.

The Principality of Monaco, on the south coast of France, has a population of 24,000 (estimated June 30, 1974) in an area of 369.9 acres, giving a density of 41,500 per square mile. This is being relieved by marine infilling which will increase her area to 447 acres.

Singapore has 2,219,000 (mid-1974 estimate) people in an inhabited area of 73 square miles.

Of countries over 1,000 square miles, the most densely populated is Bangladesh with a population of 74,991,000 (mid-1974 estimate) living in 55,126 square miles at a density of 1,359 per square mile.

The Indonesian island of Java (with an area of 48,763 square miles) had a population of 69,037,000 (estimate for 1973), giving a density of 1,415 per square mile.

Sparsest. Antarctica became permanently occupied by relays of scientists from October, 1956. The population varies seasonally and reaches 1,500 at times.

The least populated territory, apart from Antarctica, is Greenland, with a population of 49,000 (estimate of mid-1974) in an area of 840,000 square miles, giving a density of one person to every 17.02 square miles. The ice-free area of the island is only 132,000 square miles.

Cities

Most Populous. The most populous city in the world is Shanghai, China, with a population in 1971 of 10,820,000, thus surpassing the figure for the 23 wards of Tokyo, Japan. At the census of October 1, 1970, the "Keihin Metropolitan Area" (Tokyo-Yokohama Metropolitan Area) of 1,081 square miles contained 14,034,074, however.

The world's largest city not built by the sea or on a river is Greater Mexico City (Ciudad de México), the capital of Mexico, with a census population of 8,589,630 (and a possible actual population of 10,000,000) in 1970.

Oldest. The oldest known walled town is Jericho, in Israeli-occupied Jordan. Radio-carbon dating on specimens from the lowest levels reached by archeologists indicate habitation there by perhaps 3,000 people as early as 7800 B.C. The village of Zawi Chemi Shanidar, discovered in 1957 in northern Iraq, has been dated to 8910 B.C. The oldest capital city in the world is Dimashq (Damascus), capital of Syria. It has been continuously inhabited since *c.* 2500 B.C.

Highest. The highest capital city in the world, before the domination of Tibet by China, was Lhasa, at an elevation of 12,087 feet above sea level.

La Paz, the administrative and *de facto* capital of Bolivia, stands at an altitude of 11,916 feet above sea level. The city was founded in 1548 by Capt. Alonso de Mendoza on the site of an Indian village named Chuquiapu. It was originally called Ciudad de Nuestra Señora de La Paz (City of Our Lady of Peace), but in 1825 was renamed La Paz de Ayacucho, its present official name. Sucre, the legal capital of Bolivia, stands at 9,301 feet above sea level.

The new town of Wenchuan, founded in 1955 on the Chinghai-Tibet road, north of the Tangla Range is the highest in the world at 16,732 feet above sea level. The highest dwellings in the world are those in Baruduksum, Tibet, at 21,000 feet.

Lowest. The settlement of Ein Bokek, which has a synagogue, on the shores of the Dead Sea, is the lowest town in the world at 1,299 feet below sea level.

Towns

Largest in Area. The world's largest town, in area, is Mount Isa, Queensland, Australia. The area administered by the City Council is 15,822 square miles.

Northernmost. The world's northernmost town with a population of more than 10,000 is the Arctic port of Dikson, U.S.S.R., at 73° 32′ N.

The northernmost village is Ny Ålesund (78° 55′ N.), a coal mining settlement on King's Bay, Vest Spitsbergen, in the Norwegian territory of Svalbard, inhabited only during the winter season.

The northernmost capital is Reykjavik, Iceland, at 64° 06′ N. Its population was estimated to be 84,772 in 1974. The northernmost permanent human occupation is the base at Alert (82° 31′ N.), on Dumb Bell Bay, on the northeast coast of Ellesmere Island, northern Canada.

Southernmost. The world's southernmost village is Puerto Williams (population about 350), on the north coast of Isla Navarino, in Tierra del Fuego, Chile, about 680 miles north of Antarctica. Wellington, North Island, New Zealand, is the southernmost capital city at 41° 17′ S. The world's southernmost administrative center is Port Stanley (51° 43′ S.), in the Falkland Islands, off southern South America.

Most Remote from Sea. The large town most remote from the sea is Wulumuchi (Urumchi) formerly Tihwa, Sinkiang, capital of the Uighur Autonomous Region of China, at a distance of about 1,400 miles from the nearest coastline. Its population was estimated to be 320,000 in 1974.

Emigration

More people emigrate from the United Kingdom than from any other country. A total of 269,000 emigrated from the U.K. in 1974, and the provisional figure for 1975 was 230,000. The largest number of emigrants in any one year was 360,000 in 1852, mainly from Ireland in the aftermath of the Great Famine.

Immigration

The country which regularly receives the most immigrants is the United States, with 400,063 in 1973. It has been estimated that, in the period 1820–1973, the U.S. received 46,317,884 *official* immigrants.

Birth Rate

Highest and Lowest. The highest 1965–70 figure is 52.3 for Swaziland. The rate for the whole world was 31.5 per 1,000 in 1975.

Excluding Vatican City, where the rate is negligible, the lowest recorded rate is 7.8 for Monaco (1973).

Death Rate

Highest and Lowest. The highest of the latest available recorded death rates is 29.9 deaths per each 1,000 of the population in Guinea-

Bissau in 1970. The rate for the whole world was 12.8 per 1,000 in 1975. The lowest of the latest available recorded rates is 3.2 deaths per 1,000 in the Tonga Islands in the South Pacific in 1971.

Natural Increase

The highest of the latest available recorded rates of natural increase is 38.3 (45.6 − 7.3) per 1,000 in the U.S. Virgin Islands in 1970. The rate for the whole world was 31.5 − 12.8 = 18.7 per 1,000 in 1973.

The lowest rate of natural increase in any major independent country is in East Germany (birth rate 10.4, death rate 13.3 with a negative figure thus of − 2.9 per 1,000 for 1974).

Marriage Ages

The country with the lowest average ages for marriage is India, with 20.0 years for males and 14.5 years for females. At the other extreme is Ireland, with 31.4 for males and 26.5 years for females. In the People's Republic of China, the recommended age for marriage for men is 28 and for women 25.

Sex Ratio

The country with the largest recorded female surplus is the U.S.S.R., with 1,169 females to every 1,000 males at January 15, 1970. The country with the largest recorded woman shortage is Pakistan, with 936 to every 1,000 males in 1972. The figures are, however, probably under-enumerated due to *purdah*, a policy that keeps women from appearing in public.

Divorces

The country with the most divorces is the United States with a total of 970,000 in 1974—a rate of 43.6 per cent on the current annual total of marriages or 4.6 per 1,000.

Infant Mortality

Based on deaths before one year of age, the lowest of the latest available recorded rates is 9.6 deaths per 1,000 live births in Iceland and in Sweden, both in 1973. The world rate in 1975 was 98.

The highest recorded infant mortality rate reported has been 195 to 300 per 1,000 live births for Burma in 1952, and 229 for Gabon.

Many countries have apparently ceased to make returns. Among these is Ethiopia, where the infant mortality rate was estimated to be nearly 550 per 1,000 live births in 1969.

Life Expectation

There is evidence that life expectation in Britain in the 5th century A.D. was 33 years for males and 27 years for females. In the decade 1890–1900 the expectation of life among the population of India was 23.7 years.

Based on the latest available data, the highest recorded expectation of life at age 12 months is 71.42 years for Norwegian males (1961–65) and 76.7 years for Dutch females (1971).

The lowest recorded expectation of life at birth is 27 years for both sexes in the Vallée du Niger area of Mali in 1957 (sample survey, 1957–58). The figure for males in Gabon was 25 years in 1960–61, but 45 for females. In Guinea-Bissau it averaged 33 years in 1965.

STANDARDS OF LIVING

National Incomes

The country with the highest income per native citizen in 1972 was Nauru, with some $8,500 each (but only $4,152 per head considering the total population). In 1975, the U.S. reached $5,590 per head, compared with $2,606 for the U.K.

Housing Units

For comparison, a dwelling unit is defined as a structurally separated room or rooms occupied by private households of one or more people and having separate access or a common passageway to the street. The country with the greatest recorded number of private dwelling units is India, with 92,558,000 occupied in 1971. These contain 97,057,000 private households.

Hospitals

Largest. The largest medical center in the world is the District Medical Center in Chicago. It covers 478 acres and includes five hospitals, with a total of 5,600 beds, and eight professional schools with more than 3,000 students.

The largest mental hospital in the world is the Pilgrim State Hospital, Long Island, New York, with 12,800 beds. It formerly contained 14,200 beds.

The largest maternity hospital in the world is the Kandang Kerbau Government Maternity Hospital in Singapore. It has 239 midwives, 151 beds for gynecological cases, 388 maternity beds and an output of 31,255 babies in 1969, compared with the record "birthquake" of 39,856 babies (more than 109 per day) in 1966.

Longest Stay. Martha Nelson was admitted to the Columbus State Institute for the Feeble-Minded in Ohio, in 1875. She died in January, 1975, aged 103 years 6 months, in the Orient State Institution, Ohio, after spending 99 years in institutions.

Physicians

The country with the most physicians is the U.S.S.R., with 831,300, or one to every 307 persons. The country with the lowest recorded proportion is Upper Volta, with 58 physicians (one for every 92,759 people) in 1970.

China has more than a million para-medical personnel known as "barefoot doctors."

David L. Bernie, M.D., of Dayton, Ohio, numbers 5 sons and a daughter and 11 other members of his family who are qualified M.D.'s.

The oldest doctor to continue practice is Frederick Walter

Whitney Dawson (b. October 22, 1876, in Hobsonville, New Zealand), who was the first doctor to receive his license in the 20th century in London, England, on January 1, 1901, and who was still practicing in Whangerai, New Zealand, in April, 1975, in his 99th year.

Dentists

The country with the most dentists is the U.S., where 122,500 were registered members of the American Dental Association in 1974.

Psychiatrists and Psychologists

The country with the most psychiatrists is the U.S. The registered membership of the American Psychiatric Association was 21,364 in 1975. The membership of the American Psychological Association was 39,000 in 1975.

ROYALTY

Oldest Ruling House. The Emperor of Japan, Hirohito (born April 29, 1901), is the 124th in line from the first Emperor, Jimmu Tenno or Zinmu, whose reign was traditionally from 660 to 581 B.C., but probably from *c.* 40 to *c.* 10 B.C.

His Imperial Majesty Muhammad Riza Shah Pahlavi of Iran (born October 26, 1919) claims Cyrus the Great (reigned *c.* 559–530 B.C.) as an ancestor.

Reigns

Longest. The longest recorded reign of any monarch is that of Pepi II, a Sixth Dynasty Pharaoh of ancient Egypt. His reign began in *c.* 2272 B.C., when he was aged 6, and lasted 91 years.

OLDEST RULING HOUSE: Emperor Hirohito is the 124th member of his family to rule Japan.

Currently the longest reigning monarch in the world is King Sobhuza II (born July, 1899), the *Ngwenyama* (Paramount Chief) of Swaziland, who began his reign at the age of 5 months. The country was placed under United Kingdom protection at that time, December, 1899, and became independent on September 6, 1968. At the last published count in 1972, he had 112 wives. Emperor Hirohito of Japan began his reign on December 25, 1926.

The longest reign in European history was that of King Louis XIV of France, who ascended the throne on May 14, 1643, aged 4 years 8 months, and reigned for 72 years 110 days until his death on September 1, 1715, four days before his 77th birthday.

Musoma Kanijo, chief of the Nzega district of western Tanganyika (now part of Tanzania), reputedly reigned for more than 98 years from 1864, when aged 8, until his death on February 2, 1963.

The 6th Japanese Emperor Koo-an traditionally reigned for 102 years (from 392 to 290 B.C.), but probably his actual reign was from about 110 A.D. to about 140 A.D. The reign of the 11th Emperor Suinin was traditionally from 29 B.C. to 71 A.D. (99 years), but probably was from 259 A.D. to 291.

Shortest. The shortest recorded reign was that of Jean I, King of France, who was born posthumously on November 15, 1316, and died, aged 4 days, on November 19, 1316.

Youngest King and Queen. Of the world's 26 monarchies, the one with the youngest king is Bhutan (in the Himalayas) where King Jigme Singye Wangchuk (b. November 11, 1955) was crowned on June 2, 1974. Queen Alia, third wife of King Hussein I of Jordan became queen on the eve of her 24th birthday (b. December 25, 1948).

Longest-Lived Royalty. The longest life among the "blood royal" of Europe is the 98 years 206 days of H.R.H. Princess Alicia of Bourbon, who was born June 29, 1876, and died on January 20, 1975.

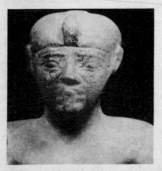

LONGEST REIGN: (Left) Pharaoh Pepi II, whose statue is in the Cairo Museum, reigned for 91 years in ancient Egypt, starting in c.2272 B.C. (Right) YOUNGEST QUEEN: Queen Alia of Jordan became queen on the eve of her 24th birthday.

The longest-lived Queen on record has been the Queen Grand-mother of Siam, Queen Sawang (born September 10, 1862), 27th daughter of King Mongkut (Rama IV), who died on December 17, 1955, aged 93 years 3 months.

Highest Regnal Number. Prince Heinrich LXXV Reuss (1800–1801) briefly enjoyed the highest post-nominal number (75). All male members of this German family are called Heinrich and are successively numbered from I upwards *each* century.

LEGISLATURES

Parliaments

Oldest. The earliest known legislative assembly was a bicameral one in Erech, Iraq, *c.* 2800 B.C. The oldest legislative body is the *Alpingi* (Althing) of Iceland, founded in 930 A.D. This body, which originally comprised 39 local chieftains, was abolished in 1800, but restored by Denmark to a consultative status in 1843 and a legislative status in 1874. The legislative assembly with the oldest continuous history is the Tynwald Court of the Isle of Man, in the Irish Channel, which is believed to have originated more than 1,000 years ago.

The earliest known use of the term "parliament" in an official English royal document, in the meaning of a summons to the King's council, dates from December 19, 1241.

Largest. The largest legislative assembly in the world is the National People's Congress of China (mainland). The fourth Congress, which met in March, 1969, had 3,500 members.

Smallest Quorum. The British House of Lords has the smallest quorum, expressed as a percentage of eligible voters, of any legislative body in the world, namely less than one-third of one per cent. To transact business there must be three peers present, including the Lord Chancellor or his deputy.

Highest-Paid Legislators. The most highly paid of all the world's legislators are U.S. Congressmen, who receive a basic annual salary of $42,500. Of this, up to $3,000 is exempt from taxation. In addition, Senators are allowed up to $157,092 per annum for office help, with a salary limit of $30,600 for any one staff member (limited to 16 in all) per annum. Senators also enjoy free travel to and from Washington, free telephones, postage, medical care, telegrams, stationery (limited to 480,000 envelopes per year), flowers and haircuts. They also are charged very low rates for filming, speech and radio transcriptions and, in the case of women Senators, beauty treatment. When abroad they have access to "counterpart funds" and on retirement to (non-contributory) pension benefits.

Filibusters. The longest continuous speech in the history of the U.S. Senate was that of Senator Wayne Morse of Oregon on April 24–25, 1953, when he spoke on the Tidelands Oil Bill for 22 hours 26 minutes without resuming his seat. Senator Strom Thurmond

(South Carolina, Democrat) spoke against the Civil Rights Bill for 24 hours 19 minutes on August 28–29, 1957, interrupted only briefly by the swearing-in of a new senator.

The record for a filibuster in any legislature is 42 hours 33 minutes by Texas State Senator Mike McKool, known as Little Hercules, at Austin, Texas, on June 26–28, 1972. He was speaking for inclusion of $17,000,000 for mental health services in the state budget.

Longest Membership. The longest span as a legislator was 83 years by József Madarász (1814–1915). He first attended the Hungarian Parliament in 1832–36 as *ablegatus absentium* (*i.e.* on behalf of an absent deputy). He was a full member in 1848–50 and from 1861 until his death on January 31, 1915.

Prime Ministers and Heads of State

Oldest. The longest-lived Prime Minister of any country is believed to have been Christopher Hornsrud, Prime Minister of Norway from January 28 to February 15, 1928. He was born on November 15, 1859 and died on December 13, 1960, aged 101 years 28 days.

El Hadji Mohammed el Mokri, Grand Vizier of Morocco, died on September 16, 1957, at a reputed age of 116 Muslim (*Hijri*) years, equivalent to 112.5 Gregorian years.

Longest Term of Office. Prof. Dr. António de Oliveira Salazar (1889–1970), was the President of the Council of Ministers (*i.e.* Prime Minister) of Portugal from July 5, 1932, for 36 years and 84 days until superseded on September 27, 1968, eleven days after going into a coma.

Oldest and Youngest Heads of State. The oldest head of state in the world is H.E. Hon. Mzce Jomo Kenyatta, born, as he says, "approximately 1889." The youngest non-royal head of state is Jean-Claude Duvalier (b. July 3, 1951), President of Haiti.

Elections

Largest. The largest election ever held was that for the Indian *Lok Sabha* (House of the People) on March 1–10, 1971. About 152,720,000 of the electorate of 272,630,000 chose from 2,785 candidates for 518 seats.

Closest. The ultimate in close general elections occurred in Zanzibar (now part of Tanzania) on January 18, 1961, when the Afro-Shirazi Party won by a single seat, after the seat of Chake-Chake on Pemba Island had been gained by a single vote.

Most One-Sided. North Korea recorded a 100 per cent turn-out of electors and a 100 per cent vote for the Workers' Party of Korea in the general election of October 8, 1962. The previous record had been set in the Albanian election of June 4, 1962, when all but seven of the electorate of 889,875 went to the polls—a 99.9992 per cent turn-out. Of the 889,868 voters, 889,828 voted for the candidates of the Albanian Party of Labor, *i.e.* 99.9955 per cent of the total poll.

The highest personal majority was 157,692 from 192,909 votes cast for H.H. Maharani of Jaipur (born May 23, 1919), in the Indian general election of February, 1962.

Most Rigged. In his book *Journey Without Maps*, Graham Greene recounts the case of the 1928 presidential election of Liberia, in which the president, Charles D. B. King, was returned to office with an officially announced majority over his opponent (Thomas J. Faulkner of the People's Party) of 600,000 votes. The total electorate at the time was less than 15,000.

Most Expensive. The cost of the 1972 Presidential election in the United States was estimated at $49,070,000 for the Republican Party (which won 49 of the 50 states), and $45,000,000 for the Democratic Party.

Communist Parties. The largest national Communist party outside the U.S.S.R. (which had 14,950,000 members in 1974) and Communist states has been the Partito Communista Italiano (Italian Communist Party), with a membership of 2,300,000 in 1946. The total fell to 1,650,000 by 1975. The membership in mainland China was estimated to be 28,000,000 in 1974.

Most Parties. The country with the greatest number of political parties is Italy, with 73 registered for the elections of May 19, 1968. These included "Friends of the Moon" with one candidate.

2. Military and Defense

WAR

Longest. The longest of history's countless wars was the "Hundred Years War" between England and France, which lasted from 1338 to 1453 (115 years), although it may be said that the Holy War, comprising nine Crusades from the First (1096–1104) to the Ninth (1270-91), extended over 195 years.

Shortest. The shortest war on record was that between the United Kingdom and Zanzibar (now part of Tanzania) from 9:02 to 9:40 a.m. on August 27, 1896. The U.K. battle fleet under Rear-Admiral (later Admiral Sir) Harry Holdsworth Rawson (1843–1910) delivered an ultimatum to the self-appointed Sultan Sa'id Khalid to evacuate his palace and surrender. This was not forthcoming until after 38 minutes of bombardment. Admiral Rawson received the Brilliant Star of Zanzibar (first class) from the new Sultan Hamud ibn Muhammad. It was proposed at one time that elements of the local populace should be compelled to defray the cost of the ammunition used.

Bloodiest. By far the most costly war in terms of human life was World War II (1939–45), in which the total number of fatalities, including battle deaths and civilians of all countries, is estimated to have been 54,800,000, assuming 25,000,000 U.S.S.R. fatalities and 7,800,000 Chinese civilians killed. The country which suffered most was Poland with 6,028,000 or 22.2 per cent of her population of 27,007,000 killed.

Most Costly. The material cost of World War II far transcended that of the rest of history's wars put together and has been estimated at $1.5 million million. In the case of the United Kingdom the cost was over five times as great as that of World War I. The total cost of World War II to the Soviet Union was estimated semi-officially in May, 1959, at 2,500,000,000,000 roubles ($280,000 million) while a figure of $530,000 million has been estimated for the United States.

Bloodiest Civil War. The bloodiest civil war in history was the T'ai-p'ing ("Peace") rebellion, in which peasant sympathizers of the Southern Ming dynasty fought the Manchu Government troops in China from 1853 to 1864. The rebellion was led by the deranged Hung Hsiu-ch'üan (poisoned himself in June, 1864), who imagined himself to be a younger brother of Jesus Christ. His force was named *T'ai-p'ing Tien Kuo* (Heavenly Kingdom of Great Peace). According to the best estimates, the loss of life was between 20,000,000 and 30,000,000 including more than 100,000 killed by Government forces in the sack of Nanking on July 19–21, 1864.

Bloodiest Battle. The battle with the greatest recorded number of fatalities was the First Battle of the Somme from July 1 to November 19, 1916, with more than 1,030,000—614,105 British and French and *c.* 420,000 (*not* 650,000) German. The gunfire was heard as far away as Hampstead Heath, London. The greatest battle of World War II and the greatest conflict ever of armor was the Battle of Kursk and Oryol which raged for 50 days from July 5 to August 23, 1943, on the Eastern front, which involved 1,300,000 Red Army troops with 3,600 tanks, 20,000 guns and 3,130 aircraft in repelling a German Army Group which had 2,700 tanks. The final invasion of Berlin by the Red Army in 1945 is, however, said to have involved 3,500,000 men; 52,000 guns and mortars; and 7,750 tanks and 11,000 aircraft on both sides.

Modern historians give no credence to the casualty figures attached to ancient battles, such as the 250,000 reputedly killed at Plataea (Greeks *vs.* Persians) in 479 B.C. or the 200,000 allegedly killed in a single day at Châlons-sur-Marne, France, in 451 A.D. This view is on the grounds that it must have been logistically quite impossible to maintain forces of such a size in the field at that time.

Greatest Invasion

Seaborne. The greatest invasion in military history was the Allied land, air and sea operation against the Normandy coasts of France on D-day, June 6, 1944. Thirty-eight convoys of 745 ships moved in on the first three days, supported by 4,066 landing craft, carrying 185,000 men and 20,000 vehicles, and 347 minesweepers. The air assault comprised 18,000 paratroopers from 1,087 aircraft. The 42 available divisions possessed an air support from 13,175 aircraft. Within a month 1,100,000 troops, 200,000 vehicles and 750,000 tons of stores were landed.

The Allied invasion of Sicily on July 10–12, 1943, involved the landing of 181,000 men in 3 days.

Airborne. The largest airborne invasion was the Anglo-American assault of three divisions (34,000 men), with 2,800 aircraft and 1,600 gliders, near Arnhem, in the Netherlands, on September 17, 1944.

Greatest Evacuation

The greatest evacuation in military history was that carried out by 1,200 Allied naval and civil craft from the beachhead at Dunkerque (Dunkirk), France, between May 27 and June 4, 1940. A total of 338,226 British and French troops were taken off.

Worst Sieges

The longest recorded siege was that of Azotus (now Ashdod), Israel, which, according to Herodotus, was besieged by Psamtik I of Egypt for 29 years in the period 664–610 B.C.

The worst siege in history was the 880-day siege of Leningrad, U.S.S.R., by the German Army from August 30, 1941, until January 27, 1944. The best estimate is that between 1.3 and 1.5 million defenders and citizens died.

Largest Armed Forces

Numerically, the country with the largest regular armed force is the U.S.S.R., with 3,575,000 at mid-1975, compared with the U.S.'s 2,130,000 at the same date. With the end of conscription in the U.S., this is likely to sink to 1,800,000 during 1976. The Chinese People's Liberation Army, which includes naval and air services, has 3,250,000 regulars, but there is also a civilian home guard militia once claimed to be 200 million strong, but regarded by the Institute of Strategic Studies to have an effective element of not more than 5,000,000.

Defense

The estimated level of spending on armaments throughout the world in 1974 was $225,000 million. This represents $56.95 per person per annum, or more than 6 per cent of the world's total production of goods and services. It was estimated in 1974 that there were 15,500,000 full-time armed force regulars or conscripts.

WORST SIEGE: Leningrad, U.S.S.R., held out against the Nazi Army for 880 days, August, 1941, to January, 1944.

The budgeted expenditure on defense by the government of the United States in the year ending June, 1977, was $101,000 million, or 6.9 per cent of the country's gross national product.

Western estimates of the U.S.S.R.'s defense expenditure in 1975 were drastically raised following an inadvertent publication in *Finanzy* SSR that the budget heading "other" included "state reserves" which in turn included military hardware. The 1975 total was revised to 60 to 63 billion roubles or some 13 per cent of her gross national product.

At the other extreme is Andorra, whose defense budget, voted in 1972, was reduced to $5.

NAVIES

Largest. The largest navy in the world is the U.S. Navy, with manpower at 536,000 and 197,000 Marines in mid-1975. The active strength in 1975 included 15 attack aircraft carriers, 64 attack nuclear submarines and 11 diesel attack submarines, 73 SAM-armed ships (9 cruisers, 29 destroyers and 26 frigates), and 65 amphibious warfare ships.

Greatest Naval Battles

The greatest number of ships and aircraft ever involved in a sea-air action was 231 ships and 1,996 aircraft in the Battle of Leyte Gulf, in the Philippines. It raged from October 22 to 27, 1944, with 166 U.S. and 65 Japanese warships engaged, of which 26 Japanese and 6 U.S. ships were sunk. In addition, 1,280 U.S. and 716 Japanese aircraft were engaged.

The greatest naval battle of modern times was the Battle of Jutland on May 31, 1916, in which 151 British Royal Navy warships were involved against 101 German warships. The Royal Navy lost 14 ships and 6,097 men and the German fleet 11 ships and 2,545 men.

The greatest of ancient naval battles was the Battle of Salamis, Greece, on September 23, 480 B.C. There were an estimated 800 vessels in the defeated Persian fleet and 310 in the victorious Greek fleet with a possible involvement of 190,000 men.

ARMIES

Largest. Numerically, the largest army is the People's Republic of China's, with a total strength of about 2,800,000 in mid-1975. The total size of the U.S.S.R.'s army in mid-1975 was estimated at 1,800,000 men, believed to be organized into about 167 divisions with a maximum strength of 12,000 each.

Oldest. The oldest army in the world is the 83-strong Swiss Guard in the Vatican City, with a regular foundation dating back to January 21, 1506. Its origins, however, extend back before 1400.

Oldest Old Soldier. The oldest old soldier of all time was probably John B. Salling of the Army of the Confederate States of America and the last accepted survivor of the U.S. Civil War

(1861–65). He died in Kingsport, Tennessee, on March 16, 1959, aged 113 years 1 day.

Tallest Soldier. The tallest soldier of all time was Väinö Myllyrinne (1909–63) who was inducted into the Finnish Army when he was 7 feet 3 inches and later grew to 8 feet 1¼ inches.

Tanks

Earliest. The first fighting tank was "Mother" or "Little Willie," built by William Forster & Co. Ltd. of England, and first tested on January 12, 1916. The tank was first taken into action by the Machine Gun Corps (Heavy Section), which later became the Royal Tank Corps, at the battle of Flers, in France, on September 15, 1916. Known as the Mark I Male, it was armed with a pair of 6-lb. guns and four machine-guns. It weighed 28 tons and, driven by a motor developing 105 horsepower, had a maximum road speed of 3 to 4 m.p.h.

Heaviest. The heaviest tank ever constructed was the German Panzer Kampfwagen Maus II, which weighed 212 tons. By 1945, it had reached only the experimental stage and was not proceeded with.

The heaviest operational tank used by any army was the 91.3-ton 13-man French Char de Rupture 2C bis of 1923. It carried a 155-mm. howitzer and had two 250-h.p. engines giving a maximum speed of 8 m.p.h. On November 7, 1957, in the annual military parade in Moscow, U.S.S.R., a Soviet tank possibly heavier than the German Jagd Tiger II (80.3 tons), built by Henschel, and certainly heavier than the Stalin III, was displayed.

Guns

Earliest. Although it cannot be accepted as proved, the best opinion is that the earliest guns were constructed in North Africa, possibly by Arabs, in *c.* 1250. The earliest representation of an English gun is contained in an illustrated manuscript dated 1326 at Oxford. The earliest anti-aircraft gun was an artillery piece on a high-angle mounting used in the Franco-Prussian War of 1870 by the French against Prussian balloons.

Largest. The remains of the most massive gun ever constructed were found near Frankfurt-am-Main, Germany, in 1945. It was the "Schwerer Gustav" or "Dora," which had a barrel 94 feet 9 inches long, with a caliber of 800 millimeters (31.5 inches), and a breech weighing 121 tons. The maximum charge was 4,409 lbs. of cordite to fire a shell weighing 5.28 tons a distance of 34 miles. The maximum projectile was one of 7.8 tons with a range of 22 miles. Each gun with its carriage weighed 1,481 tons and required a crew of 1,500 men.

Greatest Range. The greatest range ever attained by a gun is by the H.A.R.P. (High Altitude Research Project) gun consisting of two 16.5-inch caliber barrels in tandem in Barbados. In 1968, a 200-lb. projectile was fired to a height of 400,000 feet (75¾ miles). The static V.3 underground firing tubes built by the

Germans in 50-degree shafts at Mimoyecques, near Calais, France, to bombard London were never operative, due to R.A.F. bombing.

The famous long-range gun which shelled Paris in World War I was the *Kaiser Wilhelm geschütz*, with a caliber of 220 mm. (8.66 inches), a designed range of 79.5 miles and an achieved range of 76 miles. The "Big Berthas" were of larger caliber but of shorter range.

Mortars

The largest mortars ever constructed were Mallets mortar (Woolwich Arsenal, London, England, 1857), and the "Little David" of World War II, made in the U.S. Each had a caliber of 36¼ inches (920 mm.), but neither was ever used in action.

Largest Cannon

The highest caliber cannon ever constructed is the *Tsar Puchka* (King of Cannons), now housed in the Kremlin, Moscow, U.S.S.R. It was built in the 16th century with a bore of 36 inches (915 mm.) and a barrel 17 feet long. It was designed to fire cannonballs weighing 2¼ tons but was never used.

The Turks fired up to seven shots per day from a bombard 26 feet long, with an internal caliber of 42 inches, against the walls of Constantinople (now Istanbul) from April 12 to May 29, 1453. It was dragged by 60 oxen and 200 men and fired a stone cannonball weighing 1,200 lbs.

Military Engines

The largest military catapults, or onagers, were capable of throwing a missile weighing 60 lbs. a distance of 500 yards.

March

Longest. The longest march in military history was the famous Long March by the Chinese Communists in 1934–35. In 368 days, of which 268 days were of movement, from October to October, their force of 90,000 covered 6,000 miles northward from Kiangsi to Yünnan. They crossed 18 mountain ranges and six major rivers and lost all but 22,000 of their force in continual rear-guard actions against Nationalist Kuo-min-tang (K.M.T.) forces.

Most Rapid. The most rapid recorded march by foot-soldiers was one of 42 miles in 26 hours on July 28–29, 1809, by the Light Brigade under Brigadier- (later Major-) General Robert Craufurd (1764–1812), coming to the relief of Lieut.-Gen. Sir Arthur Wellesley, later Field Marshal the 1st Duke of Wellington (1769–1852), after the Battle of Talavera (Talavera de la Reina, Toledo, Spain) in the Peninsular War.

AIR FORCES

The earliest autonomous air force is the Royal Air Force of Great Britain, whose origins began with the Royal Flying Corps (created May 13, 1912); the Air Battalion of the Royal Engineers (April 1, 1911) and the Corps of Royal Engineers Balloon Section (1878) which was first operational in Bechuanaland (now Botswana) in 1884.

Largest. The greatest air force of all time was the U.S. Army Air Corps (now called the U.S. Air Force), which had 79,908 aircraft in July, 1944, and 2,411,294 personnel in March, 1944. The U.S. Air Force, including strategic air forces, had 645,000 personnel and 5,000 combat aircraft in mid-1974. The U.S.S.R. Air Force, including Air Defense Forces with about 900,000 men in mid-1974, had about 8,000 combat aircraft. In addition, the U.S.S.R.'s Offensive Strategic Rocket Forces had about 350,000 operational personnel in mid-1974.

Bombs

The heaviest conventional bomb ever used operationally was the British Royal Air Force's "Grand Slam," weighing 22,000 lbs. and measuring 25 feet 5 inches long, dropped on Bielefeld railway viaduct, Germany, on March 14, 1945. In 1949, the U.S. Air Force tested a bomb weighing 42,000 lbs. at Muroc Dry Lake, California.

Atomic. The two atom bombs dropped on Japan by the U.S. in 1945 each had an explosive power equivalent to that of 20,000 tons (20 kilotons) of trinitrotoluene, called T.N.T. The one dropped on Hiroshima, known as "Little Boy," was 10 feet long and weighed 9,000 lbs.

The most powerful thermonuclear device so far tested is one with a power equivalent to 57,000,000 tons of T.N.T., or 57 megatons, detonated by the U.S.S.R. in the Novaya Zemlya area at 8:33 a.m. G.M.T. on October 30, 1961. The shock wave was detected to have circled the world three times, taking 36 hours 27 minutes for the first circuit. Some estimates put the power of this device at between 62 and 90 megatons. On August 9, 1961, Nikita Khrushchev, then the Chairman of the Council of Ministers of the U.S.S.R., declared that the Soviet Union was capable of constructing a 100-megaton bomb, and announced the possession of one in East Berlin, Germany, on January 16, 1963. It has been estimated that such a bomb would make a crater 19 miles in diameter and would cause serious fires at a range of from 36 to 40 miles.

The atom bomb became inevitable with the meso-thorium experiments of Otto Hahn, Fritz Strassman, and Lise Meitner on December 17, 1938. Work started in the U.S.S.R. on atomic bombs in June, 1942, although their first chain reaction was not achieved until December, 1945, by Dr. Igor Vaslyevich Kurchatov.

The patent for the fusion or H-bomb was filed in the U.S. on May 26, 1946, by Dr. Janos (John) von Neumann (1903–57), a Hungarian-born mathematician, and Dr. Klaus Julius Emil Fuchs (born in Germany, 1911), the physicist who defected to Russia from England.

Largest Nuclear Arsenal

The International Institute for Strategic Studies estimates that if 3 of the 4 known new ICBM (Intercontinental Ballistic Missiles) systems now being developed in the U.S.S.R. are fully deployed, their capacity would be to deliver 7,000 separately-targeted nuclear warheads in the megaton range.

No official estimate has been published of the potential power of the device known as Doomsday, but this far surpasses any tested weapon. A 50,000-megaton cobalt-salted device has been discussed which could kill the entire human race except those who were deep underground and who stayed there for more than five years.

Largest "Conventional" Explosion. The largest use of conventional explosive was for the demolition of German U-boat pens at Heligoland, Germany, on April 18, 1947. A charge of 4,476 tons was detonated by E. C. Jellis aboard H.M.S. *Lassoe* lying 9 miles out to sea.

3. Judicial

LEGISLATION AND LITIGATION

Statutes

Oldest. The earliest known judicial code was that of King Urnammu during the Third Dynasty of Ur, Iraq, in c. 2145 B.C.

Most. It was computed in March, 1959, that the total number of laws on Federal and State statute books in the U.S. was 1,156,644. The Illinois State Legislature only discovered in April, 1967, that in 1907 it had made the sale of cigarettes illegal and punishable by a $100 fine for a second offense.

Most Protracted Litigation

The longest contested lawsuit ever recorded ended in Poona, India, on April 28, 1966, when Balasaheb Patloji Thorat received a favorable judgment on a suit filed by his ancestor Maloji Thorat 761 years earlier in 1205.

Longest Impeachment

The British Parliament's impeachment of Warren Hastings (1732–1818), for maladministration of India, began in 1788 and dragged on for seven years, until his acquittal on April 23, 1795. The trial itself lasted only 149 days.

Most Inexplicable Statute

Certain passages in several laws have always defied interpretation and the most inexplicable must be a matter of opinion. A judge of the Court of Session of Scotland has sent the editors of this book his candidate which reads, "In the Nuts (unground), (other than ground nuts) Order, the expression nuts shall have reference to such nuts, other than ground nuts, as would but for this amending Order not qualify as nuts (unground) (other than ground nuts) by reason of their being nuts (unground)."

Best-Attended Trial

The greatest attendance at any trial was at that of Major Jesús Sosa Blanco, aged 51, for an alleged 108 murders. At one point in the 12½-hour trial (5:30 p.m. to 6 a.m., January 22–23, 1959), 17,000 people were present in the Havana Sports Palace, Cuba.

Highest Bail

The highest amount ever demanded as bail was $46,500,000 against Antonio De Angelis in a civil damages suit by the Harbor Tank Storage Co. filed in the Superior Court, Jersey City, New Jersey, on January 16, 1964. He was released on June 4, 1973.

Greatest Damages

Loss of Life. The highest damages ever actually paid have been $14,387,674 following upon the crash of a private aircraft at South Lake Tahoe, California, on February 21, 1967, to the sole survivor Ray Rosendin, 45, by the Santa Clara Superior Court on March 8, 1972. Rosendin received $1,069,374 for the loss of both legs and disabling arm injuries; $1,213,129 for the loss of his wife and $10,500,000 punitive damages against Avco-Lycoming Corporation which allegedly violated Federal regulations when it rebuilt the aircraft engine owned by Rosendin Corporation.

Breach of Contract. The greatest damages ever awarded for a breach of contract were £610,392 ($1,709,000), awarded on July 16, 1930, to the Bank of Portugal against the printers Waterlow & Sons, Ltd., of London, arising from their unauthorized printing of 580,000 five-hundred escudo notes in 1925. This award was upheld in the House of Lords on April 28, 1932. One of the perpetrators, Arthur Virgilio Alves Reis, served 16 years (1930–46) in jail.

Personal Injury. The greatest damages for personal injury ever awarded went to Larry Miedema, Jr., aged 3, in Pomona, California, on June 4, 1973, against Glendora Community Hospital and Dr. Robert Reinke for malpractice resulting in his becoming mentally retarded and a quadraplegic. If he lives to the average expected age of 68, the payments will total $21,000,000.

The single payment personal injuries record was $6,300,000, awarded to Thomas Hooks, 18, of Venice, Illinois, for diving off a faultily constructed board in a hotel swimming pool and thereby paralyzing himself, in Washington, D.C., on May 27, 1975.

Divorce. The highest alimony awarded by a court has been $2,261,000 against George Storer, Sr., 74, in favor of his third wife Dorothy, 73, in Miami, Florida, on October 29, 1974. Mr. Storer, a broadcasting executive, was also ordered to pay his ex-wife's attorney $200,000 in fees.

Defamation. A sum of $16,800,000 was awarded to Dr. John J. Wild, 58, at the Hennepin District Court of Minnesota on November 30, 1972, against the Minnesota Foundation and others for defamation, bad-faith termination of a contract, interference with professional business relationships, plus $10,800,000 in punitive damages. These amounts have not to date been appealed.

Greatest Compensation

On August 12, 1975, William De Palma (born 1938) of Whittier, California, agreed to a $750,000 settlement for 16 months' wrongful imprisonment in McNeil Island Federal Prison, Washington. He had been given a 15-year sentence for armed robbery in Buena Park, California, on forged fingerprint evidence in 1968.

Highest Settlement

Divorce. The greatest amount ever paid in a divorce settlement is $9,500,000, paid by Edward J. Hudson to Mrs. Cecil Amelia Blaffer Hudson, aged 43. This award was made on February 28, 1963, at the Domestic Relations Court, Houston, Texas. Mrs. Hudson was, reputedly, already worth $14,000,000.

Patent Case. The greatest settlement ever made in a patent-infringement suit is $9,250,000, paid in April, 1952, by the Ford Motor Company to the Ferguson Tractor Co. for a claim filed in January, 1948.

Income Tax Reward. The greatest amount paid for information concerning a case of income tax delinquency was $79,999.93, paid by the U.S. Internal Revenue Service to a group of informers. Payments are limited to 10 per cent of the amount recovered as a direct result of information laid. Informants are often low-income accountants or women scorned. The total of payments in 1965 was $597,731.

The greatest lien ever imposed by a court is 40,000,000,000 lire ($64,800,000) on April 9, 1974, in Milan, upon Vittorio and Ida Riva for back taxes allegedly due on a chain of cotton mills around Turin, Italy, inherited by their brother Felice (now safe in Beirut) in 1960.

Most Literal Legal Interpretation

Eugene Schneider of Carteret, New Jersey, allegedly cut his $80,000 home in half with a chain saw in July, 1976, after his wife sued him for divorce, thus fulfilling in his eyes the equal division of property required by New Jersey law.

Most Successful Complainer

Ralph Charell, a New York network television executive, claims to have been successful in collecting for every misadventure that has damaged him. His total receipts in settlement for such complaints as poor telephone and car rental service, gas and electric overcharges, failure to deliver on time, imperfect goods, improper installation, landlord disputes, and the like, have come to $79,843.82 as of July 22, 1976—and he is still complaining! His latest complaint is against the *Guinness Book* for failing to list his 51 consecutive profitable transactions in "option trading," a category this book does not cover.

Largest Suit

The highest amount of damages ever sought is $675,000,000,000,000 (equivalent to the U.S. Government revenue for 3,000 years) in a suit by Mr. I. Walton Bader brought in the U.S. District Court, New York City on April 14, 1971, against General Motors and others for polluting all 50 States.

Wills

Shortest. The shortest valid will in the world is "Vse zene," the Czech for "All to wife," written and dated January 19, 1967, by Herr Karl Tausch of Langen, Hesse, Germany. The shortest will contested but subsequently admitted to probate in English law was the case of *Thorn v. Dickens* in 1906. It consisted of the three words "All for Mother."

Longest. The longest will on record was that of Mrs. Frederica Cook (U.S.), in the early part of the century. It consisted of four bound volumes containing 95,940 words.

Oldest and Youngest Judge

The oldest recorded active judge was Judge Albert R. Alexander (born November 8, 1859), of Plattsburg, Missouri, magistrate and probate judge of Clinton County. He retired on July 9, 1965, at the age of 105 years 8 months, and died on March 30, 1966.

No collated records on the ages of judicial appointments exist. However, Thomas J. Boynton (born Amherst, Ohio, on August 31, 1838) is known to have been appointed Federal Judge at Key West, Florida, on January 20, 1864, aged 25 years 142 days.

Highest-Paid Lawyer

It was estimated that Jerry Geisler (1886–1962), an attorney in Los Angeles, averaged $50,000 in fees for each case which he handled during the latter part of his career. Currently, the most highly paid lawyer is generally believed to be Louis Nizer of New York City.

Most Successful Criminal Lawyer

Sir Lionel Luckhoo, senior partner of Luckhoo and Luckhoo, of Georgetown, Guyana, succeeded in getting his 191st successive murder charge acquittal by January 31, 1976. He has one appeal pending.

CRIME AND PUNISHMENT

Greatest Mass Killings

China. The greatest massacre in human history ever attributed to any nation is that of 26,300,000 Chinese during the régime of Mao Tse-tung between 1949 and May, 1965. This accusation was made by an agency of the U.S.S.R. Government in a radio broadcast on April 7, 1969. The broadcast broke down the figure into four periods: 2.8 million (1949–52); 3.5 million (1953–57); 6.7 million (1958–60); and 13.3 million (1961–May, 1965). The highest reported death figures in single monthly announcements on Peking radio were 1,176,000 in the provinces of Anhwei, Chekiang, Kiangsu, and Shantung, and 1,150,000 in the Central South Provinces. Po I-po, Minister of Finance, is alleged to have stated in the organ *For a lasting peace, for a people's democracy* "in the past three years (1950–52) we have liquidated more than 2 million bandits." General Jacques Guillermaz, a French diplomat, estimated the total executions between February, 1951, and May, 1952, at between 1 million and 3 million. In April, 1971, the Executive *Yuan* or cabinet of the implacably hostile government of The Republic of China in Taipei, Taiwan, announced its official estimate of the mainland death roll in the period 1949–69 as "at least 39,940,000." This figure, however, excluded "tens of thousands" killed in the Great Proletarian Cultural Revolution, which began in late 1966. The Walker Report published by the U.S. Senate Committee of the Judiciary in July, 1971, placed the total death roll since 1949 between 32.25 and 61.7 million.

U.S.S.R. The death roll in the Great Purge, or *Yezhovshchina*, in the U.S.S.R., in 1936–38, has never been published, though evidence of its magnitude may be found in population statistics which show a deficiency of males from before the outbreak of the 1941–45 war. The reign of terror was administered by the *Narodny Kommissariat Vnutrennykh Del* (N.K.V.D.), or People's Commissariat of Internal Affairs, the Soviet security service headed by Nikolay Ivanovich Yezhov (1895–?1939), described by Nikita Khrushchev in 1956 as "a degenerate." S. V. Utechin, an expert on Soviet affairs, regards estimates of 8,000,000 or · 10,000,000 victims as "probably not exaggerations."

Nazi Germany. At the S.S. (*Schutzstaffel*) extermination camp known as Auschwitz-Birkenau (Oswiecim-Brzezinka), near Oswiecim, in southern Poland, where a minimum of 920,000 people (Soviet estimate is 4,000,000) were exterminated from June 14, 1940 to January 18, 1945. The greatest number killed in a day was 6,000. The man who operated the release of the "Zyklon B" cyanide pellets into the gas chambers there during this time was Sergeant-Major Moll (or Mold). The Nazi Commandant during the period 1940–43 was Rudolf Franz Ferdinand Höss, who was tried in Warsaw from March 11 to April 2, 1947, and hanged, aged 47, at Oswiecim on April 15, 1947.

Obersturmbannführer (Lt.-Col.) Otto Adolf Eichmann (born 1906) of the S.S. was hanged in a small room inside Ramleh Prison, near Tel Aviv, Israel, at just before midnight (local time) on May 31, 1962, for his complicity in the deaths of an indeterminably massive number of Jews during World War II, under the instruction given in April, 1941, by Adolf Hitler (1889–1945) for the "Final Solution" (*Endlösung*).

Forced Labor

No official figures have been published of the death roll in Corrective Labor Camps in the U.S.S.R., first established in 1918. The total number of such camps was known to be more than 200 in 1946, but in 1956 many were converted to less severe Corrective Labor Colonies. An estimate published in the Netherlands puts the death roll between 1921 and 1960 at 19,000,000. The camps were administered by the *Cheka* until 1922, the O.G.P.U. (1922–34), the N.K.V.D. (1934–1946), the M.V.D. (1946–1953) and the K.G.B. since 1953. Solzhenitsyn's best estimate is an aggregate number of 66 million inmates.

In China, there are no published official figures on the numbers undergoing *Lao Jiao* (Education through Labor) nor *Lao Dong Gai Zao*

(Reform through Manual Labor). An estimate published by Bao Ruo-wang, who was released in 1964 because his father was a Corsican, was 16,000,000, which is almost 3 per cent of the population.

Largest Criminal Organization

The largest syndicate of organized crime is the Mafia (meaning "swank," from a Sicilian word) or La Cosa Nostra ("our thing") which is said to have infiltrated the executive, judiciary and legislative branches of the U.S. Government. It consists of some 3,000 to 5,000 individuals in 24 "families" federated under "The Commission," with an estimated annual turnover in vice, gambling, protection rackets and rigged trading of $30,000 million per annum of which some 25 per cent is profit. The biggest Mafia killing was on September 11–13, 1931, when the topmost man Salvatore Maranzano, *Il Capo di Tutti Capi*, and 40 allies were liquidated.

The Mafia is said to have got its start in the U.S. after the lynching of 11 Mafiosi in New Orleans in 1890, for which a naive U.S. government paid $30,000 compensation to the widows. This money was seized and used as the initial funding to prime the whole operation.

Murder

Highest Rate. The country with the highest recorded murder rate is Mexico with 46.3 registered homicides per 100,000 of the population in 1970. It has been estimated that the total number of murders in Colombia during *La Violencia* (1945–62) was about 300,000, giving a rate over a 17-year period of nearly 48 per day. A total of 592 deaths was attributed to one bandit leader, Teófilo ("Sparks") Rojas, aged 27, between 1948 and his death in an ambush near Armenia on January 22, 1963. Some sources attribute 3,500 slayings to him.

The highest homicide rates recorded in New York City have been 58 in a week in July, 1972, and 13 in a day in August, 1972. In 1973, the total for Detroit, Michigan (population 1,500,000) was 751.

Lowest Rate. The country with the lowest officially recorded rate in the world is Spain, with 39 murders (a rate of 1.23 per million population) in 1967, or one murder every 9 days. In the Indian protectorate of Sikkim, in the Himalayas, murder is, however, practically unknown, while in the Hunza area of Kashmir, in the Karakoram, only one definite case by a Hunzarwal has been recorded since 1900.

Most Prolific Murderers. It was established at the trial of Buhram, the Indian Thug, that he had strangled at least 931 victims with his yellow and white cloth *ruhmal* in the Oudh district between 1790 and 1840. It has been estimated that at least 2,000,000 Indians were strangled by Thugs (*burtotes*) during the reign of the Thugee cult (pronounced "tugee") from 1550 until its final suppression by the British *raj* in 1852.

The greatest number of victims ascribed to a murderess has been 610 in the case of Countess Erszébet Báthory (1560–1614) of Hungary. At her trial which began on January 2, 1611, a witness testified to seeing a list of her victims in her own handwriting totaling this number. All were alleged to be young girls from the neighborhood of her castle at Csejthe, where she died on August 21, 1614. She was walled up in her room for 3½ years, after being found guilty.

This century's top candidate is the German, Bruno Lüdke, who confessed to 85 murders of women between 1928 and January 29, 1943. He was executed by injection without trial in a hospital in Vienna on April 8, 1944.

On September 8, 1974, a person or persons unknown placed explosives aboard a TWA Boeing 707 Athens-to-Rome flight. The resultant explosion over the Ionian Sea caused the deaths of 88 people. Sabotage was suggested as the cause of the loss of the Super Constellation over the western Pacific on March 16, 1962, when 107 were killed.

Gang Murders. During the period of open gang warfare in Chicago, the peak year was 1926, when there were 76 unsolved killings. The 1,000th gang murder in Chicago since 1919 occurred on February 1, 1967. Only 13 cases have ended in convictions.

Suicide

The estimated daily total of suicides throughout the world surpassed 1,000 in 1965. The country with the highest recorded suicide rate is Hungary, with 33.1 per 100,000 of the population in 1971. The country with the lowest recorded rate is Jordan, with a single case in 1970 and hence a rate of 0.04 per 100,000.

Capital Punishment

Capital punishment was first abolished *de facto* in Liechtenstein in 1798.

Between the 5-to-4 U.S. Supreme Court decision against capital punishment in June, 1972, and April, 1975, 32 of the 50 states have voted to restore the death penalty.

Last Guillotinings

The last person to be publicly guillotined in France was the murderer Eugen Weidmann before a large crowd at Versailles, near Paris at 4:50 a.m. on June 17, 1939.

The last person guillotined in a French prison was a 22-year-old child murderer named Christian Ranucci at Marseilles on July 28, 1976.

Dr. Joseph Ignace Guillotin (1738–1812) died a natural death. He had advocated the use of the machine designed by Dr. Antoine Louis in 1789 in the French constituent assembly.

"Smelling-Out." The greatest "smelling-out" (ritualistic execution) recorded in African history occurred before Shaka (chief of the Zulu tribes, 1787–1828) and 30,000 of his subjects near the Umhlatuzana River, Zululand (now Natal, South Africa) in March, 1824. After 9 hours, over 300 were "smelt-out" as guilty of smearing the Royal *Kraal* with blood. Their "discoverers" were 150 witch-finders led by the hideous female *isangoma* Nobela. The victims were declared innocent when Shaka admitted to having the smearing done himself to expose the falsity of the power of his diviners. Nobela poisoned herself with atropine ($C_{17}H_{23}NO_3$), but the other 149 witchfinders were thereupon skewered or clubbed to death.

Largest Hanging

The most people hanged from one gallows was 38 Sioux Indians by William J. Duly outside Mankato, Minnesota, for the murder of unarmed citizens on December 26, 1862.

Most Hanging Attempts

In 1803 it was reported that Joseph Samuels was reprieved in Sydney, Australia, after three unsuccessful attempts to hang him in which the rope broke twice.

Slowest Executions

The longest stay on "death row" in the U.S. has been one of more than 14 years by Edgar Labat, aged 44, and Clifton A. Paret, aged 38, in Angola Penitentiary, Louisiana. In March, 1953, they were sentenced to death, after being found guilty of rape in 1950. They were released on May 5, 1967, only to be immediately re-arrested on an indictment arising from the original charge.

Caryl Whittier Chessman, aged 38, convicted of 17 felonies, was executed on May 2, 1960, in the gas chamber at the California State Prison, San Quentin, California. In 11 years 10 months and one week on "death row," Chessman had won eight stays of execution.

Longest Sentences

The longest recorded prison sentences were ones of 7,109 years, awarded to two confidence tricksters in Iran (formerly Persia) on June 15, 1969. The duration of sentences is proportional to the amount of the defalcations involved. A sentence of 384,912 years was demanded at the prosecution of Gabriel March Grandos, 22, at Palma de Mallorca, Spain, on March 11, 1972, for failing to deliver 42,768 letters.

Juan Corona, a Mexican-American, was sentenced to 25 consecutive life terms for murdering 25 migrant farm workers he had hired, killed and buried in 1970–71 near Feather River, Yuba City, California, on February 5, 1973, at Fairfield, California.

Longest Time Served

Johnson VanDyke Grigsby, who began serving a life sentence for second-degree murder on August 5, 1908, was discharged from Indiana State Prison on December 9, 1974, after 66 years 127 days. He believed he was 89 or 90. He complained of the bad language of "modern" prisoners.

Oldest Prisoner

The oldest known prisoner in the U.S. is John Weber, 95, at the Chillicothe Correctional Institute, Ohio, who began his 44th year in prison on October 29, 1970.

Most Parking Tickets

Henry Rabin, 40, of Skokie, Illinois, was arrested in July, 1975, for failing to pay 468 parking tickets in 2½ years. This top "scofflaw" was fined $5,000.

Most Appearances in Court

There are no collected records on the greatest number of convictions on an individual, but the highest recently reported is 1,433 for the gentlemanly but alcoholic Edward Eugene Ebzery, who died in Brisbane Jail, Queensland, Australia, on September 23, 1967.

Lynchings

The worst year in the 20th century for lynchings in the U.S. was 1901, with 130 lynchings (105 Negroes, 25 Whites), while the first year with no reported cases was 1952.

Longest Prison Escape

The longest recorded escape from prison was that of Leonard T. Fristoe, 77, who escaped from Nevada State Prison, on December 15, 1923, and was turned in by his son on November 15, 1969, at Compton, California. He had 46 years of freedom under the name Claude R. Willis. He had killed two sheriff's deputies in 1920.

Greatest Jail Break

The greatest jail break occurred on April 19, 1974, when 50 prisoners escaped from Rio de Janeiro Jail, Brazil. Thirty-one were immediately recaptured.

Robbery

The greatest recorded robbery by market valuation was the removal of 19 paintings, valued at $19,200,000, taken from Russborough House, Blessington, Ireland, the home of Sir Alfred and Lady Beit, by 4 men and a woman, on April 26, 1974. The paintings were recovered on May 4, 1974, near Glandore, Ireland. Dr. Rose Bridgit Dugdale (born 1941) was subsequently convicted.

It is arguable that the value of the *Mona Lisa* at the time of its theft from The Louvre, Paris, on August 21, 1911, was greater than this figure. It was recovered in Italy in 1913, and Vicenzo Perruggia was charged with its theft. On September 1, 1964, antiquities reputedly worth $24,000,000 were recovered from 3 warehouses near the Pyramids in Egypt.

Bank. During the extreme civil disorder prior to January 22, 1976, in Beirut, Lebanon, a guerilla force blasted the vaults of the British Bank of the Middle East in Bab Idriss and cleared out safety deposit boxes with contents valued by former Finance Minister Lucien Dahadah at $50,000,000, and by another source as an "absolute minimum" of $20,000,000. As much as $20,000,000 (more likely $10,000,000 to $15,000,000) is being claimed as the maximum loss in a robbery of the Société Générale bank of Nice, France, on July 17 or 18, 1976, when 200 safety deposit boxes were rifled by a gang.

LARGEST TRAIN ROBBERY occurred when this Royal Mail train was ambushed in England in 1963. More than $6,000,000 was taken and less than $1,000,000 recovered.

Industrial Espionage. It has been alleged that a division of the American Cyanamid Company about 1966 lost some papers and vials of micro-organisms through industrial espionage, allegedly organized from Italy, which data had cost them $24,000,000 in research and development.

Jewel. The greatest recorded theft of jewels occurred on November 13, 1969, in Freetown, Sierra Leone, when an armed gang stole diamonds belonging to the Sierra Leone Selection Trust, worth $4,200,000.

Jewels are believed to have constituted a major part of the Hotel Pierre, New York City, "heist" on December 31, 1971. An unofficial estimate ran as high as $5,000,000.

Train. The greatest recorded train robbery occurred between 3:03 a.m. and 3:27 a.m. on August 8, 1963, when a General Post Office mail train from Glasgow, Scotland, was ambushed at Sears Crossing and robbed at Bridego Bridge at Mentmore, near Cheddington, Buckinghamshire, England. The gang escaped with about 120 mailbags containing £2,631,784 ($6,053,103) worth of bank notes being taken to London for pulping. Only £343,448 ($961,654) had been recovered by December 9, 1966.

Greatest Kidnapping Ransom

Historically, the greatest ransom paid was that for their chief, Atahualpa, by the Incas to the Spanish conquistador, Francisco Pizarro, in 1532–33 at Cajamarca, Peru, which constituted a hall full of gold and silver worth in modern money some $170 million. Pizarro killed his prisoner anyway.

The greatest ransom ever extorted is $60,000,000 for the release of two businessmen, the brothers Jorge Born, 40, and Juan Born, 39,

of Argentina, paid to the left-wing urban guerrilla group Montoneros in Buenos Aires on June 20, 1975.

The youngest person ever kidnapped has been Carolyn Wharton who was born at 12:46 p.m. on March 19, 1955, in the Baptist Hospital, Beaumont, Texas, and kidnapped by a woman disguised as a nurse at 1:15 p.m., aged 29 minutes.

Greatest Hijack Ransom

The highest amount ever paid to hijackers has been $4,800,000 in small denomination notes by the West German government to Popular Front for the Liberation of Palestine representatives 30 miles outside Beirut, Lebanon, on February 23, 1972. In return a Lufthansa Boeing 747, hijacked an hour out of New Delhi and bound for Athens, which had been forced down at Aden and its 14 crew members were released.

The longest air piracy has been one of 8,800 miles by three Filipino Moslem separatists from the southern Philippines in a BAC 111, changing to a DC8 at Bangkok, Thailand, and arriving at Benghazi, Libya, a week later on April 14, 1976.

Longest Search

In 1972, Frank Jones of Lowestoft, Suffolk, England, ended a 68-year-long search by locating his missing brother, Arthur Jones.

Largest Narcotics Haul

The heaviest recorded haul of narcotics was made in the Bahamas on August 16, 1975, when 1,049 sacks (43.14 tons) of high-grade Colombian marijuana were discovered, worth an estimated $24,000,000. The most valuable haul was of 937 lbs. of pure heroin worth $106¼ million retail seized aboard the 60-ton shrimp boat *Caprice des Temps* at Marseilles, France, on February 28, 1972. The captain, Louis Boucan, 57, tried to commit suicide, but was sentenced to 15 years on January 5, 1973.

It was revealed on January 31, 1973, that 398 lbs. of heroin and cocaine with a street value of $73,000,000 had been stolen from safe-keeping by the New York City Police Department—a record for any law enforcement agency.

Largest Bribe

, An alleged bribe of $84,000,000 offered to Shaikh Zaid ibn Sultan of Abu Dhabi, Trucial Oman, by a Saudi Arabian official in August, 1955, is the highest on record. The affair concerned oil concessions in the disputed territory of Buraimi on the Persian Gulf.

Greatest Forgery

The greatest recorded forgery was the German Third Reich government's forging operation, code name "Bernhard," engineered by Alfred Naujocks in 1940–41. It involved £150,000,000 (now about $375,000,000) worth of Bank of England £5 notes.

Greatest Swindle

In April, 1974, preliminary reports were made of a computerized-insurance swindle involving approximately $1 billion.

Welfare Swindle

The greatest welfare swindle yet worked was that of the gypsy, Anthony Moreno, on the French Social Security in Marseilles. By forging birth certificates and school registration forms, he invented 197 fictitious families and 3,000 children on which he claimed benefits from 1960 to mid-1968. Moreno, nicknamed "El Chorro" (the fountain), was last reported free of extradition worries and living in luxury in his native Spain having absquatulated with an estimated $6,440,000.

Biggest Fraud

The largest amount of money named in a defalcation case has been a gross £33,000,000 ($75,900,000) at the Lugano, Switzerland, branch of Lloyd's Bank International Ltd., on September 2, 1974. Mark Colombo was arrested pending charges including falsification of foreign currency accounts and suppression of evidence.

Passing Bad Checks

Mrs. Ann Lorraine Ohlschlager, *alias* Ann Kosak, of Los Angeles, was charged in January, 1974, with writing $37,000,000 in bad checks between January and October, 1973, netting a total of $463,000 from the United California Bank.

Fines

A fine equivalent to $25,646,400 was levied on Jean Pierre Pilato of France by a court in Valencia, Spain, on February 6, 1972, for attempting to smuggle 250 pounds of heroin worth $38,400,000 from France via Spain to the U.S. He was arrested on June 5, 1971, and is serving a 10-year sentence plus 4 years if the fine is unpaid.

Largest Court

The largest judicial building in the world is the Johannesburg Central Magistrate's Court, opened in 1941, at the junction of Fox and West Streets, Johannesburg, South Africa. There are 42 court-rooms (8 civil and 34 criminal), with a further seven criminal court-rooms under construction. The court has a panel of 70 magistrates and deals with an average of 2,500 criminal cases every week, excluding petty cases in which guilt has been admitted in writing.

Penal Camps

The largest penal camp systems in the world were those near Karaganda and Kolyma, in the U.S.S.R., each with a population estimated in 1958 at between 1,200,000 and 1,500,000. The largest labor camp in the U.S.S.R. is now said to be the Dubrovlag Complex of 15 camps centered on Pot'ma, Mordovian, U.S.S.R. The official N.A.T.O. estimate for all Soviet camps was "more than one million" in March, 1960, compared with a peak of probably 12 million during the Stalinist era.

Devil's Island. The largest French penal settlement was that of St. Laurent du Maroni, which included the notorious Île du Diable, off the coast of French Guiana, South America. It remained in operation for 99 years from 1854 until the last group of repatriated prisoners, including Théodore Rouselle, who had served 50 years, was returned to Bordeaux on August 22, 1953. It has been estimated that barely 2,000 of the 70,000 deportees ever returned. These included the executioner Ladurelle (imprisoned 1921–37), who was murdered in Paris in 1938.

Prisons

Largest. The largest prison in the world is Kharkhov Prison, in the U.S.S.R., which has at times accommodated 40,000 prisoners.

Most Secure. After it became a maximum security Federal prison in 1934, no convict was known to have lived to tell of a successful escape from the prison on Alcatraz ("Pelican") Island in

MOST SECURE PRISON was Alcatraz, on an island in San Francisco Bay, which was closed in 1963. No convict ever escaped although 23 tried. The Golden Gate Bridge is in the background.

San Francisco Bay. A total of 23 men attempted it, but 12 were recaptured, 5 shot dead, one drowned and 5 presumed drowned. On December 16, 1962, three months before the prison was closed, one man reached the mainland alive, only to be recaptured on the spot. John Chase was imprisoned for a record 26 years on Alcatraz.

Longest Siege. The longest prison siege has been one of 10 days 8 hours 58 minutes at the Texas State Penitentiary from July 24 to August 3, 1974. There were 4 fatalities.

4. Economic

MONETARY AND FINANCE

Largest Budget

The greatest annual budget expenditure of any country has been $394,200 million by the U.S. Government (federal expenditure) in fiscal year ending June 30, 1977. The highest budgeted revenue in the U.S. was $331,300 million in 1976–77.

In the U.S., the greatest surplus was $8,419,469,844 in 1947–48, and the greatest deficit was $57,420,430,365 in 1942–43.

Foreign Aid

The total net foreign aid given by the U.S. Government between July 1, 1945, and January 1, 1975, was $156,951 million.

The country which received most U.S. aid in 1975 was South Vietnam with $585,000,000. U.S. foreign aid began with $50,000 to Venezuela for earthquake relief in 1812. Foreign aid was the subject of a 4-month-long debate in the Senate, ending in favor of continuation on March 2, 1972.

Taxation

Most Taxed. The major national economy with the highest rate of central and local government expenditure is that of the United Kingdom with 60.8 per cent of her Gross National Product in 1975–76. The lowest proportion for any advanced national economy in 1973 was 19.5 per cent in Japan, which then enjoyed the highest economic growth rate.

Highest Tax Rates. The country with the most confiscatory taxation is Norway, where in January, 1974, the Labor Party and Socialist Alliance abolished the 80 per cent limit so that some 2,000 citizens have to pay more than 100 per cent of their taxable income. The shipping magnate Hilmar Reksten was assessed at 491 per cent. The second highest marginal rate is in the United Kingdom, where the 1976–77 rate for taxable incomes over £20,000 ($46,000) is 83 per cent with an additional surcharge on investment income in excess of £2,000 ($4,600) of 15 per cent, making a total rate of 98 per cent.

National Debt

The largest national debt of any country in the world is that of the U.S., where the gross federal public debt surpassed the half-trillion dollar mark in 1975. It is budgeted to reach $719,500,000,000 by September, 1977. This amount in dollar bills would make a pile 42,594 miles high, weighing 666,939 tons.

National Wealth

The richest large nation, measured by Gross National Product per head is Kuwait, with $11,000 per head. The U.S., which took the lead in 1910, is now (1974) fifth, following Kuwait, Switzerland, Sweden and Denmark. It has been estimated that the value of all physical assets in the U.S. in 1968 was $3,078,000,000,000 or $15,255 per head.

Poorest Country

According to World Bank calculations, revised in 1972, the three countries with the lowest annual income per capita are Rwanda, Upper Volta and Burundi each with $60. The U.N. General Assembly using a "category" system places Rwanda as the least of the "Least Advanced" nations.

Gross National Product

The estimated free world aggregate of Gross National Products in 1973 was about $3,800,000,000,000. The country with the largest Gross National Product is the U.S., with $1,601,000,000,000 in 1975.

MOST GOLD: The Federal Reserve Bank in New York City houses $17,000 million worth of gold bars.

Gold Reserves

The country with the greatest monetary gold reserve is the U.S. The Treasury had $11,238 million on hand in January, 1976. The Bullion Depository at Fort Knox, 30 miles southwest of Louisville, Kentucky, is the principal depository. Gold is stored in standard mint bars of 400 troy ounces (439 oz. avoirdupois), measuring 7 inches by 3⅝ inches by 1⅝ inches, and each worth $16,888.

The greatest accumulation of the world's central banks' $49,795 million of gold bullion is now in the Federal Reserve Bank at 33 Liberty Street, New York City. Some $17,000 million or 14,000 tons is stored 80 feet below street level, in a vault 50 feet by 100 feet behind a steel door weighing 89 tons.

Worst Inflation

The world's worst inflation occurred in Hungary in June, 1946, when the 1931 gold pengö was valued at 130 trillion (1.3×10^{20}) paper pengös. Notes were issued for szazmillio billion (100 trillion or 10^{20}) pengös on June 3 and withdrawn on July 11, 1946. Notes for 1,000 trillion or 10^{21} pengös were printed but not circulated. On November 6th, 1923, the circulation of Reichsbank marks reached 400,338,326,350,700,000,000. The inflation in Chile from 1950 to 1973 has been 423,100 per cent compared with 199 per cent in Great Britain in the same period.

The United Kingdom's worst rate in a year has been for May, 1974 to May, 1975 when inflation ran at a rate of 22.2 per cent. The worst single increase in a month was May over April 1975 at 4.2 per cent.

Currency

Paper money is an invention of the Chinese and, although the date of 119 B.C. has been suggested, the innovation is believed to date from the T'ang dynasty of the 7th century A.D. The world's earliest bank notes were issued by the Stockholms Banco, Sweden, in July, 1661. The oldest surviving bank note is one for 5 dalers dated December 6, 1662.

Largest and Smallest. The largest paper money ever issued was the one kwan note of the Chinese Ming dynasty issue of 1368–99, which measured 9 inches by 13 inches. The smallest bank note ever issued was the 10 bani note of the Ministry of Finance of Rumania, issued in 1917. It measured (printed area) 1.09 inches by 1.49 inches.

Highest Denominations. The highest denomination of paper currency ever authorized in the world are U.S. gold certificates for $100,000, bearing the head of former President Thomas Woodrow Wilson (1856–1924), issued by the U.S. Treasury in 1934.

The highest denomination notes in circulation are U.S. Federal Reserve Bank notes for $10,000. They bear the head of Salmon Portland Chase (1808–73). None has been printed since July, 1944, and the U.S. Treasury announced in 1969 that no further notes

HIGHEST DENOMINATION CURRENCY ever issued was this $100,000 bill, used formerly in bank transactions.

HIGHEST EXISTING DENOMINATION CURRENCY is this $10,000 bill with the portrait of Salmon P. Chase. Only 400 are circulating today.

higher than $100 would be issued. By 1974, only 400 $10,000 bills were in circulation, reputedly concentrated in Texas around Christmas time.

Lowest Denomination. The 1-cent Hong Kong note is worth one-fifth of a U.S. cent.

Highest Denomination Bond

There exists a U.S. Treasury note for $500,000,000 bearing interest at $6\frac{1}{4}$ per cent for 14 years. Each annual interest payment is $31,250,000. An example is held by the Bureau of Engraving and Printing in Washington, D.C.

Largest Check

The greatest amount paid by a single check in the history of banking was one equivalent to $2,046,700,000, handed over by Daniel P. Moynihan, the U.S. Ambassador to India, in New Delhi on February 18, 1974.

An internal U.S. Treasury check for $4,176,969,623.57 was drawn on June 30, 1954.

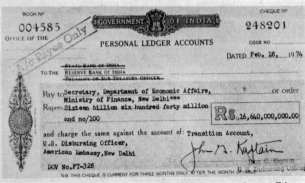

LARGEST CHECK: This check for 16,640,000,000 Indian rupees, drawn on February 18, 1974, is equivalent to more than $2 billion U.S.

COINS

Oldest. The earliest certainly dated coins are the electrum (alloy of gold and silver) staters of Lydia, in Asia Minor (now Turkey), which were coined in the reign of King Gyges (*c.* 685–652 B.C.). Primitive uninscribed "spade" money of the Chou dynasty of China is now believed to date from *c.* 770 B.C. A discovery at Tappah Nush-i-jan, Iran, of silver ingot currency in 1972 has been dated to as early as 760 B.C.

Smallest. The smallest coins in the world have been the Nepalese ¼ dam or Jawa, struck *c.* 1740 in silver in the reign of Jeya Prakash Malla. The Jawa, which weighed between 0.008 and 0.014 of a gram and measured about 2 × 2 mm., was sometimes cut into ½ and even ¼ Jawa, thus weighing 0.002 of a gram, and 14,000 coins presumably weighing 1 ounce.

Heaviest. The Swedish copper 10 daler coin of 1644 attained a weight of 43 lbs. 7¼ oz. Of primitive exchange tokens, the most massive are the holed stone discs, or *Fé*, from the Yap Islands, in the western Pacific Ocean, with diameters of up to 12 feet, weighing up to 185 pounds. A medium-sized one was worth one Yapese wife or an 18-foot canoe.

Coinless Countries. Paraguay and Laos are the only countries presently without coins (paper money only).

Denominations

Highest. The 1654 Indian gold 200 mohur ($1,400) coin of the Mughal Emperor Khurram Shihab-ud-din Muhammad, Shah Jahan (reigned 1628–57), is both the highest denomination coin, and that of the greatest intrinsic worth ever struck. It weighed 33,600 grains (70 troy oz.) and hence has an intrinsic worth of $2,462. It had a diameter of 5⅜ inches. The only known example disappeared in Patna, Bihar, India, in *c.* 1820, but a plaster cast of this coin exists in the British Museum, London.

Lowest. Lowest in face value today is the 5 aurar piece of Iceland issued in 1971 with a face value equal to 0.1311 of a U.S. cent.

MOST MASSIVE COINS: The larger of these holed stone discs, used for money in the Yap Islands of the western Pacific, is worth one wife or a canoe.

Quarter farthings (sixteen to the British penny) were struck in copper at the Royal Mint, London, in the Imperial coinage for use in Ceylon, in 1839 and 1851–53.

Most Expensive Coin

The highest price paid at auction for a single coin is $272,000 or $314,000 inclusive of commission for an Athenian silver decadrachm in Zurich, Switzerland, on June 30, 1974, by Constantinople Fine Arts Inc.

Among the many unique coins, the one which might logically attract the greatest price on the market would be the unique 1873 U.S. dime with the CC mint mark, since dimes are the most avidly collected series of any coins in the world.

Rarest

A number of coins are unique. An example of a unique coin of threefold rarity is one of the rare admixture of bronze with inlaid gold of Kaleb I of Axum (c. 500 A.D.) owned by Richard A. Thorud of Bloomington, Minnesota. Only 700 Axumite coins of any sort are known.

An unissued silver crown (5 shilling) piece of Edward VIII, owned by Richard Lobel & Co., London, is the most valuable in a set of similar coins, minted in 1937, and now insured for $500,000.

Greatest Collection

The highest price paid for a coin collection is $7,300,000 by Steve Markoff of A-Mark Coin Co. Inc. of Beverly Hills, California, for a hoard of 407,000 U.S. silver dollars from the La Vere Redfield estate in a courtroom auction in Reno, Nevada, on January 27, 1976.

Largest Coin Auction

The largest coin auction staged was one of 3,804 lots for $3,375,000 by Superior Stamp & Coin Co. Inc. of Los Angeles, August 19–23, 1975.

Largest Treasure Trove

The largest hoard ever found was one of about 80,000 aurei in Brescello near Modena, Italy, in 1814, believed to have been deposited c. 37 B.C.

The greatest hoard of gold of unknown ownership ever recovered is one valued at about $3,000,000, from the lost $8,000,000, carried in 10 ships of a Spanish bullion fleet which was sunk by a hurricane off Florida, on July 31, 1715. The biggest single haul was by the diver Kip Wagner on May 30, 1965.

Largest Mint

The largest mint in the world is the U.S. Mint built in 1965–69 on Independence Mall, Philadelphia, covering 500,000 square feet (11½ acres) with an annual capacity on a 3-shift 7-day-a-week production of 8,000 million coins. A single stamping machine can produce coins at a rate of 10,000 per minute.

TRADE UNIONS

The world's largest union is the Industrie-Gewerkschaft Metall (Metal Workers' Union) of West Germany, with a membership of 2,559,482 on April 1, 1974. The union with the longest name is probably the F.N.O.M.M.C.F.E.T.M.F., the National Federation of Officers, Machinists, Motormen, Drivers, Firemen and Electricians in Sea and River Transportation of Brazil.

Longest Working Week. The longest working week (maximum possible 168 hours) is up to 139 hours at times by some housemen and registrars in some hospitals in England.

Labor Disputes

Earliest. The earliest recorded strike was one by an orchestra leader from Greece named Aristos in Rome $c.$ 309 B.C. The cause was meal breaks. A labor dispute concerning monotony of diet and working conditions was recorded in 1153 B.C. in Thebes, Egypt.

Longest. The world's longest recorded strike ended on January 4, 1961, after 33 years. It concerned the employment of barbers' assistants in Copenhagen, Denmark. The longest recorded major strike was one at the plumbing fixtures factory of the Kohler Co. in Sheboygan, Wisconsin, between April, 1954, and October, 1962. The strike is alleged to have cost the United Automobile Workers' Union about $12,000,000 to sustain.

Working and Jobs. The longest recorded working career in one job was that of Miss Polly Gadsby who started at the age of 9 and worked 86 years wrapping elastic for the same company until she died in 1932 at the age of 95.

Ernest Turner of Ramsgate, Kent, England has been working since 1886 (minding sheep at a salary of 60¢ per week then) and in June, 1976, aged 96, was working as a canteen cleaner for Volkswagen. His son gets up at 6:30 a.m. to drive him to work. His son is on an old age pension.

The greatest number of different paid jobs recorded in a working life is the 112 accumulated by D. H. "Nobby" Clarke, the yachting author of Ipswich, Suffolk, England.

FOOD CONSUMPTION

The figures relating to net food consumption per person are based on gross available food supplies, at retail level, less waste, animal feed and that used for industrial purposes, divided by the total population. The figures given are the latest available.

Calories. Of all countries in the world, based on the latest available data, Ireland has the largest available total of calories per person. The net supply averaged 3,450 per day in 1968. The highest calorific value of any foodstuff is that of pure animal fat, with 930 calories per 100 grams (3.5 oz.). Pure alcohol provides 710 calories per 100 grams.

Protein. Australia and New Zealand have the highest recorded consumption of protein per person, an average of 106 grams (3.79 oz.) per day in 1969.

The lowest *reported* figures are 1,730 calories per day in the Libyan Arab Republic in 1960–62 and 33 grams (1.47 oz.) of protein per day in Zaïre in 1964–66.

Cereals. The greatest consumers of cereal products—flour, milled rice, etc.—are the people of Egypt, with an average of 510 lbs. per person annually (600 grams per day) in 1966–67.

Starch. The greatest eaters of starchy food (e.g., bananas, potatoes, etc.) are the people of Gabon, who consumed 4.02 lbs. per head per day in 1964–66.

Sugar. The greatest consumers of sugars are the people of Israel, with an average of 7.10 oz. per person per day in 1973. The lowest consumption is 0.45 oz. per day reported for China.

Meat. The greatest meat eaters in the world—figures include organs and poultry—are the people of Uruguay, with an average consumption of 10.93 oz. per person per day in 1964–66. The lowest consumption is 0.16 oz. in Sri Lanka (formerly Ceylon) in 1968.

Soft Drinks. The people of the U.S. undoubtedly consume more carbonated soft drinks than any other people—30.3 gallons per person in 1972, up from 16.8 gallons in 1962. Coffee consumption in the U.S. in the same period dropped from 39.2 gallons to 35.6 gallons per person in 1972, but tea increased from 6.1 to 7.2 gallons. Cold juices (not included in the soft drink totals) reached 5 gallons per person in 1972.

Beer

Of reporting countries, the nation with the highest beer consumption per person is West Germany, with 38.8 U.S. gallons per person in 1975. In the Northern Territory of Australia, however, the annual intake has been estimated to be as high as 62.4 U.S. gallons per person. A society for the prevention of alcoholism in Darwin had to disband in June, 1966, for lack of support.

Prohibition. The longest-lasting imposition of prohibition against consumption of alcoholic beverages has been 26 years in Iceland (1908–34). Other prohibitions have been Russia, later the U.S.S.R. (1914–24) and the United States (1920–33).

Largest Dish

The largest single dish in the world is roasted camel, prepared occasionally for Bedouin wedding feasts. Cooked eggs are stuffed in fish, the fish stuffed in cooked chickens, the chickens stuffed into a roasted sheep carcass and the sheep stuffed into a whole camel.

Largest Banquet

The greatest banquet ever staged was that by President Loubet, President of France, in the gardens of the Tuileries, Paris, on September 22, 1900. He invited every one of the 22,000 mayors in France and their deputies.

The largest indoor banquet was one for 10,158 at $15 a plate in support of Mayor Richard J. Daley of Chicago at the McCormick Place Convention Hall on the Lake, March 3, 1971.

The menu for the main 5½-hour banquet at the Imperial Iranian 2,500th anniversary gathering at Persepolis in October, 1971 (see also *Party Giving,* page 477.), was probably the most expensive ever compiled. It comprised quail eggs stuffed with Iranian caviar, a mousse of crayfish tails in Nantua sauce, stuffed rack of roast lamb, with a main course of roast peacock stuffed with *foie gras,* fig rings, and raspberry sweet champagne sherbet. Wines included *Château Lafite Rothschild* 1945 at $100 per bottle from the cellars of Maxim's, Paris.

Most Expensive Food

The most expensive food is white truffle of Alba, Italy, which sells according to the season for as high as $200 per lb. in the market. Truffles in the Périgord district of France require drought between mid-July and mid-August. Only 7 of Europe's 70 species of this hypogeous mycorrhizal fungus are considered edible.

Largest Pies

The largest apple pie was baked in a 16½-foot diameter steel pie tin weighing 1,800 lbs. at the Orleans County Junior Fair, New York, in August, 1976. It weighed 10 tons, including 4½ tons of apples, and had to be pushed by tractor into a 20-square-foot oven of concrete blocks to be baked.

The largest cherry pie weighed 6¼ tons and contained 4,950 lbs. of cherries. It measured 14 feet 4 inches in diameter, 24 inches in depth and was baked on the grounds of the Medusa Cement Corporation, Charlevoix, Michigan, on May 15, 1976, as part of the town's Bicentennial celebration.

Biggest Barbecue

The most monumental barbecue was one for over 4,000 people at Brisbane, California, on September 16, 1973, with a rotisserie with a 12-foot spit length impaling 7 buffaloes with a dressed weight of 3,755 lbs. John De Marco supervised the 26-hour roast.

Longest Bread

The longest one-piece loaf ever baked was one of 464 feet baked by Leonard W. Gentien on 4th Street, Taft, California, October 17, 1975. The baker used more than 1,000 lbs. of charcoal, and the finished sandwich made from the loaf weighed 1,494 lbs.

Largest Cakes

The largest cake ever baked was made for the Bicentennial celebration in Philadelphia, Pennsylvania, on July 3, 1976, by the kitchens of Sara Lee. The chocolate cake weighed 40,000 lbs., stood 50 feet tall and was 42 feet wide at the base. It provided more than 200,000 servings.

The largest confection ever assembled was the Baltimore City, Maryland, Bicentennial Cake of July 4, 1976, with ingredients weighing 69,860 lbs. It contained an estimated 10,000 eggs, 21,600 lbs. of sugar, and a 415-lb. pinch of salt.

LARGEST DOUGHNUT: This chocolate-covered doughnut is 100 times larger than standard. Baked by Dunkin' Donuts especially for the opening of the Guinness World Records Exhibit Hall in New York, it weighed 11 lbs., was 24 inches in diameter, and had a 9-inch hole. Cutting the doughnut are "Guinness" co-author Norris McWhirter and his twin brother's widow, Rosemary.

Largest Easter Egg

The largest Easter egg ever made was one of more than 2,000 lbs. made by Messrs. Buszard of Oxford Street, London, in 1897, for the trousseau of a South African millionaire's daughter. It was 9 feet high and 18 feet in circumference.

Largest Beefburger

The largest beefburger on record is one of 2,859 lbs., 27½ feet in circumference, exhibited by Tip Top Butcher's and Noonan's Bakery Pty. Ltd. at the Perth Royal Show, Western Australia, on September 24, 1975.

LONGEST HOT DOG: Measuring 1,776 inches long and containing 40 lbs. of beef and pork, this red hot was used to celebrate the Bicentennial at the South Coast Plaza Hotel in Costa Mesa, California.

Largest Omelette

The largest verified omelette made was one made with 6,720 eggs in a frying pan 16 feet 5 inches in diameter in 8 gallons of oil by 6 chefs in 2 hours 18 minutes at Kruishoutem, Belgium, on April 19, 1976.

There was a report in February, 1974, of a 10,000-egg omelette made in Washington, D.C., but details are lacking.

Largest Pancake

The largest pancake ever flipped intact on any griddle was one of 4 feet 9 inches in diameter at the St. Paul Winter Carnival, St. Paul, Minnesota, on January 27, 1974.

Largest Pizza

The largest pizza ever baked was one measuring 25 feet 1 inch in diameter, 494 square feet in area, and 1,200 lbs. in weight at the Pizza Inn, Little Rock, Arkansas, on September 4, 1974. It was commissioned by radio station KARN.

Largest Popsicle

The largest popsicle was an 8-foot-high, 2,800-lb. cherry-flavored popsicle served by the Trinity Baptist Temple, Middletown, Ohio, on March 21, 1976.

LARGEST PIZZA: More than 25 feet in diameter, this pizza in Little Rock, Arkansas, weighed 1,200 lbs.

LONGEST BANANA SPLIT: Constructed by Farrell's Ice Cream Parlour Restaurant in St. Paul, Minnesota, on January 28, 1973, this mile-long split used 33,000 scoops of ice cream and 10,580 bananas.

Biggest Salami

The largest salami on record is one 11 feet long with a circumference of 20 inches, weighing 142½ lbs., made at St. Kilda, Melbourne, Australia, in November, 1974.

Longest Sausage

The longest sausage ever recorded was one 3,124 feet long, made on June 29, 1966, by 30 butchers in Scunthorpe, Lincolnshire, England. It was made from 6½ cwt. of pork and 1½ cwt. of cereal and seasoning.

Largest Sundae

The most monstrous ice cream sundae ever concocted is one of 3,956 lbs. 12 oz. by Farrell's Ice Cream Parlour Restaurant built under the direction of Al Belmont, in front of a crowd estimated at 10,000, at Tysons Corner Center, McLean, Virginia, on July 13, 1975. It contained 777 gallons of ice cream and was covered with 6 gallons of chocolate topping, 1¼ gallons of whipped cream, one case of chocolate sprinkles, and a dish of cherry halves, representing a total of 2,099,895 calories.

Spices

Most Expensive. The most expensive of all spices is Mediterranean saffron (*Crocus sativus*). It takes 96,000 stigmas and therefore 32,000 flowers to make a pound. Packets of 1.9 grams are retailed in England for about 24 cents—equivalent to $780 per pound.

"Hottest." The hottest of all spices is the capsicum hot pepper known as Tabasco, first reported in 1868 by Edmund McIlhenny on Avery Island, Louisiana.

Rarest Condiment. The world's most prized condiment is Ca Cuong, a secretion recovered in minute amounts from beetles in North Vietnam. Owing to war conditions, the price rose to $100 per ounce before supplies virtually ceased.

Candy

The biggest candy eaters in the world are the people of Britain, with 7.8 oz. of confectionery per person per week in 1971. The figure for Scotland alone is more than 9 oz. in 1968.

The world's top-selling candies are Life Savers, with 25,000 million rolls between 1913 and November 14, 1973. The aggregate depth of the "hole in the middle" exceeds 1,000,000 miles. One has been made to last 87 minutes.

Oldest Recipe

The oldest known surviving written recipe is one dated 1657 handed down from Bernice Bardolf of the Black Horse Tavern, Barnsley, Yorkshire, England, found buried in September, 1969, in the yard of the Alhambra Hotel, Barnsley. Barnsley Bardolf, a variant, is now on the menu.

Coffee

The world's greatest coffee drinkers are the people of Sweden, who consumed 29.85 lbs. of coffee per person per year in 1973.

The rarest coffee is Jamaica Blue Mountain, which is sold in only two stores in the U.S. because only 60 bags of it are produced every year.

Tea

The most expensive tea marketed is "Oolong," specially imported by Fortnum and Mason of Piccadilly, London, where in 1974 it retailed for $13 per lb. It is blended from very young Formosan leaves.

The per capita consumption of tea in Britain (114.4 oz. in 1973) has now been exceeded by the people of Ireland (135.1 oz.).

Fresh Water

The world's greatest consumers of fresh water are the people and industrial users of the U.S., whose average consumption was 1,855 gallons per person per day in 1974.

ENERGY

To express the various forms of available energy (coal, liquid fuels and water power, etc., but omitting vegetable fuels and peat), it is the practice to convert them all into terms of coal. On this basis the world average consumption was the equivalent of 4,510 lbs. of coal, or its energy equivalents, per person in 1973. The highest consumption in the world is in the U.S., with an average of 26,312 lbs. per person in 1973. The lowest recorded average for 1972 was 22 lbs. per person in Burundi.

COMMUNICATION AND TRANSPORTATION

Merchant Shipping

The world total of merchant shipping (excluding vessels of less than 100 tons gross, sailing vessels and barges) was 63,724 vessels of 342,162,363 tons gross on July 1, 1975. The largest merchant fleet in the world as at mid-1975 was under the flag of Liberia with 2,520 ships of 65,820,414 tons gross.

Largest and Busiest Ports

Physically, the largest port in the world is New York Harbor. The port has a navigable waterfront of 755 miles (460 miles in New York State and 295 miles in New Jersey) stretching over 92 square miles. A total of 261 general cargo berths and 130 other piers give a total berthing capacity of 391 ships at one time. The total warehousing floor space is 18,400,000 square feet (422.4 acres).

The world's busiest port and largest artificial harbor is the Rotterdam-Europoort in the Netherlands, which covers 38 square miles. It handled 33,296 sea-going vessels and about 300,000 barges in 1974. It is able to handle 310 sea-going vessels simultaneously, up to 250,000 tons and 65 feet draught.

BUSIEST PORT: Rotterdam in the Netherlands is where most of the barges from Europe's network of canals and rivers load onto ocean-going vessels.

Airlines

The country with the busiest airlines system is the U.S., where 162,917,214,000 revenue passenger miles were flown on scheduled services in 1974. This was equivalent to an annual trip of 770.6 miles for every inhabitant of the U.S.

Railroads

The country with the greatest length of railroad is the U.S., with 201,067 miles of track on January 1, 1974.

Highest Speed

The official air speed record is 2,070.102 m.p.h. by Col. Robert L. Stephens and Lt.-Col. Daniel André (U.S.) in a Lockheed YF-12A over Edwards Air Force Base, California, on May 1, 1965, over a 9–15 mile course.

The fastest fixed-wing aircraft in the world was a North American Aviation X-15A-2, which flew for the first time (after modification) on June 28, 1964, powered by a liquid oxygen and ammonia rocket propulsion system. Ablative materials on the airframe enabled a temperature of 3,000°F. to be withstood. The landing speed was 210 knots (242 m.p.h.) momentarily. The highest speed attained was 4,534 m.p.h. (Mach 6.72) when piloted by Major William J. Knight, U.S.A.F. (b. 1930) on October 3, 1967. An earlier version piloted by Joseph A. Walker (1920–66) reached 354,200 feet (67.08 miles) also over Edwards Air Force Base, California, on August 22, 1963. The program was suspended after the final flight of October 24, 1968.

The U.S. Air Force Lifting Body X-24B is expected to reach supersonic speeds between Mach 5 and Mach 10.

PROGRESSIVE FIXED-WING AIRCRAFT SPEED RECORDS

m.p.h.	Mach No.	Pilot	Date
2,111	3.19	J. A. Walker	May 12, 1960
2,196	3.31	J. A. Walker	Aug. 4, 1960
2,275	3.50	R. M. White	Feb. 7, 1961
2,905	4.43	R. M. White	Mar. 7, 1961
3,074	4.62	R. M. White	Apr. 21, 1961
3,300	4.90	J. A. Walker	May 25, 1961
3,603	5.27	R. M. White	June 23, 1961
3,614	5.25	J. A. Walker	Sept. 12, 1961
3,620	5.30	F. S. Petersen	Sept. 28, 1961
3,647	5.21	R. M. White	Oct. 11, 1961
3,900	5.74	J. A. Walker	Oct. 17, 1961
4,093	6.04	R. M. White	Nov. 9, 1961
4,104	>6.06	J. A. Walker	June 27, 1962
4,250	6.33	W. J. Knight	Nov. 18, 1966
4,534	6.72	W. J. Knight	Oct. 3, 1967

> more than

Fastest Jet. The world's fastest jet aircraft is the Lockheed SR-71 reconnaissance aircraft (a variant of the YF-12A, above) which first flew on December 22, 1964, and is reportedly capable of attaining a speed of 2,200 m.p.h. and an altitude ceiling of close to 100,000 feet. The SR-71 has a span of 55.6 feet and a length of 107.4 feet and weighs 170,000 lbs. at takeoff. Its reported range is 2,982 miles at Mach 3 at 78,750 feet. Only 27 are believed to have been built and 9 had been lost by April, 1969.

The fastest Soviet jet aircraft in service is the Mikoyan MIG-25 *alias* E-266 fighter (code name "Foxbat") with a speed of Mach 3.2 (2,110 m.p.h.). It is armed with air-to-air missiles known to N.A.T.O. as "Acrid."

Fastest Biplane. The fastest recorded biplane was the Italian Fiat C.R.42B, with 1,010-h.p. Daimler-Benz DB601A engine, which attained 323 m.p.h. in 1941. Only one was built.

Fastest Piston-Engined Aircraft. The fastest speed at which a piston-engined plane has ever been measured was for a cut-down privately owned Hawker *Sea Fury* which attained 520 m.p.h. in level flight over Texas in August, 1966, piloted by Mike Carroll (d. 1969) of Los Angeles. The official record is 482.462 m.p.h. over Edwards Air Force Base, California, by Darryl C. Greenamyer, 33, in a Grumman F8F-2 Bearcat on August 16, 1969.

Fastest Propeller-Driven Aircraft. The Soviet Tu-114 turbo-prop transport is the world's fastest propeller-driven airplane. It has achieved average speeds of more than 545 m.p.h. carrying heavy payloads over measured circuits. It is developed from the Tupolev Tu-95 bomber, known in the West as the "Bear," and has 14,795-horsepower engines. The Republic XF-84H prototype U.S. Navy fighter which flew on July 22, 1955, had a top design speed of 670 m.p.h., but was abandoned.

Largest Propeller

The largest aircraft propeller ever used was the 22-foot 7½-inch diameter Garuda propeller, fitted to the Linke-Hofmann R II built in Breslau, Germany, which flew in 1919. It was driven by four 260-h.p. Mercedes engines and turned at only 545 r.p.m.

PROGRESSIVE FIXED-WING AIRCRAFT ALTITUDE RECORDS

Feet	Miles	Pilot	Date
136,500	25.85	R. M. White	Aug. 12, 1960
169,600	32.13	J. A. Walker	Mar. 30, 1961
217,000	41.11	R. M. White	Oct. 11, 1961
246,700	46.72	J. A. Walker	Apr. 30, 1962
246,700	46.72	R. M. White	June 21, 1962
314,750	59.61	R. M. White	July 17, 1962
347,000	65.88	J. A. Walker	July 19, 1963
354,200	67.08	J. A. Walker	Aug. 22, 1963

Greatest Altitude

The official altitude record by an aircraft which took off from the ground under its own power is 118,897 feet (22½ miles) by Aleksandr Fedotov (U.S.S.R.) in a Mikoyan E-266 (MIG-25) aircraft, powered by two 24,250-lb. turbojet engines on July 25, 1973.

The greatest recorded height by any pilot without a pressure cabin or even a pressure suit has been 49,500 feet by British Squadron Leader G. W. H. Reynolds, D.F.C., in a Spitfire Mark 5C over Libya in 1942.

Flight Duration

The flight duration record is 64 days, 22 hours, 19 minutes and 5 seconds, set by Robert Timm and John Cook in a Cessna 172 "Hacienda." They took off from McCarran Airfield, Las Vegas, Nevada, just before 3:53 p.m. local time on December 4, 1958, and landed at the same airfield just before 2:12 p.m. on February 7, 1959. They covered a distance equivalent to six times around the world with continued refueling without landing.

1970. She spent $720 on driving lessons and could no longer afford to buy a car.

Most Durable Driving Examiner

Vincent W. Jones (1913–75) of the California Department of Motor Vehicles, gave a lifetime total of more than 134,140 driving tests. He met his death when his examinee, a 23-year-old female, hit a bus.

Telephones

There were an estimated 358,590,000 telephones in the world at January 1, 1975, it was estimated by the American Telephone and Telegraph Co. The country with the greatest number was the U.S., with 143,972,000 instruments, equivalent to 676.5 for every 1,000 people. The territory with fewest is Pitcairn Island with 29.

The country with the most telephones per head of population is Monaco, with 824.5 per 1,000 of the population at January 1, 1975. The country with the least was Bhutan with 0.5 of a telephone per 1,000 people.

The greatest total of calls made in any country is in the U.S., with 200,011 million (940 calls per year per person) in 1974.

The city with most telephones is New York City, with 5,913,942 (769 per 1,000 people) at January 1, 1975. In 1974, Washington, D.C., reached the level of 1,358 telephones per 1,000 people, though in some small areas there are still higher densities, such as Beverly Hills, part of Los Angeles, with about 1,600 per 1,000.

Busiest Phone. The pay phone with the heaviest usage in the world is one in the Greyhound bus terminal in Chicago, which averages 270 calls a day, and is thus used each 5 minutes 20 seconds around the clock all year.

Longest Call. The longest telephone connection on record was one of 1,000 hours from March 12 to April 23, 1975, on the campus of Western Michigan University, Kalamazoo, Michigan. Students worked one-hour shifts for the 41½ days, raising funds for a unit in a medical center that is used to treat burns.

Longest Cable. The world's longest submarine telephone cable is the Commonwealth Pacific Cable (COMPAC), which runs for more than 9,000 miles from Australia *via* Auckland, New Zealand, and the Hawaiian Islands to Port Alberni, Canada. It cost about $98,000,000 and was inaugurated on December 2, 1963.

Largest Incorrect Bill. On August 18, 1975, the landlord of the Blue Bell Inn, Lichfield, Staffordshire, England, received a telephone bill for $4,386,800,000. It was later found that this bill contained "an arithmetical error."

Postal Services

The country with the largest mail in the world is the U.S., whose people posted 901,000 million letters and packages in 1974. The U.S. Postal Services then employed 710,000 people.

The U.S. also takes first place in the average number of letters which each person posts during one year. The figure was 413 in 1971. Of all countries, the greatest discrepancy between incoming and outgoing mails is for the U.S. where, in 1970, only 887 million items were mailed abroad in comparison with 1,477 million items received from foreign sources.

Postage Stamps

Earliest. The earliest adhesive postage stamps ever issued were the "Penny Blacks" of the United Kingdom, bearing the head of Queen Victoria, placed on sale on May 1 for use on May 6, 1840. A total of 68,158,080 were printed. The British National Postal Museum possesses a unique full proof sheet of 240 stamps, printed in April, 1840, before the corner letters, plate numbers or marginal inscriptions were added.

Largest. The largest stamps ever issued were the 1913 Express Delivery stamps of China, which measured $9\frac{3}{4}$ inches by $2\frac{3}{4}$ inches. The largest postage stamp ever printed was the 8 RLS (royal) airmail stamp issued by the former Trucial State of Fujeira (Fujairah) measuring $2\frac{5}{8} \times 4\frac{1}{8}$ inches on April 5, 1972 for the 1972 Olympic Games. The Universal Postage Union does not regard this issue as bona fide postal stamps.

Smallest. The smallest stamps ever issued were the 10 cents and 1 peso of the Colombian State of Bolívar in 1863–66. They measured 0.31 of an inch (8 mm.) by 0.37 of an inch (9.5 mm.).

The imperforate 4/4 schilling red of Mecklenburg-Schwerin issued on July 1, 1856, printed in Berlin, was divisible into four quarters. Thus a 1/4 section measured fractionally over 0.394 of an inch (10 mm.) square.

Highest and Lowest Denominations. The highest denomination stamp ever issued was a red and black stamp for £100 ($280) issued in Kenya in 1925–27. Although valid for postage, it was essentially for collection of revenue.

Owing to demonetization and inflation it is difficult to determine

HIGHEST
DENOMINATION
STAMP: Red and Black,
this can be used for postage
but is mostly for revenue.

MOST VALUABLE STAMP: Only a single specimen exists today and it is worth about $300,000.

the lowest denomination stamp but it was probably the 1946 3000 pengö Hungarian stamp, worth at the time 1.6×10^{-14} parts of a cent.

Largest Collection. The greatest private stamp collection ever auctioned was that of Maurice Burrus (died 1959) of Alsace, France, which realized between $3,250,000 and $4,000,000. He himself valued the collection at $10,000,000.

The largest national collection in the world is that at the British Museum, London, which has had the General Post Office collection on permanent loan since March, 1963. The British Royal collection, housed in 400 volumes, is also believed to be worth well in excess of £1,000,000 ($2,500,000). The collection of the Universal Postal Union (founded October 9, 1874) in Berne, Switzerland, started in 1878, has received 155,000 issued stamps and 2,400 miniature sheets, all of them different, from its member nations. The largest international collection open to the public is in the Swiss Postal Museum in Berne.

Most Valuable. There are a number of stamps of which but a single specimen is known. Of these the most celebrated is the one cent black on magenta issued in British Guiana (now Guyana) in February, 1856. It was originally bought for 84 cents (6/–) from L. Vernon Vaughan, a schoolboy, in 1873. This is the world's most renowned stamp, for which £A16,000/$35,768 was paid in 1940, when it was sold by Mrs. Arthur Hind. It was insured for £200,000 ($560,000) when it was displayed in 1965 at the Royal Festival Hall, London. It was sold on March 24, 1970, by auction in New York City for $280,000 by Irwin Weinberg. It is now catalogued at £120,000 ($300,000). It was alleged in October, 1938, that Hind had, in 1928, purchased and burned his stamp's twin.

The rarest British stamp which is not an error is the King Edward VII 6-pence dull purple Inland Revenue official stamp issued and withdrawn on May 14, 1904. Only 11 or 12 are known, and the only unused example in private hands was auctioned at Stanley Gibbons, London, on October 27, 1972, for £10,000 ($25,000) and reputedly resold in a private transaction in Germany in 1975 for £15,000 ($34,500).

Highest Price. The highest price ever paid for a single philatelic item is $380,000 for two 1-penny orange "Post Office" Mauritius stamps of 1847 on a cover bought at H. R. Harmer's Inc., New York City, by Raymond H. Weill, Co. of New Orleans, for their own account from the Lichtenstein-Dale collection on October 21, 1968. The item was discovered in 1897 in an Indian bazaar by a Mr. Charles Williams who paid less than $5 for it.

Postal Addresses

Earliest Numbering. The practice of numbering houses began in 1463 on the Pont Notre Dame, Paris, France.

Post Boxes. Pillar boxes were introduced at the suggestion of the English novelist Anthony Trollope (1815–82). The oldest original site still in service is one dating from February 8, 1853, at Union Street, St. Peter Port, Guernsey, Channel Islands. The present box is not the original.

Telegrams

The country where most telegrams are sent is the U.S.S.R., whose population sent about 404,918,000 telegrams in 1973.

Inland Waterways

The country with the greatest length of inland waterways is Finland. The total length of navigable lakes and rivers is about 31,000 miles.

Longest Navigable River. The longest navigable natural waterway in the world is the Amazon River, which sea-going vessels can ascend as far as Iquitos, in Peru, 2,236 miles from the Atlantic seaboard.

On a National Geographic Society expedition ending on March 10, 1969, Helen and Frank Schreider navigated downstream from San Francisco, Peru, 3,845 miles up the Amazon, by a balsa raft named *Mamuri*, 249 miles to Atalaya, then 356 miles to Pucallpa by outboard motor dug-out canoe, and then the last 3,240 miles towards Belém in the 30-foot gasoline-engined cabin cruiser, *Amazon Queen*.

5. Education

Illiteracy

Literacy is variously defined as "ability to read simple subjects" and "ability to read and write a simple letter." The looseness of definition and the scarcity of data for many countries preclude anything more than approximations, but the extent of illiteracy among adults (15 years old and over) is estimated to have been 34.7 per cent in 1969.

The continent with the greatest proportion of illiterates is Africa, where 81.5 per cent of adults were illiterate. The last published figure for Mali in 1960 showed 97.8 per cent of people over 15 were unable to read.

University

Oldest. Probably the oldest educational institution in the world is the University of Karueein, founded in 859 A.D. in Fez, Morocco. The European university with the earliest date of foundation is that of the University of Oxford, which came into being in c. 1167.

Greatest Enrollment. The university with the greatest enrollment in the world is the City University of New York, with 271,930 students and 17,542 appointed teachers in 1975. It was founded in 1847 and has ten colleges. In May, 1976, it ran into an economic crisis.

Largest Building. The largest university building in the world is the M. V. Lomonosov State University on the Lenin Hills, south of Moscow, U.S.S.R. It stands 787.4 feet tall, has 32 stories and contains 40,000 rooms. It was constructed in 1949–53.

Professors

Youngest. The youngest at which anybody has been elected to a chair (full professorship) in a major university is 19, in the case of Colin MacLaurin (1698–1746), who was admitted to Marischal College, Aberdeen, Scotland, as Professor of Mathematics on September 30, 1717. In 1725 he was made Professor of Mathematics at Edinburgh University on the recommendation of Sir Isaac Newton.

In July, 1967, Dr. Harvey Friedman, Ph.D., was appointed Assistant Professor of Mathematics at Stanford University, California, when aged just 19 years.

Most Durable. The longest period for which any professorship has been held is 63 years in the case of Thomas Martyn (1735–1825), Professor of Botany at Cambridge University, England, from 1762 until his death. His father, John Martyn (1699–1768), had occupied the chair from 1733 to 1762.

Youngest Undergraduate

The most extreme recorded case of academic juvenility was that of William Thomson (1824–1907), later Lord Kelvin, who entered Glasgow University aged 10 years 4 months in October, 1834, and matriculated on November 14, 1834.

Dr. Merrill Kenneth Wolf (born August 28, 1931) of Cleveland, Ohio, took his B.A. in music from Yale University in September, 1945, aged 14 years.

Schools

Largest. The largest school in the world was the De Witt Clinton High School in the Bronx, New York City, where the enrollment attained a peak of 12,000 in 1934. It was founded in 1897 and now has an enrollment of 6,000.

Most Expensive. The most expensive school in the world is the Oxford Academy (established 1906) in Pleasantville, New Jersey. It is a private college-preparatory boarding school for boys with "academic deficiencies." The school has 15 masters and each of the 47 boys is taught individually in each course. The tuition fee for the school year is $9,600.

Most Schools Attended

The documented record for the greatest number of schools attended by a pupil is 265 by Wilma Williams, now Mrs. R. J. Horton, from 1933 to 1943 when her parents were in show business in the U.S.

Lecture Agency

The world's largest lecture agency is the American Program Bureau of Boston with 400 personalities on 40 topics and a turnover of some $5,000,000. The top rate is $4,000 per hour commanded by Ralph Nader, equivalent to $66.66 per minute.

6. Religions

Largest. Religious statistics are necessarily the roughest approximate. The test of adherence to a religion varies widely in rigor, while many individuals, particularly in China and Japan, belong to two or more religions.

Christianity is the world's prevailing religion, with over 1,025 million adherents in 1975. The Vatican computer reported that for 1971 there were 665,700,000 Roman Catholics including priests and nuns. The largest non-Christian religions are Islam (Muslim) and Hindu, with about 535,000,000 followers each.

Largest Clergy. The world's largest religious organization is the Roman Catholic Church, with 664,388,000 active members, 425,000 priests and 900,000 nuns. The total number of cardinals, patriarchs, metropolitans, archbishops, bishops, abbots and superiors is 4,000. There are about 420,000 churches.

The total number holding Aaronic and Melchizek priesthood in the Church of Latter Day Saints (Mormon Church) on January 1, 1976 was 873,793.

Jews. The total of world Jewry was estimated to be 14,600,000 in 1975. The highest concentration was in the U.S., with 5,900,000

LARGEST RELIGIOUS BUILDING: Angkor Wat in Cambodia (now called Khmers), built in the 12th century, covers 402 acres.

of whom 1,870,000 were in New York City. The total in Israel was 3,450,000, in Britain 460,000 (of whom 285,000 are in Greater London). The total in Tokyo, Japan, is less than 1,000.

Earliest Shrine

The earliest known shrine dates from the proto-neolithic Natufian culture in Jericho, where a site on virgin soil has been dated to the 9th millennium B.C. A simple rectilinear red-plastered room with a niche housing a stone pillar, believed to be the shrine of a pre-pottery fertility cult dating from *c.* 6500 B.C., was also uncovered in Jericho (also called Ariha) in Israeli-occupied West Bank of Jordan. The oldest surviving Christian church in the world is Qal 'at es Salihige in eastern Syria, dating from 232 A.D.

Largest Temple. The largest religious building ever constructed is Angkor Wat (City Temple), covering 402 acres, in Cambodia, now Khmers. It was built to the God Vishnu by the Khmer King Suryavarman II in the period 1113–1150. Its curtain wall measures 1,400 yards by 1,400 yards and its population, before it was abandoned in 1432, was at times 80,000.

The largest Buddhist temple is Borobudur, near Joyjakarta, Indonesia, built in the 8th century.

Largest Mosque. The largest mosque ever built was the now ruined al-Malawiya mosque of al-Mutawakil in Samarra, Iraq, built in 842–852 A.D. and measuring 401,408 square feet (9.21 acres) with dimensions of 784 feet by 512 feet.

The world's largest mosque in use is the Jama Masjid (1644–58) in Delhi, India, with an area of more than 10,000 square feet and two 108-foot-tall minarets.

The largest mosque will be the Merdeka Mosque in Djakarta, Indonesia, which was begun in 1962. The cupola will be 147.6 feet in diameter and the capacity in excess of 50,000 people.

Largest Synagogue. The largest synagogue in the world is the Temple Emanu-El on Fifth Avenue at 65th Street, New York City. The temple, completed in September, 1929, has a frontage of 150 feet on Fifth Avenue and 253 feet on 65th Street. The sanctuary proper can accommodate 2,500 people, and the adjoining Beth-El Chapel seats 350. When all the facilities are in use, more than 6,000 people can be accommodated.

Cathedrals

Largest. The world's largest cathedral is the cathedral church of the Episcopalian Diocese of New York, St. John the Divine, with a floor area of 121,000 square feet and a volume of 16,822,000 cubic feet. The cornerstone was laid on December 27, 1892, and the Gothic building was still uncompleted in 1976. In New York it is referred to as "Saint John the Unfinished." The nave is the longest in the world, 601 feet in length, with a vaulting 124 feet in height.

The cathedral covering the largest area is that of Santa María de la Sede in Seville, Spain. It was built in Spanish Gothic style between 1402 and 1519 and is 414 feet long, 271 feet wide and 100 feet high to the vault of the nave. (See photo on next page.)

See also *Largest Church,* below.

HIGHEST CHURCH SPIRE (left) is on the Sky Chapel of the First Methodist Church on Clark St., Chicago, which rises 568 feet above street level. LARGEST CATHEDRAL (above): Santa Maria de la Sede in Seville, Spain, covers the largest area of any cathedral in the world.

Smallest. The smallest cathedral in the world is the Pro-Cathedral Church of St. John the Baptist, Murray Bridge, South Australia. It was dedicated on February 2, 1887, and has had the cathedra of the Bishop of the Murray since April 16, 1970. It measures 1,025 square feet and has a capacity of only 130.

Churches

Largest. The largest church in the world is the basilica of St. Peter, built between 1492 and 1612 in the Vatican City, Rome. Its length, measured from the apse, is 611 feet 4 inches. Its area is 18,110 square yards. The inner diameter of the famous dome is 137 feet 9 inches and its center is 390 feet 5 inches high. The external height is 457 feet 9 inches.

The elliptical Basilique of St. Pie X at Lourdes, France, completed in 1957 at a cost of $5,600,000, has a capacity of 20,000 under its giant span arches and a length of 659 feet.

The crypt of the underground Civil War Memorial Church in the Guadarrama Mountains, 28 miles from Madrid, Spain, is 853 feet in length. It took 21 years (1937–58) to build, at a reported cost of $392,000,000 and is surmounted by a cross 492 feet tall.

Smallest. The world's smallest church is the Union Church at Wiscasset, Maine, with a floor area of $31\frac{1}{2}$ square feet (7 feet by $4\frac{1}{2}$ feet). Les Vauxbalets Church in Guernsey, Channel Islands, has an area of 16 feet by 12 feet, room for one priest and a congregation of two.

Tallest Spires. The tallest cathedral spire in the world is that of the Protestant Cathedral of Ulm in Germany. The building is early Gothic and was begun in 1377. The tower, in the center of the west façade, was not finally completed until 1890 and is 528 feet high.

The world's tallest church spire is that of the Chicago Temple of the First Methodist Church on Clark Street, Chicago. The building consists of a 22-story skyscraper (erected in 1924) surmounted by a parsonage at 330 feet, a "Sky Chapel" at 400 feet and a steeple cross at 568 feet above street level.

Tallest Minaret. The world's tallest minaret is the Qutb Minar, south of New Delhi, India, built in 1194 to a height of 238 feet.

Tallest Pagoda. The world's tallest pagoda is the 326-foot-tall Shwe Dogon Pagoda in Rangoon, Burma, which was increased to its present height by Hsinbyushin, King of Ava (1763–1776). The tallest Chinese temple is the 13-story Pagoda of the Six Harmonies

(*Liu he t'a*) outside Hang-chow. It is "nearly 200 feet high." (See color photograph on color page F.)

Saints

There are 1,848 "registered" Saints, of whom 628 are Italians, 576 French and 271 from the British Isles. The total includes 15 Popes. The first U.S.-born saint is Mother Elizabeth Ann Bayley Seton (1774–1821) who was canonized on September 14, 1975.

Most and Least Rapidly Canonized. The shortest interval that has elapsed between the death of a Saint and his canonization was in the case of St. Anthony of Padua, Italy, who died on June 13, 1251, and was canonized 352 days later on May 30, 1252.

The other extreme is represented by St. Bernard of Thiron, for 20 years Prior of St. Sabinus, who died in 1117 and was made a Saint in 1861—744 years later. The Italian monk and painter, Fra Giovanni da Fiesole (*né* Guido di Pietro), called *Il Beato* ("The Blessed") Fra Angelico (*c.* 1400–1455), is still in the first stage of canonization.

Popes

Longest Reign. The longest reign of any of the 262 Popes has been that of Pius IX (Giovanni Maria Mastai-Ferretti), who reigned for 31 years 236 days from June 16, 1846, until his death, aged 85, on February 7, 1878.

Shortest Reign. Pope Stephen II was elected on March 24, 752, and died two days later.

Oldest. It is recorded that Pope St. Agatho (reigned 678–681) was elected at the age of 103 and lived to 106, but recent scholars have expressed doubts. The oldest of recent Pontiffs has been Pope Leo XIII (Gioacchino Pecci), who was born on March 2, 1810, elected Pope at the third ballot on February 20, 1878, and died on July 20, 1903, aged 93 years 140 days.

Youngest. The youngest of all Popes was Pope Benedict IX (Theophylact), who had three terms as Pope: in 1032–44; April to May, 1045; and November 8, 1047 to July 17, 1048. It would appear that he was aged only 11 or 12 in 1032, though the Catalogue of the Popes admits only to his "extreme youth." He died in 1056.

Last Married. The last married Pope was Adrian II (867–872). Rodrigo Borgia was the father of at least four children before being elected Pope Alexander VI in 1492. The first 37 Popes had no specific obligation to celibacy. Pope Hormisdas (514–523) was the father of Pope Silverius (536–537).

Last Non-Italian Pope. The last non-Italian Pope was the Utrecht-born Cardinal Priest Adrian Dedel (1459–1523) of the Netherlands. He was elected on January 9, 1522, crowned Pope Adrian VI on August 31, 1522, and died on September 14, 1523.

Last Non-Cardinalate Pope. The last Pope elected from outside the College of Cardinals was Bartolomeo Prignano (1318–89), Archbishop of Bari, who was elected Pope Urban VI on April 8, 1378.

Slowest and Quickest Election. After 31 months without declaring "We have a Pope," the cardinals were subjected to a bread and water diet and the removal of the roof of their conclave by the Mayor of Viterbo before electing Tabaldo Visconti (*c.* 1210–76), the Archbishop of Liege, as Pope Gregory X at Viterbo, near Rome, on September 1, 1271. The papacy was, however, vacant for at least 3 years 214 days in 304–308.

The shortest conclave was that of October 21, 1503, for the election of Pope Julius II on the first ballot.

Cardinals

Oldest. On February 2, 1973, the College of Cardinals contained a record 145 declared members—compared with 138 in June, 1976. The oldest is 96-year-old Cardinal José da Costa Nuñes (b. Cardelaria, Portugal, March 15, 1880). The record length of service of any Cardinal has been 60 years 10 days by the Cardinal York, a grandson of James VII of Scotland and II of England, from July 3, 1747, to July 13, 1807. The oldest Cardinal of all time was probably Giorgio da Costa (born Portugal, 1406) who died in Rome on September 18, 1508, aged 102.

Youngest. The youngest Cardinal of all time was Luis Antonio de Borbon (born July 25, 1727), created on December 19, 1735, aged 8 years 147 days. His son Luis was also made a Cardinal, but at age 23.

The youngest Cardinal today is Emile Biayenda, Archbishop of Brazzaville, who was born in 1927. Antonio Ribiero, patriarch of Lisbon, Portugal, was named on February 2, 1973, aged 45.

Bishops

Oldest. The oldest Roman Catholic bishop in recent years was Mgr. Alfonso Carinci (born November 9, 1862), who was titular Archbishop of Seleucia, in Isauria, from 1945 until his death on December 6, 1963, at the age of 101 years 27 days. He had celebrated Mass about 24,800 times.

Bishop Herbert Welch of the United Methodist Church who was elected a bishop for Japan and Korea in 1916 died on April 4, 1969, aged 106.

Youngest. The youngest bishop of all time was H.R.H. The Duke of York and Albany, the second son of King George III of England, who was elected Bishop of Osnabrück through his father's influence as Elector of Hanover, at the age of 196 days (less than 7 months old) on February 27, 1764. He resigned after 39 years enjoyment.

Church Attendance

The most extreme recorded case of perfect Sunday School Church attendance is that of Roland E. Daab, currently the Vice President of the Consistory of St. Paul United Church of Christ, Columbia, Illinois, who on May 23, 1976, attended service on his 3,000th consecutive Sunday, an unbroken period of more than 57 years.

Stained Glass

Oldest. The oldest stained glass in the world represents the Prophets in a window of the cathedral of Augsburg, Bavaria, Germany, dating from *c.* 1050.

Largest. The largest stained glass window is the complete mural of The Resurrection Mausoleum, Justice, Illinois, measuring 22,381 square feet in 2,448 panels completed in 1971.

Monumental Brasses

The world's oldest monumental brass is that commemorating Bishop Ysowilpe in St. Andrew's Church, Verden, near Hanover, West Germany, dating from 1231.

Largest Crowd

The greatest recorded number of human beings assembled with a common purpose was more than 5,000,000 at the 21-day Hindu feast of Kumbh-Mela, which is held every 12 years at the confluence of the Yamuna (formerly called the Jumna), the Ganges and the invisible "Sarasviti" at Allahabad, Uttar Pradesh, India, on January 21, 1966. According to the Jacobs' Formula for estimating the size of crowds, the allowance of area per person varies from 4 square feet (tight) to $9\frac{1}{2}$ square feet (loose). Thus, such a crowd must have occupied an area of more than 700 acres.

Largest Funeral

The greatest attendance at any funeral is the estimated 4 million who thronged Cairo, Egypt (United Arab Republic), for the funeral of President Gamal Abdel Nasser (b. January 15, 1918) on October 1, 1970.

LARGEST FUNERAL: An estimated 4,000,000 people attended the ceremony when President Nasser of Egypt died in Cairo in 1970.

Biggest Demonstrations

A figure of 2,700,000 was published from China for the demonstration against the U.S.S.R. in Shanghai on April 3–4, 1969, following border clashes, and one of 10 million for the May Day celebrations of 1963 in Peking.

WORST ACCIDENTS AND DISASTERS IN THE WORLD

	Deaths		
Pandemic	75,000,000	The Black Death (bubonic, pneumonic and septicaemic plague)	1347–51
	21,640,000	Influenza	April–Nov. 1918
Famine	9,500,000[1]	Northern China Feb. 1877–Sept. 1878	
Flood	3,700,000	Yellow (Hwang-ho) River, China	Aug. 1931
Circular Storm	>1,000,000*	Ganges Delta islands, Bangladesh	Nov. 13–14, 1970
Earthquake	830,000	Shensi Province, China Jan. 23, 1556	
Landslide	200,000	Kansu Province, China Dec. 16, 1920	
Conventional Bombing[2]	135,000	Dresden, Germany Feb. 13–15, 1945	
Atomic Bomb	91,223[3]	Hiroshima, Japan	Aug. 6, 1945
Marine (single ship)	c. 7,700	*Wilhelm Gustloff* (25,484 tons) torpedoed off Danzig by U.S.S.R. submarine S-13	Jan. 30, 1945
Snow Avalanche	c. 5,000[7]	Huaras, Peru	Dec. 13, 1941
Panic	c. 4,000	Chungking, China (air raid shelter)	c. June 8, 1941
Dam Burst	2,209	Johnstown, Pennsylvania (South Fork dam)	May 31, 1889
Explosion	1,963[5]	Halifax, Nova Scotia, Canada	Dec. 6, 1917
Fire[4] (single building)	1,670	The Theatre, Canton, China May, 1845	
Mining[6]	1,572	Honkeiko Colliery, Manchuria, China (coal dust explosion)	April 26, 1942
Riot	c. 1,200	New York City (anti-conscription riots) July 13–16, 1863	

* The figure published in 1972 of 1,000,000 was from Dr. Afzal, Principal Scientific Officer of the Atomic Energy Authority Centre, Dacca. One report asserted that less than half of the population of the 4 islands of Bhola, Charjabbar, Hatia and Ramagati (1961 Census 1.4 million) survived.

The most damaging hurricane recorded was the billion dollar Betsy (name now retired) in 1965 with an estimated insurance pay-out of $750 million.

WORST ROAD ACCIDENT: 127 people died when this bus plunged into an Egyptian canal in August, 1973.

Fireworks	>800	Dauphine's wedding, Seine, Paris	May 16, 1770
Tornado	689	South Central States, U.S.	Mar. 18, 1925
Railroad	543[8]	Modane, France	Dec. 12, 1917
Man-Eating Animal	436[9]	Champawat district, India, tigress shot by Col. Jim Corbett	1907
Hail	246	Moradabad, Uttar Pradesh, India	April 30, 1888
Aircraft (Civil)	346	Turkish Airlines DC-10, Ermenonville Forest, outside Paris, France	March 3, 1974
Submarine	129	U.S.S. *Thresher* off Cape Cod, Mass.	April 10, 1963
Road[10] (Single Vehicle)	127	A bus plunged into a canal at Sayyoum, Egypt	August 9, 1973
Mountaineering	40[11]	U.S.S.R. Expedition on Mount Everest	Dec., 1952
Ski Lift (Cablecar)	42	Cavalese resort, Northern Italy	March 9, 1976
Lightning (Single Bolt)	21	Hut in Chinamasa Kraal near Umtali, Rhodesia	Dec. 23, 1975

Space   3   Apollo oxygen fire, Cape
                                  Kennedy, Fla.   Jan. 27, 1967

                             3   Soyuz II re-entry over
                                  U.S.S.R.   June 29, 1971

Notes.   1.—In 1770 the great Indian famine carried away a proportion of the popu-
            lation estimated as high as one third, hence a figure of tens of millions.
            The figure for Bengal alone was probably about 10 million.
            It has been estimated that more than 5,000,000 died in the post-
            World War I famine, in the U.S.S.R. The U.S.S.R. government in
            July, 1923, informed Mr. (later President) Herbert Hoover that the
            A.R.A. (American Relief Administration) had since August, 1921,
            saved 20,000,000 lives from famine and famine diseases.

         2.—The number of civilians killed by the bombing of Germany has been put
            variously as 593,000 and "over 635,000." A figure of c. 140,000 deaths
            in U.S.A.C. fire raids on Tokyo of May 10, 1945, has been attributed.

         3.—United States Casualty Commission figure in 1960 was 79,400, while the
            Hiroshima Peace Memorial Museum gives a figure of 240,000,
            excluding later deaths.

         4.—The worst ever hotel fire killed 162 at the Hotel Taeyokale, Seoul,
            South Korea, December 25, 1971.

         5.—Some sources maintain that the final death toll was over 3,000.

         6.—The worst gold mining disaster in South Africa was 152 killed due to
            flooding in the Witwatersrand Gold Mining Co. gold mine in 1909.

         7.—A total of 10,000 Austrian and Italian troops is reputed to have been lost
            in the Dolomite valley of Northern Italy on Dec. 13, 1916, in more
            than 100 avalanches. The total is probably exaggerated though
            bodies were still being found in 1952.

         8.—There were between 500 and 800 dead in the Léon Province train
            disaster on January 16, 1944.

         9.—In the period 1941–42 c. 1,500 Kenyans were killed by a pride of 22 man-
            eating lions. Eighteen of these were shot by a hunter named Rushby.

        10.—The worst year ever for road deaths in the U.S. has been 1969 (about
            56,000). The world's highest death rate is said to be in Queensland,
            Australia, but global statistics are not available. The U.S.'s 2 millionth
            victim since 1899 died in January, 1973. The global total dead by
            September, 1975, was put at 25,000,000.

        11.—According to Polish sources, not confirmed by the U.S.S.R. On Mt.
            Fuji, Japan, 23 died in blizzard and avalanche on March 20, 1972.

PROGRESSIVE ABSOLUTE HUMAN ALTITUDE RECORDS

Feet	Pilot		Place	Date
80	Jean Francois Pilâtre de Rozier (France)	Hot Air Balloon (tethered)	Fauxbourg, Paris	Oct. 15 & 17, 1783
200	J. F. Pilâtre de Rozier (France)	Hot Air Balloon (tethered)	Fauxbourg, Paris	Oct. 19, 1783
250	J. F. Pilâtre de Rozier (France)	Hot Air Balloon (tethered)	Fauxbourg, Paris	Oct. 19, 1783
c. 330	de Rozier and the Marquis Francois Laurent d'Arlandes	Hot Air Balloon (free flight)	La Muette, Paris	Nov. 21, 1783
c. 3,000	Jacques Alexander César Charles and Ainé Robert (France)	Hydrogen Balloon	Tuileries, Paris	Dec. 1, 1783
c. 9,000	J. A. C. Charles (France)	Hydrogen Balloon	Nesles, France	Dec. 1, 1783
c. 20,000	E. G. R. Robertson (U.K.) and Loest (Germany)	Hydrogen Balloon	Hamburg, Germany	July 18, 1803
27,950	H. T. Sivel, J. E. Crocé-Spinelli, Gaston Tissandier	Coal gas Balloon *Zenith*	La Villette, Paris	Apr. 15, 1875
31,500	Prof. A. Berson (Germany)	Hydrogen Balloon *Phoenix*	Strasbourg, France	Dec. 4, 1894
36,565	Sadi Lecointe (France)	Nieuport aircraft	Issy, France	Oct. 30, 1923
43,166	Lt. Apollo Soucek (U.S. Army)	U.S.N. Wright *Apache*	Washington, D.C.	June 4, 1930
51,961	Prof. Auguste Piccard (Switzerland) and Paul Kipfer	*F.N.R.S.* I Balloon	Augsburg, Germany	May 27, 1931
53,139	Piccard and Dr. Max Cosyns (Belgium)	*F.N.R.S.* I Balloon	Dübendorf nr. Zurich	Aug. 18, 1932
72,078[1]	Raul F. Fedoseyenko, A. B. Vasenko and E. D. Ususkin	*Osoaviakhim* Balloon	Moscow	Jan. 30, 1934
72,395	Capts. Orvill Anderson and Albert Stevens (U.S. Army)	U.S. *Explorer* II Helium Balloon	Rapid City, S.D.	Nov. 11, 1935
79,600	William Barton Bridgeman (U.S.)	U.S. Douglas D558-II *Skyrocket*	California	Aug. 15, 1951
83,235	Lt.-Col. Marion Carl, U.S.M.C.	U.S. Douglas D558-II *Skyrocket*	California	Aug. 21, 1953
c.93,000	Major Arthur Murray (U.S.A.F.)	U.S. *Bell X-1A* Rocket Plane	California	1954
126,200	Capt. Iven C. Kincheloe (U.S.A.F.)	U.S. *Bell X-2* Rocket Plane	California	Sept. 7, 1956
136,500	Major Robert M. White (U.S.A.F.)	U.S. X-15 Rocket Plane	California	Aug. 12, 1960
169,600	Joseph A. Walker (U.S.)	U.S. X-15 Rocket Plane	California	Mar. 30, 1961

Miles	Pilot		Place	Date
203.2	Fl. Major Yuriy A. Gagarin (U.S.S.R.)	*Vostok I* capsule	Orbital flight	Apr. 12, 1961
253.5	Col. Vladimir M. Komarov, Lt. Boris B. Yegorov and Konstantin P. Feoktistov (U.S.S.R.)	*Voskhod I* capsule	Orbital flight	Oct. 12, 1964
309.2	Col. Pavel I. Belyayev and Lt.-Col. Aleksey A. Leonov (U.S.S.R.)	*Voskhod II* capsule	Orbital flight	Mar. 18, 1965
474.4	Cdr. John W. Young (U.S.N.) and Major Michael Collins (U.S. Army)	U.S. *Gemini X* capsule	Orbital flight	July 19, 1966
850.7	Cdr. Charles Conrad, Jr., and Lt.-Cdr. Richard F. Gordon, Jr. (U.S. Army)	U.S. *Gemini XI* capsule	Orbital flight	Sept. 14, 1966
234,672	Col. Frank Borman, Capt. James A. Lovell, William A. Anders (U.S.A.F.)	U.S. *Apollo VIII* Command Module	Circum-lunar flight	Dec. 25, 1968
248,433*	Cdr. Eugene A. Cernan (U.S.N.) and Lt.-Col. Thomas P. Stafford (U.S.A.F.)	U.S. *Apollo X* Lunar Module	Circum-lunar flight	May 22, 1969
248,665	Capt. James Arthur Lovell (U.S.N.), John L. Swigert (U.S.N.), and Frederick W. Haise	U.S. *Apollo XIII*	Circum-lunar flight	April 15, 1970

[1] All died on descent. *Note: The moon was 6,150 miles *less* distant at the time of the lunar landing of July 20-21, 1969.

LUNAR CONQUEST:
The greatest human
achievement of the century was
the landing of man on the
moon. This is Col. Edwin Aldrin
stepping down from the lunar
module, as photographed by
Neil Armstrong, fellow
astronaut and the first to land.

Chapter Eleven

HUMAN ACHIEVEMENTS

1. Endurance and Endeavor

Lunar Conquest

Neil Alden Armstrong (born Wapakoneta, Ohio, of Scotch-Irish-German ancestry, on August 5, 1930) command pilot of the Apollo XI mission, became the first man to set foot on the moon on the Sea of Tranquillity at 02:56 and 15 secs. a.m. G.M.T. on July 21, 1969. He was followed out of the Lunar Module *Eagle* by Col. Edwin Eugene Aldrin, Jr. (born Montclair, New Jersey, of Swedish, Dutch and British ancestry, on January 20, 1930), while the Command Module *Columbia* piloted by Lt.-Col. Michael Collins (born Rome, Italy, of Irish and pre-Revolutionary American ancestry, on October 31, 1930) orbited above.

Eagle landed at 20:17 hrs. 42 secs. G.M.T. on July 20 and blasted off at 17:54 G.M.T. on July 21, after a stay of 21 hours 36 minutes. The *Apollo XI* had blasted off from Cape Kennedy, Florida at

13:32 G.M.T. on July 16 and was a culmination of the U.S. space program, which, at its peak, employed 376,600 people and attained in the year 1966–67 a peak budget of $5,900,000,000.

Altitude

Manned Flight. The greatest altitude attained by man was when the crew of the ill-fated *Apollo XIII* were at apocynthion (*i.e.* their furthest point behind the moon) 158 miles above its surface and 248,665 miles above the earth's surface at 1:21 a.m. B.S.T. on April 15, 1970. The crew were Capt. James Arthur Lovell, U.S.N. (b. Denver, Colorado, August 30, 1931); John L. Swigert, Jr., U.S.N. (b. Biloxi, Mississippi, November 14, 1933); and Frederick W. Haise, Jr. (b. Cleveland, Ohio, March 25, 1928).

Woman. The greatest altitude attained by a woman is 143.5 miles by Jr. Lt. (now Lt. Col.) Valentina Vladimirovna Tereshkova-Nikolayev (born March 6, 1937), of the U.S.S.R., during her 48-orbit flight in *Vostok VI* on June 16–19, 1963. The record for a woman in an aircraft is 79,842 feet by Natalya Prokhanova (U.S.S.R.) (b. 1940) in an E-33 jet, on May 22, 1965.

Speed
Space

Man. The fastest speed at which any human has traveled is 24,791 m.p.h. when the Command and Service Module (C.S.M.) of *Apollo X* carrying Col. Thomas P. Stafford, U.S.A.F. (b. Weatherford, Okla., September 17, 1930), and Commanders Eugene Andrew Cernan (b. Chicago, March 14, 1934) and John Watts Young, U.S.N. (b. San Francisco, September 24, 1930) reached their maximum speed on their trans-earth return flight at an altitude of 400,000 feet on May 26, 1969. It was widely but incorrectly reported that the stricken *Apollo XIII* attained the highest recorded speed on its return on April 17, 1970. Its maximum was in fact 24,689.2 m.p.h.

Woman. The highest speed ever attained by a woman is 17,470 m.p.h. by Jr. Lt. (now Lt. Col.) Valentina Vladimirovna Tereshkova-Nikolayev (born March 6, 1937), of the U.S.S.R., during her 48-orbit flight in *Vostok VI* on June 16–19, 1963.

The highest speed ever achieved in an airplane is 1,669.89 m.p.h. by Svetlana Savitskaya (U.S.S.R.), reported on June 2, 1975.

Land

Man. The highest speed ever achieved on land is 650 m.p.h. momentarily during the 627.287-m.p.h. run of *The Blue Flame* driven by Gary Gabelich (b. San Pedro, California, August 29, 1940) on Bonneville Salt Flats, Utah, on October 23, 1970 (see *Mechanical World*). The car built by Reaction Dynamics Inc. of Milwaukee, Wisconsin, is designed to withstand stresses up to 1,000 m.p.h. while the tires have been tested to speeds of 850 m.p.h.

Woman. The highest land speed recorded by a woman is 335.070 m.p.h. by Mrs. Lee Breedlove (*née* Roberts) (born 1937) of Los Angeles, driving her husband's *Spirit of America—Sonic I* on the Bonneville Salt Flats, Utah, on November 3, 1965.

PROGRESSIVE· HUMAN SPEED RECORDS

The progression of the *voluntary* human speed record has been as listed below. It is perhaps noteworthy that the gasoline-engined motor car does not feature in this compilation.

m.p.h.	Vehicle	Date
<25	Running	before 6500 B.C.
>25	Sledging, southern Finland	c. 6500 B.C.
>35	Skiing, Fenno-Scandia	c. 3000 B.C.
>35	Horse riding, Near East	c. 1400 B.C.
<45	Mountain sledding, Hawaii	before 1500 A.D.
<50	Ice Yachts, Netherlands	c. 1550 A.D.
<60	Surfboard riding, Hawaiian Islands	c. 1700 A.D.
56½	*Lucifer* engine, Madeley Bank, Staffordshire, England	Nov. 13, 1839
87.8	Tommy Todd, skier, La Porte, California	March, 1873
89.48	Crompton No. 604 engine, Champigny-Pont sur Yonne, France	June 20, 1890
	(thence 5 further railroad records, 1897–1903)	
130.61	Siemens und Halske electric train, Marienfeld-Zossen, near Berlin	Oct. 27, 1903
c. 150	Frederick C. Marriott in Stanley Steamer automobile at Ormond Beach, Florida.	Jan. 25, 1907
>210	World War I fighters in dives, including Nieuport Nighthawks	1918–19
210.64	Sadi Lecointe (France), Nieuport aircraft	Sept. 26, 1921
	(thence 17 new world air speed records)	
243.94	Brig.-Gen. William Mitchell (U.S. Army) (†1879–1936) Curtis R-6, Detroit	Oct. 18, 1922
270.5	Lt. Alford J. Williams (U.S.N.) Curtis R2 C1, Mitchell Field, L.I., N.Y.	Nov. 4, 1923
274.2	Lt. Harold J. Brow (U.S.N.) Curtis H5-D12, Mitchell Field, L.I., N.Y.	Nov. 4, 1923
486	Flug Kapt. Fritz Wendel (Germany) aircraft, Augsburg	Apr. 26, 1939
c. 525	He 176 test flight, Peenemünde, Germany	July 3, 1939
652.6	Turner F. Caldwell (U.S.) Douglas Skystreak*	Aug. 20, 1947
653.4	Marion E. Carl (U.S.) Douglas Skystreak*	Aug. 25, 1947
670	Capt. Charles E. Yeager (U.S.) Bell XS-1	Oct. 14. 1947
967	Capt. Charles E. Yeager (U.S.) Bell XS-1	1948
1,135	Wm. Bridgeman (U.S.)	May 18, 1951
1,181	Wm. Bridgeman (U.S.)	June 11, 1951
1,221	Wm. Bridgeman (U.S.)	June 23, 1951
1,238	Wm. Bridgeman (U.S.) Douglas Skyrocket	Aug. 7, 1951
1,241	Wm. Bridgeman (U.S.) 558-II	Dec., 1951
1,272	A. Scott Crossfield (U.S.)	Oct. 14, 1953
1,328	A. Scott Crossfield (U.S.)	Nov. 20, 1953
1,612	Maj. Charles Yeager (U.S.) Bell X-1A	Dec. 12, 1953
1,934	Lt.-Col. Frank Everest (U.S.) Bell X-2	July 23, 1956
2,094	Capt. Milburn Apt (U.S.) Bell X-2	Sept. 27, 1956
2,111	Joseph A. Walker, North American X-15	May 12, 1960
2,196	Joseph A. Walker (U.S.) X-15	Aug. 4, 1960
2,275	Major Robert M. White (U.S.) X-15	Feb. 7, 1961
2,905	Major Robert M. White (U.S.) X-15	Mar. 7, 1961
17,560†	Fl. Major Y. A. Gagarin (U.S.S.R.) Vostok I	Apr. 12, 1961
17,558	Cdr. Walter M. Schirra (U.S.N.) Sigma 7	Oct. 3, 1962
17,600†	Komarov, Feoktistov and Yegorov (U.S.S.R.)	Oct. 12–13, 1964
17,750†	Col. Pavel I. Belyayev and Lt.-Col. Aleksey A. Leonov (U.S.S.R.) Voskhod II	Mar. 18–19, 1965
17,943	Cdr. Charles Conrad, Jr., and Lt.-Cdr. Richard F. Gordon, Jr. (U.S.N.) Gemini XI	Sept. 14, 1966
24,226	Col. Frank Borman, Capt. James A. Lovell and William A. Anders (U.S.) Apollo VIII	Dec. 21, 1968
24,752	Same crew on return flight of Apollo VIII	Dec. 27, 1968
24,790.8	Cdrs. Eugene A. Cernan and John W. Young (U.S.N.), Lt.-Col. Thomas P. Stafford (U.S.A.F.), Apollo X	May 26, 1969

N.B.—New research in the U.S. confirms that ice yacht speeds included in earlier editions are exaggerated.

* Average of two flights in opposite directions, hence one flight is faster.

† Plus or minus 20 m.p.h.   > more than   < less than

Water

The highest speed ever achieved on water is 328 m.p.h. by Donald Malcolm Campbell (born March 23, 1921), of the U.K., on his last and fatal run in the turbo-jet-engined 2¼-ton *Bluebird* K7, on Coniston water, Lancashire, England, on January 4, 1967.

The official record is 285.213 m.p.h. (average of two 1-mile runs) by Lee Taylor, Jr. (born 1934) of Downey, California, in the hydroplane *Hustler* on Lake Guntersville, Alabama, on June 30, 1967. He is currently experimenting with his 38-foot, jet-powered *U.S. Discovery*.

The world record for propeller-driven craft is 202.42 m.p.h. by Larry Hill in the supercharged *"Mr. Ed"* at Long Beach, California, in August, 1971. On a one-way run, the *Climax* reached a speed of 205.19 m.p.h.

Most Traveled Man

The man who has visited more countries than anyone is J. Hart Rosdail (born 1914) of Elmhurst, Illinois. Since 1934 he has visited 154 sovereign countries and 67 non-sovereign territories of the world, making a total of 221. He estimates his mileage as 1,482,729 miles by July, 1975. The only sovereign countries which he has not visited are China (People's Republic), Cuba, North Korea, North Vietnam and the French Antarctic Territories.

The most countries visited by a disabled person is 119 by Lester Nixon of Sarasota, Florida, who is confined to a wheelchair.

The Methodist preacher, Francis Asbury of Birmingham, England, traveled 264,000 miles by horseback in North America from 1771 to 1815, preaching 16,000 sermons.

Most Traveled in Space

The most traveled men in history are the third crew of *Skylab 4,* the space station, with 34,469,696 miles.

Fastest Round-the-World Trip

The fastest time for a round-the-world journey on commercial flights for a true circumnavigation is 47 hours 48 minutes (flying time) by Victor Kovens, 29, and Frank Barbehenn, 43, two employees of T.W.A., who passed through the necessary antipodal points near Bangkok, Thailand, and Lima, Peru, in May, 1975.

On May 1–3, 1976, a Pan American World Airways 747 SP, the "Clipper Liberty Bell," carrying 98 passengers and a 15-man cockpit team, flew around the world starting and ending in New York City (23,230.231 miles) in an elapsed time of 46 hours 50 seconds. It required fuel twice, in Delhi, India, and Tokyo, Japan.

According to the F.A.I., any flight taking off and landing at the same point, which is as long as the Tropic of Cancer (22,858.754 miles), is a circumnavigation.

Most Hours Flown

Max Conrad (U.S., b. 1905), between 1928 and mid-1974 totaled 52,929 hours 40 minutes logged flight time—more than 6 years.

Polar Conquests

South Pole. The first ship to cross the Antarctic circle (latitude 66° 30′ S.) was the *Resolution* (517 tons), under Capt. James Cook (1728–79), the English navigator, on January 17, 1773.

The first person to sight the Antarctic *mainland*—on the best available evidence and against claims made for British and Russian explorers—was Nathaniel Brown Palmer (U.S.) (1799–1877). On November 17, 1820, he sighted the Orleans Channel coast of the Palmer Peninsula from his 45-ton sloop *Hero*.

The South Pole was first reached on December 14, 1911, by a Norwegian party, led by Roald Amundsen (1872–1928), after a 53-day march with dog sleds from the Bay of Whales, to which he had penetrated in the *Fram*. Olav Bjaaland, the first to arrive, was the last survivor, dying in June, 1961, aged 88. The others were the late Helmer Hanssen, Sverre Hassel and Oskar Wisting.

SOUTH POLE CONQUERED: Helmer Hanssen was one of the Norwegians led by Roald Amundsen who first reached the South Pole in 1911.

MARINE CIRCUMNAVIGATION RECORDS (Compiled by Sq. Ldr. D. H. Clarke)

A true circumnavigation entails passing through two antipodal points (which are at least 12,429 statute miles apart).

CATEGORY	VESSEL	NAME	START	FINISH
Earliest	*Vittoria* Expedition of Ferzao de Magalhaes (Magellan) c. 1480–1521	Juan Sebastian de Eleano (d. 1526) and 17 crew	Seville, Spain Sept. 20, 1519	San Lucur, Spain Sept. 6, 1521, 30,700 miles
Earliest British	*Golden Hind* (ex *Pelican*) 100 tons	Francis Drake (c. 1540–1596) (Knighted April 4, 1581)	Plymouth, England, Dec. 13, 1577	Sept. 26, 1580
Earliest Woman	*La Bordeuse*	Crypto-female valet of M. de Commerson		1764
Earliest Solo	*Spray*, 36½-foot gaff yawl	Capt. Joshua Slocum, 51 (U.S.) (a non-swimmer)	Newport, R.I. *via* Magellan Straits, Apr. 24, 1895	July 3, 1898, 46,000 miles
Earliest Solo Eastabout *via* Cape Horn	*Lehg II*, 31¼-foot Bermuda ketch	Vito Dumas (Argentina)	Buenos Aires, June 27, 1942	Sept. 7, 1943 (272 days)
Smallest Boat	*Ahadori II*, 20-foot-8-inch Bermuda yawl	Hiroshi Aoki (Japan)	Osaka, Japan, June 13, 1972	July 29, 1974
Earliest Submarine	*U.S.S. Triton*	Capt. Edward L. Beach, U.S.N. plus 182 crew	New London, Connecticut, Feb. 16, 1960	May 10, 1960, 30,708 miles
Fastest Solo	*Manureva*, 70-foot trimaran	Alain Colas (France)	St. Malo *via* Sydney	March 29, 1974, 168 days
Earliest Non-stop Solo	*Suhaili*, 32.4-foot Bermuda ketch	Robin Knox-Johnston (G.B.) (b. 1939)	Falmouth, England, June 14, 1968	Apr. 22, 1969 (313 days)
Earliest Non-stop Solo Westabout	*British Steel*, 59-foot ketch (largest solo)	Charles "Chay" Blyth (G.B.) (b. 1940)	The Hamble, Oct. 18, 1970	Aug. 6, 1971, 292 days

The first woman to set foot on Antarctica was Mrs. Klarius Mikkelsen on February 20, 1935. No woman stood on the South Pole until November 11, 1969, when Lois Jones, Kay Lindsay, Eileen McSavenay, Jean Pearson, Tarry Lee Tickhall and Pam Young, all of the U.S., arrived by air.

Antarctic Crossing. The first crossing of the Antarctic continent was completed at 1:47 p.m. on March 2, 1958, after a 2,158-mile trek lasting 99 days from November 24, 1957, from Shackleton Base to Scott Base *via* the Pole. The crossing party of 12 was led by Dr. (now Sir) Vivian Ernest Fuchs (born February 11, 1908).

North Pole. The claims of neither of the two U.S. Arctic explorers, Dr. Frederick Albert Cook (1865–1940) nor Rear Admiral Robert Edwin Peary, U.S.N. (1856–1920) in reaching the North Pole are subject to positive proof. Cook, accompanied by the Eskimos, Ah-pellah and Etukishook, two sledges and 26 dogs, struck north from a point 60 miles north of Svartevoeg, on Axel Heiberg Is., Canada, 460 miles from the Pole on March 21, 1908, allegedly reaching Lat. 89° 31′ N. on April 19, and the Pole on April 21. Peary, accompanied by his Negro assistant, Matthew Alexander Henson (1866–1955) and the four Eskimos, Ooqueah, Eginwah, Seegloo, and Ootah (1875–1955), struck north from his Camp Bartlett (Lat. 87° 44′ N.) at 5 a.m. on April 2, 1909. After traveling another 134 miles, he allegedly established his final camp, Camp Jessup, in the proximity of the Pole at 10 a.m. on April 6, and marched a further 42 miles quartering the sea ice before turning south at 4 p.m. on April 7. On excellent pack ice, Herbert's 1968–69 Expedition (see below) attained a best day's route mileage of 23 miles in 15 hours. Cook claimed 26 miles twice, while Peary claimed a surely unsustainable average of 38 miles for 8 consecutive days.

The earliest indisputable attainment of the North Pole over the sea ice was at 3 p.m. (Central Standard Time) on April 19, 1968, by Ralph Plaisted (U.S.) and three companions after a 42-day trek in four snowmobiles. Their arrival was independently verified 18 hours later by a U.S. Air Force weather aircraft.

Circum-Polar Flight. The first woman to fly over both poles was Flight Nurse Mrs. Helen Beetton Dustin in the transpolar flight of the Convair 990 *Polar Byrd I* on November 9 (North) and November 22 (South) in 1968.

Arctic Crossing. The first crossing of the Arctic sea ice was achieved by the British Trans-Arctic Expedition which left Point Barrow, Alaska, on February 21, 1968, and arrived at the Seven Island Archipelago northeast of Spitzbergen 464 days later on May 29, 1969, after a haul of 2,920 statute miles and a drift of 700 miles, compared with a straight-line distance of 1,662 miles. The team was Wally Herbert (leader), 34, Major Ken Hedges, 34, R.A.M.C., Allan Gill, 38, and Dr. Roy Koerner (glaciologist), and 34 huskies. This was the longest sustained (sled) journey ever made on polar pack ice and the first undisputed conquest of the North Pole by sled. Temperatures sank to —47° F. during the trek.

Longest Sled Journey. The longest polar sled journey was 3,720 miles by Herbert's Expedition (see above), when it continued

TRANSATLANTIC MARINE RECORDS (Compiled by Sq. Ldr. D. H. Clarke)

CATEGORY	CAPTAIN	VESSEL & SIZE	START	FINISH	DURATION	DATE
Earliest Crossing (2 men)	C. R. Webb + 1 crew	Charter Oak, 43 ft.	New York (June 4)	Liverpool	35 days	1857
Earliest Trimaran	John Mikes+2 crew (U.S.)	Non Pareil, 25 ft.	New York	Southampton, England	43 days	1868
Earliest Sailing	Alfred Johnson (Denmark)	Centennial, 20 ft.	Nova Scotia	Newlyn, Wales	46 days	1876
Earliest Woman Sailing	Mrs. Joanna Crapo (Scot.)	New Bedford, 20 ft.	Chatham, Mass.	Newlyn, England	51 days	1877
Earliest Single-handed race	J. W. Lawlor (U.S.)	Sea Serpent, 15 ft.	Boston (June 17)	Coverack, England	47 days	1891
Earliest and Fastest Rowing	Six British deserters	Ship's boat, c. 20 ft.	St. Helena (June 10)	Belmonte, Brazil	28 days (83 m.p.d.)	1794
Fastest Sailing Ship	Captain and crew	Lancing, 4 masts	New York	Cape Wrath	6¾ days	1916
Fastest Solo Sailing West-East	J. V. T. McDonald (G.B.)	Inverarity, 38 ft.	Nova Scotia	Ireland	16 days	1922
Earliest Canoe (with sail)	F. Romer (Germany)	Deutscher Sport, 22½ ft.	Las Palmas (June 2)	St. Thomas, V.I.	58 days	1928
Fastest Solo Sailing East-West (Northern Route)	Cdr. R. D. Graham (G.B.)	Emanuel, 30 ft.	Bantry, Ireland	St. John's, Newfoundland	24.35 days	1934
Earliest Woman Solo-Sailing West-East	Gladys Gradely (U.S.)	Lugger, 18 ft.	Nova Scotia		60 days	1903
Earliest Woman Solo-Sailing East-West	Mrs. Ann Davison (G.B.)	Felicity Ann, 23 ft.	Plymouth, Eng. (May 18, 1952)	Miami, Florida (Aug. 13, 1953)	454 days	1952-53
Earliest Rowing (G.B.)	Capt. John Ridgway (G.B.) Sgt. Charles Blyth (G.B.)	English Rose III, 22 ft.	Cape Cod (June 4)	Inishmore, Ireland (Sept. 3)	91 days	1966
Fastest Crossing Sailing	Eric Tabarly (France) +2 crew	Pen Duick IV, 68 ft.	Tenerife, Madeira	Martinique	251.4 miles/day (10 days 12 hrs.)	1968
Fastest Solo East-West (Northern)	Jean-Yves Ter Pain (France)	Vendredi 13, 128 ft.	Plymouth, Eng. (June 13)	Newport, R.I. (July 8)	21 days 5¼ hrs.	1972
Fastest Solo Rowing East-West	Sidney Genders, 51 (G.B.)	Khaggavisana, 19¾ ft.	Sennen Cove, Eng.	Miami, Florida via Antigua	37.3 miles/day	1970
Earliest Solo Rowing East-West	John Fairfax (G.B.)	Britannia, 22 ft.	Las Palmas, Canary Is. (Jan. 20)	Ft. Lauderdale, Florida (July 19)	180 days	1969
Fastest Solo East-West (Southern)	Sir Francis Chichester (G.B.)	Gipsy Moth V, 57 ft.	Portuguese Guinea	Nicaragua	179.1 miles/day (22.4 days)	1970
Earliest Solo Rowing West-East	Tom McClean (Ireland)	Super Silver, 20 ft.	St. John's, Newfoundland (May 17)	Black Sod Bay, Ireland (July 27)	70.7 days	1969
Fastest Solo East-West Northern (multi-hull)	Prof. Alain Colas (France)	Pen Duick IV, 68 ft. trimaran	Plymouth, Eng. (June 17)	Newport, R.I. (July 7)	20 days	1972
Smallest East-West (Southern)	Hugo S. Vihlen (U.S.)	The April Fool, 5 ft. 11½ in.	Casablanca	Ft. Lauderdale, Florida	13¾ hrs. 180 days	1969

FIRST ATLANTIC ROW WEST-TO-EAST was made in this 20-foot dory, "Super Silver," by Tom McClean, who rowed for 70 days 17 hours from Newfoundland to Ireland.

for 12 more days to June 10, 1969. The longest totally self-supporting polar sled journey ever made was one of 1,080 miles from west to east across Greenland, June 18–September 5, 1934, by Capt. M. Lindsay, Lt. Arthur Godfrey, and Andrew Croft and 49 dogs, as the British Trans-Greenland Expedition.

The same crossing was first made with man-hauled sledges by the Inter Services 1974 Trans-Greenland Expedition, led by Flight Lt. D. R. Gleed, in 36 days.

The longest dog-hauled sled journey in history has been by the Japanese mountaineer and adventurer Naomi Uemara (born 1941) from Greenland across northern Canada to Kotzebue, Alaska, a distance of more than 4,000 miles. He started on the west coast of Greenland in January, 1975, and reached Alaska in early May, 1976.

SMALLEST
TRANSATLANTIC
BOAT: Hugo S. Vihlen
navigated the 5-foot
11½-inch "April Fool"
from Casablanca, Morocco
to Florida in 180 days.

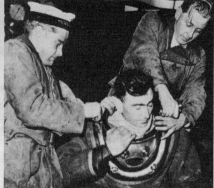

EVEREST CONQUERED: Tenzing Norkhay (left), a Sherpa, was with Sir Edmund Hillary in 1953 on this historic climb. DEEPEST DIVER (right): George Wookey (U.K.), in this diving suit descended to a then record 600 feet.

Mountaineering

The conquest of the highest point on earth, Mount Everest (29,028 feet) was first achieved at 11:30 a.m. on May 29, 1953, by Edmund Percival Hillary (New Zealand) and the Sherpa, Tenzing Norkhay (see *Mountaineering*, Chapter 12).

The female record was set by Mrs. Junko Tabei, 34, of Japan, on reaching Everest's summit on May 16, 1975.

Deep Diving Records

In his record-setting dive of 285 feet (see table), Enzo Maiorca surfaced unconscious. At 282 feet, the previous record holder, Jacques Mayol, felt a pressure on his thorax of 136.5 lbs. per square inch, and his pulse fell to 36. Breath-holding diving is an extremely dangerous activity. Some scuba divers have survived free swimming for short intervals at 1,400 feet.

Underwater Rescue

The deepest underwater rescue achieved was of the *Pisces III* in which Roger R. Chapman, 28, and Roger Mallinson, 35, were trapped for 76 hours when it sank to 1,575 feet, 150 miles southeast of Cork, Ireland, on August 29, 1973. She was hauled to the surface by the cable ship *John Cabot* after preliminary work by *Pisces V*, *Pisces II* and the remote control recovery vessel U.S. C.U.R.V., on September 1, 1973.

The greatest depth of an actual escape without any equipment has been from 198 feet by Sub. Lt. W. Morrison of the British Royal Navy and E. R. A. Swatton from H.M. Submarine X.E.11 in Loch Striven, Scotland, on March 6, 1945.

Deep Sea Diving

The world's record depth for a salvage observation chamber was established by the British Admiralty salvage ship *Reclaim* on June 28,

DEEP DIVING—PROGRESSIVE RECORDS

BREATH-HOLDING

Feet	Divers	Location	Date
198	Jacques Mayol (France)	off Grand Bahama	July, 1966
212½	P.O. Robert Croft, U.S.N.,	Florida coast	Feb. 8, 1967
125	Evelyn Patterson (Zambia)	off Freeport	1967
§147½	Guiliana Treleani (Italy)	off Cuba	Sept., 1967
217½	P.O. Robert Croft, U.S.N.	off Ft. Lauderdale	Dec. 19, 1967
231	Jacques Mayol (France)	Mediterranean	Jan. 14, 1968
240	P.O. Robert Croft, U.S.N.	Florida coast	Aug. 12, 1968
242.7	Enzo Maiorca (Italy)		1969
249.3	Jacques Mayol (France)	off Japanese coast	
250	Enzo Maiorca (Italy)	Syracuse, Sicily	Aug. 11, 1971
282	Jacques Mayol (France)	off Elba, Italy	Nov. 9, 1973
285	Enzo Maiorca (Italy)	off Sorrento, Italy	Sept. 27, 1974

BREATHING AIR

Feet	Divers	Location	Date
162[1]	A. Lambert (U.K.)	Grand Canary Is.	1885
190[1]	Greek and Swedish divers	off Patras, Greece	1904
210[1]	Lt. G. C. C. Damant, R.N. (U.K.)	Loch Striven, Scotland	1906
274[2]	Chief Gunner S. J. Drellifsak, U.S.N.	from U.S.S. *Walke*	Oct. 9, 1914
304[2]	F. Crilley, W. F. Loughman, F. C. L. Nielson, U.S.N.	off Hawaii	1915
344[2]	Diver Hilton, R.N. (U.K.)	British waters	1932
307	Frederick Dumas (France)	Mediterranean	1947
†396[3]	Lt. Maurice Farques (France)	Mediterranean	1947
††400[3]	Hope Root (U.S.)	U.S. waters	1953
350[3]	Jean Clarke-Samazen	off S. Catalina, Calif.	Aug., 1954
§320[3]	Katherine Troutt (Australia)	Sydney, Aust.	Sept. 7, 1964
355[3]	Hal D. Watts and Herb Johnson (U.S.)	off Loo Key, Fla.	Sept. 4, 1966
380[3]	Hal D. Watts, Arthur J. Muns (U.S.)	off Miami Beach	Sept. 3, 1967
§325[3]	Kitty Giesler (U.S.)	off Freeport	Oct. 31, 1967
437[3]	John J. Gruener and R. Neal Watson (U.S.)	off Freeport, Grand Bahama	Oct. 14, 1968

BREATHING GAS MIXTURES

Feet	Divers	Location	Date
420[4]	M. G. Nohl (U.S.)	Lake Michigan	Dec. 1, 1937
440[5]	R. M. Metzger and Claude Conger, U.S.N.	Portsmouth, N.H.	June 22, 1941
†528[5]	A. Zetterström (Sweden)	Baltic	Aug. 7, 1945
450[4]	Wilfred H. Bollard and W. Soper, R.N. (U.K.)	Loch Fyne, Scotland	Aug. 26, 1948
540[4]	W. H. Bollard, R.N. (U.K.)	Loch Fyne	Aug. 28, 1948
550	Diver J. E. Johnson	Hauriki Gulf, N.Z.	1949
600[4]	Lt.-Cdr. George A. M. Wookey, R.N. (U.K.)	Oslo Fjord, Norway	Oct. 13, 1956
728[6]	Hannes Keller (Switzerland) and Kenneth MacLeish (U.S.)	Lake Maggiore, Italy	June 30, 1961
*1,000[6]	H. Keller (Switzerland) and Peter Small† (U.K.)	off Santa Catalina, Calif.	Dec. 3, 1962
**1,025[4]	U.S. Navy Aquanauts		Feb., 1968
**1,100[4]	Carl Deckman (Int. Underwater Contractors, Inc.)	Murray Hill, N.J.	Mar. 12, 1968
**1,197[4]	Ralph W. Brauer (U.S.) and Réné Veyrunes (France)	Comex Chamber, Marseilles, France	June 27, 1968
**1,500[4]	John Bevan and Peter Sharphouse (U.K.)	Alverstoke, Hampshire	Mar. 11, 1970
**1,706	Patrice Chemin and Bernard Reiuller (France)	Comex Chamber, Marseilles, France	Nov. 19, 1970
**2,001[4]	Patrice Chemin and Robert Gauret (France)	Comex Chamber	June, 1972

§ Female record.
† Died on the ascent.
†† Died on the descent.
* Emerged from a diving bell.
** Simulated chamber dive.

[1] Surface supplied, helmet.
[2] Surface supplied, flexible dress.
[3] Scuba (self-contained underwater breathing apparatus).
[4] Oxygen-helium.
[5] Oxygen-hydrogen.
[6] Oxygen-helium plus an additive.

1956. In an observation chamber measuring 7 feet long and 3 feet internal diameter, Senior Commissioned Boatswain (now Lt.-Cdr.) George A. M. Wookey, descended to a depth of 1,060 feet in Oslo Fjord, Norway.

OCEAN DESCENTS—PROGRESSIVE RECORDS

Feet	Vehicle	Divers	Location	Date
c.245	Steel Sphere	Ernest Bazin (France)	Belle Ile, France	1865
c.830	Diving Bell	Balsamello Bella Nautica (Italy)		1889
c.1,650	Hydrostat	Hartman		1911
2,200	Bathysphere	Dr. C. W. Beebe and Dr. Otis Barton (U.S.)	S.E. Bermuda	Sept. 22, 1932
2,510	Bathysphere	Dr. C. W. Beebe and Dr. Otis Barton (U.S.)	S.E. Bermuda	Aug. 11, 1934
3,028	Bathysphere	Dr. C. W. Beebe and Dr. Otis Barton (U.S.)	S.E. Bermuda	Aug. 15, 1934
7,850	Converted U-boat	Heinz Sellner (Germany) (unwitnessed)	Murmansk, U.S.S.R.	Aug. 1947
4,500	Benthoscope	Dr. Otis Barton (U.S.)	Santa Cruz, Calif.	Aug. 16, 1949
5,085	Bathyscaphe F.N.R.S. 3	Lt.-Cdr. Georges S. Houet and Lt. Pierre-Henri Willm (France)	off Toulon, France	Aug. 12, 1953
6,890	Bathyscaphe F.N.R.S. 3	Lt.-Cdr. G. S. Houet and Lt. P.-H. Willm (France)	off Cap Ferrat, Fr.	Aug. 14, 1953
10,335	Bathyscaphe Trieste	Prof. Auguste and Dr. Jacques Piccard (Switzerland)	Ponza Is., Italy	Sept. 30, 1953
13,287	Bathyscaphe F.N.R.S. 3	Lt.-Cdr. G. S. Houet and Eng.-Offr. P.-H. Willm (France)	off Dakar, Senegal	Feb. 15, 1954
18,600	Bathyscaphe Trieste	Dr. J. Piccard (Switz.) and Andreas B. Rechnitzer (U.S.)	Marianas Trench	Nov. 14, 1959
24,000	Bathyscaphe Trieste	Dr. J. Piccard (Switz.) and Lt. D. Walsh, U.S.N.	Marianas Trench	Jan. 7, 1960
35,820	Bathyscaphe Trieste	Dr. J. Piccard (Switz.) and Lt. D. Walsh, U.S.N.	Marianas Trench	Jan. 23, 1960

Greatest Ocean Descent

The record ocean descent was achieved in the Challenger Deep of the Marianas Trench, 250 miles southwest of Guam, when the Swiss-built U.S. Navy bathyscaphe *Trieste*, manned by Dr. Jacques Piccard (b. 1914) and Lt. Donald Walsh, U.S.N., reached the ocean bed 35,820 feet (6.78 miles) down, at 1:10 p.m. on January 23, 1960. The pressure of the water was 16,883 lbs. per square inch (1,215.6 tons per square foot), and the temperature 37.4° F. The descent required 4 hours 48 minutes and the ascent 3 hours 17 minutes.

Salvaging

Deepest. The greatest depth at which salvage has been achieved is 16,500 feet by the bathyscaphe *Trieste II* (Lt. Commander Mel Bartels, U.S.N.) to attach cables to an "electronics package" on the sea bed 400 miles north of Hawaii on May 20, 1972.

By Divers. The deepest salvage by flexible dress divers was on the wreck of the S.S. *Niagara*, sunk by a mine in 1940, 438 feet down off Bream Head, Whangarei, North Island, New Zealand. All but 6 per cent of the $6,300,000 of gold in her holds was recovered in

7 weeks. The record recovery was from the White Star Liner *Laurentic*, which was torpedoed in 114 feet of water off Malin Head, Donegal, Ireland, in 1917, with $14,000,000 of gold ingots in her Second Class baggage room. By 1924, 3,186 of the 3,211 gold bricks had been recovered with immense difficulty.

Largest. The largest vessel ever salvaged was the U.S.S. *Lafayette*, formerly the French liner *Normandie* (83,423 tons), which keeled over during fire-fighting operations at the West 49th Street Pier, Hudson River, New York City, on February 9, 1942. She was righted in October, 1943, at a cost of $4,500,000, and was broken up at Newark, New Jersey, beginning in September, 1946.

Mining Depths

Man's deepest penetration made into the ground is in the Western Deep Levels Mine at Carletonville, Transvaal, South Africa. By May, 1975, a record depth of 12,600 feet had been attained. The rock temperature at this depth is 126° F.

Shaft-Sinking Record. The one-month (31-day) world record is 1,251 feet for a standard shaft 26 feet in diameter at Buffelsfontein Mine, Transvaal, South Africa, in March, 1962.

Marriage and Divorce

Longest Engagement. The longest engagement on record is one of 67 years between Octavio Guillen, 82, and Adriana Martinez, 82. They finally took the plunge in June, 1969, in Mexico City.

DEEPEST MINE: The Western Deep Levels Mine at Carletonville, South Africa, reaches a depth of 12,600 feet. Miners must work in refrigerated air since the rock temperature reaches 126°F. at such extreme depth.

Engagement "Faux Pas." If measured by financial consequence, the greatest *faux pas* on record was that of the young multi-millionaire, James Gordon Bennett, committed on January 1, 1877, at the family mansion of his demure fiancée, one Caroline May, on Fifth Avenue, New York City. Bennett arrived late in a two-horse cutter and obviously in wine. By dint of intricate footwork, he gained the portals to enter the living room, where he was the cynosure of all eyes. He mistook the fireplace for a plumbing fixture more usually reserved for another purpose. The May family broke the engagement and Bennett was obliged to spend the rest of his footloose and fancy-free life based in Paris with the resultant non-collection of millions of tax dollars by the U.S. Treasury.

Most Divorces and Marriages. Mrs. Beverly Nina Avery, then aged 48, a barmaid from Los Angeles, set a monogamous world record in October, 1957, by obtaining her 16th divorce, this one from Gabriel Avery, her 14th husband. She alleged outside the court that five of the 14 had broken her nose.

The greatest number of marriages in the monogamous world is 19 by Mr. Glynn de Moss Wolfe (U.S.) (b. 1908) who married, for the 19th time since 1931, his 17th wife Gloria, aged 23, on February 22, 1969. He believes he has 34 children. He keeps two wedding dresses (different sizes) in his closet for ready use. He has suffered 16 mothers-in-law.

The most often-marrying millionaire, Thomas F. Manville (1894–1967), contracted his 13th marriage to his 11th wifeⵔChristine Erdlen Papa (1940–71) in New York City, on January 11, 1960, when aged 65. His shortest marriage (to his seventh wife) effectively lasted only 7½ hours. His fortune of $20,000,000 came from asbestos, which he unfortunately could not take with him.

Oldest Bride and Bridegroom. The oldest bridegroom on record was Ralph Cambridge, 105, who married Mrs. Adriana Kapp, 70, at Knysna, South Africa, on September 30, 1971. Dyura Avramovich, 101, married Yula Zhivich, 95, in Belgrade, Yugoslavia, in November, 1963.

Longest Marriage. The longest recorded marriage is one of 86 years between Sir Temulji Bhicaji Nariman and Lady Nariman from 1853 to 1940 resulting from a cousin marriage when both were five. Sir Temulji (born September 3, 1848) died, aged 91 years 11 months, in August, 1940.

The only reliable instance of an 83rd anniversary celebrated by a couple marrying at normal ages is that between the late Edd (105) and Margaret (99) Hollen (U.S.) who celebrated their 83rd anniversary on May 7, 1972. They were married in Kentucky on May 7, 1889.

The only known example of a marriage with both partners over the age of 100 was that of John Downham (born May 16, 1861) and his wife Mary (born November, 1860) of Nottingham, England, who celebrated their 77th anniversary in April, 1961.

Most Married. James and Mary Grady of Illinois have married each other 27 times in the period 1964–69, as a protest against the existence of divorce. They have married in 25 different states, 3 times in a day (December 16, 1968), twice in an hour and twice on television.

Fastest Wedding

The fastest wedding on record was one on September 22, 1939, between Mr. and Mrs. T. G. Franklin. Only 7½ hours after the proposal, and two hours after obtaining a special license, the wedding was solemnized at St. Mary's Church, Acocks Green, Birmingham, England.

Mass Ceremony. The largest mass wedding ceremony was one of 1,800 couples officiated over by Sun Myung Moon of the Holy Spirit Association for the Unification of World Christianity in Seoul, South Korea, on February 14, 1975. The response to the question "Will you swear to love your spouse for ever?" is "Ye."

STUNTS AND MISCELLANEOUS ENDEAVORS

Apple Peeling. The longest single unbroken apple peel on record is 155 feet 1¾ inches peeled by Kathy Wafler, 16, of Wolcott, New York, in 11 hours at the Long Ridge Mall, Rochester, N.Y., on October 11, 1975. The apple was 18½ inches in circumference.

Apple Picking. The greatest recorded performance is 270 U.S. bushels picked in 8 hours by Harold Oaks, 22, at his father's orchard, Hood River, Oregon, on September 30, 1972.

Baby Carriage Pushing. The greatest distance covered in 24 hours in pushing a perambulator is 319 miles on a track by a 60-man team from the White Horse Sports and Social Club, Stony Stratford, England, on May 19–20, 1973. A team of 10 with an adult "baby" from "Flore Moderns" covered 226.1 miles at Flore, Northamptonshire, England, in 24 hours on June 28–29, 1975.

Bagpipes. The longest bagpipe performance was 80 hours by Jim Menzies, Jack Taylor, Angus Clarke, and Alan MacDonald of Aberdeen University Officers Training Corps, Scotland, April 19–22, 1975.

Balancing on One Foot. The longest recorded duration for continuous balancing on one foot is 8 hours 46 minutes by Don Carter of Hill McCloy High School, Montrose, Michigan, May 30, 1975. The disengaged foot may not be rested on the standing foot nor may any sticks be used for support or balance.

Frank Norman of Gosport, England, went 12 hours 32 minutes on December 6, 1975. He took a 5-minute rest break every hour.

Balloon Racing. The largest balloon release on record has been one of 100,000 helium balloons at the opening of "Transpo 72" at Dulles Airport, Washington, D.C., on May 27, 1972. The longest reported toy balloon flight is one of 9,000 miles from Atherton, California (released by Jane Dorst on May 21, 1972) and found on June 10, 1972 at Pietermaritzburg, South Africa.

Tammy Brunetti, a 5th-grader at West Street School in Newburgh, N.Y., released a helium-filled balloon on April 28, 1976, which was found in Strathaven, Scotland, 2 days later—a distance of 4,800 miles. The U.S. Weather Bureau estimated that the balloon traveled at speeds of up to 500 m.p.h.

Ball Punching. Ron Renaulf (Australia) equaled his own world duration ball-punching record of 125 hours 20 minutes at 10:20 p.m. on December 31, 1955, at the Esplanade, Southport, Queensland, Australia.

Band, One-Man. The greatest number of musical instruments played continuously is 49 by Werner Hirzel (b. 1919) (known as Schnickelgruber), who performed on ABC-TV with the David Frost Show on April 5, 1974. For 3 minutes Christopher Critchlow of Darlington, England, played 58 instruments at the Cockerton Band Club on December 18, 1975.

Don Davis of Hollywood, California, is the only one-man band able to play 4 melody and 2 percussion instruments simultaneously. For a rendition of Beethoven's Fifth Symphony, he utilizes an 8-prong pendular perpendicular piano pounder and a semi-circular chromatic radially operated centrifugally sliding left-handed glockenspiel.

MOST COMPLEX ONE-MAN BAND: Don Davis is able to play 4 melody and 2 percussion instruments simultaneously.

ONE-MAN BAND:
As Werner Hirzel struts around, he plays 49 instruments, including the accordion, flute, saxophone, gong, duck, fox and goose callers, siren, oogal and cow horns, tambourines, cymbals, washboard, musical hose, toilet brush, bass drum and balloon pump.

Band Marathons. The longest recorded "blow-in" is 76 hours 1 minute by the Watsonville High School Wildcatz Band, California, February 12–15, 1976. Each bandsman was allowed 5 minutes per hour to regain his wind.

The marathon record for a one-man band is 16 hours (no breaks) by Joe Littlefield of McNavy High School, Salem, Oregon, on November 10, 1974.

Band, Pop. The duration record for a 4-man pop group is 140 hours 34 minutes by "The Animation" in St. Andrews Church Hall, Liverpool, England, on July 22–28, 1974. The group at no time sank below a trio.

Barrel Jumping. The greatest number of barrels jumped by a skater is 17 (total length 28 feet 8 inches) by Kenneth LeBel at the Grossinger Country Club, Liberty, New York, on January 9, 1965. Roger Wood leaped 29 feet 2 inches on December 14, 1972.

Barrel Rolling. The record for rolling a 43.2-gallon metal beer barrel over a measured mile is 12 minutes 29.5 seconds by "The Fletch A" team in Coventry, England, on October 13, 1975.

Bathtub Racing. The record for the annual 36-mile Nanaimo to Vancouver, British Columbia, bathtub race is 1 hour 36 minutes 4 seconds by Phil Holt (Australia) on July 18, 1976. Tubs are limited to 75 inches and 6-h.p. motors. The greatest distance for a hand-propelled bathtub in 24 hours is 36 miles 1,072 yards by 25 Venture Scouts at Priory Park, Malvern, Gloucestershire, England, on May 10–11, 1975.

BED PUSH: This is part of the team of 12 from the Greensburg Recreational Board, Greensburg, Pennsylvania, as they completed their epic 1,776-mile push of a wheeled hospital bed in August, 1975.

Baton Twirling. Five Portland (Maine) High School majorettes, Lucinda Haney, Sharon Harkins, Diane Heal, Susan Leiter and Laurie Orfaly twirled for 44 hours accompanied by their school band on June 26–28, 1975. (See photo on page 701.)

Bedmaking. The record time set under the rigorous rules of the Australian Bedmaking Championships is 35.7 seconds by Jill Donnelly of Newport, New South Wales, Australia, on May 6, 1976.

Bed of Nails. The duration record for non-stop lying on a bed of nails (needle-sharp 6-inch nails, 2 inches apart) is 25 hours 20 minutes by Vernon E. Craig (Komar, the Hindu *fakir*) at Wooster, Ohio, July 22–23, 1971. Mike Pimble, 24, of Gwent, Wales, endured 28 hours (with 5-minute rests per hour) June 27–28, 1976. The feminine record (with 5-minute rests per hour) is 25 hours 30 minutes by Ruth Marie Porter, 18, at Springfield, Virginia, on February 13–14, 1975.

Much longer durations are claimed by unwitnessed *fakirs*—the most extreme case being *Silki* who claimed 111 days in São Paulo, Brazil, ending on August 24, 1969.

The highest weight recorded for an "iron maiden" is 1,371 lbs. endured by Master Chi (Ronald Champlain) who lay between two beds of 6-inch nails, 2 inches apart at McCoy Stadium, Pawtucket, Rhode Island on June 23, 1976.

Bed Pushing. The longest recorded push of a normally stationary object is 1,776 miles in the case of a wheeled hospital bed by a team of 12 at the Greensburg Recreational Board, Greensburg, Pennsylvania, August 10–27, 1975.

Bed Racing. The record time for the annual Knaresborough Bed Race (established 1966) in Yorkshire, England is 14 minutes 9.0 seconds for the 2½-mile course crossing the River Nidd by the Harrogate Athletic Club on June 14, 1975.

Bell Ringing. Seven members of the Hussite Bell Ringers, Winston-Salem, North Carolina, held a handbell ringing recital for 28 hours 2 minutes on April 17–18, 1976.

Best Best Man. The world's champion "best man" is Wally Gant, a bachelor fishmonger from Wakefield, Yorkshire, England, who officiated for the 50th time since 1931 in December, 1964.

Billiard Table Jumping. Joe Darby (1861–1937) cleared a 12-foot billiard table lengthwise, taking off from a 4-inch-high solid wooden block, at Wolverhampton, England, on February 5, 1892.

Bomb Defusing. The highest reported number of unexploded bombs defused by any individual is 8,000 by Werner Stephan in West Berlin, Germany, in the 12 years from 1945 to 1957. He was killed by a small grenade on the Grünewald blasting site on August 17, 1957.

Bond Signing. The greatest feat of bond signing was performed by L. E. Chittenden (died 1902), the Registrar of the United States Treasury. In 48 hours (March 20–22, 1863), he signed 12,500 bonds worth $10,000,000, which had to catch a steam packet to England. He suffered years of pain thereafter and the bonds were never used.

Boomerang Throwing. The earliest mention of a word similar to "boomerang" is "wo-mur-rang" in Collins *Account N.S. Wales Vocabulary*, published in 1798. The earliest Australian certain account of a returning boomerang (term established in 1827) was in 1831 by Major (later Sir Thomas) Mitchell.

Curved throwing sticks for hunting wild fowl were found in the tomb of Tutankhamen, dating from the mid-14th century B.C. World championships and codified rules were not established until 1970. Jeff Lewry has won the world title in 1970–71–72–73, and the Australian title in 1974. The Boomerang Association of Australia's official record for distance reached before the boomerang returns is 89.66 yards by Jeff Lewry at Albury, N.S.W., Australia, on July 16, 1972. Bob Burwell, 32, won a contest at Albany Creek, Queensland, Australia, with a throw of 110 yards in 1976.

Braille Writing. Braille was invented in 1825 by Louis Braille. The highest speed recorded by a braillist (using contracted braille) is 100 words per minute using repetitive copy on a Stainsby writer by William P. Rowland at Claremont Civic Centre, Cape Town, South Africa, on June 19, 1975.

Brick Carrying. The record for carrying a brick (8¾ lbs.) without dropping or resting is 43.57 miles by Ken Gormley and Paul Schweibinz of Pittsburgh, Pennsylvania, on July 5, 1975. The wire-cut semi-pressed brick has to be carried in a downward position with a nominated ungloved hand.

CIRCUS RECORDS

The following circus acrobatic feats represent the greatest performed, either for the first time, or if marked with an asterisk, uniquely. A "mechanic" is a safety harness.

Category	Feat	Performer(s)	Place	Date
Flying Trapeze	Earliest Act	Jules Leotard (France)	Circus Napoleon, Paris	1859
	Double back somersault	Eddie Silbon	Paris Hippodrome	1879
	Triple back somersault (female)	Lena Jordan (Latvia) to Lew Jordan (U.S.)	Sydney, Australia	1897
	Triple back somersault (male)	Ernest Clarke to Charles Clarke	Publiones Circus, Cuba	1909
	Triple and a half back somersault	Tony Steele to Lee Strath Marliees	Durango, Mexico	1962
	Quadruple back somersault (in practice)	*Ernest Clarke to Charles Clarke	Orrin Bros. Circus, Mexico City, Mexico	1915
	Triple back somersault with 1½ twist (female)	Terry Cavarette Lemus	Circus Circus Hotel, Las Vegas, Nevada	1969
	Head to head stand on swinging bar (no holding)	*Ed. and Ira Millette (née Wolf)	Various	1910–20
Horseback	Running leaps on and off	*26 by "Poodles" Hanneford	New York City	1915
	Three-high column without "mechanic"	*Willy, Baby and Rene Fredianis	Nouveau Cirque, Paris	1908
	Double back somersault mounted	(John or Charles) Frederic Clarke	Various	c. 1905
	Double back somersault from a 2-high to a trailing horse with "mechanic"	Aleksandr Sergey	Moscow Circus	1956
Fixed Bars	Pass from 1st to 3rd bar with a double back somersault	Phil Shevette, Andres Atayde	Woods Gymnasium, New York City-European tours	1925–27
	Triple flyaway to ground (male)	Phil Shevette	Folies Bergère, Paris	1896
	Triple flyaway to ground (female)	Loretto Twins, Ora and Pauline	Los Angeles	1914
Giant Springboard	Running forward triple back somersault	John Cornish Worland (1855–1933) of the U.S.	St. Louis, Missouri	1874
Risley (Human Juggling)	Back somersault feet to feet	Richard Risley Carlisle (1814–74) and son (U.S.)	Theatre Royal, Edinburgh	1844
Acrobatics	Quadruple back somersault to a chair	Sylvester Mezzetti (voltigeur) to Butch Mezzetti (catcher)	New York Hippodrome	1915–17
Aerialist	One arm swings 125 (no net) 32 feet up	Vicky Unus (La Toria) (U.S.)	Ringling Bros., Barnum & Bailey circuit	1962
Teeter Board	Seat to seat triple back somersault	The 5 Draytons	Madison Square Garden, N.Y.C.	1896
Wire-Walking	16 hoops (hands and feet)	Ala Naito (Japan) (female)	Empire Theatre, Johannesburg	1937
Low Wire (7 feet)	Feet to feet forward somersault	Con Colleano	Madison Square Garden, N.Y.C.	1923
		Ala Naito (Japan) (female)	Moscow Circus	1937
High Wire (30–40 feet)	Four high column (with mechanic)	*The Solokhin Brothers (U.S.S.R.)	Moscow Circus	1962
	Three layer, 7-man pyramid	Great Wallendas (Germany)	U.S.	1961
	Stationary double back somersault	Francois Gouleau (France)		1905
	Four high column	The-Picchianis (Italy)		1905
Ground Acrobatics	Five high pyramids	The Yacopis (Argentina) with 3 understanders, 3 second layer understanders, 1 middleman, 1 upper middleman and a top mounter	Ringling Bros., Barnum & Bailey circuit	1941

CIRCUS FEAT: Terry Lemus performs a difficult triple back somersault with 1½ twists in her trapeze act at Circus Circus Hotel in Las Vegas, Nevada.

The feminine record for an 8-lb. 15-oz. brick is 5.9 miles by Cynthia Ann Smolko of Denville, New Jersey, on May 31, 1975.

Bricklaying. Kevin Temple, 28, of Alnwick, England, laid 6,429 rough-pressed bricks in an 8-hour shift at Acklington, England, on April 30, 1976. He was aided by a gang of 5 men.

Brick Throwing. The greatest reported distance for throwing a standard 5-lb. building brick is 142 feet 6 in. by Robert Gardner at Stroud, Gloucestershire, England, in a 1971 contest.

Burial Alive. In June, 1951, two men emerged from an underground bunker at Babie Doly, near Gdynia, Poland, which had been demolished by the retreating German army in January, 1945. One died immediately.

The longest recorded *voluntary* burial alive is one of 101 days 37 minutes by Hendrik Louis Alexander Luypaerts (born May 9, 1931) at Hechtel, Belgium, in a coffin measuring 6 feet 6 inches by 25½ inches by 33½ inches, 9 feet 10 inches deep, from April 13 to July 23, 1974. The case of a 119-day claim in the U.S. is, however, now under investigation.

Camping Out. Graham Hurry of Coventry, England, and Richard Markham of Rugby, England, won a *Camping* magazine contest by sleeping outdoors 365 nights in 1975. Hurry completed two years of outdoor life on June 19, 1976.

Car Stunting. (See *Motorcycle and Car Stunting*.)

Cat's Cradle. Maryann and Rita Di Vona and Geneva Hultenius completed 21,200 cat's cradles in 21 hours at Chula Vista California, on August 17–18, 1974.

Champagne Fountain. The tallest successfully filled column of champagne glasses is one 18 high, filled from the top by Frank Dettmer of Oakland, California, on August 2, 1975.

Circus. (See Circus Stunt records, page 458.)

Clapping. The duration record for continuous clapping (sustaining an average 140 claps per minute audible at 100 yards) is 35 hours 29 minutes by Lawrence Cratty, Jr., T. Utterback, Jack Wolfkill, Kenneth Clark, Bruce Cockshoot, Amy Smith and Benjamin Rogers, Jr., all of Des Moines, Iowa, May 1–2, 1976.

Club Swinging. Bill Franks set a world record of 17,280 revolutions (4.8 per second) in 60 minutes at Webb's Gymnasium, Newcastle, N.S.W., Australia, on August 2, 1934. M. Dobrilla swung continuously for 144 hours at Cobar, N.S.W., Australia, finishing on September 15, 1913.

Coal Carrying. The record time for the annual "World Coal Carrying Championship" over the uphill, 1,080-yard course at Ossett cum Gawthorpe, Yorkshire, England, with a 112-lb. sack is 4 minutes 36 seconds by Tony Nicholson, 26, on April 3, 1972.

Coal Shoveling. The record for filling a 1,120-lb. hopper with coal is 47.4 secs. by R. Hughes of Westport, New Zealand, in February, 1974.

Coin Balancing. The greatest recorded feat of coin balancing is the stacking of 126 coins on top of a silver U.S. dollar on edge by Alex Chervinsky, 65, of Lock Haven, Pennsylvania, on September 16, 1971, after 23 years' practice.

Coin Snatching. The greatest number of 25-cent-sized coins caught by the same hand after being flipped from a pile or piles balanced on the back of the forearm is 65 by Gerry Berg in North Vancouver, British Columbia, Canada, on June 18, 1975.

Contest Winnings. The largest recorded individual prize won was $307,500 by Herbert J. Idle, 55, of Chicago in an encyclopedia contest run by Unicorn Press, Inc., on August 20, 1953.

Crawling. The longest crawl (at least one knee always on the ground) is 8½ miles by Mark Hunt and Mark Donnelly of Olympia High School, Rochester, New York, on August 1, 1975.

Hormoz Tabar Heydar of Iran crawled about 30 miles from Swindon to Oxford, England, in 43 hours, March 28–30, 1971.

Crochet. The longest recorded crocheted chain is one of 4-ply wool measuring 2.46 miles completed between December 3, 1974, and May 3, 1975, by Lisa Zwelinski and Chris Kuchalla of Meriden, Connecticut.

Cucumber Slicing. Norman Johnson of the Blackpool College of Art and Technology, England, sliced 12 inches of a 1½-inch-diameter cucumber into 20 slices to the inch in 24.2 seconds, on the BBC-TV *Record Breakers* program, on September 28, 1973.

Custard Pie Throwing. The most-times champion in the annual World Custard Pie Championship at Coxheath, Kent, England

CHAMPAGNE FOUNTAIN (left): Frank Dettmer successfully filled an 18-glass-high column. DANCE MARATHON (right): Tony Alteriri and Vera Mikus went almost 25 weeks in 1932 to win a prize of $1,000.

(instituted 1967) has been the Birds and the Coxheath Men, each with 3 wins. The target (face) must be 8 feet 3⅝ inches from the thrower, who must throw a pie no more than 10¾ inches in diameter. Six points are scored for a square hit full in the face.

Dancing. Marathon dancing must be distinguished from dancing mania, which is a pathological condition. The worst outbreak of dancing mania was at Aachen, Germany, in July, 1374, when hordes of men and women broke into a frenzied dance in the streets which lasted for hours till injury or complete exhaustion ensued.

The most severe marathon dance (staged as a public spectacle in the U.S.) was one lasting 4,152½ hours (24 weeks 5 days). This was completed by Tony Alteriri and Vera Mikus (now Mrs. Oglesby of Springfield,, Pennsylvania) at Motor Square Garden, Pittsburgh, from June 6 to November 30, 1932. The rest allowance was progressively cut from 15 minutes per hour to only 3 minutes until this Marathon Dance "Classic" was finally stopped by the authorities. The prize of $1,000 was equivalent to 24 cents per hour.

Largest Dance. The largest dance ever held was that put on by the Houston Livestock Show at the Astro Hall, Houston, Texas, on February 8, 1969. The attendance was 16,500, with 4,000 turned away.

Dancing, Ballet. In the *entrechat* (a vertical spring from the fifth position with the legs extended criss-crossing at the lower calf), the starting and finishing position each count as one, such that in the *entrechat douze* there are *five* crossings and uncrossings. This was performed by Wayne Sleep for the BBC-TV *Record Breakers* program on January 7, 1973. He was in the air for 0.71 of a second.

The greatest number of spins called for in classical ballet choreography is the 32 *fouettés rond de jambe en tournant* in "Swan Lake" by Pyotr Ilyich Chaykovskiy (Tschaikovsky) (1840–93). Rowena Jackson (b. 1926) of New Zealand, achieved 121 such turns at her class in Melbourne, Victoria, Australia, in 1940.

The greatest recorded number of curtain calls ever received by ballet dancers is 89 by Dame Peggy Arias, *née* Hookham (born in Reigate, Surrey, England, May 18, 1919) *alias* Margot Fonteyn and Rudolf Hametovich Nureyev (born in a train near Irkutsk, U.S.S.R., March 17, 1938) after a performance of "Swan Lake" at the Vienna Staatsoper, Austria, in October, 1964.

The largest cast of ballet dancers used in a production has been 2,000 in the London Coster Ballet of 1962, directed by Lillian Rowley, at the Royal Albert Hall, London.

Dancing, Ballroom. The individual continuous world record is 106 hours 5 minutes 10 seconds by Carlos Sandrini in Buenos Aires, Argentina, in September, 1955. Three girls worked shifts as his partner.

The world's most successful professional ballroom dancing champions have been Bill Irvine and Bobbie Irvine, of London, who won 13 world titles, 1960–72.

Dancing, Belly. The longest recorded belly dance was one of 38 hours 22 minutes by "Phaedra" (Linda Long) in Philadelphia, Pennsylvania, July 2–4, 1976.

Dancing, Charleston. The Charleston duration record is 37½ hours by Terri Fry, Roberta Gatto, Mary McPeak, and Scotty Parker, all of Parkrose High School, Portland, Oregon, May 28–30, 1976.

Dancing, Conga. The longest recorded conga line was a "snake" of 3,376 students from Bowling Green State University in Ohio, on October 24, 1975.

Dancing, Flamenco. The fastest flamenco dancer ever measured is Solero de Jerez, aged 17, who, in Brisbane, Australia, in September, 1967, in an electrifying routine attained 16 heel taps per second or a rate of 1,000 a minute.

Dancing, Go-Go. The duration record for go-go dancing (Boogaloo or Reggae) is 110 hours (with 5-minute breaks each hour) by Patricia Glenister at Bailey's Nightclub, Leicester, England, May 12–16, 1975.

Dancing, High Kicking. The world record for high kicks is 8,005 in 4 hours 40 minutes by Veronica Evans (*née* Steen) (b. Liverpool, February 20, 1910) at the Pathétone Studios, Wardour Street, London, in the summer of 1939.

Dancing, Jive. The duration record for non-stop jiving is 53 hours by John and Olwen Abbott at Tiffany's, Shrewsbury, England, June 20–22, 1976. Breaks of 5 minutes per hour were permitted for massage.

Dancing, Limbo. The lowest height for a flaming bar under which a limbo dancer has passed is 6⅛ inches at Port of Spain Pavilion, Toronto, on June 24, 1973, by Marlene Raymond, 15.

Strictly no part of the body other than the sole or side of the foot should touch the ground, though brushing the shoulder blade does not, in fact, usually result in disqualification.

Dancing, Modern. The longest recorded dancing marathon (50 minutes per hour) in modern style is 114 hours 27½ minutes by Chris Rodriguez and Louisa Marquez of Sydney, Australia, October 28–November 2, 1975.

Dancing, Tap. The fastest *rate* ever measured for any tap dancer has been 1,440 taps per minute (24 per second) by Roy Castle on the BBC-TV *Record Breakers* program on January 14, 1973.

Dancing the Twist. The duration record for the twist is 102 hours 28 minutes 37 seconds by Roger Guy English at La Jolla, California, on July 11–16, 1973.

Dance Band. The most protracted session is one of 321 hours (13 days 9 hours) by the Black Brothers of Bonn, West Germany, ending on January 2, 1969. Never less than a quartet were in action during the marathon.

Demolition. Fifteen members of the International Budo Association led by Phil Milner (3rd dan karate) demolished a 6-room early Victorian house at Idle, Bradford, Yorkshire, England, by head, foot and empty hand in 6 hours on June 4, 1972. On completion they bowed to the rubble.

Dining Out. The world champion for dining out is Fred E. Magel of Chicago, who, between 1928 and March, 1976, dined in 39,000 restaurants in 60 nations as a restaurant grader.

He asserts the restaurant serving the largest helpings is Zehnder's Hotel, Frankenmuth, Michigan. Mr. Magel's favorite dishes are South African rock lobster and mousse of fresh English strawberries.

Disc Jockey. The longest continuous period of acting as a disc jockey is 800 hours by Mark Gondelman of Woodstock, New York, July 4–August 7, 1975. L.P.'s are limited to 50 per cent of total playing time.

Diving, High. The highest regularly performed dive is that of professional divers from La Quebrada ("the break in the rocks") at Acapulco, Mexico, a height of 118 feet. The leader of the 27 divers in the exclusive Club de Clavadistas is Raul Garcia (born 1928) with more than 35,000 dives. The base rocks are 21 feet out from the take-off, necessitating a leap 27 feet out. The water is only 12 feet deep.

On the *Wide World of Sports* television program, a record of 130 feet 6 inches, was set jointly by Donnie Vick, Pat Sucher, and John Tobler in March, 1974.

On May 18, 1885, Sarah Ann Henley, aged 24, jumped from the Clifton Suspension Bridge across the Avon, England. Her 250-foot fall was slightly cushioned by her voluminous dress and petticoat acting as a parachute. She landed, bruised and bedraggled, in the mud on the Gloucestershire bank and was carried to hospital by four policemen.

On February 11, 1968, Jeffrey Kramer, 24, leaped off the George Washington Bridge 250 feet above the Hudson River, New York City, and survived. Of the 511 people who have made suicide dives from the Golden Gate Bridge, San Francisco, California, 1937 to April 25, 1974, only 7 have survived.

On July 10, 1921, a stuntman named William H. Bailey leapt from a seaplane into the Ohio River at Louisville. The alleged altitude was 310 feet.

The celebrated dive, allegedly of 203 feet, made in 1919, by Alex Wickham, from a rock into the Yarra River in Melbourne, Victoria,

SHALLOW HIGH DIVE SPECIALIST: Henri La Mothe, 70, shows how he dives from 40 feet up the Flatiron Building in New York City into a 12½-inch deep plastic wading pool of water.

Australia, was in fact from a height of 96 feet 5 inches. Samuel Scott (U.S.) is reputed to have made a dive of 497 feet at Pattison Fall (now Manitou Falls) in Wisconsin, in 1840, but this would have entailed an entry speed of 86 m.p.h. The actual height was probably 165 feet. Col. Harry A. Froboess (Switzerland) jumped 360 feet into the Bodensee from the airship *Graf Hindenburg* on June 22, 1936.

Diving, Highest Shallow. Henri La Mothe (b. 1904) set a record by diving 40 feet from the Flatiron Building, New York City, into 12½ inches of water in a child's wading pool on April 5, 1974.

The greatest height reported for a dive into a flaming tank is 100 feet into 7½ feet of water by Bill McGuire, 48, at the Holiday Inn in Chicago City Center, Michigan, on August 14, 1975.

DOMINO THEORETICIAN: Bob Speca relaxes before setting his 22,221 dominoes in action.

Dominoes. The greatest row of dominoes ever toppled at one time is one of 22,221 by Bob Speca of the University of Pennsylvania, in the Spring of 1976. (See color photograph on color page G. Speca's tumble of 15,000 dominoes on the David Frost-Guinness TV show can be seen on a video tape monitor in the Guinness Exhibit Halls in New York and Las Vegas.)

Drumming. The world's duration drumming record is 270 hours by Jim Moore of McCall, Idaho, June 11–22, 1975, with 5-minute breaks per hour.

Ducks and Drakes. The best accepted ducks and drakes (stone-skipping) record is 24 skips (including both plinkers and pitty-pats) by Warren Klope, 20, of Troy, Michigan, with a 4-inch thin flat limestone at the annual Mackinac Island, Michigan, stone-skipping tournament on July 5, 1975.

Egg Drop. The greatest height from which fresh eggs landed without breaking was from 600 feet from a helicopter by David Donaghue and John Cartwright, on February 8, 1974.

Egg and Spoon Racing. Len Dean and Mike O'Kane of Bournemouth College, England, completed a 27-mile fresh egg and dessert spoon marathon in 5 hours 38 minutes on October 25, 1972.

Egg-Shelling. Two kitchen hands, Harold Witcomb and Gerald Harding, shelled 1,050 dozen eggs in a 7¼-hour shift at Bowyers, Trowbridge, Wiltshire, England on April 23, 1971. Both are blind.

Egg Throwing. The longest recorded distance for throwing a fresh hen's egg without breaking it is 316 feet 5¾ inches at their 11th exchange by David Barger and Craig Finley at Lamar High School, Missouri, on May 2, 1974.

Escapology. The most renowned of all escape artists has been Ehrich Weiss *alias* Harry Houdini (1874–1926), who pioneered underwater escapes from locked, roped and weighted containers while handcuffed and shackled with irons. Paul Denver of Rhyl, Wales, performed an escape from a straitjacket when suspended from a helicopter 1,200 feet from the ground over Makati, near Manila, Philippines, on November 13, 1975.

The fastest reported time for an escape from a standardized straitjacket is 24 seconds by Herbie Becker (The Great) Kardeen of Orange City, Florida, in 1975.

Reynir Oern Léosson (b. 1938) succeeded in breaking out of a prison in Iceland in 1972 from a cell in which he had been locked with three handcuffs behind his back and his hands tied by 5 mm. chains, each able to withstand a force of 2,800 lbs. His feet were fastened with footcuffs and he was further loaded with 5 mm. and 10 mm. (tensile strength 13,310 lbs.) chains weighing in all 44 lbs. Léosson broke out in 5 hours 50 minutes and emerged through a 28-mm.-thick 9-inch-wide glass window which he had "extended" by breaking some of the adjoining brickwork. In a laboratory on May 24, 1974, he demonstrated the ability of parting 10 mm. chain which had a tensile strength of 13,448 lbs.

Family Tree. The largest family tree on record is the Borton tree, measuring 18 feet by 15 feet, compiled by Nelleray Borton Holt of Union Gap, Washington, over 16 years. It contains 6,820 names of relatives extending back to 1562.

Fashion Show. The longest fashion show ever recorded was one which lasted for 27 hours 2 minutes at Eastland Shopping Center, West Covina, California, September 13–14, 1975. Tammy Warren, Cristi Stevenson and Sandy Teal all completed 16 miles on the runway.

Adalene Ross of Palo Alto, California, has produced and served as the commentator in more than 4,000 fashion shows to mid-1975.

Feminine Beauty. Female pulchritude, being qualitative rather than quantitative, does not lend itself to records. It has been suggested that, if the face of Helen of Troy (c. 1200 b.c.) was capable of launching 1,000 ships, then a unit of beauty sufficient to launch one ship should be called a millihelen.

The pioneer beauty contest was staged at Atlantic City, New Jersey, in 1921, and was won by a blue-eyed blonde with a 30-inch bust, Margaret Gorman. The Miss World contest, begun in 1951, had a winner in 1954, Miss Egypt (Antigone Costander), who had the Junoesque measurements of 40–26–38.

The world's largest beauty pageant is the annual Miss Universe contest, inaugurated in Long Beach, California, in 1952. The number of countries represented on July 10, 1976, in Hong Kong was 75. The U.S. has been most successful, winning in 1954, 1956, 1960 and 1967.

Ferris Wheel Riding. Endurance record for big wheel riding is 22 days 4 hours 2 minutes by David Chabira and John Benaka in Joyland Park Amusement Park, Topeka, Kansas, May 31–June 22, 1975.

Fire Pump Pulling. The longest unaided tow of a fire appliance was one of 123.4 miles, July 26–27, 1974 from Winchester Guildhall, Hampshire, to Littlehampton, West Sussex, England, and back, by a team of 32 Winchester firemen in 24 hours 2 minutes.

Flute Marathon. The longest recorded time is 43 hours by flautist Ken Munson of Stamford, Connecticut, June 1–2, 1976.

Frisbee Throwing. Competitive Frisbee throwing began in 1958. The longest outdoor throw claimed is one of 420 feet in February, 1976, by the professional Victor Malafronte (U.S.). The International Frisbee Association records are: men, 412 feet by David Johnson; women, 283 feet 6 inches by Susanne Lempert. The throw, run, and catch records are: men, 234 feet by John Kirkland; women, 143 feet by Monika Lou. The marathon record is 76 hours by 3 pairs simultaneously in June, 1976.

Gold Panning. The fastest time recorded for "panning" 8 planted gold nuggets is 15.4 seconds by Larry Bertles of Fallon, Nevada, in the 1976 World Gold Panning Championships held at Tropico Gold Mine, Rosamond, California, on March 7, 1976. Ms. Lilly Szcrupa, a schoolteacher, took the award for "the world's worst gold panner" in 1974.

Golf Ball Balancing. On November 21, 1974, Mark Baumann of Grand Island, Nebraska, succeeded in balancing 5 new golf balls vertically without using any adhesive.

Grape Catching. The longest recorded distance for catching a thrown grape in the mouth is 204 feet by Arden Chapman at Northeast Louisiana University on April 26, 1974.

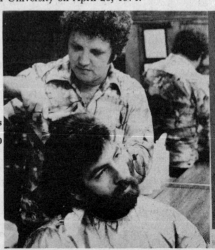

CHAMPION HAIRDRESSER: Louis Sanft of Fall River, Massachusetts spent 200 hours behind the chair.

HANDSHAKE CHAMPION: Teddy Roosevelt shook hands everywhere he went and set a world record on New Year's Day, 1907, when he shook 8,513 hands.

Grave Digging. It is recorded that Johann Heinrich Karl Thieme, sexton of Aldenburg, Germany, dug 23,311 graves during a 50-year career. In 1826, his understudy dug *his* grave.

Guitar Playing. The longest recorded solo guitar playing marathon is one of 122 hours by Mike Palmer at Tiffany's, Merthyr Tydfil, Wales, May 22–27, 1976.

Hairdressing. The world record for non-stop styling, cutting and setting hair is 200 hours by Louis Sanft of Fall River, Massachusetts, from May 27 to June 4, 1976.

The most expensive men's hairdresser is Tristan of Hollywood, who charges any "client" $200 on a first visit. This consists of a "consultation" followed by "remedial grooming."

Hair Splitting. The greatest reported achievement in hair splitting has been that of Alfred West (born London, April 14, 1901) who has succeeded in splitting a human hair 13 times into 14 parts. This hair is on permanent display in the Guinness World Records Exhibit Hall in the Empire State Building in New York City.

Handshaking. The world record for handshaking was set by President Theodore Roosevelt (1858–1919), who shook hands with 8,513 people at a New Year's Day White House Presentation in Washington, D.C., on January 1, 1907. Outside public life the record has become meaningless because aspirants merely arrange circular queues and shake the same hands repetitively.

Handwriting. The longest recorded handwriting marathon was one of 125 hours and more than 2,000 letters by Raymond L. Cantwell of Oxford, England (trying to raise money for the Oxford Animal Sanctuary), December 1–6, 1975.

Hiking. The longest recorded hike is one of 18,500 miles through 14 countries from Singapore to London by David Kwan, aged 22, which occupied 81 weeks from May 4, 1957, or an average of 32 miles a day.

Hitchhiking. The title of world champion hitchhiker is claimed by Devon Smith who from 1947 to 1971 thumbed lifts totaling 291,000 miles. In 1957, he covered all the then 48 U.S. states in 33 days. It was not till his 6,013th hitch that he got a ride in a Rolls Royce.

Hoop Rolling. In 1968 it was reported that Zolilio Diaz (Spain) had rolled a hoop 600 miles from Mieres to Madrid and back in 18 days.

Hopscotch. The longest recorded hopscotch marathon is one of 36 hours 19 minutes by Hilary Manning and Ruth Wilson-Croome of Royal Holloway College, University of London, February 20–21, 1976.

HOT WATER BOTTLE BLOW: Englishman Stuart Hughes is one of two masters of this esoteric art. The bottles can measure more than 5 feet long before they burst.

House of Cards. The greatest number of stories achieved in building houses of cards is 39 in the case of a tower using 1,240 cards by John Wilson, 15, of Port Credit, Ontario, Canada. The highest house with alternate 8- and 6-card stories is 30, achieved by Julian Bardo in St. John's College, Cambridge, England, on June 14, 1974. He used 4 packs and a plumb-line.

Joe E. Whitlam of Deborah Scaffolding Ltd., Barnsley, South Yorkshire, England, by exercise of professional skill, built a structure of 73 stories to a height of 13 feet 10¼ inches with 1,440 cards, July

HUMAN CANNONBALL: Emanuel Zacchini and his daughter Florinda were regularly shot 175 feet from a cannon.

4–5, 1974. Added strength was given to the structure by bending some cards into angle supports.

Hula Hooping. The record for sustaining gyrating hoops is 28, set by De Ann Deluna of Los Angeles, when she won the U.S. National championship on May 27, 1974.

Hula hoops have been the most successful toy ever marketed, with sales in the 1950's once reaching 100 million in a six-month period.

Human Cannonball. The record distance for firing a human from a cannon is 175 feet in the case of Emanuel Zacchini in the Ringling Bros. and Barnum & Bailey Circus, in 1940. His muzzle velocity was estimated at 54 m.p.h. On his retirement the management was fortunate in finding that his daughter, Florinda, was of the same caliber.

In the Halifax explosion of December 6, 1917 (see *Worst Accidents*), William Becker (d. 1969) was blown some 1,600 yards, and found, still alive, in a tree.

MOST KISSES: Roger Guy English claims to have kissed 3,000 girls in 8 hours. Here he demonstrates his patented two-hand technique.

Ice Encasement. Jim Randi, 46, entombed himself unclad in an ice igloo under medical surveillance for 43 minutes 8 seconds in Boston on August 31, 1974.

Ironing. The longest recorded ironing marathon was one won by Mrs. J. Maassen, 37, after 89 hours 32 minutes in Melbourne, Australia, on March 9, 1973.

Joke Telling. Johnny Kay cracked jokes unremittingly at Poynton Social Centre, Cheshire, England, for 8 hours on February 15, 1975.

The duo duration record is 52 hours by Wayne Malton and Mike Hamilton at the Howard Johnson Motor Hotel, Toronto Airport, Canada, November 13–16, 1975.

Juggling. The only juggler in history able to juggle—as opposed to "shower"—10 balls or 8 plates was the Italian Enrico Rastelli, who was born in Samara, Russia, on December 19, 1896, and died in Bergamo, Italy, on December 13, 1931.

Kissing. The most prolonged osculatory marathon in cinematic history is one of 185 seconds by Regis Toomey and Jane Wyman in *You're In the Army Now*, released in 1940.

In a "smouchathon" at Pretoria, South Africa, Inge Ordendaal and Billy Van Der Westhuizen kissed for 119 hours 12 minutes.

Roger Guy English of La Jolla, California, claims to have kissed 3,000 girls in 8 hours—a sustained rate of one every 9.6 seconds.

Kite Flying. The greatest reported height attained by kites is 35,530 feet by a train of 19 flown near Portage, Indiana, by 10 Gary high school boys. The flight took 7 hours, used 56,457 feet of line, and was assessed by telescopic triangulation.

The solo record is 22,500 feet (minimum) to 28,000 feet (maximum) by Philip R. Kunz of the University of Wyoming on November 21, 1967.

The longest officially recorded flight is one of 168 hours by Walter Scott at Briny Breezes, Florida, in 1967, and recorded in the American Kitefliers Association magazine.

The most kites flown on a single line is 1,050 by Kazuhiko Asaba, 52, at Kamakura, Japan, on April 4, 1976. The topmost kite reached an estimated 4,000 feet.

The largest kite on record was built in Naruto City, Japan in 1936, of 3,100 panes of paper weighing 9½ tons. The largest hand-launched kite was one 83 feet long and 820 square feet in area, by Robert Bartlett, flown at Grant Park, Chicago, on April 28, 1974.

Knitting. The longest recorded non-stop knitting marathon is one of 100 hours (with 5-minute time-out allowances per hour) by Mrs. Ann Whitbrown of Market Drayton, Salop, England, April 11–15, 1976.

The most prolific hand-knitter of all time is Mrs. Gwen Matthew-man (b. 1927) of Featherstone, Yorkshire, England, who in 1975 knitted 885 garments involving 10,530 oz. of wool (equivalent to the fleece of 85 sheep). She had been timed to average 108 stitches per minute in a 30-minute test. Her technique has been filmed by the world's only Professor of Knitting—a Japanese.

Mrs. Margaret Collins of Bournemouth, England, knitted 139 rows (3,336 stitches) in 45 minutes in 1976 to set a speed record.

Knot Tying. The fastest recorded time for tying the six Boy Scout Handbook knots (square knot, sheet bend, sheep shank, clove hitch, round turn and two half hitches and bowline) on individual ropes is 10.9 seconds by Kenneth L. Purnell, 13, of Calgary, Canada, on February 23, 1974.

Leap Frogging. Fourteen students of the Hoover Apprentices Association, Merthyr Tydfil, Wales, covered 399¼ miles in 96 hours, August 11–15, 1975.

Lecture. Ronald Lackey, of Chopticon High School, Morganza, Maryland, lectured for 50 hours 6 minutes on April 25–27, 1974. He took a 2-minute break every 2 hours.

Life Saving. In November, 1974, the City of Galveston, Texas, and the Noon Optimist Club unveiled a plaque to the deaf-mute lifeguard Leroy Colombo (1905–74), who saved 907 people from drowning in the waters around Galveston Island, from 1917 to his death.

LIGHTNING-STRUCK: Roy Sullivan has lived to tell 6 tales.

Lightning-Struck. The only living man in the world to be struck by lightning 6 times is Shenandoah Park Ranger Roy C. Sullivan (U.S.), the human lightning-conductor of Virginia. His attraction for lightning began in 1942 (lost big toe nail), and was resumed in July, 1969 (lost eyebrows), in July, 1970 (left

CHAMPION LION-TAMER: Alfred Schneider is the only man to have tackled 40 lions simultaneously.

shoulder seared), on April 16, 1972 (hair set on fire), and, *finally* he hoped, on August 7, 1973: as he was driving along a bolt came out of a small, low-lying cloud, hit him on the head through his hat, set his hair on fire again, knocked him 10 feet out of his car, went through both legs, and knocked his left shoe off. He had to pour a pail of water over his head to cool off. Then, on June 6, 1976, he was struck again for the *sixth* time, and injured but recovered. He can offer no explanation for his magnetism, but he has donated his lightning-burnt Ranger hats to the Guinness World Records Exhibits in New York City and Las Vegas.

Lion Taming. The greatest number of lions mastered and fed in a cage simultaneously by an unaided lion-tamer was 40, by "Captain" Alfred Schneider in 1925.

Clyde (Raymond) Beatty (1903–65) likewise handled more than 40 "cats" (mixed lions and tigers) simultaneously. Beatty, top of the bill for 40 years, insisted on being called a lion-trainer. Twenty-one lion-tamers have died of injuries since 1900.

Log Rolling. The most protracted log-rolling contest on record was one in Chequamegon Bay, Ashland, Wisconsin, in 1900, when Allan Stewart dislodged Joe Oliver from a 24-inch diameter log after 3 hours 15 minutes birling.

Message in a Bottle. The longest recorded interval between drop and pick-up is 64 years, between August 7, 1910 ("please write to Miss Gladys Potter") in Grand Lake, and August, 1974, from Lake Huron. Miss Potter was traced and found to be Mrs. Oliver Scheid, 76, of Columbus, Ohio.

A bottle apparently bearing a message written on November 19, 1899, by Captain Charles Weieerishen of the S.S. *Crown Princess Cecilia* off Varberg, Sweden, was reportedly picked up on the coast of Victoria, B.C., Canada, on December 9, 1936.

Milk Bottle Balancing. The greatest distance walked by a person continuously balancing an empty pint milk bottle on the head is 15 miles 1,738 yards by William Charlton at Davenport, Tasmania, on June 4, 1972.

Morse Code. The highest recorded speed at which anyone has received Morse code is 75.2 words per minute—over 17 symbols per second. This was achieved by Ted R. McElroy (U.S.) in a tournament at Asheville, North Carolina, on July 2, 1939.

Motorcycle and Car Stunting. The greatest number of "bodies" cleared in a motorcycle ramp jump is 41 by Sgt.-Maj. Thomas Gledhill, 41, of the Royal Artillery Motorcycle Display Team on a 441-c.c. B.S.A. Victor GP at Woolwich, Greater London, on June 4, 1971. Tony Yeates cleared 84 feet (*equivalent* to 55 men) at Swindon, England, in 1970.

The so-called T-bone diver or Dive Bomber crashes by cars off ramps over and onto parked cars are measured by the number of cars but, owing to their variable size, and because their purpose in landing on cars is purely to cushion the shock, distance is more significant.

LARGEST GAME OF MUSICAL CHAIRS started with 1,082 contestants and 991 chairs.

The longest recorded distance is 176 feet by Dusty Russell in a 1963 Ford Falcon in Athens, Georgia, in April, 1973.

The longest distance claimed for motorcycle long jumping over cars is 171 feet over 22 cars by Bob Gill (born in St. Petersburg, Florida, September 26, 1945) at the Seattle International Raceway, Washington, on July 17, 1973.

Evel Knievel (Robert Craig Knievel) (b. October 17, 1938, at Butte, Montana) suffered 433 bone fractures by his 1975 season. His abortive attempt to cross the Snake River Canyon, Idaho, on September 8, 1974, in a rocket, reputedly increased his lifetime earnings by $6,000,000. He made a motorcycle jump of reputedly 150 feet, landing on bus No. 14 at Kings Mills, Ohio, October 25, 1975.

The longest recorded jump in a car is one of 203 feet into water by stuntman Roland van de Putte (Belgium) in a Volkswagen on August 11, 1968.

The greatest endurance feat on a "wall of death" was 3 hours 4 minutes by the motorcyclist Louis W. "Speedy" Babbs on a 32-foot diameter silo, refuelling in motion, at the Venice Amusement Pier, California, on October 11, 1929. In 1934, Babbs performed 1,003 consecutive loop-the-loops, sitting side-saddle in an 18-foot-diameter globe at Ocean Park Pier, California. In a life of stunting, Babbs, who proclaims "Stuntmen are not fools," has broken 56 bones.

The greatest number of cars wrecked in a stunt career is 1,031 by April, 1975, by Dick Sheppard of Gloucester, England.

Also see *Tunnel of Fire*.

Musical Chairs. The longest game on record was one starting with 1,082 participants and 991 chairs and ending with Catherine Wood on the last chair at Joaquin Moraga Intermediate School, Moraga, California, on April 30, 1976.

Needle Threading. The record number of strands of cotton threaded through a number 13 needle (eye $\frac{1}{2}$ of an inch by $\frac{1}{16}$ of an inch) in 2 hours is 3,795 by Brenda Robinson of the College of Further Education, Chippenham, Wiltshire, England, on March 20, 1971.

Noodle Making. Stephen Yim (b. Shanghai, China, 1949) made 256 noodle strips (exceeding 5 feet) in 63 seconds on the BBC-TV *Record Breakers* program on October 21, 1973.

Omelette Making. Jeffrey Neese, a short-order cook at the Palace Restaurant, Taylor, Michigan, made 188 2-egg omelettes in 30 minutes on December 23, 1975. He used 6 pans and 6 burners. The single pan record is 105 in 26 minutes 25 seconds by Clement Rapphael Freud at The Victoria in Nottingham, England, on July 15, 1971.

Onion Peeling. Conrad Gerster, 18, peeled 39 lbs. 10¾ oz. of onions in the annual onion peeling contest in Bern, Switzerland, on November 24, 1975.

Pancake Tossing. Brenda ("Angel") Lavisso of the Village Inn Pancake House, Fort Worth, Texas, flipped a pancake (circumference of 9½ inches) 8,960 times in 65½ minutes on December 20, 1975.

Paper Airplanes. A paper airplane was reported to have been flown 1,126 yards by Greg Ruddue, 11, at San Geronimo Valley Elementary School, California, on May 31, 1973.

Paper Chains. The longest recorded paper link chain (limit 12 inches per link) made in under 24 hours has been one of 13 miles 925 yards by 75 students from Herbert Hoover High School, San Jose, California, February 7–8, 1976, using 93,800 links and 200,000 staples. They used back issues of the *San Jose Mercury News* for paper.

Parachute, Longest Fall Without Parachute. The greatest altitude from which anyone has bailed out without a parachute and survived is 21,980 feet. This occurred in January, 1942, when Lt. (now Lt.-Col.) I. M. Chisov (U.S.S.R.) fell from an Ilyushin 4 which had been severely damaged. He struck the ground a glancing blow on the edge of a snow-covered ravine and slid to the bottom. He suffered a fractured pelvis and severe spinal damage. It is estimated that the human body reaches 99 per cent of its low-level terminal velocity after falling 1,880 feet. This is 117–125 m.p.h. at normal atmospheric pressure in a random posture, but up to 185 m.p.h. in a head-down position.

Vesna Vulovic, 23, a Jugoslavenski Aerotransport hostess, survived when her DC-9 blew up at 33,330 feet over the Czechoslovak village of Ceska Kamenice on January 26, 1972. She fell inside a section of tail unit and was hospitalized for 17 months.

Party Giving. The most expensive private party ever thrown was that of Mr. and Mrs. Bradley Martin of Troy, N.Y. It was staged at the Waldorf-Astoria Hotel, New York City, in February, 1897. The cost to the host and hostess was estimated to be $369,200 in the days when dollars were made of gold.

Piano Playing. The longest piano-playing marathon has been one of 1,091 hours (45 days 11 hours) playing 22 hours every day from October 11 to November 24, 1970, by James Crowley, Jr., 30, in Scranton, Pennsylvania.

The women's world record is 133 hours non-stop (5 days 13 hours) by Mrs. Marie Ashton, aged 40, in a theatre at Blyth, Northumberland, England, on August 18–23, 1958. This category has since Leen discontinued.

PARACHUTING RECORDS

First from Tower	Sébastian Lenormund	quasi-parachute	Lyons, France	1783
First from Balloon	André-Jacques Garnerin (1769–1823)	2,230 ft.	Monceau Park, Paris	Oct. 22, 1797
First from Aircraft (man)	Capt. Albert Berry	U.S. Army	St. Louis	Mar. 1, 1912
(woman)	Mrs. "Tiny" Broadwick (b. 1893)		Griffith Park, Los Angeles	June 21, 1913
First Free Fall	Mrs. "Tiny" Broadwick (pilot, Glenn L. Martin)		North Island San Diego, California	Sept. 13, 1914
Lowest Escape	Squad. Leader T. Spencer, R.A.F.	30–40 ft.	Wismar Bay, Baltic Sea	Apr. 19, 1945
Longest Duration Fall	Lt. Col. Wm. H. Rankin, U.S.M.C.	40 mins., due to thermals	North Carolina	July 26, 1956
Highest Escape	Flt. Lt. J. de Salis and Fg. Off. P. Lowe, R.A.F.	56,000 ft.	Monyash, Derby, Eng.	Apr. 9, 1958
Longest Delayed Drop (man)	Capt. Joseph W. Kittinger*	84,700 ft. (16.04 miles) from balloon at 102,800 ft.	Tularosa, New Mexico	Aug. 16, 1960
(woman)	O. Kommissarova (U.S.S.R.)	46,250 ft.	over U.S.S.R.	Sept. 21, 1965
Most Southerly	Tech. Sgt. Richard J. Patton	Operation Deep Freeze	South Pole	Nov. 25, 1956
Most Northerly	Ray Munro (Canada)	−39° F.	89° 39' N.	Mar. 31, 1969
Career Total (man)	Lt.-Col. Ivan Savkin (U.S.S.R.)	More than 5,000	over U.S.S.R.	to Aug. 12. 1967
(woman)	Patty Wilson	More than 1,000	Elsinore paracenter, California	to Nov., 1973
Highest Landing	Ten U.S.S.R. parachutists†	23,405 ft.	Lenina Peak	May, 1969
Heaviest Load	U.S.A.F. C-130 Hercules	25.22 tons steel plates 6 parachutes	El Centro, California	Jan. 28, 1970
Highest from Bridge	Donald R. Boyles	1,053 ft.	Royal Gorge, Colorado	Sept. 7, 1970
Highest Tower Jump	Herb Schmidtz (U.S.)	KTUL-TV Mast 1,984 ft.	Tulsa, Okla.	Oct. 4, 1970
Connected Free Fall	29 "National Enquirer" Skydivers	3-seconds connected	Zephyr Hill, Florida	Mar. 25, 1974
Most Traveled	Kevin Seaman from a Cessna Skylane (pilot, Charles Merritt)	12,186 miles	Jumps in all 50 U.S. States	July 26– Oct. 15, 1972
Oldest Man	Archie McFarland (Great Britain) aged 75		Shabdon, England	Feb. 16, 1973
Oldest Woman	Mrs. Cecilia Reeser (U.S.), aged 62		Flint, Michigan	Aug. 15, 1972
24-Hour Total	Jean-Pierre Blanchet	232 in 24 hours	Quebec, Canada	Sept. 9–10, 1972

*Maximum speed in rarified air was 614 m.p.h. †Four were killed.

Piano Smashing. The record time for demolishing an upright piano and passing the entire wreckage through a circle 9 inches in diameter is 2 minutes 26 seconds by six men representing Ireland led by Johnny Leydon of Sligo, at Merton, Surrey, England, on September 7, 1968.

Dave Gibbons, Les Hollis and "Ginger" O'Regan smashed a piano with bare hands in 13 minutes 23 seconds in Guernsey, Channel Islands, on July 20, 1974.

Piano Tuning. The record time for pitch raising (almost two semi-tones) and then returning a piano to a musically acceptable quality is 30 minutes 9 seconds by Steve Fairchild at the Nassau Chapter of the Piano Technicians Guild Inc., New York, on November 12, 1974.

Pipe Smoking. The duration record for keeping a pipe (3.3 grams of tobacco) continuously alight with only an initial match is 253 minutes 28 seconds by Yrjö Pentikäinen of Kuopio, Finland, on March 15–16, 1968.

Plate Spinning. The greatest number of plates spun simultaneously is 44 by Holley Gray on the *Blue Peter* TV show in London on May 18, 1970.

Pogo Stick Jumping. The greatest number of jumps achieved is 64,649 in 8 hours 35 minutes by Douglas K. Ziegler of Allentown, Pennsylvania, on May 15, 1976.

Scott Spencer, 13, of Wilmington, Delaware, covered 6 miles in 6½ hours in September, 1974.

Pole Sitting. There being no international rules, the "standards of living" atop poles vary widely. The record squat is 399 days by Frank Perkins from June 1, 1975, to July 4, 1976, in an 8 by 8 foot box atop a 50-foot telegraph pole in San Jose, California. He was observed by motorists passing by.

Modern records do not, however, compare with that of St. Daniel (409–493 A.D.), called Stylites (Greek, *stylos*=pillar), a monk who spent 33 years 3 months on a stone pillar on Wonderful Mountain, Syria. This is probably the earliest example of record setting.

Psychiatrist, Fastest. The world's fastest "psychiatrist" was Dr. Albert L. Weiner of Erlton, New Jersey, who dealt with up to 50 patients a day in four treatment rooms. He relied heavily on narco-analysis, muscle relaxants and electro-shock treatments. In December, 1961, he was found guilty on 12 counts of manslaughter from using unsterilized needles. He had been trained in osteopathy but not in psychiatry.

Quoit Throwing. The world's record for rope quoit throwing is an unbroken sequence of 4,002 pegs by Bill Irby, Sr., of Australia in 1968.

Longest on a Raft. The longest recorded survival alone on a raft is 133 days (4½ months) by Second Steward Poon Lim (born Hong

Kong) of the U.K. Merchant Navy, whose ship, the S.S. *Ben Lomond*, was torpedoed in the Atlantic 565 miles west of St. Paul's Rocks at Lat. 00° 30′ N. and Long. 38° 45′ W. at 11:45 a.m. on November 23, 1942. He was picked up by a Brazilian fishing boat off Salinópolis, Brazil, on April 5, 1943, and was able to walk ashore. In July, 1943, he was awarded the British Empire Medal.

Maurice and Maralyn Bailey survived 118¼ days in an inflatable dinghy 4½ feet in diameter in the northeast Pacific from March 4 to June 30, 1973.

Riding in Armor. The longest recorded ride in full armor is one of 146 miles from Glasgow to Dumfries, via Lanark and Peebles, Scotland, in 3 days 3 hours 40 minutes by Dick Brown, 42, on June 12–15, 1973.

Riveting. The world's record for riveting is 11,209 in 9 hours by J. Moir at the Workman Clark Ltd. shipyard, Belfast, Northern Ireland, in June, 1918. His peak hour was his seventh with 1,409, an average of nearly 23½ per minute.

Rocking Chair. The longest recorded duration of a "Rockathon" is 336 hours by Mark Pauga of the Brunswick Recreation Center, Lombard, Illinois, July 27–August 10, 1975.

Roller Coasting. The endurance record is 72 hours (873 miles) by James Bruse and Leroy Harrison on the Swamp Fox Roller Coaster, Grand Strand Amusement Park, Myrtle Beach, South Carolina, June 11–14, 1976.

Rolling Pin. The record distance for a woman to throw a 2-lb. rolling pin is 157 feet 6 inches by Janet Thompson at West London Stadium, Wormwood Scrubs, London, England, on July 6, 1975.

SEE-SAW MARATHON: Charles "Sir Walter" Ryan (left) and Philip Duiett (right) rode this see-saw for 820 hours in 1976.

Rope Jumping. The greatest number of turns ever performed without a break or fault is 50,000 in 5 hours 15 minutes by Rabbi Barry Silberg in Milwaukee, Wisconsin, in May, 1976.

Other rope-jumping records made without a break:

Most turns in one jump	5	Katsumi Suzuki (Japan) Tokyo	early 1968
Most turns in 1 minute	286	J. Rogers (Aust.) Melbourne	Nov. 10, 1937
		T. Lewis (Aust.) Melbourne	Sept. 16, 1939
Most turns in 10 seconds	57	Lu Ann Stolt (U.S.) Bloomer, Wisconsin	1972
Double turns	2,736	Kaori Sumitani (Japan) Tokyo	April 14, 1976
Treble turns	110	Katsumi Suzuki (Japan) Tokyo	Nov. 28, 1975
Duration	1,264 miles	Tom Morris (Aust.) Brisbane–Cairns	1963
Most children, single rope (4 turns)	35	Hawthorne Jr. H.S., Lorvin, Ohio	Oct. 31, 1975

Rope Tricks. The only man ever able to spin 12 ropes simultaneously has been Roy Vincent (b. 1910) of Gloversville, New York. His prime years were 1933 to 1953.

Rummage Sale. The largest known rummage sale is that staged annually at Rockford, Illinois. In 1974, it used 847 volunteer workers and raised $21,830.23.

See-Saw. The most protracted session for see-sawing indoors is one of 820 hours by Charles Ryan and Philip Duiett of Theodore High School, Theodore, Alabama, February 23–March 28, 1976. Georgi Chaffin and Tammy Adams of Goodhope Junior High School, Cullman, Alabama, completed 730½ hours outdoors from June 25–July 25, 1975.

Sermon. The longest sermon on record was delivered by Robert Marshall, 55, minister of the Birmingham Unitarian Church, Birmingham, Michigan, January 1–3, 1976, for 60 hours 31 minutes.

From May 31 to June 10, 1969, the Dalai Lama, the exiled ruler of Tibet, completed a sermon on Tantric Buddhism for five to seven hours per day to total 60 hours.

Shaving. The fastest demon barber on record is Gerry Harley, who shaved 130 men in 60 minutes with a cut-throat razor at The Plough, Gillingham, Kent, England, on April 1, 1971. In setting a marathon record he ran out of volunteer subjects.

Sheaf Tossing. The world's best performance for tossing an 8-lb. sheaf is 56 feet by C. R. Wiltshire of Geelong, Victoria, Australia, in 1956. Contests date from 1914.

Shoe Shining. In this category, limited to teams of 4 teenagers, an 8-hour time limit, and all shoes "on the hoof," the record is 5,303 pairs by the Churchdown Scout Group, Gloucestershire, England, on April 24, 1976.

Shorthand, Fastest. The highest recorded speeds ever attained under championship conditions are: 300 words per minute (99.64

per cent accuracy) for five minutes and 350 w.p.m. (99.72 per cent accuracy, that is, two insignificant errors) for two minutes by Nathan Behrin (U.S.), in New York City in December, 1922. Behrin (born 1887) used the Pitman system invented in 1837. Morris I. Kligman, official court reporter at the U.S. Court House, New York City, has taken 50,000 words in five hours (a sustained rate of 166.6 w.p.m.). Rates are dependent upon the nature, complexity, and syllabic density of the material.

G. W. Bunbury of Dublin, Ireland, held the unique distinction of writing at 250 w.p.m. for 10 minutes on January 23, 1894.

Showering. The most prolonged continuous shower bath on record is one of 200 hours by Bernard Beatty of Beaverton, Oregon, October 3–10, 1975.

The feminine record is 98 hours 1 minute by Paula Glenn, 18, and Margaret Nelson, 20, in Britain on November 24, 1971.

Singing. The longest recorded solo singing marathon is one of 105 hours by Eamonn McGirr at The Bower Club, Stalybridge, Manchester, England, on August 5–10, 1974.

The marathon record for a choir is 40 hours by the Cleveland High School choir of Seattle, Washington, April 9–11, 1976.

The last performance in the now-discontinued category of singing without 5-minute breaks was one of 9 hours by Robert Manderson of Great Shalford, Cambridgeshire, England, on February 2, 1975.

Skateboarding. Sam Puccio, 25, a 225-lb. longshoreman from San Pedro, California, reached a speed of 54 m.p.h. on a skateboard on Signal Hill, Inlong Beach, California, on June 26, 1976.

The high jump record from a skateboard was set by the professional Tom Sims, 25, of Santa Barbara, California, at the New York World Masters Contest on June 19, 1976, when he cleared a bar set at a height of 4 feet $5\frac{1}{2}$ inches. Sims has been skateboarding for 15 years.

On September 21, 1975, Steve Brown, 17, of San Pedro, California, took off from a moving skateboard, jumped over 16 barrels (12-inch diameters) and landed on another skateboard.

Slinging. The greatest distance recorded for a slingshot is 1,147 feet 4 inches using a 34-inch-long sling and a $7\frac{1}{3}$-oz. stone by Melvyn Gaylor on the Newport Golf Course, Shide, Isle of Wight, England, on September 25, 1970.

Smoke-Ring Blowing. The highest recorded number of smoke rings formed from a single pull of a cigarette is 175 by Vince Tresaloni of Lexington, Kentucky, on March 3, 1976. An unsubstantiated claim of 203 was made from Denmark in November, 1975.

Snowshoe Travel. The fastest officially recorded time for covering a mile is 6 minutes 23.8 seconds by Richard Lemay (Frontenac Club of Quebec, Canada) at Manchester, New Hampshire, in 1973.

HIGH JUMP ON SKATEBOARD: Tom Sims jumped 4 feet 5½ inches on June 19, 1976.

Speech-Listening. The Guild of Professional Toastmasters (founded 1962) has only 12 members. Its founder, Ivor Spencer, listened to a speech in excess of 2 hours by the maudlin subject of a retirement luncheon. The Guild also elects the most boring speaker of the year, but for professional reasons will not publicize the winner's name.

Spinning. The duration record for spinning a clock balance wheel by hand is 5 minutes 26.8 seconds by Philip Ashley, aged 16, of Leigh, Lancashire, England, on May 20, 1968.

Spitting. The greatest distance achieved at the annual (July) tobacco-spitting classic (instituted 1955) at Raleigh, Mississippi, is 31 feet 1 inch by Don Snyder, 28, on July 26, 1975. In the 3rd International Spittin', Belchin', and Cussin' Triathlon, Harold Fielden reached 34 feet ¼ inch at Central City, Colorado, on July 13, 1973. Distance is dependent on the quality of salivation, absence of cross wind, two-finger pressure, and the co-ordination of the quick hip and neck snap. Sprays or wads smaller than a dime are not measured.

The record for projecting a melon seed under WCWSSCA rules is 57 feet 8½ inches by Russ Foster of Weatherford, Oklahoma, on August 4, 1973. The highest reported distance for a cherrystone spat from a sitting position is 42 feet 5½ inches by John Crosby near Harrogate, North Yorkshire, England, on June 5, 1976. Spitters who care about their image wear 12-inch block-ended boots so practice spits can be measured without a tape.

Stair Climbing. The 100-story record for stair climbing was set by Dr. Randolph W. Seed in the John Hancock Building in Chicago, Illinois, on February 27, 1972, in 14 minutes 29 seconds. He had previously set the record for the vertical mile—5 round trips—2 hours 53 minutes, 16 seconds, on November 15, 1970.

Standing Up. Swami Maujgiri Maharij stood up continuously for 17 years, from 1955 to November, 1973, while performing the Tapasya or penance in Shahjahanpur, India. He leaned against a plank to sleep.

Stilt Walking. The highest stilts ever successfully mastered were 21 feet from the ankle to the ground by Henry Edward Yelding ("Harry Sloan") (1902–71) of Great Yarmouth, England.

Hop pickers use stilts up to 15 feet. In 1892, M. Garisoain of Bayonne, France, stilt-walked the last 4.97 miles into Biarritz in 42 minutes to average 7.1 m.p.h. In 1891, Sylvain Dornon stilt-walked from Paris to Moscow *via* Vilno in 50 stages for the 1,830 miles. Another source gives his time as 58 days.

Stretcher Bearing. The longest recorded carry of a stretcher case with a 140-lb. "body" is 80.4 miles in 24 hours 25 minutes by two 4-man teams from 1 Field Ambulance, Canadian Forces Base, Calgary, Alberta, June 24–25, 1975.

String Ball, Largest. The largest balls of string on record are 11 feet in diameter weighing 5 tons, one of which was amassed by Francis A. Johnson of Darwin, Minnesota, since 1950, and another by Frank Stoeber of Cawker City, Kansas, since at least 1962.

Submergence. The longest submergence under water (excluding the use of diving bells) is 126 hours 30 minutes, established at the 1961 Canadian National Sportsmen's Show, Toronto, Ontario, by Patrick Morrison of Toronto, Joe Mangus of Ohio, and Mrs. Alberta Jones of Miami, Florida.

ONE OF TWO LARGEST BALLS OF STRING: Francis Johnson of Darwin, Minnesota, began this string ball in 1950. It now measures 11 feet in diameter and weighs 5 tons.

IN THE SWING: Kitty Brown had a wonderful time as she set a record mark of 122½ hours.

Suggestion Box. The most prolific suggestion box stuffer on record is John Drayton (born September 13, 1907) of Pontypool, Gwent, Wales, who plied British Rail and the companies from which it was formed with a total of 27,500 suggestions from 1924 to April, 1976. One out of every seven was accepted.

The U.S. Postal Service champion John Kingston has an acceptance rate of one in 5.3 (284 out of 1,500) to January, 1976.

Swinging. The record duration for continuous swinging is 122½ hours by Kitty Brown of Anaheim, California, December 29, 1975, to January 5, 1976.

Talking. The world record for non-stop talking is 144 hours 4 minutes by Tim Harty of Coon Rapids, Minnesota, January 27–February 2, 1975.

The longest continuous political speech on record was one of 29 hours 5 minutes by Gerard O'Donnell in Kingston-upon-Hull, Yorkshire, on June 23–24, 1959.

The women's non-stop talking record was set by Mrs. Mary E. Davis, who, on September 2–7, 1958, started talking at a radio station in Buffalo, New York, and did not stop until 110 hours 30 minutes 5 seconds later in Tulsa, Oklahoma.

The longest after-dinner speech was 3 hours, delivered by Rev. Henry Whithead (d. March, 1896) at the Rainbow Tavern in London, England, on January 16, 1874.

TEETH PULL TRAIN: John Massis of Belgium gets two Long Island passenger cars weighing 80 tons moving along the tracks by pulling them with his teeth. He later pulled two railway cars in Belgium weighing 124 tons (U.S.).

Pulling with Teeth. The "strongest teeth in the world" belong to "Hercules" John Massis of St. Amandsberg, Belgium, who in April, 1976, demonstrated the ability to pull two Belgian Railway cars weighing 124 tons along the rails with a bit in his teeth. At Evry, France, on March 27, 1976, he raised a weight of 498¼ lbs. from the ground with a bit in his teeth.

FIRST TO CROSS NIAGARA FALLS was Charles Blondin (left) who walked across on a 3-inch rope on July 30, 1885. **185 DAYS (AND NIGHTS) ON A TIGHT-ROPE** 82 feet up in the air was the record set by Henri Rochetain of France (right). Doctors cannot understand how he could sleep on the high wire.

HIGHEST TIGHTROPE WALK: Philippe Petit (France) walking 1,350 feet above street level between the twin towers of the World Trade Center of New York City on August 7, 1974.

Tightrope Walking. The greatest 19th century tightrope walker was Jean François Gravelet, *alias* Charles Blondin (1824–1897), of France, who made the earliest crossing of Niagara Falls on a 3-inch rope, 1,100 feet long, 160 feet above the Falls on July 30, 1855. He also made a crossing with Harry Colcord, pickaback on September 15, 1860, though other artists find it difficult to believe. Colcord was his agent.

The world tightrope endurance record is 185 days by Henri Rochetain (born 1926) of France on a wire 394 feet long, 82 feet above a supermarket in St. Etienne, France, from March 28 to September 29, 1973. His ability to sleep on the wire has left doctors puzzled. During this time, he walked some 310 miles on the wire to keep fit.

The longest tightrope walk by any funambulist was achieved by Rochetain on a wire 3,790 yards long slung across a gorge at Clermont-Ferrand, France, on July 13, 1969. He required 3 hours 20 minutes to negotiate the crossing.

The tightrope walk over the highest drop occurred when Philippe Petit, 24, of Nemours, France, crossed on a wire 1,350 feet above the street in New York City between the newly constructed twin towers of the World Trade Center on August 7, 1974. He shot the wire across by bow and arrow. He was charged with criminal trespass after a 75-minute display of at least 7 crossings. The police psychiatrist's verdict was, "Anyone who does this 110 stories up can't be entirely right."

Treasure Finding. The most successful treasure hunter has been C. Fred Ahrendt of Dayton, Ohio, who, by August, 1974, had found with his metal detector 158 class rings (earliest, 1908) and 149

TREE SITTING: Jim Sparks, 14, was continuously up a tree for 61 days in the summer of 1975.

wedding rings of 14 or more carats. Employees of crematoria are officially excluded from the competition.

Tree Climbing. The fastest tree-climbing record is one of 36 seconds for a 90-foot pine by Kelly Stanley (Canada) at the Toowoomba Show, Queensland, Australia, in 1968.

Tree Sitting. The duration record for sitting in a tree is 61 days 21 hours 56 minutes by Jim Sparks, 14, in a fruitless mulberry tree in his father's back yard in Visalia, California, from June 25 to August 25, 1975.

Tunnel of Fire. The significance of the length of a tunnel of fire depends largely upon the dimensions. A height and width of 6 feet 8 inches is now becoming standard. All previous records were eclipsed in February, 1974, near Johannesburg, South Africa, when the stuntman Ed Kannemeyer (born 1950) forsook the usual motorcycle for a regular bicycle. Blinded by flames after 137 feet, he ran the final 84½ feet on foot, emerging after 15 seconds.

Typing, Fastest. The highest recorded speeds attained with a ten-word penalty per error on a manual machine are:

One Minute: 170 words, Margaret Owen (U.S.) (Underwood Standard), New York City, October 21, 1918.

One Hour: 147 words (net rate per minute), Albert Tangora (U.S.) (Underwood Standard), October 22, 1923.

The official hour record on an electric machine is 9,316 words (40 errors) on an I.B.M. machine, giving a net rate of 149 words per minute, by Margaret Hamma, now Mrs. Dilmore (U.S.), in Brooklyn, New York City, on June 20, 1941. Mrs. Barbara Blackburn of Lee's Summit, Missouri, has sustained speeds of 170 w.p.m. using the Dvorak Simplified Keyboard (D.S.K.) system.

In an official test in 1946, Stella Pajunas, now Mrs. Garnand, attained a speed of 216 words in a minute on an I.B.M. machine.

Typing, Slowest. Chinese typewriters are so complex that even the most skilled operator cannot select characters from the 1,500 offered at a rate of more than 11 words a minute. The Hoang typewriter produced in 1962 now has 5,850 Chinese characters. The keyboard is 2 feet long and 17 inches wide.

Typing, Longest. The world duration record for typing on an electric machine is 162 hours 1 minute by Robin Heil of Sherman E. Burroughs High School, Ridgecrest, California, April 6–13, 1976.

Mrs. Marva Drew, 51, of Waterloo, Iowa, between 1968 and November 30, 1974, typed the numbers 1 to 1,000,000 on a manual typewriter. She used 2,473 pages. When asked why, she replied, "But I love to type."

The longest duration typing marathon on a manual machine is 120 hours 15 minutes by Mike Howell, a 23-year-old blind office

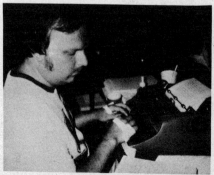

UNSUPPORTED CIRCLE: 1,817 students at Huntington Beach High School, California, sat in each other's laps on March 30, 1976.

worker from Greenfield, Lancashire, England, on November 25–30, 1969, on an Olympia manual typewriter in Liverpool. In aggregating 561,006 strokes he performed a weight movement of 2,780 tons plus a further 174 tons on moving the carriage on line spacing.

Unsupported Circle. The highest recorded number of people who have demonstrated the physical paradox of all being seated without a chair in an unsupported circle is 1,817 by students of Huntington Beach High School, California, on March 30, 1976.

HANDSTAND RACER: Rick Sorrell "ran" a 50-yard sprint in 24.2 seconds.

Walking-on-Hands. The duration record for walking-on-hands is 871 miles by Johann Hurlinger, who, in 55 daily 10-hour stints, averaged 1.58 m.p.h. from Vienna to Paris in 1900.

Rick Sorrell, 17, of Franklin High School, Franklin, Ohio, completed a 50-yard sprint on his hands in 24.2 seconds on July 1, 1975.

Wallpapering. Mike Young, 34, of Cheshunt, Hertfordshire, England, demonstrated the ability to hang 20 rolls of patterned wallpaper in 4 hours in April, 1976. This is an average of 165 feet per hour.

Wheelbarrow Pushing. The heaviest loaded wheelbarrow pushed for a minimum 20 feet is one loaded with 290 bricks weighing 1,740 lbs. by Peter King at Ventnor on the Isle of Wight, England, in November, 1975.

Whip Cracking. The longest stock whip ever "cracked" (*i.e.* the end made to travel above the speed of sound—760 m.p.h.) is one of 80 feet, first cracked by Frank Dean (U.S.) at the North Dakota State Fair in 1939.

Wood Cutting. The earliest competitions date from Tasmania in 1874. The best times ever recorded on Australian hardwoods in competition on 12-inch logs are:

Underhand	20.0 sec.	Gus De Blano	1921
Standing Block	13.7 sec.	C. Stewart	1965
Hard Hitting	17 hits	G. Parker, Tom Kirk	1958
Tree Felling	1 m. 20.0 sec.	Bill Youd	1970

The fastest time ever recorded for double-handed sawing an 18-inch block of Lombardy poplar is 8.0 seconds by Merv Reed and Nelson Thorburn at Hukerenui, New Zealand, on February 8, 1958.

Writing under Handicap. The ultimate feat in "funny writing" would appear to be the ability to write extemporaneously and decipherably backwards, upside down, laterally inverted (mirror-style) while blindfolded with both hands simultaneously. Several close approaches to this are under investigation.

Writing Small. Larry Yates of McMinnville, Oregon, has manually engraved the Lord's Prayer within a square millimeter (one 645th of a square inch) with a pivot-arm device of his own invention.

William R. Woodbridge, 46, of Harrow, England, demonstrated in November, 1974, the ability, without mechanical or optical aids, to write the Lord's Prayer 10 times (2,700 words) within the size of a definitive postage stamp (0.84 × 0.71 of an inch).

Yodeling. The most protracted yodel on record is that of Richard Baker, for 5 hours 24 minutes in Lexington, Kentucky, on April 3, 1976.

Yo-Yo. The yo-yo originates from a Filipino jungle fighting weapon recorded in the 16th century weighing 4 lbs. with a 20-foot cord. The word means "come-come." The modern toy was first marketed by Donald F. Duncan of Chicago in 1926 and popularized nationwide by the toy manufacturer, Louis Marx (U.S.) in 1929. A device like it, called a bandilore, had previously been illustrated in a book in 1891. The most difficult modern yo-yo trick is the "whirlwind," incorporating both inside and outside horizontal loop-the-loops. The greatest reported number of consecutive loop-the-loops is 7,351 by Tony Flor (born 1902) on August 23, 1975. The individual continuous endurance record is 79 hours 58 minutes by Robert Neales, 16, of Portland, Maine, June 25–28, 1975.

The highest number of oscillations recorded in 60 minutes is 5,269 by Peter Ballantyre of England on July 12, 1975.

GASTRONOMIC RECORDS

Records for eating and drinking by trenchermen do not match those suffering from the rare disease of bulimia (morbid desire to eat) and polydipsia (pathological thirst). Some bulimia patients have to spend 15 hours a day eating, with an extreme consumption of 384 lbs. 2 oz. of food in six days by Matthew Daking, aged 12, in 1743 (known as Mortimer's case). Some polydipsomaniacs have been said to be unsatisfied by less than 96 pints of liquid a day. Miss Helge Andersson (b. 1908) of Lindesberg, Sweden, was reported in January, 1971, to have been drinking 40 pints of water a day since 1922—a total of 87,600 gallons.

The world's greatest trencherman is Edward Abraham ("Bozo") Miller (born 1909) of Oakland, California. He consumes up to 25,000 calories per day, or more than 11 times that recommended. He stands 5 feet 7½ inches tall but weighs from 280 to 300 lbs., with a 57-inch waist. He has been undefeated in eating contests since 1931 (see below).

The bargees (barge sailors) on the Rhine are reputed to be the world's heaviest eaters, with 5,200 calories per day. However, the New Zealand Sports Federation of Medicine reported in December, 1972, that a long-distance road runner consumed 14,321 calories in 24 hours.

While no healthy person has been reported to have succumbed in any contest for eating or drinking non-alcoholic or non-toxic drinks, such attempts, from a medical point of view, must be regarded as *extremely* inadvisable, particularly among young people. Gastronomic record attempts should aim at improving the *rate* of consumption, rather than the volume. *Guinness* will not list any records involving the consumption of more than 2 liters (approximately 2 quarts) of beer nor any at all involving liquor. Nor will this book list records for potentially dangerous categories as consuming live ants, quantities of chewing gum or marshmallows, or raw eggs in shells.

Specific records have been claimed as follows:

Baked Beans. 1,823 cold beans one by one, with a cocktail stick in 30 minutes by Nigel Moore at the P.O. Social Club, Manchester, England on June 19, 1974.

Bananas. 63 in 10 minutes by Michael Gallen, 23, in Cairns, Australia, on October 11, 1972.

Beer. Peter G. Dowdeswell (born in London, July 29, 1940) of Earl's Barton, Northamptonshire, England, in 1975 broke all the beer-drinking records: 2½-pint yard of ale in 5 seconds on May 4; 3-pint yard of ale in 6.5 seconds on May 4; 2 pints (40 fluid oz.) in 2.3 seconds on June 11.

Champagne. 1,000 bottles per annum by Bobby Aclan of the "Black Raven," Bishopsgate, London, England.

Cheese. 16 oz. of hard English cheddar in 3 minutes 17 seconds by John Wharton in Aurora, Colorado, on June 28, 1975.

Chicken. 27 (2-lb. pullets) by "Bozo" Miller (see above) at a sitting at Trader Vic's, San Francisco, California, in 1963.

Clams. 424 in 8 minutes by Dave Barnes at Port Townsend Bay, Washington, on May 3, 1975.

Doughnuts. 29 (total of 2 lbs. 12½ oz.) in 7 minutes 16 seconds by Hany Rizk of Melbourne, Australia, on April 10, 1976.

Eels. 1 lb. of elvers (1,300) in 43 seconds by Leslie Cole, 37, at Frampton-on-Severn, Gloucestershire, England on April 13, 1971.

Eggs. (Hard-boiled) 14 in 100 seconds by Mike Laskouskí of New York on February 14, 1976. (Soft-boiled) 32 in 130 seconds by Douglas L. Burch at Korbets Restaurants, Mobile, Alabama, on May 9, 1975. (Raw, without shells) 13 in 3.8 seconds by James Lindop in Manchester, England, on September 29, 1973.

Frankfurters. 20 (2 oz.) in 3 minutes 33 seconds by Jimmy Davenport of Lexington, Kentucky, on March 3, 1976.

Gherkins. 1 lb. in 43.6 seconds by Rex Barker of Elkhorn, Nebraska, on October 30, 1975.

Grapes. 3 lbs. 1 oz. in 34.6 seconds by Jim Ellis of Montrose, Michigan, on May 30, 1976.

Hamburgers. 17 1.6-oz. hamburgers (with 3½-inch diameter buns) in 30 minutes by Ronald Sloan in Cincinnati, Ohio, on April 15, 1976.

Ice Cream. 8 lbs. (51 2½-oz. scoops) in 12 minutes by Ronald C. Long at Friendly's Ice Cream Shop, North Adams, Massachusetts, on May 2, 1975.

Lemons. 12 quarters (3 lemons) whole (including skin and seeds) in 35 seconds by Bob Blackmore of Lexington, Kentucky, on March 3, 1976.

Meat. One whole roast ox in 42 days by Johann Ketzler of Munich, Germany, in 1880.

Milk. 1.2 quarts in 3.2 seconds by Peter Dowdeswell at Dudley Top Rank Club, West Midlands, England, on May 31, 1974.

Oysters. 588 in 17 minutes 32 seconds by Vernon Bass, 48, at Walt's Fish Market, Sarasota, Florida, on November 23, 1975.

The record for opening oysters is 100 in 3 minutes 1 second by Douglas Brown, 26, at Christchurch, New Zealand, on April 29, 1974.

Pancakes. 61 (size 6 inches in diameter, buttered and with syrup) in 7 minutes by Mark Mishon, 19, at The Obelix Creperie, London, England, on February 11, 1973.

Peanuts. 100 (unshelled) singly in 59.2 seconds by Chris Ambrose in Clerkenwell, London, on April 3, 1973.

Pickled Onions. 91 in 2 minutes by D. A. Dase of Cincinnati, Ohio, on May 31, 1975.

Potatoes. 3 lbs. in 4 minutes 45 seconds by Ian Cameron of Dudley, Worcestershire, England, on June 10, 1976.

Potato Chips. 30 2-oz. bags in 24 minutes 33.6 seconds, without a drink, by Paul G. Tully of Brisbane University, Australia, in May, 1969.

The largest single potato chip on record is one measuring 5 inches by 3 inches, found at Reeds School, Cobham, Surrey, England, on February 2, 1971. Another with the same dimensions was reported by Mr. and Mrs. David J. Buja of Gardner, Massachusetts, on May 4, 1974.

Prunes. 130 (without pits) in 105 seconds by Dave Man at Eastbourne, England, on June 16, 1971.

Ravioli. 324 (first 250 in 70 minutes) by "Bozo" Miller (see above) at Rendezvous Room, Oakland, California, in 1963.

Sandwiches. 40 (jam and butter $6 \times 3\frac{3}{4} \times \frac{1}{2}$ inch) in 39 minutes by Steve Street in Edmonton, London, England, April 10, 1974.

Sausages. $89\frac{1}{2}$ Danish 1 oz. sausages in 6 minutes by Lee Hang in Hong Kong, on May 3, 1972.

Shellfish. 81 (unshelled) whelks in 15 minutes by William Corfield at Helyar Arms, East Coker, Somerset, England, on September 6, 1969.

Shrimps. $2\frac{1}{4}$ lbs. in 15 minutes by Myron Gavant at Long John Silver's Shoppe, Jackson, Mississippi, on February 4, 1976.

Snails. 124 (Moroccan snails) in 15 minutes by Mrs. Nicky Bove at the 6th Great Escargot Eating Contest, Houston, Texas, April 1, 1974. The style prize was won by Rex Miller.

Spaghetti. 100 yards in 67 seconds by Bill Simpson of Lexington, Kentucky, on March 3, 1976.

Tortillas. 74 by Tom Nall in the 2nd World Championship at Marciano's Mexican Restaurant, Dallas, Texas, October 16, 1973.

WEALTH AND POVERTY

The measurement of extreme personal wealth is beset with intractable difficulties. Quite apart from reticence and the element of approximation in estimating the valuation of assets, as Jean Paul Getty (see below) once said: "If you can count your millions, you are not a billionaire." The term, millionaire, was invented in *c.* 1740 and billionaire in 1861.

The earliest dollar billionaires were John Davison Rockefeller (1839-1937); Henry Ford (1863-1947); and Andrew William Mellon (1855-1937).

Living Billionaires. There are currently two surviving U.S. dollar billionaires: John Donald MacArthur (b. Pittston, Pennsylvania, 1897); and Daniel K. Ludwig (b. South Haven, Michigan, June, 1897). H. Ross Perot (b. Texarkana, Texas, 1930) was in December, 1969, worth in excess of a billion dollars on paper.

Fortune magazine in May, 1968, assessed the wealth of Jean Paul Getty (1892–1976) at $1.338 billion and re-assessed Howard R. Hughes (1905–1976) at $1.200 billion in December, 1973. Mr. Ludwig was, in January, 1972, stated to be richer than either. On proven oil reserve revaluations, however, Mr. Getty would appear to be unsurpassable and early indications were that his personal assets and trust funds at the time of his death were in excess of $1,750,000,000.

Because there are fewer people to share the wealth, the richest oil sheiks are the rulers of Kuwait, a nation which in 1974 received $8,000 million in oil export revenues.

Europeans with family assets in excess of the equivalent of a billion dollars include the Wallenburg family in Sweden and the wealthiest United Kingdom citizen, Sir John Reeves Ellerman (1909–1973), whose fortune was once estimated at £600 million ($1.5 billion). Ellerman's will, the largest ever probated in Britain, left only £53,238,370, however.

Highest Income. The greatest income is derived from the collection of royalties per barrel by rulers of oil-rich sheikdoms, who have not abrogated personal entitlement. Before his death in 1965, H.H. Shaikh Sir Abdullah as-Salim as-Sabah (b. 1895), the 11th Amir of Kuwait, was accumulating royalties payable at the rate of £2.6 million ($6.5 million) per week or £135 million ($337.5 million) a year.

Highest Gross. The highest gross income ever achieved in a single year by a private citizen is an estimated $105,000,000 in 1927 by the Chicago gangster Alphonse ("Scarface Al") Capone (1899–1947). This was derived from illegal liquor trading and alky-cookers (illicit stills), gambling establishments, dog tracks, dance halls, "protection" rackets and vice. On his business card, Capone described himself as a "Second Hand Furniture Dealer."

Millionairesses. The world's wealthiest woman was probably Princess Wilhelmina Helena Pauline Maria of Orange-Nassau (1880–1962), formerly Queen of the Netherlands (from 1890 to her abdication, September 4, 1948), with a fortune which was estimated at over $550,000,000.

The youngest person ever to accumulate a million dollars was the child film actor Jackie Coogan (born Los Angeles, 1914) co-star with Sir Charles Chaplin (born London, 1889) in "The Kid," made in 1920. Shirley Temple (born April 23, 1928), now Mrs. Charles Black, accumulated wealth in excess of $1,000,000 before she was 10 years old. Her child actress career spanned the years 1934–39.

The earliest recorded self-made millionairess was Madame Charles Joseph Walker (*née* Sarah Breedlove on December 23, 1867) a black, whose fortune was founded on a hair straightener. She had been a scrubwoman and a laundress.

Greatest Miser. An estate of $95,000,000 was left by the notorious miser Henrietta (Hetty) Howland Green (*née* Robinson) (1835–1916). She had a balance of over $31,400,000 in one bank alone. She was so mean that her son had to have his leg amputated because of the delays in finding a *free* medical clinic. She herself lived off cold oatmeal because she was too mean to heat it, and died of apoplexy in an argument over the virtues of skimmed milk.

Richest Families. It has been tentatively estimated that the combined value of the assets controlled by the Du Pont family of some 1,600 members may be of the order of $150,000 million. The family arrived penniless in the U.S. from France on January 1, 1800.

Biggest Dowry. The largest recorded dowry was that of Elena Patiño, daughter of Don Simón Iturbi Patiño (1861–1947), the Bolivian tin millionaire, who in 1929 bestowed $22,400,000 from a fortune at one time estimated to be worth $350,000,000.

Longest Pension. Miss Millicent Barclay, daughter of Col. William Barclay of Great Britain was born posthumously on July 10, 1872, and became eligible for a Madras Military Fund pension to continue until her marriage. She died unmarried on October 26, 1969, having drawn the pension for every day of her life of 97 years 3 months.

Highest Earnings. The highest salary paid in the U.S. in 1974 was $1,595,000 to Michel C. Bergerac, president of the Revlon cosmetics company.

The highest-salaried woman executive was believed to be Mary Wells Lawrence, chairman of the advertising firm, Wells, Rich, Greene, Inc., of New York City, who received $385,000 in 1973. Her husband, Harding L. Lawrence, also earns a salary as chairman of Braniff Airways.

Lowest Incomes. The poorest people in the world are the Tasaday tribe of cave-dwellers of central Mindanao, the Philippines, who were "discovered" in 1971, and live without any domesticated animals, agriculture, pottery, wheels or clothes.

Biggest Loss. The biggest recorded personal paper loss in one

24-hour period on stock values was taken by Ray A. Kroc, chairman of McDonald's Corporation, $64,901,718 on July 8, 1974, and Edwin H. Land, president of the Polaroid Corporation, $59,397,355 on May 28–29, 1975, when Polaroid stock closed down $12.12 at 43¼.

Return of Cash. The largest amount of cash ever found and returned to its rightful owners was $500,000 found by Lowell Elliott, 61, on his farm at Peru, Indiana. It had been dropped in June, 1972, by a parachuting skyjacker.

Greatest Bequests. The greatest bequests in a lifetime of a millionaire were those of the late John Davison Rockefeller (1839–1937), who gave away sums totaling $750,000,000.

The Scottish-born U.S. citizen, Andrew Carnegie (1835–1919), is estimated to have made benefactions totaling $350,000,000 in the last 18 years of his life. These included 7,689 church organs and 2,811 libraries. He had started in a bobbin factory at $1.20 per week.

The largest bequest made in the history of philanthropy was the $500,000,000 gift, announced on December 12, 1955, to 4,157 educational and other institutions by the Ford Foundation (established 1936) of New York City. The assets of the Foundation had a book value of $3,370,521,943 in 1971.

2. Honors, Decorations and Awards

Eponymous Record. The largest object to which a human name is attached is the super cluster of galaxies known as Abell 7, after the astronomer Dr. George O. Abell of the University of California. The group of clusters has an estimated linear dimension of 300,000,000 light-years and was announced in 1961.

The human who has had the most objects named after him is William Prout (1785–1850) who, in 1815, enunciated (the incorrect) Prout's Law that all the atomic weights of all the elements are multiples of the atomic weight of hydrogen. Ernest (later Lord) Rutherford, in 1911, named the positively charged nucleus of the atom a Proton (after Prout). It is estimated that there are some 10^{85} protons in the observable universe.

Orders and Decorations

Oldest. The earliest of the orders of chivalry is the Venetian order of St. Marc, reputedly founded in 831 A.D. The Castilian order of Calatrava has an established date of foundation in 1158. The prototype of the princely Orders of Chivalry is the Most Noble Order of the Garter founded by King Edward III of England in c. 1348.

Most Titles. The most titled person in the world is the 18th Duchess of Alba (Albade Termes), Doña María del Rosario Cayetana Fitz-James Stuart y Silva. She is 8 times a duchess, 15 times a marchioness, 21 times a countess and is 19 times a Spanish grandee.

U.S. The highest U.S. decoration is the Congressional Medal of Honor. Five marines received both the Army and Navy Medals of

WAR ACE WITH HIGHEST HONORS: Captain Edward Rickenbacker (left) shot down 26 planes in World War I and received Distinguished Service Cross with 9 clusters (see table). **TOP JET ACE:** Captain Joseph McConnell, U.S.A.F. (right) shot down 16 jets in the Korean War.

Honor for the same acts in 1918 and 14 officers and men from 1863 to 1915 have received the medal on two occasions.

MOST CLUSTERS AND GOLD STARS

Navy Cross	4 gold stars	Brig. Gen. Lewis B. Puller, U.S.M.C.
		Cdr. Ray M. Davenport, U.S.N.
Distinguished Service Cross	9 clusters	Capt. Edward Rickenbacker (died 1973)
Silver Star	8 clusters	Col. David H. Hackworth, U.S.A.
	2 gold stars	Lt. Col. Raymond L. Murray, U.S.M.C.
Distinguished Flying Cross	11 clusters	Col. Francis S. Gabreski, U.S.A.F.
	8 gold stars	Capt. Howard J. Finn, U.S.M.C.
Distinguished Service Medal (Army)	4 clusters	Gen. of the Army Douglas MacArthur (also one Naval award)
		Gen. of the Army Dwight D. Eisenhower
Distinguished Service Medal (Navy)	3 gold stars	Fleet Admiral William F. Halsey
Legion of Merit	5 clusters	Maj. Gen. Richard Steinbach
	3 gold stars	Lt. Gen. Claire E. Hutchin
		Major Gen. Field Harris, U.S.M.C.
		Col. William H. Patterson, Jr.
Purple Heart	9 clusters	Sgt. Raymond E. Tirva

Top Jet Ace. The greatest number of kills in jet-to-jet battles is 16 by Capt. Joseph Christopher McConnell (U.S.A.F.) in the Korean War (1950–53). He was killed on August 25, 1954. It is possible that an Israeli ace may have surpassed this total in the period 1967–70, but the identity of pilots is subject to strict security.

Top Scoring Air Aces

Country	World War I 1914–1918	World War II 1939–1945
World	80 Rittm. Manfred, Freiherr (Baron) von Richthofen (Germany)	352[1] Major Erich Hartman (Germany)
U.S.	26 Capt. Edward Vernon Rickenbacker, M.H., D.S.C. (9 o.l.c.), L. d'H., C. de G.	40 Major Richard I. Bong, M.H., D.S.C., S.S., D.F.C. (6 o.l.c.), A.M. (11 o.l.c.).
Canada	72 Lt.-Col. William Avery Bishop, V.C., C.B., D.S.O. and bar, M.C., D.F.C., L. d'H., C. de G.	31½ Sq.-Ldr. George F. Beurling, D.S.O., D.F.C., D.F.M. and bar.

[1] Only one of these aircraft on the Eastern Front in 1942–45, in this unrivalled total was an obsolescent Soviet transport plane.

Top Woman Ace. The record score for any woman fighter pilot is 13 by Jr. Lt. Lila Litvak (U.S.S.R.) in the Eastern Front campaign of 1941–45.

Most Successful U-Boat Captain. The most successful of all World War II submarine commanders was Leutnant Herbert Schultze, captain of the U.48, who up to June, 1941, sank one escort vessel and 51 Allied merchantmen totaling 310,000 gross registered tons. In World War I, Kapitan-Leutnant Lothar von Arnauld de la Periere, in the U.35 and U.139, sank 194 Allied ships totalling 453,716 gross tons.

The most successful boats were the U.48, which in World War I sank 54 ships of 90,350 g.r.t. in a single voyage and 535,900 g.r.t. all told, and the U.53, which sank 53 ships of 318,111 g.r.t. in World War II.

Most Bemedalled. The most bemedalled chest was that of H.I.M. Haile Selassie (born, as Ras Tafari Makonnen) (1892–1975), ex-Emperor of Ethiopia, who had over 50 medal ribbons worn in up to 14 rows.

Most Statues. The world record for raising statues to oneself was set by Generalisimo Dr. Rafael Leónidas Trujillo y Molina (1891–1961), former President of the Dominican Republic. In March, 1960, a count showed that there were "over 2,000." The country's highest mountain was named Pico Trujillo (now Pico Duarte). One province was called Trujillo and another Trujillo Valdez. The capital was named Ciudad Trujillo (Trujillo City) in 1936, but reverted to its old name of Santo Domingo on November 23, 1961. Trujillo was assassinated in a car ambush on May 30, 1961, and May 30 is now celebrated annually as a public holiday.

The man to whom most statues have been raised is undoubtedly Vladimir Ilyich Ulyanov, *alias* Lenin (1870–1924), busts of whom have been mass-produced. Busts of Mao Tse-tung (b. December 26, 1893) and Ho Chi Minh (1890–1969) have also been mass-produced.

Greatest Reception. The greatest ticker-tape reception ever given in New York City was that for Lt.-Col. (now Col.) John Herschel Glenn, Jr. (born July 18, 1921), on March 1, 1962, after

GREATEST TICKER-TAPE PARADE: Given on Lower Broadway, New York City, to Lt.-Col. John H. Glenn, Jr. on his return from 3 orbits in space, March, 1962. It was estimated that 3,474 tons of paper were tossed out of windows.

his return from his tri-orbital flight. (See photo.) The New York Street Cleaning Department estimated that 3,474 tons of paper descended. This total compared with 3,249 tons for General of the Army Douglas MacArthur (1880–1964) in 1951, and 1,800 tons for Col. Charles Augustus Lindbergh (born February 4, 1902), in June, 1927.

Most Honorary Degrees. The greatest number of honorary degrees awarded to any individual is 89, given to Herbert Clark Hoover (1874–1964), former President of the United States (1929–33).

Nobel Prizes

The Nobel Foundation of $8,960,000 was set up under the will of Alfred Bernhard Nobel (1833–96), the unmarried Swedish chemist and chemical engineer who invented dynamite in 1866. The Nobel Prizes are presented annually on December 10, the anniversary of Nobel's death and the festival day of the Foundation. Since the first Prizes were awarded in 1901, the highest cash value of the award, in the fields of Physics, Chemistry, Medicine and Physiology, Literature, Peace and Economics was $123,000 in 1974.

Most Awards by Countries. The U.S. has shared in the greatest number of awards (including those made in 1975) with a total of 89, made up of 22 for Physics, 15 for Chemistry, 26 for Medicine-Physiology, 6 for Literature, 15 for Peace and 5 for Economics.

By classes, the U.S. holds the records for Medicine-Physiology with 26, for Physics with 22 and for Peace with 15; Germany for Chemistry with 22; and France for Literature with 12.

Individuals. Individually the only person to have won two Prizes outright is Dr. Linus Carl Pauling (born February 28, 1901),

Professor of Chemistry since 1931 at the California Institute of Technology, Pasadena, California. He was awarded the Chemistry Prize for 1954 and the Peace Prize for 1962. Only two others have won two Prizes. One was Madame Marie Curie (1867–1934), who was born in Poland as Marja Sklodowska. She shared the 1903 Physics Prize with her husband Pierre Curie (1859–1906) and Antoine Henri Becquerel (1852–1908), and won the 1911 Chemistry Prize outright. The other was Professor John Bardeen (b. May 23, 1908) who shared the Physics Prize in 1956 and 1972. The Peace Prize has been awarded three times to the International Committee of the Red Cross (founded October 29, 1863), of Geneva, Switzerland, namely in 1917, 1944 and in 1963, when it was shared with the International League of Red Cross Societies.

Oldest. The oldest prizeman was Professor Francis Peyton Rous (b. in Baltimore, Maryland, 1879, d. 1970), who worked at the Rockefeller Institute, New York City. He shared the Medicine Prize in 1966, at the age of 87.

Youngest. The youngest laureate has been Professor Sir William Lawrence Bragg (born in Adelaide, South Australia, March 31, 1890), of the U.K., who, at the age of 25, shared the 1915 Physics Prize with his father, Sir William Henry Bragg (1862–1942), for work on X-rays and crystal structures. Bragg and also Theodore William Richards (1868–1928) of the U.S., who won the 1914 Chemistry Prize, carried out their prize work when aged 23. The youngest Literature prizeman was Rudyard Kipling (U.K.) (1865–1936) at the age of 41, in 1907. The youngest Peace prizewinner was the Rev. Dr. Martin Luther King, Jr. (born January 15, 1929, assassinated April 4, 1968), of the U.S., in 1964.

Who's Who

The longest entry of the 66,000 entries in *Who's Who in America* is that of Prof. Richard Buckminster Fuller (b. 1895) whose all-time record of 139 lines compares with the 23-line sketch on Richard M. Nixon.

EVOLUTION OF SPORTS RECORDS IN THE 20TH CENTURY

	Start of the Century—January 1, 1901	*Middle of the Century—January* 1, 1951	*Present-Day Record—August*, 1976
Greatest Weight Lift	4,133 lbs.—Louis Cyr (Canada), 1896	4,133 lbs.—Louis Cyr (Canada), 1896	6,270 lbs.—Paul Anderson (U.S.), 1957
Fastest 100 yards	9.8 secs.—John Owen (U.S.) and 12 others, 1890–1899	9.3 secs.—Mel Patton (U.S.), 1948	9.0 secs.—Ivory Crockett (U.S.), 1974 Houston McTear (U.S.) 1975
Fastest One Mile	4m 12.8s—W. G. George (U.K.), 1886	4m 01.3s—Gunder Hägg (Sweden), 1945	3m 49.4 s—John Walker (N.Z.) 1975
One Hour Running	11 miles 932 yds.—W. G. George (U.K.), 1884	12 miles 29 yds.—Viljo Heino (Finland), 1945	13 miles 24¾ yards—J. Hermens (Netherlands), 1976
Highest High Jump	6′ 5⅝″—M. Sweeney (U.S.), 1895	6′ 11″—Lester Steers (U.S.), 1941	7′ 7¼″—D. Stones (U.S.), 1976
Highest Pole Vault	11′ 10½″—R. Clapp (U.S.), 1898	15′ 7¾″—Cornelius Warmerdam (U.S.), 1942	18′ 8¼″—David Roberts (U.S.), 1976
Long Jump	24′ 7¾″—P. O'Conner (U.K.), 1900	26′ 8¼″—Jesse Owens (U.S.), 1935	29′ 2½″—R. Beamon (U.S.), 1968
Longest Shot Put	48′ 2″—D. Horgan (U.K.), 1897	58′ 10¾″—Jim Fuchs (U.S.), 1950	72′ 2½″—A. Baryshnikov (U.S.S.R.), 1976
Longest Discus Throw	122′ 3½″—R. Sheldon (U.S.), 1899	186′ 11″—Fortune Gordien (U.S.), 1949	232′ 6″—M. Wilkins (U.S.), 1976
Longest Hammer Throw	169′ 4″—J. J. Flanagan (U.S.), 1900	196′ 5″—Imre Németh (Hungary), 1950	260′ 2″—Walter Schmidt (W. Germany), 1975
Longest Javelin Throw	161′ 9¾″—E. Lemming (Sweden), 1899	258′ 2″—Yrjo Nikkanen (Finland), 1938	310′ 4″—M. Nemeth (Hungary), 1976
One Hour Walking	8 miles 270 yds.—W. J. Sturgess (U.K.), (Amateur), 1895	8 miles 1,025 yds.—John Mikaelsson (Sweden), 1945	8 miles 1,294 yds.—G. Panichkin (U.S.S.R.), 1959
Longest Ski Jump	116½′—O. Tanberg (Norway), 1900	442¾′—Dan Netzell (Sweden), 1950	577′ 5″—T. Innauer (Austria), 1976
Fastest 500 meters Ice Skating	45.2 sec.—P. Ostlund (Norway), 1900	41.8 sec.—Hans Engnestangen (Norway), 1938	37.0 sec—Evgeni Kulikov (U.S.S.R.), 1975
Fastest 100 meters Swim (long course)	1m 14.0s (no turn)—J. Nutall (U.K.), 1893	55.8 sec.—Alexandre Jany (France), 1947	49.44 sec.—Jonty Skinner (S. Africa), 1976
Cycling (m.p.h.) Paced	62.27—C. M. Murphy (U.S.), 1899	>80—L. Vanderstuyft (Belgium), 1928	140.5—Allan V. Abbott (U.S.), 1973
Fastest 1 mile Race Horse (excluding straightaways)	1m 35.5s—*Salvator*, in U.S., 1890	1m 33.4s—*Citation* in U.S., 1950	1m 32.2s.—*Dr. Fager* in U.S., 1968
Highest Mountain Climbed (feet)	22,834—Aconcagua, Argentina, 1897	26,492—Annapurna I, Nepal, 1950	29,028—Everest, Nepal-Tibet, 1953

Chapter Twelve

SPORTS, GAMES AND PASTIMES

Earliest. The origins of sport stem from the time when self-preservation ceased to be the all-consuming human preoccupation. Archery was a hunting skill in Mesolithic times (by *c.* 8000 B.C.), but did not become an organized sport until about 300 A.D., among the Genoese. The earliest dated evidence for sport is *c.* 2450 B.C. for fowling with throwing sticks and hunting. Ball games by girls, depicted on Middle Kingdom murals at Ben Hasan, Egypt, have been dated to *c.* 2050 B.C.

Fastest. The governing body for aviation, *La Fédération Aéronautique Internationale,* records maximum speeds in lunar flight of up to 24,791 m.p.h. However, these achievements, like all air speed records since 1923, have been para-military rather than sporting.

The highest speed reached in a non-mechanical sport is in sky-diving, in which a speed of 185 m.p.h. is attained in a head-down free-falling position, even in the lower atmosphere. In delayed drops, a speed of 614 m.p.h. has been recorded at high rarefied altitudes. The highest projectile speed in any moving ball game is *c.* 160 m.p.h. in pelota (jai-alai). This compares with 170 m.p.h. (electronically-timed) for a golf ball driven off a tee.

Slowest. In amateur wrestling, before the rules were modified toward "brighter wrestling," contestants could be locked in holds for so long that single bouts could last for 11 hours 40 min. In the extreme case of the 2 hours 41 minutes pull in the regimental tug o'war in Jubbulpore, India, on August 12, 1889, the winning team moved a net distance of 12 feet at an average speed of 0.00084 m.p.h.

Longest. The most protracted sporting test was an automobile duration test of 222,618 miles by Appaurchaux and others in a Ford Taunus. This was contested over 142 days in 1963. The distance was equivalent to 8.93 times around the equator.

The most protracted non-mechanical sporting event is the *Tour de France* cycling race. In 1926, this was over 3,569 miles, lasting 29 days. The total damage to the French national economy of this annual event, now reduced to 23 days, is immense. If it is assumed that one-third of the total working population works for only two-thirds of the time during *Le Tour* this would account for a loss of more than three-quarters of one per cent of the nation's annual Gross National Product. In 1973 this loss would have been some $1,836,000,000.

Largest Field. The largest field for any ball game is that for polo with 12.4 acres, or a maximum length of 300 yards and a width, without side-boards, of 200 yards.

Most Participants. The annual Nijmegen Vierdaagse march in the Netherlands over distances up to 50 kilometers (31 miles 120 yards) attracted 16,667 participants in 1968. The greatest number of competitors in any competitive event is for the "Vasa Lopp" Nordic skiing race in Sweden. There were 9,500 starters in 1976.

According to a report issued in April, 1971, 28,400,000 men and 15,200,000 women are actively involved in 209,000 physical culture and sports groups in the U.S.S.R. There are 6.1 million track athletes, 5.6 million volleyball players, 3.9 million soccer players and 891,000 weightlifters. The report also lists 2,918 stadiums and 430 indoor and 475 outdoor swimming pools for 791,000 swimmers.

Worst Disasters. The worst disaster in recent history was when an estimated 604 were killed after some stands at the Hong Kong Jockey Club race course collapsed and caught fire on February 26, 1918. During the reign of Antoninus Pius (138–161 A.D.) the upper wooden tiers in the Circus Maximus, Rome, collapsed during a gladiatorial combat, killing some 1,100 spectators.

Youngest and Oldest Sports Record Breakers. The youngest age at which any person has broken a world record is 12 years 328 days in the case of Karen Yvette Muir (born September 16, 1952), of Kimberley, South Africa, who broke the women's 110-yard backstroke world record with 1 minute 08.7 seconds at Blackpool, England, on August 10, 1965.

The oldest person to hold a world record is Gerhard Weidner (W. Germany) (b. March 15, 1933) who broke the 20-mile track walking record in Hamburg on May 25, 1974, when he was 41 years 71 days old.

Youngest and Oldest Internationals. The youngest age at which any person has won international honors is 8 years in the case of Joy Foster, the Jamaican singles and mixed-doubles table tennis champion in 1958. It would appear that the greatest age at which anyone has actively competed for his country is 72 years 280 days in the case of Oscar G. Swahn (Sweden) (born October 20, 1847), who won a silver medal for shooting in the Olympic Games at Antwerp on July 26, 1920. He qualified for the 1924 Games, but was unable to participate because of illness.

Youngest and Oldest Champions. The youngest person to have successfully participated in a world title event was a French boy, whose name is not recorded, who coxed the winning Netherlands pair at Paris on Aug. 26, 1900. He was not more than 10 and may have been as young as 7. The youngest individual Olympic winner was Marjorie Gestring (U.S.), who took the springboard diving title at the age of 13 years 9 months at the Olympic Games in Berlin in 1936. Sir Eyre Massey Shaw (G.B.) (1830–1908) won an Olympic gold medal in yachting in the 1900 Games at the age of 70 years 4 months.

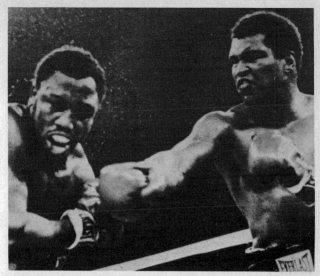

LARGEST PURSE OF ALL TIME: Muhammad Ali (right) defeated Joe Frazier in his successful defense of the heavyweight title in Manila, Philippines, on October 1, 1975. In the process, he collected $6 million—the largest purse for a single event in sports history.

The longest reign as a world champion is 27 years (1928–55) by the Basque tennis player, Pierre Etchbaster (born in France, 1893), who retired undefeated at age 62 in 1955 as world amateur real (royal) tennis champion, to set a record for age.

Greatest Earnings. The greatest fortune amassed by an individual in sport is an estimated $47,500,000 by Sonja Henie (1912–69), of Norway, the triple Olympic figure skating champion (1928–32–36) as a professional ice skating promoter starring in her own ice shows and 11 films. The most for a single event is a purse of $6,000,000 won by Muhammad Ali Haj in his title fight against Joe Frazier, fought in Manila, Philippines, on October 1, 1975. The gross purse was reportedly $9,000,000, but the true figure will never be known.

The highest-paid woman athlete in the world is ice skater Janet Lynn (*née* Nowicki) (U.S.) (born April 6, 1953) who in 1974 signed a $1,500,000 three-year contract. In 1974 she earned more than $750,000.

Heaviest Sportsmen. The heaviest sportsman of all time was the wrestler William J. Cobb of Macon, Georgia, who in 1962 was billed as the 802-lb. "Happy Humphrey." The heaviest player of a ball game was Bob Pointer, the 487-lb. tackle, formerly on the 1967 Santa Barbara High School team, and still playing in California in 1972 at 480 lbs.

Most Expensive. The most expensive of all sports is the racing of large yachts—"J" type boats and International 12-meter boats. The owning and racing of these is beyond the means of individual millionaires and is confined to multi-millionaires or syndicates.

Largest Crowd. The greatest number of live spectators for any sporting spectacle is the estimated 1,000,000 (more than 20 per cent of the population) who line the route of the annual San Sylvestre road race of 8,600 meters (5 miles 605 yards) through the streets of São Paulo, Brazil, on New Year's night. However, spread over 23 days, it is estimated that more than 10,000,000 see the annual *Tour de France* along the route.

The largest crowd traveling to any sporting event is "more than 400,000" for the annual *Grand Prix d'Endurance* motor race on the Sarthe circuit near Le Mans, France. The record stadium crowd was one of 199,854 for the Brazil *vs.* Uruguay match in the Maracanã Municipal Stadium, Rio de Janeiro, Brazil, on July 16, 1950.

Best Attended Sports Funeral

A crowd estimated between 60,000 and 70,000 people attended the funeral of the 1960 and 1964 Olympic marathon champion Abebe Bikila (Ethiopia), at Addis Ababa, in October, 1973.

Archery

Earliest References. The discovery of stone arrowheads at Border Cave, Northern Natal, South Africa, in deposits exceeding the Carbon 14 dating limit, indicates that the bow was invented *ante* 46,000 B.C. Archery developed as an organized sport at least as early as the 4th century A.D. The world governing body is the *Fédération Internationale de Tir à l'Arc* (FITA), founded in 1931.

Flight Shooting. The longest flight shooting records are achieved in the footbow class. In the unlimited footbow division, the professional Harry Drake of Lakeside, California, holds the record at 1 mile 268 yards, shot at Ivanpah Dry Lake, California, on October 24, 1971. The unlimited handbow class (*i.e.* standing stance with bow of any weight) record is 922 yards 16 inches by Bruce Odle at Wendover, Utah, on August 12, 1975. The crossbow record is 1,359 yds. 29 inches, held by Drake and set at same venue on October 14–15, 1967.

Sultan Selim III shot an arrow 1,400 Turkish *pikes* or *gez* near Istanbul, Turkey, in 1798. The equivalent English distance is somewhere between 953 and 972 yards.

Highest Scores. The world records for a single FITA Round are: men, 1,316 points (of a possible 1,440) by Darrell Pace (U.S.) at Oxford, Ohio, August 5–6, 1975; and women, 1,256 points (possible 1,440) by Irene Lorensen (U.S.) at Oxford, Ohio, August 5–6, 1975.

There are no world records for Double FITA rounds, but the highest scores achieved in either a world or Olympic championship were posted at the 1976 Olympics at Montreal, Canada, July 27–30, 1976: men, 2,571 points (possible 2,880) by Darrell Pace (U.S.); women, 2,499 by Luann Ryon (U.S.).

HOLDER OF TWO FLIGHT-SHOOTING RECORDS: Harry Drake is the master with the footbow (1 mile 268 yards), and crossbow. Here he is trying to break his own unlimited footbow record.

Most Titles. The greatest number of world titles (instituted 1931) ever won by a man is four by H. Deutgen (Sweden) in 1947–48–49–50. The greatest number won by a woman is seven by Mrs. Janina Spychajowa-Kurkowska (Poland) in 1931–32–33–34, 1936, 1939 and 1947.

Oscar Kessels (Belgium) has participated in 21 world championships since 1931.

Marathon. The highest recorded score over 24 hours by a pair of archers is 45,454 during 42 Portsmouth Rounds (60 arrows at 20 yards with a 2-inch diameter 10 ring) shot by Stan Kiehl and Greg Shumaker at the S. & R. Sports Haven, Greentown, Ohio, June 21–22, 1975.

Auto Racing

Earliest Races. The first automobile trial was one of 20 miles in France, from Paris to Versailles and back on April 20, 1887, won by Georges Bouton (1847–1938) of France in his steam quadricycle in 74 minutes, at an average of 16.22 m.p.h.

The first "real" race was from Paris to Bordeaux and back (732 miles) on June 11–13, 1895. The winner was Emile Lavassor (d. 1897) (France) driving a Panhard-Lavassor two-seater with a 2.1-liter Daimler engine developing $3\frac{1}{2}$ h.p. His time was 48 hours 47 min.

(average speed 15.01 m.p.h.). The first closed circuit race was held at the Circuit du Sud-Ouest, Paris, in 1900.

The oldest auto race in the world, still being regularly run, is the R.A.C. Tourist Trophy (38th race held in 1974), first staged on the Isle of Man on September 14, 1905. The oldest continental race is the French Grand Prix (53rd in 1975) first held on June 26–27, 1906.

Fastest Circuits. The highest average lap speed attained on any closed circuit is 221.160 m.p.h. by Mark Donohue, Jr. (1937–75) (U.S.) who lapped the 2.66-mile 33-degree banked tri-oval at Alabama International Motor Speedway, Talladega, Alabama, in 43.299 seconds, driving a 5,374-c.c. turbocharged Porsche 917/30 Can-Am car on August 9, 1975.

The highest average race lap speed for a closed circuit is more than 195 m.p.h. by Richard Brickhouse (U.S.) driving a 1969 Dodge Daytona Charger powered by a 6,981-c.c. 600-b.h.p. V8 engine, during a 500-mile race on the tri-oval at Alabama International Motor Speedway, Talladega, Alabama, on September 14, 1969.

The fastest road circuit is the Francorchamps circuit near Spa, Belgium. It is 14.10 kilometers (8 miles 1,340 yards) in length and was lapped in 3 minutes 13.4 seconds (average speed of 163.086 m.p.h.) during the Francorchamps 1,000-kilometer sports car race on May 6, 1973, by Henri Pescarolo (b. Paris, France, September 25, 1942) driving a 2,933-c.c. V12 Matra-Simca MS 670 Group 5 sports car. The practice lap record is 3 minutes 12.7 seconds (average speed 163.678 m.p.h.) by Jacques-Bernard "Jacky" Ickx (b. Brussels, Belgium, January 1, 1945) driving a 2,998.5-c.c. flat-12 Ferrari 312 P Group 5 sports car on May 4, 1973.

Fastest Races. The fastest race in the world is the NASCAR Grand National 125-mile event on the 2½-mile 31-degree banked tri-oval at Daytona International Speedway, Daytona Beach, Florida. The record time is 40 minutes 55 seconds (average speed 183.295 m.p.h.) by William Caleb "Cale" Yarborough (born March 27, 1939) of Timmonsville, South Carolina, driving a 1969 Mercury V8, on February 19, 1970.

The fastest road race was the 1,000-kilometer (621-mile) sports car race held on the Francorchamps circuit (8 miles 1,340 yards) near Spa, Belgium. The record time for this 71-lap (622.055-mile) race is 4 hours 1 minute 9.7 seconds (average speed 154.765 m.p.h.) by Pedro Rodriguez (1940–71) of Mexico and Keith Jack "Jackie" Oliver (b. Chadwell Heath, Essex, England, Aug. 14, 1942), driving a 4,998-c.c. flat-12 Porsche 917K Group 5 sports car on May 9, 1971.

Toughest Circuits. The Targa Florio (first run 1906) was widely acknowledged to be the most arduous race. Held on the Piccolo Madonie Circuit in Sicily, it covered eleven laps (492.126 miles) and involved the negotiation of 9,350 corners, over severe mountain gradients, and narrow rough roads.

The record time was 6 hours 27 minutes 48.0 seconds (average speed 76.141 m.p.h.) by Arturo Francesco Merzario (b. Civenna, Italy, March 11, 1943) and Sandro Munari (Italy) driving a

2,995.5-c.c. flat-12 Ferrari 312 P Group 5 sports car in the 56th race on May 21, 1972. The lap record was 33 minutes 36.0 seconds (average speed 79.890 m.p.h.) by Leo Juhani Kinnunen (born Tampere, Finland, Aug. 5, 1943) on lap 11 of the 54th race in a 2,997-c.c. flat-8 Porsche 908/3 Spyder Group 6 prototype sports car on May 3, 1970. The race was last held on May 13, 1973.

The most difficult Grand Prix circuit is generally regarded to be that for the Monaco Grand Prix (first run on April 14, 1929), run through the streets and around the harbor of Monte Carlo. It is 3,312 meters (2.058 miles) in length and has 11 pronounced corners and several sharp changes of gradient. The race is run over 78 laps (160.522) miles and involves on average about 1,600 gear changes.

The record for the race is 1 hour 59 minutes 51.47 seconds (average speed 80.356 m.p.h.) by Andreas-Nikolaus "Niki" Lauda (b. Vienna, Austria, February 22, 1949), driving a 2,998.5-c.c. flat-12 Ferrari 312T2 on May 30, 1976. The race lap record is 1 minute 38.28 seconds (average speed 82.064 m.p.h.) by Gianclaudio Giuseppe "Clay" Regazzino (b. Lugano, Switzerland, September 5, 1939), driving a similar Ferrari on lap 60 of the race on May 30, 1976. The practice lap record is 1 minute 27.65 seconds (average speed 84.641 m.p.h.) by Lauda on May 29, 1976.

Le Mans

The greatest distance ever covered in the 24-hour *Grand Prix d'Endurance* (first held on June 26–27, 1923) on the Sarthe circuit (8 miles 650 yards) at Le Mans, France, is 3,315.210 miles (average speed 138.134 m.p.h.) by Dr. Helmut Marko (b. Graz, Austria, April 27, 1943) and Jonkheer Gijs van Lennep (b. Bloemendaal, Netherlands, March 16, 1942) driving a 4,907-c.c. flat-12 Porsche 917K Group 5 sports car on June 12–13, 1971. The race lap record is 3 minutes 18.7 seconds (151.632 m.p.h.) by Pedro Rodriguez (1940–71) driving a Porsche 917L on June 12, 1971. The practice lap record is 3 minutes 13.6 seconds (average speed 155.627 m.p.h.) by Jackie Oliver driving a similar car on April 18, 1971. The prewar record average speed was 86.85 m.p.h. by a 3.3-liter Bugatti in 1939.

Most Wins. The race has been won by Ferrari cars nine times, in 1949, 1954, 1958 and 1960–61–62–63–64–65. The most wins by one man is four by Oliver Gendebien (Belgium), who won in 1958 and 1960–61–62.

Indianapolis 500

The Indianapolis 500-mile race (200 laps) was inaugurated on May 30, 1911. The most successful drivers have been Warren Wilbur Shaw (1902–1954), who won in 1937, 1939, and 1940; Louis Meyer, who won in 1928, 1933 and 1936, and Anthony Joseph "A.J." Foyt, Jr., who won in 1961, 1964 and 1967. Mauri Rose won in 1947 and 1948 and was the co-driver with Floyd Davis in 1941.

The record time is 3 hours 4 minutes 5.54 seconds (average speed 162.962 m.p.h.) by Mark Donohue (b. Summit, New Jersey, March 18, 1937) driving a 2,595-c.c. 900-b.h.p. turbocharged Sunoco

MOST SUCCESSFUL DRIVER: Juan-Manuel Fangio of Argentina won the World Drivers' Championship five times and 24 Grand Prix races before retiring in 1958.

McLaren M16B-Offenhauser on May 27, 1972. The record prize fund was $1,037,775.96 for the 60th race on May 30, 1976. The individual prize record is $271,697.72 by Al Unser (b. Albuquerque, New Mexico, May 29, 1939) on May 30, 1970.

The race lap record is 47.02 seconds (average speed 191.408 m.p.h.) by Wally Dallenbach of New Brunswick, New Jersey, driving a 2.6-liter turbocharged Eagle-Offenhauser on lap 2 of the race held on May 26, 1974. The practice lap record is 45.21 (average speed 199.071 m.p.h.) by Johnny Rutherford (b. 1938) of Fort Worth, Texas, driving a 2,595-c.c. 900-b.h.p. turbocharged Gulf-McLaren M16B-Offenhauser on lap 3 of his 4-lap qualification run on May 12, 1973.

The slowest finish was by the winner of the 1915 race, Ralph De Palma, who had to push his Mercedes the final 1½ miles.

Fastest Pit Stop. Bobby Unser (U.S.) took 4 seconds to take on fuel on lap 10 of the Indianapolis 500 on May 30, 1976.

Duration Record

The greatest distance ever covered in one year is 400,000 kilometers (248,548.5 miles) by François Lecot (1879–1949), an innkeeper from Rochetaillée, France, in a 1,900-c.c. 66-b.h.p. Citroën 11 sedan mainly between Paris and Monte Carlo, from July 22, 1935 to July 26, 1936. He drove on 363 of the 370 days allowed.

The world's duration record is 185,353 miles 1,741 yards in 133 days 17 hours 37 minutes 38.6 seconds (average speed 58.07 m.p.h.) by Marchand, Presalé and six others in a Citroën on the Montlhéry track near Paris, during March–July, 1933.

Most Successful Drivers

Based on the World Drivers' Championships, inaugurated in 1950, the most successful driver is Juan-Manuel Fangio (born Balcarce, Argentina, June 24, 1911), who won five times in 1951–54–55–56–57. He retired in 1958, after having won 24 Grand Prix races (2 shared).

The most successful driver in terms of race wins is Richard Lee Petty (born Randleman, North Carolina, July 2, 1937) with 177 NASCAR Grand National wins from 1960 to November 2, 1975. His best year was 1967 with 27 victories.

The most Grand Prix victories is 27 by Jackie Stewart of Scotland between September 12, 1965 and August 5, 1973. Jim Clark, O.B.E. (1936–1968) of Scotland holds the record of Grand Prix victories in one year with 7 in 1963. He won 61 Formula One and Formula Libre races between 1959 and 1968. The most Grand Prix starts is 176 (out of a possible 184) between May 18, 1958, and Jan. 26, 1975, by Norman Graham Hill, O.B.E. (b. London, England, February 15, 1929). He took part in 90 *consecutive* Grands Prix between November 20, 1960 and October 5, 1969.

Oldest and Youngest World Champions. The oldest was Juan-Manuel Fangio, who won his last World Championship on August 18, 1957, aged 46 years 55 days. The youngest was Emerson Fittipaldi (Brazil) who won his first World Championship on September 10, 1972, aged 25 years 273 days.

Oldest and Youngest Grand Prix Winners and Drivers. The youngest Grand Prix winner was Bruce Leslie McLaren (1937–70) of New Zealand, who won the U.S. Grand Prix at Sebring, Florida, on December 12, 1959, aged 22 years 104 days. The oldest Grand Prix winner was Tazio Giorgio Nuvolari (1892–1953) of

GRAND PRIX CHAMPION (left): Jackie Stewart of Scotland (#5) has won 27 Grand Prix races. LAND SPEED HOLDER (right): Gary Gabelich has driven "The Blue Flame" at 650 m.p.h. (see next page).

Italy, who won the Albi Grand Prix at Albi, France, on July 14, 1946, aged 53 years 240 days. The oldest Grand Prix driver was Louis Alexandre Chiron (born Monaco, August 3, 1899), who finished 6th in the Monaco Grand Prix on May 22, 1955, aged 55 years 292 days.

The youngest Grand Prix driver was Christopher Arthur Amon (b. Bulls, New Zealand, July 20, 1943) who took part in the Belgian Grand Prix on June 9, 1963, aged 19 years 324 days.

Land Speed Records

The highest speed ever recorded by a wheeled vehicle was achieved by Gary Gabelich (b. San Pedro, California, August 29, 1940), at Bonneville Salt Flats, Utah, on October 23, 1970. He drove the Reaction Dynamics *The Blue Flame*, weighing 4,950 lbs. and measuring 37 feet long, powered by a liquid natural gas-hydrogen peroxide rocket engine developing a maximum static thrust of 22,000 lbs. On his first run, at 11:23 a.m. (local time), he covered the measured kilometer in 3.543 seconds (average speed 631.367 m.p.h.) and the mile in 5.829 seconds (617.602 m.p.h.). On the return run, at 12:11 p.m. his times were 3.554 seconds for the kilometer (629.413 m.p.h.) and 5.739 seconds for the mile (627.287 m.p.h.). The average times for the two runs were 3.5485 seconds for the kilometer (630.388 m.p.h.) and 5.784 seconds for the mile (622.407 m.p.h.). During the attempt only 13,000 lbs. s.t. was used and a peak speed of 650 m.p.h. was momentarily attained.

The most successful land speed record breaker was Major Sir Malcolm Campbell (1885–1948) (U.K.). He broke the official record nine times between September 25, 1924, with 146.157 m.p.h. in a Sunbeam, and September 3, 1935, when he achieved 301.129 m.p.h. in the Rolls-Royce-engined *Bluebird*.

The world speed record for compression-ignition-engined cars is 190.344 m.p.h. (average of two runs over measured mile) by Robert Havemann of Eureka, California, driving his *Corsair* streamliner, powered by a turbocharged 6,981-c.c. 6-cylinder GMC 6-71 diesel engine developing 746 b.h.p., at Bonneville Salt Flats, Utah, in August, 1971. The faster run was made at 210 m.p.h.

Dragging

Piston-Engined. The lowest elapsed time recorded by a piston-engined dragster is 5.637 seconds by Donald Glenn "Big Daddy" Garlits (born 1932) of Seffner, Florida, driving his rear-engined AA-F dragster, powered by a 7,948-c.c. supercharged Dodge V8 engine during the National Hot Rod Association's Supernationals at Ontario Motor Speedway, California, on October 11, 1975. On this run, he reached a record 250.69 m.p.h.

The world record for two runs in opposite directions over 440 yards from a standing start is 6.70 seconds by Dennis Victor Priddle (b. 1945) of Yeovil, Somerset, England, driving his 6,424-c.c. supercharged Chrysler dragster, developing 1,700 b.h.p. using nitromethane and methanol, at Elvington Airfield, England, on October 7, 1972. The faster run took 6.65 seconds.

Rocket or Jet-Engined. The highest terminal velocity recorded by any dragster is 377.754 m.p.h. (elapsed time 4.65 seconds) by Norman Craig Breedlove (b. March 23, 1938) of Los Angeles,

EARLIEST AUTO RALLY: Prince Scipione Borghese arrives in Paris 61 days after leaving Peking—10 days ahead of his nearest rival.

California driving his *English Leather Special* rocket dragster at Bonneville Salt Flats, Utah, in Sept. 1973. The lowest elapsed time recorded by any dragster is 4.55 seconds by Sam Miller of Wayne, New Jersey, at Seattle International Raceway, Kent, Washington, on May 31, 1975.

Terminal velocity is the speed attained at the end of a 440-yard run made from a standing start and elapsed time is the time taken for the run.

Stock Car Racing

Richard Petty of Randleman, North Carolina, was the first stock car driver to attain $1,000,000 lifetime earnings on August 1, 1971.

Rallies

Earliest. The earliest long rally was promoted by the Parisian daily *Le Matin* in 1907 from Peking, China to Paris, over a route of about 7,500 miles. Five cars left Peking on June 10. The winner, Prince Scipione Borghese, arrived in Paris on August 10, 1907 in his 40 h.p. Itala.

Longest. The world's longest ever rally event was the £10,000 ($24,000) London *Daily Mirror* World Cup Rally run over 16,243 miles starting from London, England, on April 19, 1970, to Mexico City via Sofia, Bulgaria and Buenos Aires, Argentina, passing through 25 countries. It was won on May 27, 1970, by Hannu Mikkola (born Joensuu, Finland, May 24, 1942) and Gunnar Palm (b. Kristinehamn, Sweden, February 25, 1937) in an 1,834-c.c. Ford Escort RS1600. The longest held annually is the East African Safari (first run 1953), run through Kenya, Tanzania and Uganda, which is up to 3,874 miles long, as in the 17th Safari held on April 8–12, 1971. It has been won a record three times by Jogindev Singh (Kenya) in 1965, 1974 and 1976.

Smallest Car. The smallest car to win the Monte Carlo rally (founded 1911) was an 841-c.c. Saab driven by Erik Carlsson (born Sweden, 1929) and Gunnar Häggbom of Sweden on January 25, 1962, and by Carlsson and Gunnar Palm on January 24, 1963.

Go-Kart Circumnavigation

The only recorded instance of a go-kart being driven around the world was a circumnavigation by Stan Mott, of New York, who drove a Lambretta-engined 175-c.c. Italkart with a ground clearance of two inches, 23,300 land miles through 28 countries from February 15, 1961, to June 5, 1964, starting and finishing in New York.

Pike's Peak Race

The Pike's Peak Auto Hill Climb, Colorado (instituted 1916) has been won by Bobby Unser 11 times between 1956 and 1969 (9 championship, 1 stock and 1 sports car title). On June 30, 1968, in the 46th race, he set a record of 11 minutes 54.9 seconds in his 5,506-c.c. Chevrolet championship car over the 12.42-mile course rising from 9,402 to 14,110 feet through 157 curves.

Badminton

Origins. The game was devised *c.* 1863 at Badminton Hall in Gloucestershire, England, the seat of the Dukes of Beaufort. The oldest club is the Newcastle Badminton Club, England, formed as the Armstrong College Club, on January 24, 1900.

International Championships. The International Championship or Thomas Cup (instituted 1948) has been won six times by Indonesia in 1957–58, 1960–61, 1963–64, 1969–70, 1972–73 and 1975–76.

MOST MEN'S TITLES:
Rudy Hartono of Indonesia has dominated men's badminton since 1968.

The Ladies International Championship or Uber Cup (instituted 1956) has been most often won by Japan (1966–69–72) and the United States (1957–60–63).

Most Titles Won. The record number of All-England Championship (instituted 1899) titles won is 21 by Sir George Thomas (d. 1972) between 1903 and 1928. The record for men's singles is 8 by Rudy Hartono of Indonesia (1968–74, 76). The most, including doubles, by women is 17, a record shared by Miss M. Lucas (1899–1910) and Mrs. G. C. K. Hashman (*née* Judy Devlin) (U.S.) from 1954 to 1967, who won 10 singles titles.

Shortest Game. In the 1969 Uber Cup in Djakarta, Indonesia, Miss N. Takagi (Japan) beat Miss P. Tumengkol in 9 minutes.

Longest Games. The longest recorded game was one of 291 hours by 5 boys from Kirkham Grammar School, Lancashire, England, July 7–19, 1972, who maintained continuous singles. The longest doubles marathon was one of 318 hours by 8 players from Muslim Youth Association, July 18 to 30, 1974, at the Mill Lane Youth Centre, Newcastle-upon-Tyne, England.

Longest Hit. Frank Rugani drove a shuttlecock 79 feet 8½ inches in tests at San Jose, California, on February 29, 1964.

Baseball

Origins. Baseball is a totally American derivative of the English game of cricket (first recorded in the U.S. in 1747) and the now-little-played English game of rounders. The game evolved about the end of the eighteenth century; as early as 1786, "baste-ball" was banned at Princeton, N.J. Haphazard versions of the so-called Town Ball Game grew up in Boston, New York and Philadelphia during the period 1820–33. Rules were first codified in 1845 in New York by Alexander Cartwright.

An English woodcut of "Base-Ball" dated 1744 is the earliest known reference.

On February 4, 1962, it was claimed in *Nedelya*, the weekly supplement to the Soviet newspaper *Izvestia*, that "Beizbol" was an old Russian game.

Earliest Games. The earliest game on record under the Cartwright rules was on June 19, 1846, in Hoboken, N.J., where the "New York Nine" defeated the Knickerbockers 23 to 1 in 4 innings. The earliest all-professional team was the Cincinnati Red Stockings in 1869.

Home Runs

Henry L. (Hank) Aaron broke the record set by George H. (Babe) Ruth (New York AL) of 714 home runs in a lifetime when he hit No. 715 on April 8, 1974. Between 1954 and 1974 he hit 733 home runs in the National League. In 1975, he switched over to the American League and hit 12 more, bringing his lifetime total to 745, the major league record.

800 HOME RUNS: Josh Gibson hit 800 lifetime home runs for the Homestead Grays of the Negro League, and 84 in one season. He was never able to play in the major leagues, but was posthumously elected to the Baseball Hall of Fame in 1972.

An all-league record of 800 in a lifetime has been claimed for Josh Gibson (1911–47) of the Homestead Grays of the Negro League, who was elected in 1972 to the Baseball Hall of Fame in Cooperstown, New York. Gibson hit 84 round-trippers in one season.

The longest home run ever measured was one of 618 feet by Roy Edward Carlyle in a minor league game at Emeryville Ball Park, California, on July 4, 1929. Babe Ruth hit a 587-foot homer at Tampa, Florida, in 1919.

Fastest Pitcher

The fastest pitcher in the world is L. Nolan Ryan of the California Angels who, on August 20, 1974, in Anaheim Stadium, was electronically clocked at a speed of 100.9 m.p.h.

Longest Throw

The longest throw of a 5-5¼-oz. baseball is 445 feet 10 inches by Glen Gorbaus on August 1, 1957. Mildred "Babe" Didrikson (later Mrs. George Zaharias) (1914–56) threw a ball 296 feet at Jersey City, New Jersey, on July 25, 1931.

Fastest Base Runner

Evar Swanson circled the bases at Columbus, Ohio, in 1932 in 13.3 seconds.

Do-Nothing Record

Toby Harrah of the Texas Rangers (AL) played an entire double-header at shortstop on June 26, 1976, without having a chance to make any fielding plays, assists or putouts.

Hit by Pitch

Ron Hunt, an infielder who played with various National League teams from 1963 to 1974, led the league in getting hit by pitched balls for a record seven consecutive years. His career total is 243, also a major league record.

Youngest Player

The youngest major league player of all time was the Cincinnati pitcher, Joe Nuxhall, who started his career in June, 1944, aged 15 years 10 months 11 days.

MAJOR LEAGUE ALL-TIME RECORDS
(including 1975 season)
*means player is active in 1976

Individual Batting

Highest percentage, lifetime (5,000 at-bats)
.367 Tyrus R. Cobb, AL: Det. 1905–26; Phil. 1927–28

Highest percentage, season (500 at-bats) (Leader in each league)
.438 Hugh Duffy, NL: Bos. 1894
.422 Napoleon Lajoie, AL: Phil. 1901

Most games played
*3,213 Henry L. Aaron, Mil. NL, 1954–65, Atl. NL, 1966–74; Mil. AL, 1975

Most consecutive games played
2,130 Henry Louis Gehrig, N.Y. AL, June 1, 1925 through Apr. 30, 1939

Most runs, lifetime
2,244 Tyrus R. Cobb, Det. AL, 1905–1926; Phil. AL, 1927–28; 24 years

Most runs, season
196 William R. Hamilton, Phil. NL, 131 games, 1894

RECORD SLUGGER: Babe Ruth (New York AL) still holds the record for 60 home runs in a 154-game season, most long hits (119), most total bases (457), and most bases on balls (170) in a season and had a lifetime slugging percentage of .690.

GREATEST BATTER of all time: Ty Cobb (Detroit AL) had highest lifetime batting average (.367), made most base hits (4,191) and scored most runs (2,244), as well as stealing the most bases (892).

Individual Batting Records (continued)

Most runs batted in, lifetime
*2,261 Henry L. Aaron, Mil. NL, 1954–65, Atl. NL, 1966–74; Mil. AL, 1975

Most runs batted in, season
190 Lewis R. (Hack) Wilson, Chi. NL, 155 games, 1930

Most runs batted in, game
12 James L. Bottomley, St. L. NL, Sept. 16, 1924

Most runs batted in, inning
7 Edward Cartwright, St. L. AA, Sept. 23, 1890

Most base hits
4,191 Tyrus R. Cobb, Det. AL, 1905–26; Phil. AL, 1927–28; 24 years

Most base hits, season
257 George H. Sisler, St. L. AL, 154 games, 1920

Most hits in succession
12 M. Frank (Pinky) Higgins, Bos. AL, June 19–21 (4 games), 1938; Walter Dropo, Det. AL, July 14, July 15, 2 games, 1952

Most base hits, consecutive, game
7 Wilbert Robinson, Balt. NL, June 10, 1892, 1st game (7-ab) 6-1b, 1-2b

Renaldo Stennett, Pitt. NL, Sept. 16, 1975 (7-ab), 4-1b, 2-2b, 1-3b

Cesar Gutierrez, Det. AL, June 21, 1970, 2nd game (7-ab) 6-1b, 1-2b (extra-inning game)

Most consecutive games batted safely, season
56 Joseph P. DiMaggio, N.Y. AL (91 hits—16-2b, 4-3b, 15 hr), May 15 to July 16, 1941

Most long hits, season
119 George H. (Babe) Ruth, N.Y. AL (44-2b, 16-3b, 59 hr), 152 games, 1921

Most total bases, lifetime
*6,756 Henry L. Aaron, Mil. NL, 1954–65, Atl. NL, 1966–74; Mil. AL, 1975

Most total bases, season
457 George H. (Babe) Ruth, N.Y. AL, 152 g. (85 on 1b, 88 on 2b, 48 on 3b, 236 on hr), 1921

Most total bases, game
18 Joseph W. Adcock, Mil. NL (1-2b, 4-hr), July 31, 1954

Sluggers' percentage
(The percentage is obtained by dividing the "times at bat" into total bases.)
Highest slugging percentage, lifetime
.690 George H. (Babe) Ruth, Bos.-N.Y. AL, 1914–34; Bos. NL, 1935

Individual Batting Records (continued)

Triple-Crown winners

(Most times leading league in batting, runs batted in and home runs.)

2   Rogers Hornsby, St. L. NL, 1922, 1925

Theodore S. Williams, Bos. AL, 1942, 1947

Most Valuable Player, as voted by Baseball Writers Association

3 times James E. Foxx, Phil. AL, 1932, 33, 38

Joseph P. DiMaggio, N.Y. AL, 1939, 41, 47

Stanley F. Musial, St. L. NL, 1943, 46, 48

Lawrence P. (Yogi) Berra, N.Y. AL, 1951, 54, 55

Roy Campanella, Bklyn. NL, 1951, 53, 55

Mickey C. Mantle, N.Y. AL, 1956, 57, 62

Most one-base hits (singles), season

202   William H. Keeler, Balt. NL, 128 games, 1898

Most two-base hits, season

67   Earl W. Webb, Bos. AL, 151 games, 1931

Most three-base hits, season

36   J. Owen Wilson, Pitts. NL, 152 games, 1912

Most home runs, lifetime

*745   Henry L. Aaron, Mil. NL, 1954 (13), 1955 (27), 1956 (26), 1957 (44), 1958 (30), 1959 (39), 1960 (40), 1961 (34), 1962 (45), 1963 (44), 1964 (24), 1965 (32); Atl. NL, 1966 (44), 1967 (39), 1968 (29), 1969 (44), 1970 (38), 1971 (47), 1972 (34), 1973 (40), 1974 (20); Mil. AL, 1975 (12).

Most home runs, season (154-game schedule)

60   George H. (Babe) Ruth, N.Y. AL (28 home, 32 away), 151 gs, 1927

Most home runs, season (162-game schedule)

61   Roger E. Maris, N.Y. AL (30 home, 31 away), 161 gs. 1961

Most home runs, one month

18   Rudolph York, Det. AL, Aug. 1937

Most consecutive games hitting home runs

8   R. Dale Long, Pitt. NL. May 19–28, 1956

Most home runs bases filled, lifetime

23   Henry Louis Gehrig, N.Y. AL, 1927–1938

HOME RUN KING: Henry L. (Hank) Aaron played in the National League for 21 seasons before switching to the American League in 1975. He adds to his home run record of 745 every time he hits another one over the fences.

Individual Batting Records (continued)

Most home runs, one double header
   5 Stanley F. Musial, St. L. NL, 1st game (3), 2nd game (2), May 2, 1954
      Nathan Colbert, S.D. NL, 1st game (2), 2nd game (3), Aug. 1, 1972

Most home runs with bases filled, season
   5 Ernest Banks, Chi. NL, May 11, 19, July 17 (1st game), Aug. 2, Sept. 19, 1955
      James E. Gentile, Balt. AL, May 9 (2), July 2, 7, Sept. 22, 1961

Most home runs, with bases filled, same game
   2 Anthony M. Lazzeri, N.Y. AL, May 24, 1936
      James R. Tabor, Bos. AL (2nd game), July 4, 1939
      Rudolph York, Bos. AL, July 27, 1946
      James E. Gentile, Balt. AL, May 9, 1961 (consecutive at-bats)
      Tony L. Cloninger, Atl. NL, July 3, 1966
      James T. Northrup, Det. AL, June 24, 1968 (consecutive at-bats)
      Frank Robinson, Balt. AL, June 26, 1970 (consecutive at-bats)

Most bases on balls, game
   6 Walter Wilmot, Chi. NL, Aug. 22, 1891
      James E. Foxx, Bos. AL, June 16, 1938

Most bases on balls, season
  170 George H. (Babe) Ruth, N.Y. AL, 152 games, 1923

Most consecutive pinch hits, lifetime
   9 David E. Philley, Phil. NL, Sept. 9, 11, 12, 13, 19, 20, 27, 28, 1958; Apr. 16, 1959

Base Running

Most stolen bases, lifetime
  937 William R. Hamilton, K.C. AA, 1888–89; Phil. NL 1890–95; Bos. NL 1896–1901

Most stolen bases, lifetime since 1900
  892 Tyrus R. Cobb, Det. AL, 1905–26; Phil. AL, 1927–28

Most stolen bases, season since 1900
  118 Louis C. Brock, St. L. NL, 153 games, 1974

Most stolen bases, game
   7 George F. (Piano Legs) Gore, Chi. NL, June 25, 1881
      William R. (Sliding Billy) Hamilton, Phil. NL, 2nd game, 8 inn., Aug. 31, 1894

Most times stealing home, game
   2 by 8 players

Most times stealing home, lifetime
  35 Tyrus R. Cobb, Det.-Phil. AL, 1905–28

Fewest times caught stealing, season (50+ attempts)
   2 Max Carey, Pitt. NL, 1922 (53 atts.)

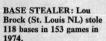

BASE STEALER: Lou Brock (St. Louis NL) stole 118 bases in 153 games in 1974.

Pitching

Most games, lifetime
1,070 J. Hoyt Wilhelm, N.Y.-St. L.-
Atl.-Chi.-L.A. NL, 1952–57, 69–
72; Clev.-Balt.-Chi.-Cal. (622)
AL, 1957–69

Most complete games, lifetime
751 Denton T. (Cy) Young, Clev.-
St. L.-Bos. NL (428); Bos.-Clev.
AL (323), 1890–1911

Most complete games, season
74 William H. White, Cin. NL, 1879

Most innings pitched, game
26 Leon J. Cadore, Bklyn. NL, May
1, 1920
Joseph Oeschger, Bos. NL, May
1, 1920

Lowest earned run average, season
0.90 Ferdinand M. Schupp, N.Y. NL,
1916 (140 inn)
1.01 Hubert B. (Dutch) Leonard, Bos.
AL, 1914 (222 inn)
1.12 Robert Gibson, St. L. NL, 1968
(305 inn)

Most games won, lifetime
511 Denton T. (Cy) Young, Clev. NL
(239) 1890–98; St. L. NL 1899–
1900; Bos. AL (193) 1901–08;
Clev. AL (29) 1909–11; Bos. NL
(4) 1911

Most games won, season
60 Charles Radbourne, Providence
NL, 1884

FASTEST PITCHER: L. Nolan Ryan
(California AL), who can throw a pitch
100.9 m.p.h., set a new modern record
with 383 strikeouts in the 1973 season.
He has also tied Sandy Koufax with
4 no-hit games.

Most consecutive games won, lifetime
24 Carl O. Hubbell, N.Y. NL, 1936
(16); 1937 (8)

Most shutout games, season
16 George W. Bradley, St. L. NL,
1876
Grover C. Alexander, Phil. NL,
1916

Most shutout games, lifetime
113 Walter P. Johnson, Wash. AL, 21
years, 1907–27

Most consecutive shutout games, season
6 Donald S. Drysdale, L.A. NL,
May 14, 18, 22, 26, 31, June 4,
1968

Most consecutive shutout innings
58 Donald S. Drysdale, L.A. NL,
May 14–June 8, 1968

Most strikeouts, lifetime
3,508 Walter P. Johnson, Wash. AL,
1907–27

Most strikeouts, season
505 Matthew Kilroy, Balt. AA, 1886
(Distance 50 ft)
383 L. Nolan Ryan, Cal. AL, 1973
(Distance 60 ft 6 in.)

LONGEST-LASTING PITCHER:
Hoyt Wilhelm, knuckleball pitcher for 9
teams in both leagues, played in 1,070
major league games between 1952 and
1972, and had a lifetime ERA of 2.52.

Most strikeouts, game (9 inn) since 1900:
19 Steven N. Carlton, St. L. NL vs N.Y., Sept. 15, 1969 (lost)
G. Thomas Seaver, N.Y. NL vs S.D., Apr. 22, 1970
L. Nolan Ryan, Cal. AL, vs Bos., Aug. 12, 1974

Most strikeouts, extra-inning game
21 Thomas E. Cheney, Wash. AL vs Balt. (16 inns), Sept. 12, 1962 (night)

Special mention
1959 Harvey Haddix, Jr., Pitt. vs Mil. NL, May 26, pitched 12 "perfect" innings, allowed hit in 13th and lost

Most no-hit games, lifetime
4 Sanford Koufax, L.A. NL, 1962–63–64–65
L. Nolan Ryan, Cal. AL, 1973(2)-74-75

Perfect game—9 innings

1880 John Lee Richmond, Worcester vs Clev. NL, June 12 ... 1–0
John M. Ward, Prov. vs Buff. NL, June 17 AM 5–0

1904 Denton T. (Cy) Young, Bos. vs Phil. AL, May 5 ... 3–0

1908 Adrian C. Joss, Clev. vs Chi. AL, Oct. 2 1–0

†1917 Ernest G. Shore, Bos. vs Wash. AL, June 23 (1st g.) 4–0

1922 C. C. Robertson, Chi. vs Det. AL, April 30 2–0

**1956 Donald J. Larsen, N.Y. AL vs Bklyn. NL, Oct. 8 2–0

1964 James P. Bunning, Phil. NL vs N.Y., June 21 (1st g.) 6–0

1965 Sanford Koufax, L.A. NL vs Chi., Sept. 9 1–0

1968 James A. Hunter, Oak. AL vs Minn., May 8 4–0

---

†Starting pitcher, "Babe" Ruth, was banished from game by Umpire Owens after giving first batter, Morgan, a base on balls. Shore relieved and while he pitched to second batter, Morgan was caught stealing. Shore then retired next 26 batters to complete "perfect" game.

**World Series game.

Club Batting

Highest percentage, season
.343 Phil. NL, 132 games, 1894
.319 N.Y. NL, 154 games, 1930

Most runs, one club, game
36 Chi. NL (36) vs Louisville (7), June 29, 1897

Most runs, one club, inning
18 Chi. NL, 7th inning, Sept. 6, 1883

Most runs, both clubs, inning
19 Wash. AA (14), Balt. (5), 1st inn., June 17, 1891

Most hits, one club, 9 inning game
36 Phil. NL, Aug.- 17, 1894

Most hits, one club, inning
18 Chi. NL, 7th inning, Sept. 6, 1883

Fewest hits, both clubs, game
1 Chi. NL (0) vs L.A. (1), Sept. 9, 1965

Most home runs, one club, season (154-game schedule)
221 N.Y. NL, 155 games, 1947
Cin. NL, 155 games, 1956

Most home runs, one club, season (162-game schedule)
240 N.Y. AL, 163 games, 1961

Fewest home runs (135 or more games), one club, season
3 Chi. AL, 156 games, 1908

Most stolen bases (1900 to date), one club, season
347 N.Y. NL, 154 games, 1911

Most stolen bases, one club, inning
8 Wash. AL, 1st inning, July 19, 1915
Phil. NL, 9th inning, 1st g., July 7, 1919

Club Fielding

Highest percentage, one club, season
.985 Balt. AL, 1964

Fewest errors, season
95 Balt. AL, 163 games, 1964

Most double plays, club, season
217 Phil. AL, 154 games, 1949

Most double plays, club, game
7 N.Y. AL, Aug. 14, 1942
Houst. NL, May 4, 1969

General Club Records

Shortest and longest game by time
51 minutes N.Y. NL (6), Phil. (1), 1st g., Sept. 28, 1919
7:23 S.F. NL (8) at N.Y. (6) 23 inn., 2nd g., May 31, 1964

General Club Records (continued)

Longest 9-inning game
4:18 S.F. NL (7) at L.A. (8), Oct. 2, 1962

Fewest times shutout, season
0 Bos. NL, 1894 (132 g.)
   Phil. NL, 1894 (127 g.)
   N.Y. AL, 1932 (155 g.)

Most consecutive innings shutting out opponents
56 Pitt. NL, June 1–9, 1903

Highest percentage games won, season
.798 Chi. NL (won 67, lost 17), 1880
.763 Chi. NL (won 116, lost 36), 1906
.721 Clev. AL (won 111, lost 43), 1954

Most games won, season (154-game schedule)
116 Chi. NL, 1906

Most consecutive games won, season
26 N.Y. NL, Sept. 7 (1st g.) to Sept. 30 (1 tie), 1916

Most pitchers used in a game, 9 innings, one club
9 St. L. AL vs Chi., Oct. 2, 1949

Managers' consecutive championship records
5 years Charles D. (Casey) Stengel, N.Y. AL, 1949–50–51–52–53

World Series Records

Most series played
14 Lawrence P. (Yogi) Berra, N.Y., 1947, 49–53, 55–58, 60–63

Highest batting percentage (20 g. min.), total series
.391 Louis C. Brock, St. L. NL, 1964, 67–68 (g-21, ab-87, h-34)

Highest batting percentage, 4 or more games, one series
.625 4-game series, George H. (Babe) Ruth, N.Y. AL, 1928

Most runs, total series
42 Mickey C. Mantle, N.Y. AL, 1951–53, 55–58, 60–64

Most runs, one series
9 George H. (Babe) Ruth, N.Y. AL, 1928
   Henry Louis Gehrig, N.Y. AL, 1932

Most runs batted in, total series
40 Mickey C. Mantle, N.Y., AL, 1951–53, 55–58, 60–64

Most runs batted in, game
6 Robert C. Richardson, N.Y. AL, (4) 1st inn., (2) 4th inn., Oct. 8, 1960

Most runs batted in, consecutive times at bat
7 James L. (Dusty) Rhodes, N.Y. NL, first 4 times at bat, 1954

Most base hits, total series
71 Lawrence P. (Yogi) Berra, N.Y. AL, 1947, 49–53, 55–58, 60–61

Most home runs, total series
18 Mickey C. Mantle, N.Y. AL, 1952 (2), 53 (2), 55, 56 (3), 57, 58 (2), 60 (3), 63, 64 (3)

Most home runs, 4-game series
4 Henry Louis Gehrig, N.Y. AL, 1928

Most home runs, game
3 George H. (Babe) Ruth, N.Y. AL, Oct. 6, 1926; Oct. 9, 1928

Pitchers' Records

Pitching in most series
11 Edward C. (Whitey) Ford, N.Y. AL, 1950, 53, 55–58, 60–64

Most victories, total series
10 Edward C. (Whitey) Ford, N.Y. AL, 1950 (1), 55 (2), 56 (1), 57 (1), 60 (2), 61 (2), 62 (1)

All victories, no defeats
6 Vernon L. (Lefty) Gomez, N.Y. AL, 1932 (1), 36 (2), 37 (2), 38 (1)

Most games won, one series
3 games in 5-game series Christy Mathewson, N.Y. NL, 1905
J. W. Coombs, Phil. AL, 1910
Many others won 3 games in series of more games.

Most shutout games, total series
4 Christy Mathewson, N.Y. NL, 1905 (3), 1913

Most shutout games, one series
3 Christy Mathewson, N.Y. NL, 1905

Most strikeouts, one pitcher, total series
94 Edward C. (Whitey) Ford, N.Y. AL, 1950, 53, 55–58, 60–64

Most strikeouts, one series

23 in 4 games Sanford Koufax, L.A. NL, 1963

18 in 5 games Christy Mathewson, N.Y. NL, 1905

20 in 6 games C. A. (Chief) Bender, Phil. AL, 1911

35 in 7 games Robert Gibson, St. L. NL, 1968

28 in 8 games W. H. Dinneen, Bos. AL, 1903

Most Series Won
20   New York AL, 1923, 1927, 1928,
     1932, 1936, 1937, 1938, 1939,
     1941, 1943, 1947, 1949, 1950,
     1951, 1952, 1953, 1956, 1958,
     1961, 1962

Most strikeouts, one pitcher, game
17   Robert Gibson, St. L. NL, Oct. 2,
     1968

Highest attendance
420,784 L.A. NL, World Champions
         vs Chi. AL, 4–2, 1959

*Baseball records by Seymour Siwoff.
Elias Sports Bureau.*

Highest Catch

Joe Sprinz (San Francisco Seals, Pacific Coast League) a former Cleveland AL catcher, caught a baseball (on his fifth attempt) dropped from an airship at about 1,000 feet over Treasure Island, in San Francisco Bay on August 3, 1939. The force of catching the ball cost him 4 front teeth.

First Rain-In

On June 16, 1976, rains fell so hard in and around Houston, Texas, that the grounds around the Houston Astrodome were completely flooded, preventing fans and umpires from getting into the ballpark, and so forcing the cancellation of the game between Houston and Pittsburgh. It was the first time any game played in a covered stadium had to be called because of rain.

Largest Stadium

The Cleveland Municipal Stadium in Cleveland, Ohio, has a seating capacity of 76,977.

Basketball

Origins. *Ollamalitzli* was a 16th-century Aztec precursor of basketball played in Mexico. If the solid rubber ball was put through a fixed stone ring placed high on one side of the stadium, the player was entitled to the clothing of all the spectators. The captain of the losing team often lost his head (by execution). Another game played much earlier, in the 10th century b.c. by the Olmecs in Mexico, called *Pok-ta-Pok*, also resembled basketball in its concept of a ring through which a round object was passed.

Modern basketball was devised by the Canadian-born Dr. James A. Naismith (1861–1939) at the Training School of the International Y.M.C.A. College at Springfield, Massachusetts, in December, 1891. The first game played under modified rules was on January 20, 1892. The first public contest was on March 11, 1892. The game is now a global activity.

The International Amateur Basketball Federation (F.I.B.A.) was founded in 1932.

Most Accurate Shooting. The greatest goal-shooting demonstration was made by an amateur, Ted St. Martin, now of

BASKETBALL PROTOTYPE: "Pok-ta-Pok" was played by the Olmec Indians in Mexico in the 10th century B.C.

Jacksonville, Florida, who, on February 28, 1975, scored 1,704 consecutive free throws.

In a 24-hour period, May 31–June 1, 1975, Fred L. Newman of San Jose, California, scored 12,874 baskets out of 13,116 attempts (98.15 per cent).

John T. Sebastian made 63 straight free throws while blindfolded at Maine Township High School East, Park Ridge, Illinois, on May 18, 1972.

Longest Field Goal. The longest recorded field goal in a game is 84 feet 11 inches by George Line, 20, of the University of Alabama against the University of North Carolina, in January, 1955, at Tuscaloosa.

In practice in 1953, Larry Slinkard of Arlington Heights High School, Arlington, Illinois, scored with a shot from 88 feet.

Tallest Players

The tallest player of all time has been Emili Rached of Brazil, 7 feet 7⅝ inches tall, who competed in the 1971 Pan American Games. The tallest woman player is Gwendalin Bachman of Inglewood, California, at 7 feet 0¼ inch. The tallest N.B.A. player is Tom Burleson, 22, of the Seattle SuperSonics. He is 7 feet 4 inches tall.

Most Expensive

In August, 1974, Moses Malone, 19, of the University of Maryland, signed a 7-year contract with the Utah Stars of the now defunct A.B.A. for a reported $3,000,000.

Greatest Attendances. The Harlem Globetrotters played an exhibition to 75,000 in the Olympic Stadium, West Berlin, Germany, in 1951. The largest indoor basketball crowd was at the Astrodome, Houston, Texas, where 52,693 watched a game on January 20, 1968, between the University of Houston and U.C.L.A.

MOST POPULAR TEAM: Since 1927 the Harlem Globetrotters have delighted basketball fans with their antics. In one year alone, they posted 333 wins against 8 losses and traveled over 75,000 miles.

The Harlem Globetrotters set unapproached attendance records in their silver jubilee season of 1951–52. They won 333 exhibitions and lost 8 before over 3,000,000 spectators and traveled over 75,000 miles. The team was founded by Abraham M. Saperstein (1903–66) of Chicago, and their first game was played at Hinckley, Illinois, on January 7, 1927.

Highest Scoring·

The highest score by an individual player occurred in a college game when Clarence (Bevo) Francis of Rio Grande College, Rio Grande, Ohio, scored 150 points in a game in 1954.

Mats Wermelin, 13, of Sweden, scored all 272 points in a 272–0 win in a regional boys' tournament in Stockholm, Sweden, on February 5, 1974.

The highest score in an international match is 164 by Rumania against Wales (50) on May 15, 1975, at Hagen, West Germany. The highest by a women's team is 153 by the U.S.S.R. against Switzerland (25) on June 4, 1956.

Olympic Champions

The U.S. won all seven Olympic titles from the time the sport was introduced to the Games in 1936 until 1968, without losing a single match. In 1972, in Munich, their run of 64 consecutive victories was broken when they lost 51–50 to the U.S.S.R. in a much-disputed final match. They regained the Olympic title in Montreal in 1976, again without losing a game.

World Champions

Brazil and the U.S.S.R. are the only countries to win the World Championship (instituted 1950) on more than one occasion. Brazil won in 1959 and 1963; the U.S.S.R. in 1967 and 1974.

In 1975, the U.S.S.R. won the women's championship (instituted 1953) for the fifth consecutive time since 1959.

Marathon

The longest recorded marathon is 61 hours by 10 players at Spartacus Camp for Boys, New Orleans, Louisiana, April 30 to May 2, 1976. This involved 2 teams of 5 without substitutes, but with 10-minute breaks between halves.

NATIONAL BASKETBALL ASSOCIATION
Regular Season Records
Including 1975–76 Season

The National Basketball Association's Championship series was established in 1947. Prior to 1949, when it joined with the National Basketball League, the professional circuit was known as the Basketball Association of America.

SERVICE

Most Games, Lifetime
1,122 Hal Greer, Syr. 1959–63; Phil. 1964–73

Most Games, Consecutive, Lifetime
844 John Kerr, Syr.-Phil.-Balt., Oct. 31, 1954–Nov. 4, 1965

Most Complete Games, Season
79 Wilt Chamberlain, Phil. 1962

Most Complete Games, Consecutive, Season
47 Wilt Chamberlain, Phil. 1962

Most Minutes, Lifetime
47,859 Wilt Chamberlain, Phil.-S.F.-L.A. 1960–73

Most Minutes, Season
3,882 Wilt Chamberlain, Phil. 1962

SCORING

Most Seasons Leading League
7 Wilt Chamberlain, Phil. 1960–62; S.F. 1963–64; S.F.-Phil. 1965; Phil. 1966

Most Points, Lifetime
31,419 Wilt Chamberlain, Phil.-S.F.-L.A. 1960–73

Most Points, Season
4,029 Wilt Chamberlain, Phil. 1962

Most Seasons 1000+ Points
14 John Havlicek, Bos. 1963–76

Most Points, Game
100 Wilt Chamberlain, Phil. vs. N.Y., Mar. 2, 1962

Most Points, Half
59 Wilt Chamberlain, Phil. vs. N.Y., Mar. 2, 1962

Most Points, Quarter
31 Wilt Chamberlain, Phil. vs. N.Y., Mar. 2, 1962

Most Points, Overtime Period
13 Earl Monroe, Balt. vs. Det., Feb. 6, 1970
Joe Caldwell, Atl. vs. Cin., Feb. 18, 1970

Highest Scoring Average, Lifetime (400 + games)
30.1 Wilt Chamberlain, Phil.-S.F.-L.A. 1960–73

Highest Scoring Average, Season
50.4 Wilt Chamberlain, Phil. 1962

Field Goals Made

Most Field Goals, Lifetime
12,681 Wilt Chamberlain, Phil.-S.F.-L.A. 1960–73

Most Field Goals, Season
1,597 Wilt Chamberlain, Phil. 1962

Most Field Goals, Consecutive, Season
35 Wilt Chamberlain, Phil. Feb. 17–28, 1967

Most Field Goals, Game
36 Wilt Chamberlain, Phil. vs. N.Y., Mar. 2, 1962

Most Field Goals, Half
22 Wilt Chamberlain, Phil. vs. N.Y., Mar. 2, 1962

Most Field Goals, Quarter
12 Cliff Hagan, St.L. vs. N.Y., Feb. 4, 1958
Wilt Chamberlain, Phil. vs. N.Y., Mar. 2, 1962

Basketball (N.B.A.) continued

Field Goals Attempted

Most Field Goal Attempts, Lifetime
23,497 Wilt Chamberlain, Phil.-S.F.-L.A. 1960–73
Most Field Goal Attempts, Season
3,159 Wilt Chamberlain, Phil. 1962
Most Field Goal Attempts, Game
63 Wilt Chamberlain, Phil. vs. N.Y., Mar. 2, 1962
Most Field Goal Attempts, Half
37 Wilt Chamberlain, Phil. vs. N.Y., Mar. 2, 1962
Most Field Goal Attempts, Quarter
21 Wilt Chamberlain, Phil. vs. N.Y., Mar. 2, 1962

Field Goal Percentage

Most Seasons Leading League
9 Wilt Chamberlain, Phil. 1961; S.F. 1963; S.F.-Phil. 1965; Phil. 1966–68; L.A. 1969, 72–73
Highest Percentage, Lifetime
.545 Kareem Abdul-Jabbar, Mil.-L.A. 1970–76
Highest Percentage, Season
.727 Wilt Chamberlain, L.A. 1973

Free Throws Made

Most Free Throws Made, Lifetime
7,694 Oscar Robertson, Cin.-Mil. 1961–74

MOST ASSISTS IN ONE GAME:
Bob Cousy, star of the Boston Celtics, made a record 28 assists in 1959.

Most Free Throws Made, Season
840 Jerry West, L.A. 1966
Most Free Throws Made, Consecutive, Season
58 Calvin Murphy, Hou. Oct. 28-Nov. 18, 1975
Most Free Throws Made, Game
28 Wilt Chamberlain, Phil. vs. N.Y., Mar. 2, 1962
Most Free Throws Made (No Misses), Game
19 Bob Pettit, St.L. vs. Bos., Nov. 22, 1961
Most Free Throws Made, Half
19 Oscar Robertson, Cin. vs. Balt., Dec. 27, 1964
Most Free Throws Made, Quarter
14 Rick Barry, S.F. vs. N.Y., Dec. 6, 1966

Free Throws Attempted

Most Free Throw Attempts, Lifetime
11,862 Wilt Chamberlain, Phil.-S.F.-L.A. 1960–73
Most Free Throw Attempts, Season
1,363 Wilt Chamberlain, Phil. 1962
Most Free Throw Attempts, Game
34 Wilt Chamberlain, S.F. vs. N.Y., Nov. 27, 1963
Most Free Throw Attempts, Half
22 Oscar Robertson, Cin. vs. Balt., Dec. 27, 1964
Most Free Throw Attempts, Quarter
16 Oscar Robertson, Cin. vs. Balt., Dec. 27, 1964
Stan McKenzie, Phoe. vs. Phil., Feb. 15, 1970
Pete Maravich, Atl. vs. Chi., Jan. 2, 1973

Free Throw Percentage

Most Seasons Leading League
7 Bill Sharman, Bos. 1953–57, 59, 61
Highest Percentage, Lifetime
.890 Rick Barry, S.F.-G.S. 1966–67, 73–76
Highest Percentage, Season
.932 Bill Sharman, Bos. 1959

REBOUNDS

Most Seasons Leading League
11 Wilt Chamberlain, Phil. 1960–62; S.F. 1963; Phil. 1966–68; L.A. 1969, 71–73
Most Rebounds, Lifetime
23,924 Wilt Chamberlain, Phil.-S.F.-L.A. 1960–73
Most Rebounds, Season
2,149 Wilt Chamberlain, Phil. 1961
Most Rebounds, Game
55 Wilt Chamberlain, Phil. vs. Bos., Nov. 24, 1960
Most Rebounds, Half
32 Bill Russell, Bos. vs. Phil., Nov. 16, 1957
Most Rebounds, Quarter
18 Nate Thurmond, S.F. vs. Balt., Feb. 28, 1965

REBOUND RECORD-HOLDER: Wilton Norman (the Stilt) Chamberlain (b. August 21, 1936) who played with various teams, is probably the greatest basketball player of all time. He made 55 rebounds in one game, 2,149 in a season. He also set records of 100 points in a game, 4,029 points in a season, most field goals (36 in a game, 35 in succession, 1,597 in a season), most free throws made in a game, (28) and other records.

Basketball (N.B.A.) continued

Highest Average (per game), Lifetime
  22.9 Wilt Chamberlain, Phil.-S.F.-L.A. 1960–73
Highest Average (per game), Season
  27.2 Wilt Chamberlain, Phil. 1961

ASSISTS

Most Seasons Leading League
  8 Bob Cousy, Bos. 1953–60
Most Assists, Lifetime
  9,887 Oscar Robertson, Cin.-Mil. 1961–74
Most Assists, Season
  910 Nate Archibald, K.C.-Omaha 1973
Most Assists, Game
  28 Bob Cousy, Bos. vs. Minn., Feb. 27, 1959
    Guy Rodgers, S.F. vs. St.L., Mar. 14, 1963
Most Assists, Half
  19 Bob Cousy, Bos. vs. Minn., Feb. 27, 1959
Most Assists, Quarter
  12 Bob Cousy, Bos. vs. Minn., Feb. 27, 1959
Highest Average (per game), Lifetime
  9.5 Oscar Robertson, Cin.-Mil. 1961–74
Highest Average (per game), Season
  11.5 Oscar Robertson, Cin. 1965

PERSONAL FOULS

Most Personal Fouls, Lifetime
  3,855 Hal Greer, Syr.-Phil. 1959–73
Most Personal Fouls, Season
  366 Bill Bridges, St.L. 1968

Most Personal Fouls, Game
  8 Don Otten, T.C. vs. Sheb., Nov. 24, 1949
Most Personal Fouls, Half
  6 By many. Last:
    Clyde Lee, Phil. vs. Port., Mar. 12, 1975
Most Personal Fouls, Quarter
  6 Connie Dierking, Syr. vs Cin., Nov. 17, 1959
    Henry Akin, Seattle vs Phil., Dec. 20, 1967
    Bud Ogden, Phil. vs Phoe., Feb. 15, 1970
    Don Smith, Hou. vs. Clev., Feb. 8, 1974

DISQUALIFICATIONS

(Fouling Out of Game)
Most Disqualifications, Lifetime
  127 Vern Mikkelsen, Minn., 1950–59
Most Disqualifications, Season
  26 Don Meineke, Ft. W. 1953
Most Games, No Disqualifications, Lifetime
  1,045 Wilt Chamberlain, Phil.-S.F.-L.A. 1960–73 (Entire Career)

TEAM RECORDS

(OT=Overtime)
Most Seasons, League Champion
  13 Boston 1957, 59–66, 68–69, 74, 76
Most Seasons, Consecutive, League Champion
  8 Boston 1959–66
Most Seasons, Division Champion
  14 Boston 1957–65, 72–76

Most Seasons, Consecutive, Division
  Champion
  9 Boston 1957–65
Most Games Won, Season
  69 Los Angeles, 1972
Most Games Won, Consecutive, Season
  33 Los Angeles Nov. 5, 1971–Jan.
    7, 1972
Most Games Won, Consecutive, Start of
  Season
  15 Washington Nov. 3–Dec. 4, 1948
Most Games Won, Consecutive, End of
  Season
  14 Milwaukee Feb. 28–Mar. 27,
    1973
Most Games Lost, Season
  73 Philadelphia 1973
Most Games Lost, Consecutive, Season
  20 Philadelphia Jan. 9–Feb. 11,
    1973
Most Games Lost, Consecutive, Start of
  Season
  15 Denver Oct. 29–Dec. 25, 1949
    Cleveland Oct. 14–Nov. 10, 1970
    Philadelphia Oct. 10–Nov. 10,
    1973
Highest Percentage, Games Won,
  Season
  .841 Los Angeles 1972
Lowest Percentage, Games Won, Season
  .110 Philadelphia 1973

Team Scoring

Most Points, Season
  10,143 Philadelphia 1967
Most Games, 100+ Points, Season
  81 Los Angeles 1972
Most Games, Consecutive, 100+ Points,
  Season
  77 New York 1967
Most Points, Game
  173 Boston vs Minn. Feb. 27, 1959
Most Points, Both Teams, Game
  316 Phil. (169) vs N.Y. (147) Mar. 2,
    1962
    Cin. (165) vs San Diego (151)
    Mar. 12, 1970
Most Points, Half
  97 Atlanta vs San Diego Feb. 11,
    1970
Most Points, Quarter
  58 Buffalo vs Bos. Oct. 20, 1972
Widest Victory Margin, Game
  63 Los Angeles (162) vs Golden
    State (99) Mar. 19, 1972

Field Goals Made

Most Field Goals, Season
  3,972 Milwaukee 1971
Most Field Goals, Game
  72 Boston vs Minn. Feb. 27, 1959
Most Field Goals, Both Teams, Game
  134 Cin. (67) vs San Diego (67)
    Mar. 12, 1970
Most Field Goals, Half
  40 Boston vs Minn. Feb. 27, 1959
    Syracuse vs Det. Jan. 13, 1963

FIELD GOAL LEADER: Kareem
Abdul-Jabbar has a shooting percentage
of .545 in his 7 years in pro basketball.

Most Field Goals, Quarter
  23 Boston vs Minn. Feb. 27, 1959
    Buffalo vs Bos. Oct. 20, 1972

Field Goals Attempted

Most Field Goal Attempts, Season
  9,295 Boston 1961
Most Field Goal Attempts, Game
  153 Philadelphia vs. L.A. Dec. 8,
    1961 (3 ot)
  150 Boston vs Phil. Feb. 3, 1960
Most Field Goal Attempts, Both Teams,
  Game
  291 Phil. (153) vs L.A. (138) Dec. 8,
    1961 (3 ot)
  274 Bos. (149) vs Det. (125) Jan. 27,
    1961
Most Field Goal Attempts, Half
  83 Philadelphia vs Syr. Nov. 4, 1959
    Boston vs Phil. Dec. 27, 1960
Most Field Goal Attempts, Quarter
  47 Boston vs Minn. Feb. 27, 1959
Highest Field Goal Percentage, Season
  .509 Milwaukee 1971

Free Throws Made

Most Free Throws Made, Season
  2,434 Phoenix 1970
Most Free Throws Made, Game
  59 Anderson vs Syr. Nov. 24, 1949
    (5 ot)
Most Free Throws Made, Both Teams,
  Game
  116 And. (59) vs Syr. (57) Nov. 24,
    1949 (5 ot)
Most Free Throws Made, Half
  36 Chicago vs Phoe. Jan. 8, 1970
Most Free Throws Made, Quarter
  24 St. Louis vs Syr. Dec. 21, 1957

Free Throws Attempted

Most Free Throw Attempts, Season
  3,411 Philadelphia 1967
Most Free Throw Attempts, Game
    86 Syracuse vs And. Nov. 24, 1949
       (5 ot)
    71 Chicago vs Phoe. Jan. 8, 1970
Most Free Throw Attempts, Both
    Teams, Game
   160 Syr. (86) vs And. (74) Nov. 24,
       1949 (5 ot)
   127 Ft.W. (67) vs Minn. (60) Dec.
       31, 1954
Most Free Throw Attempts, Half
    48 Chicago vs Phoe. Jan. 8, 1970
Most Free Throw Attempts, Quarter
    30 Boston vs Chi. Jan. 9, 1963
Highest Free Throw Percentage, Season
   .821 K.C.-Omaha 1975

Rebounds

Most Rebounds, Season
  6,131 Boston 1961
Most Rebounds, Game
   112 Philadelphia vs Cin. Nov. 8,
       1959
       Boston vs Det. Dec. 24, 1960
Most Rebounds, Both Teams, Game
   215 Phil. (110) vs L.A. (105) Dec. 8,
       1961 (3 ot)
   196 Bos. (106) vs Det. (90) Jan. 27,
       1961
Most Rebounds, Half
    62 Boston vs Phil. Nov. 16, 1957
       New York vs Phil. Nov. 19, 1960
       Philadelphia vs Syr. Nov. 9,
       1961
Most Rebounds, Quarter
    40 Philadelphia vs Syr. Nov. 9,
       1961

Assists

Most Assists, Season
  2,320 Boston 1973
Most Assists, Game
    60 Syracuse vs Balt. Nov. 15, 1952
       (1 ot)
    52 Chicago vs Atl. Mar. 20, 1971
Most Assists, Both Teams, Game
    89 Det. (48) vs Clev. (41) Mar. 28,
       1973 (1 ot)
    88 Phoe. (47) vs San Diego (41)
       Mar. 15, 1969
Most Assists, Half
    29 Chicago vs Atl. Mar. 20, 1971
Most Assists, Quarter
    16 Boston vs Minn. Feb. 27, 1959
       Chicago vs Atl. Mar. 20, 1971

Personal Fouls

Most Personal Fouls, Season
  2,372 Seattle 1968
Most Personal Fouls, Game
    66 Anderson vs Syr. Nov. 24, 1949
       (5 ot)
Most Personal Fouls, Both Teams,
    Game
   122 And. (66) vs Syr. (56) Nov. 24,
       1949 (5 ot)
    97 Syr. (50) vs N.Y. (47) Feb. 15,
       1953
Most Personal Fouls, Half
    30 Rochester vs Syr. Jan. 15, 1953
Most Personal Fouls, Quarter
    16 Syracuse vs Bos. Dec. 26, 1950
       Rochester vs Syr. Jan. 15, 1953
       Chicago vs Bos. Jan. 9, 1963
       Philadelphia vs San Diego Nov.
       19, 1969
       Portland vs. Atl. Mar. 8, 1973
       New York vs. Chi. Nov. 30, 1973

Bicycling

Earliest Race. The earliest recorded bicycle race was a veloci-
pede race over two kilometres (1.24 miles) at the Parc de St. Cloud,
Paris, on May 31, 1868 won by James Moore (G.B.).

Slow Cycling. Slow cycling records came to a virtual end in
1968 when Tsugunobu Mitsuishi, aged 39, of Tokyo, Japan, balanced
while staying stationary without support for 5 hours 25 minutes.

Highest Speed. The highest speed ever achieved on a bicycle is
140.5 m.p.h. by Dr. Allan V. Abbott, 29, of San Bernardino, California, behind a windshield mounted on a 1955 Chevrolet over ¾ of
a mile at Bonneville Salt Flats, Utah, on August 25, 1973. His speed
over a mile was 138.674 m.p.h. Considerable help is provided by the
slipstreaming effect of the lead vehicle. Charles Minthorne Murphy

(born 1872) achieved the first mile-a-minute behind a pacing loco-motive on the Long Island Railroad on June 30, 1899. He took only 57.8 seconds, so averaging 62.28 m.p.h.

Alan Abbott recorded an unofficial unpaced 9.36 sec. for 200 meters (47.80 m.p.h.) at Irwindale Raceway, California, on April 24, 1976.

The greatest distance ever covered in one hour is 76 miles 604 yards by Leon Vanderstuyft (Belgium) on the Montlhéry Motor Circuit, France, on September 30, 1928. This was achieved from a standing start paced by a motorcycle. The 24-hour record behind pace is 860 miles 367 yards by Hubert Opperman in Australia in 1932.

Most Olympic Titles. Cycling has been on the Olympic program since the revival of the Games in 1896. The greatest number of gold medals ever won is four by Marcus Hurley (U.S.) over the $\frac{1}{4}$, $\frac{1}{3}$, $\frac{1}{2}$ and 1 mile in 1904.

Tour de France

The greatest number of wins in the Tour de France (inaugurated 1903) is five by Jacques Anquetil (born January 8, 1934) of France, who won in 1957, 1961, 1962, 1963, and 1964, and Eddy Merckx (b. Belgium, 1945) who won five titles (1969–70–71–72–74).

The closest race ever was that of 1968 when after 2,898.7 miles over 25 days (June 27–July 21) Jan Janssen (Netherlands) (born 1940) beat Herman van Springel (Belgium) in Paris by 38 seconds. The longest course was 3,569 miles on June 20–July 18, 1926. The length of the course is usually about 3,000 miles, but varies from year to year.

World Titles

The only four cyclists to have won 7 world titles in any of the world championship events are Leon Meredith (G.B.) who won the Amateur 100-kilometer paced event in 1904–05–07–09–11–13; Jeff Scherens (Belgium); Antonio Maspes (Italy) who won the Professional sprint title in 1932–33–34–35–36–37 and 1947 and in 1955–56–59–60–62–64–65; and Daniel Morelon (France) who won the amateur sprint title in 1966–67–69–70–71–73–75.

One Hour and 24 Hour Records

The greatest distance covered in 60 minutes unpaced is 30 miles 125 yards by Eddy Merckx at Mexico City, Mexico, on October 25, 1972. The 24-hour record on the road is 507.00 miles by Roy Cromack in Cheshire, England, on July 26–27, 1969.

Endurance

Tommy Godwin (G.B.) in the 365 days of 1939 covered 75,065 miles or an average of 205.65 miles per day. He then completed 100,000 miles in 500 days on May 14, 1940.

The duration record for cycling on a track is 168 hours (7 days) by Syed Muhammed Nawab, aged 22, of Lucknow, India, in Addis Ababa, Ethiopia, in 1964. The monocycle duration record

TOUR DE FRANCE CHAMPION: Eddy Merckx of Belgium has won this classic race five times.

is 23½ hours by Steve McPeak in 1969. The longest cycle tour on record is the more than 270,000 miles amassed by Walter Stolle (b. Czechoslovakia), an itinerant lecturer. Since January 24, 1959 he has covered 140 countries, had 5 bicycles stolen and suffered 21 other robberies.

Ray Reece, 41, of Alverstoke, England, circumnavigated the world by bicycle (13,325 road miles) between June 14 and November 5 (143 days) in 1971.

Most on One Cycle. The Chinese Acrobatic Theatre from Shanghai regularly performs tricks involving up to 12 members simultaneously riding one bicycle.

Coast to Coast

The transcontinental record is 13 days 5 hours 20 minutes from San Francisco to New York (City Hall) by Paul Cornish, 25, March 4–17, 1973. He averaged 225 miles a day.

David Martin (born January 3, 1957) and Scott Parcel (born August 16, 1957) set out from San Francisco on February 4, 1973, on a tandem bicycle and pedaled 4,837 miles around the United States, finishing in Washington, D.C., on June 5, 1973.

EARLY BILLIARDS MATCH: St. James's Hall in London was filled for the championship game in 1870.

Billiards

Earliest Mention. The earliest recorded mention of billiards was in France in 1429, and it was mentioned in England in 1588 in inventories of the Duke of Norfolk's Howard House and the Earl of Leicester's property in Essex. The first recorded public room for billiards in England was the Piazza, Covent Garden, London, in the early part of the 19th century.

Rubber cushions were introduced in 1835 and slate beds in 1836.

Highest Breaks. Tom Reece (England) made an unfinished break of 499,135, including 249,152 cradle cannons (2 points each), in 85 hours 49 minutes against Joe Chapman at Burroughes' Hall, Soho Square, London, between June 3 and July 6, 1907. This was not recognized because press and public were not continuously present. The highest certified break made by the anchor cannon is 42,746 by W. Cook (England) from May 29 to June 7, 1907. The official world record under the then baulk-line rule is 1,784 by Joe Davis in the United Kingdom Championship on May 29, 1936. Walter Lindrum (Australia) made an official break of 4,137 in 2 hours 55 minutes against Joe Davis at Thurston's, London, on January 19–20, 1932, before the baulk-line rule was in force. The amateur record is 859 by Mohammed Lafir (Sri Lanka) versus Eric Simons (New Zealand) in the World Amateur Championship in Bombay, India, on December 5, 1973.

Fastest Century. Walter Lindrum (1898–1960) of Australia made an unofficial 100 break in 27.5 seconds in Australia on October 10, 1952. His official record is 100 in 46.0 seconds, set in Sydney, 1941.

Most World Titles. The greatest number of world championship titles (instituted 1870) won by one player is eight by John Roberts, Jr. (England) in 1870 (twice), 1871, 1875 (twice), 1877 and 1885 (twice).

Willie Hoppe (U.S.) won 51 "world" titles in the U.S. variant of the game between 1906 and 1952.

Most Amateur Titles. The record for world amateur titles is four by Robert Marshall (Australia) in 1936–38–51–62. The record number for women's titles is 9 by Maureen Baynton (*née* Barrett) between 1955 and 1968.

Pool

Pool or championship pocket billiards with numbered balls began to become standardized *c.* 1890. The greatest exponents were Ralph Greenleaf (U.S.) (1899–1950), who won the "world" professional title 19 times (1919–1937), and William Mosconi (U.S.), who dominated the game from 1941 to 1957.

The greatest number of balls pocketed in 24 hours is 5,688 (a rate of 1 every 15.19 seconds) by Bruce Christopher in New York City, September 12–13, 1974.

The longest recorded game by 3 players is one of 280 hours in Nelson, Lancashire, England, April 16–28, 1976.

3-Cushion Billiards

This pocketless variation dates back to 1878. The most successful exponent, 1906–52 was William F. Hoppe (b. October 11, 1887, Cornwall-on-Hudson, New York; d. February 1, 1959) who won 51 billiards championships in all forms.

Bobsledding

Origins. The oldest known sled is dated *c.* 6500 B.C. and came from Heinola, southern Finland. The word toboggan comes from the Micmac American Indian word *tobaakan*. The oldest bobsledding club in the world is at St. Moritz, Switzerland, home of the Cresta Run, founded in 1887. Modern world championships were inaugurated in 1924. Four-man bobs were included in the first Winter Olympic Games at Chamonix, France, in 1924 and two-man boblets from the third Games at Lake Placid, New York, in 1932.

Olympic and World Titles. The Olympic four-man bob has been won four times by Switzerland (1924–36–56–72). The U.S. (1932, 1936), Italy (1956, 1968) and West Germany (1952 and 1972) have won the Olympic boblet event twice. The most medals won by an individual is 6 (two gold, two silver, two bronze) by Eugenio Monti (Italy) from 1956 to 1968.

The world four-man bob has been won 12 times by Switzerland (1924–36–39–47–54–55–56–57–71–72–73–75). Italy won the 2-man title 14 times (1954–56–57–58–59–60–61–62–63–66–68–69–71–75). Eugenio Monti (Italy) (b. January 23, 1928) has been a member of 11 world championship crews.

Tobogganing

The skeleton one-man toboggan dates, in its present form, from 1892. On the 1,325-yard-long Cresta Run at St. Moritz, Switzerland, dating from 1884, the record from the Junction (2,868 feet) is 42.96

TOBOGGAN CHAMPION: Nino Bibbia of Italy has won 8 Grand National titles, 8 Curzon Cup titles, and the gold medal in the 1948 Olympic Games.

seconds (average 63.08 m.p.h.) by Poldi Birchtold of Switzerland in January, 1975. The record from Top (3,981 feet) is 53.24 seconds, also by Birchtold in January, 1975. Momentary speeds of 85 m.p.h. have been attained.

The greatest number of wins in the Cresta Run Grand National (instituted 1885) is eight by the 1948 Olympic champion Nino Bibbia (Italy) (b. September 9, 1924) in 1960–61–62–63–64–66–68–73. The greatest number of wins in the Cresta Run Curzon Cup (instituted in 1910) is eight by Bibbia in 1950–57–58–60–62–63–64–69 who hence won the Double in 1960–62–63–64. The greatest number of descents made in a season is 7,749 during the 65 racing days of 1975.

Lugeing

In lugeing the rider adopts a sitting, as opposed to a prone position. It was largely developed by British tourists at Klosters, Switzerland, from 1883. The first European championships were at Reichenberg (now East) Germany, in 1914 and the first world championships at Oslo, Norway, in 1953. The International Luge Federation was formed in 1957. Lugeing became an Olympic sport in 1964.

Most World Titles. The most successful rider in the world championships is Thomas Köhler (East Germany) (b. June 25, 1940), who won the single-seater title in 1962, 1964 (Olympics), 1966, and 1967, and shared in the two-seater title in 1967 and 1968 (Olympics). Miss Otrum Enderlein (East Germany) (b. January 12, 1943) has won 4 times—1964 (Olympics), 1965, 1966, and 1967. Margi Schumann (East Germany) has equalled this mark, winning in 1973, 1974, 1975, and 1976 (Olympics).

Highest Speed. The fastest luge run is at Krynica, Poland, where speeds of more than 80 m.p.h. have been recorded.

Bowling

Origins. Bowling can be traced to articles found in the tomb of an Egyptian child of 5200 B.C. where there were nine pieces of stone to be set up as pins at which a stone "ball" was rolled. The ball first had to roll through an archway made of three pieces of marble. There is also resemblance to a Polynesian game called *ula maika* which utilized pins and balls of stone. The stones were rolled a distance of 60 feet. In the Italian Alps about 2,000 years ago, the underhand tossing of stones at an object is believed the beginnings of *bocci*, a game still widely played in Italy and similar to bowling. Bowling at pins probably originated in ancient Germany as a religious ceremony. Martin Luther is credited with the statement that nine was the ideal number of pins. In the British Isles, lawn bowls was preferred to bowling at pins. In the 16th century, bowling at pins was the national sport in Scotland. How bowling at pins came to the United States is a matter of controversy. Early British settlers probably brought lawn bowls and set up what is known as Bowling Green at the tip of Manhattan Island in New York but perhaps the Dutch under Henry Hudson were the ones to be credited. Some historians say that in Connecticut the tenth pin was added to evade a legal ban against the nine-pin game in 1845 but others say that ten pins was played in New York City before this and point to Washington Irving's "Rip Van Winkle" written about 1818 as evidence.

Lanes. In the U.S. there are 8,577 bowling establishments with 140,741 lanes in 1975 and about 65,000,000 bowlers. The world's largest bowling hall is the Tokyo World Lanes Bowling Center in Tokyo, Japan, with 252 lanes.

Organizations. The American Bowling Congress (ABC) comprises 4,200,000 men who bowl in leagues and tournaments. The Women's International Bowling Congress (WIBC) has a membership of 3,500,000.

World Championships

The Fédération Internationale des Quilleurs world championships were instituted in 1954. The highest pinfall in the individual men's event is 5,963 for 28 games by Ed Luther (U.S.) at Milwaukee, Wisconsin, in 1971.

In the women's event (instituted 1963) the record is 4,615 pins in 24 games by Annedore Haefker (West Germany) at Tolworth, Surrey, England, in 1975.

Highest Game. The greatest altitude at which a game has taken place is 25,000 feet, when Dick Weber played Sylvia Wene in a Boeing 707 "Starstream Astrojet" freighter of American Airlines on January 7, 1964.

League Scores

Highest Men's. The highest individual score for three games is 886 by Allie Brandt of Lockport, New York, in 1939. Maximum

FIRST TEAM EVENT PERFECT GAME: Les Schissler of Denver claps his hands as his 12th ball scatters the pins for the first 300 game in the team event in the history of the American Bowling Congress Tournament, at Miami Beach, Florida, in 1967.

possible is 900 (three perfect games). Highest team score is 3,858 by Budweisers of St. Louis in 1958.

Highest Women's. The highest individual score for three games is 818 by Bev Ortner (now of Tucson, Arizona) in Galva, Iowa in 1968. Highest team score is 3,379 by Freeway Washer of Cleveland in 1960. (Highest in WIBC tournament play is 737 by D. D. Jacobson in 1972.)

Consecutive Strikes. The record for consecutive strikes in sanctioned match play is 33 by John Pezzin (born 1930) at Toledo, Ohio, on March 4, 1976.

Most Perfect Scores. The highest number of sanctioned 300 games is 26 (to 1975) by Elvin Mesger of Sullivan, Missouri. The maximum 900 for a three-game series has been recorded three times in unsanctioned games—by Leo Bentley at Lorain, Ohio, on March 26, 1931; by Joe Sargent at Rochester, New York, in 1934; and by Jim Murgie in Philadelphia, on February 4, 1937.

ABC Tournament Scores

Highest Individual. Highest three-game series in singles is 775 by Lee Jouglard of Detroit in 1951. Best three-game total in any ABC event is 792 by Jack Winters of Philadelphia in doubles in 1962. Jim Godman of Vero Beach, Florida, holds the record for a nine-game All-Events total with 2,184 (731–749–704) set in Indianapolis, Indiana, in 1974. Jim Stefanich of Joliet, Illinois, and Bill Lillard of Houston, Texas, have won the most championships with 6 each. Stefanich won the team in 1963 and 1968, the doubles in 1966 and 1969, the singles in 1969, and All-Events in 1968. Lillard won the team in 1955–56–62–71, the doubles in 1956, and All-Events in 1956.

Highest Doubles. The ABC record of 544 was set in 1946 by Joseph Gworek (279) and Henry Kmidowski (265) of Buffalo. The record score in a doubles series is 1,453, set in 1952 by John Klares (755) and Steve Nagy (698) of Cleveland.

Perfect Scores. Les Schissler of Denver scored 300 in the Classic team event in 1967, and Ray Williams of Detroit scored 300 in Regular team play in 1974. In all, there have been only twenty-nine 300 games in the ABC tournament. There have been 16 perfect games in singles, 11 in doubles, and two in team play.

Best Finishes in One Tournament. Les Schissler of Denver won the singles, All-Events, and was on the winning team in 1966 to tie Ed Lubanski of Detroit and Bill Lillard of Dallas as the only man to win three ABC crowns in one year. The best four finishes in one ABC tournament were third in singles, second in doubles, third in team and first in All-Events by Bob Strampe, Detroit, in 1967, and first in singles, third in team and doubles and second in All-Events by Paul Kulbaga, Cleveland, in 1960.

Attendance. Largest attendance on one day for an ABC tournament was 5,257 in Milwaukee in 1952. Total attendance record was also set at that tournament with 147,504 in 85 days.

Prize Winnings

Largest individual prize winner in an ABC tournament was Tom Hennessey of St. Louis, with $4,000 in 1965. Highest prize fund in one tournament was $796,912 in Dayton, Ohio, in 1975.

Youngest and Oldest Winners. The youngest champion was Harold Allen of Detroit who was a 1915 doubles winner at the age of 18. The oldest champion was E.D. (Sarge) Easter of Detroit, who, at the age of 67, was a winner in the 1950 team event. The oldest doubles team in ABC competition totaled 165 years in 1955: Jerry Ameling (83) and Joseph Lehnbeutter (82), both from St. Louis.

Strikes and Spares in a Row

In the greatest finish to win an ABC title, Ed Shay set a record of 12 strikes in a row in 1958, when he scored a perfect game for a total of 733 in the series.

The most spares in a row is 23, a record set by Lt. Hazen Sweet of Battle Creek, Michigan, in 1950.

Oldest Bowler. Tom Fatherson of the Long Beach Club, California, was still playing daily after his 103rd birthday in October, 1973.

Marathon

Thomas Mogavero of Leroy, New York, bowled for 130 hours 50 minutes at the WOKR-TV lanes in Rochester, N.Y., October 22–28, 1975. He bowled 861 games using a 16-lb. ball.

Richard Dewey, 46, of Omaha, Nebraska, bowled 1,472 consecutive games in 114½ hours, June 5–10, 1975. He bowled with both his right and left hands, averaged 159 through his first 750 games and 126 for all 1,472.

LONGEST AS CHAMPION: Joe Louis (left) was the heavyweight champion of the world for 11 years 8 months 7 days.

Boxing

Earliest References. Boxing with gloves was depicted on a fresco from the Isle of Thera, Greece, which has been dated 1520 B.C. The earliest prize-ring code of rules was formulated in England on August 16, 1743, by the champion pugilist Jack Broughton (1704–89), who reigned from 1729 to 1750. Boxing, which had in 1867 come under the Queensberry Rules, formulated for John Sholto Douglas, 9th Marquess of Queensberry, was not established as a legal sport in Britain until after a ruling of Mr. Justice Grantham following the death of Billy Smith (Murray Livingstone) as the result of a fight on April 24, 1901, at Covent Garden, London.

Longest Fight. The longest recorded fight with gloves was between Andy Bowen of New Orleans and Jack Burke in New Orleans, on April 6–7, 1893. The fight lasted 110 rounds and 7 hours 19 minutes from 9:15 p.m. to 4:34 a.m., but was declared a no contest when both men were unable to continue. The longest recorded bare knuckle fight was one of 6 hours 15 minutes between James Kelly and Jack Smith at Fiery Creek, Dalesford, Victoria, Australia, on December 3, 1855. The greatest recorded number of rounds is 276 in 4 hours 30 minutes, when Jack Jones beat Patsy Tunney in Cheshire, England, in 1825.

Shortest Fight. There is a distinction between the quickest knockout and the shortest fight. A knockout in 10½ seconds (including a 10-second count) occurred on September 29, 1946, when Al Couture struck Ralph Walton while the latter was adjusting a gum shield in his corner at Lewiston, Maine. If the time was accurately taken it is clear that Couture must have been more than half-way across the ring from his own corner at the opening bell.

The shortest fight on record appears to be one in a Golden Gloves tournament in Minneapolis, Minnesota, on November 4, 1974, when Mike Collins floored Pat Brownson with his first punch and the contest was stopped, without a count, 4 seconds after the bell.

The shortest world heavyweight title fight occurred when Tommy Burns (1881–1955) (né Noah Brusso) of Canada knocked out Jem Roche in 1 minute 28 seconds in Dublin, Ireland, on March 17, 1908. The duration of the Clay vs. Liston fight at Lewiston, Maine, on May 25, 1965, was 1 minute 52 seconds (including the count) as timed from the video tape recordings despite a ringside announcement giving a time of 1 minute. The shortest world title fight was when Al McCoy knocked out George Chip in 45 seconds for the middleweight crown in New York on April 6, 1914.

Tallest and Heaviest. The tallest and heaviest boxer to fight professionally was Gogea Mitu (born 1914) of Rumania in 1935. He was 7 feet 4 inches and weighed 327 lbs. John Rankin, who won a fight in New Orleans, in November, 1967, was reputedly also 7 feet 4 inches.

World Heavyweight Champions

Longest and Shortest Reigns. The longest reign of any world heavyweight champion is 11 years 8 months and 7 days by Joe Louis (born Joseph Louis Barrow, at Lafayette, Alabama, May 13, 1914), from June 22, 1937, when he knocked out James J. Braddock in the 8th round at Chicago until announcing his retirement on March 1, 1949. During his reign Louis made a record 25 defenses of his title. The shortest reign was by Primo Carnera (Italy) for 350 days from June 29, 1933 to June 14, 1934. However, if the disputed title claim of Marvin Hart is allowed, his reign from July 3, 1905, to February 23, 1906, was only 235 days.

Heaviest and Lightest. The heaviest world champion was Primo Carnera (Italy) (1906–67), the "Ambling Alp," who won the title from Jack Sharkey in 6 rounds in New York City, on June 29, 1933. He scaled 267 lbs. for this fight but his peak weight was 270 lbs. He had the longest reach at 85½ inches (fingertip to fingertip) and also the largest fists with a 14¾-inch circumference. He had an expanded chest measurement of 53 inches. The lightest champion was Robert Prometheus Fitzsimmons (1862–1917), who was born at Helston, Cornwall, England, and, at a weight of 167 lbs., won the title by knocking out James J. Corbett in 14 rounds at Carson City, Nevada, on March 17, 1897.

The greatest differential in a world title fight was 86 lbs. between Carnera (270 lbs.) and Tommy Loughran (184 lbs.) of the U.S., when the former won on points at Miami, Florida, on March 1, 1934.

Tallest and Shortest. The tallest world champion was the 6-foot-5.4-inch-tall Carnera, who was measured by the Physical Education Director at the Hemingway Gymnasium of Harvard. Jess Willard (1881–1968), who won the title in 1915, often stated as 6 feet 6¼ inches tall, and widely reported and believed to be up to 6 feet 8½

RETIRED UNDEFEATED HEAVYWEIGHT CHAMPION: Rocky Marciano (left) shares this honor with Gene Tunney.

inches, was in fact 6 feet 5.25 inches. The shortest was Tommy Burns (1881–1955) of Canada, world champion from February 23, 1906, to December 26, 1908, who stood 5 feet 7 inches, and weighed 179 lbs.

Oldest and Youngest. The oldest man to win the heavyweight crown was Jersey Joe Walcott (born Arnold Raymond Cream, January 31, 1914, at Merchantville, New Jersey), who knocked out Ezzard Charles on July 18, 1951, in Pittsburgh, when aged 37 years 5 months 18 days. Walcott was the oldest title holder at 38 years 7 months 23 days when he lost to Rocky Marciano on September 23, 1952. The youngest age at which the world title has been won is 21 years 331 days by Floyd Patterson (born Waco, North Carolina, January 4, 1935). After the retirement of Rocky Marciano, Patterson won the vacant title by beating Archie Moore in 5 rounds in Chicago, on November 30, 1956. Patterson and Muhammad Ali Haj (formerly Cassius Clay) (born in Louisville, Kentucky, January 17, 1942) are the only two men ever to regain the heavyweight championship. Patterson defeated Ingemar Johansson (Sweden) on June 20, 1960, having lost to him on June 26, 1959. Muhammad Ali defeated George Foreman on October 30, 1974, having been stripped of his title on April 28, 1967.

Undefeated. Only James Joseph (Gene) Tunney (1926–28) and Rocky Marciano (1952–56) *finally* retired as undefeated champions.

Longest-Lived. Jess Willard was born December 29, 1881, at St. Clere, Kansas, and died in California, on December 15, 1968, aged 86 years 351 days.

Earliest Title Fight. The first world heavyweight title fight, with gloves and 3-minute rounds, was between John L. Sullivan (1858–1918) and "Gentleman" James J. Corbett (1866–1933) in New Orleans, on September 7, 1892. Corbett won in 21 rounds.

World Champions (any weight)

Longest and Shortest Reign. Joe Louis's heavyweight duration record stands for all divisions. The shortest reign has been 54 days by the French featherweight Eugène Criqui from June 2 to July 26, 1923. The disputed flyweight champion Emile Pladner (France) reigned only 47 days from March 2, to April 18, 1929, as did the disputed featherweight champion Dave Sullivan from September 26, to November 11, 1898.

Youngest and Oldest. The youngest at which any world championship has been claimed is 17 years 180 days by Wilfredo Benitez (born September 8, 1958) of Puerto Rico, who won the light-welterweight title in San Juan on March 6, 1976.

The oldest world champion was Archie Moore (b. Archibald Lee Wright, Collinsville, Illinois, December 13, 1913 or 1916), who was recognized as a light-heavyweight champion up to February 10, 1962, when his title was removed. He was then between 45 and 48. Bob Fitzsimmons (1872–1917) had the longest career of any official world titleholder with over 32 years from 1882 to 1914. He won his last world title aged 41 years 174 days in San Francisco on November 25, 1903. He was an amateur from 1880 to 1882.

Longest Fight. The longest world title fight (under Queensberry Rules) was between the lightweights Joe Gans (1874–1910), of the U.S., and Oscar "Battling" Nelson (1882–1954), the "Durable Dane," at Goldfield, Nevada, on September 3, 1906. It was terminated in the 42nd round when Gans was declared the winner on a foul.

Most Recaptures. The only boxer to win a world title five times at one weight is Sugar Ray Robinson (b. Walker Smith, Jr., in Detroit, May 3, 1920) who beat Carmen Basilio (U.S.) in the Chicago Stadium on March 25, 1958, to regain the world middleweight title for the fourth time. The other title wins were over Jake LaMotta (U.S.) in Chicago on February 14, 1951, Randy Turpin (U.K.) in New York on September 12, 1951, Carl "Bobo" Olson (U.S.) in Chicago on December 9, 1955, and Gene Fullmer (U.S.) in Chicago on May 1, 1957. The record number of title bouts in a career is 33 or 34 (at bantam and featherweight) by George Dixon (1870–1909), *alias* Little Chocolate, of Canada, between 1890 and 1901.

Most Titles Simultaneously. The only man to hold world titles at three weights simultaneously was Henry ("Homicide Hank") Armstrong (born December 12, 1912), now the Rev. Henry Jackson, of the U.S., at featherweight, lightweight and welterweight from August to December, 1938.

Greatest "Tonnage." The greatest "tonnage" recorded in any fight is 700 lbs., when Claude "Humphrey" McBride of Oklahoma at 340 lbs. knocked out Jimmy Black of Houston at 360 lbs. in the 3rd round at Oklahoma City on June 1, 1971.

The greatest "tonnage" in a world title fight was 488¾ lbs. when Carnera (259¼ lbs.) fought Paolino Uzcudem (229½ lbs.) of Spain in Rome, Italy, on October 22, 1933.

Smallest Champions. The smallest man to win any world title has been Pascual Perez (b. Mendoza, Argentina, on March 4, 1926) who won the flyweight title in Tokyo on November 26, 1954, at 107 lbs. and 4 feet 11½ inches tall. Jimmy Wilde (b. Merthyr Tydfil, 1892, d. 1969, U.K.) who held the flyweight title from 1916 to 1923 was reputed never to have fought above 108 lbs.

Most Knockdowns in Title Fights. Vic Toweel (South Africa) knocked down Danny O'Sullivan of London 14 times in 10 rounds in their world bantamweight fight at Johannesburg, on December 2, 1950, before the latter retired.

All Fights

Largest Purse. Muhammad Ali Haj (born Cassius Marcellus Clay, in Louisville, Kentucky, January 17, 1942) won a reported $6,000,000 in his successful defense of the heavyweight title against Joe Frazier (U.S.), held in Manila, Philippines, on October 1, 1975.

The largest stake ever fought for in the bare-knuckle era was $22,500 in a 27-round fight between Jack Cooper and Wolf Bendoff at Port Elizabeth, South Africa, on July 29, 1889.

Highest Attendances. The greatest paid attendance at any boxing fight has been 120,757 (with a ringside price of $27.50) for the Tunney vs. Dempsey world heavyweight title fight at the Sesquicentennial Stadium, Philadelphia, on September 23, 1926. The indoor record is 37,321 at the Clay vs. Terrell fight in the Astrodome, Houston, Texas, on February 6, 1967. The highest non-paying attendance is 135,132 at the Tony Zale vs. Billy Pryor fight at Juneau Park, Milwaukee, Wisconsin, on August 18, 1941.

Lowest. The smallest attendance at a world heavyweight title fight was 2,434 at the Clay vs. Liston fight at Lewiston, Maine, on May 25, 1965.

Greatest Receipts. The greatest total receipts from any boxing fight have been those from the Frazier-Ali fight in Madison Square Garden, New York City, on March 8, 1971. The gate was $1,352,951 (20,455 paid attendance) but the total gross, including T.V. closed circuit transmissions and all other rights have been estimated at more than $20,000,000. The highest *gate* receipts were those for the Tunney-Dempsey fight of 1927 when 104,943 paid $2,658,660 with a ringside price of $40.

Highest Earnings in Career. The largest known fortune ever made in a fighting career is an estimated $46,500,000 amassed by Muhammad Ali to September, 1976.

Including earnings for refereeing and promoting, Jack Dempsey had grossed over $10,000,000 to 1967.

Most Knockouts. The greatest number of knockouts in a career is 141 by Archie Moore (1936 to 1963). The record for consecutive

K.O.'s is 44, set by Lamar Clark of Utah at Las Vegas, Nevada, on January 11, 1960. He knocked out 6 in one night (5 in the first round) in Bingham, Utah, on December 1, 1958.

Most Fights. The greatest recorded number of fights in a career is 1,309 by Abraham Hollandersky, *alias* Abe the Newsboy (U.S.), in the fourteen years from 1905 to 1918. He filled in the time with 387 wrestling bouts (1905–16).

Most Fights Without Loss. Hal Bagwell, a lightweight, of Gloucester, England, was reputedly undefeated in 180 consecutive fights, of which only 5 were draws, between August 15, 1938, and November 29, 1948. His record of fights in the wartime period (1939–46) is very sketchy, however. Of boxers with complete records, Packy McFarland (1888–1936) went undefeated in 97 fights from 1905 to 1915.

Greatest Weight Difference. The greatest weight difference recorded in a major bout is 140 lbs., between Bob Fitzsimmons (172 lbs.) and Ed Dunkhorst (312 lbs.) at Brooklyn, New York City, on April 30, 1900. Fitzsimmons won in two rounds.

Longest Career. The heavyweight Jem Mace, known as "the gypsy" (born at Norwich, England, April 8, 1831), had a career lasting 35 years from 1855 to 1890, but there were several years in which he had only one fight. He died, aged 79, in Jarrow on November 30, 1910. Walter Edgerton, the "Kentucky Rosebud," knocked out John Henry Johnson, aged 45, in 4 rounds at the Broadway A.C., New York City, on February 4, 1916, when aged 63.

Most Olympic Gold Medals. The only amateur boxer ever to win three Olympic gold medals is the southpaw László Papp (born 1926 in Hungary), who took the middleweight (1948) and the light-middleweight titles (1952 and 1956). The only man to win two titles in one meeting was O. L. Kirk (U.S.), who took both the bantam and featherweight titles at St. Louis, Missouri, in 1904, when the

TWICE OLYMPIC CHAMPION: Teofilio Stevenson (right) of Cuba became the first heavyweight ever to repeat as gold medallist in the 1972 and 1976 Games.

U.S. won all the titles. Harry W. Mallin (Great Britain) was in 1924 the first boxer ever to successfully defend an Olympic title when he retained the middleweight crown.

The oldest man to win an Olympic gold medal in boxing was Richard K. Gunn (born 1870) of Great Britain who won the featherweight title on October 27, 1908, in London, aged 38.

Bridge (Contract)

Earliest References. Bridge (corruption of Biritch) is thought to be of Levantine origin, similar games having been played there in the early 1870's. The game was known in London in 1886 under the title of "Biritch or Russian Whist." Whist, first referred to in 1529, was the world's premier card game until 1930. Its rules had been standardized in 1742.

Auction bridge (highest bidder names trump) was introduced in 1904, but was swamped by contract bridge, which was devised by Harold S. Vanderbilt (U.S.) on a Caribbean voyage in November, 1925. The new version became a world-wide craze after the U.S. vs. Great Britain challenge match between Ely Culbertson (born in Rumania, 1891) and Lt.-Col. Walter Thomas More Buller (1886–1938) at Almack's Club, London, on September 15, 1930. The U.S. won the 54-hand match by 4,845 points.

Highest Possible Scores (excluding penalties for rules infractions)

Opponents bid 7 of any suit or no trump, doubled and redoubled and vulnerable. Opponents make no trick.		Bid 1 no trump, doubled and redoubled, vulnerable	
Above Line 1st undertrick	400	*Below Line* 1st trick (40×4)	160
12 subsequent under-		*Above Line* 6 overtricks (400×6)	2,400
tricks at 600 each	7,200	2nd game of 2-Game	
All Honors	150	Rubber	*350
		All Honors (4 aces)	150
		Bonus for making redoubled	
		contract	50
	7,750	(Highest Possible Positive Score)	3,110

* In practice, the full bonus of 700 points is awarded after the completion of the second game, rather than 350 after each game.

Perfect Deals. The mathematical odds against dealing 13 cards of one suit are 158,753,389,899 to 1, while the odds against receiving a "perfect hand" consisting of all 13 spades are 365,013,559,599 to 1. The odds against each of the 4 players receiving a complete suit are 2,235,197,406,895,366,368,301,559,999 to 1. Instances of this are reported frequently but the chances of it happening genuinely are extraordinarily remote—in fact if all the people in the world were grouped in bridge fours, and each four were dealt 120 hands a day, it would require 62×10^{12} years before one "perfect" deal could be expected to recur.

A "perfect" perfect deal with the dealer (South) with 13 clubs, round to East with 13 spades was the subject of affidavits by Mrs. E. F. Gyde (dealer), Mrs. Hennion, David Rex-Taylor and Mrs. P. Dawson at Richmond Community Centre, Surrey, England, on August 25, 1964. This deal, 24 times more remote than a "perfect deal," the second of the rubber, was with a pack not used for the first deal.

In view of the fact that there should be 31,201,794 deals with two perfect hands for each deal with four perfect hands, and that reports of the latter far outnumber the former, it can be safely assumed that reported occurrences of perfect deals are, almost without exception, phony.

World Titles. The World Championship (Bermuda Bowl) has been won most often by Italy's "Blue Team" (Squadra Azzura) (1957–58–59, 1961–62–63, 1965–66–67, 1969, 1973–74–75), which also won the Olympiad in 1964, 1968 and 1972. Giorgio Belladonna was on all 16 winning teams. The team retired in 1969, but came back to defeat the Dallas Aces (1970–71 World Champions) 338–254 in Las Vegas in December, 1971, and take the Olympiad in Miami in June, 1972, followed by wins in the Bermuda Bowl at Guaruja, Brazil, in 1973, at Venice, Italy, in 1974, and at Bermuda in 1975.

Longest Session. The longest recorded session is one of 180 hours by four students at Edinburgh University, Scotland, on April 21–28, 1972.

Most Master Points. In 1971, a new World Ranking List based on Master Points was instituted. The leading male player is Giorgio Belladonna (see above) with 1,765 points, followed by 5 more Italians.

The world's leading woman player is Mrs. Rixi Markus (G.B.) with 229 points to June, 1976.

Bull Fighting

The first renowned professional *espada* (bull fighter) was Francisco Romero of Ronda, in Andalusia, Spain, who introduced the *estoque* and the red muleta *c.* 1700. Spain now has some 190 active matadors. Since 1700, 42 major matadors have died in the ring.

Largest Stadiums and Gate. The world's largest bull-fighting ring is the Plaza, Mexico City, with a capacity of 48,000. The largest of Spain's 312 bullrings is Las Ventas, Madrid, with a capacity of 26,000.

Most Successful Matadors. The most successful matador measured by bulls killed was Lagartijo (1841–1900), born Rafael Molina, whose lifetime total was 4,867.

The longest career of any 20th-century *espada* was that of Juan Belmonte (1892–1962) of Spain, who survived 29 seasons from 1909 to 1937 killing 3,000 bulls and being gored 50 times. In 1919, he killed 200 bulls in 109 *corridas*. (Recent Spanish law requires compulsory retirement at age 55.)

Most Kills in a Day. In 1884, Romano set a record by killing 18 bulls in a day in Seville, and in 1949 El Litri (Miguel Báes) set a Spanish record with 114 *novilladas* in a season.

Highest Paid Matadors. The highest paid bull fighter in

history is El Cordobés (born Manuel Benitez Pérez, probably on May 4, 1936, in Palma del Rio, Spain), who became a multi-millionaire in 1966, during which year he fought 111 *corridas* up to October 4, receiving over $15,000 for each half hour in the ring. In 1970, he received an estimated $1,800,000 for 121 fights.

Currently, Paco Camino receives $36,800 per *corrida*.

Canoeing

Origins. The acknowledged pioneer of canoeing as a sport was John Macgregor, a British barrister, in 1865. The Canoe Club was formed on July 26, 1866.

Most Olympic Gold Medals. Gert Fredriksson (b. November 21, 1919) of Sweden has won the 1,000-meter Kayak singles in 1948, 1952 and 1956, the 10,000-meter Kayak singles in 1948 and 1956, and the 1,000-meter Kayak doubles in 1960. In addition to his 6 Olympic titles he has won 3 other world titles in non-Olympic years: 1,000-meter K.1 in 1950 and 1954, and 500-meter K.1 in 1954.

The Olympic 1,000-meter best performance of 3 minutes 8.71 seconds represents an average speed of 11.85 m.p.h. and a striking rate of about 125 strokes per minute.

Longest Journey

The longest canoe journey in history was one of 7,165 miles from New York City to Nome, Alaska, by Geoffrey W. Pope, aged 24, and Sheldon P. Taylor, 25, from April 25, 1936 arriving on August 11, 1937. The journey was made entirely on the North American river system by paddle and portage.

The longest journey without portage is one of 6,102 miles by Richard H. Grant and Ernest Lassy circumnavigating the eastern U.S. from Chicago to New Orleans to Miami to New York, returning back to Chicago *via* the Great Lakes, from September 22, 1930, to August 15, 1931.

Downstream Canoeing

River	Miles	Canoers	Location	Duration
Mississippi	2,250	Dr. Gerald Capers, Charles Saunders, Joseph Tagg	Lake Itasca, Minnesota, 1937	49 days
Amazon	3,400	Stephan Z. Bezuk (U.S.) (kayak)	Atalaya to Ponta des Céu, June 21–Nov. 4, 1970	4½ mths.
Nile (Egypt)	4,000	John Goddard (U.S.), Jean Laporte and André Davy (France)	Kagera to the Delta, Nov., 1954–July, 1955	9 months
Congo (Zaïre)	2,500	John and Julie Batchelor (G.B.)	Moasampanga to Banana, May 8– Sept. 12, 1974	128 days

Eskimo Rolls. The record for Eskimo rolls is 1,004 in 107 minutes 12 seconds by David Ansell, 19, at Bedford, England, on May 29,

1972. A "hand-rolling" record of 100 rolls in 3 minutes 58.7 seconds was set in the Bootham School Pool, York, England, on June 14, 1975, by David A. Clapham, 15.

English Channel Crossing. David Shankland (born 1929) paddled his homemade N.C.K.I. canoe (named "Jelly Roll") from Dover, England, to Cap Gris-Nez, France, in 3 hours 36 minutes on June 21, 1965.

Transatlantic. In 1928 E. Romer (Germany) crossed the North Atlantic from Lisbon to the West Indies in a 19½-foot canvas sailing Kayak named *Deutsches Sport* in 58 days.

Cave Exploration *(Spelunking)*

PROGRESSIVE CAVING DEPTH RECORDS

Feet	Cave	Cavers	Date
210	Lamb Lair, Somerset, England	John Beaumont (explored)	c. 1676
453	Macocha, Moravia	Nagel	May, 1748
741	Grotta di Padriciano, Trieste, Italy	Antonio Lindner, Svetina	1839
1,076	Grotta di Trebiciano, Trieste	Antonio Lindner	April 6, 1841
1,293	Nidlenloch, Switzerland	—	1909
1,509	Geldloch, Austria	—	1923
1,574	Antro di Corchia, Tuscany, Italy	E. Fiorentino Club	1934
1,978	Trou du Glaz, Isère, France	F. Petzl, C. Petit-Didier	May 4, 1947
2,418	Gouffre de la Pierre St. Martin, Básses-Pyrénées, France	*Georges Lépineux	Aug. 15, 1953
2,962	Gouffre Berger, Isère, France	*F. Petzl and 6 men	Sept. 25, 1954
3,123	Gouffre Berger, Isère, France	L. Potié, G. Garby *et al.*	July 29, 1955
3,681	Gouffre Berger, Isère, France	F. Petzl and others	July, 1956

N.B.—The Reseau de la Pierre St. Martin has been explored via a number of entrances, and has never been entirely descended at any one time. Consequently, after July, 1956, the "sporting" records for greatest descent into a cave should read:

3,707	Gouffre Berger, Isère, France	K. Pearce	Aug., 1967
3,743	Gouffre Berger, Isère, France	Spéléo Club de Seine	July, 1968
3,842	Reseau de la Pierre Saint Martin	Ass. de Rech. Spéléo Internationale	Aug., 1956
4,370	Reseau de la Pierre Saint Martin	A.R.S.I.P.	Aug., 1975

* Leader

Duration. The endurance record for staying in a cave is 463 days by Milutin Veljkovic (b. 1935) (Yugoslavia) in the Samar Cavern, Svrljig Mountains, northern Yugoslavia from June 24, 1969, to September 30, 1970.

Checkers

Origins. Checkers, known as draughts in some countries, has origins earlier than chess. It was played in Egypt in the first millenium B.C. The earliest book on the game was by Antonio Torquemada of Valencia, Spain in 1547.

The earliest U.S. *vs.* Great Britain international match was in 1905, and was won by the Scottish Masters, 73–34, with 284 draws. The U.S. won in 1927 in New York, 96–20 with 364 draws.

The only man to win 5 titles has been J. Marshall (Fife, Scotland) in 1948–50–52–54–66. The longest tenure of invincibility in freestyle play was that of Melvin Pomeroy (U.S.), who was internationally undefeated from 1914 until his death in 1933.

Longest Game. In competition, the prescribed rate of play is not less than 30 moves per hour with the average game lasting about 90 minutes. In 1958 a match between Dr. Marian Tinsley (U.S.) and Derek Oldbury (G.B.) lasted 7½ hours.

Most Opponents. Newell W. Banks (b. Detroit, October 10, 1887) played 140 games simultaneously, winning 133 and drawing 7 in Chicago in 1933. His playing time was 145 minutes so averaging about one second per move.

Chess

Origins. The name chess is derived from the Persian word *shah*. It is a descendant of the game *Chaturanga*. The earliest reference is from the Middle Persian Karnamak (*c.* 590–628), though there are grounds for believing its origins are from the 2nd century, owing to the discovery, announced in December, 1972, of two ivory chessmen, in the Uzbek Soviet Republic, datable to that century. The game reached Britain in *c.* 1255. The *Fédération Internationale des Echecs* was established in 1924. There were an estimated 7,000,000 registered players in the U.S.S.R. in 1973.

It has been calculated that the four opening moves can be made in 197,299 ways, leading to some 72,000 different positions. The approximate number of different games possible is 25×10^{116}—a number astronomically higher than the number of atoms in the observable universe.

World Champions. François André Danican, *alias* Philidor (1726–95), of France claimed the title of "world champion" from 1747 until his death. World champions have been generally recognized since 1886. The longest tenure has been 27 years by Dr. Emanuel Lasker (1868–1941) of Germany, from 1894 to 1921. Robert J. (Bobby) Fischer (b. Chicago, March 9, 1943) is reckoned on the officially adopted Elo system to be the greatest Grandmaster of all time. He has an I.Q. of 187 and became at 15 the youngest ever International Grandmaster.

The women's world championship has been most often won by Vera Menchik-Stevenson in 1927–30–31–33–35–37–39, and Nona Gaprindashvili (U.S.S.R.) from 1963 to 1976.

Winning Streak. Bobby Fischer (see above) won 20 games in succession in grandmaster chess from December 2, 1970 (*vs.* Jorge Rubinetti of Argentina) to September 30, 1971 (*vs.* Tigran Petrosian of the U.S.S.R.).

Longest Games. The most protracted chess game on record was one drawn on the 191st move between H. Pilnik (Argentina) and Moshe Czerniak (Israel) at Mar del Plata, Argentina, in April, 1950. The total playing time was 20 hours. A game of 21½ hours, but drawn on the 171st move (average over 7½ minutes per move), was played between Makagonov and Chekhover at Baku, U.S.S.R., in 1945.

Marathon. The longest recorded session is one of 130 hours

between Raymond Cantwell and Stephen Fitzgerald in Little
Milton, Oxfordshire, England, November 18–23, 1975.

The slowest recorded move (before modern rules) was one of
more than 11 hours between Paul Morphy, the U.S. champion
of 1852–62, and the chessmaster Louis Paulsen.

Shortest Game. The shortest recorded game between masters
was one of four moves when Lazard (Black) beat Gibaud in a Paris
chess café in 1924. The moves were: 1. P–Q4, N–KB3; 2. N–Q2,
P–K4; 3. PxP, N–N5; 4. P–KR3, N–K6. White then resigned because
if he played 5. PxN there would have followed Q–KR5 check and
the loss of his Queen for a Knight by any other move.

Most Opponents. Records by chessmasters for numbers of
opponents tackled simultaneously depend very much on whether or
not the opponents are replaced as defeated, are in relays, or whether
they are taken on in a simultaneous start. The greatest number
tackled on a replacement basis is 400 (379 defeated) by the late
Swedish master Gideon Stůhlberg in 36 hours of play in Buenos
Aires, Argentina, in 1940. The greatest number tackled in a simultaneous start is 179 by Jude Acers (U.S.) at the Mid Island Plaza,
Hicksville, New York, July 2–3, 1976. He won 160 of the games,
lost 15 and drew 4 in 19 hours. Georges Koltanowski (Belgium, later
of U.S.) tackled 56 opponents "blindfold" and won 50, drew 6, lost 0
in 9¾ hours at the Fairmont Hotel, San Francisco, on December 13,
1960.

Curling

Origins. The earliest illustration of the sport was in one of the
winter scenes by the Flemish painter, Pieter Brueghel, *c.* 1560. The
club with the earliest records, dating back to 1716, is that at Kilsyth,
Scotland. Organized administration began in 1838 with the formation of the Royal Caledonian Curling Club, the international
legislative body based in Edinburgh. The first indoor ice rink to
introduce curling was at Southport, England, in 1879.

The U.S. won the first Gordon International Medal series of
matches, between Canada and the U.S., at Montreal in 1884. The
first Strathcona Cup match between Canada and Scotland was won
by Canada in 1903. Although demonstrated at the Winter Olympics
of 1924, 1932 and 1964, curling has never been included in the
official Olympic program.

Largest Rink. The world's largest curling rink is the Big Four
Curling Rink, Calgary, Alberta, Canada, opened in 1959 at a cost
of Can. $2,250,000. Each of the two floors has 24 sheets of ice,
accommodating 96 teams and 384 players.

Most Titles. The record for international team matches for the
Scotch Cup and Air Canada Silver Broom (instituted 1959) is 12
wins by Canada, in 1959–60–61–62–63–64–66–68–69–70–71–72.
The most Strathcona Cup wins is seven by Canada (1903–09–12–23–
38–57–65) against Scotland.

Marathon. The longest recorded curling match is one of 60 hours by 8 members of the Glendale Golf and Curling Club, Hamilton, Ontario, Canada, April 2–4, 1976. Duration record for 2 curlers is 14 hours 23 minutes by Timothy Moreton and Robert Maddock at Toronto, Canada, April 16–17, 1973. The weight handled was 10.8 tons each.

Most Durable Player. In 1972, Howard "Pappy" Wood competed in his 65th consecutive annual *bonspiel* since 1908 at the Manitoba Curling Association.

Longest Bonspiel. The longest bonspiel in the world is the Alcan Employees' Bonspiel held in Arvida, Quebec, Canada. The tournament lasts 22 days, 396 games, and involves 200 teams of 4 players.

Equestrian Sports

Origin. Evidence of horse riding dates from an Anatolian statuette dated *c.* 1400 B.C. Pignatelli's academy of horsemanship at Naples dates from the sixteenth century. The earliest show jumping was in Paris in 1886. Equestrian events have been included in the Olympic Games since 1912.

Most Olympic Medals. The greatest number of Olympic gold medals is 5 by Hans Günter Winkler (West Germany), who won 4 team gold medals as captain in 1956, 1960, 1964 and 1972, and won the individual Grand Prix in 1956. The most team wins in the Prix de Nations is 5 by Germany in 1936, 1956, 1960, 1964, and 1972.

The lowest score obtained by a winner was no faults, by Frantisek Ventura (Czechoslovakia) on *Eliot* in 1928. Pierre Jonqueres d'Oriola (France), is the only two-time winner of the individual gold medal, in 1952 and 1964. Richard John Hannay Meade (G.B.) (b. December 4, 1938) is the only 3-day event rider to win 3 gold medals—the individual in 1972 and the team in 1968 and 1972.

World Titles. The men's world championship (instituted 1953) has been won twice by Hans Winkler of West Germany in 1954 and 1955, and Raimondo d'Inzeo of Italy in 1956 and 1960. The women's title (instituted 1965) has been won twice by Janou Tissot (*née* Lefebvre) of France on *Rocket* in 1970 and 1974.

Jumping Records. The official *Fédération Equestre Internationale* high jump record is 8 feet 1¼ inches by *Huaso*, ridden by Capt. A. Larraguibel Morales (Chile) at Santiago, Chile, on February 5, 1949, and 27 feet 2¾ inches for long jump over water by *Amado Mio* ridden by Lt.-Col. Lopez del Hierro (Spain), at Barcelona, Spain, on November 12, 1951. *Heatherbloom*, ridden by Dick Donnelly was reputed to have covered 37 feet in clearing an 8-foot-3-inch *puissance* jump at Richmond, Virginia, in 1903. H. Plant on *Solid Gold* cleared 36 feet 3 inches over water at the Wagga Show, N.S.W., Australia, in August, 1936. *Jerry M* allegedly cleared 40 feet over water at Aintree, Liverpool, England, in 1912.

At Cairns, Queensland, *Golden Meade* ridden by Jack Martin cleared an unofficially measured 8 feet 6 inches on July 25, 1946. *Ben Bolt* was credited with clearing 9 feet 6 inches at the 1938 Royal

HIGHEST EQUESTRIAN JUMP: Captain Morales leaped 8 feet 1½ inches on "Huasó" at Santiago, Chile, in 1949.

Horse Show, Sydney, Australia. The Australian record however is 8 feet 4 inches by C. Russell on *Flyaway* in 1939 and A. L. Payne on *Golden Meade* in 1946. The world's unofficial best for a woman is 7 feet 5½ inches by Miss B. Perry (Australia) on *Plain Bill* at Cairns, Queensland, Australia, in 1940.

The greatest recorded height reached bareback is 6 feet 7 inches by *Silver Wood* at Heidelberg, Victoria, Australia, on December 10, 1938.

Longest Ride. In 1911, two Texans, Temple and Louis Abernathy, rode 3,619 miles from Coney Island, New York City, to San Francisco, in 62 days. Temple was aged 9 and Louis was 11, and had they taken two days less they would have won a $10,000 prize. One of their horses, *Wylie Haynes*, finished the trip. The other, *Sam Bass* (the oldest member of the party at 16), died in Wyoming and was replaced by another horse.

Marathon. The duration record in the saddle is 178 hours 8 minutes by Rani Kolbaba, 15, and Ethelyn Larsen, 14, of White Salmon, Washington, June 14–21, 1974. Marathons of this kind stipulate that mounts must be changed at least every 6 hours.

Joseph Roberts of Newport Pagnell, Buckingham, England, rode at all paces (including jumping) for 48 hours 25 minutes at the Allerton Equitation Centre, Huntingdon, England, September 20–22, 1974.

Fencing

Origins. Fencing (fighting with single sticks) was practiced as a sport in Egypt as early as *c.* 1360 B.C. The first governing body for fencing in Britain was the Corporation of Masters of Defence founded by Henry VIII before 1540 and fencing was practiced as sport,

TWO OLYMPIC GOLD MEDALS have been won by Rudolf Karpati (left) in the sabre competitions of 1956 and 1960.

notably in prize fights, since that time. The foil was the practice weapon for the short court sword from the 17th century. The épée was established in the mid-19th century and the light sabre was introduced by the Italians in the late 19th century.

Most Olympic and Most World Titles

Event	Olympic Gold Medals	World Championships (not held in Olympic years)
Men's Foil, Individual	2 Christian d'Oriola (France) b. Oct. 3, 1928 (1952, 56)	4 Christian d'Oriola (France) (1947, 49, 53, 54)
	2 Nedo Nadi (Italy) (1894–1952) 1912, 20	
Men's Foil, Team	5 France (1924, 32, 48, 52, 68)	12 Italy (1929–31, 33–35, 37, 38, 49, 50, 54, 55)
Men's Epée, Individual	2 Ramón Fonst (Cuba) b. 1883 d. 1959 (1900, 04)	3 Georges Buchard (France) b. Dec. 21, 1893 (1927, 31, 33)
		3 Aleksey Nikanchikov (U.S.S.R.) b. July 30, 1940 (1966, 67, 70)
Men's Epée, Team	6 Italy (1920, 28, 36, 52, 56, 60)	10 Italy (1931, 33, 37, 49, 50, 53–55, 57, 58)
Men's Sabre, Individual	2 Dr. Jenö Fuchs (Hungary) b. Oct. 29, 1882 (1908, 12)	3 Aladar Gerevich (Hungary) (1935, 51, 55)
	2 Rudolf Kárpáti (Hungary) b. July 17, 1920 (1956, 60)	3 Jerzy Pawlowski (Poland) b. Oct. 25, 1932 (1957, 65, 66)
		3 Yacov Rylsky (U.S.S.R.) (1958, 61, 63)
Men's Sabre, Team	9 Hungary (1908, 12, 28, 32, 36, 48, 52, 56, 60)	14 Hungary (1930, 31, 33–35, 37, 51, 53–55, 57, 58, 66, 73)
Women's Foil, Individual	2 Ilona Schacherer-Elek (Hungary) b. 1907 (1936, 48)	3 Helene Mayer (Germany) 1910–53 (1929, 31, 37)
		3 Ilona Schacherer-Elek (Hungary) b. 1907 (1934, 35, 51)
		3 Ellen Müller-Preiss (Austria) b. May 6, 1912 (1947, 49, 50 (shared))
Women's Foil, Team	4 U.S.S.R. (1960, 68, 72, 76)	11 Hungary (1933–35, 37, 53–55, 59, 62, 67, 73)

Most Olympic Titles. The greatest number of individual Olympic gold medals won is three by Ramón Fonst (Cuba) (b. 1883) in 1900 and 1904 (2) and Nedo Nadi (Italy) (1894–1952) in 1912 and 1920 (2). Nadi also won three team gold medals in 1920 making an unprecedented total of five gold medals at one Olympic meet.

Edoardo Mangiarotti (Italy) (born April 7, 1919) holds the record of 13 Olympic medals (6 gold, 5 silver, 2 bronze), won in the foil and épée competitions from 1936 to 1960.

The women's record is 7 medals (2 gold, 3 silver, 2 bronze) by Ildiko Sagine Rejto (formerly Ujlaki-Rejto) (Hungary) (b. May 11, 1937) from 1960 to 1976.

Most World Titles. The greatest number of individual world titles won is four by d'Oriola (see table, above), but note that d'Oriola also won 2 individual Olympic titles. Likewise, of the three women foilists with 3 world titles (Helene Meyer, Ellen Müller-Preiss and Ilona Schacherer-Elek) only Elek also won 2 individual Olympic titles.

Ellen Müller-Preiss (Austria) won the women's foil in 1947 and 1949 and shared it in 1950. She also won the Olympic title in 1932.

Italy won the men's foil team 12 times; Hungary the ladies' foil teams 11 times; Italy the épée team 10 times and Hungary the sabre team 13 times.

Field Hockey

Origin. A representation of two hoop players with curved snagging sticks apparently in an orthodox "bully" position was found in Tomb No. 17 at Beni Hasan, Egypt, and has been dated to *c.* 2050 B.C. There is a reference to the game in Lincolnshire, England, in 1277. The first country to form a national association was England (The Hockey Association) in 1886.

Earliest International. The first international match was the Wales *vs.* Ireland match on January 26, 1895. Ireland won 3–0.

Highest International Score. The highest score in international field hockey was when India defeated the U.S. 24–1 at Los Angeles, in the 1932 Olympic Games. The Indians were Olympic Champions from the re-inception of Olympic hockey in 1928 until 1960, when Pakistan beat them 1–0 at Rome. They had their seventh win in 1964. Of the 6 Indians who have won 3 Olympic gold medals, two have also won a silver medal—Leslie Claudius in 1948, 1952, 1956 and 1960 (silver), and Udham Singh in 1952, 1956, 1969 and 1960 (silver).

The greatest scoring feat occurred when M. C. Marckx (Bowdon 2nd XI) scored 19 goals (score 23–0) against Brooklands on December 31, 1910.

The highest score in a women's international match occurred when England defeated France 23–0 at Merton, Surrey, on February 3, 1923.

The World Cup was won by Pakistan at Barcelona in 1971, and by the Netherlands at Amsterdam in 1973.

Fishing

(Sea fish records taken by tackle as ratified by the International Game Fish Association to January 1, 1976. Fresh-water fish are marked *.)

Species	Weight in lbs.	oz.	Name of Angler	Location	Date
Amberjack	149	0	Peter Simons	Bermuda	June 21, 1964
Barracuda	83	0	K. J. W. Hackett	Lagos, Nigeria	Jan. 13, 1952
Bass (Californian Black Sea)	563	8	James D. McAdam	Anacapa Island, California	Aug. 20, 1968
Bass (Giant Sea)	680	0	Lynn Joyner	Fernandina Beach, Florida	May 20, 1961
*Carp†	55	5	Frank J. Ledwein	Clearwater Lake, Minnesota	July 10, 1952
Cod	98	12	Alphonse J. Bielevich	Isle of Shoals, Massachusetts	June 8, 1969
Marlin (Black)	1,560	0	Alfred C. Glassell, Jr.	Cabo Blanco, Peru	Aug. 4, 1953
Marlin (Blue)	1,142	0	Jack Herrington	Nags Head, North Carolina	July 26, 1974
Marlin (Pacific Blue)	1,153	0	Greg D. Perez	Ritidian Point, Guam	Aug. 21, 1969
Marlin (Striped)	415	0	B. C. Bain	Cape Brett, New Zealand	Mar. 31, 1964
Marlin (White)	159	8	W. E. Johnson	Pompano Beach, Florida	Apr. 25, 1953
*Pike (Northern)	46	2	Peter Dubuc	Sacandaga Reservoir, New York	Sept. 15, 1940
Sailfish (Atlantic)	128	1	Harm Steyn	Luanda, Angola	Mar. 27, 1974
Sailfish (Pacific)	221	0	C. W. Stewart	Santa Cruz I., Galapagos Is.	Feb. 12, 1947
*Salmon (Chinook)§	92	0	H. Wichmann	Skeena River, B.C., Canada	July 19, 1959
Sawfish	890	8	Jack Wagner	Fort Amador, Canal Zone	May 26, 1960
Shark (Blue)	410	0	Richard C. Webster	Rockport, Massachusetts	Sept. 1, 1960
Shark (Mako)	1,061	0	James B. Penwarden	Mayor Island, New Zealand	Feb. 17, 1970
**Shark (White or Man-Eating)	2,664	0	Alfred Dean (See photo)	Ceduna, South Australia	Apr. 21, 1959
Shark (Porbeagle)	430	0	Desmond Bougourd	South of Jersey, England	June 29, 1969
Shark (Thresher)‡	739	0	Brian Galvin	Tutukaka, New Zealand	Feb. 17, 1975
Shark (Tiger)	1,780	0	Walter Maxwell	Cherry Grove, South Carolina	June 14, 1964
*Sturgeon (White)	360	0	Willard Cravens	Snake River, Idaho	Apr. 24, 1956
Swordfish	1,182	0	L. E. Marron	Iquique, Chile	May 7, 1953
Tarpon	283	0	M. Salazar	Lago de Maracaibo, Venezuela	Mar. 19, 1956
*Trout (Lake)‖	65	0	Larry Daunis	Great Bear Lake, Northwest Terr., Canada	Aug. 8, 1970
Tuna (Allison or Yellowfin)	308	0	Harold J. Tolson	San Benedicto Island, Mexico	Jan. 18, 1973
Tuna (Atlantic Big-eyed)	335	1	Wilhelm Rapp	Mogan, Canary Islands	July 11, 1975
Tuna (Pacific Big-eyed)	435	0	Dr. Russel V. A. Lee	Cabo Blanco, Peru	Apr. 17, 1957
Tuna (Bluefin)	1,120	0	Lee Coffin	North Lake, Prince Edward Is., Canada	Oct. 19, 1973
Wahoo	149	0	John Pirovano	Cat Cay, Bahamas	June 15, 1962

† A carp weighing 83 lbs. 8 oz. (not by rod) was taken near Pretoria, South Africa. A 60 lb. specimen was taken by bow and arrow by Ben A. Topham in Wythe Co., Virginia, on July 5, 1970. § A salmon weighing 126 lbs. 8 oz. was taken (not by rod) near Petersburg, Alaska. ‖ A 102-lb. trout was taken from Lake Athabasca, northern Saskatchewan, Canada, on August 8, 1961. ** A 1,295-lb. specimen was taken by two anglers off Natal, South Africa, on March 17, 1939, and a 1,500-lb. specimen harpooned inside Durban Harbour, South Africa, in 1933. ‡ W. W. Dowding caught a 922-lb. thresher shark in 1937 on an untested line.

Longest Game. The longest international game on record was one of 145 minutes (into the sixth period of extra time), when Netherlands beat Spain 1–0 in the Olympic tournament at Mexico City on October 25, 1968.

Attendance. The highest attendance at a women's hockey match was 65,000 for the match between England and Wales at the Empire Stadium, Wembley, Greater London, on March 8, 1969.

Fishing

Largest Catches. The largest fish ever caught on a rod is an officially ratified man-eating great white shark (*Carcharodon carcharias*) weighing 2,664 lbs., and measuring 16 feet 10 inches long, caught by Alf Dean at Denial Bay, near Ceduna, South Australia, on April 21, 1959. Capt. Frank Mundus (U.S.) harpooned and landed a 17-foot-long 4,500-lb. white shark, after a 5-hour battle, off Montauk Point, Long Island, New York, in 1964.

THE ULTIMATE IN ANGLING: Alf Dean (Australia) with his record 2,664-lb. white shark.

The largest marine animal ever killed by *hand* harpoon was a blue whale 97 feet in length, killed by Archer Davidson in Twofold Bay, New South Wales, Australia, in 1910. Its tail flukes measured 20 feet across and its jaw bone 23 feet 4 inches. To date this has provided the ultimate in "fishing stories."

Smallest Catch. The smallest full-grown fish ever caught is the *Schindleria praematurus*, weighing 1/14,000th of an ounce found near Samoa, in the central Pacific.

The smallest mature shark is the rare *Squalidus laticaudus,* found off the Philippines, which measures only 6 inches in length.

Spear-fishing. The largest fish ever taken underwater was an 804-lb. giant black grouper by Don Pinder of the Miami Triton Club, Florida, in 1955.

Freshwater Casting. The longest freshwater cast ratified under I.C.F. (International Casting Federation) rules is 574 feet 2 inches by Walter Kummerow (West Germany), for the Bait Distance Double-Handed 30-gram event held at Lenzerheide, Switzerland, in the 1968 Championships.

Surf Casting. The longest surf casting distance ever reported is one of 1,000 feet achieved on a beach in South Africa.

Longest Fight. The longest recorded fight with a fish is 32 hours 5 minutes by Donal Heatley (b. 1938) (New Zealand) with a broadbill (estimated length 20 feet and weight 1,500 lbs.) off Mayor Island off Tauranga, New Zealand, January 21–22, 1968. It towed the 13½-ton launch 50 miles before breaking the line.

Marathon. Roy Wyeth of Kingsland, Southampton, Hampshire, England, fished for 336 hours, May 3–16, 1975.

Football

Origins. The origin of modern football stems from the "Boston Game" as played at Harvard. Harvard declined to participate in the inaugural meeting of the Intercollegiate Football Association in New York City in October, 1873, on the grounds that the proposed rules were based on the non-handling "Association" code of English football. Instead, Harvard accepted a proposal from McGill University of Montreal, Canada, who played the more closely akin English Rugby Football. The first football match under the Harvard Rules was thus played against McGill at Cambridge, Mass., in May, 1874. In November, 1876, a New Intercollegiate Football Association, based on modern football, was inaugurated at Springfield, Mass., with a pioneer membership of five colleges.

Professional football dates from the Latrobe, Pa. *vs.* Jeannette, Pa. match at Latrobe, in August, 1895. The National Football League was founded in Canton, Ohio, in 1920, although it did not adopt its present name until 1922. The year 1969 was the final year in which professional football was divided into separate National and American Leagues, for record purposes.

Longest Service Coach

The longest service head coach was Amos Alonzo Stagg, who served Springfield in 1890–91, Chicago from 1892 to 1932 and College of Pacific from 1933 to 1946, making a total of 57 years.

All-Star Games

The reigning N.F.L. Champions first met an All-Star College selection in the annual August series in Chicago in 1934. The highest scoring match was that of 1940 in which Green Bay beat the All-Stars 45–28. The biggest professional win was in 1949 when Philadelphia won 38–0, and the biggest All-Stars win was in 1943 when Washington was defeated 27–7.

College Series Records

The oldest collegiate series is that between Princeton and Rutgers dating from 1869, or 7 years before the passing of the Springfield rules. The most regularly contested series is between Lafayette and Lehigh, who have met 109 times between 1884 and the end of 1973.

MODERN MAJOR-COLLEGE INDIVIDUAL RECORDS

Points

Most in a Game	43	Jim Brown (Syracuse)	1956
Most in a Season	174	Lydell Mitchell (Penn State)	1971
Most in a Career	354	Glenn Davis (Army)	1943–46

Touchdowns

Most in a Game	7	Arnold Boykin (Mississippi)	1951
Most in a Season	29	Lydell Mitchell (Penn State)	1971

Field Goals

Most in a Game	6	Frank Nester (West Virginia)	1972
	6	Charley Gogolak (Princeton)	1965
Most in a Season	21	Don Bitterlich (Temple)	1975
Most in a Career	51	Dave Lawson (Air Force)	1972–75

SEASON RECORDS

Total Offense	3,343 yds.	Bill Anderson (Tulsa)	1965
Most Rushing and Passing Plays	580	Bill Anderson (Tulsa)	1965
Most Times Carried	358	Steve Owens (Oklahoma)	1969
Yards Gained Rushing	1,881 yds.	Ed Marinaro (Cornell)	1971
Highest Average Gain per Rush	9.35 yds.	Greg Pruitt (Oklahoma)	1971
Most Passes Completed	296	Bill Anderson (Tulsa)	1965
Most Touchdown Passes	39	Dennis Shaw (San Diego St.)	1969
Highest Completion Percentage	69.3%	Chris Kupec (North Carolina)	1974
Most Yards Gained Passing	3,464 yds.	Bill Anderson (Tulsa)	1965
Most Passes Caught	134	Howard Twilley (Tulsa)	1965
Most Yards Gained on Catches	1,779 yds.	Howard Twilley (Tulsa)	1965
Most Touchdown Passes Caught	18	Tom Reynolds (San Diego St.)	1969
Most Passes Intercepted by	14	Al Worley (Washington)	1968

Longest Streaks

The longest winning streak is 47 straight by Oklahoma. The longest unbeaten streak is 63 games (59 won, 4 tied) by Washington from 1907 to 1917.

Highest Score

The most points ever scored in a college football game was 222 by Georgia Tech, Atlanta, Georgia, against Cumberland University of Lebanon, Tennessee, on October 7, 1916. Tech also set records for the most points scored in one quarter (63) most touchdowns (32) and points after touchdown (30) in a game, and the largest victory margin (Cumberland did not score). There were no first downs.

All-America Selections

The earliest All-America selections were made in 1889 by Caspar Whitney of *The Week's Sport* and later of *Harper's Weekly*.

ALL-TIME PROFESSIONAL INDIVIDUAL RECORDS

Service

Most Seasons, Active Player
26 George Blanda, Chi. Bears 1949–58; Balt. 1950; AFL: Hou. 1960–66; Oak. 1967–75

Most Games Played, Lifetime
340 George Blanda, Chi. Bears 1949–58; Balt. 1950; AFL: Hou. 1960–66; Oak. 1967–75

Most Consecutive Games Played, Lifetime
224 George Blanda, Hou. 1960–66; Oak. 1960–75
Jim Otto, Oak. 1960–75

Most Seasons, Head Coach
40 George Halas, Chi. Bears 1920–29, 33–42, 46–55, 58–67

Scoring

Most Seasons Leading League
5 Don Hutson, Green Bay 1940–44
Gino Cappelletti, Bos. 1961, 63–66 (AFL)

Most Points, Lifetime
2,002 George Blanda, Chi. Bears 1949–58; Balt. 1950; AFL: Hou. 1960–66; Oak. 1967–75 (9-td, 943-pat, 335-fg)

Most Points, Season
176 Paul Hornung, Green Bay 1960 (15-td, 41-pat, 15-fg)

Most Points, Rookie, Season
132 Gale Sayers, Chi. 1965 (22-td)

Most Points, Game
40 Ernie Nevers, Chi. Cards vs Chi. Bears, Nov. 28, 1929 (6-td, 4-pat)

Most Points, One Quarter
29 Don Hutson, Green Bay vs Det., Oct. 7, 1945 (4-td, 5-pat) 2nd Quarter

Touchdowns

Most Seasons Leading League
8 Don Hutson, Green Bay, 1935–38, 41–44

Most Touchdowns, Lifetime
126 Jim Brown, Cleve. 1957–65 (106-r, 20-p)

Most Touchdowns, Season
23 O. J. Simpson, Buff. 1975 (16-r, 7-p.)

Most Touchdowns, Rookie Season
22 Gale Sayers, Chi. 1965 (14-r, 6-p, 1-prb, 1-krb)

Most Touchdowns, Game
6 Ernie Nevers, Chi. Cards vs Chi. Bears, Nov. 28, 1929 (6-r)
William (Dub) Jones, Cleve. vs Chi. Bears, Nov. 25, 1951 (4-r, 2-p)
Gale Sayers, Chi. vs S. F., Dec. 12, 1965 (4-r, 1-p, 1-prb)

Most Consecutive Games Scoring Touchdowns
18 Lenny Moore, Balt. 1963–65

ENDURANCE RECORDS as well as scoring and field goal records were set in 1975 by George Blanda (Oakland) who was still starring at the age of 48.

MOST EFFICIENT PASSER:
Sammy Baugh (Wash.) had a 70.3
percentage for the season in 1945.
Baugh also holds punting records.

N.F.L. Records (continued)

Points after Touchdown

Most Seasons Leading League
8 George Blanda, Chi. Bears 1956;
   AFL: Hou. 1961–62; Oak. 1967–
   69, 72, 74

Most Points After Touchdown, Lifetime
943 George Blanda, Chi. Bears 1949–
     58; Balt. 1950; AFL: Hou.
     1960–66; Oak. 1967–75

Most Points After Touchdown, Season
64 George Blanda, Hou. 1961 (AFL)

Most Points After Touchdown, Game
9 Marlin (Pat) Harder, Chi. Cards
   vs N. Y., Oct. 17, 1948
   Bob Waterfield, L. A. vs Balt.,
   Oct. 22, 1950
   Charlie Gogolak, Wash. vs N. Y.,
   Nov. 27, 1966

Most Consecutive Points After Touchdown
234 Tommy Davis, S. F. 1959–65

Most Points After Touchdown (no
misses), Season
56 Danny Villanueva, Dall. 1966

Most Points After Touchdown (no
misses), Game
9 Marlin (Pat) Harder, Chi. Cards
   vs N. Y., Oct. 17, 1948
   Bob Waterfield, L. A. vs Balt.,
   Oct. 22, 1950

Field Goals

Most Seasons Leading League
5 Lou Groza, Cleve., 1950, 52–54,
   57

Most Field Goals, Lifetime
335 George Blanda, Chi. Bears 1949–
     58; Balt. 1950; AFL: Hou.
     1960–66; Oak. 1967–75

Most Field Goals, Season
34 Jim Turner, N.Y. 1968 (AFL)

Most Field Goals, Game
7 Jim Bakken, St. L. vs Pitt., Sept.
   24, 1967

Most Consecutive Games, Field Goals
31 Fred Cox, Minn. 1968–70

Most Consecutive Field Goals
16 Jan Stenerud, K.C. 1969 (AFL)
    Don Cockroft, Clev. 1974–75

Longest Field Goal
63 yds. Tom Dempsey, New Orl. vs Det.
   Nov. 8, 1970

Rushing

Most Seasons Leading League
8 Jim Brown, Cleve. 1957–61, 63–65

Most Yards Gained, Lifetime
12,312 Jim Brown, Cleve., 1957–65

Most Yards Gained, Season
2,003 O. J. Simpson, Buff., 1973

Most Yards Gained, Game
250 O. J. Simpson, Buff. vs N.E.,
     Sept. 16, 1973

Longest Run from Scrimmage
97 yards Andy Uram, Green Bay vs
          Chi. Cards, Oct. 8, 1939 (td)
          Bob Gage, Pitt. vs Chi. Bears,
          Dec. 4, 1949 (td)

Highest Average Gain, Lifetime (700 att.)
5.2 Jim Brown, Cleve. 1957–65
     (2,359–12,312)

Highest Average Gain, Season (100 att.)
9.9 Beattie Feathers, Chi. Bears,
     1934 (101–1004)

Highest Average Gain, Game (10 att.)
17.1 Marion Motley, Cleve. vs Pitt.,
      Oct. 29, 1950 (11–188)

Most Touchdowns Rushing, Lifetime
106 Jim Brown, Cleve., 1957–65

Most Touchdowns Rushing, Season
19 Jim Taylor, Green Bay, 1962

Most Touchdowns Rushing, Game
6 Ernie Nevers, Chi. Cards vs Chi.
   Bears, Nov. 28, 1929

Passing

Most Seasons Leading League
6 Sammy Baugh, Wash., 1937, 40,
   43, 45, 47, 49

Most Passes Attempted, Lifetime
5,225 Fran Tarkenton, Minn. 1961–65,
       72–75; N.Y. Giants 1967–71
       (2,931 completions)

Most Passes Attempted, Season
508 C. A. (Sonny) Jurgensen, Wash.
1967 (288 completions)

Most Passes Attempted, Game
68 George Blanda, Hou. vs Buff.,
Nov. 1, 1964 (AFL) (37 completions)

Most Passes Completed, Lifetime
2,931 Fran Tarkenton, Minn. 1961–66,
72–75; N.Y. Giants 1967–71
(5,225 attempts)

Most Passes Completed, Season
288 C. A. (Sonny) Jurgensen, Wash.,
1967 (508 attempts)

Most Passes Completed, Game
37 George Blanda, Hou. vs Buff.,
Nov. 1, 1964 (AFL) (68
attempts)

Most Consecutive Passes Completed
17 Bert Jones, Balt. vs. N.Y. Jets,
Dec. 15, 1974

Passing Efficiency, Lifetime (1,000 att.)
57.4 Bart Starr, Green Bay, 1956–71
(3,149–1,808)

Passing Efficiency, Season (100 att.)
70.3 Sammy Baugh, Wash., 1945
(182–128)

Passing Efficiency, Game (20 att. or more)
90.9 Ken Anderson, Cin. vs. Pitt.,
Nov. 10, 1974 (20–22)

Longest Pass Completion (all TDs)
99 Frank Filchock (to Farkas),
Wash. vs Pitt., Oct. 15, 1939
George Izo (to Mitchell), Wash.
vs Cleve., Sept. 15, 1963
Karl Sweetan (to Studstill), Det.
vs Balt., Oct. 16, 1966
C. A. Jurgensen (to Allen), Wash.
vs Chi., Sept. 15, 1968

Shortest Pass Completion for Touchdown
2″ Eddie LeBaron (to Bielski), Dall.
vs Wash., Oct. 9, 1960

Most Yards Gained Passing, Lifetime
40,239 John Unitas, Balt. 1956–72;
S.D. 1973

Most Yards Gained Passing, Season
4,007 Joe Namath, N. Y. 1967 (AFL)

Most Yards Gained Passing, Game
554 Norm Van Brocklin, L. A. vs
N. Y. Yanks, Sept. 28, 1951
(41–27)

Most Touchdown Passes, Lifetime
291 Fran Tarkenton, Minn. 1961–66,
72–75; N.Y. Giants 1967–71

Most Touchdown Passes, Season
36 George Blanda, Hou. 1961 (AFL)
Y. A. Tittle, N. Y. 1963

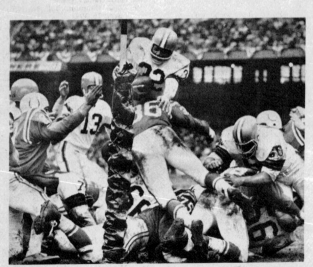

GREATEST ALL-TIME RUSHER: Jim Brown (Cleve.) holds the record for 12,312 yards gained in a lifetime and has the highest lifetime rushing average per carry. Here he is vaulting over a few Baltimore Colts in the 1964 championship game.

Most Touchdown Passes, Game
7   Sid Luckman, Chi. Bears vs N. Y.
    Nov. 14, 1943
    Adrian Burk, Phil. vs Wash.,
    Oct. 17, 1954
    George Blanda, Hou. vs N. Y.,
    Nov. 19, 1961 (AFL)
    Y. A. Tittle, N. Y. vs Wash.,
    Oct. 28, 1962
    Joe Kapp, Minn. vs Balt., Sept.
    28, 1969

Most Consecutive Games, Touchdown
    Passes
47   John Unitas. Balt., 1956–60

    Passes Had Intercepted

Fewest Passes Intercepted, Season (100
    att.)
1   Bill Nelsen, Pitt., 1966 (112
    attempts)

Most Consecutive Passes Attempted,
    None Intercepted
294 Bryan (Bart) Starr, Green Bay,
    1964–65

Most Passes Intercepted, Game
8   Jim Hardy, Chi. Cards vs Phil.,
    Sept. 24, 1950 (39 attempts)

Lowest Percentage Passes Intercepted,
    Lifetime (1,000 att.)
3.34 Roman Gabriel, L. A., 1962–72;
    Phil. 1973–75

Lowest Percentage Passes Intercepted,
    Season (100 att.)
0.89 Bill Nelsen, Pitt., 1966 (1–112)

    Pass Receptions

Most Seasons Leading League
8   Don Hutson, Green Bay, 1936–
    37, 39, 41–45

Most Pass Receptions, Lifetime
635 Charley Taylor, Wash. 1964–75

Most Pass Receptions, Season
101 Charley Hennigan, Hou. 1964
    (AFL)

Most Pass Receptions, Game
18   Tom Fears, L. A. vs Green Bay,
    Dec. 3, 1950 (189 yds.)

Longest Pass Reception (all tds)
99   Andy Farkas (Filchock), Wash.
    vs Pitt., Oct. 15, 1939
    Bobby Mitchell (Izo), Wash. vs
    Cleve., Sept. 15, 1963
    Pat Studstill (Sweetan), Det. vs
    Balt., Oct. 16, 1966
    Gerry Allen (Jurgensen), Wash.
    vs Chi., Sept. 15, 1968

Shortest Pass Reception for Touchdown
2"   Dick Bielski (LeBaron), Dall. vs
    Wash., Oct. 9, 1960

Most Consecutive Games, Pass Re-
    ceptions
105 Dan Abramowicz, N.O. 1967–73;
    S.F. 1973–74

**THREW MOST TOUCHDOWN
PASSES (one game):** Sid Luckman
(Chi.) shares record of 7 with
George Blanda and 3 others.

    Touchdowns Receiving

Most Touchdown Passes, Lifetime
99   Don Hutson, Green Bay, 1935–45

Most Touchdown Passes, Season
17   Don.Hutson, Green Bay, 1942
    Elroy (Crazy Legs) Hirsch, L. A.,
    1951
    Bill Groman, Hou. 1961 (AFL)

Most Touchdown Passes, Game
5   Bob Shaw, Chi. Cards vs Balt.,
    Oct. 2, 1950

Most Consecutive Games, Touchdown
    Passes
11   Elroy (Crazy Legs) Hirsch, L.A.,
    1950–51
    Gilbert (Buddy) Dial, Pitt., 1959–
    60

    Pass Interceptions

Most Interceptions by, Lifetime
79   Emlen Tunnell, N. Y. (74), 1948–
    58; Green Bay (5), 1959–61

Most Interceptions by, Season
14   Richard (Night Train) Lane,
    L. A., 1952

Most Interceptions by, Game
4   By many players

    Interception Yardage

Most Yards Gained, Lifetime
1,282 Emlen Tunnell, N. Y., 1948–58;
    Green Bay, 1959–61

Most Yards Gained, Season
349 Charley McNeil, San Diego 1961
    (AFL)

LONGEST PUNTER: Steve O'Neal (N.Y. Jets) kicked 98 yards in the AFL in 1969.

N.F.L. Records (continued)

Most Yards Gained, Game
177 Charley McNeil, San Diego vs Hou., Sept. 24, 1961 (AFL)

Longest Gain (all TDs)
102 Bob Smith, Det. vs Chi. Bears, Nov. 24, 1949
Erich Barnes, N. Y. vs Dall., Oct. 22, 1961

Touchdowns on Interceptions

Most Touchdowns, Lifetime
9 Ken Houston, Hou. 1967–71

Most Touchdowns, Season
4 Ken Houston, Hou. 1971
Jim Kearney, K.C. 1972

Punting

Most Seasons Leading League
4 Sammy Baugh, Wash., 1940–43
Jerrel Wilson, K.C., 1965, 68, 72–73

Most Punts, Lifetime
970 Bobby Joe Green, Pitt. 1960–61; Chi. 62–73

Most Punts, Season
105 Bob Scarpitto, Den. 1967 (AFL)

Most Punts, Game
14 Dick Nesbitt, Chi. Cards. vs Chi. Bears, Nov. 30, 1933
Keith Molesworth, Chi. Bears vs G.B., Dec. 10, 1933
14 Sammy Baugh, Wash. vs Phil., Nov. 5, 1939
John Kinscherf, N. Y. vs Det., Nov. 7, 1943
George Taliaferro, N. Y. Yanks vs L. A., Sept. 28, 1951

Longest Punt
98 yards Steve O'Neal, N. Y. Jets vs. Den., Sept. 21, 1969 (AFL)

Average Yardage Punting

Highest Punting Average, Lifetime (300 punts)
45.1 yards Sammy Baugh, Wash., 1937–52 (338)

Highest Punting Average, Season (20 punts)
51.4 yards Sammy Baugh, Wash., 1940 (35)

Highest Punting Average, Game (4 punts)
61.8 yards Bob Cifers, Det. vs. Chi. Bears, Nov. 24, 1946

Kickoffs

Yardage Returning Kickoffs

Most Yards Gained, Lifetime
6,922 Ron Smith, Chi. 1965, 70–72; Atl. 1966–67; L.A. 1968–69; S.D. 1973; Oak. 1974

Most Yards Gained, Season
1,317 Bobby Jancik, Hou. 1963 (AFL)

Most Yards Gained, Game
294 Wally Triplett, Det. vs L. A., Oct. 29, 1950 (4)

Longest Kickoff Return for Touchdown
106 Al Carmichael, Green Bay vs. Chi. Bears, Oct. 7, 1956
Noland Smith, K.C. vs Den., Dec. 17, 1967 (AFL)

Average Yardage Returning Kickoffs

Highest Average, Lifetime (75 returns)
30.6 Gale Sayers, Chi. 1965–71

Highest Average, Season (15 returns)
41.1 Travis Williams, Green Bay, 1967 (18)

Highest Average, Game (3 returns)
73.5 Wally Triplett, Det. vs L. A., Oct. 29, 1950 (4-294)

Touchdowns Returning Kickoffs

Most Touchdowns, Lifetime
6 Ollie Matson, Chi. Cards. 1952 (2), 54, 56, 58 (2)
Gale Sayers, Chi., 1965, 66 (2), 67 (3)
Travis Williams, G.B., 1967 (4), 69, 71

Most Touchdowns, Season
4 Travis Williams, Green Bay, 1967
Cecil Turner, Chi. 1970

Most Touchdowns, Game
2 Thomas (Tim) Brown, Phil. vs Dall., Nov. 6, 1966
Travis Williams, Green Bay vs Cleve., Nov. 12, 1967

Fumbles

Most Fumbles, Lifetime
96 Roman Gabriel, L.A. 1962–72; Phil. 1973–75

Most Fumbles, Season
17 Dan Pastorini, Hou., 1973

Most Fumbles, Game
7   Len Dawson, K.C. vs San Diego,
    Nov. 15, 1964 (AFL)

Most Own Fumbles Recovered, Lifetime
38 Jack Kemp, Pitt. 1957; AFL:
    L. A./San Diego 1960–62; Buff.
    1962–67, 69

Most Own Fumbles Recovered, Season
8   Paul Christman, Chi. Cards, 1945;
    Bill Butler, Minn., 1963

Most Own Fumbles Recovered, Game
4   Otto Graham, Cleve. vs N. Y.,
    Oct. 25, 1953
    Sam Etcheverry, St. L. vs N. Y.,
    Sept. 17, 1961
    Roman Gabriel, L. A. vs S. F.,
    Oct. 12, 1969

Most Opponents' Fumbles Recovered,
Lifetime
26 Jim Marshall, Clev. 1960; Minn.
    1961–75

Most Opponents' Fumbles Recovered,
Season
9   Don Hultz, Minn., 1963

Most Opponents' Fumbles Recovered,
Game
3   Corwin Clatt, Chi. Cards vs Det.,
    Nov. 6, 1949
    Vic Sears, Phil. vs Green Bay,
    Nov. 2, 1952
    Ed Beatty, S. F. vs L. A., Oct. 7,
    1956
    Ron Carroll, Hou. vs Cin., Oct.
    27, 1974

Longest Fumble Run
104 Jack Tatum, Oak. vs G.B., Sept.
    24, 1972

**MOST FUMBLES: Roman Gabriel
has fumbled the ball 96 times,
1962-75.**

Miscellaneous

Most Drop Kick Field Goals, Game
4   John (Paddy) Driscoll, Chi. Cards
    vs Columbus, Oct. 11, 1925 (23,
    18, 50, 35 yards)
    Elbert Bloodgood, Kansas City
    vs Duluth, Dec. 12, 1926 (35, 32,
    20, 25 yards)

Longest Drop Kick Field Goal
50 Wilbur (Pete) Henry, Canton vs
    Toledo, Nov. 13, 1922
    John (Paddy) Driscoll, Chi. Cards
    vs Milwaukee, Sept. 28, 1924;
    vs Columbus, Oct. 11, 1925

Most Yards Returned Missed Field
Goal
101 Al Nelson, Phil. vs Dall., Sept. 26,
    1971 (TD)

SEASON RECORDS—OFFENSE

Most Seasons League Champion
11 Green Bay, 1929–31, 36, 39, 44,
    61–62, 65–67

Most   Consecutive   Games   Without
Defeat (Regular Season)
24 Canton, 1922–23 (Won–21, Tied–
    3)
    Chicago Bears, 1941–43 (Won–
    23, Tied–1)

Most Consecutive Victories (All Games)
18 Chicago Bears (1933–34; 1941–
    42)
    Miami (1972–73)

Most Consecutive Victories (Regular
Season)
17 Chicago Bears, 1933–34

Most Consecutive Victories, One Season
(All Games)
17 Miami, 1972

Most Consecutive Shutout Games Won
7   Detroit, 1934

Scoring

Most Seasons Leading League
9   Chicago Bears, 1934–35, 39, 41–
    43, 46–47, 56

Most Points, Season
513 Houston, 1961 (AFL)

Most Points, Game
72 Washington vs N. Y., Nov. 27,
    1966

Most Touchdowns, Season
66 Houston, 1961 (AFL)
Most Touchdowns, Game
10 Philadelphia vs Cin., Nov. 6, 1934
    Los Angeles vs Balt., Oct. 22,
    1950
    Washington vs N. Y., Nov. 27,
    1966
Most Touchdowns, Both Teams, Game
16 Washington (10) vs N. Y. (6),
    Nov. 27, 1966

Most Points After Touchdown, Season
65 Houston, 1961 (AFL)

Most Points After Touchdown, Game
10 Los Angeles vs Balt., Oct. 22, 1950

Most Points After Touchdown, Both Teams, Game
14 Chicago Cards (9) vs N. Y. (5), Oct. 17, 1948
    Houston (7) vs Oakland (7), Dec. 22, 1963 (AFL)
    Washington (9) vs N. Y. (5), Nov. 27, 1966

Most Field Goals Attempted, Season
49 Los Angeles, 1966
    Washington, 1971

Most Field Goals Attempted, Game
9 St. Louis vs Pitt., Sept. 24, 1967

Most Field Goals Attempted, Both Teams, Game
11 St. Louis (6) vs Pitt. (5), Nov. 13, 1966
    Washington (6) vs Chi. (5), Nov. 14, 1971
    Green Bay (6) vs Det. (5), Sept. 29, 1974

Most Field Goals, Season
34 New York, 1968 (AFL)

Most Field Goals, Game
7 St. Louis vs Pitt., Sept. 24, 1967

Most Field Goals, Both Teams, Game
8 Cleveland (4) vs St. L. (4), Sept. 20, 1964
    Chicago (5) vs Phil. (3), Oct. 20, 1968
    Washington (5) vs Chi. (3), Nov. 14, 1971
    Kansas City (5) vs. Buff. (3), Dec. 19, 1971
    Detroit (4) vs G.B. (4), Sept. 29, 1974
    Cleveland (5) vs Den. (3), Oct. 19, 1975
    New England (4) vs S.D. (4), Nov. 9, 1975

Most Consecutive Games Scoring Field Goals
31 Minnesota, 1968–70

First Downs

Most Seasons Leading League
9 Chicago Bears, 1935, 39, 41, 43, 45, 47–49, 55

Most First Downs, Season
318 Buffalo, 1975

Most First Downs, Game
38 Los Angeles vs N. Y., Nov. 13, 1966

Most First Downs, Both Teams, Game
58 Los Angeles (30) vs Chi. Bears (28), Oct. 24, 1954
    Denver (34) vs K.C. (24), Nov. 18, 1974

Most First Downs, Rushing, Season
177 Los Angeles, 1973

Most First Downs, Rushing, Game
25 Philadelphia vs Wash., Dec. 2, 1951

Most First Downs, Passing, Season
186 Houston, 1964 (AFL)
    Oakland, 1964 (AFL)

Most First Downs, Passing, Game
25 Denver vs K.C., Nov. 18, 1974

Net Yards Gained (Rushes and Passes)

Most Seasons Leading League
12 Chicago Bears, 1932, 34–35, 39, 41–44, 47, 49, 55–56

Most Yards Gained, Season
6,288 Houston, 1961 (AFL)

Most Yards Gained, Game
735 Los Angeles vs N. Y. Yanks, Sept. 28, 1951 (181-r, 554-p)

Most Yards Gained, Both Teams, Game
1,133 Los Angeles (636) vs N. Y. Yanks (497), Nov. 19, 1950

Rushing

Most Seasons Leading League
11 Chicago Bears, 1932, 34–35, 39–42, 51, 55–56, 68

Most Rushing Attempts, Season
659 Los Angeles, 1973

Most Rushing Attempts, Game
72 Chicago Bears vs Brk., Oct. 20, 1935

Most Rushing Attempts, Both Teams, Game
108 Chicago Cards (70) vs Green Bay (38), Dec. 5, 1948

Most Yards Gained Rushing, Season
3,088 Buffalo 1973

Most Yards Gained Rushing, Game
426 Detroit vs Pitt., Nov. 4, 1934

Most Yards Gained Rushing, Both Teams, Game
595 L. A. (371) vs N. Y. Yanks (224), Nov. 18, 1951

Highest Average Gain Rushing, Season
5.7 Cleveland, 1963

Most Touchdowns Rushing, Season
36 Green Bay, 1962

Most Touchdowns Rushing, Game
6 By many teams. Last: N. Y. Jets vs Boston, Oct. 27, 1968 (AFL)

Most Touchdowns Rushing, Both Teams, Game
8 Los Angeles (6) vs N. Y. Yanks (2), Nov. 18, 1951
    Cleveland (6) vs L. A. (2), Nov. 24, 1957

Passing

Most Seasons Leading League
10 Washington, 1937, 39–40, 42–45, 47, 67, 74

Most Passes Attempted, Season
592 Houston, 1964 (AFL)

Most Passes Attempted, Game
68 Houston vs Buffalo, Nov. 1, 1964 (AFL) (37 comp.)

Most Passes Attempted, Both Teams, Game
98 Minn. (56) vs Balt. (42), Sept. 28, 1969

Most Passes Completed, Season
301 Washington, 1967 (527-att.)

Most Passes Completed, Game
37 Houston vs Buffalo, Nov. 1, 1964 (AFL) (68 att.)

Most Passes Completed, Both Teams, Game
56 Minn. (36) vs Balt. (20), Sept. 28, 1969

Most Yards Gained Passing, Season
4,392 Houston, 1961 (AFL)

Most Yards Gained Passing, Game
554 Los Angeles vs N. Y. Yanks, Sept. 28, 1951

Most Yards Gained Passing, Both Teams, Game
834 Philadelphia (419) vs St. L. (415), Dec. 16, 1962

Most Seasons Leading League (Completion Pct.)
11 Washington, 1937, 39–40, 42–45, 47–48, 69–70

Most Touchdowns Passing, Season
48 Houston, 1961 (AFL)

Most Touchdowns Passing, Game
7 Chicago Bears vs N. Y., Nov. 14, 1943
Philadelphia vs. Wash., Oct. 17, 1954
Houston vs N. Y., Nov. 19, 1961 and Oct. 14, 1962 (AFL)
New York vs Wash., Oct. 28, 1962
Minnesota vs Balt., Sept. 28, 1969

Most Touchdowns Passing, Both Teams, Game
12 New Orleans (6) vs St. Louis (6), Nov. 2, 1969

Most Passes Had Intercepted, Season
48 Houston, 1962 (AFL)

Fewest Passes Had Intercepted, Season
5 Cleveland, 1960 (264-att.)
Green Bay, 1966 (318-att.)

Most Passes Had Intercepted, Game
9 Detroit vs Green Bay, Oct. 24, 1943
Pittsburgh vs Phil., Dec. 12, 1965

Punting

Most Seasons Leading League (Avg. Distance)
6 Washington, 1940–43, 45, 58

Highest Punting Average, Season
47.6 Detroit, 1961

Punt Returns

Most Seasons Leading League
8 Detroit, 1943–45, 51–52, 62, 66, 69

Most Yards Gained Punt Returns, Season
781 Chicago Bears, 1948

Most Yards Gained Punt Returns, Game
231 Detroit vs S. F., Oct. 6, 1963

Highest Average Punt Returns, Season
20.2 Chicago Bears, 1941

Most Touchdowns Punt Returns, Season
5 Chicago Cards, 1959

Most Touchdowns Punt Returns, Game
2 Detroit vs L. A., Oct. 14; vs Green Bay, Nov. 22, 1951
Chicago Cards vs Pitt., Nov. 1; vs N. Y., Nov. 22, 1959
New York Titans vs Den., Sept. 24, 1961 (AFL)

Kickoff Returns

Most Seasons Leading League
6 Washington, 1942, 47, 62–63, 73–74

Most Yards Gained Kickoff Returns, Season
1,824 Houston, 1963 (AFL)

Most Yards Gained Kickoff Returns, Game
362 Detroit vs L. A., Oct. 29, 1950

Most Yards Gained Kickoff Returns, Both Teams, Game
560 Detroit (362) vs L. A. (198), Oct. 29, 1950

Highest Average Kickoff Returns, Season
29.4 Chicago, 1972

Most Touchdowns Kickoff Returns, Season
4 Green Bay, 1967
Chicago, 1970

Most Touchdowns Kickoff Returns, Game
2 Chicago Bears vs Green Bay, Sept. 22, 1940–Nov. 9, 1952
Philadelphia vs Dall., Nov. 6, 1966
Green Bay vs Cleve., Nov. 12, 1967

Fumbles

Most Fumbles, Season
56 Chicago Bears, 1938

Fewest Fumbles, Season
8 Cleveland, 1959

Most Fumbles, Game
10 Phil/Pitts vs N. Y., Oct. 9, 1943
    Detroit vs Minn., Nov. 12, 1967
    Kansas City vs Hou., Oct. 12,
    1969 (AFL)

Most Fumbles, Both Teams, Game
14 Chicago Bears (7) vs Cleve. (7),
    Nov. 24, 1940
    St. Louis (8) vs N. Y. (6), Sept. 17,
    1961
    Kansas City (10) vs Hou. (4),
    Oct. 12, 1969 (AFL)

Most Opponents' Fumbles Recovered,
Season
31 Minnesota, 1963 (50 fumbles)

Most Opponents' Fumbles Recovered,
Game
7 Buffalo vs Cinci., Nov. 30, 1969
   (AFL)

Most Own Fumbles Recovered, Season
37 Chicago Bears, 1938 (56 fumbles)

Most Fumbles (Opponents' and Own)
Recovered, Season
58 Minnesota, 1963 (95 fumbles)

Most Fumbles (Opponents' and Own),
Recovered, Game
10 Denver vs Buff., Dec. 13, 1964
    (AFL)
    Pittsburgh vs Hou., Dec. 9, 1973

Penalties

Most Seasons Leading League, Fewest
Penalties
9 Pittsburgh, 1946–47, 50–52, 54,
   63, 65, 68

Fewest Penalties, Season
19 Detroit, 1937 (139 yards)

Most Penalties, Game
22 Brooklyn vs Green Bay, Sept. 17,
    1944 (170 yards)
    Chicago Bears vs Phil., Nov. 26,
    1944 (170 yards)

Fewest Penalties, Game
0 By many teams.

Fewest Penalties, Both Teams, Game
0 Brooklyn vs Pitt., Oct. 28, 1934;
   vs Bos., Sept. 28, 1936
   Cleveland Rams vs Chi. Bears,
   Oct. 9, 1938
   Pittsburgh vs Phil., Nov. 10, 1940

Most Yards Penalized, Season
1,274 Oakland, 1969 (AFL)

Fewest Yards Penalized, Season
139 Detroit, 1937 (19 pen.)

Most Yards Penalized, Game
209 Cleveland vs Chi. Bears, Nov. 25,
     1951 (21 pen.)

DEFENSE

Fewest Points Allowed, Season (since
1932)
44 Chicago Bears, 1932

Fewest Touchdowns Allowed, Season
(since 1932)
6 Chicago Bears,1932
   Brooklyn, 1933

Fewest First Downs Allowed, Season
77 Detroit, 1935

Fewest First Downs Allowed, Rushing,
Season
35 Chicago Bears, 1942

Fewest First Downs Allowed, Passing,
Season
33 Chicago Bears, 1943

Fewest Yards Allowed, Season
1,539 Chicago Cards, 1934

Fewest Yards Allowed Rushing, Season
519 Chicago Bears, 1942

Fewest Touchdowns Allowed, Rushing,
Season
2 Detroit, 1934
   Dallas, 1968
   Minnesota, 1971

Fewest Yards Allowed Punt Returns,
Season
22 Green Bay, 1967

Fewest Yards Allowed Kickoff Returns,
Season
225 Brooklyn, 1943

Fewest Yards Allowed Passing, Season
545 Philadelphia, 1934

Most Opponents Tackled Attempting
Passes, Season
67 Oakland, 1967 (AFL)

Fewest Touchdowns Allowed, Passing,
Season
1 Portsmouth, 1932
   Philadelphia, 1934

Most Seasons Leading League, Interceptions Made
9 New York Giants, 1933, 1937–39,
   44, 48, 51, 54, 61

Most Pass Interceptions Made, Season
49 San Diego, 1961 (AFL)

Most Yards Gained, Interceptions,
Season
929 San Diego, 1961 (AFL)

Most Yards Gained, Interceptions, Game
314 Los Angeles vs S. F., Oct. 18, 1964

Most Touchdowns, Interception Returns, Season
9 San Diego, 1961 (AFL)

Most Touchdowns, Interception Returns, Game
3 Baltimore vs Green Bay, Nov. 5, 1950
Cleveland vs Chi., Dec. 11, 1960
Philadelphia vs Pitt., Dec. 12, 1965
Baltimore vs Pitt., Sept. 29, 1968
Buffalo vs N. Y., Sept. 29, 1968 (AFL)
Houston vs S.D., Dec. 19, 1971
Cincinnati vs Hou., Dec. 17, 1972

Gliding

Emanuel Swedenborg (1688–1772) of Sweden made sketches of gliders *c.* 1714.

The earliest man-carrying glider was designed by Sir George Cayley (1773–1857) and carried his coachman (possibly John Appleby) about 500 yards across a valley near Brompton Hall, Yorkshire, England, in the summer of 1853. Gliders now attain speeds of 168 m.p.h. and the Jastrzab acrobatic sailplane is designed to withstand vertical dives at up to 280 m.p.h.

Most World Titles

World individual championships (instituted 1948) have been 5 times won by West Germans. Heinz Huth (W. Germany), was the first pilot to win 2 world individual titles.

Hang-Gliding

In the 11th century, the monk Elmer is reported to have flown from the 60-foot-tall tower of Malmesbury Abbey, Wiltshire, England. Professor Francis Rogallo of the U.S. National Space Agency developed a "wing" in the 1950's from his research into space capsule re-entries.

WORLD TITLE HOLDER: Heinz Huth of West Germany was the first pilot to win 2 world individual titles.

Rudy Kishazy took off from Mont Damavand, Iran, glided 13.6 miles out and 15,324 feet down and landed 41 minutes later.

The longest recorded flight duration for hang-gliding is one of 10 hours 18 minutes by John Hughes and David Lane (U.S.) at Makapun, Oahu, Hawaii, on July 14, 1974.

The greatest altitude from which a hang-glider has descended is 26,155 feet by Wayne Mulgrew, 23, who was released from a balloon over Pope Valley, California, on August 11, 1975, and landed 44 minutes 23 seconds later.

Parasailing

The longest reported flight after being mechanically launched is 15 hours 3 minutes 50 seconds by Bill Flewellyn (New Zealand) over Lake Bonney, South Australia, January 10, 1972.

GLIDING WORLD RECORDS

DISTANCE

Single seaters — 907.7 miles — Hans-Werner Grosse (W. Germany) in an ASW-12 on April 25, 1972.

DECLARED GOAL FLIGHT

765.4 miles — Hans-Werner Grosse (W. Germany) in an ASW-17 on April 16, 1974, from Lubeck, Germany, to Marmande, France.

ABSOLUTE ALTITUDE

46,266 feet — Paul F. Bikle, Jr. (U.S.) in a Schweizer SGS-1-23E over Mojave, Calif. (released at 3,963 feet) on Feb. 25, 1961 (also record altitude gain—42,303 feet).

GOAL AND RETURN

1,298.969 miles — Karl H. Striedieck (U.S.) in an ASW-17 and Leonard Royal McMaster (U.S.) in a Standard Cirrus on March 17, 1976.

SPEED OVER TRIANGULAR COURSE

100 km. — 108.73 m.p.h. — Klaas Goudriaan (S. Africa) in an ASW-17 over South Africa on Nov. 22, 1975.

300 km. — 95.95 m.p.h. — Walter Neubert (W. Germany) in a Kestrel 604 over Kenya on March 3, 1972.

500 km. — 87.19 m.p.h. — Malcolm Jinks (Australia) in a Nimbus 2 over Australia on Jan. 31, 1975.

Golf

Origins. The earliest mention of golf occurs in a prohibiting law passed by the Scottish Parliament in March, 1457, under which "golfe be utterly cryed downe." The Romans had a cognate game called *paganica*, which may have been carried to Britain before 400 A.D. In February, 1962, the Soviet newspaper *Izvestiya* claimed that the game was of 15th-century Danish origin, while the Chinese National Golf Association claims the game is of Chinese origin from the 3rd or 2nd century B.C. Gutta percha balls succeeded feather balls in 1848, and were in turn succeeded in 1902 by rubber-cored balls, invented in 1899 by Haskell (U.S.). Steel shafts were authorized in 1929.

Clubs

Oldest. The oldest club of which there is written evidence is the Gentleman Golfers (now the Honourable Company of Edinburgh

Golfers) formed in March, 1744—10 years prior to the institution of the Royal and Ancient Club of St. Andrews, Fife, Scotland. The oldest existing club in North America is the Royal Montreal Club (1873) and the oldest in the U.S. is St. Andrews, Westchester County, New York (1888). An older claim is by the Foxbury Country Club, Clarion County, Pennsylvania (1887).

Largest. The only club in the world with 15 courses is the Eldorado Golf Club in California. The club with the highest membership in the world is the Wentworth Club, Virginia Water, Surrey, England, with 1,850 members, compared with 1,750 members of the Royal and Ancient Golf Club at St. Andrews (see above).

Courses

Highest. The highest golf course in the world is the Tuctu Golf Club in Morococha, Peru, which is 14,335 feet above sea level at its lowest point. Golf has, however, been played in Tibet at an altitude of over 16,000 feet.

Lowest. The lowest golf course in the world was that of the Sodom and Gomorrah Golfing Society at Kallia, on the northeastern shores of the Dead Sea, 1,250 feet below sea level. The clubhouse was burnt down in 1948 but the game is now played on the nearby Kallia Hotel course.

Longest Hole. The longest hole in the world is the 17th hole (par 6) of 745 yards at the Black Mountain Golf Club, North Carolina. It was opened in 1964. In August, 1927, the 6th hole at Prescott Country Club in Arkansas, measured 838 yards.

Largest Green. Probably the largest green in the world is the 5th green at Runaway Brook G.C., Bolton, Massachusetts, with an area greater than 28,000 square feet.

Biggest Bunker. The world's biggest trap is Hell's Half Acre on the 7th hole of the Pine Valley course, New Jersey, built in 1912 and generally regarded as the world's most trying course.

Longest "Course." Floyd Satterlee Rood used the whole United States as a course when he played from the Pacific surf to the Atlantic surf from September 14, 1963 to October 3, 1964, in 114,737 strokes. He lost 3,511 balls on the 3,397.7-mile trip.

Lowest Scores

9 holes and 18 holes—Men. The lowest recorded score on any 18-hole course with a par of 70 or more is 55 first achieved by A. E. Smith, the English professional, at Woolacombe on January 1, 1936. The course measured 4,248 yards. The detail was 4, 2, 3, 4, 2, 4, 3, 4, 3=29 out, and 2, 3, 3, 3, 3, 2, 5, 4, 1=26 in.

E. F. Staugaard (U.S.) also carded a 55 on the 6,419-yard Monticello Park (California) Golf Club in 1935.

Nine holes in 25 (4, 3, 3, 2, 3, 3, 1, 4, 2) was recorded by A. J. "Bill" Burke in a round of 57 (32+25) on the 6,389-yard par 71 Normandie course in St. Louis on May 20, 1970. This equalled the score of Daniel E. Cavin (3, 3, 3, 3, 3, 3, 2, 3, 2) on the par 36 Bill Brewer Course, Greggton, Texas, on September 27, 1959.

The United States P.G.A. tournament record for 18 holes is 60 by Al Brosch (30+30) in the Texas Open on February 10, 1951; William Nary in the El Paso Open, Texas, on February 9, 1952; Ted Kroll (born August, 1919) in the Texas Open on February 20, 1954; Wally Ulrich in the Virginia Beach Open on June 11, 1954; Tommy Bolt (b. March 31, 1918) in the Insurance City Open on June 25, 1954; Mike Souchak (see below) in the Texas Open on February 17, 1955; and Samuel Jackson Snead (born May 27, 1912) in the Dallas Open, on September 14, 1957.

In non-P.G.A. tournaments, Sam Snead had 59 in the Greenbrier Open (now called the Sam Snead Festival), at White Sulphur Springs, West Virginia, on May 16, 1959, and Gary Player (South Africa) (born November 1, 1936) also carded 59 in the second round of the Brazilian Open in Rio de Janeiro on November 29, 1974.

36 holes. The record for 36 holes is 122 (59 + 63) by Sam Snead in the 1959 Greenbrier Open (now called the Sam Snead Festival) (non-P.G.A.) (see above) May 16–17, 1959. Horton Smith (see below) scored 121 (63+58) on a short course on December 21, 1928.

72 holes. The lowest recorded score on a first-class course is 257 (27 under par) by Mike Souchak (born May 10, 1927) in the Texas Open at San Antonio in February, 1955, made up of 60 (33 out and 27 in), 68, 64, 65 (average 64.25 per round), exhibiting, as one critic said, his "up and down form." The late Horton Smith (1908–63), a U.S. Masters Champion, scored 245 (63, 58, 61 and 63) for 72 holes on the 4,700-yard course (par 64) at Catalina Country Club, California, to win the Catalina Open on December 21–23, 1928.

The lowest 72 holes in a national championship is 262 by Percy Alliss (1897–1975) of Britain, with 67, 66, 66 and 63 in the Italian Open Championship at San Remo in 1932, and by Liang Huan Lu (b. 1936) (Taiwan) in the 1971 French Open at Biarritz.

Women. The lowest recorded score on an 18-hole course (over 6,000 yards) for a woman is 62 (30+32) by Mary (Mickey) Kathryn Wright (born February 14, 1935), of Dallas, on the Hogan Park Course (6,282 yards) at Midland, Texas, in November, 1964.

Wanda Morgan recorded a score of 60 (31+29) on the Westgate-on-Sea and Birchington Golf Club course (England) over 18 holes (5,002 yards) on July 11, 1929.

Highest Round Score. It is recorded that Chevalier von Cittern went round 18 holes at Biarritz, France, in 1888 in 316 strokes—an average of 17.55 shots per hole.

Highest Single-Hole Scores. The highest score for a single hole in a tournament (the British Open) is 21 by a player in the inaugural meeting at Prestwick in 1860. Double figures have been recorded on the card of the winner only once, when Willie Fernie (1851–1924) scored a 10 at Musselburgh, Lothian, Scotland, in 1883. Ray Ainsley of Ojai, California, took 19 strokes for the par-4 16th hole during the second round of the U.S. Open at Cherry Hills Country Club, Denver, Colorado, on June 10, 1938. Most of the strokes were used in trying to extricate the ball from a brook. Hans Merrell of Mogadore, Ohio, took 19 strokes on the par-3 16th (222 yards) during the third round of the Bing Crosby National Tournament at the Cypress Point course, Del Monte, California, on January 17, 1959.

Most Shots—Women. A woman player in the qualifying round of the Shawnee Invitational for Ladies at Shawnee-on-

Delaware, Pennsylvania, in *c.* 1912, took 166 strokes for the 130-yard 16th hole. Her tee shot went into the Binniekill River and the ball floated. She put out in a boat with her exemplary, but statistically minded, husband at the oars. She eventually beached the ball 1½ miles downstream, but was not yet out of the woods. She had to play through a forest on the home stretch.

Most Rounds in a Day

The greatest number of rounds played on foot in 24 hours is 22 rounds plus 5 holes (401 holes) by Ian Colston, 35, at Bendigo G.C., Victoria, Australia (6,061 yards) on November 27–28, 1971. He covered more than 100 miles.

Raymond A. Lasater, 44, played 1,530 holes (85 rounds) in 62 hours 20 minutes on the 6,155-yard par-72 Hunter Point course, Lebanon, Tennessee, June 19–21, 1973. He used a golf cart and luminous balls.

Fastest and Slowest Rounds

With such variations in the lengths of courses, speed records, even for rounds under par, are of little comparative value.

Bob Williams at Eugene, Oregon, completed 18 holes (6,010 yds.) in 27 minutes 48.2 seconds in 1971, but this test permitted him to stroke the ball while it was still moving. The record for a still ball is 31 minutes 22 seconds by Len Richardson, the South African Olympic athlete, at Mowbray, Cape Town, over a 6,248-yard course in November, 1931.

On June 11, 1976, forty-three players representing Borger High School, Huber, Texas, completed the 18-hole 6,109-yard Huber Golf Course in 10 minutes 11.4 seconds.

The slowest stroke-play-tournament round was one of 6 hours 45 minutes when South Africa won their first round of the 1972 World Cup at the Royal Melbourne Golf Club, Australia. This was a 4-ball medal round, everything holed out.

Longest Drive

In long-driving contests 330 yards is rarely surpassed at sea level. The United States P.G.A. record is 341 yards by Jack William Nicklaus (born Columbus, Ohio, January 21, 1940), then weighing 206 lbs., in July, 1963.

The world record is 392 yards by a member of the Irish P.G.A., Tommie Campbell, made at Dun Laoghaire, Co., Dublin, in July, 1964.

Bill Calise, 32, won the McGregor contest at Wayne Country Club, New Jersey, on June 20, 1954, with 365 yards.

The greatest recorded drive is one of 515 yards by Michael Hoke Austin (born February 17, 1910) of Los Angeles, in the U.S. National Seniors Open Championship at Las Vegas, Nevada, on September 25, 1974. Aided by an estimated 35-m.p.h. tailwind, the 6-foot-2-inch 210-lb. golfer drove the ball on the fly to within a yard of the green on the par-4 450-yard 5th hole. The ball rolled 65 yards past the hole.

Perhaps the longest recorded drive on level ground was one of an estimated 430 yards by Craig Ralph Wood (1901–68) (U.S.) on

GOLF CHAMPIONS: Jack Nicklaus (left) has won the Masters Championship 5 times and also claims a record 16 major tournament wins. The late Bobby Jones (right) won the U.S. Open 4 times and the U.S. Amateur title 5 times.

the 530-yard 5th hole at the Old Course, St. Andrews, Fife, Scotland, in the Open Championship in June, 1933. The ground was parched and there was a strong following wind.

Arthur Lynskey claimed a drive of 200 yards out and 2 miles down off Pike's Peak, Colorado, on June 28, 1968.

A drive of 2,640 yards (1½ miles) across ice was achieved by an Australian meteorologist named Nils Lied at Mawson Base, Antarctica, in 1962. On the moon, the energy expended on a mundane 300-yard drive would achieve, craters permitting, a distance of a mile.

Longest Hitter. The golfer regarded as the longest consistent hitter the game has ever known is the 6-foot-5-inch-tall, 230-lb. George Bayer (U.S.), the 1957 Canadian Open Champion. His longest measured drive was one of 420 yards at the fourth in the Las Vegas Invitational in 1953. It was measured as a precaution against litigation since the ball struck a spectator. Bayer also drove a ball pin high on a 426-yard hole in Tucson, Arizona. Radar measurements show that an 87-m.p.h. impact velocity for a golf ball falls to 46 m.p.h. in 3.0 seconds.

Most Tournament Wins

The record for winning tournaments in a single season is 19 (out of 31) by Byron Nelson (born February 4, 1912), of Fort Worth, Texas, in 1945. Of these 11 were consecutive, including the U.S. Open,

P.G.A., Canadian P.G.A. and Canadian Open, from March 16 to August 15. He was a money prize winner in 113 consecutive tournaments.

Kathy Whitworth (U.S.) won 76 professional tournaments up to August, 1976.

Most Titles

U.S. Open	Willie Anderson (1880–1910)	4	1901–03–04–05
	Robert Tyre Jones, Jr. (1902–71)	4	1923–26–29–30
	Ben W. Hogan (b. Aug. 13, 1912)	4	1948–50–51–53
U.S. Amateur	R. T. Jones, Jr.	5	1924–25–27–28–30
British Open	Harry Vardon (1870–1937)	6	1896–98–99, 1903, 1911, 1914
British Amateur	John Ball (1861–1940)	8	1888–90–92–94–99, 1907–10, 1912
P.G.A. Championship (U.S.)	Walter C. Hagen (1892–1969)	5	1921–24–25–26–27
Masters Championship (U.S.)	Jack W. Nicklaus (b. Jan. 21, 1940)	5	1963–65–66–72–75
U.S. Women's Open	Miss Elizabeth (Betsy) Earle-Rawls (b. May, 1928)	4	1951–53–57–60
	Miss "Mickey" Wright (b. Feb. 14, 1935)	4	1958–59–61–64
U.S. Women's Amateur	Mrs. Glenna Vare (née Collett) (b. June 20, 1903)	6	1922–25–28–29–30–35

Jack Nicklaus (U.S.) is the only golfer who has won five major titles, including the U.S. Amateur, twice, and a record total 16 major tournaments (1962–75).

The Open (British)

The Open Championship was inaugurated in 1860 at Prestwick, Strathclyde, Scotland. The lowest score for 9 holes is 29 by Tom Haliburton (Wentworth) and Peter W. Thomson (Australia), in the first round at the Open on the Royal Lytham and St. Anne's course at Lytham St. Anne's, Lancashire, England, on July 10, 1963. Tony Jacklin (Great Britain) also shot a 29 in the first round of the 1970 Open at St. Andrews, Scotland.

The lowest scoring round in the Open itself is 65 by 6 different players: (Thomas) Henry Cotton (G.B.) at Royal St. George's, Kent, England, in the 2nd round on June 27, 1934; Eric Chalmers Brown (G.B.) at Royal Lytham and St. Anne's, Lancashire, England, in the 3rd round on July 3, 1958; Christy O'Connor (Ireland) at Lytham in the 2nd round on July 10, 1969; Neil C. Coles on the Old Course, St. Andrews, Scotland, in the 1st round on July 8, 1970; Jack Nicklaus (U.S.) at Troon, Scotland, in the 4th round on July 14, 1973; and Jack Newton (Australia) at Carnoustie, Tayside, Scotland, in the 3rd round on July 11, 1975. The lowest 72-hole aggregate is 276 (71, 69, 67, 69) by Arnold Daniel Palmer (born September 10, 1929) of Latrobe, Pennsylvania, at Troon, Strathclyde, Scotland, ending on July 13, 1962 and by Tom Weiskopf (b. November 9, 1942) also at Troon on July 11–14, 1973 with 68–67–71–70.

SHARES U.S. OPEN RECORD: When Lee Trevino shot a total of 275 in the 1968 Open, he tied a record set by Jack Nicklaus the year before.

U.S. Open

This championship was inaugurated in 1894. The lowest 72-hole aggregate is 275 (71, 67, 72 and 65) by Jack Nicklaus on the Lower Course (7,015 yards) at Baltusrol Golf Club, Springfield, New Jersey, on June 15–18, 1967, and by Lee Trevino (b. Horizon City, Texas, December 1, 1939) at Oak Hill Country Club, Rochester, New York, on June 13–16, 1968. The lowest score for 18 holes is 63 by John Miller (b. April 29, 1947) of California on the 6,921-yard, par-71 Oakmont (Pennsylvania) course on June 17, 1973.

U.S. Masters

The lowest score in the U.S. Masters (instituted at 6,980-yard Augusta National Golf Course, Georgia, in 1934) was 271 by Jack Nicklaus in 1965 and Raymond Floyd (born 1943) in 1976. The lowest rounds have been 64 by Lloyd Mangrum (1914–74) (1st round, 1940), Jack Nicklaus (3rd round, 1965), and Maurice Bembridge (G.B.) (b. February 21, 1945) (4th round, 1974).

U.S. Amateur

This championship was inaugurated in 1893. The lowest score for 9 holes is 30 by Francis D. Ouimet (1893–1967) in 1932.

British Amateur

The lowest score for nine holes in the British Amateur Championship (inaugurated in 1885) is 29 by Richard Davol Chapman (born March 23, 1911) of the U.S. at Sandwich in 1948. Michael Francis Bonallack (b. 1924) shot a 61 (32+29) on the 6,905-yard par-71 course at Ganton, Yorkshire, on July 27, 1968, on the 1st 18 of the 36 holes in the final round.

Longest Tie

The longest delayed result in any National Open Championship occurred in the 1931 U.S. Open at Toledo, Ohio. George von Elm and Billy Burke tied at 292, then tied the first playoff at 149. Burke won the second playoff by a single stroke after 72 extra holes.

Highest Earnings

The greatest amount ever won in official golf prizes is $2,548,394 by Jack Nicklaus to December 31, 1975.

The record for a year is $353,000 by Johnny Miller in 1974.

The highest career earnings by a woman is $784,766 by Kathy Whitworth (b. September 27, 1938) through August, 1976.

Youngest and Oldest Champions. The youngest winner of the British Open was Tom Morris, Jr. (b. 1850, d. December 25, 1875) at Prestwick, Ayrshire, Scotland, in 1868, aged 18. The youngest winner of the British Amateur title was John Charles Beharrel (born May 2, 1938) at Troon, Strathclyde, Scotland, on June 2, 1956, aged 18 years 1 month. The oldest winner of the British Amateur was the Hon. Michael Scott at Hoylake, Cheshire, England, in 1933, when 54. The oldest British Open Champion was "Old Tom" Morris (b. 1821) who was aged 46 when he won in 1867. In modern times, the 1967 champion Roberto de Vicenzo (b. Buenos Aires, Argentina, April 14, 1923) was aged 44 years 93 days. The oldest U.S. Amateur Champion was Jack Westland (born 1905) at Seattle, Washington, in 1952, aged 47.

Shooting Your Age

The record for scoring one's age in years over an 18-hole round is held by Weller Noble, who between 1955 (scoring 64 when aged 64) and December 31, 1971, has amassed 644 "age scores" on the Claremont Country Club, Oakland, California (par 68) of 5,735 yards. The course is provenly harder than many of 6,000 yards or more on which to produce low scores.

The oldest player to score his age is C. Arthur Thompson (1869–1975) of Victoria, British Columbia, Canada, who scored 103 on the Uplands course of 6,215 yards when aged 103 in 1973. He was still regularly playing until a few weeks before his death.

The youngest player to score his age is Robert Leroy Klingaman (born October 22, 1914) who shot a 58 when aged 58 on the 5,654-yard course at the Caledon Golf Club, Fayetteville, Pennsylvania, on August 31, 1973.

Throwing the Golf Ball

The lowest recorded score for throwing a golf ball around 18 holes (over 6,000 yards) is 82 by Joe Flynn, 21, at the 6,228-yard Port Royal Course, Bermuda, on March 27, 1975.

Longest Putt

The longest recorded holed putt in a major tournament was one of 86 feet on the vast 13th green at the Augusta National, Georgia, by Cary Middlecoff (b. January, 1921) in the 1955 Masters Tournament.

Richest Prize

The greatest first place prize money was $100,000 (total purse $500,000) in the 144-hole "World Open" played at Pinehurst, North Carolina, on November 8–17, 1973, won by Miller Barber, 42, of Texas.

Holes-in-One

In 1975, *Golf Digest* was notified of 26,267 holes-in-one, so averaging over 71 per day.

Longest. The longest straight hole shot in one is the 10th hole (444 yards) at Miracle Hills Golf Club, Omaha, Nebraska. Robert Mitera achieved a hole-in-one there on October 7, 1965. Mitera, aged 21 and 5 feet 6 inches tall, weighed 165 lbs. A two-handicap player, he normally drove 245 yards. A 50-m.p.h. gust carried his shot over a 290-yard drop-off. The group in front testified to the remaining 154 yards.

The longest dogleg achieved in one is the 480-yard 5th hole at Hope Country Club, Arkansas, by L. Bruce on November 15, 1962.

The women's record is 393 yards by Marie Robie of Wollaston, Massachusetts, on the first hole of the Furnace Brook Golf Club, September 4, 1949.

Most. The greatest number of holes-in-one in a career is 40 by Art Wall, Jr. (born November 23, 1923), between 1936 and 1973.

Douglas Porteous, 28, aced 4 holes over 36 consecutive holes—the 3rd and 6th on September 26 and the 5th on September 28 at Ruchill Golf Club, Glasgow, Scotland, and the 6th at the Clydebank and District Golf Club Course on September 30, 1974. Robert Taylor holed the 188-yard 16th hole at Hunstanton, Norfolk, England, on three successive days—May 31, June 1 and 2, 1974. Joe Lucius, 59, aced the 138-yard 15th at the Mohawk Golf Club, Tiffin, Ohio, for the eighth time on November 16, 1974.

Consecutive. There is no recorded instance of a golfer performing three consecutive holes-in-one, but there are at least 15 cases of "aces" being achieved in two consecutive holes of which the greatest was Norman L. Manley's unique "double albatross" on two par-4 holes (330-yard 7th and 290-yard 8th) on the Del Valle Country Club course, Saugus, California, on September 2, 1964.

Youngest and Oldest. The youngest golfer recorded to have shot a hole-in-one was Tommy Moore (6 years 36 days) of Hagerstown, Maryland, on the 145-yard 4th at the Woodbrier Golf Course, Martinsburg, West Virginia, on March 8, 1968. The oldest golfers to have performed the feat are George Miller, 93, at the 11th at Anaheim Golf Club, California, on December 4, 1970, and Charles Youngman, 93, at the Tam O'Shanter Club, Toronto, in 1971.

World Cup (formerly Canada Cup)

The World Cup (instituted 1953) has been won most often by the U.S. with 12 victories in 1955–56, 1960–61–62–63–64–66–67–69–71–73. The only men to have been on six winning teams have been

Arnold Palmer (1960, 62–64, 66–67) and Jack Nicklaus (1963–4, 66–67, 71, 73). The only man to take the individual title three times is Jack Nicklaus (U.S.) in 1963–64–71. The lowest aggregate score for 144 holes is 545 by Australia (Bruce Devlin and David Graham) at San Isidro, Buenos Aires, Argentina, on November 12–15, 1970, and the lowest score by an individual winner was 269 by Roberto de Vicenzo, 47, on the same occasion.

Walker Cup

The U.S. versus Great Britain-Ireland series instituted in 1921 (for the Walker Cup since 1922), now biennial, has been won by the U.S. 23½–2½ to date (July, 1975). Joe Carr (G.B.-I.) played in 10 contests (1947–67).

Ryder Trophy

The biennial Ryder Cup (instituted 1927) professional match between the U.S. and G.B., has been won by the U.S. 17½–3½ to date (July, 1976). Billy Casper has the record of winning most matches, with 20 won (1961–75).

Greyhound Racing

Earliest Meeting. In September, 1876, a greyhound meeting was staged at Hendon, North London, England, with a railed hare operated by a windlass. Modern greyhound racing originated with the perfecting of the mechanical hare by Owen P. Smith at Emeryville, California, in 1919.

Fastest Dog. The highest speed at which any greyhound has been timed is 41.72 m.p.h. (410 yards in 20.1 secs.) by *The Shoe* for a track record at Richmond, New South Wales, Australia, on April 25, 1968. It is estimated that he covered the last 100 yards in 4.5 seconds or at 45.45 m.p.h. The fastest *photo*-timing is 28.17 seconds over 525 yards or 38.12 m.p.h. by *Easy Investment* on June 30, 1973. The fastest photo-timing over 525-yard hurdles is 29.10 seconds (36.90 m.p.h.) by *Sherry's Prince* on May 8, 1971.

Gymnastics

Earliest References. Gymnastics were widely practiced in Greece during the period of the ancient Olympic Games (776 B.C. to 393 A.D.), but they were not revived until *c.* 1780.

World Championships. The greatest number of individual titles won by a man in the World Championships is 10 by Boris Shakhlin (U.S.S.R.) between 1954 and 1964. He was also on three winning teams. The women's record is 10 individual wins and 5 team titles by Larissa Semyonovna Latynina (born December 27, 1934, retired 1966) of the U.S.S.R., between 1956 and 1964.

Olympic Games. Japan has won the most men's titles with 5 victories. The U.S.S.R. has won 7 women's team titles.

PERFECT ROUTINES: Nadia Comaneci (left), a 14-year-old Rumanian, received 7 perfect marks in the 1976 Olympics. **MOST MEDALS:** Boris Shakhlin (right) is the only man ever to win 6 Olympic individual gold medals.

The only man to win six individual gold medals is Boris Shakhlin (U.S.S.R.), with one in 1956, four (two shared) in 1960 and one in 1964.

The most successful woman has been Vera Caslavska-Odlozil (Czechoslovakia), with seven individual gold medals, three in 1964 and four (one shared) in 1968. Larissa Latynina of the U.S.S.R. won six individual and three team gold medals, five silver, and four bronze for an all-time record total of 18 Olympic medals.

Nadia Comaneci (b. 1962, Rumania) became the first gymnast to be awarded a perfect score of 10.00 in the Olympic Games, in the 1976 Montreal Olympics. She ended the competition with a total of seven such marks (four on the uneven parallel bars, three on the balance beam).

World Cup

In the first World Cup Competition in London in 1975, Ludmilla Tourisheva (born October 7, 1952) of the U.S.S.R. won all five available gold medals.

Chinning the Bar. The record for 2-arm chins from a dead hang position is 106 by William D. Reed (University of Pennsylvania) on June 23, 1969. The women's record for one-handed chin-ups is 27 in Hermann's Gym, Philadelphia, in 1918, by Lillian Leitzel (Mrs. Alfredo Codona) (U.S.), who was killed in Copenhagen, Denmark, on March 15, 1931. Her total would be unmatched by any male, but it is doubtful if they were achieved from a "dead hang" position. It is believed that only one person in 100,000 can chin a bar one-handed. Francis Lewis (born 1896) of Beatrice, Nebraska, in May, 1914, achieved 7 consecutive chins using only the middle finger of his left hand. His bodyweight was 158 lbs.

Rope Climbing. The U.S. Amateur Athletic Union records are tantamount to world records: 20 feet (hands alone) 2.8 secs., Don Perry, at Champaign, Illinois, on April 3, 1954; 25 feet (hands alone), 4.7 secs., Garvin S. Smith at Los Angeles, on April 19, 1947.

Push-Ups. The greatest recorded number of consecutive push-ups is 7,026 in 3 hours 56 minutes by Robert Louis Knecht, 13, of Minneapolis, Minnesota, on February 5, 1976. Father Leo Coote did 1,247 push-ups in 29 minutes 10 seconds in Everton Park, Brisbane, Australia, on February 23, 1976. Henry Marshall, 28, of San Antonio, Texas, did 124 one-arm push-ups on his right arm in 65 seconds, and 103 on his left arm in 65 seconds on September 12, 1974. James Ullrich (U.S.) achieved 140 fingertip push-ups in 80 seconds on March 11, 1974.

Sit-ups. The greatest recorded number of consecutive sit-ups on a hard surface without feet pinned or knees bent is 25,222 in 11 hours 14 minutes by Richard John Knecht, aged 8, at the Idaho Falls High School Gymnasium on December 23, 1972. On November 20, 1975, Dr. David G. Jones recorded 123 sit-ups at Bolling A.F.B., Maryland, in 2 minutes.

Jumping Jacks. The greatest number of side-straddle hops is 15,025, performed in 3 hours 32 minutes (better than 1 per sec.) by Steven Welsher of Long Beach, California, on July 27, 1974.

Vertical Jump. The greatest height reached in a vertical jump (the difference between standing and jumping fingertip reach) is 42 inches by David Thompson (6 feet 4 inches) of North Carolina in 1972. Mary E. Peters (G.B.) reportedly jumped 30 inches in California in 1972.

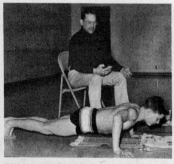

TUMBLING BROTHERS: Robert Louis Knecht (above) and his brother Richard John Knecht (right) of Minneapolis, Minnesota, have set remarkable endurance records for push-ups and sit-ups.

BALANCING STUNT: From 1908 to 1917, Harry Berry and Nelson Soule performed this exciting dive to a hand-to-hand stand.

Greatest Tumbler. The only tumbler to have achieved a running triple back somersault on the ground is V. Bindler (U.S.S.R.), 16, in Kiev in March, 1974.

James Chelich (born Fairview, Alberta, Canada, March 12, 1957) performed 8,450 forward rolls in 8.3 miles on September 21, 1974.

Hand-to-Hand Balancing. The longest horizontal dive achieved in any hand-to-hand balancing act is 22 feet by Harry Berry (top mounter) and the late Nelson Soule (understander) of the Bell-Thazer Brothers from Kentucky, who played at state fairs and in vaudeville from 1908 to 1917. Berry used a 10-foot tower and trampoline for impetus.

Largest Gymnasium. The world's largest gymnasium is Yale University's Payne Whitney Gymnasium at New Haven, Connecticut, completed in 1932 and valued at $18,000,000. The building, known as the "Cathedral of Muscle," has nine stories with wings of five stories each. It is equipped with 4 basketball courts, 3 rowing tanks, 28 squash courts, 12 handball courts, a roof jogging track and a 25-yard by 42-foot swimming pool on the first floor and a 55-yard long pool on the third floor.

Largest Crowd. The largest recorded crowd was some 18,000 people who packed the Forum, Montreal, Canada for the finals of the women's individual apparatus competitions at the XXI Olympic Games on July 22, 1976.

Handball (Court)

Origin. Handball is a game of ancient Celtic origin. In the early 19th century only a front wall was used, but later side and back walls were added. The court is now standardized 60 feet by 30 feet in Ireland and Australia, and 40 feet by 20 feet in Canada, Mexico and the U.S. The game is played with both a hard and soft ball in Ireland, and a soft ball only elsewhere.

The earliest international contest was in New York City in 1887, between the champions of the U.S. and Ireland.

Championship. World championships were inaugurated in New York in October, 1964, with competitors from Australia, Canada, Ireland, Mexico and the U.S. The U.S. beat Canada for the team title.

HANDBALL MASTER: Jim Jacobs of New York City has won a total of 12 U.S. National titles.

In November, 1967, Canada and the U.S. shared the team title and in October, 1970, it was won by Ireland.

Most Titles. The most successful player in the U.S.H.A. National Four-Wall Championships has been James Jacobs (U.S.), who won 6 singles titles (1955–56–57–60–64–65) and shared in 6 doubles titles (1960–62–63–65–67–68).

Handball (Field)

Origins. Field handball was first played *c.* 1895. The earliest international match was when Sweden beat Denmark on March 8, 1935. It was introduced into the Olympic Games at Berlin in 1936 as an 11-a-side outdoor game. The standard size of team for the indoor version has been 7 since 1952. Field handball is played somewhat like soccer but with hands instead of feet.

By 1975 there were 65 countries affiliated with the International Handball Federation, a World Cup competition, and an estimated 10,000,000 participants.

Harness Racing

Origins. The trotting gait (the simultaneous use of the diagonally opposite legs) was first recorded in England in *c.* 1750. The sulky first appeared in harness racing in 1829. Pacers thrust out their fore and hind legs simultaneously on one side.

RECORDS AGAINST TIME

TROTTING

World (mile track)	1:54.8	Nevele Pride (U.S.), Indianapolis	Aug. 31, 1969
Australia	2:01.8	Gramel, Harold Park, Sydney	1964
New Zealand	2:02.4	Control, Addington, Christchurch	1964

PACING

World (mile track)	1:52.0	Steady Star, Lexington, Ky.	Oct. 1, 1971
Australia	1:57.0	Young Quinn, Harold Park, Sydney	1975
New Zealand	1:56.2	Cardigan Bay, Wellington	1963

RECORDS SET IN RACES

Trotting	1:55.6	Noble Victory (U.S.) at Du Quoin, Illinois	Aug. 31, 1966
Pacing	1:54.6	Albatross (U.S.) at Sportsman's Park, Cicero, Illinois	July 1, 1972

Highest Price. The highest price paid for a trotter is $3,000,000 for *Nevele Pride* by the Stoner Creek Stud of Lexington, Kentucky, from Louis Resnick and Nevele Acres in 1969. The highest for a pacer is $3,600,000 for *Nero* in March, 1976.

Greatest Winnings. The greatest amount won by a trotting horse is $1,660,627 by *Une de Mai* to retirement at the end of the 1973 season. The record for a pacing horse is $1,201,470 by *Albatross*, who was retired to stud in December, 1972.

Most Successful Driver

The most successful sulky driver in North America has been Herve Filion (Canada) (b. Quebec, February 1, 1940) who reached a record of 5,396 wins at the end of the 1975 season, after a record 637 victories in the 1974 season.

Hockey

Origins. There is pictorial evidence of hockey being played on ice in the Netherlands in the 17th century. The game probably was first played in 1860 at Kingston, Ontario, Canada, but Montreal and Halifax also lay claim to priority.

Olympic Games. Canada has won the Olympic title six times (1920–24–28–32–48–52) and the world title 19 times, the last being at Geneva in 1961. The longest Olympic career is that of Richard Torriani (Switzerland) from 1928 to 1948. The most gold medals

HOCKEY originated in Holland in the 17th century, as this picture proves.

won by any player is three; this was achieved by four U.S.S.R. players in the 1964–68–72 Games—Vitaliy Davidov, Aleksandr Ragulin, Anatoliy Firssov and Viktor Kuzkin. Davidov and Ragulin had played on nine World Championship teams prior to the 1972 Games.

Stanley Cup. This cup, presented by the Governor-General Lord Stanley (original cost $48.67), became emblematic of world professional team supremacy several years after the first contest at Montreal in 1893. It has been won most often by the Montreal Canadiens, with 19 wins in 1916, 1924, 1930, 1931, 1944, 1946, 1953, 1956, 1957, 1958, 1959, 1960, 1965, 1966, 1968, 1969, 1971, 1973, and 1976. Henri Richard played in his eleventh finals in 1973.

Longest Match. The longest match was 2 hours 56 minutes 30 seconds when the Detroit Red Wings eventually beat the Montreal Maroons 1–0 in the sixth period of overtime at the Forum, Montreal, at 2:25 a.m. on March 25, 1936.

Longest Career. Gordie Howe skated a record 25 years for the Detroit Red Wings from 1946–47 through the 1970–71 season, playing in a record total of 1,687 N.H.L. games. During that time he also set records for most career goals, assists, and scoring points, and collected 500 stitches in his face.

Most Consecutive Games. Garry Unger, playing for both the Detroit Red Wings and the St. Louis Blues, skated in 643 consecutive games without a miss—8 complete seasons from 1968–69 through 1975–76. The most consecutive complete games by a goaltender is 502, set by Glenn Hall (Detroit, Chicago), beginning in 1955 and ending when he suffered a back injury in a game against Boston on November 7, 1962.

Longest Season. The only man ever to play 82 games in a 78-game season is Ross Lonsberry. He began the 1971–72 season with the Los Angeles Kings where he played 50 games. Then, in January, he was traded to the Philadelphia Flyers (who had played only 46 games at the time) where he finished out the season (32 more games).

Most Wins and Losses

The Boston Bruins had the winningest season in N.H.L. history in 1970–71. They ended the regular 78-game season with a record 121 points earned, with an all-time record of 57 victories and 7 ties against only 14 losses. They also scored a record 399 goals and 697 assists in that season.

The Washington Capitols set the record for seasonal losses with 67 in their maiden season in the league (1974–75). They won only 8 games.

Longest Winning Streak. In the 1929–30 season, the Boston Bruins won 14 straight games. The longest a team has ever gone without a defeat is 23 games, again set by Boston. From December 22, 1940, to February 25, 1941, they won 15 games and tied 8.

Longest Losing Streak. The Washington Capitols went from February 18 to March 26, 1975, without gaining a point—a total

HIGH SCORING CENTER: Phil Esposito (left) (Boston Bruins) put in a record 76 goals in the 1970-71 season. Added to his 76 assists, he totaled 152 points, also a N.H.L. record.

of 17 straight defeats. The longest time a team has gone without a win was when the New York Rangers played 25 games, over two seasons, before scoring a victory—starting January 23, 1944, they lost 21 games and tied 4 games before ending the drought on November 11, 1944.

Team Scoring

Most Goals. The greatest number of goals recorded in a World Championship match has been 47–0 when Canada beat Denmark on February 12, 1949.

The N.H.L. record for both teams is 21 goals, scored when the Montreal Canadiens beat Toronto St. Patricks at Montreal 14–7 on January 10, 1920. The most goals ever scored by one team in a single game was set by the Canadiens, when they defeated the Quebec Bulldogs on March 3, 1920 by a score of 16–3.

Fastest Scoring. Toronto scored 8 goals against the New York Americans in 4 minutes 52 seconds on March 19, 1938.

The fastest goal that has ever been scored from the opening whistle came at 6 seconds of the first period by Henry Boucha of the Detroit Red Wings on January 28, 1973, against Montreal. Claude Provost of the Canadiens scored a goal against Boston after 4 seconds of the opening of the second period on November 9, 1957.

The fastest scoring record is held by Bill Mosienko (Chicago) who scored 3 goals in 21 seconds against the New York Rangers on March 23, 1952.

Individual Scoring

Most Goals and Points. The career record in the N.H.L. for goals is 786 by Gordie Howe of the Detroit Red Wings. Howe has scored 1,809 points in his career, with 1,023 assists.

Reggie Leach (Philadelphia Flyers) scored a total of 80 goals in the 1975–76 season including the playoffs.

Phil Esposito (Boston Bruins) scored 76 goals in the 1970–71 regular season. Esposito also holds the record for most points in a season at 152 (76 goals, 76 assists) in the same season.

Phil Esposito has also scored 100 or more points in 7 different seasons, and 50 or more goals in 5 consecutive years. Bobby Orr has 6 consecutive 100-or-more-point seasons since 1969–70. Bobby Hull (Chicago) had five 50-or-more-goal years when he left the N.H.L.

The most goals ever scored in one game is 7 by Joe Malone of the Quebec Bulldogs against the Toronto St. Patricks on January 31, 1920. Four different men have scored 4 goals in one period—Harvey Jackson (Toronto), Max Bentley (Chicago), Clint Smith (Chicago), and Red Berenson (St. Louis).

The most points scored in one N.H.L. game is 10, a record set by Darryl Sittler of the Toronto Maple Leafs, on February 7, 1976, against the Boston Bruins. He had 6 goals and 4 assists.

In 1921–22, Harry (Punch) Broadbent of the Ottawa Senators scored 25 goals in 16 consecutive games to set an all-time "consecutive game goal-scoring streak" record.

Most Assists. Bobby Orr of Boston assisted on 102 goals in the 1970–71 season for a record. His average of 1.31 assists per game is a league record.

The most assists recorded in one game is 7 by Billy Taylor of Detroit on March 16, 1947 against Chicago. Detroit won 10–6.

Most 3-Goal Games. In his 15-year N.H.L. career, Bobby Hull of Chicago scored 3 or more goals in 28 games. Four of these were 4-goal efforts. The term "hat-trick" properly applies when 3 goals are scored consecutively by one player in a game without interruption by either an answering score by the other team or a goal by any other player on his own team. In general usage, a "hat-trick" is any 3-goal effort by a player in one game.

Goaltending

The longest any goalie has gone without a defeat is 33 games, a record set by Gerry Cheevers of Boston in 1971–72. The longest a goalie has ever kept successive opponents scoreless is 460 minutes 49 seconds by Alex Connell of the Ottawa Senators in 1927–28. He registered 6 consecutive shutouts in this time.

The most shutouts ever recorded in one season is 22 by George Hainsworth of Montreal in 1928–29 (this is also a team record). This feat is even more remarkable considering that the season was only 44 games long at that time, compared to the 78-game season currently used.

Terry Sawchuk registered a record 103 career shutouts in his 20 seasons in the N.H.L. He played for Detroit, Boston, Toronto, Los Angeles, and the New York Rangers during that time.

Most Penalties

The most any team has been penalized in one season is the 1,980 minutes assessed against the Philadelphia Flyers in 1975–76.

Ted Lindsay, playing for Detroit and Chicago, set an individual career record for penalties with 1,808 minutes over a period of 17 seasons. Dave Schultz of Philadelphia was called for a record 472 minutes in the 1974–75 season.

Jim Dorey of the Toronto Maple Leafs set an all-time record in Toronto on October 16, 1968, in a game against the Pittsburgh Penguins. He was whistled down for a total of 9 penalties in the game, 7 of which came in the second period (also a record). The 4 minor penalties, 2 major penalties, 2 10-minute misconducts, and 1 game misconduct added up to a record total of 48 minutes for one game.

Penalty Shots. "Scotty" Bowman of the old St. Louis Eagles was the first player in the N.H.L. to attempt a penalty shot on November 13, 1934. He scored. Since 1963, when records on penalty shots were first kept, 35.7 per cent of those awarded have resulted in goals. The most penalty shots called in a single season was 9 in both 1963–64 and 1971–72.

MOST PENALIZED:
During his 17 seasons
with Chicago and
Detroit, Ted Lindsay
(No. 15) was slapped with
1,808 minutes in penalties.

Fastest Player. The highest speed measured for any player is 29.7 m.p.h. for Bobby Hull (Chicago Black Hawks) (b. January 3, 1939). The highest puck speed is also attributed to Hull, whose left-handed slap shot has been measured at 118.3 m.p.h.

Horse Racing

Origins. Horsemanship was an important part of the Hittite culture of Anatolia, Turkey, dating from about 1400 B.C. The 23rd ancient Olympic Games of 624 B.C. featured horse racing. The earliest horse race recorded in England was one held in *c.* 210 A.D. at Netherby, Yorkshire, among Arabians brought to Britain by Lucius Septimius Severus (146–211 A.D.), Emperor of Rome. The oldest race still being run annually is the Lanark Silver Bell, instituted in Scotland by William Lion (1165–1214). Organized horse racing began in New York State at least as early as March, 1668.

The original Charleston Jockey Club, Virginia, was the first in the world, organized in 1734. Racing colors (silks) became compulsory in 1889.

Racecourses. The world's largest racecourse is the Newmarket course in England (founded 1636), on which the Beacon Course, the longest of the 19 courses, is 4 miles 397 yards long and the Rowley Mile is 167 feet wide. The border between Suffolk and Cambridgeshire runs through the Newmarket course. The world's largest racecourse grandstand was opened in 1968 at Belmont Park, Long Island, N.Y., at a cost of $30,700,000. It is 110 feet tall, 440 yards long and contains 908 mutuel windows. The greatest seating capacity at any racetrack is 40,000 at the Atlantic City Audit, New Jersey. The world's smallest is the Lebong racecourse, Darjeeling,

West Bengal, India (altitude 7,000 feet), where the complete lap is 481 yards. It was laid out *c.* 1885 and used as a parade ground.

Most Entrants. The most horses entered in a single race was 66, in the Irish Grand National Sweepstakes of March 22, 1929.

Longest Race

The longest recorded horse race was one of 1,200 miles in Portugal, won by a horse *Emir*, bred from Egyptian-bred Blunt Arab stock. The holder of the world's record for long distance racing and speed is *Champion Crabbet*, who covered 300 miles in 52 hours 33 minutes, carrying 245 lbs., in 1920.

In 1831, Squire George Osbaldeston (1787–1866), M.P. of East Retford, England, covered 200 miles in 8 hours 42 minutes at Newmarket, using 50 mounts, so averaging 22.99 m.p.h.

Victories. The horse with the best recorded win-loss record was *Kincsem*, a Hungarian mare foaled in 1874, who was unbeaten in 54 races (1876–79), including the English Goodwood Cup of 1878.

Camarero, owned by Don José Coll Vidal of Puerto Rico, foaled in 1951, had a winning streak of 56 races, 1953–55, and 73 wins in 77 starts altogether.

Greatest Winnings. The greatest amount ever won by a horse is $1,977,896 by *Kelso* (foaled in 1957) in the U.S., between 1959 and his retirement on March 10, 1966. In 63 races he won 39, came in second in 12 and third in 2.

UNBEATEN HORSE: The Hungarian mare foaled in 1874, "Kincsem," was the only horse to remain unbeaten in all her 54 races.

GREATEST MONEY-WINNING HORSE: Kelso, who retired in 1966, won almost $2,000,000 in prizes. In 63 races, he won 39 and placed second in 12 of them.

The most won by a filly is $1,512,943 by *Dahlia*, up to June, 1976.

The most won in a year is $860,404 by *Secretariat* in 1973. His total winnings were $1,316,808.

Tallest. The tallest horse ever to race is *Fort d'Or*, owned by Lady Elizabeth (Eliza) Nugent (*née* Guinness) of Berkshire, England, which stands 18.2 hands. He was foaled in April, 1963.

Most Valuable Horse

The highest price ever paid for a horse is $8,000,000 for the 11-year-old American stallion *What a Pleasure* in early 1976. He was syndicated in 32 shares, valued at $250,000 each.

Horses   Speed Records

Distance	Time	m.p.h.	Name	Course	Date
¼ mile	20.8s.	43.26	*Big Racket* (U.S.)	Mexico City, Mex.	Feb. 5, 1945
½ mile (stra.)	45.0s.	40.00	*Gloaming* (N.Z.)	Wellington, N.Z.	Jan. 12, 1921
½ mile	44.8s.	40.17	*Tamran's Jet* (U.S.)	Sunland, N.M.	Mar. 22, 1968
	44.8s.	40.17	*Crimson Saint* (U.S.)	Hot Springs, Ark.	Apr. 1, 1971
	44.8s.	40.17	*Mighty Mr. A* (U.S.)	Cicero, Ill.	Nov. 1, 1971
	44.8s.	40.17	*Thief of Baghdad* (U.S.)	Cicero, Ill.	Nov. 5, 1971
⅝ mile	53.6s.	41.98	*Indigenous* (G.B.)	Epsom, England	June 2, 1960
¾ mile	1m. 07.2s.	40.18	*Grey Papa* (U.S.)	Longacres, Wash.	Sept. 4, 1972
	1m. 06.2s.	40.78	*Broken Tindril* (G.B.)	*Brighton, England	Aug. 6, 1929
Mile	1m. 31.8s.	39.21	*Soueida* (G.B.)	*Brighton, England	Sept. 19, 1963
	1m. 31.8s.	39.21	*Loose Cover* (G.B.)	*Brighton, England	June 9, 1966
	1m. 32.2s.	39.04	*Dr. Fager* (U.S.)	Arlington, Ill.	Aug. 24, 1968
1½ miles	2m. 23.0s.	37.76	*Fiddle Isle* (U.S.)	Arcadia, Calif.	Mar. 21, 1970
2 miles**	3m. 15.0s.	36.93	*Polazel* (G.B.)	Salisbury, England	July 8, 1924
3 miles	5m. 15.0s.	34.29	*Farragut* (Mex.)	Agua Caliente, Mex.	Mar. 9, 1941

* Course downhill for 2/3rd of a mile.

** A more reliable modern record is 3m. 16.75 secs. by *Il Tempo* (N.Z.) at Trentham, Wellington, New Zealand, on January 17, 1970.

Funeral Wreath. The largest floral piece honoring a horse was the tribute to the racehorse *Ruffian*, an 8½-foot-high, 8-foot-wide horseshoe made of 1,362 white carnations. It was made by Jay W. Becker Florist Inc. of Floral Park, New York, and decorated the grave of the horse in the infield at Belmont Race Track where she was buried in July, 1975.

Dead Heats

There is no recorded case in turf history of a quintuple dead heat. The nearest approach was in the Astley Stakes, at Lewes, England, on August 6, 1880, when *Mazurka, Wandering Nun* and *Scobell* triple dead-heated for first place, just ahead of *Cumberland* and *Thora*, who dead-heated for fourth place. Each of the five jockeys thought he had won. The only three known examples of a quadruple dead heat were between *Honest Harry, Miss Decoy, Beningbrough* and *Peteria* at Bogside, England, on June 7, 1808; between *The Defaulter, Squire of Malton, Reindeer* and *Pulcherrima* in the Omnibus Stakes at The Hoo, England, on April 26, 1851; and between *Overreach, Lady Go-Lightly, Gamester* and *The Unexpected* at the Houghton Meeting at Newmarket, England, on October 22, 1855.

Since the introduction of the photo-finish, the highest number of horses in a dead heat has been three, on several occasions.

Jockeys

The most successful jockey of all time is Willie Shoemaker (b. weighing 2½ lbs. on August 19, 1931) now weighing 98 lbs. and standing 4 feet 11½ inches, who beat Johnny Longden's lifetime record of 6,032 winners on September 7, 1970. From March 19, 1949, to March 14, 1976, he rode 7,000 winners. His winnings have aggregated some $54,000,000.

Chris McCarron (U.S.), 19, won a total of 546 races in 1974.

The greatest amount ever won by any jockey in a year is $4,251,060 by Laffit Pincay, Jr. in the U.S. in 1974.

The oldest jockey was Levi Barlingame (U.S.), who rode his last race at Stafford, Kansas, in 1932, aged 80. The youngest jockey was Frank Wootton (English Champion jockey 1909–12), who rode his first winner in South Africa aged 9 years 10 months. The lightest recorded jockey was Kitchener (died 1872), who won the Chester Cup in England on *Red Deer* in 1844 at 49 lbs. He was said to have weighed only 40 lbs. in 1840.

Victor Morley Lawson won his first race at Warwick, England, on *Ocean King*, October 16, 1973, aged 67.

The greatest number of winners ridden on one card is 8 by Hubert S. Jones at Caliente, California, on June 11, 1944, of which 5 were photo-finishes.

Trainers. The greatest number of wins by a trainer in one year is 352 by Dick Dutrow (U.S.) in 1975. The greatest amount by a trainer in one year is $2,456,250 by Eddie Neloy (U.S.) in 1966.

Shortest Odds

The shortest odds ever quoted for any racehorse are 10,000 to 1 on for *Dragon Blood*, ridden by Lester Piggott (G.B.) in the Premio

Naviglio in Milan, Italy, on June 1, 1967. He won. Odds of 100 to 1 on were quoted for the American horse *Man o' War* (foaled March 29, 1917, died November 1, 1947) on three separate occasions in 1920. In 21 starts in 1919–20 he had 20 wins and one second (on August 13, 1919, in the Sanford Memorial Stakes).

Pari-Mutuel Record

The U.S. pari-mutuel record pay-off is $941.75 to $1 on *Wishing Ring* at Latonia track, Kentucky, in 1912.

Largest Prizes. The richest race ever held was the 1972 All-American Futurity, a race for quarter-horses over 440 yards at Ruidoso Downs, New Mexico. The prizes in that year totaled $1,035,900.

The richest first prize was 1,497,400 francs ($382,651) won by *Rheingold* in the 1973 *L'Arc de Triomphe* race at Longchamps, Paris, France.

Horseshoe Pitching

Origin. This sport was derived by military farriers and is of great antiquity. The first formal World Championships were staged at Bronson, Kansas, in 1909.

Most Titles. The record for men's titles is 10 by Ted Allen (Boulder, Colorado) in 1933–34–35–40–46–53–55–56–57–59. The women's record is 9 titles by Vicki Chapelle Winston (LaMonte, Missouri) in 1956–58–59–61–63–66–67–69–75.

Highest Percentage. The record for percentage of ringers in one game is 95 by Ruth Hangen (Getzville, N.Y.) in 1973. The record for consecutive ringers is 72 by Ted Allen in 1951 for men, and 42 by Ruth Hangen in 1974 for women.

Most Ringers. The most ringers in a single game is 175 by Glen Henton of Maquoketa, Iowa, in 1965.

Marathon. The longest continuous session is 100 hours by a team of 6 playing in shifts in Allentown, Pennsylvania, August 6–10, 1973.

Ice Skating

Origins. The earliest reference to ice skating is in Scandinavian literature of the 2nd century, although its origins are believed, on archeological evidence, to be 10 centuries earlier still. The earliest English account of 1180 refers to skates made of bone. The earliest known illustration is a Dutch woodcut of 1498. The earliest skating club was the Edinburgh Skating Club, Scotland, formed in 1742. The earliest artificial ice rink in the world was the "Glaciarium," built in Chelsea, London, in 1876. The International Skating Union was founded in 1892.

Longest Race. The longest race regularly held is the "Elfstedentocht" ("Tour of the Eleven Towns") in the Netherlands. It covers

WORLD RECORD HOLDER AT 3,000 METERS: Ard Schenk of the Netherlands, winning here, completed this distance in 4 minutes 8.3 seconds.

200 kilometers (124 miles 483 yards) and the fastest time is 7 hours 35 minutes by Jeen van den Berg (born January 8, 1928) on February 3, 1954.

Largest Rink. The world's largest artificial ice rink is the quadruple rink at Burnaby, British Columbia, Canada, completed in December, 1972, which has an ice area of 68,000 sq. ft. The largest artificial outdoor rink is the Fujikyu Highland Promenade Rink, Japan, opened at a cost of $938,000 in 1967 with an area of 165,750 square feet (3.8 acres).

Figure Skating

World. The greatest number of men's figure skating titles (instituted 1896) is ten by Ulrich Salchow (born August 7, 1877), of Sweden, in 1901–05 and 1907–11. The women's record (instituted 1906) is ten titles by Sonja Henie (April 8, 1912–October 12, 1969), of Norway, between 1927 and 1936. Irena Rodnina (born September 12, 1949), of the U.S.S.R., has won eight pairs titles (instituted 1908)—four with Aleksiy Ulanov (1969–72) and four with Aleksandr Zaitsev (1973–76). The most ice dance titles (instituted 1950) won is six by Aleksandr Gorshkov (born December 8, 1946) and Ludmilla Pakhomova (born December 31, 1946), both of the U.S.S.R.

Olympic. The most Olympic gold medals won by a figure skater is three by Gillis Grafström (born June 7, 1893), of Sweden, in 1920, 1924, and 1928 (also silver medal in 1932); and by Sonja Henie (see above) in 1928, 1932 and 1936.

Most Difficult Jump. The triple Axel has been performed by only one man, Gordon McKellen (b. September 26, 1953), the 1973 and 1974 U.S. champion.

Highest Marks. The highest number of maximum six marks awarded for one performance in an international championship was

11 to Aleksandr Zaitsev and Irena Rodnina (U.S.S.R.) in the European pairs competition in Zagreb, Yugoslavia, in 1974.

Donald Jackson (Canada) was awarded 7 "sixes" in the world men's championship at Prague, Czechoslovakia, in 1962.

Most Titles Speed Skating

World. The greatest number of world speed skating titles (instituted 1893) won by any skater is five by Oscar Mathisen (Norway) in 1908–09 and 1912–14, and Clas Thunberg (born April 5, 1893) of Finland, in 1923, 1925, 1928–29 and 1931. The most titles won by a woman is four by Mrs. Inga Voronina, *née* Artomonova (1936–66) of Moscow, U.S.S.R., in 1957, 1958, 1962 and 1965, and Mrs. Atje Keulen-Deelstra of the Netherlands (b. 1938) in 1970 and 1972–73–74.

Olympic. The most Olympic gold medals won in speed skating is six by Lidia Skoblikova (born March 8, 1939), of Chelyaminsk, U.S.S.R., in 1960 (2) and 1964 (4). The male records are by Ivar Ballangrud of Norway (b. March 7, 1904) who won 4 gold, 2 silver and 1 bronze medal in 1928–32–36, and by Clas Thunberg (see above) with 4 gold, 1 tied gold, 1 silver and 1 tied bronze in 1924–28.

WORLD SPEED SKATING RECORDS

Distance	mins. secs.	Name and Nationality	Place	Date
Men				
500 meters	37.00	Evgeni Kulikov (U.S.S.R.)	Medeo, U.S.S.R.	Mar. 29, 1975
1,000 meters	1:15.70	Evgeni Kulikov (U.S.S.R.)	Medeo, U.S.S.R.	Mar. 20, 1976
1,500 meters	1:55.61	Hans van Helden (Neth.)	Inzell, W. Ger.	Mar. 13, 1976
3,000 meters	4:08.30	Ard Schenk (Neth.)	Inzell, W. Ger.	Mar. 2, 1972
5,000 meters	7:02.38	Piet Kleine (Neth.)	Inzell, W. Ger.	Mar. 12, 1976
10,000 meters	14:38.08	Stan Stensen (Norway)	Medeo, U.S.S.R.	Mar. 21, 1976
Women				
500 meters	40.68	Sheila Young (U.S.)	Inzell, W. Ger.	Mar. 13, 1976
1,000 meters	1:23.46	Tatiana Averina (U.S.S.R.)	Medeo, U.S.S.R.	Mar. 29, 1975
1,500 meters	2:09.90	Tatiana Averina (U.S.S.R.)	Medeo, U.S.S.R.	Mar. 11, 1975
3,000 meters	4:31.00	Galina Stepanskaya (U.S.S.R.)	Medeo, U.S.S.R.	Mar. 23, 1976

Longest Marathon. The longest recorded skating marathon is one of 101 hours by Eben Gouws of Port Elizabeth, South Africa, February 13–17, 1976. The fastest time to complete 100 miles is 5 hours 34 minutes 1.45 seconds by Kirt Barnes, 22, on February 26, 1971, at Fuller Recreation Facility Ice Rink, Ann Arbor, Michigan.

Ice and Sand Yachting

Origin. The sport originated in the Low Countries (earliest patent is dated 1600) and along the Baltic coast. The earliest authentic record is Dutch, dating from 1768. The largest ice yacht built was *Icicle*, built for Commodore John E. Roosevelt for racing on the Hudson River, New York, *c.* 1870. It was 68 feet 11 inches long and carried 1,070 square feet of canvas.

Highest Speed. The highest speed officially recorded is 143 m.p.h. by John D. Buckstaff in a Class A stern-steerer on Lake Winnebago, Wisconsin, in 1938. Such a speed is possible in a wind of 72 m.p.h.

Sand Yachting. Land or sand yachts of Dutch construction were first reported on beaches (now in Belgium) in 1595. The earliest international championship was staged in 1914.

The fastest recorded speed for a sand yacht is 57.69 m.p.h. (measured mile in 62.4 secs.) by *Coronation Year Mk. II*, owned by R. Millett Denning and crewed by J. Halliday, Bob Harding, J. Glassbrook and Cliff Martindale at Lytham St. Anne's, England, in 1956.

A speed of 77.47 m.p.h. was attained by Jan Paul Lowe (born April 15, 1936) (U.S.) in *Sunkist*, at Ivanpaugh Dry Lake, California, on March 25, 1975.

Jai-Alai *(Pelota)*

The game, which originated in Italy as *longue paume* and was introduced into the Basque country between Spain and France in the 13th century, is said to be the fastest of all ball games with speeds of up to 160 m.p.h. Gloves were introduced *c.* 1840 and the *chisterak* (basket-like glove) was invented *c.* 1860 by Gantchiki Dithurbide of Sainte Pée. The long *chistera* was invented by Melchior Curuchage of Buenos Aires, Argentina, in 1888. Games are played in a *fronton* (playing court), with both leather and rubber balls. The sport is governed by the International Federation of Basque Pelote.

The world's largest *fronton* was built for $12,000,000 in Macau, China, with a seating capacity of 4,000 and a floor area of 365,970 square feet.

An electronically measured speed of 131.7 m.p.h. was recorded in August, 1976, at the *fronton* in Bridgeport, Conn.

Longest Domination. The longest domination as the world's No. 1 player was enjoyed by Chiquito de Cambo (*né* Joseph Apesteguy) (France) (b. May 10, 1881–d. 1955), from the beginning of the century until succeeded in 1938 by Jean Urruty (France) (b. October 19, 1913).

Judo

Origin. Judo is a modern combat sport which developed out of an amalgam of several old Japanese fighting arts, the most popular of which was *ju-jitsu* (*jiu jitsu*), which is thought to be of pre-Christian Chinese origin. Judo has developed greatly since 1882, when it was first devised by Dr. Jigoro Kano. World Championships were inaugurated in Tokyo on May 5, 1956.

Highest Grade. The efficiency grades in Judo are divided into pupil (*kyu*) and master (*dan*) grades. The highest awarded is the extremely rare red belt *Judan* (10th *dan*), given only to seven men. The Judo protocol provides for a *Juichidan* (11th *dan*), who also would wear a red belt, and even a *Junidan* (12th *dan*), who would wear a white belt twice as wide as an ordinary belt, and even a *Shihan* (the highest of all), but these have never been bestowed.

Marathon. The longest recorded Judo marathon with con-

JUDO WINNER: Holland's Willem Ruska has won 4 world and Olympic titles. Here he has brought down Russia's Vitali Kusnezov in the 1972 Olympics.

tinuous play by two of six Judoka in 5-minute stints is 70 hours by members of the BP Judo Club, Hull, England, July 10–12, 1976.

Champions. The only man to have won 4 world titles is Willem Ruska of the Netherlands who won the 1967 and the 1971 heavyweight and the 1972 Olympic heavyweight and Open titles.

Karate

Origins. Originally *karate* (empty hand) is known to have been developed by the unarmed populace as a method of attack on, and defense against, armed Japanese aggressors in Okinawa, Ryukyu Islands, based on techniques devised from the 6th century Chinese art of *Chuan-fa* (Kempo). Transmitted to Japan in the 1920's by Funakoshi Gichin, the founder of modern *karate*, this method of combat was further refined and organized into a sport with competitive rules.

The five major schools of *karate* in Japan are *Shotokan*, *Wado-ryu*, *Goju-ryu*, *Shito-ryu*, and *Kyokushinkai*, each of which places different emphasis on speed, power, etc. The military form of *Tae-kwan-do* with 9 *dans* is a Korean equivalent of *karate*. *Kung fu* is believed to have originated in Nepal or Tibet but was adopted within Chinese temples *via* India.

Wu shu is a comprehensive term embracing all Chinese martial arts.

Most Titles. The only winner of 3 All-Japanese titles has been Takeshi Oishi, who won in 1969–70–71.

The highest *dan* among karetekas is Yamaguchi Gogen (b. 1907), a 10th *dan* of the *Goju-ryu* Karate Do.

Greatest Force. Considerably less emphasis is placed on *Tamashiwara* (wood breaking, etc.) than is generally supposed. Most styles use it only for demonstration purposes. However, the force needed to break a brick with the abductor *digiti quinti* muscle of the hand is normally 130–140 lbs. The highest measured impact is 196 lbs. force.

Brick Breaking. The greatest feat of brick breaking by hand was 4,487 by Tom Slaven, of Seven Hills, N.S.W., Australia, in November, 1975.

Lacrosse

Origin. The game is of American Indian origin, derived from the inter-tribal game *baggataway*, and was played by Iroquois Indians in lower Ontario, Canada, and upper New York State, before 1492. The game was included in the Olympic Games of 1908.

World Championship. The first World Tournament was held at Toronto, Canada, in 1967 and the second at Melbourne, Australia, in 1974. The U.S. won both.

Longest Throw. The longest recorded throw is 162.86 yards, by Barney Quinn of Ottawa, Canada, on September 10, 1892.

Highest Score. The highest score in any international match was U.S. over Canada, 26–15, at Melbourne in 1974.

Motorcycling

Earliest Races. The first motorcycle race was one from Paris to Dieppe, France, in 1897. The oldest motorcycle races in the world are the Auto-Cycle Union Tourist Trophy (T.T.) series, first held on the 15.81-mile "Peel" ("St. John's") course on the Isle of Man on May 28, 1907, and still run on the island, on the "Mountain" circuit (37.73 miles).

The first closed-circuit race was held at the Parc des Princes, Paris cycle track, in 1903.

Longest Circuits. The 37.73-mile "Mountain" circuit, over which the two main T.T. races have been run since 1911, has 264 curves and corners and is the longest used for any motorcycle race.

Fastest Circuit. The highest average lap speed attained on any closed circuit is 182 m.p.h. by a Kawasaki racer powered by a 748-c.c. three-cylinder two-stroke engine on a banked circuit in Tokyo, Japan, in December, 1971.

The fastest road circuit is the Francorchamps circuit near Spa, Belgium. It is 14.10 kilometers (8 miles 1,340 yards) in length and was lapped in 3 minutes 52.2 seconds (average speed of 135.752 m.p.h.) by Barry Sheene (born Holborn, London, England, September 11, 1950) on a 500-c.c. four-cylinder Suzuki during the 500-c.c. Belgian Grand Prix on July 6, 1975.

Fastest Race. The fastest race in the world was held at Grenzlandring, West Germany, in 1939. It was won by Georg Meier (b. Germany, 1910) at an average speed of 134 m.p.h. on a supercharged 495-c.c. flat-twin B.M.W.

The fastest road race is the 500-c.c. Belgian Grand Prix on the Francorchamps circuit (see above). The record time for this 10-lap 87.56-mile race is 39 minutes 22.8 seconds (average speed of 133.405 m.p.h.) by John Glyn Williams (U.K.) on a 495-c.c. four-cylinder Suzuki on July 4, 1976.

Longest Race. The longest race is the Liège 24 hours. The greatest distance ever covered is 2,523.26 miles (average speed 105.136 m.p.h.) by Jean-Claude Chemarin and Gerard Debrock of France on a 860-c.c. four-cylinder Honda on the Francorchamps circuit (8 miles 1,340 yards) near Spa, Belgium, August 17–18, 1974.

World Championships. Most world championship titles (instituted by the Fédération Internationale Motorcycliste in 1949) won are 15 by Giacomo Agostini (Italy) in the 350-c.c. class 1968, 69, 70, 71, 72, 73, 74 and in the 500-c.c. class 1966, 67, 68, 69, 70, 71, 72, 75. Agostini (b. 1942) is the only man to win two world championships in five consecutive years (350- and 500-c.c. titles in 1968–69–70–71–72). Agostini won 121 races in the world championship series between April 24, 1965, and June 26, 1976, including a record 19 in 1970, also achieved by Stanley Michael Bailey "Mike" Hailwood, M.B.E., G.M. (b. Oxford, England, April 2, 1940) in 1966.

Alberto "Johnny" Cecotto (born Caracas, Venezuela, January, 1956) was the youngest person to win a world championship. He was aged 19 years 7 months when he won the 350-c.c. title on August 24, 1975.

The oldest was Eric Staines Oliver (b. Crowborough, Sussex, England, April 13, 1911) who won the sidecar title in 1953, aged 42.

Most Successful Machines. Italian M.V.-Agusta motorcycles won 37 world championships between 1952 and 1973 and 274 world championship races between 1952 and 1975. Japanese Honda machines won 29 world championship races and five world championships in 1966. In the seven years Honda contested the championship (1961–67) its annual average was 20 race wins.

Speed Records

Official world speed records must be set with two runs over a measured distance within a time limit (one hour for F.I.M. records, two hours for A.M.A. records).

Don Vesco (born 1939) of El Cajon, California, recorded an average speed of 303.810 m.p.h. over the measured mile at Bonneville Salt Flats, Utah, on September 28, 1975, to establish an A.M.A. record. Riding a 21-foot-long *Silver Bird* Streamliner powered by two 750-c.c. Yamaha TZ750 4-cylinder engines developing 180 b.h.p., he covered the first mile in 11.817 seconds (304.646 m.p.h.). On the second run his time was 11.882 seconds (302.979 m.p.h.). The average time for the two runs was 11.8495 (303.810 m.p.h.) for the A.M.A. record. On the same day, he set an F.I.M. record at an average speed of 302.928 m.p.h. Also on the same day, he covered a flying quarter mile in 2.925 seconds (307.692 m.p.h.), the highest speed ever achieved on a motorcycle.

The world record average speed for two runs over one kilometer (1,093.6 yards) from a standing start is 122.77 m.p.h. (18.22 seconds) by David John Hobbs (b. Woodford, Essex, England, June 3, 1947) on his supercharged Triumph *Olympus II* powered by two twin-cylinder 500-c.c. engines, each developing 100 b.h.p., using methanol and nitromethane, at Elvington Airfield, Yorkshire, England, on September 30, 1972.

The world record for two runs over 440 yards from a standing start is 94.687 m.p.h. (9.505 seconds) by Keith Parnell (born Cornwall, England, October 8, 1936) on his supercharged 750-c.c. Triumph *Rouge et Noir* at Elvington Airfield, North Yorkshire, England, on October 5, 1974. The faster run was made in 9.40 seconds.

The fastest time for a single run over 440 yards from a standing start is 7.86 seconds (terminal velocity 178.92 m.p.h.) by Russ Collins of Gardena, California, riding his 3,246-c.c. *Atchison, Topeka & Santa Fé*, powered by three Honda engines, during the National Hot Rod Association's U.S. Supernationals at Ontario Motor Speedway, Ontario, California, on October 10, 1975.

The highest terminal velocity recorded at the end of a 440-yard run from a standing start is 182.55 m.p.h. (elapsed time 8.12 seconds) by Joe Smith of West Covina, California, riding his supercharged 3,736-c.c. twin-engined Harley Davidson, at the 1975 U.S. Supernationals at Ontario, California, October 12, 1975.

Marathon. The longest time a solo motorcycle has been kept in continuous motion is 114 hours by Michael Shirley, Brian Shirley, and Shane McLachlan riding a 900-c.c. Kawasaki Z900 at Oran Park Raceway, N.S.W., Australia, February 2–7, 1976, covering 4,535.3 miles.

Mountaineering

Origins. Although bronze-age artifacts have been found on the summit (9,605 feet) of the Riffelhorn, Switzerland, mountaineering, as a sport, has a continuous history dating back only to 1854. Isolated instances of climbing for its own sake exist back to the 14th century. The Atacamenans built sacrificial platforms near the summit of Llullaillaco in South America (22,058 feet) in late pre-Columbian times, *c.* 1490.

Rock Climbing. The world's most demanding free climbs are in the Yosemite Valley, California, with a severity rating of 5.12.

Warren Harding and Dean Caldwell averaged 80 vertical feet a day in their record 27 days on the Wall of the Early Morning Light on Yosemite's El Capitan in November, 1971.

Greatest Fall. The greatest recorded fall survived by a mountaineer was when Christopher Timms (Christchurch University) slid

7,500 feet down an ice face into a crevasse on Mt. Elie de Beaumont (10,200 feet), New Zealand on December 7, 1966. His companion was killed, but he survived with concussion, bruises and a hand injury.

Mount Everest. Mount Everest (29,028 feet) was first climbed at 11:30 a.m. on May 29, 1953, when the summit was reached by Edmund Percival Hillary (born July 20, 1919), of New Zealand, and the Sherpa, Tenzing Norgay (born, as Namgyal Wangdi, in Nepal in 1914, formerly called Tenzing Khumjung Bhutia). The successful expedition was led by Col. (later Brigadier Lord) Henry Cecil John Hunt (born June 22, 1910).

Subsequent ascents of Mount Everest are as follows:

Climbers	Date
Ernst Schmidt, Jurg Marmet (Switz.)	May 23, 1956
Hans Rudolf von Gunten, Adolf Reist (Switz.)	May 24, 1956
Wang Fu-chou, Chu Yin-hua (China), Konbu	May 25, 1960
James Warren Whittaker (U.S.), Sherpa Nawang Gombu	May 1, 1963
Barry C. Bishop, Luther G. Jerstad (U.S.)	May 22, 1963
Dr. William F. Unsoeld, Dr. Thomas F. Hornbein (U.S.)	May 22, 1963
Capt. A. S. Cheema (India), Sherpa Nawang Gombu	May 20, 1965
Sonam Gyaltso, Sonam Wangyal	May 22, 1965
C. P. Vohra (India), Sherpa Ang Kami	May 24, 1965
Capt. H. P. S. Ahluwalia, H. C. S. Rawat (India), Phu Dorji	May 29, 1965
Nomi Uemura, Tero Matsuura (Japan)	May 11, 1970
Katsutoshi Harabayashi (Japan) and Sherpa Chotari	May 12, 1970
Sgt. Mirko Minuzzo, Sgt. Rinaldo Carrel (Italy) with Lapka Tenzing and Samba Tamang	May 5, 1973
Capt. Fabrizio Innamorati, W. O. Virginio Epis and Sgt. Maj. Claudio Benedetti (Italy) with Sonam Gallien	May 7, 1973
Hisashi Ishiguro, Yasuo Kato (Japan)	Oct. 26, 1973
Mrs. Junko Tabei, Ang Tserang	May 16, 1975
Mrs. Phanthog, Sodnam Norbu, Lotse Samdrub, Darphuntso, Kunga Pasang, Tsering Tobgyal, Ngapo Khyen (Tibet), Hou Sheng-Fu (China)	May 27, 1975
Doug Scott, Dougal Haston (U.K.)	Sept. 24, 1975
Peter Boardman (U.K.), Pertember (Nepal)	Sept. 26, 1975
Sgt. John Stokes, Cpl. Michael Lane (U.K.)	May 17, 1976

Greatest Wall. The highest final stage in any wall climb is that on the south face of Annapurna I (26,545 feet). It was climbed by the British expedition led by Christian Bonington April 2–May 27, 1970, when Donald Whillans, 36, and Dougal Haston, 27, scaled to the summit.

The longest wall climb is on the Rupal-Flanke from the base camp at 11,680 feet to the South Point (26,384 feet) of Nanga Parbat—a vertical ascent of 14,704 feet. This was scaled by the Austro-Germano-Italian Expedition led by Dr. Herrligkoffer in April, 1970.

Greatest Alpine Wall. Europe's greatest wall is the 6,600-foot (2,000-m.) north face of the Eigerwand (Ogre Wall) first climbed on August 20, 1932, by Hans Lauper, Alfred Zurcher, Alexander Graven and Josef Knubel. The first direct ascent was by Heinrich Harrar and Fritz Kasparek of Austria and Andreas Heckmair and Ludvig Vörg of Germany on July 21–24, 1938. The greatest alpine solo climb was that of Walter Bonatti (Italy) of the South West Pillar of the Dru, Montenvers, now called the Bonatti Pillar in 126 hrs. 7 min. with 5 bivouacs on August 17–22, 1955.

African Record. The climbing of Africa's two highest mountains, Kilimanjaro (19,340 feet) and Mount Kenya (17,058 feet) from summit to summit in 24 hours, was achieved on February 9–10, 1964, by Rusty Baillie (Rhodesia) and Barry Cliff (G.B.). The descent of 15,300 feet, the 250-mile drive, and the 8,500-foot ascent of Mount Kenya were achieved in 21 hours 50 minutes.

Olympic Games

Note: These records now include the un-numbered Games held at Athens in 1906, which some authorities ignore. Although inserted between the regular IIIrd Games in 1904 and the IVth Games in 1908, the 1906 Games were both official and were of a higher standard than all three of those that preceded them.

Origins. The earliest celebration of the ancient Olympic Games of which there is a certain record is that of July, 776 B.C. (when Coroibos, a cook from Elis, won a foot race), though their origin probably dates from *c.* 1370 B.C. The ancient Games were terminated by an order issued in Milan in 393 A.D. by Theodosius I, "the Great" (*c.* 346–395), Emperor of Rome. At the instigation of Pierre de Fredi, Baron de Coubertin (1863–1937), the Olympic Games of the modern era were inaugurated in Athens on April 6, 1896.

Most Medals

In the ancient Olympic Games, victors were given a chaplet (head garland) of olive leaves. Milo (Milon of Kroton) won 6 titles at *palaisma* (wrestling), 540–516 B.C.

Individual. The most individual gold medals won by a male competitor in the modern Games is 10 by Raymond Clarence Ewry (U.S.) (b. October 14, 1874, at Lafayette, Indiana; d. September 27, 1937), a jumper (see *Track and Field*). The female record is seven by Vera Caslavska-Odlozil (b. May 3, 1942) of Czechoslovakia (also see *Gymnastics*).

Al Oerter of the U.S. dominated the discus competition in 4 consecutive Olympic meetings (1956 to 1968), a unique achievement in Olympic track and field.

The only Olympian to win 4 consecutive individual titles has been Alfred A. Oerter (b. September 19, 1936, New York City) who won the discus title in 1956–60–64–68.

Most Olympic Gold Medals at One Games. Mark Spitz (U.S.), the swimmer who won 2 relay golds at Mexico in 1968, won 7 more (4 individual and 3 relay) at Munich in 1972. The latter figure is an absolute Olympic record for one celebration at any sport.

National. The total figures for most medals and most gold medals for all Olympic events (including those now discontinued) for the Summer (1896–1976) and Winter Games (1924–1976) and for the Art Competitions (1912–1948) are:—

	Gold	Silver	Bronze	Total
1. U.S.A.	658*	511½	437½	1,607
2. U.S.S.R. (formerly Russia)	309	257	244	810
3. G.B. (including Ireland to 1920)	165½	202½	178	546

* The A.A.U. (U.S.) reinstated James F. Thorpe (1888–1953), the disqualified high scorer in the 1912 decathlon and pentathlon events on October 12, 1973, but no issue of medals has yet been authorized by the International Olympic Committee. If allowed, this would give the U.S. 2 more gold medals.

Oldest and Youngest Gold Medalists. The oldest recorded winner is Sir Eyre Massey Shaw (Great Britain) (1830–1908) who was over 70 when he won the 2–3 ton class in the 1900 yachting regatta in *Ollé* on May 25, 1900. The youngest woman to win gold medals is Marjorie Gestring (U.S.) (b. November 18, 1922, now Mrs. Bowman) aged 13 years 9 months, in the 1936 women's springboard event. The youngest winner ever was a French boy (whose name is not recorded) who coxed the Netherlands coxed pair in 1900. He was not more than 10 and may have been as young as 7. He substituted for Dr. Hermanus Brockmann, who coxed in the heats but proved too heavy.

Longest Span. The longest competitive span of any Olympic competitor is 40 years by Dr. Ivan Osiier (Denmark), who competed as a fencer in 1908, 1912 (silver medal), 1920, 1924, 1928, 1932 and 1948, totaling seven celebrations. He refused to compete in the 1936 Games on the grounds that they were Nazi-dominated. The longest span for a woman is 24 years (1932–56) by the Austrian fencer Ellen Müller-Preiss. Janice Lee York Romary, the U.S. fencer, competed in all six Games from 1948 to 1968, and Lia Manoliu (Rumania) competed from 1952 to 1972, winning the discus title in 1968.

Largest Crowd. The largest crowd at any Olympic site was 150,000 at the 1952 ski-jumping at the Holmenkollen, outside Oslo, Norway. Estimates of the number of spectators of the marathon race through Tokyo, Japan, on October 21, 1964, have ranged from 500,000 to 1,500,000.

Most Competitors. The greatest number of competitors in any summer Olympic Games up to 1976 has been 7,147 (including 1,070 women) from a record 122 countries at Munich in 1972. The fewest was 285 competitors from 12 countries in 1896. In 1904 only 11 countries participated. The largest team was 880 men and 4 women from France at the 1900 Games in Paris.

Most Participations. Five countries have never failed to be represented at the 21 Celebrations of the Games: Australia, Greece, Great Britain, Switzerland and the United States of America.

Pentathlon, Modern

The Modern Pentathlon (Riding, Fencing, Shooting, Swimming and Running) was inaugurated into the Olympic Games at Stockholm in 1912.

Point scores in riding, fencing, cross country and hence overall scores have no comparative value between one competition and another. In shooting and swimming (300 meters), where measurements are absolute, the point scores are of record significance.

	Points			
Shooting	1,088	Mario Medda (Italy)	Munich, W. Germ.	Aug. 29, 1972
Swimming	1,288	John Alexander (Canada)	London, Eng.	Sept. 8, 1973

Most World Titles. The record number of world titles won is 6 by András Balczó (Hungary) in 1963, 1965, 1966, 1967 and 1969, and the Olympic title in 1972, which also rates as a world title.

Olympic Titles. The greatest number of Olympic gold medals won is three by Balczó, a member of Hungary's winning team in 1960 and 1968, and the 1972 individual champion. Lars Hall (Sweden) uniquely has won two individual Championships (1952 and 1956). Balczó has won a record number of five medals (3 gold and 2 silver).

SIX-TIME WORLD CHAMPION András Balczó of Hungary has also won 3 Olympic gold medals.

SPRINT RACE: On July 30, 1976, these birds were released from the 86th Floor Observatory of the Empire State Building in New York City. One 2-month-old hen proceeded to fly the 6 miles to the New Jersey Meadowlands Sports Complex in 5 minutes 40 seconds—just over a mile a minute.

Pigeon Racing

Earliest References. Pigeon Racing was the natural development of the use of homing pigeons for the carrying of messages—a quality utilized in the ancient Olympic Games (776 B.C.–393 A.D.). The sport originated in Belgium. The earliest major long-distance race was from Crystal Palace, South London, England, in 1871.

Longest Flights. The greatest recorded homing flight by a pigeon was made by one owned by the 1st Duke of Wellington (1769–1852). Released from a sailing ship off the Ichabo Islands, West Africa, on April 8, it dropped dead a mile from its loft at Nine Elms, London, England, on June 1, 1845, 55 days later, having flown an airline route of 5,400 miles, but an actual distance of possibly 7,000 miles to avoid the Sahara Desert. It was reported on November 27, 1971, that an exhausted pigeon bearing a Hanover (Germany) label was found 10,000 miles away at Cunnamulla, Queensland, Australia.

Highest Speeds. In level flight in windless conditions it is very doubtful if any pigeon can exceed 60 m.p.h. The highest race speed recorded is one of 3,229 yards per minute (110.07 m.p.h.) in East Anglia, England, on May 8, 1965, when 1,428 birds were backed by a powerful southwest wind. The winner was A. Vidgeon & Son.

The highest race speed recorded over a distance of more than 1,000 kilometers is 82.93 m.p.h. by a hen pigeon in the Central Cumberland Combine Race over 683 miles 147 yards from Murray Bridge, South Australia, to North Ryde, Sydney, on October 2, 1971.

The world's longest reputed distance in 24 hours is 803 miles (velocity 1,525 yards per minute) by E. S. Peterson's winner of the 1941 San Antonio (Texas) Racing Club event.

Lowest Speed. *Blue Chip,* a pigeon belonging to Harold Hart, released in Renres, France, arrived home in its loft in Leigh,

England, on September 29, 1974, 7 years 2 months later. It had covered the 370 miles at an average speed of 0.00589 m.p.h., which is slower than the world's fastest snail (see page 105).

Highest-Priced Bird. £10,500 ($24,150) was paid by Louis Massarella of Leicester, England, on December 31, 1975, for *De Blicksen*.

Polo

Earliest Games. Polo is usually regarded as being of Persian origin, having been played as *Pula c.* 525 B.C. Other claims have come from Tibet and the Tang dynasty of China 250 A.D.

Stone goalposts (probably 12th century), 8 yards wide and 300 yards apart, still stand at Isfahan, Iran. The earliest club of modern times was the Kachar Club (founded in 1859) in Assam, India. The game was introduced into England from India in 1869 by the 10th Hussars at Aldershot, Hampshire, and the earliest match was one between the 9th Lancers and the 10th Hussars on Hounslow Heath, west of London, in July, 1871. The earliest international match between England and the U.S. was in 1886.

Playing Field. The game is played on the largest field of any ball game in the world. The ground measures 300 yards long by 160 yards wide with side-boards or, as in India, 200 yards wide without boards.

Highest Handicap. The highest handicap based on eight 7½-minute "chukkas" is 10 goals, introduced in the U.S. in 1891 and in the United Kingdom and in Argentina in 1910. The most recent additions to the select ranks of the 38 players to have received 10-goal handicaps are A. Heguy and A. Harriot of Argentina.

Highest Score. The highest aggregate number of goals scored in an international match is 30, when Argentina beat the U.S. 21–9 at Meadow Brook, Long Island, New York, in September, 1936.

Most Olympic Medals. Polo has been part of the Olympic program on five occasions: 1900, 1908, 1920, 1924 and 1936. Of the 21 gold medalists, a 1920 winner, John Wodehouse, the 3rd Earl of Kimberly (b. 1883–d. 1941) uniquely also won a silver medal (1908).

Most Internationals. Thomas Hitchcock, Jr. (1900–44) played five times for the U.S. vs. England (1921–24–27–30–39) and twice vs. Argentina (1928–36).

Most Expensive Pony. The highest price ever paid for a polo pony was $22,000, paid by Stephen Sanford for Lewis Lacey's *Jupiter* after the 1928 U.S. vs. Argentina international.

Largest Trophy. Polo claims the world's largest sporting trophy —the Bangalore Limited Handicap Polo Tournament Trophy. This massive cup standing on its plinth is 6 feet tall and was presented in 1936 by the Indian Raja of Kolanke.

Largest Crowd. Crowds of more than 50,000 have watched flood-lit matches at the Sydney, Australia, Agricultural Shows.

A crowd of 40,000 watched a game played at Jaipur, India, in 1976, when elephants were used instead of ponies. The length of the polo sticks used has not been ascertained.

Powerboat Racing

Origins. The earliest application of the gasoline engine to a boat was Gottlieb Daimler's experimental powerboat on the Seine River, Paris, in 1887. The sport was given impetus by the presentation of a championship cup by Sir Alfred Harmsworth of England in 1903, which was also the year of the first offshore race from Calais to Dover.

Harmsworth Cup. Of the 25 contests from 1903 to 1961, the U.S. has won 16, the United Kingdom 5, Canada 3 and France 1.

The greatest number of wins has been achieved by Garfield A. Wood (U.S.) with 8 (1920–21, 1926, 1928–29–30, 1932–33). The only boat to win three times is *Miss Supertest III*, owned by James G. Thompson (Canada), in 1959–60–61. This boat also achieved the record speed of 115.972 m.p.h. at Picton, Ontario, Canada, in 1960.

Gold Cup. The Gold Cup (instituted 1903) has been won 5 times by Bill Muncey (1956–57–61–62–72). The record speed attained is 120.356 m.p.h. for a 3-mile lap by the Rolls-Royce-engined *Miss Exide*, owned by Milo Stoen, and driven by Bill Brow at Seattle, Washington, on August 4, 1965.

Highest Offshore Speed. The highest speed attained is 93.1 m.p.h. by L. Sonny Kay (U.S.) in his 36-foot *Aeromarine II*, powered by two 7,669-c.c. 600-h.p. Kiekhaefer Aeromarine engines. This average speed was recorded over the 63 statute miles of the

LONGEST POWERBOAT JUMP: Jerry Comeaux jumped his boat 110 feet in the air for the film "Live and Let Die."

Cleveland Yachting Club's Firecracker 50 race on Lake Erie, Cleveland, Ohio, on June 30, 1973.

Longest Race. The longest race has been the Port Richborough (London) to Monte Carlo Marathon Offshore International Event. The race extended over 2,947 miles in 14 stages on June 10–25, 1972. It was won by *H.T.S.* (G.B.), driven by Mike Bellamy, Eddie Chater and Jim Brooks in 71 hours 35 minutes 56 seconds (average 41.15 m.p.h.).

Longest Jump. The longest jump achieved by a powerboat has been 110 feet by Jerry Comeaux, 29, in a Glastron GT-150 with a 135-h.p. Evinrude Starflite off a greased ramp on an isolated waterway in Louisiana, in mid-October, 1972. The take-off speed was 56 m.p.h. The jump was required for a sequence in the eighth James Bond film *Live and Let Die*.

Dragsters. The first drag boat to attain 200 m.p.h. was Sam Kurtovich's *Crisis* which attained 200.44 m.p.h. in California in October, 1969, at the end of a one-way run.

Longest Journey. The Dane, Hans Tholstrup, 25, circumnavigated Australia in a 17-foot Caribbean Cougar fiberglass runabout with a single 80-h.p. Mercury outboard motor from May 11 to July 25, 1971.

Rodeo

Origins. Rodeo came into being with the early days of the North American cattle industry. The earliest references to the sport are from Sante Fe, New Mexico, in 1847. Steer wrestling began with

Bill Pickett (Texas) in 1900. The other events are calf roping, bull riding, saddle and bareback bronco riding.

The largest rodeo in the world is the Calgary Exhibition and Stampede at Calgary, Alberta, Canada. The record attendance has been 993,777 on July 5–14, 1973. The record for one day is 141,670 on July 13, 1974.

Champion Bull. The top bucking bull is *Tiger*, a 7-year-old 1,400-lb. brindle-colored cross-bred bull with horns, owned by the Cervi Championship Rodeo Co. of Sterling, Colorado. He is seldom ridden successfully, but, in 1974, Don Gay scored 94 points on him. *Tiger* is notorious for "hooking" fallen cowboys.

Champion Bronc. Currently the greatest bronc is *Checkmate*, a 10-year-old stout animal weighing 1,200 lbs. He belongs to Christensen Bros. Rodeo Co., Eugene, Oregon, and during the 1974 season he threw 18 out of 24 of his riders, including 1974 world champion bronc rider, John McBeth. He was voted 1974 "Bucking Horse of the Year." Traditionally a bronc called *Midnight* owned by Jim McNab of Alberta, Canada, was never ridden in 12 appearances at the Calgary Stampede.

Most World Titles. The record number of all-round titles is 6 by Larry Mahan (b. November 21, 1943) (1966–67–68–69–70–73). The record figure for prize money in a single season is $66,929 by

CHAMPION COWBOY: Larry Mahan (U.S.) won the all-round world title six times.

Tom Ferguson, the 1974 all-round champion from Miami, Oklahoma.

Time Records. Records for timed events, such as calf roping and steer wrestling, are meaningless, because of the widely varying conditions due to the size of arenas and amount of start given the stock. The fastest time recently recorded for roping a calf is 7.5 seconds by Junior Garrison of Marlow, Oklahoma, at Evergreen, Colorado, in 1967, and the fastest time for overcoming a steer is 2.4 seconds by James Bynum of Waxahachie, Texas, at Marietta, Oklahoma, in 1955.

The standard required time to stay on in bareback, saddle bronc and bull riding events is 8 seconds. In the now obsolete ride-to-a-finish events, rodeo riders have been recorded to have survived 90 minutes or more, until the mount had not a buck left in it.

Roller Skating

Origin. The first roller skate was devised by Joseph Merlin of Huy, Belgium, in 1760. Several "improved" versions appeared during the next century, but a really satisfactory roller skate did not materialize before 1866, when James L. Plimpton of New York City produced the present four-wheeled type, patented it, and opened the first public rink in the world at Newport, Rhode Island, that year. The great boom periods were 1870–75, 1908–12 and 1948–54, each originating in the U.S.

LONGEST SKATE:
Clint Shaw of Victoria, Canada, skated across Canada in 1967 and across the U.S. in 1974.

Largest Rink. The largest indoor rink ever to operate was located in the Grand Hall, Olympia, London, England. It had an actual skating area of 68,000 square feet. It first opened in 1890, for one season, then again from 1909 to 1912.

Roller Hockey. Roller hockey was first introduced in England as Rink Polo, at the old Lava rink, Denmark Hill, London, in the late 1870's. The Amateur Rink Hockey Association was formed in 1905, and in 1913 became the National Rink Hockey (now Roller Hockey) Association. Britain won the inaugural World Championship in 1936, and since then Portugal has won the most with 11 titles from 1947 to 1973.

Most Titles. Most world speed titles have been won by Miss A. Vianello (Italy) with 16 between 1953 and 1965. Most world pair titles have been taken by Dieter Fingerle (W. Germany) with four in 1959–65–66–67. The records for figure titles are 5 by Karl Heinz Losch in 1958–59–61–62–66 and 4 by Astrid Bader, also of West Germany, in 1965 to 1968.

Speed Records. The fastest speed (official world's record) is 25.78 m.p.h. by Giuseppe Cantarella (Italy) who recorded 34.9 seconds for 440 yards on a road at Catania, Italy, on September 28, 1963. The mile record on a rink is 2 minutes 25.1 seconds by Gianni Ferretti (Italy). The greatest distance skated in one hour on a rink by a woman is 21.995 miles by Marisa Danisi at Inzell, West Germany, on September 27, 1968. The men's record on a closed road circuit is 23.133 miles by Alberto Civolani (Italy) at Inzell, West Germany, on September 27, 1968. He went on to skate 50 miles in 2 hours 20 minutes 33.1 seconds.

Marathon Record. The longest recorded continuous roller skating marathon was one of 183 hours 7 minutes by Clinton Shaw at Sherman Square Roller Rink, Reseda, California, August 23–30, 1975. The longest reported skate was also by Shaw from Victoria, British Columbia, to St. John's, Newfoundland (4,900 miles) on the Trans-Canadian Highway *via* Montreal from April 1 to November 11, 1967. On May 4, 1974, he started his New York–California skate, arriving in Santa Monica, California, on July 20, 1974, after 3,100 miles. His longest stint in a day was 106 miles from Clines Corners to Laguna, both in New Mexico. Shaw is planning to donate his skates when he retires to the Guinness World Records Exhibit in Las Vegas, Nevada.

Rowing

Oldest Race. The earliest established sculling race is the Doggett's Coat and Badge, first rowed on August 1, 1716, on a 5-mile course from London Bridge to Chelsea. It is still being rowed every year over the same course, under the administration of the Fishmongers' Company. The first English regatta probably took place on the Thames by the Ranelagh Gardens, near Putney, London, in

SCULLS CHAMPION: Vyacheslav Ivanov (U.S.S.R.) shares the record for 3 gold Olympic medals. Here (in shell at top) he has just won the singles in an international regatta.

1775. Boating began at Eton, England, in 1793. The oldest club, the Leander Club, was formed in *c.* 1818.

Olympic Games. Since 1900 there have been 118 Olympic finals of which the U.S. has won 26, Germany (now West Germany) 15 and Great Britain 14. Four oarsmen have won 3 gold medals: John B. Kelly (U.S.) (1889–1960), father of Princess Grace of Monaco, in the sculls (1920) and double sculls (1920 and 1924); his cousin Paul V. Costello (U.S.) (b. December 27, 1899) in the double sculls (1920, 1924 and 1928); Jack Beresford, Jr. (G.B.) (b. January 1, 1899) in the sculls (1924), coxless fours (1932) and double sculls (1936) and Vyacheslav Ivanov (U.S.S.R.) (b. July 30, 1938) in the sculls (1956, 1960 and 1964).

Sculling. The record number of wins in the Wingfield Sculls (instituted 1830) is seven by Jack Beresford, Jr., from 1920 to 1926. The record number of world professional sculling titles (instituted 1831) won is seven by W. Beach (Australia) between 1884 and 1887. Stuart A. Mackenzie (Great Britain and Australia) performed the unique feat of winning the Diamond Sculls at Henley for the sixth consecutive occasion on July 7, 1962. In 1960 and 1962 he was in Leander colors. The fastest time (Putney to Mortlake) has been 21 minutes 11 seconds by Leslie Southwood in 1933.

Highest Speed. Speeds in tidal or flowing water are of no comparative value. The highest recorded speed for 2,000 meters by an eight is 5 mins. 32.54 secs. (13.45 m.p.h.) by East Germany in the European Championships at Copenhagen, Denmark, on August 21, 1971. The highest speed in the Olympic Games has been 5 mins. 54.02 secs. (12.64 m.p.h.) by Germany, at Toda, Japan, on October 12, 1964.

Henley Royal Regatta. The annual regatta at Henley-on-Thames, Oxfordshire, England, was inaugurated on March 26, 1839.

Since 1839 the course, except in 1923, has been about 1 mile 550 yards, varying slightly according to the length of boat. In 1967, the shorter craft were "drawn up" so all bows start level. Prior to 1922, there were two slight angles. Classic Records (year in brackets indicates the date instituted):

			mins. secs.	
Grand Challenge Cup (1839)	8 oars	Harvard University (U.S.)	6:13	July 5, 1975
		Leander & Thames Tradesmen's R.C. (U.K.)	6:13	July 5, 1975
Ladies' Challenge Plate (1845)	8 oars	Trinity College (U.S.)	6:24	July 2, 1976
Thames Challenge Cup (1868)	8 oars	Christiana Roklub (Norway)	6:25	July 2, 1976
Princess Elizabeth Challenge (1946)	8 oars	Ridley College (Canada)	6:35	July 5, 1975
Stewards' Challenge (1841)	4 oars	Potomac B.C. (U.S.)	6:50	July 6, 1975
Prince Philip Cup (1963)	4 oars	Northeastern University Rowing Association (U.S.)	7:00	July 6, 1973
Visitors' Challenge (1847)	4 oars	University of London (U.K.)	7:07	July 2, 1976
Wyfold Challenge (1855)	4 oars	Thames Tradesmen's R.C. (U.K.)	6:57	July 6, 1975
Britannia Challenge (1969)	4 oars	Tideway Scullers (U.K.)	7:11	July 2, 1976
Silver Goblets and Nickalls' Challenge Cup (1895)	Pair oar	Peter Gorny and Gunther Bergau (ASK Vorwaerts Rostock, East Germany)	7:35	July 1, 1965
Double Sculls (1939)	Sculls	M. J. Hart and C. L. Baillieu (Leander Club and Cambridge Univ., U.K.)	6:59	July 6, 1973
Diamond Challenge (1844)	Sculls	Sean Drea (Neptune R.C., Ireland)	7:40	July 5, 1975

Highest Rate. The highest rate of stroking recorded in international competition is 56 per minute by the Japanese Olympic eight at Henley, England, in 1936.

Marathon. George Ellem of Brisbane, Australia, rowed 100 miles in 9 hours 18 minutes on the Brisbane River, Jan. 25–26, 1975.

Shooting

Earliest Club. A target shooting club in Geneva, Switzerland, has records since 1474.

Olympic Games. The record number of gold medals won is five by seven marksmen: Carl Osburn (U.S.) (1912–1924); Konrad Stäheli (Switz.) (1900 and 1906); Willis Lee (U.S.) (1920); Louis Richardet (Switz.) (1900 and 1906); Ole Andreas Lilloe-Olsen (Norway) (1920–1924); Alfred Lane (U.S.) (1912 and 1920) and Morris Fisher (U.S.) (1920 and 1924). Osburn also won 4 silver and 2 bronze medals to total 11. The only marksman to win 3 individual gold medals has been Gulbrandsen Skatteboe (Norway) (b. July 18, 1875) in 1906–1908–1912.

Most world titles have been won by S. De Lumniczer (Hungary) in 1929, 1933 and 1939. The only woman to win two world titles has been Gräfin von Soden (West Germany) in 1966–67.

WORLD RECORDS
Possible Score

Free Pistol	50 m. 6 × 10 shot series	600—	579	Karl Heinz Smieszek (W. Ger.) Montreal, 1976
Free Rifle	300 m. 3 × 40 shot series	1,200—1,157		Gary L. Anderson (U.S.) Mexico City, 1968
Small-Bore Rifle	50 m. 3 × 40 shot series	1,200—1,167		Lones W. Wigger, Jr. (U.S.) Mexico City, 1973 K. Bulan (Czech.) Thun, Switzerland, 1974
Small-Bore Rifle	50 m. 60 shots prone	600—	599	Ho Jun Li (N. Korea) Munich, 1972 K. Bulan (Czech.) Thun, Switzerland, 1974 Mircea Ilca (Rumania) Bucharest, 1975
Rapid-Fire Pistol	25 m. silhouettes 60 shots	600—	598	Giovanni Liverzani (Italy) Phoenix, Ariz., 1970
Running (Boar) Target	50 m. 60 shots "normal runs"	600—	577	H. Bellingrodt (Colombia) Thun, Switzerland, 1974 V. Postoianov (U.S.S.R.) Thun, Switzerland, 1974
Trap	200 birds	200—	199	Angelo Scalzone (Italy) Munich, 1972 Michel Carrega (France) Thun, Switzerland, 1974
Skeet	200 birds	200—	200	Yevgeniy Petrov (U.S.S.R.) Phoenix, Ariz., 1970
		200—	200	Yuri Tzuranov (U.S.S.R.) Bologna, Italy, 1971
		200—	200	Tariel Zhgenti (U.S.S.R.) Turin, Italy, 1973
		200—	200	Kield Rasmussen (Denmark) Vienna, 1975
		200—	200	Wieslaw Gawlikowski (Poland) Vienna, 1975

Record Heads. The world's finest head is the 23-pointer stag head in the Maritzburg collection, Germany. The outside span is 75½ inches, the length 47½ inches and the weight 41½ lbs. The greatest number of points is probably 33 (plus 29) on the stag shot in 1696 by Frederick III (1657–1713), the Elector of Brandenburg, later King Frederick I of Prussia.

Largest Shoulder Guns. The largest bore shoulder guns made were 2 bores. Less than a dozen of these were made by two English wildfowl gunmakers in *c.* 1885. Normally the largest guns made are double-barrelled 4-bore weighing up to 26 lbs. which can be handled only by men of exceptional physique. Larger smooth-bore guns have been made, but these are for use as punt-guns.

Bench Rest Shooting. The smallest group on record at 1,000 yards is 6.125 inches by Kenneth A. Keefer, Jr., with a 7 m.m.-300 Remington Action in Williamstown, Pennsylvania, on September 22, 1974.

FREE-RIFLE CHAMP (left): Gary Anderson scored 1,157 out of a possible 1,200 at Mexico City in 1968. FASTEST GUN (right): Bob Munden can draw his pistol and shoot in .02 of a second.

Block Tossing. Using a pair of auto-loading Remington Nylon 66 .22 caliber guns, Tom Frye (U.S.) tossed 100,010 blocks (2¼-inch pine cubes) and hit 100,004—his longest run was 32,860—on October 5–17, 1959.

Clay Pigeon Shooting. The record number of clay birds shot in an hour is 1,904 by Tom Kreckman, 36, at Cresco, Pennsylvania, on September 28, 1975.

Biggest Bag. The largest animal ever shot by any big game hunter was a bull African elephant (*Loxodonta africana*) shot by J. J. Fénykövi (Hungary), 48 miles north-northwest of Macusso, Angola, on November 13, 1955. It required 16 heavy caliber bullets from a 0.416 Rigby and weighed an estimated 24,000 lbs., standing 13 feet 2 inches at the shoulders. In November, 1965, Simon Fletcher, 28, a Kenyan farmer, claims to have killed two elephants with one 0.458 bullet.

The greatest recorded lifetime bag is 556,000 birds, including 241,000 pheasants, by the 2nd Marquess of Ripon (1867–1923) of England. He himself dropped dead on a grouse moor after shooting his 52nd bird on the morning of September 22, 1923.

Quickest Draw. The super-star of fast drawing and described as The Fastest Gun Ever Alive is Bob Munden (b. Kansas City, Missouri, February 8, 1942). His single-shot records include Walk and Draw Level Blanks in 15/100ths sec. at Arcadia, California, on June 4, 1972, and Standing Reaction Blanks (4-inch balloons at 8 feet) in 16/100ths sec. at Norwalk, California, on January 21, 1973, and Self Start Blanks in 2/100ths sec. at Baldwin Park, California, on August 17, 1968. His fastest shot with live ammunition is 21/100ths sec. at 21 feet, hitting a man-sized silhouette, in 1963. Munden also holds the 5 shot at balloons at 8 feet record at 1.06 seconds.

Revolver Shooting. The greatest rapid-fire feat was that of Ed McGivern (U.S.), who twice fired from 15 feet 5 shots which could be covered by a silver half dollar piece in 0.45 of a second at the Lead Club Range, South Dakota, on August 20, 1932.

McGivern also, on September 13, 1932, at Lewiston, Montana, fired 10 shots in 1.2 seconds from two guns at the same time double action (no draw), all 10 shots hitting two $2\frac{1}{4}$ by $3\frac{1}{2}$ inch playing cards at 15 feet.

Air Weapons. The individual world record for air rifle (40 shots at 10 meters) is 393 by Olegario Vazquez (Mexico) at Mexico City in 1973, and for air pistol (40 shots at 10 meters) is 393 by Harald Vollmar (East Germany) at Paris in February, 1976.

Trick Shooting. The most renowned trick shot of all time was Annie Oakley (*née* Mozee) (1860–1926). She demonstrated the ability to shoot 100 ex 100 in trap shooting for 35 years, aged between 27 and 62. At 30 paces she could split a playing card end-on, hit a dime in mid-air or shoot a cigarette from the lips of her husband—one Frank Butler.

Skiing

Origins. The earliest dated skis found in Fenno-Scandian bogs have been dated to *c.* 2500 B.C. A rock carving of a skier at Rodoy, northern Norway, dates from 2000 B.C. The earliest recorded isolated military competition was in Oslo, Norway, in 1767, though it did not grow into a sport until 1843 at Tromsø. The Trysil Shooting and Skiing Club (founded 1861), in Norway, claims to be world's oldest. Skiing was not introduced into the Alps until 1883, though there is some evidence of earlier use in the Carniola district. The earliest formal downhill race was staged at Montana, Switzerland, in 1911. The first Slalom event was run at Mürren, Switzerland, on January 6, 1921. The International Ski Federation (F.I.S.) was founded on February 2, 1924. The Winter Olympics were inaugurated on January 25, 1924.

Highest Speed. The highest speed ever claimed for any skier is 120.784 m.p.h. by Pino Meynet of Italy, on the Kilometro Lanciato (Flying Kilometer) at Cervinia, Italy, in July, 1975.

The average race speed by the 1976 Olympic Downhill champion on the Iglis-Patscherkofel course, Innsbruck, Austria, by Franz Klammer (born December 3, 1953) of Austria, was 66.838 m.p.h.

Duration. The longest non-stop overland skiing marathon was one that lasted 48 hours by Onni Savi, aged 35, of Padasjoki, Finland, who covered 305.9 kilometers (190.1 miles) between noon on April 19 and noon on April 21, 1966.

Chris Vaness and Rick Napurski of Maple Lake, Minnesota, completed 50 hours 17 minutes of Alpine skiing at Powder Ridge, Minnesota, on March 13–15, 1976.

Most World Titles. The World Alpine Championships were inaugurated at Mürren, Switzerland, in 1931. The greatest number

HIGHEST SKIING SPEED: Pino Meynet of Italy was clocked at more than 120 m.p.h. in 1975.

of titles won is 12 by Christel Cranz (born July 1, 1914), of Germany, with four Slalom (1934–37–38–39), three Downhill (1935–37–39) and five Combined (1934–35–37–38–39). She also won the gold medal for the Combined in the 1936 Olympics. The most titles won by a man is seven by Anton ("Toni") Sailer (born November 17, 1935), of Austria, who won all four in 1956 (Giant Slalom, Slalom, Downhill and the non-Olympic Alpine Combination) and the Downhill, Giant Slalom and Combined in 1958.

MOST TITLED SKIER: Toni Sailer (Austria) won 7 world alpine titles, including all four events in 1956.

WORLD CUP: Gustav Thoni of Italy has won this prize 4 times.

In the Nordic events Sixten Jernberg (Sweden) won eight titles, 4 at 50 km., one at 30 km., and 3 in relays, in 1956–64. Johan Gröttumsbraaten (born February 24, 1899), of Norway, won six individual titles (two at 18 kilometers and four Combined) in 1926–32. The record for a jumper is five by Birger Ruud (born August 23, 1911), of Norway, in 1931–32 and 1935–36–37.

The World Cup, instituted in 1967, has been won four times by Gustav Thoni (Italy) (b. February 28, 1931) in 1971–72–73–75. The women's cup has been won five times by the 5-foot-6-inch 150-lb. Annemarie Moser *née* Proell (Austria) in 1971–72–73–74–75. In 1973, she completed a record sequence of 11 consecutive downhill victories.

Most Olympic Victories. The most Olympic gold medals won by an individual for skiing is four (including one for a relay) by Sixten Jernberg (born February 6, 1929), of Sweden, in 1956–60–64. In addition, Jernberg has won three silver and two bronze medals. The only woman to win four gold medals is Galina Koulakova (b. 1942) of U.S.S.R., who won the 5 kilometers and 10 kilometers (1972) and was a member of the winning 3 × 5 kilometers relay team in 1972 and again in 1976.

The most Olympic gold medals won in men's alpine skiing is three, by Anton ("Toni") Sailer in 1956 and Jean-Claude Killy in 1968.

Longest Jump. The longest ski jump ever recorded is one of 176 meters (577 feet 5 inches) by Toni Innauer (Austria) at Oberstdorf, West Germany, on March 6, 1976. The record for a 70-meter hill is 280½ feet by Tauno Käyhkö at Falun, Sweden, on

February 19, 1973, when scoring 247.8 points for distance and style.

The women's record is 321 feet 5 inches by Anita Wold of Norway, at Okura, Sapporo, Japan, on January 14, 1975.

Cross-Country. The world's greatest Nordic ski race is the "Vasa Lopp," which commemorates an event of 1521 when Gustavus Vasa (1496–1560), later King of Sweden, skied 85 kilometers (52.8 miles) from Mora to Sälen, Sweden. The re-enactment of this journey in reverse direction is now an annual event, with 9,397 starters on March 4, 1970. The record time is 4 hours 39 minutes 49 seconds by Janne Stefansson on March 3, 1968.

Greatest Descent. The greatest reported elevation descended in 12 hours is 416,000 feet by Sarah Ludwig, Scott Ludwig, and Timothy B. Gaffney, at Mt. Brighton, Michigan, on February 16, 1974.

Highest Altitude. Yuichiro Miura (Japan) skied 1.6 miles down Mt. Everest starting from 26,200 feet. In a run from a height of 24,418 feet he reached speeds of 93.6 m.p.h. on May 6, 1970. Sylvain Saudan (Switzerland) became the first man to ski down Mount McKinley (20,320 feet) on June 10, 1972. He took 7 hours to reach the 7,000 foot level and made 2,700 jump turns on the 50–55° top slopes.

Longest Run. The longest all-downhill ski run in the world is the Weissfluhjoch-Küblis Parsenn course (7.6 miles long), near Davos, Switzerland. The run from the Aiguille du Midi top of the Chamonix lift (vertical lift 8,176 feet) across the Vallée Blanche is 13 miles.

WINNER OF 9 OLYMPIC MEDALS AND 8 WORLD TITLES: Sixten Jernberg of Sweden, cross-country skier, is here finishing a 50-km. run at Sapporo, Japan, in 1972.

STEEPEST DESCENT:
Sylvain Saudan has skied
down hills with a gradient
in excess of 60 degrees.

Steepest Descent. Sylvain Saudan (b. Lausanne, Switzerland, September 23, 1936) achieved a descent of Mont Blanc on the northeast side down the Couloir Gervasutti from 13,937 feet on October 17, 1967, skiing gradients in excess of 60 degrees.

Hot-Dog Skiing. Nineteen members of the Sunset Sports Center's "Hot Dog" team at Grand Targhee Ski Resort, Wyoming, performed a simultaneous back somersault while holding hands on February 9, 1975.

Longest Lift. The longest chair lift in the world is the Alpine Way to Kosciusko Châlet lift above Thredbo, near the Snowy Mountains, New South Wales, Australia. It takes from 45 to 75 minutes to ascend the 3.5 miles, according to the weather. The highest is at Chactaltaya, Bolivia, rising to 16,500 feet.

Skijoring. The record speed reached in aircraft skijoring (being towed by an aircraft) is 109.23 m.p.h. by Reto Pitsch on the Silsersee, St. Moritz, Switzerland, in 1956.

Ski Parachuting. The greatest recorded vertical descent in parachute ski-jumping is 2,300 feet by Rick Sylvester, 29 (U.S.), who on

NINETEEN AT ONCE: This "Hot-Dog" stunt was accomplished in Wyoming.

January 31, 1973, skied off the 3,200-foot sheer face of El Capitan, Yosemite Valley, California. His parachute opened at 1,500 feet.

Ski-Bob. The ski-bob was invented by a Mr. Stevens of Hartford, Connecticut, and patented (No. 47334) on April 19, 1892, as a "bicycle with ski-runners." The Fédération Internationale de Skibob was founded on January 14, 1961, in Innsbruck, Austria. The first World Championships were held at Bad Hofgastein, Austria, in 1967.

The highest speed has been 103.4 m.p.h. by Erick Brenter (Austria) at Cervinia, Italy, in 1964. The only ski-bobbers to retain world championships are Gerhilde Schiffkorn (Austria) who won the women's title in 1967 and 1969, Gertrude Geberth, who won in 1971 and 1973 and Alois Fischbauer (Austria) who won the men's title in 1973 and 1975.

Snowmobiling. The record speed for a snowmobile stood at 127.3 m.p.h. by Yvon Duhamel (Canada) on a Ski Doo XR-2 on February 10, 1973.

Soccer

Origins. A game with some similarities termed *Tsu-chin* was played in China in the 3rd and 4th centuries B.C. The earliest clear representation of the game is in a print from Edinburgh, Scotland, dated 1672–73. The game became standardized with the formation of the Football Association in England on October 26, 1863. A 26-a-side game, however, existed in Florence, Italy, as early as 1530, for which rules were codified in *Discorsa Calcio* in 1580. The world's oldest club was Sheffield F.C. of England, formed on October 24, 1857. Eleven on a side was standardized in 1870.

Highest Scores

Teams. The highest score recorded in any first-class match is 36. This occurred in the Scottish Cup match between Arbroath and Bon Accord on September 5, 1885, when Arbroath won 36–0 on their home ground. But for the lack of nets, the playing time might have been longer and the score possibly even higher.

The highest goal margin recorded in any international match is 17. This occurred in the England vs. Australia match at Sydney on June 30, 1951, when England won 17–0. This match is not listed by England as a *full* international.

Individuals. The most goals scored by one player in a first-class match is 16 by Stains for Racing Club de Lens vs. Aubry-Asturies, in Lens, France, on December 13, 1942.

The record number of goals scored by one player in an international match is 10 by Gottfried Fuchs for Germany, which beat Russia 16–0 in the 1912 Olympic tournament in Sweden.

Artur Friedenreich (b. 1892) is believed to have scored an undocumented 1,329 goals in Brazilian football, but the greatest total of goals scored in a specified period is 1,216 by Edson Arantes do Nascimento (b. Baurú, Brazil, October 23, 1940), known as Pelé, the Brazilian inside left, from September 7, 1956, to October 2, 1974 (1,254 games). His best year was 1958 with 139, as well as his *milesimo* (1,000th) which came in a penalty for his club, Santos, in the Maracanã Stadium, Rio de Janeiro, when he was playing in his 909th first-class match. He came out of retirement in 1975 to add to his total with the New York Cosmos of the North American Soccer League. By June, 1976, his total had reached 1,249. Franz ("Bimbo") Binder (b. 1911) scored 1,006 goals in 756 games in Austria and Germany between 1930 and 1950. (See color photograph on color page H.)

Fastest Goals

The record for an international match is 3 goals in 3½ minutes by Willie Hall (Tottenham Hotspur) for England against Ireland on November 16, 1938, at Old Trafford, Manchester, England.

Most Appearances

Robert ("Bobby") Moore of West Ham United set a new record of full international appearances by playing in his 108th game for England vs. Italy on November 14, 1973 at Wembley, London. His first appearance was vs. Peru on May 20, 1962.

Most Successful Coach

George Raynor (born England, 1907) coached Sweden to the 1948 Olympic title, second place in the 1958 World Cup, and third place in the 1950 World Cup and 1952 Olympics.

Longest Match

The world duration record for a first-class match was set in the Copa Libertadores championship in Santos, Brazil, on August 2–3, 1962, when Santos drew 3–3 with Penarol F.C. of Montevideo, Uruguay. The game lasted 3½ hours (with interruptions), from 9:30 p.m. to 1 a.m.

It is claimed that a match between the Dallas Tornado and the Rochester Lancers lasted 3 hours 59 minutes (176 minutes playing time) in September, 1971.

Crowds

The greatest recorded crowd at any football match was 205,000 (199,854 paid) for the Brazil vs. Uruguay World Cup final in Rio de Janeiro, Brazil, on July 16, 1950.

Transfer Fees

The world's highest reported transfer fee is £922,300 ($2,305,750) for the Amsterdam Ajax striker Johan Cruyff, signed by F.C. Barcelona of Spain, announced on August 20, 1973.

It is reported that Naples, Italy, paid Bologna, Italy, $3,220,000 for center-forward Giuseppe Savoldi on July 11, 1975. Two other players were included in this deal.

World Cup

The *Fédération Internationale de Football* (F.I.F.A.) was founded in Paris on May 21, 1904, and instituted the World Cup Competition in 1930, two years after the four British Isles' associations had

LARGEST GOALKEEPER: Willie J. ("Fatty") Foulke (England) covered a large part of the goal at 6 feet 3 inches and 311 lbs.

resigned. The record attendance was for the 1966 competition, which totaled 5,549,521.

The only country to win three times has been Brazil (1958–1962–1970). Brazil was also third in 1938 and second in 1950, and is the only one of the 45 participating countries to have played in all 10 competitions.

The record goal scorer has been Just Fontaine (France) with 13 goals in 6 games in the final stages of the 1958 competition. The most goals scored in a final is 3 by Geoffrey Hurst (West Ham United) for England vs. West Germany on July 30, 1966. Gerd Müller (West Germany) scored 14 goals in two World Cup finals (1970 and 1974).

Antonio Carbajal (b. 1923) played for Mexico in goal in the competitions of 1950–54–58–62 and 1966.

Receipts

The greatest receipts at a World Cup final were £204,805 ($573,454) from an attendance of 96,924 for the match between England and West Germany at the Empire Stadium, Wembley, Greater London, on July 30, 1966.

Heaviest Goalkeeper

The biggest goalie on record was Willie J. ("Fatty") Foulke of England (1874–1916) who stood 6 feet 3 inches and weighed 311 lbs. By the time he died, he tipped the scales at 364 lbs. He once stopped a game by snapping the cross bar.

Soccer (Amateur)

Most Olympic Wins. The only country to have won the Olympic football title three times is Hungary in 1952, 1964 and 1968. The United Kingdom won in 1908 and 1912 and also the unofficial tournament of 1900. These contests have now virtually ceased to be amateur. The highest Olympic score is Denmark 17 vs. France "A" 1 in 1908.

Largest Crowd. The highest attendance at any amateur match is 100,000 at the English Football Association Amateur Cup Final between Pegasus and Bishop Auckland at Wembley, London, on April 21, 1951.

Heading. The highest recorded number of repetitions for heading a ball is 12,100 in 54 minutes 22 seconds by Michael Helliwell, 17, of Elland, England, on December 14, 1973.

Marathons. The longest recorded 11-a-side soccer marathon played without substitutes under Football Association rules is 37 hours by teams from Toccoa Falls, Georgia, April 25–26, 1975, and equalled by teams from Tenney High School, Methuen, Massachusetts, June 7–8, 1975, and South Cobb High School, Austell, Georgia, May 15–16, 1976.

The longest recorded authenticated 5-a-side games have been (outdoors) 57 hours by two teams (no substitutes) from the Fossa Youth Club, County Kerry, Ireland, August 1–3, 1975, and (indoors) 73 hours 50 minutes by two teams (no substitutes) from Mallow Youth Centre, Ireland, April 13–16, 1976.

Table Football. The most protracted game of 2-a-side table football on record was one of 341 hours maintained by 6 members of Burrow on Soar Youth Club, Leicestershire, England, April 10–24, 1976.

Squash

(Note: "1971," for example, refers to the 1971–72 season.)

Earliest Champion. Although racquets with a soft ball was evolved in *c.* 1850 at Harrow School (England), there was no recognized champion of any country until J. A. Miskey of Philadelphia won the American Amateur Singles Championship in 1906.

World Title. The inaugural Amateur International Federation championships were staged in Australia in August, 1967. Australia has won the team title four times. Geoffrey Hunt (Australia) took the individual title in 1967, 1969 and 1971.

The inaugural world professional championship, held at Wembley, London, England, in February, 1976, was won by Geoffrey Hunt (Australia).

Most Victories

Open Championship. The most wins in the Open Championship (amateur or professional), held annually in Britain, is seven by Hashim Khan (Pakistan) in 1950–51–52–53–54–55 and 1957.

Amateur Championship. The most wins in the Amateur Championship is six by Abdel Fattah Amr Bey (Egypt), later appointed Ambassador in London, who won in 1931–32–33 and 1935–36–37.

OPEN SQUASH
CHAMPION:
Hashim Khan
of Pakistan has
won 7 times.

Longest Championship Match. The longest recorded championship match was .one of 2 hours 13 minutes in the final of the Open Championship of the British Isles in Birmingham in December, 1969, when Jonah P. Barrington (Ireland) beat Geoffrey B. Hunt (Australia) 9–7, 3–9, 3–9, 9–4, 9–4, with the last game lasting 37 minutes.

Most Victories in the Women's Championship. The most wins in the Women's Squash Rackets Championship is 15 by Mrs. Heather McKay (*née* Blundell) of Australia, 1961 to 1976.

Marathon Record. In squash marathons a rest interval of 1 minute is allowed between games and 2 minutes between the 4th and 5th games with 5 minutes additional rest per hour. The rate of play must not exceed 11 games per hour.

The longest recorded squash marathon (under these competition conditions) has been one of 76 hours 36 minutes by Garth Madden and Lawrie Cook at Johannesburg, South Africa, April 1–4, 1976. Tony Taylor of Victoria, Australia, played for 80 hours 10 minutes against 89 opponents on June 11–14, 1976. He won 255 games out of 538 played.

Surfing

Origins. The traditional Polynesian sport of surfing in a canoe (*ehorooe*) was first recorded by the British explorer, Captain James Cook (1728–79) on his third voyage to Tahiti in December, 1771. Surfing on a board (*Amo Amo iluna ka lau oka nalu*) was first described ("most perilous and extraordinary . . . altogether astonishing, and is scarcely to be credited") by Lt. (later Capt.) James King of the Royal Navy in March, 1779, at Kealakekua Bay, Hawaii Island. A surfer was first depicted by this voyage's official artist John Webber.

The sport was revived at Waikiki by 1900. Australia's first club, the Bondi Surf Bathers Lifesaving Club, was formed in February, 1906. Hollow boards came in in 1929 and the plastic-foam type in 1956.

Highest Waves Ridden. Makaha Beach, Hawaii, provides reputedly the best consistently high waves for surfing, often reaching the rideable limit of 30–35 feet. The highest wave ever ridden was the *tsunami* of "perhaps 50 feet," which struck Minole, Hawaii, on April 3, 1868, and was ridden to save his life by a Hawaiian named Holua.

Longest Ride. About 4 to 6 times each year rideable surfing waves break in Matanchen Bay near San Blas, Nayarit, Mexico, which make rides of *c.* 5,700 feet possible.

World Champions. World Championships were inaugurated in 1964 at Sydney, Australia. The first surfer to win two titles has been Joyce Hoffman (U.S.) in 1965 and 1966.

Swimming

Earliest References. It is recorded that inter-school swimming contests in Japan were ordered by Imperial edict of Emperor Go-Yoozei as early as 1603. Competitive swimming originated in London *c.* 1837, at which time there were five or more pools, the earliest of · which had been opened at St. George's Pier Head, Liverpool, in 1828.

Largest Pools. The largest swimming pool in the world is the salt-water Orthlieb Pool in Casablanca, Morocco. It is 480 meters (1,574.8 feet) long and 75 meters (246 feet) wide, an area of 8.9 acres.

WORLD'S LARGEST SWIMMING POOL: The Orthlieb Pool in Casablanca, Morocco, is 1,575 feet long and 246 feet wide.

The largest land-locked swimming pool with heated water was the Fleishhacker Pool on Sloat Boulevard, near Great Highway, San Francisco. It measures 1,000 feet by 150 feet (3.44 acres), is up to 14 feet deep, and can contain 7,500,000 gallons of water. It was opened on May 2, 1925, but has now been abandoned to a few ducks.

The world's largest competition pool is at Osaka, Japan. It accommodates 25,000 spectators.

Fastest Swimmer. Excluding relay stages with their anticipatory starts, the highest speed reached by a swimmer is 5.09 m.p.h. by John Trembley (U.S.), who recorded 20.06 seconds for 50 yards in a 25-yard pool at Long Beach, California, on March 28, 1974.

Most World Records. Men: 32, Arne Borg (Sweden) (b. 1901), 1921–29. Women: 42, Ragnhild Hveger (Denmark) (b. December 10, 1920), 1936–42.

Most Difficult Dives. Those with the highest tariff (degree of difficulty 3.0) are the "3½ forward somersault in tuck position and the 1½ forward triple-twisting somersault from the 1-meter board; the backward 2½ somersault piked, the reverse 2½ piked, and the forward 3½ piked from the 3-meter board." Joaquín Capilla of Mexico has performed a 4½-somersault dive from a 10-meter board, but this is not on the international tariff.

Olympic Swimming Records

Most Olympic Gold Medals. The greatest number of Olympic gold medals won is 9 by Mark Andrew Spitz (U.S.) (b. February 10, 1950), as follows:

100 meter free-style	1972
200 meter free-style	1972
100 meter butterfly	1972
200 meter butterfly	1972
4 × 100 meter free-style relay	1968 and 1972
4 × 200 meter free-style relay	1968 and 1972
4 × 100 meter medley relay	1972

All but one of these performances (the 4×200 meter relay of 1968) were also world records at the time.

The record number of gold medals won by a woman is 4 shared by Mrs. Patricia McCormick (*née* Keller) (U.S.) (b. May 12, 1930) with the High and Springboard Diving double in 1952 and 1956 (also the women's record for individual golds); by Dawn Fraser (now Mrs. Gary Ware) (Australia) (b. September 4, 1937) with the 100 meter free-style (1956–60–64) and the 4 × 100 meter free-style relay (1956); and by Kornelia Ender (East Germany) with the 100 and 200 meter free-style (1976), the 100 meter butterfly (1976) and the 4 × 100 meter medley relay (1976). (See photo on page 633.)

Most Olympic Medals. The most medals won is 11 by Spitz, who in addition to his 9 golds (see above), won a silver (100 m. butterfly) and a bronze (100 m. free-style) both in 1968.

The most medals won by a woman is 8 by Dawn Fraser, who in addition to her 4 golds (see above) won 4 silvers (400 m. free-style 1956, 4×100 m. free-style relay 1960 and 1964, 4×100 m. medley relay 1960), and by Shirley Babashoff (U.S.) who won 2 golds

MOST OLYMPIC GOLD MEDALS (left): Mark Spitz (U.S.) won 9 in two meetings. **LONG DISTANCE SWIMMER (right):** Mihir Sen of India has swum from India to Ceylon, across the Dardanelles, and the length of the Panama Canal.

(4 × 100 m. free-style relay 1972 and 1976) and 6 silvers (100 m. free-style 1972, 200 m. free-style 1972 and 1976, 400 m. and 800 m. free-style 1976, and 400 m. medley 1976).

Most Individual Gold Medals. The record number of individual gold medals won is 4 shared by four swimmers: Charles M. Daniels (U.S.) (b. July 12, 1884) (100 m. free-style 1906 and 1908, 220 yard free-style 1904, 440 yard free-style 1904); Roland Matthes (E. Germany) (b. November 17, 1950) with 100 m. and 200 m. backstroke 1968 and 1972 and Spitz and McCormick (see above).

Closest Verdict. The closest victory in the Olympic Games was in the Munich 400-meter individual medley final on August 30, 1972, when Gunnar Larsson (Sweden) won by 2/1,000ths of a second in 4 minutes 31.98 seconds over Tim McKee (U.S.)—a margin of less than ⅛ inch, or the length grown by a finger nail in 3 weeks.

Long Distance Swimming

A unique achievement in long distance swimming was established in 1966 by the cross-channel swimmer Mihir Sen of Calcutta, India. These were the Palk Strait from India to Ceylon (in 25 hours 36 minutes on April 5–6); the Straits of Gibraltar (Europe to Africa in 8 hours 1 minute on August 24); the Dardanelles (Gallipoli, Europe, to Sedulbahir, Asia Minor, in 13 hours 55 minutes on September 12) and the entire length of the Panama Canal in 34 hours 15 minutes on October 29–31. He had earlier swum the English Channel in 14 hours 45 minutes on September 27, 1958.

Longest Distance Ocean Swim

The longest recorded ocean swim is one of 122½ miles by Walter Poenisch (U.S.) in the Florida Straits (in a shark cage) in 25 hours 8 minutes on June 19–20, 1976.

The greatest recorded distance ever swum is 1,826 miles down the Mississippi from Ford Dam, near Minneapolis, to Carrollton Avenue, New Orleans, July 6 to December 29, 1930, by Fred P. Newton, then 27, of Clinton, Oklahoma. He was in the water a total of 742 hours, and the water temperature fell as low as 47° F. He protected himself with petroleum jelly. Mr. Newton, now of Gainesville, Texas, became the inventor of the famous Relaxo-Bak support.

The longest duration swim ever achieved was one of 168 continuous hours, ending on February 24, 1941, by the legless Charles Zibbelman, *alias* Zimmy (born 1894) of the U.S., in a pool in Honolulu, Hawaii.

The longest duration swim by a woman was 87 hours 27 minutes in a pool by Mrs. Myrtle Huddleston of New York City, in 1931.

The greatest distance covered in a continuous swim is 288 miles by Clarence Giles from Glendive, Montana, to Billings, in the Yellowstone River in 71 hours 3 minutes, June 30 to July 3, 1939.

Channel Swimming

Earliest Man. The first man to swim across the English Channel (without a life jacket) was the merchant navy captain Matthew Webb (1848–83) (G.B.), who swam breast stroke from Dover, England, to Cap Gris Nez, France, in 21 hours 45 minutes on August 24–25, 1875. Webb swam an estimated 38 miles to make the 21-mile crossing. Paul Boyton (U.S.) had swum from Cap Gris Nez to the South Foreland in his patent lifesaving suit in 23 hours 30 minutes on May 28–29, 1875. There is good evidence that Jean-Marie Saletti, a French soldier, escaped from a British prison hulk off Dover by swimming to Boulogne in July or August, 1815. The first crossing from France to England was made by Enrique Tiraboschi, a wealthy Italian living in Argentina, who crossed in 16 hours 33 minutes on August 11, 1923, to win a $5,000 prize.

Woman. The first woman to succeed was Gertrude Ederle (U.S.) who swam from Cap Gris Nez, France, to Dover, England, on August 6, 1926, in the then record time of 14 hours 39 minutes. The first woman to swim from England to France was Florence Chadwick of California, in 16 hours 19 minutes on September 11, 1951. She repeated this on September 4, 1953, and October 12, 1955.

Youngest. The youngest conqueror is Abla Khairi (Egypt) who swam from Dover to Cap Gris Nez in 12 hours 30 minutes on August 18, 1974, aged 13 years 10 months.

Oldest. The oldest conqueror of the 21-mile crossing has been William E. (Ned) Barnie, who was 55 when he swam from France to England in 15 hours 1 minute on August 16, 1951.

Fastest. The official Channel Swimming Association record is

SWIMMING—WORLD RECORDS—MEN

At distances recognized by the Federation Internationale de Natation Amateur as of August 1, 1976. F.I.N.A. no longer recognizes any records made for non-metric distances. Only performances set up in 50-meter pools are recognized as World Records.

Distance	min. sec.	Name and Nationality	Place	Date
		FREE-STYLE		
100 meters	49.44	Jonty Skinner (South Africa)	Philadelphia, Pennsylvania	Aug. 14, 1976
200 meters	1:50.29	Bruce Furniss (U.S.)	Montreal, Canada	July 19, 1976
400 meters	3:51.93	Brian Goodell (U.S.)	Montreal, Canada	July 22, 1976
800 meters	8:01.54	Bobby Hackett (U.S.)	Long Beach, California	June 21, 1976
1,500 meters	15:02.40	Brian Goodell (U.S.)	Montreal, Canada	July 20, 1976
4 × 100 Relay	3:24.85	U.S. National Team	Cali, Colombia	July 23, 1975
		(Bruce Furniss, James Montgomery, Andrew Coan, John Murphy)		
4 × 200 Relay	7:23.22	U.S. National Team	Montreal, Canada	July 22, 1976
		(Bruce Furniss, Michael Bruner, James Montgomery, John Naber)		
		BREAST STROKE		
100 meters	1:03.11	John Hencken (U.S.)	Montreal, Canada	July 20, 1976
200 meters	2:15.22	David Wilkie (G.B.)	Montreal, Canada	July 24, 1976
		BUTTERFLY STROKE		
100 meters	54.27	Mark Spitz (U.S.)	Munich, West Germany	Aug. 31, 1972
200 meters	1:59.23	Michael Bruner (U.S.)	Montreal, Canada	July 18, 1976
		BACK STROKE		
100 meters	55.46	John Naber (U.S.)	Montreal, Canada	July 19, 1976
200 meters	1:59.19	John Naber (U.S.)	Montreal, Canada	July 24, 1976
		INDIVIDUAL MEDLEY		
200 meters	2:06.08	Bruce Furniss (U.S.)	Kansas City, Kansas	Aug. 23, 1975
400 meters	4:23.68	Rod Strachan (U.S.)	Montreal, Canada	July 25, 1976
		MEDLEY RELAY		
		(Back Stroke, Breast Stroke, Butterfly Stroke, Free-Style)		
4 × 100 meters	3:42.22	U.S. National Team	Montreal, Canada	July 22, 1976
		(John Naber, John Hencken, Matthew Vogel, James Montgomery)		

FASTEST WOMAN CHANNEL SWIMMER: Lynne Cox (U.S.) at age 16 on August 10, 1973, made the 21-mile crossing in 9 hours 36 minutes.

9 hours 35 minutes by Barry Watson, 25, of Yorkshire, England, who swam from France to England, August 15–16, 1964. The fastest time ever by a woman is 9 hours 36 minutes by Lynne Cox (U.S.), 16, who swam from England to France on August 10, 1973.

Slowest. The slowest crossing was the third ever made, when Henry Sullivan (U.S.) swam from England to France in 26 hours 50 minutes, August 5–6, 1923.

Relays. The fastest crossing by a relay team is one of 8 hours 51 minutes by Hetzel's Volunteers on August 13–14, 1974.

First Double Crossing. Antonio Abertondo (Argentina), aged 42, swam from England to France in 18 hours 50 minutes (8:35 a.m. on September 20 to 3:25 a.m. on September 21, 1961) and after about 4 minutes rest returned to England in 24 hours 16 minutes, landing at St. Margaret's Bay at 3:45 a.m. on September 22, 1961, to complete the first "double crossing" in 43 hours 10 minutes.

Fastest Double Crossing. The fastest double crossing, and only the fourth ever achieved, was one of 30 hours by Jon Erikson on August 14–15, 1975. He shaved 3 minutes off the previous record, set in September, 1965, by his father, Edward (Ted) Erikson.

FIRST DOUBLE CROSSING OF ENGLISH CHANNEL was swum by Antonio Abertondo of Argentina in 1961.

SWIMMING—WORLD RECORDS—WOMEN

(As of August 1, 1976)

Distance	min. sec.	Name and Nationality	Place	Date
		FREE-STYLE		
100 meters	56.65	Kornelia Ender (E. Germany)	Montreal, Canada	July 19, 1976
200 meters	2:02.26	Kornelia Ender (E. Germany)	Montreal, Canada	July 22, 1976
400 meters	4:09.89	Petra Thumer (E. Germany)	Montreal, Canada	July 20, 1976
800 meters	8:37.14	Petra Thumer (E. Germany)	Montreal, Canada	July 25, 1976
1,500 meters	16:33.94	Jenny Turrall (Australia)	Concord, California	Aug. 25, 1974
4×100 Relay	3:44.82	U.S. National Team	Montreal, Canada	July 25, 1976
		(Kim Peyton, Wendy Boglioli, Jill Sterkel, Shirley Babashoff)		
		BREAST STROKE		
100 meters	1:11.16	Hannelore Anke (E. Germany)	Montreal, Canada	July 24, 1976
200 meters	2:33.35	Marina Koshevaya (U.S.S.R.)	Montreal, Canada	July 21, 1976
		BUTTERFLY STROKE		
100 meters	1:00.13	Kornelia Ender (E. Germany)	East Berlin, E. Germany	June 4, 1976
200 meters	2:11.22	Rosemarie Kother (E. Germany)	East Berlin, E. Germany	June 5, 1976
		BACK STROKE		
100 meters	1:01.51	Ulrike Richter (E. Germany)	East Berlin, E. Germany	June 5, 1976
200 meters	2:12.47	Birgit Treiber (E. Germany)	East Berlin, E. Germany	June 4, 1976
		INDIVIDUAL MEDLEY		
200 meters	2:17.14	Kornelia Ender (E. Germany)	East Berlin, E. Germany	June 5, 1976
400 meters	4:42.77	Ulrike Tauber (E. Germany)	Montreal, Canada	July 24, 1976
		MEDLEY RELAY		
		(Back Stroke, Breast Stroke, Butterfly Stroke, Free-Style)		
4×100 meters	4:07.95	East German National Team	Montreal, Canada	July 18, 1976
		(Ulrike Richter, Hannelore Anke, Andrea Pollack, Kornelia Ender)		

Most Conquests. The greatest number of Channel conquests is 9 by Desmond Renford (born 1928) (Australia) from 1970 to September 1, 1975. Greta Andersen-Sonnichsen (U.S.) has swum the Channel five times (1957–65).

Underwater. The first underwater cross-Channel swim was achieved by Fred Baldasare (U.S.), aged 38, who completed the distance from France to England with scuba in 18 hours 1 minute on July 10–11, 1962. Simon Paterson, aged 20, a frogman from Egham, Surrey, England, traveled underwater from France to England with an airhose attached to his pilot boat in 14 hours 50 minutes on July 28, 1962.

BUTTERFLY CHAMPION: Rosemarie Kother, a member of the lightning-fast East German women's team, holds the record for the 200-meter butterfly at 2 minutes 11.22 seconds.

Ice Swimming

The "Human Polar Bear," Gustave A. Brickner (b. 1912) went for his daily dip in the Monongahela River of Pennsylvania on February 10, 1953, when the water temperature was 32°F., the air temperature —18°F., and the wind speed 40 m.p.h. (chill factor —85°F.). The river was ice-clogged at the time.

Most Dangerous Swim

One of the most dangerous swims on record was the unique crossing of the Potaro River in Guyana, South America, just above the 741-foot-high Kaieteur Falls by Private Robert Howatt (U.K.) (the Black Watch) on April 17, 1955. The river is 464 feet wide at the lip of the falls.

Odd Swimming Records

The longest recorded mileage in a 24-hour relay swim (team of 5) is 73 miles 245 yards by a team from St. James's Swimming Club, Dulwich, England, at London, May 11–12, 1974.

The fastest time recorded for 100 miles by a team of 20 swimmers is 25 hours 55 minutes 8.2 seconds by a high school team in Dundee, Scotland, December 14–15, 1974.

A team of 6 boys, aged 13 to 15, covered 300 miles in 230 hours 39 minutes, July 18–28, 1968, in Buttermere, England.

The longest recorded underground swim is one of 3,402 yards in 87 minutes by David Stanley Gale through the Dudley Old Canal Tunnel, West Midlands, England, in August, 1967.

Treading Water

The duration record for treading water (vertical posture in an 8-foot square without touching the lane markers) without rest breaks is 41 hours 11 minutes by Pete Bahn, Jr. at Herrin City Park, Illinois, August 15–16, 1975.

Table Tennis

Earliest Reference. The earliest evidence relating to a game resembling table tennis has been found in the catalogues of London sporting goods manufacturers in the 1880's. The old Ping-Pong Association was formed there in 1902, but the game proved only a temporary craze until resuscitated in 1921.

Fastest Rallying. The record number of returns in 60 seconds is 159 by Nicky Jarvis and Jim Walker at Barrow-in-Furness, England, on October 24, 1975.

Marathon Records. In the Swaythling Cup final match between Austria and Rumania in Prague, Czechoslovakia, in 1936, the play lasted for 25 or 26 hours, spread over three nights. In this same 1936 tournament, Alex Ehrlich (Poland) and Paneth Farcas (Rumania) had an opening rally that lasted 2 hours 12 minutes. On April 14, 1973, Nick Krajancie and Graham Lassen *staged* a 2 hour 31 minute rally in Auckland, New Zealand.

The longest recorded time for a marathon singles match by two players is 100 hours 30 minutes by M. Rowe and N. Franklyn of the Lindisfarne T.T.C., Westcliff-on-Sea, Essex, England, October 30–November 2, 1975. David Thoman of Blue Springs, Nebraska, played a series of opponents for 105 hours, August 19–23, 1974.

The longest doubles marathon by 4 players is 72 hours 15 minutes by players from the Lindisfarne T.T.C., Essex, England, October 30–November 2, 1975.

The longest recorded marathon by 4 players maintaining continuous singles is 682 hours by players from the Lindisfarne T.T.C., Essex, England, October 11–November 8, 1975.

Highest Speed. No conclusive measurements have been published, but in a lecture M. Sklorz (W. Germany) stated that a smashed ball had been measured at speeds up to 105.6 m.p.h.

Youngest International. The youngest international (probably in any sport) was Joy Foster, aged 8, the 1958 Jamaican singles and mixed doubles champion.

Most Wins in Table Tennis World Championships
(Instituted 1926–27)

Event	Name and Nationality	Times	Date
Men's Singles (St. Bride's Vase)	G. Viktor Barna (Hungary)	5	1930, 32, 33, 34, 35
Women's Singles (G. Geist Prize)	Angelica Rozeanu (Rumania)	6	1950, 51, 52, 53, 54, 55
Men's Doubles	G. Viktor Barna (Hungary) with two different partners	8	1929, 30, 31, 32, 33, 34, 35, 39
Women's Doubles	Maria Mednyanszky (Hungary) with three different partners	7	1928, 30, 31, 32, 33, 34, 35
Mixed Doubles (Men)	Ferenc Sido (Hungary) with two different partners	4	1949, 50, 52, 53
(Women)	M. Mednyanszky (Hungary) with three different partners	6	1927, 28, 30, 31, 33, 34

G. Viktor Barna gained a personal total of 15 world titles, while 18 have been won by Miss Mednyanszky.

Note: With the staging of championships biennially, the breaking of the above records would now be virtually impossible.

Men's Team (Swaythling Cup)	Hungary	11	1927, 28, 29, 30, 31, 33, 34, 35, 38, 49, 52
Women's Team (Marcel Corbillon Cup)	Japan	8	1952, 1954, 1957, 1959, 1961, 1963, 1967, 1971

Tennis

Origins. The modern game of lawn tennis is generally agreed to have evolved as an outdoor form of Royal Tennis, and to have first become organized with the court and equipment devised, and patented in February, 1874, by Major Walter Clopton Wingfield, of England (1833–1912). This was introduced as "sphairistike," but the game soon became known as lawn tennis.

Amateurs were permitted to play with and against professionals in Open tournaments starting in 1968.

Oldest Courts. The oldest court for Royal Tennis is one built in Paris in 1496. The oldest of 16 surviving tennis courts in the British Isles is the Royal Tennis Court at Hampton Court Palace, which was built by order of King Henry VIII in 1529–30, and rebuilt by order of Charles II in 1660.

Greatest Crowd. The greatest crowd at a tennis match was the 30,472 who came to the Houston Astrodome in Houston, Texas, on September 20, 1973, to watch Billie Jean King beat Bobby Riggs, over 25 years her senior, in straight sets in the so-called "Tennis Match of the Century."

The record for an orthodox match is 25,578 at Sydney, Australia, on December 27, 1954, in the Davis Cup Challenge Round vs. the U.S. (1st day).

Davis Cup

Most Victories. The greatest number of wins in the Davis Cup (instituted 1900) has been (inclusive of 1975) the United States with 24 over Australia's 23 wins.

Individual Performance. Nicola Pietrangeli (Italy) played 164 rubbers, 1954 to 1972, winning 120. He played 110 singles (winning 78) and 54 doubles (winning 42). He took part in 66 ties.

Greatest Domination. The earliest occasion upon which any player secured all four of the world's major titles was in 1935 when Frederick John Perry (U.K.) (b. 1909) won the French title, having won Wimbledon (1934), the U.S. title (1933–34) and the Australian title (1934).

GRAND SLAM WINNERS: The only men to win all four major titles in the same year were Rod Laver (left) of Australia who performed the feat twice in 1962 and 1969, and Don Budge (right) of the U.S. who did it once in 1937-38.

WOMEN'S GRAND SLAM: Margaret Smith Court (Australia) won all four major tournaments in 1970.

The first player to hold all four titles simultaneously was J. Donald Budge (U.S.) (b. 1915), who won the championships of Wimbledon (1937), the U.S. (1937), Australia (1938), and France (1938). He subsequently retained Wimbledon (1938) and the U.S. (1938). Rodney George Laver (Australia) (b. August 9, 1938) achieved this grand slam in 1962 as an amateur and repeated as a professional in 1969 to become the first two-time grand slammer.

Two women players also have won all these four titles in the same tennis year. The first was Maureen Catherine Connolly (U.S.). She won the United States title in 1951, Wimbledon in 1952, retained the U.S. title in 1952, won the Australian in 1953, the French in 1953 and Wimbledon again in 1953. She won her third U.S. title in 1953, her second French title in 1954, and her third Wimbledon title in 1954. Miss Connolly (later Mrs. Norman Brinker) was seriously injured in a riding accident shortly before the 1954 U.S. championships; she died in June, 1969, aged only 34.

The second woman to win the "grand slam" was Margaret Smith Court (Australia) (b. July 16, 1942) in 1970. (See photo above).

Wimbledon Records

(The first Championship was in 1877. Professionals first played in 1968.) From 1971 the tie-break system was introduced, which effactully prevents sets proceeding beyond a 17th game, i.e. 9–8.

Most Appearances. Arthur W. Gore (1868–1928) of the U.K. made 36 appearances between 1888 and 1927, and was in 1909 at 41 years the oldest singles winner ever. In 1964, Jean Borotra (born August 13, 1898) of France made his 35th appearance since 1922. In 1975, he appeared in the Veterans' Doubles, aged 76.

MOST GAMES AND LONGEST MATCHES

Note: The increasing option since 1970 by tournament organizers to use various "tie-break" systems, which are precisely designed to stop long sets, is reducing the likelihood of these records being broken and they may shortly become of mere historic interest.

	No. of Games	Players and score	Place and Date
Any match	147	Dick Leach–Dick Dell (U. of Mich.) bt. Tommy Mozur–Lenny Schloss 3–6, 49–47, 22–20	Newport, R.I., August 18–19, 1967
Any singles	126	Roger Taylor (G.B.) bt. Wieslaw Gasiorek (Poland) 27–29, 31–29, 6–4 (4 hrs. 35 mins.)	King's Cup, Warsaw, Poland, November 5, 1966
Any women's singles	62	Kathy Blake (U.S.) bt. Elena Subirats (Mexico) 12–10, 6–8, 14–12	Piping Rock, Locust Valley, N.Y., 1966
Any women's match	81	Nancy Richey–Carole Graebner (née Caldwell) bt. Justina Bricka–Carol Hanks (all U.S.) 31–33, 6–1, 6–4	South Orange, N.J., 1964
Any mixed doubles	71	William F. Talbot–Margaret du Pont (née Osborne) bt. Robert Falkenburg–Gertrude Moran (all U.S.) 27–25, 5–7; 6–1	Forest Hills, N.Y., 1948
Any set	96	See middle set of any match above	
Longest time for any match	6 hrs. 23 mins.	Mark Cox–Robert K. Wilson (U.K.) bt. Charles M. Pasarell–Ron E. Holmburg (U.S.) 26–24, 17–19, 30–28	U.S. Indoor Championships, Salisbury, Md., August 18–19, 1967
Any Wimbledon match	112	R. A. (Pancho) Gonzales (U.S.) bt. Charles M. Pasarell (U.S.) 22–24, 1–6, 16–14, 6–3, 11–9	First round, June 24–25, 1969
Any Wimbledon doubles	98	Eugene L. Scott (U.S.)–Nicola Pilic (Yugoslavia) bt. G. Cliff Richey (U.S.)–Torben Ulrich (Denmark) 19–21, 12–10, 6–4, 4–6, 9–7	First round, June 22, 1966
Any Wimbledon set	62	Pancho Segura (Ecuador)–Alex Olmedo (Peru) bt. Abe A. Segal–Gordon L. Forbes (S. Africa) 32–30	Second round, June 1968
Longest time for any Wimbledon match	5 hrs. 12 mins.	See any Wimbledon match above	
Wimbledon men's final	58	Jaroslav Drobny (then Egypt) bt. Kenneth R. Rosewall (Australia) 13–11, 4–6, 6–2, 9–7	Final, July 1954
Wimbledon men's doubles final	70	John D. Newcombe–Anthony D. Roche (Australia) bt. Kenneth R. Rosewall–Frederick S. Stolle (Australia) 3–6, 8–6, 5–7, 14–12, 6–3	Final, July 1968
Wimbledon women's final	46	Margaret Smith Court (Australia) bt. Billie Jean Moffitt King (U.S.) 14–12, 11–9 (2 hrs. 25 mins.)	Final, July 1970
Wimbledon women's doubles final	38	Mme. Simone Mathieu (France)–Elizabeth Ryan (U.S.) bt. Freda James (now Hammersley)–Adeline Maud Yorke (both G.B.) 6–2, 9–11, 6–4	Final, July 1933
		Rosemary Casals–Billie Jean King (both U.S.) bt. Maria E. Bueno (Brazil)–Nancy Richey (U.S.) 9–11, 6–4, 6–2	Final, July 1963

MOST GAMES AND LONGEST MATCHES (continued)

Wimbledon mixed doubles final	48	Eric W. Sturgess–Mrs. Sheila Summers (S. Africa) bt. John E. Bromwich (Australia)–Alice Louise Brough (U.S.) 9–7, 9–11, 7–5	Final, July 1949
Any Davis Cup rubber	122	Stanley Smith–Erik Von Dillen (U.S.) bt. Jaime Fillol–Pat Cornejo (Chile) 7–9, 37–39, 8–6, 6–1, 6–3	American Zone Tie, 1973
Any Davis Cup singles	86	Arthur Ashe (U.S.) bt. Christian Kuhnke (Germany) 6–8, 10–12, 9–7, 13–11, 6–4	Challenge Round, Cleveland, O. 1970
Any Davis Cup tie i.e. 5 rubbers	327	India bt. Australia 3–2	East Zone Final, Calcutta, May 10–14, 1974

LONGEST WIMBLEDON MATCH: Pancho Gonzales (U.S.) played 112 games in 5 hours 12 minutes in 1969, and finally beat Charles Pasarell (U.S.).

YOUNGEST WIMBLEDON CHAMPION: When Dennis Ralston won the men's doubles title with Rafael Osuna in 1960, he was only 17 years old.

WIMBLEDON CHAMPION Billie Jean King (U.S.) in her moment of victory.
She has won a total of 19 titles.

Most Wins. Elizabeth (Bunny) Ryan (U.S.) (b. 1894) won her
first title in 1914 and her nineteenth in 1934 (12 women's doubles
with 5 different partners and 7 mixed doubles with 5 different
partners). Her total of 19 championships was equaled by Billie Jean
King (*née* Moffitt) (U.S.) with 6 singles, 9 women's doubles, and
4 mixed doubles, 1961–75.

The greatest number of singles wins was eight by Mrs. F. S. Moody
(*née* Helen Wills) (b. October 6, 1905) (U.S.), who won in 1927,
1928, 1929, 1930, 1932, 1933, 1935 and 1938.

The greatest number of singles wins by a man was seven by
William C. Renshaw in 1881–2–3–4–5–6–9. He also won 7 doubles
titles (1880–1–4–5–6–8–9) partnered by his twin brother (James)
Ernest. His total of 14 titles is also a men's record.

The greatest number of doubles wins by men was 8 by the
brothers Doherty (G.B.)—Reginald Frank (1872–1910) and Hugh
Lawrence (1875–1919). They won each year from 1897 to 1905
except for 1902.

The most wins in women's doubles were the 12 by Elizabeth
Ryan (U.S.), mentioned above.

The greatest number of mixed doubles wins was 7 by Elizabeth
Ryan (U.S.), as noted before. The men's record is four wins, shared
by Elias Victor Seixas (b. August 30, 1923) (U.S.) in 1953–54–55–56,
and Kenneth N. Fletcher (b. June 15, 1940) (Australia) in 1963–65–
66–68.

Youngest Champions. The youngest champion ever at Wimbledon was Charlotte Dod (1871–1960), who was 15 years 8 months
old when she won in 1887.

The youngest male singles champion was Wilfred Baddeley (born January 11, 1872), who won the Wimbledon title in 1891 at the age of 19.

Richard Dennis Ralston (born July 27, 1942), of Bakersfield, California, was 25 days short of his 18th birthday when he won the men's doubles with Rafael H. Osuna (1938–69), of Mexico, in 1960. (See photo on page 639.)

Greatest Attendance. The record crowd for one day at Wimbledon is 37,290 on June 27, 1975. The total attendance record was set at the 1975 Championships with 338,591.

Professional Tennis

Highest Prize Money. The greatest reward for playing a single match is the $500,000 won by Jimmy Connors (U.S.) (born September 2, 1952) when he beat John Newcombe (Australia) (born May 23, 1944) in a challenge match at Caesars Palace, Las Vegas, Nevada, April 26, 1975.

Tennis Marathons

The longest doubles is one of 72 hours by 4 players from Shu Lin Kou Air Station (U.S.A.F.), Taiwan, March 11–14, 1976.

The duration record for singles is 76 hours 10 minutes by Joseph Grzych and Kenneth Ross at Bogan Park, Chicago, Illinois, October 10–13, 1975. Douglas Clark of Kingsgate Racket Club, Kings Mills, Ohio, played singles against a number of opponents for 83 hours, December 20–24, 1975.

Fastest Service. The fastest service ever *measured* was one of 154 m.p.h. by Michael Sangster (U.K.) in June, 1963. Crossing the net the ball was traveling at 108 m.p.h. Some players consider the service of Robert Falkenberg (U.S.), the 1948 Wimbledon champion, as the fastest ever produced.

Longest Career. The championship career of C. Alphonso Smith (born March 18, 1909) of Charlottesville, Virginia, extended from winning the U.S. National Boy's title at Chicago on August 14, 1924, to winning the National 65-and-over title at Aptos, California (exactly 50 years to the day later) on August 14, 1974.

Track and Field

Earliest References. Track and field athletics date from the ancient Olympic Games. The earliest accurately known Olympiad dates from July 21 or 22, 776 B.C., at which celebration Coroibos won the foot race. The oldest surviving measurements are a long jump of 23 feet 1½ inches by Chionis of Sparta in *c.* 656 B.C. and a discus throw of 100 cubits (*c.* 152 feet) by Protesilaus.

Fastest Runners. Robert Lee Hayes (born December 20, 1942), of Jacksonville, Florida, was timed between the 60- and the 75-yard marks at St. Louis, on June 21, 1963, at 27.89 m.p.h. in his world record 9.1 sec. 100 yards. Wyomia Tyus (U.S.) was timed at 23.78 m.p.h. in Kiev, U.S.S.R., on July 31, 1965.

Earliest Landmarks. The first time 10 seconds ("even time") was bettered for 100 yards under championship conditions was when John Owen recorded 9⅘ seconds in the A.A.U. Championships at Analostan Island, Washington, D.C., on October 11, 1890. The first recorded instance of 6 feet being cleared in the high jump was when Marshall Jones Brooks jumped 6 feet 0⅛ inch at Marston, near Oxford, England, on March 17, 1876. The breaking of the "4 minute barrier" in the one mile was first achieved by Dr. Roger Gilbert Bannister (born Harrow, England, March 23, 1929), when he recorded 3 minutes 59.4 seconds on the Iffley Road track, Oxford, at 6:10 p.m. on May 6, 1954.

Cross-Country. The earliest recorded international cross-country race took place over 9 miles 18 yards from Ville d'Avray, outside Paris, on March 20, 1898, between France and England. England won.

The largest recorded field was one of 1,815 starters (1,020 completed the course) at Gosforth Park, Newcastle, England, in the summer of 1916.

World Record Breakers

Oldest. The greatest age at which anyone has broken a standard world record is 35 years 255 days in the case of Dana Zátopkova, (*née* Ingrova) (born September 19, 1922), of Czechoslovakia, who broke the women's javelin record with 182 feet 10 inches at Prague, Czechoslovakia, on June 1, 1958.

On June 20, 1948, Mikko Hietanen (Finland) (born September 22, 1911) bettered his own world 30,000-meter record with 1 hour 40 minutes 46.4 secs. at Jyväskylä, Finland, when aged 36 years 272 days.

Youngest. Ulrike Mayforth (b. May 4, 1956) (W. Germany) equaled the world record for the women's high jump at 6 feet 3½ inches at the Munich Olympics, 1972, aged 16 years 4 months.

Most Records in a Day. The only athlete to have his name entered in the record book 6 times in one day was J. C. "Jesse" Owens (U.S.) who at Ann Arbor, Michigan, on May 25, 1935, equaled the 100-yard running record with 9.4 secs. at 3:15 p.m.; long-jumped 26 feet 8¼ inches at 3:25 p.m.; ran 220 yards (straight away) in 20.3 secs. at 3:45 p.m.; and 220 yards over low hurdles in 22.6 secs. at 4 p.m. The two 220-yard runs were also ratified as 200-meter world records.

Running Backwards. The fastest time recorded for running 100 yards backwards is 13.5 secs. by the tap dancer, Bill Robinson (1878–1949), in the U.S. early in the century.

Three-Legged Race. The fastest recorded time for a 100-yard three-legged race is 11.0 seconds by Harry L. Hillman and Lawson Robertson at Brooklyn, New York City, on April 24, 1909.

Ambidextrous Shot Put. Allan Feuerbach (U.S.) has put a 16-lb. shot a total of 121 feet 6¾ inches (51 feet 5 inches with his left hand and 70 feet 1¾ inches with his right) at Malmö, Sweden, in 1974.

SIX TIMES IN ONE
DAY: Jesse Owens
(U.S.) broke six world
records on May 25, 1935.

Standing Long Jump. Joe Darby (1861–1937), the famous
Victorian professional jumper from Dudley, Worcestershire,
England, jumped a measured 12 feet 1½ inches *without* weights at
Dudley Castle, on May 28, 1890. Johan Christian Evandt (Norway)
achieved 11 feet 11¾ inches as an amateur in Reykjavik, Iceland, on
March 11, 1962.

Standing High Jump. The best amateur standing high jump is
5 feet 10½ inches by Rune Almen (Sweden) at Örebro, Sweden, on
December 8, 1974. Joe Darby (see above), the professional, reportedly cleared 6 feet with his ankles tied at Church Cricket
Ground, Dudley, England, on June 11, 1892.

Highest Jumper. There are several reported instances of high
jumpers exceeding the official world record height of 7 feet 7¼ inches.
The earliest of these came from unsubstantiated reports of Watusi
tribesmen in Central Africa clearing up to 8 feet 2½ inches, definitely
however, from inclined take-offs. The greatest height cleared above
an athlete's own head is 20¼ inches by Ron Livers (U.S.), who
cleared 7 feet 4¼ inches despite a physical height of only 5 feet 8 inches
at Provo, Utah, on July 23, 1975.

The greatest height cleared by a woman above her own head is
8¼ inches by Rosemarie Witschas (now Ackermann) (East
Germany) who stood 5 feet 8¾ inches when she jumped 6 feet 5
inches at Dresden, East Germany, on May 8, 1976.

Longest Career. Duncan McLean (born Gourock, Scotland,
December 3, 1884) won the South African 100-yard title in February,
1904, in 9.9 seconds, and was fifth in a heat in 13.2 seconds in the
Veterans' 100-meter handicap at Hurlingham, London, England, on
September 7, 1974—more than 70 years later.

Blind 100 Meters. The fastest time recorded for 100 meters by a
blind man is 11.5 seconds by Kozuck, a Polish runner, in 1976.

WORLD RECORDS—MEN

The complete list of World Records for the 54 scheduled men's events (excluding the 6 walking records, see under Walking) passed by the International Amateur Athletic Federation as of August 1, 1976. Those marked with an asterisk* are awaiting ratification. Note: On July 27, 1976, I.A.A.F. eliminated all records for races measured in yards, except for the mile (for sentimental reasons). All distances up to (and including) 400 meters must be professionally timed to be records. When a time is given to one-hundredth of a second, it represents the official electrically timed record. In two cases, performances have bettered or equaled the I.A.A.F. mark, but the same highly rigorous rules as to timing, measuring and weighing are not necessarily applied.

RUNNING

Event	min. secs.	Name and Nationality	Place	Date
100 yards	9.0	Ivory Crockett (U.S.)	Knoxville, Tennessee	May 11, 1974
	9.0	Houston McTear (U.S.)	Long Beach, California	May 4, 1975
220 yards (straight)	19.5	Tommie C. Smith (U.S.)	San Jose, California	May 7, 1966
220 yards (turn)	19.9	Donald O'Riley Quarrie (Jamaica)	Eugene, Oregon	June 7, 1975
	19.9	Steve Williams (U.S.)	Eugene, Oregon	June 7, 1975
440 yards	44.5	John Smith (U.S.)	Eugene, Oregon	June 26, 1971
880 yards	1:44.1	Richard Wohlhuter (U.S.)	Eugene, Oregon	June 8, 1974
1 mile	3:49.4	John Walker (N.Z.)	Gothenburg, Sweden	Aug. 12, 1975
2 miles	8:13.8	Brendan Foster (U.K.)	London, England	Aug. 27, 1973
3 miles	12:47.8	Emiel Puttemans (Belgium)	Brussels, Belgium	Sept. 20, 1972
6 miles	26:47.0	Ronald William Clarke (Australia)	Oslo, Norway	July 14, 1965
10 miles	45:57.2	Jos Hermens (Netherlands)	Papendal, Netherlands	Oct. 13, 1975
15 miles	1H 11:52.6	Pekka Paivarinta (Finland)	Oulu, Finland	May 15, 1975
100 meters	9.96	James Ray Hines (U.S.)	Mexico City, Mexico	Oct. 14, 1968
200 meters (straight)	19.5	Tommie C. Smith (U.S.)	San Jose (U.S.)	May 7, 1966
200 meters (turn)	19.81	Donald O'Riley Quarrie (Jamaica)	Cali, Colombia	Aug. 3, 1971
400 meters	43.86	Lee Edward Evans (U.S.)	Mexico City, Mexico	Oct. 18, 1968
800 meters	1:43.50	Alberto Juantareno (Cuba)	Montreal, Canada	July 25, 1976
1,000 meters	2:13.9	Richard Wohlhuter (U.S.)	Oslo, Norway	July 30, 1974

FASTEST HUMANS EVER: Tommie Smith (U.S.) (left) holds world records at 220 yards and 200 metres. James Ray Hines (U.S.) (right) has run 100 metres in 9.96 seconds.

SURPRISE RECORDBREAKER: Alberto Juantareno of Cuba (left) came out of the field in the 1976 Olympics, won 2 gold medals, and set a new world record for 800 meters.

WORLD RECORDS—MEN (Continued)

RUNNING (continued)

Event	mins. secs.	Name and Nationality	Place	Date
1,500 meters	3:32.2	Filbert Bayi (Tanzania)	Christchurch, New Zealand	Feb. 2, 1974
2,000 meters	4:51.4*	John Walker (N.Z.)	Oslo, Norway	June 30, 1976
3,000 meters	7:35.2	Brendan Foster (G.B.)	Gateshead, England	Aug. 3, 1974
5,000 meters	13:13.0	Emiel Puttemans (Belgium)	Brussels, Belgium	Sept. 20, 1972
10,000 meters	27:30.8	David Colin Bedford (U.K.)	London, England	July 13, 1973
20,000 meters	57:24.2	Jos Hermens (Netherlands)	Papendal, Netherlands	May 1, 1976
25,000 meters	1H 14:16.8	Pekka Paivarinta (Finland)	Oulu, Finland	May 15, 1975
30,000 meters	1H 31:30.4	James Noel Carroll Alder (U.K.)	Crystal Palace, London	Sept. 5, 1970
1 hour	13 miles 24⅓ yards	Jos Hermens (Netherlands)	Papendal, Netherlands	May 1, 1976

HURDLING

Event	mins. secs.	Name and Nationality	Place	Date
120 yards (3' 6" hurdles)	13.0	Rodney Milburn (U.S.)	Eugene, Oregon	June 25, 1971
	13.0	Rodney Milburn (U.S.)	Eugene, Oregon	June 20, 1973
	13.0	Guy Drut (France)	Berlin, West Germany	Aug. 22, 1975
220 yards (2' 6") (straight)	21.9	Donald Augustus Styron (U.S.)	Baton Rouge, Louisiana	Apr. 2, 1960
440 yards (3' 0")	48.7	James Bolding (U.S.)	Turin, Italy	July 24, 1974
110 meters (3' 6")	13.24	Rodney Milburn (U.S.)	Munich, West Germany	Sept. 7, 1972
200 meters (2' 6") (straight)	21.9	Donald Augustus Styron (U.S.)	Baton Rouge, Louisiana	Apr. 2, 1960
200 meters (2' 6") (turn)	22.5	Karl Martin Lauer (West Germany)	Zurich, Switzerland	July 7, 1959
	22.5	Glenn Ashby Davis (U.S.)	Bern, Switzerland	Aug. 20, 1960
400 meters (3' 0")	47.64	Edwin Moses (U.S.)	Montreal, Canada	July 25, 1976
3,000 meters Steeplechase	8:08.0	Anders Garderud (Sweden)	Montreal, Canada	July 28, 1976

5,000-METER CHAMPION (left): Emiel Puttemans of Belgium ran this distance in 13 minutes 13 seconds. FASTEST 1,500 METERS (right): Filbert Bayi (Tanzania) (#613) on his way to his record time of 3 minutes 32.2 seconds. John Walker of New Zealand (#483), who came in second, also bettered the previous record time and, in 1975, set a new world record for the mile run.

Longest Race. The longest race ever staged was the 1929 Transcontinental Race (3,665 miles) from New York City to Los Angeles. The Finnish-born Johnny Salo (killed October 6, 1931) was the winner in 79 days, from March 31 to June 17. His elapsed time of 525 hours 57 minutes 20 seconds gave a running average of 6.97 m.p.h.

The United States "go as you please" (running or walking) record is 53 days 7 hours 45 minutes from New York to Los Angeles by E. Gordon Brooks, 28, from June 21 to August 13, 1974.

HURDLING RECORD HOLDER at 120 yards and 110 meters is Rodney Milburn (U.S.) (center).

WORLD RECORDS—MEN (Continued)

FIELD EVENTS

Event	ft.	ins.	Name and Nationality	Place	Date
High Jump	7	7¼	Dwight Stones (U.S.)	Philadelphia, Pa.	Aug. 4, 1976
Pole Vault	18	8¼	David Roberts (U.S.)	Eugene, Oregon.	June 23, 1976
Long Jump	29	2½	Robert Beamon (U.S.)	Mexico City, Mexico.	Oct. 18, 1968
Triple Jump	58	8¼	Joao Oliveira (Brazil)	Mexico City, Mexico.	Oct. 15, 1975
Shot Put	72	2½	Aleksandr Baryshnikov (U.S.S.R.)	Paris, France	July 11, 1976
Discus Throw	232	6	Mac Wilkins (U.S.)	San Jose, California	May 1, 1976
Hammer Throw	260	2	Walter Schmidt (West Germany)	Frankfurt, West Germany	Aug. 14, 1975
Javelin Throw	310	4	Miklos Nemeth (Hungary)	Montreal, Canada	July 26, 1976

Note: The two professional performances which were equal or superior to the I.A.A.F. marks, but where the same highly rigorous rules as to timing, measuring and weighing were not necessarily applied, were the 120-yards hurdles in 13.0 secs. by Rodney Milburn (U.S.) and the Shot Put of 75 feet by Brian Ray Oldfield (U.S.), both at El Paso, Texas, on May 10, 1975.

RELAYS

Event	min. secs.	Team	Place	Date
4×110 yards (two turns)	38.6	University of Southern California (U.S.) (Earl Ray McCullouch, Fred Kuller, Orenthal James Simpson, Lennox Miller (Jamaica))	Provo, Utah	June 17, 1967
4×220 yards	1:21.7†	Texas Agricultural and Mechanical College (U.S.) (James Donald Rogers, Herbert Woods, Marvin Mills, Curtis Mills)	Des Moines, Iowa	Apr. 24, 1970
	1:21.7	University of Tennessee (U.S.) (Lamar Preyor, Ronnie Harris, Jerome Morgan, Reggie Jones)	Knoxville, Tennessee	Apr. 10, 1976
4×440 yards	3:02.4	U.S. National Team (Ronald Ray, Robert Taylor, Maurice Peoples, Stan Vinson)	Durham, N. Carolina	July 19, 1975
4×880 yards	7:10.4	University of Chicago Track Club (U.S.) (Tom Bach, Ken Sparks, Lowell Paul, Richard Wohlhuter)	Durham, N. Carolina	May 12, 1973
4×1 mile	16:02.8	New Zealand (Kevin Ross, Anthony Polhill, Richard Taylor, T. J. L. Quax)	Auckland, N.Z.	Feb. 3, 1972

† The time of 1:20.7 achieved by the University of Southern California team (Edesel Garrison, Lee Brown, William Deckard and Donald O'Riley Quarrie) at Fresno, California, on May 13, 1972, is not eligible because Quarrie is a Jamaican national, but this rule was not applied in the case of Miller in the 4×110.

HIGH JUMPER: Using his version of the Fosbury Flop, Dwight Stones of the United States leaped 7 feet 7¼ inches in Philadelphia in August, 1976.

GREATEST JUMP: Bob Beamon (U.S.) startled everyone when he exceeded the previous record long (broad) jump by 2 feet. No one has come close to his 29 feet 2½ inches, set in 1968.

WORLD RECORDS—MEN (Continued)

RELAYS (continued)

Event	mins. secs.	Team	Place	Date
4×100 meters	38.19	United States Olympic Team (Larry Black, Robert Taylor, Gerald Tinker, Eddie Hart)	Munich, West Germany	Sept. 10, 1972
4×200 meters	1:21.5	Italian Team (Franco Ossala, Pasqualino Abeti, Luigi Benedetti, Pietro Mennea)	Barletta, Italy	July 21, 1972
	1:21.5	University of Tennessee (U.S.) (Lamar Preyor, Ronnie Harris, Jerome Morgan, Reggie Jones)	Philadelphia, Pa.	Apr. 24, 1976
4×400 meters	2:56.1	United States Olympic Team (Vincent Matthews, Ronald Freeman, G. Lawrence James, Lee Edward Evans)	Mexico City, Mexico	Oct. 20, 1968
4×800 meters	7:08.6	West Germany "A" Team (Manfred Kinder, Walter Adams, Dieter Bogatzki, Franz-Josef Kemper)	Weisbaden, West Germany	Aug. 13, 1966
4×1,500 meters	14:40.4	New Zealand (Anthony Polhill, John Walker, Rodney Dixon, T. J. L. Quax)	Oslo, Norway	Aug. 22, 1973

DECATHLON

8,618 points		Bruce Jenner (U.S.)	Montreal, Canada	July 19–20, 1976

THE MARATHON

There is no official marathon record because of the varying severity of courses. The best time over 26 miles 385 yards (standardized in 1924) is 2 hours 08 minutes 33.6 seconds (av. 12.24 m.p.h.) by Derek Clayton (b. 1942 at Barrow-in-Furness, England) of Australia, at Antwerp, Belgium, on May 30, 1969.

The fastest time by a female is 2 hours 38 minutes 19 seconds (av. 9.93 m.p.h.) by Jackie Hansen (U.S.) at Eugene, Oregon, on October 12, 1975.

DECATHLON CHAMPION: Bruce Jenner (U.S.) won the gold medal in Montreal by giving the best all-around performance of all time.

Endurance. Mensen Ernst (1799–1846), of Norway, is reputed to have run from Istanbul, Turkey, to Calcutta, in West Bengal, India, and back in 59 days in 1836, so averaging an improbable 94.2 miles per day. The greatest non-stop run recorded is 131 miles 440 yards in 22 hours 20 minutes by Max Telford (b. Scotland, 1935) of New Zealand, September 2–3, 1975.

The 24-hour running record is 161 miles 545 yards by Ron Bentley, 43, at Walton-on-Thames, Surrey, England, November 3–4, 1973.

The fastest recorded time for 100 miles is 11 hours 27 minutes 58 seconds by Richard A. Rose of Granite City, Illinois, on May 30, 1976.

The greatest distance covered by a man in six days (*i.e.* the 144 permissible hours between Sundays in Victorian times) was 623¾ miles by George Littlewood (England), who required only 139 hours 1 min. for this feat in December, 1888, at the old Madison Square Garden, New York City.

The greatest lifetime mileage recorded by any runner is 184,202 miles by Earle Littlewood Dilks (b. 1884) of New Castle, Pennsylvania, through 1975.

Most Olympic Gold Medals. The most Olympic gold medals won is 10 (an absolute Olympic record) by Ray C. Ewry (U.S.) (b. October 14, 1873, d. September 29, 1937) with:

Standing High Jump	1900, 1904, 1906, 1908
Standing Long Jump	1900, 1904, 1906, 1908
Standing Triple Jump	1900, 1904

The most gold medals won by a woman is 4, a record shared by Francina E. Blankers-Koen (Netherlands) (b. April 26, 1918) with 100 m., 200 m., 80 m. hurdles and 4×100 m. relay (1948) and

WORLD RECORDS—WOMEN

RUNNING

Event	mins.secs.	Name and Nationality	Place	Date
100 yards	10.0	Chi Cheng (Republic of China)	Portland, Oregon	June 13, 1970
220 yards (turn)	22.6	Chi Cheng (Republic of China)	Los Angeles, California	July 3, 1970
440 yards	52.2	Kathy Hammond (U.S.)	Urbana, Illinois	Aug. 12, 1972
	52.2	Debra Sapenter (U.S.)	Bakersfield, California	June 29, 1974
880 yards	2:02.0	Dixie Willis (Australia)	Perth, Australia	Mar. 3, 1962
	2:02.0	Judith Florence Pollock (née Amoore) (Australia)	Helsinki, Finland	June 28, 1967
1 mile	4:29.5	Paola Cacchi (née Pigni) (Italy)	Viareggio, Italy	Aug. 8, 1973
60 meters	7.2	Betty Cuthbert (Australia)	Sydney, N.S.W., Australia	Feb. 21, 1960
	7.2	Irina Robertovna Bochkaryova (née Turova) (U.S.S.R.)	Moscow, U.S.S.R.	Aug. 28, 1960
	7.2	Andrea Lynch (U.K.)	London, England	June 22, 1974
	7.2*	Lea Alaerts (Belgium)	Namour, Belgium	Aug. 2, 1975
	7.2*	Denise Robertson (Australia)	Melbourne, Australia	Dec. 16, 1975
100 meters	11.01	Annegret Richter (West Germany)	Montreal, Canada	July 25, 1976
200 meters (turn)	22.21	Irena Szewinska (née Kirszenstein) (Poland)	Potsdam, Poland	June 13, 1974
400 meters	49.29	Irena Szewinska (née Kirszenstein) (Poland)	Montreal, Canada	July 29, 1976
800 meters	1:54.9	Tatyana Kazankina (U.S.S.R.)	Montreal, Canada	July 26, 1976
1,500 meters	3:56.0*	Tatyana Kazankina (U.S.S.R.)	Podolsk, U.S.S.R.	June 28, 1976
3,000 meters	8:27.1	Lyudmila Bragina (U.S.S.R.)	College Park, Maryland	Aug. 7, 1976

HURDLES

Event	mins.secs.	Name and Nationality	Place	Date
100 meters	12.59	Annelie Ehrhardt (East Germany)	Munich, West Germany	Sept. 8, 1972
400 meters (2' 6")	56.51	Krystyna Kacperczyk (Poland)	Augsburg, West Germany	July 13, 1974

FIELD EVENTS

Event	ft.	ins.	Name and Nationality	Place	Date
High Jump	6	5	Rosemarie Ackermann (née Witschas) (East Germany)	Dresden, East Germany	May 8, 1976
Long Jump	22	11¼	Sigrun Siegl (née Thon) (East Germany)	Dresden, East Germany	May 20, 1976
Shot Put	71	10	Ivanka Khristova (Bulgaria)	Belmeken, Bulgaria	July 4, 1976
Discus Throw	231	3	Faina Melnik (U.S.S.R.)	Sochi, U.S.S.R.	Apr. 24, 1976
Javelin Throw	226	9	Ruth Fuchs (née Gamm) (East Germany)	East Berlin, E. Germany	July 11, 1976

200 AND 400 METER CHAMPION: Irena Szewinska of Poland has hit her top form at the age of 30.

JAVELIN THROW: Ruth Fuchs (East Germany) repeated her 1972 gold medal performance in Montreal in 1976. She also holds the world record throw of 226 feet 9 inches.

WORLD RECORDS—WOMEN (Continued)

PENTATHLON

		Place	Date
4,932 points	Burglinde Pollak (East Germany) (100 meter hurdles, 13.21 sec.; shot, 52 ft.; high jump, 5 ft. 10 in.; long jump, 21 ft. 2¼ in.; 200-meter dash, 23.35 sec.)	Bonn, West Germany	Sept. 22, 1973

RELAYS

Event	mins. secs.	Team	Place	Date
4×110 yards	44.07	West German National Team (Inge Helten, Birgit Wilkes, Annegret Kroniger, Maren Gang)	Durham, N. Carolina	July 18, 1975
4×220 yards	1:35.8	Australia (Marian R. Hoffman, Raelene Boyle, Pamela Kilborn, Jennifer F. Lamy)	Brisbane, Australia	Nov. 9, 1969
4×440 yards	3:30.3	West German National Team (Christiane Krause, Dagmar Jost-Fuhrmann, Erika Weinstein, Elke Barth)	Durham, N. Carolina	July 19, 1975
4×100 meters	42.50*	East Germany (Marlies Oelsner, Renate Stecher, Carla Bodendorf, Martina Blos)	Karl Marx Stadt, E. Ger.	May 29, 1976
4×200 meters	1:33.8†	United Kingdom National Team (Maureen Dorothy Tranter, Della P. James, Janet Mary Simpson, Valerie Peat (née Wild))	London, England	Aug. 24, 1968
4×400 meters	3:19.2	East German National Team (Doris Maletski, Brigitte Rohde, Eilen Streidt, Christina Bremer)	Montreal, Canada	July 31, 1976
4×800 meters	8:05.2	Bulgarian National Team (Nikolina Chtereva, Lilyana Tomova, Rosita Peckhlivanova, Sveta Zlateva)	Sofia, Bulgaria	Aug. 30, 1975

† The time of 1:32.6 achieved by the Australian team of Denise Robertson, Raelene Boyle, Barbara Jordan-Wilson and Susan Jowett at Brisbane, Australia, on January 26, 1976, was not ratified as Jowett is a citizen of New Zealand.

WOMEN'S 100 METER HURDLING CHAMPION: Annelie Ehrhardt of East Germany set the mark to beat in Munich with 12.59 seconds.

Betty Cuthbert (Australia) (b. April 20, 1938) with 100 m., 200 m., 4×100 m. relay (1956) and 400 m. (1964).

Most Olympic Medals. The most medals won is 12 (9 gold and 3 silver) by Paavo Johannes Nurmi (Finland) (1897–1973) with:

1920   Gold: 10,000 m.; Cross Country, Individual and Team; silver: 5,000 m.
1924   Gold: 1,500 m.; 5,000 m.; 3,000 m. Team; Cross Country, Individual and Team.
1928   Gold: 10,000 m.; silver: 5,000 m.; 3,000 m. steeplechase.

The most medals won by a woman athlete is 7 by Shirley de la Hunty (*née* Strickland) (Australia) (b. July 18, 1925) with 3 gold, 1 silver and 3 bronze in the 1948, 1952 and 1956 Games. A recently discovered photo-finish indicates that she finished third, not fourth, in the 1948 200 m. event, thus increasing her total to 8.

Most Wins at One Games. The most gold medals at one celebration is 5 by Nurmi in 1924 (see above) and the most individual is 4 by Alvin C. Kraenzlein (U.S.) (1876–1928) in 1900 with 60 m., 110 m. hurdles, 200 m. hurdles and long jump.

Mass Relay Record. The record for 100 miles by 100 runners belonging to one club is 8 hours 5 minutes 24.8 seconds by the Sale Harriers at Crystal Palace, London, England, on June 29, 1975.

The women's mark is 13 hours 40 minutes 54.4 seconds by a team from Southern Regional High School, Manahawkin, N.J., on June 9, 1976.

The best time for a 100×400 meter relay is 1 hour 34 minutes

00.6 seconds by the Tarnverein Länggasse, Bern, Switzerland, on April 19, 1975.

A 13-man relay team from the Los Angeles Police Revolver and Athletic Club ran from the steps of the Capitol, Washington, D.C., to Los Angeles City Hall (3,871.6 miles) in 20 days 5 hours 20 minutes in May, 1974.

Pancake Race Record. The annual Housewives Pancake Race at Olney, Buckinghamshire, England, was first mentioned in 1445. The record for the winding 415-yard course (three tosses mandatory) is 61.0 seconds, set by Sally Ann Faulkner, 16, on February 26, 1974. The record for the counterpart race at Liberal, Kansas, is 59.1 seconds by Kathleen West, 19, on February 10, 1970.

Trampolining

Origin. The sport of trampolining (from the Spanish word *trampolin*, a springboard) dates from 1936, when the prototype "T" model trampoline was developed by George Nissen (U.S.). Trampolines were used in show business at least as early as "The Walloons" of the period, 1910–12.

Most Difficult Maneuvers. The most difficult maneuver yet achieved is the triple back somersault with a double twist, known as a Luxon after the first trampolinist able to achieve it—Paul Luxon (U.K.), the 1972 world amateur and 1973 world professional champion—achieved at the University of Southwest Louisiana in February, 1972. The women's record is the Wills (5½ twisting back somersault) named after the five-time world champion, Judy Wills (U.S.) (born 1948), of which no analyzable film exists.

Marathon Record. The longest recorded trampoline bouncing marathon is one of 1,248 hours (52 days) set by a team of 6 in Phoenix, Arizona, from June 24 to August 15, 1974. The solo record is 105 hours (with 5-minute breaks per hour permissible) by Cpl. Leslie Hammond (R.A.F.) near Haverfordwest, Wales, July 1–5, 1976.

Most Titles. The only men to win a world title (instituted 1964) twice have been Dave Jacobs (U.S.) the 1967–68 champion, Wayne Miller (U.S.) the 1966 and 1970 champion, and Richard Tison (France) in 1974 and 1976. Judy Wills won 5 women's titles (1964–65–66–67–68).

Volleyball

Origin. The game was invented as Minnonette in 1895 by William G. Morgan at the Y.M.C.A. gymnasium at Holyoke, Massachusetts. The International Volleyball Association was formed in Paris in April, 1947. The ball travels at a speed of up to 70 m.p.h. when smashed over the net, which measures 7 feet 11½ inches. In the women's game it is 7 feet 4¼ inches.

ONE-MAN VOLLEYBALL TEAM: Bob Schaffer of Suffern, New York, regularly beats complete 6-man contingents—singlehandedly!

World Titles. World Championships were instituted in 1949. The U.S.S.R. has won five men's titles (1949, 1952, 1960, 1962 and 1968). The U.S.S.R. won the women's championship in 1952, 1956, 1960, 1968, 1970, and 1973. The record crowd is 60,000 for the 1952 world title matches in Moscow, U.S.S.R.

Most Olympic Medals. The sport was introduced to the Olympic Games for both men and women in 1964. The only women volleyball players to win three medals are Ludmila Bouldakova (U.S.S.R.) (b. May 25, 1938) and Inna Ryskal (U.S.S.R.) (b. June 15, 1944), who both won a silver medal in 1964 and golds in 1968 and 1972.

The record for medals for men is held by Yury Poyarkov (U.S.S.R.), who won gold medals in 1964 and 1968, and a bronze in 1972.

Marathon. The longest recorded volleyball marathon is one of 30 hours played by two teams of six (no substitutes) from Carlsbad High School, Carlsbad, California, March 27–28, 1976. They took a 5-minute break every hour.

One-Man Team. Bob L. Schaffer of Suffern, New York, specializes in taking on 6-man teams singlehandedly. His won-lost record since August 16, 1963 is 1,985 wins to only 3 losses.

Walking

Longest Annual Race. The Strasbourg-Paris event (instituted in 1926 in the reverse direction) over 313 to 344 miles is the world's longest annual walk event. Gilbert Roger (France) has won 6 times (1949–53–54–56–57–58).

Longest in 24 Hours. The best performance is 133 miles 21 yards by Huw Neilson (G.B.) at Walton-on-Thames, England, October 14–15, 1960.

Most Olympic Medals. Walking races have been included in the Olympic schedule since 1906. The 20-kilometer event in Montreal in 1976 was the 25th Olympic race. The only walker to win three gold medals has been Ugo Frigerio (Italy) (b. September 16, 1901) with the 3,000 m. and 10,000 m. in 1920 and the 10,000 m. in 1924. He also holds the record of most medals with four (having additionally won the bronze medal in the 50,000 m. in 1932), which total is shared with Vladimir Golubnitschyi (U.S.S.R.) (b. June 2, 1936), who won gold medals for the 20,000 m. in 1960 and 1968, the silver in 1972 and the bronze in 1964.

OFFICIAL WORLD RECORDS (Track Walking)
(As recognized by the International Amateur Athletic Federation)

Distance	hrs. mins. secs.	Name and Nationality	Date	Place
20,000 meters	1 24 45	Bernd Kannenberg (West Germany)	May 25, 1974	Hamburg
30,000 meters	2 12 51	S. Zschiegner (East Germany)	Oct. 13, 1974	Giorico-Bellinzona
20 miles	2 27 38	Vittorio Visini (Italy)	Nov. 1, 1975	Vicenza
30 miles	3 48 23.4	Bernd Kannenberg (West Germany)	Nov. 16, 1975	Milan
50,000 meters	3 56 51.4	Bernd Kannenberg (West Germany)	Nov. 16, 1975	Milan
2 hours 16 miles 1,517 yards		Bernd Kannenberg (West Germany)	May 11, 1974	Kassel

UNOFFICIAL WORLD BEST PERFORMANCES (Track Walking)
(Best valid performances over distances or times for which records are no longer recognized by the I.A.A.F.)

5 miles	34 21.2	Kenneth Joseph Matthews (U.K.)	Sept. 28, 1960	London
10 miles	1 09 40.6	Kenneth Joseph Matthews (U.K.)	June 6, 1964	Walton-on-Thames
50,000 meters (road)	3 52 44.6	Bernd Kannenberg (West Germany)	1972	West Germany
1 hour 8 miles 1,294 yards		Grigoriy Panichkin (U.S.S.R.)	Nov. 1, 1959	Stalinabad

Walking on Crutches. David Ryder, 21, a polio victim from Essex, England, left Los Angeles on March 30 and arrived at New York City on August 14, 1970, after covering 2,960 miles on his crutches.

Walking "Marathon." Frederick Jago, 38, of Great Britain, walked 308.5 miles at Vivary Park, Taunton, England, in 143 hours 3 minutes December 19–25, 1975. He did not permit himself any stops for resting and was moving 98.33 per cent of the time.

WALKING CHAMPIONS: Bernd Kannenberg (West Germany) (left) holds 4 records. Plennie Wingo (right) walked 8,000 miles backwards in 1931-32. He used special glasses to see where he was going.

Walking Around the World. The first person recorded to have "walked around the world" is David Kunst, who started with his brother John from Waseca, Minnesota, on June 10, 1970. John was killed by Afghani bandits in 1972. David arrived home after walking 14,500 miles on October 5, 1974.

The Trans-Asia record is 238 days for 6,800 miles from Riga, Latvia, to Vladivostok, U.S.S.R., by Georgyi Bushuyev, 50, in 1973–74.

Walking Across America. John Lees, 27, of Brighton, England, on April 11–June 3, 1972, walked 2,876 miles across the U.S. from City Hall, Los Angeles, to City Hall, New York City, in 53 days 12 hours 15 minutes (53.746 miles per day). This bettered the time of 53 days 23 hours 12½ minutes (average 53.29 miles a day) for *running* the distance by John Ball (South Africa), 45, between March 5 and April 28, 1972.

Walking Across Canada. The record Trans-Canada (Halifax to Vancouver) walk of 3,764 miles is 96 days by Clyde McRae, 23, from May 1 to August 4, 1973.

Walking Backwards. The greatest exponent of reverse pedestrianism has been Plennie L. Wingo (b. 1895) then of Abilene, Texas, who started on his 8,000-mile transcontinental walks on April 15, 1931, from Santa Monica, California, to Istanbul, Turkey, and arrived on October 24, 1932.

The longest distance reported for walking backwards in 24 hours is 80 miles by Lindsay R. Dodd (England), April 9–10, 1976.

Water Polo

Origins. Water polo was developed in England as "Water Soccer" in 1869 and was first included in the Olympic Games in Paris in 1900.

Olympic Victories. Hungary has won the Olympic tournament most often with six wins, in 1932, 1936, 1952, 1956, 1964 and 1976. Five players share the record of three gold medals: George Wilkinson (b. 1880) in 1900–08–12; Paulo (Paul) Radmilovic (1886–1968), and Charles Sidney Smith (b. 1879) all G.B. in 1908–12–20; and the Hungarians Deszö Gyarmati (b. October 23, 1927) and György Kárpáti (b. June 23, 1935) in 1952–56–64.

Radmilovic also won a gold medal for the 4×200 m. relay in 1908.

Most Caps. The greatest number of internationals is 244 by Ozren Bonacic for Yugoslavia between 1964 and September, 1975.

Marathon. The longest match on record is one of 45 hours 17 minutes between two teams of 15 from the Kitimat water polo team, British Columbia, Canada, June 5–7, 1976. Breaks and substitutions were in accordance with N.C.A.A. regulations.

Water Skiing

Origins. The origins of water skiing lie in plank gliding or aquaplaning. A photograph exists of a "plank-riding" contest in a regatta won by a Mr. S. Storry at Scarborough, Yorkshire, England, on July 15, 1914. Competitors were towed on a *single* plank by a motor launch. The present-day sport of water skiing was pioneered by Ralph W. Samuelson on Lake Pepin, Minnesota, on two curved pine boards in the summer of 1922, though claims have been made for the birth of the sport on Lake Annecy (Haute Savoie), France, in 1920. The first World Water Ski Organization was formed in Geneva, Switzerland, on July 27, 1946.

Jumps. The first recorded jump on water skis was by Ralph W. Samuelson, off a greased ramp at Miami Beach, Florida, in 1928. The longest jump recorded is one of 180 feet by Wayne Grimditch, 20 (U.S.), at Callaway Gardens, Pine Mountain, Georgia, July 13, 1975. A minimum margin of 8 inches is required for sole possession of the world record.

The women's record is 125 feet by Elizabeth Allan-Shetter (U.S.) at Callaway Gardens, Georgia, on August 25, 1974.

Slalom. The world record for slalom is 40 buoys (with a 75-foot rope shortened by 36 feet) by Kris La Point (U.S.).

The highest recorded point score for figures is 5,740 points by Russ Stiffler (U.S.) in 1974.

MOST WORLD CHAMPIONSHIPS: Mike Suyderhoud (U.S.) is one of 3 men who have repeated as world champion.

Longest Run. The greatest distance traveled non-stop is 1,000 miles by Ray de Fir of Portland, Oregon, in 33 hours 27 minutes, August 22–23, 1958, on the Columbia River between Portland and Astoria.

Highest Speed. The water skiing speed record is 125.69 m.p.h. recorded by Danny Churchill (U.S.) at the Oakland Marine Stadium, California, in 1971. Sally Younger, 17, set a feminine record of 105.15 m.p.h. at Perris, California, on June 17, 1970.

Most Titles. World championships (instituted 1949) have been twice won by Alfredo Mendoza (U.S.) in 1953–55, Mike Suyderhoud (U.S.) in 1967–69, and George Athans (Canada) in 1971 and 1973, and three times by Mrs. Willa McGuire (*née* Worthington) of the

FASTEST WOMAN WATER SKIER: Sally Younger, at the age of 17, sped 105.15 m.p.h. in June, 1970.

U.S., in 1949–50 and 1955 and Elizabeth Allan-Shetter (U.S.) in 1965, 1969, and 1975.

Water Ski Kite Flying. The altitude record is 4,750 feet by Bill Moyes (Australia) on March 14, 1972. He was towed by a 435-h.p. Hamilton Jet Boat over Lake Ellesmere, New Zealand. The duration record is 15 hours 3 minutes by Bill Flewellyn (N.Z.) over Lake Bonney, South Australia, in 1971.

Barefoot. The barefoot duration record is 2 hours 37 minutes by Paul McManus (Australia). The backwards barefoot record is 39 minutes by McManus. A barefoot jump of 54 feet has been reported from Australia. The barefoot speed records are 98.9 m.p.h. by Gordon Eppling at Long Beach, California, on August 18, 1974, and for women 61 m.p.h. by Haidee Jones (Australia).

Weightlifting

Origins. Amateur weightlifting is of comparatively modern origin, and the first world championship was staged at the Café Monico, Piccadilly, London, on March 28, 1891. Prior to that time, weightlifting consisted of professional exhibitions in which some of the advertised poundages were open to doubt. The first to raise 400 lbs. was Charles Rigoulot (1903–62), a French professional, with 402½ lbs. on February 1, 1929, but his barbell would not now be regarded as acceptable.

Greatest Lift. The greatest weight ever raised by a human being is 6,270 lbs. in a back lift (weight raised off trestles) by the 364-lb. Paul Anderson (U.S.) (b. 1932), the 1956 Olympic heavyweight champion, at Toccoa, Georgia, on June 12, 1957. (The heaviest Rolls-Royce, the Phantom VI, weighs 5,936 lbs.) The greatest by a woman is 3,564 lbs. with a hip and harness lift by Mrs. Josephine Blatt (*née* Schauer) (U.S.) (1869–1923) at the Bijou Theatre, Hoboken, New Jersey, on April 15, 1895.

The greatest overhead lifts made from the ground are the clean and jerks achieved by super-heavyweights which now exceed 560 lbs. (see table on page 664).

The greatest overhead lift ever made by a woman, also professional, is 286 lbs. in a Continental jerk by Katie Sandwina, *née* Brummbach (Germany) (born January 21, 1884, died as Mrs. Max Heymann in New York City, in 1952) in *c.* 1911. This is equivalent to seven 40-pound office typewriters. She stood 5 feet 11 inches tall, weighed 210 lbs., and is reputed to have unofficially lifted 312½ lbs. and to have once shouldered a 1,200-lb. cannon taken from the tailboard of a Barnum & Bailey circus wagon. (See photo on page 666.)

Power Lifts. Paul Anderson as a professional has bench-pressed 627 lbs., achieved 1,200 lbs. in a deep-knee bend, and dead-lifted 820 lbs. making a career aggregate of 2,647 lbs.

International Powerlifting Federation records in the Superheavy-weight division have all been set by Donald C. Reinhoudt (U.S.) in Chattanooga, Tennessee, with a squat of 934 lbs. (April 10, 1976),

LIFTS MORE THAN THREE TONS: Paul Anderson of Toccoa, Georgia, who weighs 364 lbs., raised the greatest weight ever lifted by a human—6,270 lbs.—in a back lift.

a bench press of 606¼ lbs. (August 31, 1975), dead lift of 885½ lbs. and total of 2,420 lbs. (May 3, 1975).

The highest official two-handed dead lift is 882 lbs. by John Kuc (U.S.). Hermann Görner performed a one-handed dead lift of 734½ lbs. in Dresden on July 20, 1920. He once raised 24 men weighing 4,123 lbs. on a plank with the soles of his feet and also carried on his back a 1,444-lb. piano for a distance of 52½ feet on June 3, 1921. Görner is also reputed to have once lifted 14 bricks weighing 123½ lbs. horizontally, using only lateral pressure.

Peter B. Cortese (U.S.) achieved a one-arm dead lift of 22 lbs. over triple his body weight with 370 lbs. at York, Pennsylvania, on September 4, 1954.

The highest competitive two-handed dead lift by a woman is 412½ lbs. by Jan Suffolk Todd (born May 22, 1952) (U.S.) at Sydney, Nova Scotia, Canada, on May 1, 1976. She weighed 165 lbs.

It was reported that a hysterical 123-lb. woman, Mrs. Maxwell Rogers, lifted one end of a 3,600-lb. car which, after the collapse of a jack, had fallen on top of her son at Tampa, Florida, on April 24, 1960. She cracked some vertebrae.

OFFICIAL WORLD WEIGHTLIFTING RECORDS

(As of August 1, 1976)

Flyweight
(114½ lb.–52 kg.)

Snatch	239	Alexander Voronin (U.S.S.R.)	E. Germany	Apr. 3, 1976
Jerk	310¾	Alexander Voronin (U.S.S.R.)	Canada	July 18, 1976
Total	534½	Alexander Voronin (U.S.S.R.)	Canada	July 18, 1976

Bantamweight
(123¼ lb.–56 kg.)

Snatch	259	Koji Miki (Japan)	Cuba	Sept. 16, 1973
Jerk	332¾	Mohamed Nassiri (Iran)	Turkey	Aug. 2, 1973
Total	578½	Norair Nourikian (Bulgaria)	Canada	July 19, 1976

Featherweight
(132¼ lb.–60 kg.)

Snatch	282	Gyorgyi Todorov (Bulgaria)	Bulgaria	Oct. 4, 1975
Jerk	354¾	Nikolai Kolesnikov (U.S.S.R.)	U.S.S.R.	July 5, 1975
Total	628½	Gyorgyi Todorov (Bulgaria)	U.S.S.R.	Sept. 17, 1975

Lightweight
(148¾ lb.–67.5 kg.)

Snatch	310	Kazimerz Czainechi (Poland)	Poland	Apr. 22, 1976
Jerk	391¼	Murkharbi Kirzhinov (U.S.S.R.)	West Ger.	Aug. 30, 1972
Total	688¾	Murkharbi Kirzhinov (U.S.S.R.)	West Ger.	Aug. 30, 1972

Middleweight
(165¼ lb.–75 kg.)

Snatch	339½	Viktor Lissenko (U.S.S.R.)	U.S.S.R.	Feb. 22, 1976
Jerk	424½	Valery Smirnov (U.S.S.R.)	U.S.S.R.	July 1976
Total	755	Valery Smirnov (U.S.S.R.)	U.S.S.R.	July 1976

Light-heavyweight
(181¾ lb.–82.5 kg.)

Snatch	364¾	Valeri Shary (U.S.S.R.)	U.S.S.R.	July 8, 1975
Jerk	457½	Rolf Milser (E. Germany)	E. Germany	Apr. 8, 1976
Total	809½	Valeri Shary (U.S.S.R.)	U.S.S.R.	Feb. 22, 1976

Middle-heavyweight
(198¼ lb.–90 kg.)

Snatch	396¾	David Rigert (U.S.S.R.)	U.S.S.R.	May 15, 1976
Jerk	487¼	David Rigert (U.S.S.R.)	U.S.S.R.	May 22, 1976
Total	882	David Rigert (U.S.S.R.)	U.S.S.R.	May 15, 1976

Heavyweight
(242½ lb.–110 kg.)

Snatch	407¾	Valentin Khristov (Bulgaria)	E. Germany	Apr. 10, 1976
Jerk	523½	Valentin Khristov (Bulgaria)	U.S.S.R.	Sept. 22, 1975
Total	920¼	Valentin Khristov (Bulgaria)	U.S.S.R.	Sept. 22, 1975

Super-heavyweight
(Over 242½ lb.–110 kg.)

Snatch	440¾	Khristo Plachkov (Bulgaria)	Bulgaria	May 1976
Jerk	562	Vasili Alexeev (U.S.S.R.)	Canada	July 27, 1976
Total	975½	Khristo Plachkov (Bulgaria)	Bulgaria	May 1976

MOST SUCCESSFUL OLYMPIC WEIGHTLIFTERS

Louis Hostin (France)	Gold, light-heavyweight 1932 and 1936; Silver, 1928.
John Davis (U.S.)	Gold, heavyweight 1948 and 1952.
Tommy Kono (Hawaii/U.S.)	Gold, lightweight 1952; Gold, light-heavyweight 1956; Silver, middleweight 1960.
Charles Vinci (U.S.)	Gold, bantamweight 1956 and 1960.
Arkady Vorobyov (U.S.S.R.)	Gold, middle-heavyweight 1956 and 1960.
Yoshinobu Miyake (Japan)	Gold, featherweight 1964 and 1968; Silver, bantamweight 1960.
Waldemar Baszanowski (Poland)	Gold, lightweight 1964 and 1968.
Leonid Schabotinsky (U.S.S.R.)	Gold, heavyweight 1964 and 1968.
Vasili Alexeev (U.S.S.R.)	Gold, super-heavyweight 1972 and 1976.
Norair Nourikian (Bulgaria)	Gold, featherweight 1972; Gold, bantamweight 1976

TWO OLYMPIC GOLD MEDALS: Vasili Alexeev (U.S.S.R.) also holds the world record for Super-heavyweight lifters in the Clean and Jerk category.

OLYMPIC GOLD MEDAL WINNER: Tommy Kono (Hawaii, U.S.) won 3 medals altogether, took home gold medals in 1952 and 1956.

Most Olympic Medals. Winner of most Olympic medals is Norbert Schemansky (U.S.) with four: gold, middle-heavyweight 1952; silver, heavyweight 1948; bronze, heavyweight 1960 and 1964. Schemansky achieved a world record (heavyweight snatch of 361½ lbs. on April 28, 1962, at Detroit) at the record age of 37 years 10 months.

Most Olympic Gold Medals. Of the 90 Olympic titles at stake, the U.S.S.R. has won 26, the U.S. 15 and France 9. Ten lifters have succeeded in winning an Olympic gold medal in successive Games. Of these, three have also won a silver medal.

Wrestling

Earliest References. The earliest depiction of wrestling holds and falls are from the walls of the tomb of Ptahhotap (Egypt) so proving that wrestling dates from *c.* 2350 B.C. or earlier. It was introduced into the ancient Olympic Games in the 18th Olympiad in *c.* 704 B.C. The Graeco-Roman style is of French origin and arose about 1860. The International Amateur Wrestling Federation (F.I.L.A.) was founded in 1912.

Sumo Wrestling. The sport's origins in Japan certainly date from *c.* 200 A.D. The heaviest performer was probably Dewagatake, a wrestler of the 1920's who was 6 feet 5 inches tall and weighed up to 420 lbs. Weight is amassed by over-eating a high protein sea food stew called *chanko-rigori*. The tallest was probably Ozora, an early

19th century performer, who stood 7 feet 3 inches tall. The most successful wrestler has been Koki Naya (born 1940), *alias* Taiho ("Great Bird"), who won 32 Emperor's Cups until his retirement in 1971. He was the *Yokozuna* (Grand Champion) in 1967. The highest *dan* is Makuuchi.

The youngest wrestler ever to attain the rank of *Yokozuna* was Toshimitsu Ogata (*alias* Kitanoumi) in July, 1974, aged 21 years 2 months.

Most Olympic Titles. Three wrestlers have won three Olympic titles. They are:

Carl Westergren (Sweden) (b. Oct. 13, 1895)		Ivar Johansson (Sweden) (b. Jan. 31, 1903)	
Graeco-Roman Middleweight A	1920	Free-style Middleweight	1932
Graeco-Roman Middleweight B	1924	Graeco-Roman Welterweight	1932
Graeco-Roman Heavyweight	1932	Graeco-Roman Middleweight	1936

Aleksandr Medved (U.S.S.R.) (b. Sept. 16, 1937)		
Free-style Light-heavyweight	1964	The only wrestler with more medals is Imre Polyák (Hungary) who won the silver medal for the Graeco-Roman featherweight class in 1952, 56–60 and the gold in 1964.
Free-style Heavyweight	1968	
Free-style Super-heavyweight	1972	

Best Record. Dan Gable (U.S.) (born October 25, 1948) won 299 bouts with only 6 losses from 1963 to 1973. He also won the 1972 free-style Olympic lightweight title.

Most World Championships. The greatest number of world championships won by a wrestler is ten by the free-styler Aleksandr Medved (U.S.S.R.), with the light-heavyweight titles in 1964 (Olympic) and 1966, the heavyweight 1967 and 1968 (Olympic), and the super-heavyweight title 1969, 1970, 1971 and 1972 (Olympic). The only other wrestler to win world titles in 6 successive years has been Abdullah Movahad (Iran) in the lightweight division in 1965–70. The record for Graeco-Roman titles is five shared by Roman Rurua (U.S.S.R.) with the featherweight 1966, 1967, 1968 (Olympic), 1969 and 1970 and Victor Igumenov (U.S.S.R.) with the welterweight 1966, 1967, 1969, 1970 and 1971.

SUMO WRESTLER: Koki Naya ("Taiho") (left) has won 32 Emperor's Cups and was the Grand Champion in 1967.

MOST SUCCESSFUL WRESTLER was Strangler Lewis (left) who won all but 33 out of 6,200 bouts.

Longest Bout. The longest recorded bout was one of 11 hours 40 minutes between Martin Klein (Estonia, representing Russia) and Armas Asikainen (Finland) in the Graeco-Roman middleweight "A" event in the 1912 Olympic Games in Stockholm, Sweden.

Professional Wrestling. Modern professional wrestling dates from 1874 in the United States. Georges Karl Julius Hackenschmidt (1877–1968) made no submissions in the period 1898–1908.

The highest paid professional wrestler ever is Antonino ("Tony") Rocca with $180,000 in 1958. The heaviest wrestler was William J. Cobb of Macon, Georgia, who was billed in 1962 as the 802-lb. "Happy" Humphrey. What he lacked in mobility he possessed in suffocating powers. By July, 1965, he had reduced to a modest 232 lbs.

Most Successful. Ed "Strangler" Lewis (1890–1966), né Robert H. Friedrich, fought 6,200 bouts in 44 years losing only 33 matches. He won world titles in 1920, 1922 and 1928.

Yachting

Origin. Yachting dates from the £100 (now $250) stake race between King Charles II of England and his brother James, Duke of York, on the Thames River, on September 1, 1661, over 23 miles, from Greenwich to Gravesend. The earliest club is the Royal Cork Yacht Club (formerly the Cork Harbour Water Club), established in Ireland in 1720. The word "yacht" is from the Dutch, meaning to hunt or chase.

Most Successful. The most successful racing yacht in history was the British Royal Yacht *Britannia* (1893–1935), owned by King Edward VII while Prince of Wales, and subsequently by King George V, which won 231 races in 625 starts.

Highest Speed. The official world sailing speed record is 31.09 knots (35.80 m.p.h.) achieved by the 55-foot proa *Crossbow* (sail area 932 square feet, designed by Rod McAlpine-Downie) with Timothy Colman as helmsman, off Portland, Dorset, England, on September 30, 1975. The U.S. Navy experimental hydrofoil craft *Monitor* is reported to have attained speeds close to 40 knots (46 m.p.h.) in 1956.

Longest Race. The longest regularly contested yacht race is the biennial Los Angeles-Tahiti Trans Pacific event which is over 3,571 miles. The fastest time has been 8 days 13 hours 9 minutes by Eric Taberley's *Pen Duick IV* (France) in 1969.

Most Competitors. 1,261 sailing boats started the 233-mile Round Zealand (Denmark) race in June, 1976.

America's Cup. The America's Cup was originally won as an outright prize by the schooner *America* on August 22, 1851, at Cowes, England, but was later offered by the New York Yacht Club as a challenge trophy. On August 8, 1870, J. Ashbury's *Cambria* (G.B.) failed to capture the trophy from the *Magic*, owned by F. Osgood (U.S.). Since then the Cup has been challenged by Great Britain in 15 contests, by Canada in two contests, and by Australia thrice, but the United States holders have never been defeated. The closest race ever was the fourth race of the 1962 series, when the 12-meter sloop *Weatherly* beat her Australian challenger *Gretel* by about $3\frac{1}{2}$ lengths (75 yards), a margin of only 26 seconds, on September 22, 1962. The fastest time ever recorded by a 12-meter boat for the triangular course of 24 miles is 2 hours 46 minutes 58 seconds by *Gretel* in 1962.

Little America's Cup. The catamaran counterpart to the America's cup was instituted in 1961 for International C-class catamarans. Great Britain has won 8 times from 1961 to 1968.

Admiral's Cup. The ocean racing series to have attracted the largest number of participating nations (three boats allowed to each nation) is the Admiral's Cup held by the Royal Ocean Racing Club in the English Channel in alternate years. Up to 1975, Britain had won 6 times, U.S. twice and Australia and West Germany once each.

In 1975, a record number of 19 nations competed.

Olympic Victories. The first sportsman ever to win individual gold medals in four successive Olympic Games has been Paul B. Elvström (b. February 25, 1928) (Denmark) in the Firefly class in 1948 and the Finn class in 1952, 1956 and 1960. He has also won 8 other world titles in a total of 6 classes.

The lowest number of penalty points by the winner of any class in an Olympic regatta is 3 points [6 wins (1 disqualified) and 1 second in 7 starts] by *Superdocius* of the Flying Dutchman class sailed by Lt. Rodney Stuart Pattison (b. August 5, 1943), British Royal Navy and Ian Somerled Macdonald-Smith (b. July 3, 1945), in Acapulco Bay, Mexico, in October, 1968.

Largest Yacht. The largest private yacht ever built was Mrs. Emily Roebling Cadwalader's *Savarona* of 5,100 gross tons, completed in Hamburg, Germany, in October, 1931, at a cost of $4,000,000. She (the yacht), with a 53-foot beam and measuring 408 feet 6 inches overall, was sold to the Turkish government in March, 1938. Operating expenses for a full crew of 107 men approached $500,000 per year. Currently, she is a Turkish navy training ship with a complement of 213.

Currently the largest reported private yacht is *Apollo*, 339 feet 7 inches long and weighing 3,288 tons, built in Northern Ireland in 1936 and registered in Panama.

The largest private sailing yacht ever built was the full-rigged 350-foot auxiliary barque *Sea Cloud* (formerly *Hussar*), owned by the oft-married Mrs. Marjorie Merriweather Post-Close-Hutton-Davies-May (1888–1973), one-time wife of the U.S. Ambassador to the U.S.S.R. Her four masts carried 30 sails with the total canvas area of 36,000 square feet.

Largest Sail. The largest sail ever made was a parachute spinnaker with an area of 18,000 square feet (more than two-fifths of an acre) for Harold S. Vanderbilt's *Ranger* in 1937.

Most Numerous. The numerically largest class of sailing boats in the world is the "Sunfish" (U.S.), with a total in excess of 140,000. Made of plastic, it is a 14-foot sailing surfboard with a single sail.

The numerically largest class of centerboard sailing dinghy is the International Optimist, a 7-foot 7-inch wooden or plastic boat intended to be used by children. 105,000 are claimed worldwide. This boat is also the smallest in size and cheapest of any recognized international yachting class.

Highest Altitude. The greatest altitude at which sailing has been conducted is 14,212 feet on Lake Pomacocha, Peru, by *Nusta*, a 19-foot Lightning dinghy owned by Jan Jacobi, reported in 1959.

PICTURE CREDITS

The editors and publishers wish to thank the following people and organizations for pictures which they supplied:

Mrs. Addison; Aero-Camera; Ernest W. Albright; American Bowling Congress; American Broadcasting Companies, Inc.; American Museum of Natural History; *Anaheim Bulletin*; Associated Newspapers Ltd.; Associated Press; Atlanta Braves; Denis Bekett; Bensen Aircraft Corp.; Lawrence Berkeley Laboratory; Bilderdienst; Birmingham Post & Mail; Peter J. Bish; B.O.A.C.; Border Press, Carlisle; Boston Garden; British Gliding Association; British Information Services; Camera Press; *Canberra Times*; J. Allan Cash; Chesapeake Bay Bridge and Tunnel Commission; Christie's; *Coffeyville Journal*; M. Colomban; *Contra Costa Suns*, California; Gerry Cranham; Crown Copyright; F. E. Curran; *Daily Mail*, London; Dept. of Supply, Antarctic Division; "Discovery" Committee, Colonial Office, London; Walt Disney Productions; Alfred Dunhill Ltd.; A. Dupont; Eljay Photo Service; Embassy of the Czechoslovak Socialist Republic; Jim England; Europix; *Evening News*, London; *Express Star*, Wolverhampton, England; *Family Doctor*; The Federal Reserve Bank of N.Y.; *Fort Worth Star Telegram*; Ford Motor Co.; Robert L. Foster; Fox Photos Ltd.; French Embassy, London; French Government Tourist Office; Marvin Frost; General Photographic Agency; Ghana Information Service; Golding Farms; Government of India; Greek Tourist Office; Bob Hagopian; Harmsworth Photo Library; Hong Kong Government Information Services; David Hossingers; *F. R. Herald News*; Herts Pictorial, Hitchin, England; Edwin G. Huffman; Huntsville Times; Ellerton M. Jette; Keystone Press Agency; E. D. Lacey; Las Vegas News Bureau; Ann Li Mongello; Loffland Drilling Co.; Mansell Collection; John Marshall; E. W. Marwick; Gary McMillin; *Minneapolis Tribune*; R. N. Misra; Monitor Press Features Ltd.; Mt. Everest Foundation; Mt. Wilson & Palomar Observatory; *Montreal Star-Canada Wide*; Museum of Science, Boston; NASA; National Baseball Hall of Fame; NCAA; *New York Daily News* Photo; *New York Times*; New York Zoological Society; New Zealand Consulate; *New Zealand Herald Weekly News*; Norsk Polarinstitutt; Norsk Telegram byrå; Nova Scotia Information; Novosti; Oak Ridge National Laboratory; Pacific Telephone & Telegraph Co.; Svante Palme; Peabody Museum of Salem; D. E. Pedgley; *The Philadelphia Inquirer*; Photo Cern; Photo-Reportage Ltd.; Picture Post; Planet News Ltd.; Hank Pollard; The Port Authority of N.Y. & N.J.; Kenneth Prater, A.I.I.P.; Elvis Presley Fan Club; Press Association Photos; Pro Football Hall of Fame; Queens Nassau Pix; Radio Times Hulton Picture Library; Reaction Dynamics, Inc.; Republican Publications; Ringsport; Bernard Ronget; Al Ruelle; Ruth Robertson; Henry Salameh; Ugo Sbaraglia; Eddie Schuurling/Frank W. Lane; H. H. Seiden; Six Flags Over Mid-America; Smithsonian Institution; Jerry Soalt; Rick Sorrell; South Africa Embassy; Spanish Tourist Office; A. G. Spalding & Bros.; Sperryn's; Triborough Bridge and Tunnel Authority; United Artists; Universal Pictorial Press; University of Denver; UPI; U.S. Air Force; U.S. Dept. of Commerce; U.S. Forest Service; U.S. Information Service; U.S. Lawn Tennis Association; U.S. National Park Service; U.S. Navy; M. T. Walters & Associates Ltd.; *Waterloo Courier*, Iowa; Westminster Press Ltd.; Ron Wheeler; Werkfoto; Western International Hotels; Charles Wherry; Wide World Photos; Wilson Sporting Goods Co.; G. L. Wood; Wyman-Gordon Press; Norman Zeisloft; Zoological Society of London.

Color photographs courtesy of British Museum of Natural History; *Garden News;* Harrah's Automobile Collection, Reno, Nevada; Tony Korody (SYGMA); E.D. Lacey; Popperfoto; Bob Speca; Sporting Pictures (U.K.) Ltd; Stanley Works Ltd.; Michael Tweedie; Universal Pictures; Van Cleef & Arpels.

INDEX

Mouse, smallest rodent 70, smallest, rarest marsupial 74
Mousing 81
Moustache, longest 39
Movies, see Motion Pictures
Murals, earliest, largest 195
Murder, greatest mass 397–398, highest rate, lowest 399, most prolific murderers 399–400, gang murders, "smelling out" 400
Muscles, largest, smallest human 37
Museums, oldest 195, largest 196
Mushroom, largest 116, largest farm 370
Music, instruments 218–221, orchestras 221, composers 221–223, national anthems, longest rendering, longest symphony 222, longest piano composition, longest silence 223, highest paid musicians 223–225, opera 224, 225, bells 225–227, songs 227, hymns 227–228; see also Records
Musical Chairs, duration 476
Musical Instrument, earliest piano, grandest piano, organ, largest and loudest 218, youngest and oldest organist, marathon, accordion marathon, largest string instruments 219, largest guitar 219, 220, most expensive, most valuable violin 219, underwater violinist 220, F, largest tuba, brass instrument, alphorn, drum 220, most players for an instrument 221, smallest violin C
Musical Notes, highest and lowest sung 47, oldest musical notation 218, highest and lowest orchestra 221
Musician, most players for an instrument 221, highest paid pianist 223, violinist 223, 224, drummer, singers 224

Nails, longest finger 39
Names, longest star 160, chemical 200, place 202–203, personal 203–205, Bible 208
Narcotics, largest haul 404
National Anthems, see Anthems
National Debt, largest 407
National Income 382
National Increase, highest, lowest 381
National Wealth 408
Natural Bridge, longest 141
Natural World, natural phenomena 124–127, 140–144, structure and dimensions 128–140, weather 144–149
Navy, largest, greatest battle 390
Necks, longest human 38
Needle Threading 476
Neon Sign, largest 279
Nerve Gas, most powerful 173
Nests, largest 86
Net, largest fishing 347
Newspapers, most, oldest 216, largest, smallest, highest circulation, most read 217
Newt, largest, smallest 92
New York Stock Exchange 351–353
Night Club, highest performance fee 230, largest, oldest 255, highest, lowest 256

Nile, longest river 136–137, subterranean river 137
Nobel Prizes, values, most awards by countries 500, individuals 500–501, oldest, youngest winners 501
Noise, intensity 47, loudest 187
Non-Fiction, best selling 211
Nonuplets 32, 33
Noodle Making 476
Northern Lights, most frequent, lowest latitudes, altitude 152
North Pole, conquest 445
Note (musical), highest and lowest human voice 47, highest electronic 186, orchestral 221
Novel, longest 207; see also Books
Novelist, most prolific, fastest 208, oldest, youngest, highest paid 209, top-selling 210
Nuclear Arsenal, largest 393
Nuclear Power, see Atomic Power
Nudist Camp, first, largest 279
Nuggets, largest gold, silver 178
Number, lowest and highest prime, lowest and highest perfect, highest named, most primitive 183, longest slide rule 184, 185, earliest measures, smallest units, most accurate version of "Pi," square root of two 184
Numeration, numbers 183–184, smallest units 184–185, time measure 185
Nut (mechanical), largest 335
Nylon, sheerest 364

Obelisks, oldest, largest 273
Object, smallest visible 46, farthest visible 161, 162, remotest 163, sharpest 188
Observatory, highest 180
Oceanarium, earliest, largest, largest marine mammal in captivity 123; see also Aquarium
Ocean Descent, progressive records, greatest descent 450
Oceans, area of earth, weight, volume, largest, longest voyage, most southerly, deepest, remotest spot 129, temperature, largest sea, gulf, bay 130, highest sea-mountain 130, 135, highest wave 130, highest tidal wave, greatest tides 131, greatest and strongest current, icebergs 132, straits 133, greatest submarine depression 136, river 137, deepest canyon 143, progressive records, record descent 450
Octopus, largest 104
Octuplets 33
Odor, smelliest substance 172
Office Building, tallest 247
Oil, longest pipeline, tank, spill 334
Oil Company, largest 348
Oil Field, largest 281, greatest gusher, greatest flare, largest gas tank 282
Oil Platform, largest 294
Oil Refinery, largest 349
Oil Tanker Wreck 294
Olympic Games, earliest 602, most gold medals 602–603, most at one Games, national, oldest and youngest gold medalists, longest span, largest crowd,

Swimming, fastest bird 84, earliest references 626, largest pools 626–627, fastest swimmer, most world records, most difficult dives, Olympic records, medals 627–628, closest verdict, long-distance swimming 628, ocean swim, longest duration, Channel swimming —first man, first woman, youngest, oldest 629, fastest 629, 631, world records, men 630, Channel—slowest, relays, first and fastest double crossings 631, world records, women 632, top woman swimmer, most conquests, underwater, butterfly champion 633, ice swimming, most dangerous, odd records, treading water 634

Swindle, greatest, welfare 405

Swinging, marathon 485

Switch, fastest 190

Sword, longest swallowed 44, highest-priced 367

Symphony, most prolific composer 221, fastest composition, longest 222–223

Synagogue, largest 429

Syndicate, largest crime 399

Tablecloth, largest 367

Table Tennis, earliest reference, fastest rallying 634, marathon records 634–635, highest speed, youngest international, most world championships 635

Take-Offs, most 321

Take-Over, largest commercial business 342

Talking, fastest 50, most talkative bird 86, lecture 473, non-stop 485

Tallest, see Giants

Tank, gas, largest 282, oil 334, (military), earliest, heaviest 391

Tanker, largest, longest 290, largest wreck 294, spill 334

Tap Dancing, fastest 463

Tapestry, earliest, most expensive, largest, longest 367

Tarantula, heaviest spider 97, rarest, longest-lived 98

Tartan, earliest 367

Taste, sweetest, bitterest 172

Tattoos, most 45

Taxation, highest rate 407

Taxi, largest fleet, longest journey 305

Tea, most expensive, highest consumption 419

Teeter-Totter, 480, 481

Teeth, decay 40, earliest, most, most extracted 45, strongest 486

Tektites 152

Telegrams, most sent 426

Telephones, most, fewest, busiest phone, longest call, cable, largest incorrect bill 423

Telescope, earliest, largest reflector 179, refractor, solar, highest observatory, first and largest radio-telescope 180, largest steerable dish 181

Television, invention 232, first public demonstration, service, first trans-mitters and sets, first transatlantic transmission, greatest audience, largest

Television continued
prizes, highest hourly rate 233, largest contracts 233–234, longest program, most televised performer, most durable show, most prolific scriptwriter 234, highest advertising rate 235, highest masts 261

Temperature, highest human, lowest human 42, highest endured 52, highest and lowest mammalian blood 73, highest and lowest sea 130, highest and lowest man-made 185

Temperature (atmospheric), maximum shade, minimum screen 144, 147, greatest range 144, most equable, humidity and discomfort 145, weather records 147–149, lunar, solar 154, comparison of planets 157

Temple, largest 428, 429

Temple Tower, largest 275

Tennis, origins 635, oldest courts, greatest crowd, Davis Cup 636, greatest domination 636–637, Wimbledon records—most appearances 637, most games and longest matches 638–639, youngest Wimbledon champions 639, 640–641, most wins 640, greatest attendance, professional tennis, marathons, fastest service, longest career 641

Tenrec, rarest animal 57, 60, largest litter 62, youngest breeder 63, longest-lived insectivore 71

Tensile Strength, greatest element 171, chemical compound 172

Tent, largest 278

Terrier, most popular dog 77

Territories, separately administered 375, most populated 378, least 379

Tern, longest bird flight 84

Text, oldest written, oldest printed, oldest mechanically printed 205

Theatre, origins, oldest, largest, largest amphitheatre, longest runs 228, one-man show, shortest runs, longest play, complete Shakespeare 229, cabaret, longest chorus lines, ice shows, shortest criticism, most ardent theatregoer 230, oldest and largest movie 237

Three-Cushion Billiards 535

Three-Legged Race 642

Thunder Days, most 148

Tick, largest and smallest 101

Ticker-Tape Reception 499–500

Tickets, most parking 402

Tidal Power Station, first 330

Tidal Wave, highest 131

Tides, greatest 131

Tiers, most opera 225

Tiger, extinct 61, largest 65

Tightrope, circus records 458, greatest walker, endurance 486, 487, longest, highest act 487

Time Capsule, largest 367

Time Measure, longest, shortest 185, most accurate 339

Tires, largest 304

Titles, most 497

Toad, largest 92, 93, smallest, highest and lowest 93

Toadstool, most poisonous 121

Index prepared by L. Jefferson Siegel

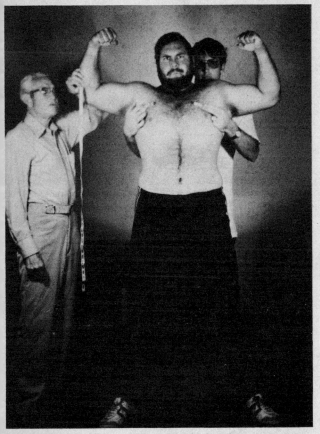

LARGEST CHEST: Gentleman Dan Bernhardt of Salt Lake City claims to measure 70 inches around his chest and 18 inches around his right forearm. Here, a five-foot tape measure stretched around his upper torso leaves a noticeable gap.

MOST EXPENSIVE COIN: Steven A. Markoff of the A-Mark Coin Company of Beverly Hills, California, paid "close to a million dollars" for a U.S. 1907 Double Eagle ($20 gold coin). Previous owners included the late King Farouk of Egypt.

WEINER TAKES ALL: This frankfurter, 8 feet long, 18 inches around, weighing 1,776 ounces, was displayed at the Hygrade Summer Festival in Central Park, New York City, on August 13, 1976. It sat on a 5¾-foot-long roll.

ONE-MAN BAND: Englishman Christopher Critchlow played 58 instruments for three minutes on December 18, 1975, thus rivaling the feats of Don Davis and Werner Hirzel (Schnickelgruber).

700

BATON TWIRLING MARATHON: Lucinda Haney, Susan Leiter, Diane Heal, Sharon Harkins and Laurie Orfaly twirled their batons for 44 hours in June, 1975, to set the record.

"IRON MAIDEN" RECORDBREAKER: Ronald Champlain (shown here during a marathon attempt) sandwiched himself between two beds of nails on June 23, 1976, in Pawtucket, Rhode Island. On top sat baseball players weighing a total of 1,371 lbs.

STONE-SKIPPING CHAMPION: Warren Klope of Troy, Michigan, topped the field in a 1975 contest with a record 24 skips. This includes both plinkers and pitty-pats.

FERRIS WHEEL RIDERS: David "Jocko" Chabira (left) and John "Bimbo" Benaka (right) rode for 22 days 4 hours 2 minutes in May and June, 1975.

DRUMMING MARATHON: Jim Purol of Livonia, Michigan, set a new mark to beat by going 320 hours from June 19 to July 2, 1976.

HOT DOG DEVOURER: Jimmy Davenport of Lexington, Kentucky, choked down 20 2-oz. franks in 3 minutes 33 seconds on March 3, 1976.

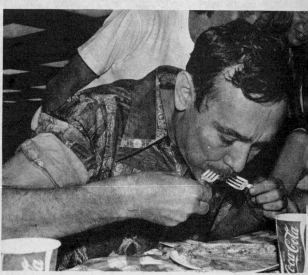

SPAGHETTI EATING CHAMPION: Bill Simpson of Lexington, Kentucky, used both hands to eat 100 yards of spaghetti in 67 seconds on March 3, 1976.